Economic Commission for Europe

ECONOMIC SURVEY OF EUROPE IN 1993-1994

Prepared by the
SECRETARIAT OF THE
ECONOMIC COMMISSION FOR EUROPE
GENEVA

New York and Geneva, 1994

NOTE

The designations employed and the presentation of the material in this publication do not imply the expression of any opinion whatsoever on the part of the Secretariat of the United Nations concerning the legal status of any country, territory, city or area, or of its authorities, or concerning the delimitation of its frontiers or boundaries.

UNITED NATIONS PUBLICATION
Sales No. E.94.II.E.1
ISBN 92-1-116594-6
ISSN 0070-8712

PREFACE

The present *Survey* is the forty-seventh in a series of reports prepared by the secretariat of the Economic Commission for Europe to serve the needs of the Commission and to help in reporting on world economic conditions.

The *Survey* is published on the responsibility of the secretariat, and the views expressed in it should not be attributed to the Commission or to its participating Governments.

The pre-publication text of this *Survey* was completed in March 1994 as a document for the 49th session of the Economic Commission for Europe. This text, finalized in April 1994, incorporates minor changes.

EXPLANATORY NOTES

The following symbols have been used throughout this *Survey*:

.. = not available or not pertinent

- = nil or negligible

* = estimate by the secretariat of the Economic Commission for Europe

In referring to a combination of years, the use of an oblique stroke (e.g., 1993/94) signifies a twelve-month period (say, from 1 July 1993 to 30 June 1994). The use of a hyphen (e.g., 1993-1994) normally signifies either an average of, or a total for, the full period of calendar years covered (including the end-years indicated).

Unless the contrary is stated, the standard unit of weight used throughout is the metric ton. The definition of "billion" used throughout is a thousand million. The definition of "trillion" used throughout is a thousand billion. Minor discrepancies in totals and percentages are due to rounding.

References to dollars ($) are to United States dollars unless otherwise specified.

The following abbreviations have been used:

CEFTA	Central European Free Trade Area
CIS	Commonwealth of Independent States
CMEA	Council for Mutual Economic Assistance
EBRD	European Bank for Reconstruction and Development
ECE	Economic Commission for Europe
EC	European Community
EEA	European Economic Area
EFTA	European Free Trade Association
EIB	European Investment Bank
EU	European Union
FDI	Foreign direct investment
GATT	General Agreement on Tariffs and Trade
GDP	Gross domestic product
GNP	Gross national product
GSP	Generalized System of Preferences
IMF	International Monetary Fund
MFN	Most Favoured Nation
NMP	Net material product
OECD	Organization for Economic Cooperation and Development
SDR	Special drawing rights
WTO	World Trade Organization

Eastern Europe, as employed in the text and tables of this publication, refers to the formerly centrally planned economies of Albania, Bulgaria, Czech Republic, Hungary, Poland, Romania and Slovakia, and the successor states of the Socialist Federal Republic of Yugoslavia. Among the now independent republics of the former *Soviet Union*, a distinction is made between the *Baltic states* (Estonia, Latvia and Lithuania) and the majority of the remaining republics which cooperate in the institutions of the Commonwealth of Independent States – the *CIS* countries.

CONTENTS

Chapter 1

Overview of the transition economies in 1993-1994

The level of output: Depression and recovery	1
Changes in the structure of output	2
The collapse of fixed investment	4
Foreign direct investment	5
Official development assistance	6
Macroeconomic stability	6
Unemployment	7
Inflation	7
External balance	8
Restructuring and privatization	9
The outlook for 1994	11

Chapter 2

The market economies

2.1	Expectations, policies, outcomes		13
	(i)	Overview of developments in 1993	13
	(ii)	Factors in recent economic performance	14
	(iii)	Crisis in the labour market	16
	(iv)	Monetary policy	18
	(v)	Fiscal policy	21
	(vi)	The short-term economic outlook	22
2.2	Output and the components of demand		24
	(i)	Output	24
	(ii)	The components of demand	27
2.3	Costs and prices		34
	(i)	Recent changes in consumer prices	34
	(ii)	World commodity prices	36
	(iii)	Input and output prices in manufacturing industry	36
	(iv)	Labour and non-labour unit costs in total economy	37
	(v)	The sources of inflation	38
2.4	Labour markets		40
	(i)	Recent changes in the demand for labour	40
	(ii)	Recent changes in the supply of labour	42
	(iii)	Unemployment	43
	(iv)	Labour market policy	45
2.5	Foreign trade and payments		48
	(i)	Trade volumes	48
	(ii)	Current account balances	48

Chapter 3

The transition economies

- 3.1 Expectations and outcomes for 1993 51
    - (i) Overview of developments in 1993 51
    - (ii) Scourges of transition: Inflation and unemployment 53
    - (iii) External imbalances 54
    - (iv) Fiscal constraints 56
    - (v) Transformation: The new sectors 56
    - (vi) Growing political instability 57

- 3.2 Output and demand 58
    - (i) Overview 58
    - (ii) Sectoral output developments 58
    - (iii) Structural change in industry 64
    - (iv) Factors behind the output changes 66
    - (v) Changes in domestic absorption 67
    - (vi) Foreign sector impact 72

- 3.3 Costs and prices 74
    - (i) Overview 74
    - (ii) Consumer prices 74
    - (iii) Producer prices and wages 77
    - (iv) Origins of inflation 81

- 3.4 Labour markets 83
    - (i) Employment 83
    - (ii) Unemployment 86
    - (iii) Vacancies 89

- 3.5 Foreign trade of the transition economies 92
    - (i) Introduction 92
    - (ii) Eastern Europe 92
    - (iii) The Commonwealth of Independent States 101
    - (iv) The Baltic states 107
    - (v) Trade imbalances and trade policies: Some tentative conclusions 109

- 3.6 Balance of payments, reserves and debt 110
    - (i) Overview 110
    - (ii) Results by country 110
    - (iii) Concluding observations 115

- 3.7 Macroeconomic policies 116
    - (i) Overview of central policy issues 116
    - (ii) Macroeconomic policies in eastern Europe and the Baltic states 116
    - (iii) Macroeconomic policies in Russia and Ukraine 122

- 3.8 Short-term outlook 129
    - (i) Constraints on emerging recovery in eastern Europe 129
    - (ii) Uncertain prospects for the CIS economies 131
    - (iii) End of recession in the Baltic states? 131

Chapter 4

External support for the transition economies

4.1 Financial flows and commitments of financial assistance 133

    (i) Overview 133
    (ii) Private capital flows 134
    (iii) Official credits 137
    (iv) Resource flows into the transition economies 141
    (v) Relations with the London and Paris Clubs 143
    (vi) Development bank sectoral lending 145

4.2 East-west cooperation agreements and market access 149

    (i) Introduction 149
    (ii) The transformation of east-west commercial relations 149
    (iii) The rise of contingent protection: A trend or a blip? 153
    (iv) Summary of trade liberalization measures and prospects 155

Chapter 5

Restructuring of state-owned enterprises in eastern Europe

5.1 The experience of enterprise restructuring in transition economies 159

    (i) Key issues and comparative perspectives 159
    (ii) Macroeconomic environment and enterprise restructuring 160
    (iii) Privatization and enterprise restructuring 161

5.2 Restructuring of state-owned enterprises in the Czech Republic 163

    (i) Key issues in the restructuring of large SOEs 163
    (ii) Developments in restructuring during the period 1989-1993 167
    (iii) Lessons from Czech restructuring 172

5.3 Enterprise restructuring in eastern Germany 174

    (i) Introduction 174
    (ii) The starting point: The conglomerate in the GDR economy 175
    (iii) Restructuring in eastern Germany: Principles, methods and results 176
    (iv) Examples from east German enterprise restructuring 182
    (v) Lessons for other transition countries 183

5.4 Restructuring of large state-owned enterprises in Hungary, 1988-1993 185

    (i) Definitions and key issues 185
    (ii) The starting point: Early enterprise reforms in Hungary 185
    (iii) Spontaneous privatization, 1988-1990: A bottom-up approach 188
    (iv) Centralized privatization, 1990-1992: Insufficient restructuring 190
    (v) Restructuring in 1992-1993: A top-down approach 192
    (vi) Some lessons from Hungarian restructuring policies 196

5.5 Enterprise transformation in Poland 199

    (i) Restructuring of large state-owned enterprises: The main approaches 199
    (ii) The starting point and first results 204
    (iii) Four years of transformation: A summary 212

References 213

LIST OF TABLES AND CHART

Chapter 2

Table		*Page*
2.1.1	Macroeconomic indicators for western Europe and the United States, 1991-1994	14
2.1.2	Geographical structure of merchandise exports of western Europe and North America, 1987 and 1992	16
2.2.1	Quarterly changes in real GDP, 1992-1993	25
2.2.2	Real GDP in western Europe and North America, 1991-1994	26
2.2.3	Industrial output in western Europe and North America, 1991-1993	27
2.2.4	Capacity utilization rates in manufacturing industry in western Europe and North America, 1982-1994 QI	28
2.2.5	Contribution of domestic demand and the net foreign balance to annual changes of real GDP, 1992-1993	29
2.2.6	Real private consumption expenditures in western Europe and North America, 1991-1993	29
2.2.7	Saving ratios of private households in western Europe and North America, 1990-1993	30
2.2.8	Real public consumption expenditures in western Europe and North America, 1991-1993	30
2.2.9	Real gross fixed capital formation in western Europe and North America, 1991-1993	31
2.2.10	Volume of trade in goods and services in western Europe and North America, 1990-1993	32
2.3.1	Annual changes in consumer price index of western Europe and North America, 1990-1993	34
2.3.2	Producer prices and average hourly earnings in manufacturing industries of western Europe and North America, 1992-1993	37
2.3.3	Labour costs and profits in western Europe and North America, 1992-1993	38
2.3.4	Contribution to the changes in the GDP and domestic demand deflators in western Europe and North America, 1992-1993	39
2.4.1	Labour market changes in western Europe and North America, 1989-1993	41
2.4.2	Employment by sector, 1982 and 1992	41
2.4.3	Changes in employment by sector, 1990-1993	42
2.4.4	Labour force participation rates in western Europe and North America: 1973, 1982 and 1992	43
2.4.5	Standardized unemployment rates in western Europe and North America, 1990-1993	44
2.4.6	Unemployment by sex, age and duration in western Europe and North America, 1993	45
2.5.1	Volume of merchandise trade in western Europe and North America, 1992-1993	48
2.5.2	Real effective exchange rates, 1988-1993	49
2.5.3	Current account balances in western Europe and North America, 1991-1993	49

Chart		*Page*
2.1.1	Consumer and business confidence in the European Community and the United States, January 1991-January 1994	15
2.1.2	Output, employment and unemployment in western Europe and the United States, 1970-1993	17
2.1.3	Nominal short-term and long-term interest rates in western Europe and the United States, January 1992-January 1994	18
2.1.4	Approximate term structure of interest rates in the four major west European economies and the United States, January 1992-January 1994: Long-term rates less short-term rates	19
2.1.5	Average monthly bilateral exchange rates between Germany, Japan and the United States, January 1992-January 1994	19
2.1.6	Average monthly bilateral exchange rates in western Europe, August 1992-January 1994	20
2.1.7	General government financial balances in western Europe and the United States, 1980-1993	21
2.2.1	Real GDP in the seven major industrialized economies, 1990-1993	25
2.2.2	Quarterly index numbers of industrial output in western Europe and the United States, 1989-1993	27
2.2.3	Outlays on EDP equipment and total machinery and equipment by the US business sector, 1980-1993	32
2.2.4	Investment-output ratios in western Europe and the United States, 1970-1993	33
2.3.1	Quarterly changes in the consumer price index of western Europe and North America, 1990-1993	35
2.3.2	World market prices of raw materials in US dollars, 1990-1993	36
2.4.1	Standardized unemployment rates in western Europe and North America, 1973-1993	47

Chapter 3

Table		*Page*
3.1.1	European transition countries: Economic activity, 1990-1993	52
3.2.1	GDP by major sectors, 1990-1992	59
3.2.2	European transition countries: Gross agricultural production, 1990-1993	63
3.2.3	Transition economies: Index of industrial output, by branch	64
3.2.4	European CIS countries: Industrial growth by branch, 1991-1993	65
3.2.5	European transition countries: Domestic production and absorption, 1990-1993	68
3.2.6	European transition countries: Gross fixed investment and construction sector activity, 1990-1993	71
3.2.7	European transition countries: Volume of foreign trade, 1990-1993	73

		Page
3.3.1	Transition countries: Changes in consumer price indices, 1991-1993	75
3.3.2	Transition countries: Monthly changes in consumer price indices, 1992-1993	76
3.3.3	Transition countries: Producer prices, 1993	77
3.3.4	Transition countries: Average nominal monthly wages, 1993	78
3.3.5	Transition countries: Real wages, 1990-1993	79
3.3.6	Introduction of the value-added tax in transition economies and rates in January 1994	82
3.4.1	Transition countries: Employment, 1985-1992	84
3.4.2	Selected transition countries: Changes in employment by broad sectors, 1989-1992	85
3.4.3	Selected transition countries: Output-employment relationship, 1990-1992	85
3.4.4	Transition countries: Unemployment, 1990-1993	86
3.4.5	Transition countries: Unemployment, 1992-1993	88
3.4.6	Selected transition countries: Unemployment rates by sex	89
3.5.1	European transition countries: Foreign trade, by direction, 1991-1993	93
3.5.2	European transition countries: Trade balances, 1990-1993	93
3.5.3	European transition countries: Change in foreign trade values and trade balances by partner region, 1991-1993	95
3.5.4	Eastern Europe: Average monthly US dollar wages, 1991-1993	100
3.5.5	Foreign trade of Commonwealth of Independent States with non-CIS countries, 1993	102
3.5.6	Russia's trade with CIS countries, 1992-1993	104
3.5.7	Russian exports of oil to CIS countries, 1991-1993	105
3.5.8	Baltic states: Foreign trade by direction, 1992-1993	107
3.6.1	Convertible currency current account balances of transition countries, 1990-1993	111
3.6.2	External debt in convertible currencies of the transition countries, 1990-1993	112
3.6.3	Foreign currency reserves and BIS deposits of transition countries, 1989-1993	113
3.6.4	Net debt-exports and reserves-imports ratios of transition countries, 1990-1993	114
3.7.1	Transition countries: Indices of monetary aggregates in December 1993	117
3.7.2	Minimum obligatory reserve requirements, selected countries, 1992 and 1993	118
3.7.3	Transition countries: Budget accounts, current prices, 1992-1993	119
3.7.4	Official exchange rates and consumer price index in transition countries, end-December 1993	122
3.7.5	Russian Central Bank's interest rates, 1991-1993	124
3.7.6	Changes in monetary aggregates and consumer prices in Russia, 1992-1993	125
3.7.7	Ukraine: Key financial indicators, 1993	128

Chart		Page
3.2.1	East European countries: Monthly indices of gross industrial output, 1992-1993	61
3.2.2	CIS countries: Monthly indices of gross industrial output, 1992-1993	62
3.3.1	Consumer prices, producer prices and average nominal wages of transition countries, 1992-1993	80
3.4.1	Selected transition countries: Unemployment rates, 1990-1993	87
3.4.2	Selected transition countries: Unemployment benefits/wage ratio and share of unemployed receiving benefits, 1990-1993	90
3.4.3	Selected transition countries: Unemployment vacancy ratio, 1990-1993	91
3.5.1	Specific western import demand facing eastern Europe and the former Soviet Union, 1990-1994	100

Chapter 4

Table		Page
4.1.1	Medium- and long-term funds raised on the international financial markets by transition countries, 1988-1993	135
4.1.2	Joint ventures and foreign direct investment in transition countries, 1990-1993	136
4.1.3	Bank and non-bank debt of transition economies *vis-à-vis* BIS and OECD reporting institutions, 1990-1993	137
4.1.4	IMF arrangements in force in transition economies in 1992-1994	138
4.1.5	Financial commitments of the development institutions to transition economies, 1990-1993	139
4.1.6	Gross disbursements by international financial institutions to the transition economies, 1991-1993	140
4.1.7	Gross financial flows to eastern Europe and the former Soviet Union/Russia, 1990-1993	141
4.1.8	Two measures of net transfer of resources into the transition countries and changes in reserves, 1991-1993	142
4.1.9	Financial commitments of the development institutions to the transition economies, by industrial sector, 1990-1993	145
4.1.10	Total financial commitments of the development institutions to the transition economies, by industrial sector, 1990-1993	146
4.2.1	Restrictive actions taken by western countries against products from transition economies	154

Chapter 5

Table		Page
5.2.1	Structure of privatization projects by originator, Czech Republic, 1992	164
5.2.2	Privatized units and property according to privatization method applied, Czech Republic, 1992-1993	166
5.2.3	Number of industrial units before and after privatization project approval, Czech republic, February 1994	166
5.2.4	Number of industrial enterprises, Czech Republic, 1989-1993	167
5.2.5	Size structure of industrial enterprises, Czech Republic, 1989-1992	168
5.2.6	Share of the largest companies in total industrial output, Czech Republic, 1989 and 1993	168
5.2.7	Small enterprises by industrial branch, Czech Republic, 1992	169
5.2.8	Shares of four largest producers in the total output of manufacturing branches, Czech Republic, 1989 and 1992	169
5.2.9	Concentration ratios comparison: Austria, 1989 and Czech Republic, 1992	170
5.2.10	Ownership structure of industrial enterprises, Czech Republic, 1992-1993	171
5.3.1	The transformation of the Treuhand portfolio, 1990-1993	176
5.3.2	Treuhand activities: Enterprise sales, revenues, job and investment guarantees, 1990-1993	177
5.3.3	The role of foreigners and east Germans in privatization, end-June 1993	177
5.3.4	East German manufacturing industry: The importance of Treuhand, 1991-1993	178
5.3.5	Investment per employee by Treuhand, privatized and newly-founded firms in east German manufacturing, 1991-1992	181
5.4.1	Structure of industrial enterprises by number of employees, Hungary, 1970-1991	186
5.4.2	Government subsidies by type, Hungary, 1987-1993	186
5.4.3	Economic organizations by legal type, Hungary, 1988-1993	187
5.4.4	Economic organizations with "legal personality" by number of employees, Hungary, 1988-1993	187
5.4.5	Structure of industrial employment in state-owned enterprises by firm size, Hungary, 1970-1991	188
5.4.6	Structure of economic units with "legal personality" by organizational form, Hungary, 1988-1993	188
5.4.7	Number of firms concerned by bankruptcy and liquidation proceedings, Hungary, 1992-1993	193
5.5.1	Structure of employment in state-owned industry, Poland, 1980-1992	205
5.5.2	State firms in Poland, by sector, 1990-1993	206
5.5.3	Private firms in Poland, by sector, 1990-1993	206
5.5.4	Private firms employing no more than five people, by sector, Poland, 1989-1993	207
5.5.5	Share of the private sector in the Polish economy, 1989-1993	207
5.5.6	Share of private enterprises in output and employment, by sector, Poland, 1989-1993	208
5.5.7	Output changes in state and private enterprises, by sector, Poland, 1990-1993	208
5.5.8	Private sector share in exports and imports, Poland, 1990-1992	208
5.5.9	Financial performance of state and private enterprises, Poland, 1991-1993	208
5.5.10	Fnancial performance in firms undergoing privatization, Poland, 1992-1993	209
5.5.11	Financial performance of joint-stock companies quoted on the Warsaw Stock Exchange, 1991-1993	210
5.5.12	Progress in the privatization process in Poland, 1990-1993	211

Chapter 1

OVERVIEW OF THE TRANSITION ECONOMIES IN 1993-1994

The level of output: Depression and recovery

Nearly four and a half years after the collapse of the communist regimes in eastern Europe and the former Soviet Union, most of the region is still in a deep economic depression. However, in most of eastern Europe the fall in output last year was generally much smaller than in 1992 and for a number of countries there are clear signs of a recovery in activity. In Poland GDP rose by 4 per cent last year, thus extending the recovery that began in 1992. There was also a significant recovery of total output in Albania where there has been a sharp increase in agricultural production.[1] GDP also increased, albeit modestly, in Romania and Slovenia, while the data on industrial production suggest that the recession is levelling out in the Czech Republic and that output has been rising in Hungary. However, output has continued to fall with little respite in the south European transition economies (excepting Slovenia and Albania) and especially in FR Yugoslavia and the FYR of Macedonia. Altogether, total output in eastern Europe last year probably fell by something of the order of 3 per cent, which is less than half the rate of decline in 1992.

In Russia and the other members of the CIS the collapse in output continued virtually unchecked last year, with an average fall of some 13 per cent following a 20 per cent drop in 1992. In the CIS the depression has been greatly intensified by the collapse of trade among the highly interdependent member states. This was largely the result of a failure to overcome the monetary and payments problems which arose in the wake of the break-up of the Soviet Union and which finally led to the break-up of the rouble zone in the latter half of 1993. Most of the CIS members are thus facing an additional "trade shock" in the form of a large deterioration in their terms of trade with Russia and other suppliers of energy, as the latter raise their prices to world market levels, as well as interruptions in deliveries (especially oil and gas) because of non-payment of debts and bureaucratic confusion in the inter-state distribution systems.

Similar problems, of higher prices and interruptions of oil and gas deliveries from Russia, were also disruptive in the Baltic states in 1990-1991, but since their departure from the rouble zone in 1992 production has been badly hit by the loss of markets in the former Soviet Union. With the introduction of tough stabilization policies, the Baltic states have experienced some of the most severe depressions of all the transition economies. Nevertheless, there does appear to have been some levelling out in the decline of total output in Estonia last year.

Although not a single post-communist country has been able to avoid the long and deep recession[2] which has followed the political and economic revolution of 1989, there are very large differences among them in the extent to which they have suffered. In eastern Europe the recession has been *relatively* less prolonged in the Czech Republic, Hungary, Poland and Slovenia where, on current indications, a gradual recovery may now be emerging. These countries have progressed further in the transformation of their economies and in their integration with the larger European economy in terms of trade and foreign investment. However, despite the considerable progress that has been achieved, this "advanced" group of transition economies still faces considerable problems in the areas of macroeconomic stabilization, the privatization of large state-owned enterprises (see below) and the reform of the banking system. Moreover, it should be emphasized that many of the achievements so far are more likely to impress professional economists and international officials than the long-suffering electorates of the countries concerned. Even in this group, with the possible exception of the Czech Republic, there is still widespread disillusionment with the transition process and dissatisfaction with the fall in living standards: the essentially political task of organizing and maintaining popular support for the ultimate objectives of market-based economies and democratic institutions remains as urgent as ever.[3]

Although this *Survey* focuses on economic questions, it should be emphasized that, for many people in eastern Europe and the former Soviet Union, the transition process

---

[1] Albania, probably the poorest country in Europe, was in a catastrophic state just two years ago and largely dependent on humanitarian aid for essential food supplies. Radical reforms were introduced very rapidly after the elections of March 1992 and Albanian farmers appear to have responded quickly to price liberalization and privatization of most of the country's agricultural land.

[2] There are many reasons for doubting the accuracy of the output and other statistics in the transition economies at present, and it is possible that the official figures overstate the depth of the fall in output. Until the national statistical offices revise the data the extent of the errors will remain essentially unknown, but it seems unlikely that the slump in output will be statistically revised into a mild recession.

[3] On the weakening support for economic reforms see United Nations Economic Commission for Europe, *Economic Survey of Europe in 1992-1993*, New York, 1993, pp.10-14.

appears as a social crisis. In seven out of nine transition economies monitored by UNICEF, the crisis "appears most pronounced and general in the fields of poverty, mortality (particularly for males in the 40-59 age group), marriage and birth rates, pre-school education and youth, and overall crime", the data showing "clear and sizeable deteriorations in each of these areas". The situation appears to have stopped deteriorating in Hungary, Slovakia and the Czech Republic, but only in the last country are there any signs of a return to normal conditions.[4]

The recent recovery of activity in some of the transition economies must also be kept in the perspective of the depth of the recession: if Poland is able to maintain its current growth rate of some 4 per cent a year it will still take until 1997 before the level of output in 1989 is surpassed. This is but a crude piece of arithmetic which ignores changes in the quality of output (and of consumption), but it nevertheless provides a broad indication of the scale of the problems facing national governments.

In the other transition economies the range and intensity of problems is rather greater, although they are difficult to place in neat categories. Some of them (Albania, Bulgaria, Romania and the Baltic states, for example) have initiated major reforms and have made significant headway, but their problems of adjustment and stabilization are such that they are even more vulnerable to setbacks than the "advanced" group discussed above. In many of the countries of the former Soviet Union and former Yugoslavia, the problems of economic transition have had to take second place while problems of political stability and national identity are addressed. Consequently, institutional transformation is held back and problems of economic stability tend to become acute.

It is sometimes tempting for observers in the western market economies (and in international institutions) to conclude that the considerable variations in progress towards the market economy reflect the degree of determination and consistency with which rigorous programmes of macroeconomic stabilization and structural reform are pursued. Political leadership and determination are, of course, very important ingredients in a successful reform, but the variation in performance among the transition economies is also greatly − if not predominantly − affected by more fundamental factors such as the weight of economic and political history, by geopolitical situations, and by the initial conditions in which the reform process began after 1989. The composition of the "advanced" group of transition economies might just as well have been predicted from their pre-1989 history as from their post-1989 efforts. Hungary and Poland had experimented with partial reforms towards more market-based incentives long before 1989; Czechoslovakia (and, later, Slovakia and the Czech Republic) started the transition with the most balanced macroeconomic situation of any of the transition countries,[5] an inheritance of the conservatism of the communist regime; while Slovenia, always the most prosperous of the Yugoslav republics and with an administration that supported the entrepreneurial drive of its population, also began the transition in relatively favourable macroeconomic conditions.[6] The "leaders" were thus already ahead before the collapse of the Berlin wall.

Changes in the structure of output

The transformation of the former centrally planned economies involves not only a radical restructuring of institutions and behavioural patterns, but also considerable changes in the distribution of economic activities.[7] The liberalization of foreign trade and the adoption of decentralized price-setting in free markets have led to large changes in the relative prices facing actual and potential producers of particular goods and services. Parts of the existing capital stock will have been rendered unprofitable and will have to contract or be retired, while other, potentially more profitable, activities will attract new investment, domestic and foreign, which will lead to an expansion in productive capacity. This process is still in its early stages, but although the limitations of the statistical data prevent any detailed examination, some of the changes are already visible.

In terms of the broadest sectors of the economy the most apparent change in eastern Europe is the expansion of *services*. In the space of just two years (1990-1992) their share of GDP has risen by 7-8 percentage points in Hungary and Poland, and by even more in Bulgaria. The expansion of the services sector is one of the most conspicuous breaks with the former, centrally planned regime and reflects not only the growth of small-scale enterprise in retail trade, restaurants etc., in part a result of successful privatization, but also the creation of new financial, legal and business services which have an essential role to play in a market economy. It is noticeable that in Belarus and Ukraine, for example, two countries where the transition process has made little progress, the share of services in total output is under half that in the more "advanced" reform countries of eastern Europe.

Changes in the relative importance of other sectors − agriculture, construction and industry − are more variable and it is difficult generalize. The *construction* industry has tended to contract rather faster than the economy as a whole in most countries, a reflection of the general collapse in fixed investment, the pressures to cut public expenditure

---

[4] UNICEF-International Child Development Centre, *Central and Eastern Europe in Transition − Public Policy and Social Conditions*, Florence, November 1993, p.3.

[5] Students of the *longue durée* will note that the Czech Republic emerged from the collapse of communism in 1989 in much the same condition as it escaped from the wreckage of the Austro-Hungarian empire in 1918, namely, with low inflation, small foreign debts and a balanced budget.

[6] Slovenia inherited a relatively high inflation rate from the former Yugoslavia but its foreign debt was small.

[7] Some aspects of changes in the structure of ownership are discussed later in this chapter; and a detailed review of four countries' experience in privatizing state-owned enterprises is contained in chapter 5 of this *Survey*.

(which in practice usually have a disproportionate effect on public investment), and a fall in housebuilding. In the medium term, this decline in the construction sector can be expected to be reversed given the potential for industrial restructuring, the need for extensive infrastructure investment, and the social pressures for a renewal of the housing stock. The sector is also suited to small and medium-sized enterprises of which a very large proportion is already in private ownership. In the meantime, the construction sector continues to be restrained, not only by the continued weakness in total fixed investment, but also by the familiar transition problems of uncertain property rights, especially on land, continued price controls on private housing and office buildings, weak financial institutions, and bureaucratic delays in obtaining construction permits.

Agricultural output throughout eastern Europe and the states of the former Soviet Union has fallen every year since the transition process got under way. Apart from the vagaries of the weather, which hit output particularly hard in 1992, delays in land privatization and uncertainty surrounding property rights have had a depressing effect on output in a number of transition economies. Lack of financial resources for farmers as well as monopolistic distribution systems, which prevent producers from benefiting from higher retail prices for food, are also among the factors which are holding back the restructuring of agriculture and the expansion of private farms. In the CIS, a highly mechanized and energy-intensive agriculture has been highly vulnerable to the adjustment of prices to world levels: large price increases for fertilizers, fuel and fodder have contributed to a considerable reduction in the output of meat and dairy products.[8] Some east European agricultural exporters have also lost market share to heavily subsidized exports from western Europe and from the EU in particular. The withdrawal of export subsidies on west European exports to the transition economies would be a helpful initiative on the part of the EU[9] and the opening of western Europe's markets to agricultural products from the eastern countries would be even more so. Demands for agricultural protectionism are already strong in eastern Europe and tariffs on imports have been raised in a number of countries, including Russia. A more liberal approach by the EU might therefore help eastern governments to avoid following the western path to agricultural protectionism, which would effectively place a heavy tax on the newly emerging activities in the industrial and service sectors.

Within the *manufacturing sector* of the transition economies there has been a general collapse of output in all industries, but some have clearly suffered much more than others. Among the hardest hit are some of the traditional "heavy" industries – iron and steel, parts of mechanical engineering and chemicals, etc. – but also a number of "high-tech" activities such as telecommunications. Among the relatively unscathed are printing and publishing, clothing and processed foods. This general impression from the output figures is supported by the data on international trade.[10] Exports of textiles, clothing and other labour-intensive products have done better than average, as have certain foodstuffs, chemicals (e.g., fertilizers), timber products and other resource-based manufactures. Czech and Polish exports of machinery or electro-engineering rose strongly last year, and they also did relatively well in Hungary.

These observations refer to such a short period that it would not be justified to use them to draw strong conclusions about changing comparative advantages. Nevertheless, the changes do suggest the following developments in the structure of industrial production in eastern Europe and the Baltic states: first, a shift away from excessive production of heavy capital goods towards more consumer goods; and secondly, an increased share in total output of labour-intensive and/or internationally standardized, intermediate products in the production of which the eastern countries are relatively competitive on international markets.[11] These changes are also likely to have been supported by changes in the pattern of domestic demand, since both relative price changes and falling real wages in most countries have probably led to an increasing proportion of household expenditure being spent on food and clothing.

The contraction of both traditional heavy industries and new, high-technology industries is not so surprising, since both were "protected" by the former central planning systems and by "soft markets" in other CMEA countries, particularly the Soviet Union. However, the contraction of the more advanced activities has come as an unpleasant surprise for some eastern policy makers who frequently emphasize the high quality of their educational systems. But the production of "high-tech" products invariably requires not just high level research and technical skills, but also a high degree of managerial competence and the ability to adapt products quickly to consumers' requirements. The production-driven culture of the centrally planned economy, where managers were protected from outside competition by the planning system and from their own shortcomings by the soft budget constraint, simply did not favour the evolution of such managerial skills or the continuous interchange between producers and consumers which is characteristic of both capital goods and "new" products in the western market economies. Restrictions on western technology exports may have had a negative impact on eastern competitiveness in "high-tech" sectors but in comparison with these managerial shortcomings their effect is likely to have been minor. This conclusion, however, in no way condemns the

---

[8] However, livestock production, based on subsidized, imported fodder, had been boosted to artificially high levels in the Soviet Union by the policies introduced under Brezhnev. The withdrawal of central government subsidies on imports of feed grains is therefore bound to lead to a fall in meat production.

[9] A small step in this direction is the Commission's decision to withdraw, temporarily, subsidies on EU exports of apples to the Czech Republic. An extension of such a policy to other products and markets is, apparently, under discussion. See *Financial Times*, 7 March 1994.

[10] See section 3.5 below.

[11] Until more detailed statistics are available it is difficult to tell whether the growth in machinery exports, noted above, conforms to this pattern of characteristics or is an exception to it.

eastern economies to a low- or medium-"tech" future. Comparative advantage is a dynamic phenomenon which evolves in line with changes in the composition of the human and physical capital stock. Those changes are brought about by investment, the composition of which, of course, can be influenced, *inter alia*, by industrial policies.

The collapse of fixed investment

The restructuring of output in the transition economies has so far been largely a "negative" process, in the sense that some activities have survived the onslaught of depression better than others. The principal exception to this generalization has been the rapid growth of services. Even "negative" restructuring has been limited insofar as many state-owned enterprises have survived with the continued supply of central government subsidies, interenterprise credits and the reluctance of governments to accept the employment consequences of illiquidity or a more rapid privatization (or closure) of large enterprises.

Eventually, restructuring must imply the expansion of activities in which the transition economies can develop existing and new comparative advantages, but this development will require a significant upturn and changes in the composition of investment in fixed and human capital. In general, economic growth in middle income countries tends to be boosted by investment in plant and equipment, and supported by inflows of foreign direct investment.[12] Recent research has also focused attention on the positive link between investment in machinery and economic growth,[13] as well as on the positive role of public infrastructure investment in raising productivity, profitability and fixed investment in the private sector.[14] In many of the transition economies, and especially in central and eastern Europe, the stock of human capital and skills is relatively high for current levels of income per head, but, as noted above, the nature of the former regimes has left gaps, particularly in the area of management skills. Also, although the formal qualifications and production skills of the labour force in many of the transition economies may be high, many of them will become obsolete with the retirement of large parts of the capital stock and the introduction of market-oriented behaviour on the part of enterprises. Training or re-training of many sections of the labour force, from managers to operatives, is therefore needed in order to encourage a recovery of investment and the optimal exploitation of new technologies in a competitive market setting. Nevertheless, the development of investment in new plant and equipment is a fundamental requirement for the long-run restructuring of the transition economies and for creating the basis for a sustained expansion in economic activity.

For most of the transition economies, however, fixed investment remains in the deep slump into which it has sunk since 1989. Since then, gross fixed investment has fallen in eastern Europe by an average 37 per cent, and by much more in Russia and Ukraine (53 and 56 per cent) and in the Baltic states (some 80 per cent). The data for 1993 are still in a very poor state and far from complete, but there does appear to have been some recovery of fixed investment in Poland – both in construction and equipment – Hungary and perhaps of investment in machinery in the Czech Republic. Investment also rose by about 11 per cent in Slovenia.

Most of the available data refer to total investment and it is difficult to separate machinery and equipment from housing and other construction. However, the trade figures show a substantial increases in the dollar value of machinery imports into Poland (23 per cent) and the Czech Republic (23 per cent) in 1993. Imports of capital goods into Slovenia also rose by some 10 per cent. Since the dollar prices of machinery exports from the principal western exporters were virtually unchanged or even falling for much of 1993, these changes in import values also indicate significant increases in volume. There was also a large increase in Hungarian imports of machinery last year, but as cars and other transport equipment are included in the figure the implication for fixed investment in Hungary is less clear. Statistics on the sectoral distribution of fixed investment are not easily available, but the recovery does appear to be taking place in industry as well as in the new service sectors, and in the Czech Republic, Hungary and Poland there have been large increases of investment in telecommunications. If a revival of fixed investment is a litmus test of whether or not the reforms are beginning to yield concrete results, then these figures for machinery imports are an encouraging development for the "advanced" group of transition economies. But in all the other transition economies – that is to say, in the majority of them – fixed investment continues to fall rapidly, especially in Russia and in the other former members of the Soviet Union.

It should not, of course, be surprising that fixed investment in the transition economies has fallen so much and that the signs of a recovery are still limited to the small group of "advanced" reformers in eastern Europe. The rapid breakdown of the old command systems and their only gradual replacement by the institutional framework of the market economy has created a situation of pervasive uncertainty in which the risks of investment are very high. In many of the transition economies there is still a lack of clarity about property rights and their enforceability and, in general, the legal framework is still too weak to support a sustained expansion in private economic activity. In addition, high rates of inflation, and uncertainty over the willingness or ability of the governments of some transition economies to take the necessary measures to lower them, will discourage all but the most short-term investments. Political instability and the perversion of "market" activities and behaviour by crime and corruption will have

---

[12] See Magnus Blomström, Robert Lipsey and Mario Zejan, *What Explains Developing Country Growth?*, NBER Working Paper No.4132, Cambridge, Mass., 1992.

[13] See J. Bradford de Long and Laurence H. Summers, "Equipment Investment and Economic Growth: How Strong is the Nexus?", *Brookings Papers on Economic Activity*, 2: 1992, pp.157-211.

[14] Alicia Munnell, "Infrastructure Investment and Economic Growth", *Journal of Economic Perspectives*, Vol.6, No.4, Fall 1992, pp.189-198. Also, the same author's "Why Has Productivity Growth Declined? Productivity and Public Investment", *New England Economic Review*, January/February 1990, pp.3-20.

a similar effect. Thus, if by the "transition process" is meant the creation of the basic legal and institutional infrastructure of a market economy and the appropriate alterations in the behaviour of economic agents, then private investment is unlikely to pick up until that process is complete or, at least, until business expectations are reasonably confident that the end of the process is in sight and is unlikely to be reversed. It is precisely the strengthening of such expectations which distinguishes the "advanced" group of transition economies from the others.

There is also a general "development" problem that arises in countries where the total capital stock is either too small or too obsolete to generate significant external economies among competing enterprises. The international competitiveness of a modern enterprise depends to a large degree on having access to a wide range of independent and specialized producers of components and materials and of business services, and where these do not exist new investments will be discouraged and, indeed, will tend to move to other locations where they are well-established. A problem with virtually all of the transition economies is that the former regimes prevented the spontaneous development of the highly specialized division of labour that characterizes the western market economies.[15] This implies not only a considerable loss of efficiency gains in the past but also a major obstacle to a sustained revival of investment in the future. One way around this problem of externalities would be to encourage the simultaneous expansion of a number of activities in order to achieve a critical mass of demand which would then "extend the market" for other producers throughout the economy and thus encourage a general expansion of investment. An earlier example of such an approach is Monnet's plan for the post-war reconstruction of the European coal and steel industries, but any suggestion of "indicative planning" is unlikely to get very far at the present time. Alternatively, investment demand could be increased via an expansion of public expenditure on the physical infrastructure (roads, railways, telecommunications, environment etc.) which is in need of considerable improvement in all the transition economies and which is currently a source of major bottlenecks to investment and economic activity in general. However, this way forward is also heavily circumscribed partly because of pressures to reduce government budget deficits and partly because of ideological antipathies to the state playing a significant role in economic development. However, the latter may now be starting to change in response to the slow rate of transition in many countries (see below).

Foreign direct investment

One of the assumptions made by western governments and some international institutions was that private foreign direct investment (FDI) would play a key role in the transition process and that this would obviate the need for official assistance on, say, the scale of the Marshall Plan. So far this has not proved to be the case. The net inflow of FDI into eastern Europe has been much less than was expected – or hoped for – by both western and eastern governments. Last year the total is estimated to have been some $3.5 billion, and since 1990 the total inflow has been under $10 billion (for nine countries). Moreover most of the investment is concentrated on just a few countries: the four "advanced" transition economies have received over 90 per cent of the total since 1990, with most (80 per cent) of it going to Hungary and the Czech Republic. Negligible amounts, if any, have gone to other transition economies in the former Soviet Union. Not all FDI necessarily adds to productive capacity: in the first instance, foreign investors often buy existing assets, but there is a reasonable presumption that this will eventually lead to restructuring, fixed investment and increased capacities.

What is surprising about this performance is that anyone should have thought it should have been so much better. Private investors do not normally get heavily involved in "transition processes" of the type under way in eastern Europe until the outcome is virtually assured. Foreign investors are deterred from making investments in the transition economies for much the same reasons as those noted above as holding back investment in general. In addition, foreign investors encounter a range of operational problems[16] which, given the high risks and uncertainty of investment at present, may tip the balance against most eastern countries as a location for FDI. Also, uncertainties over the macroeconomic outlook and the future level of demand in the transition economies add to the risks of long-term investment.[17]

Once the uncertainties over the market infrastructure are removed, the flow of FDI is likely to strengthen and, depending on the extent to which problems such as training are overcome, may play an important role in sustaining growth over the medium term. Nevertheless, foreign investors will be reluctant to move in before they see a reasonably high probability of success for the transition. Even in the countries which have received most of the FDI so far, a cautious "wait-and-see" approach is suggested by the fact that most individual investments have involved the commitment of only small amounts of capital. This limits

---

[15] This is reflected, for example, in the fact that the level of intra-industry trade among the members of the CMEA remained very much lower than that among the countries of western Europe and, especially, the EU. See Z. Drabek and D. Greenaway, "Economic Integration and Intra-Industry Trade: the CMEA and the EEC Compared", *Kyklos*, 37, 1984. A political scientist has remarked that "unlike liberal capitalist democracies, Leninist regimes 'parcel' rather than 'divide' labour ... The net effect was a division of labour that in important respects resembled Durkheim's *mechanical* division of labour, a 'ringworm' division of labour in which each institution attempted to replicate the self-sufficiency of all the others". See Ken Jowett, *New World Disorder. The Leninist Extinction*, University of California Press, Berkeley 1992, pp.289-290.

[16] These differ considerably from country to country. For a very useful survey of the problems facing foreign companies in eastern Europe, including an attempt to weight the various factors increasing the risk of investment, see Pietro Genco, Siria Taurelli and Claudio Viezzoli, "Private investment in central and eastern Europe: Survey results", European Bank for Reconstruction and Development, *Working Paper*, No.7, July 1993.

[17] The uncertainty over the level of demand was one factor which was removed in the former east Germany by massive transfers from the Federal Government and this provided an incentive to invest, especially in activities devoted to the local market.

the exposure of the foreign company to current risks while securing a market position on which expansion can be based when the outlook becomes less uncertain. The exceptions to this pattern usually occur when foreign companies are able to "buy" dominating positions in the domestic markets of the transition economies, the attractions of monopoly or oligopoly reducing the risks of current investment.[18]

One reaction to the "disappointing" inflow of FDI into the transition economies might be for individual countries to offer special incentives to attract foreign investors. Such a response would almost certainly be a mistake. Numerous OECD studies of tax incentives for attracting FDI have failed to show any clear impact, although many countries believe they have to introduce them for defensive reasons because other countries are doing the same. The main beneficiary in such a situation is usually the foreign investor who receives a windfall profit. Another "incentive" to foreign investors is to offer them protection in the host country's market with import quotas or high tariffs. This has already occurred in some of the transition economies and sometimes has been negotiated *after* the foreign investor has proved to have been over-optimistic about sales. Clearly such action undermines the basic objective of the transition process which is to create efficient market economies. Moreover, such measures are likely to create costly distortions which will be difficult to remove once the foreign company is installed. The most appropriate response to weak FDI flows is to concentrate on the basic tasks of establishing sound macroeconomic policies and of creating the essential infrastructure of the market economy, including an appropriate, non-discriminatory legal framework for foreign investment.[19] Also, as many transition economies are relatively small, the foreign investor is not so much attracted by the size of the host country's domestic market as by its attractiveness as a base for reaching the much larger markets of eastern Europe and the former Soviet Union as a whole. The avoidance of restrictions on, as well as measures to facilitate, intraregional trade can therefore have an important influence in attracting FDI into the transition countries.

Official development assistance

In the absence of a significant boost to domestic fixed investment from FDI, it might be expected that official assistance and development bank lending would step in to fill the gap and to offset the lack of private foreign investment in individual countries. Official multilateral flows of new finance to the transition economies have in fact been generally larger than private capital since 1990, although private funds to eastern Europe last year were much larger than official. In the four years since 1990, the development banks' disbursement of funds to eastern Europe has totalled some $5 billion, to which some $5.9 billion of official grants from western governments can be added. So official flows, excluding bilateral credits, were roughly equal to the total for FDI into eastern Europe. However, although details of disbursement are not available, just over 70 per cent of development bank *commitments* to eastern Europe were to the four "advanced" transition economies. The only "compensation" for FDI flows occurred mainly within this group, insofar as Poland received the largest share of the development banks' funds. Very few resources have gone to the countries of the former Soviet Union. In other words, the countries that have achieved most progress in the transition process have succeeded in not only attracting most of the private foreign investment available for the transition economies but also most of the official funds as well. They are also the eastern countries with the highest levels of income per head. However, the needs of the less well-off countries are just as urgent and much less likely to be met by private investment. It should also be remembered that IMF approval of short-run stabilization programmes is often necessary before development bank funds can be released for essential infrastructure investments. If the argument that their difficulties in getting an effective transition programme under way only reflects a lack of political will or determination is rejected, then a review of the scale and distribution of official assistance is urgently needed.

Macroeconomic stability

The weakness of fixed investment in the transition economies is both a reflection and a cause of many of the rigidities which are holding back or slowing down the transition process in many of the eastern economies. Without a strong recovery in fixed investment it will not be possible to achieve the extensive restructuring of the supply side of the economies which is essential for a sustained reduction of inflation to rates broadly comparable with those in western Europe. At the same time, investment and the expansion of new activities is essential for creating new jobs to replace those destroyed in the course of restructuring uncompetitive, state-owned enterprises. Labour mobility is often low and so adjustment will require the help of training programmes and other active labour market policies, as well as a socially acceptable level of unemployment benefits. However, because the traditional instruments of fiscal and monetary policy are still deficient or inadequate in most of the transition economies, a reflection of their transitional state, most of the burden of stabilization policy is being placed on reductions in *government expenditure*. Given the absence or narrow scope of domestic bond markets and limited access to foreign borrowing, large budget deficits are therefore likely to exacerbate inflationary pressures. Increasing tax revenue is inhibited by underdeveloped tax collection systems and widespread tax avoidance,

---

[18] Some foreign investors, however, might be deterred from entering countries where domestic investors are thin on the ground since this would make them more vulnerable to possibly hostile action by governments. This consideration might be more important for long-term bond markets where the absence of domestic holders may increase the risk of default.

[19] A warning of the dangers of encouraging inflows of foreign investment *before* the basic structures of the market economy were in place and functioning was given in the United Nations Economic Commission for Europe, *Economic Survey of Europe in 1989-1990*, New York, 1990, pp.15-16 and p.23.

especially by the new private sector. But cutting expenditure presents governments with painful dilemmas: public infrastructure investment is already very low and further cuts would reduce the contribution of the international development banks' expenditure in this area;[20] reducing social security benefits at a time of sharply rising unemployment is politically dangerous; and a sharp cut in subsidies to ailing state-owned enterprises will lead to a large increase in unemployment with further demands for unemployment benefit and the risk of social instability. The challenge for both domestic and international policy makers is thus to find ways of spreading the burden of adjustment among a wider range of policy instruments and of easing the resolution of some of these dilemmas.

Unemployment

Unemployment reacted slowly to the introduction of reforms in 1989 and 1990, but since 1991 it has risen sharply and is now a major economic and social problem in the transition economies. In eastern Europe there were about 7.5 million persons officially registered as unemployed at the end of 1993, nearly a threefold increase since the end of 1990. As a proportion of the labour force, the average unemployment rate is around 14 per cent, although individual values range from 3.5 per cent in the Czech Republic[21] to 30 per cent or so in the FYR of Macedonia.

In Russia, the other CIS countries, and also in the Baltic states, official unemployment rates are still exceptionally low given the large falls in output – although unemployment has started to increase sharply in the Baltic states. These low levels of official unemployment, which range between 0.2 and 1.3 per cent in the CIS (except in Armenia where the rate was 6.2 per cent), reflect to some extent the slow rate of structural change in many parts of the former Soviet Union,[22] but there are also grounds for believing that the statistics are greatly distorted. In Russia the unemployment rate at the end of last year, based on the number of people classified as "having the official status of being unemployed", was 1.1 per cent of the labour force, but on the ILO definition of unemployment (those out of work and actively seeking employment) it was just over 5 per cent. If the count is extended to include partial unemployment and workers on "unpaid leave", the estimate of the unemployment rate increases to over 10.4 per cent.[23]

Unemployment on the present scale in eastern Europe would be a serious problem in any country, but it is particularly disturbing when previous experience of it is virtually non-existent and where governments are still without an effective strategy for industrial and labour market restructuring. At the same time governments are being forced to reduce the social protection given to the unemployed because of the macroeconomic pressures to reduce overall spending. Not only has unemployment benefit as a proportion of the average wage fallen considerably in all the transition economies since 1991, but the proportion of the unemployed actually entitled to benefit has also been sharply reduced. Rough estimates for six east European countries suggest that, on average, only about 30-40 per cent of the unemployed are entitled to a benefit which is equivalent to about one third of the average wage.[24] In Russia the unemployment benefit is equivalent to about 30 per cent of the official minimum subsistence income. This helps to explain why workers are prepared to accept periods of unpaid leave, since they remain attached to the labour force and retain access to the social support system of the enterprise,[25] and why the government is reluctant to face the social consequences of a more rapid restructuring of the large state-owned enterprises.

Inflation

The slow pace of restructuring and privatization of large state-owned enterprises is one of the factors behind the persistence of high inflation rates in all the transition economies. Price liberalization generally went ahead rapidly while monopolistic structures remained in place to provide a persistent source of inflationary pressure. At the same time, the range and efficacy of the instruments available to transition economy governments has been limited.[26] Nevertheless, there has been some success in either avoiding hyperinflation[27] (Poland in 1990, Estonia and Latvia in 1992 and Russia in 1993) or containing the after-shocks of price liberalization (most notably the Czech Republic). However, inflation rates still remain high even in countries where there has been most success in lowering

---

[20] The banks usually fund 50-60 per cent of infrastructure projects, but the balance has to be met from domestic resources. Of their total commitments to eastern Europe since 1990, about 25 per cent is for infrastructure projects in roads, other transport and telecommunications.

[21] The low rate of Czech unemployment, given the fall in aggregate output, continues to intrigue observers, but no one has yet provided a fully satisfactory explanation. Among the factors suggested are: a loss of jobs among a large number of workers already above retirement age, who then left the labour force rather than joining the unemployment register; very tight eligibility rules for unemployment benefit, as well as the introduction of youth training schemes, have also kept down the numbers on the unemployment register; low real wages and the slow rate of restructuring large SOEs have encouraged enterprises to retain labour; and a substantial increase of output and employment in small private enterprises (in services, tourism, etc.) may not be fully reflected in the official statistics.

[22] But for evidence that the changes in Russian industry have been greater than is often assumed see Guy Standing, *Labour Market Dynamics in Russia in 1993: Results from the Third Round of the RLFS*, ILO, Central and East European Team, Budapest, February 1994.

[23] RF Goskomstat started publishing all three estimates in November 1993.

[24] Although not strictly comparable, this latter figure is considerably lower than the replacement ratios (of unemployment benefit to previous disposable income) to be found in the countries of western Europe and North America. See Economic Commission for Europe, "The Cost of Unemployment, 1972-1982", *Economic Bulletin for Europe*, Pergamon Press for the United Nations, Vol.35, No.3, 1983, pp.289-306, table 3.1.

[25] See United Nations Economic Commission for Europe, *Economic Survey of Europe in 1992-1993*, New York, 1993, p.14. Unpaid leave, rather than unemployment, also carries with it the hope of regaining one's job. Guy Standing, loc.cit., p.22. There is also the prospect of sharing in the distribution of free shares in the event of privatization.

[26] See section 3.7 below.

[27] Conventionally defined as a monthly rate of increase of 50 per cent.

them and in none of the transition economies have annual rates been established in single digits. In the four "advanced" transition economies, prices rose by just over 20 per cent in 1993 in the Czech Republic and Hungary, and by some 37 and 33 per cent in Poland and Slovenia. These figures represent a slight improvement for Poland, hardly any for Hungary, and a considerable one for Slovenia. Slovakia was the only other transition economy with an inflation rate within this 20-37 per cent range. Changes in the trend of inflation are difficult to establish because of the introduction of, or increases in, value-added taxes during the course of 1993, in some cases accompanied by temporary price controls: but for these five countries the underlying rate has perhaps stabilized at around 15-20 per cent a year, maybe somewhat higher in Poland. This stickiness of the rate of inflation raises the question – or the dilemma – of whether to continue attempts to reduce it further at the cost of more unemployment or to try to revive growth and investment in the hope that rising productivity and a faster rate of structural change will help to reduce inflationary pressure. To some extent Poland has attempted to follow the latter course, with some success, although how far the acceleration in the rate of inflation towards the end of 1993 was due to seasonal rather than more fundamental factors is unclear. One important aspect of the current situation, particularly in the "advanced" group of reformers, is that having seriously underestimated both the costs and the duration of the transition period, governments now have an increasing credibility problem with workers whose resistance to further cuts in real wages is growing.

In all the other transition economies the inflation problem was markedly worse than in the central European countries and in general tended to worsen during the course of 1993. In FR Yugoslavia hyperinflation continued unchecked. Inflation in the other Balkan states for which data are available last year ranged from just over 70 per cent in Bulgaria to 350 per cent in the FYR of Macedonia.

Despite widespread fears a year or so ago, Russia has managed to avoid the descent into hyperinflation. The monthly rate of inflation during much of 1993 ranged between 20 and 26 per cent per month, although there was a sharp deceleration at the end of the year as a result of a tightening of monetary policy.[28] In virtually all the other CIS states inflation in 1993 was over 1,000 per cent and was generally deteriorating throughout the year, especially in the second half after the collapse of the rouble zone. Although in some cases special factors such as price liberalization created sharp jumps in the price level, by the middle of the year a number of republics were dangerously close to the threshold of hyperinflation or had passed it (Georgia and Ukraine).

External balance

An unexpected development in 1993 was the sharp deterioration in the current account balances of all the central and east European countries except the Czech Republic. The principal source of the deterioration was located in the trade balance where, in general, export growth fell while imports grew, in many cases substantially.[29] All the eastern exporters were faced with much weaker demand in western Europe, now their largest single market, but the variation in performance (from falls of 13 and 16 per cent in value for Bulgaria and Hungary to growth of 7 and 17 per cent in Poland and the Czech Republic) suggests that domestic supply-side factors, including the extent of exchange rate overvaluation, have played a major role.[30]

The growth of imports also varied considerably, from under 1 per cent in Bulgaria to about 25 per cent in Poland, but here the changes are more closely related to differences in the growth of output and domestic demand. The growth of imports of capital goods has already been noted in a number of countries but there was also a rapid growth of consumer goods as well, particularly in Poland and Slovenia where personal consumption grew by some 10 per cent or so.

With the exception of the Czech Republic, all the east European countries had current account deficits last year, the largest being Hungary ($3.5 billion), Poland ($2.3 billion) and Romania ($1.5 billion). In the immediate future there does not appear to be an urgent problem in financing these deficits, although Hungary may find it difficult to finance another deficit of the size of last year's. The recent debt reduction arrangements for Bulgaria and Poland should make it easier for them to obtain financing. But the question of sustainability is likely to become more urgent in the course of 1994, particularly for countries where export performance has been weakening and where private consumption has been pulling in increasing volumes of consumer goods. For countries entering a period of restructuring and development it is perfectly normal, indeed desirable, to run current account deficits, and as long as the foreign borrowing is being seen to be used to expand productive capacity there should be few difficulties in sustaining the deficit over a number of years. However, perceptions of country and area risk may still deter private lending and so the international financial institutions must be ready to move quickly to meet any shortfall in funding. In assessing the justification of particular deficits some sensitivity to the needs of the domestic population is required. Not all consumer goods can be regarded as "unnecessary" for promoting development, but eventually some of the transition economies will have to give greater attention to policies designed to shift domestic demand in favour of investment.

The situation in Russia is very different to that in eastern Europe. Russian exports continued to rise a little last year while imports fell by some 27 per cent, and the current account moved into a surplus of some $15 billion.

---

[28] See sections 3.3 and 3.7 below.

[29] There are still considerable problems surrounding the collection and estimation of trade data in the eastern countries, and the published figures have been subject to considerable revisions in the past year. See section 3.5 below.

[30] The current account balances of a number of countries – especially Bulgaria, Romania, Hungary and Slovenia – were also adversely affected by international sanctions against FR Yugoslavia.

A number of factors were behind the fall in imports, including weak domestic demand and the depreciation of the rouble, but the main reason was a large reduction in "centralized" (and subsidized) imports due to the squeeze on government expenditure. The implied sharp cuts in the supply of subsidized imports to Russian enterprises is likely to have had a significant negative effect on the level of domestic output.

Restructuring and privatization

The process of privatization is central to the entire process of transforming the former centrally planned economies into decentralized market economies. (Although a market economy without private ownership is possible, this has never been considered as politically feasible in the transition economies.) "Privatization" is as much a description of the objective of the transition process as a means of achieving it. The progress of privatization – and especially of privatization policies – has closely reflected the changes in mood and thinking that have marked the transition programmes since 1989: an initial euphoria and expectations of rapid change based on an oversimplified analysis of the likely obstacles, followed by disappointment and disillusion when progress proved to be much slower than expected and the costs of adjustment more painful, leading gradually to a more pragmatic approach to highly complex and interdependent problems.

In the immediate aftermath of the revolutions of 1989 the quickest route to the market economy was seen in the rapid transfer of state-owned enterprises to private owners. The government's role would be to ensure macroeconomic stability – employing "shock therapy", if necessary, to deal with inflation and government deficits – and the construction of the legal and institutional framework required for a market economy to function efficiently. In this framework, the government would promote allocative efficiency by cutting subsidies to enterprises, liberalizing prices, and opening the economy to foreign trade and competition. The improvement of productive efficiency within individual enterprises would result from the restructuring and investment activities of the new private owners among whom, it was hoped, would be a significant number of foreign companies who would bring with them new technology, a new managerial ethos, and capital to supplement the limited supply of domestic savings. Thus, from the point of view of government, privatization and restructuring were regarded as virtually synonymous.

This non-interventionist approach to restructuring former centrally planned economies, with a strategic role for FDI, was widely supported in the early stages of the transition by both eastern and western governments. The presumption that the creation of new incentives for capital, labour and management would be sufficient to lead to rapid change was naturally attractive to the new governments in eastern Europe who, not surprisingly, wished to distance themselves as quickly as possible from the institutions and behaviour patterns of the former regimes. Even when advisers were less sanguine about the likely rate of progress, there was considerable reluctance to contemplate an active role for government in the restructuring process: at best, the bureaucracy was judged incompetent to judge the future viability of individual enterprises and the nature and scale of the required restructuring; at worst, it might be tempted to frustrate the reforms and turn the clock back. These attitudes reflected the more general antagonism between the official and private realms which characterized the former communist regimes throughout eastern Europe and the former Soviet Union.[31] Western governments also found this approach attractive: not only did it agree with the anti-interventionist spirit of the 1980s but it also played down the need for large amounts of official financial assistance. The emphasis would, instead, be on technical assistance, especially for creating the institutions and skills required for the private business sector to operate, which in turn would increase its attractiveness to foreign investors.

Thus the initial approach to privatization in the former GDR, the Czech Republic, Hungary and Poland,[32] was to sell state-owned enterprises as quickly as possible, preferably as entities, and to keep the state out of any form of microeconomic intervention. The mood was caught by a Polish minister when he declared that "the best industrial policy was no industrial policy".[33]

There is no doubt that considerable progress has been made with privatization in most of the transition economies. "Small" privatization, together with the creation of new private businesses, many of them small family concerns, has led to a rapid expansion of private enterprise. In terms of total output and employment the share of the private sector is rather smaller than its share in the *number* of enterprises, but its growth is still impressive: from 29 per cent of GDP in Poland to 47 per cent in 1992; and from virtually zero in the Czech Republic to around 50 per cent in 1993.

Although attention is often focused on the "advanced" group of transition economies, this should not disguise the fact that there has been significant progress elsewhere, although it is often uneven. In Albania and Romania a significant proportion of agricultural land has been returned to private ownership and about half the number of state farms have been privatized in Albania. But in neither country has there been any significant progress in privatizing the industrial sector, although in Romania the legislative framework is in place. In Bulgaria, land reform has moved slowly and few state-owned enterprises have been privatized although, as in Romania, the relevant enabling laws have been passed. In all three countries, private ownership has progressed quickly in retailing and services, although most concerns are very small. But, apart from the fairly common problems such as the high levels of indebtedness of many SOEs, a major reason for the slowness of privatization in the industrial sector is either lack of popular support or a lack of agreement among the governing parties.

---

[31] Ken Jowett, op.cit., pp.284-294.

[32] These are the four countries for which case studies of restructuring are presented in chapter 5 of this *Survey*.

[33] See section 5.5 below.

Although there has been much pessimism over the progress of reforms in Russia, the privatization programme has in fact been moving very quickly and is one of the most successful elements in the transformation process. The first wave of privatization in 1992 concentrated on small enterprises (employing less than 200 people) and 85 per cent of these are estimated to have been privatized by the end of 1993.[34] In 1993 the mass privatization of medium-sized and large enterprises got under way on the basis of voucher auctions[35] and more than 2,200 were auctioned in the first half of the year. Many of the enterprises are now owned by their managers and workers who obtained their companies' assets at very low prices. This may eventually give rise to problems of corporative governance, but for the present the privatization agency[36] is achieving its objective of a rapid transformation of property rights.

The success of "small" privatization in the transition economies has had a major impact on the lives of private citizens and the appearance of public places: the availability, range and quality of goods in the shops and of personal services have greatly improved, even if a significant proportion of the population is unable to afford them; and encouragement has been given to the emergence (or re-emergence) of an entrepreneurial middle class. Nevertheless, the share of output and employment accounted for by large state-owned enterprises remains considerable and they continue to dominate the industrial sectors. While the initial, "model" approach to privatization worked well enough with small enterprises, it has had relatively little success with large SOEs: the problems of turning them over to private ownership are proving exceptionally difficult and this is one reason for a general slow-down in the overall pace of privatization. This slow-down, in turn, has complicated the problems of macroeconomic stability, not least in the area of public expenditure, and is a brake on the recovery of fixed investment.

The original plan to sell or close down SOEs quickly soon ran into a number of major obstacles: it proved difficult to find buyers for large enterprises, many of which were unwieldy conglomerates, with high levels of debt and considerable structural problems; second, the application of western-style bankruptcy and liquidation procedures, even when the necessary legislation had been passed, turned out to be inappropriate in a situation where the bankruptcy of one enterprise could set off a chain reaction of failures because of the high levels of interenterprise debt; and in any case, the number of potentially non-viable enterprises was often so large that governments were simply unwilling – or, rather, unable – to accept the political and budgetary implications of a sudden and massive rise in unemployment. Given the specialized regional division of labour under many of the former communist regimes, single enterprises often dominate a town or a locality so that their bankruptcy would threaten to devastate a region. Since most of the large SOEs were also the biggest clients of the banks under the old regime, the latter now have balance sheets which are so full of bad debts that many of them would probably be declared insolvent under western banking rules. The banks are therefore unable to play a constructive role in the restructuring of industry and of the economy as a whole.

Governments (or the relevant privatization agencies) have tended to run into these problems one after the other and consequently have been drawn, often reluctantly, into a direct and active role in the financial restructuring of individual enterprises and, from there, into broader industrial and regional policies. The Hungarian and Polish governments and the German Treuhand have all travelled down this road. The dangers of a piecemeal approach to the problems of restructuring is that governments will become too responsive to political and sectional pressures and thus risk undermining the reforms by sustaining non-viable enterprises and non-entrepreneurial behaviour. On the other hand, if government policy is *too* tough, the hard-budget constraints will still be put at risk by threatening too many bankruptcies and encouraging management and labour to stiffen their resistance to change. The experience of the Treuhandanstalt in privatizing SOEs in eastern Germany is both instructive and salutary for the other transition economies. Among the important lessons appear to be the following: first, financial restructuring is necessary before privatization, but debt reduction should not go beyond the normal gearing ratios in a market economy; clear and specific policies are needed to identify the potentially viable components of large SOEs; *persistent* effort to examine alternative routes to viability is important in order to retain employee support for restructuring and can lead to innovations such as the Management KG;[37] a clear distinction needs to be made between the minimal degree of financial and organizational restructuring required to find buyers for the enterprise and *strategic* restructuring (decisions about net investments, new products etc.) which should be the responsibility of the new owners. The Treuhand experience demonstrates not only that the hardening of enterprise budget constraints is *not* synonymous with no government involvement but also that effective restructuring is unlikely to occur without the intervention of government or its agents.[38]

Restructuring and privatization in the former GDR has been much more extensive and carried out more quickly than in any other transition economy. But the lessons for other countries may also be difficult to apply. The Treuhand's efforts were supported by massive infrastructure investments in the eastern *Länder* by the federal government which improved the locational attractiveness of the east for west German firms; financial restructuring involved a shift of a proportion of enterprise debt to the federal budget and the German taxpayer; and

---

[34] *PlanEcon Report*, Vol.IX, Nos.44-45, p.39.

[35] For a description of this programme, see Bozidar Djelic and Natalie Tsukanova, "Voucher Auctions: A Crucial Step towards Privatization, *RFE/RL Research Report*, Vol.2, No.30, 23 July 1993, pp.10-18.

[36] The State Committee for the Administration of State Property (Goskomimushchestvo).

[37] See section 5.3 below.

[38] On the need for transparent industrial policies in transition economies see United Nations Economic Commission for Europe, *Economic Survey of Europe in 1992-1993*, United Nations, New York, 1993, pp.15-17.

even in Germany, the Treuhand has had to face a shortage of managerial talent. Of course, the scale of the problems facing the Treuhand was greatly increased by the speed at which German monetary union took place: east German wages rose rapidly towards western levels while productivity remained at the previous, relatively low level, thus making much of the capital stock unprofitable. Nevertheless, the success of the Treuhand, as well as the current difficulties of other transition economies, suggests the need for a coordinated strategy incorporating: a clear, de-politicized policy towards enterprise and industrial restructuring, including specific measures to reduce the burden of accumulated enterprise debt; a programme to re-capitalize the banks and to privatize them; and a significant increase in infrastructure spending on transport and communications. Since most of the transition economies would need outside help to pursue these objectives, they effectively constitute a set of priorities for revised programmes of official assistance.

The outlook for 1994

The recovery that got under way in 1993 in several countries of eastern Europe now seems very likely to continue in 1994. Growth is set to continue in Poland at around 4 per cent and a recovery is expected to emerge in Slovenia and the Czech Republic with growth rates of perhaps 1 to 2 per cent. The outlook is more problematic for Hungary, where forecasts range between a continued fall in output and a mild recovery, and for Romania where the recent austerity programme agreed with the IMF seems likely to produce zero growth this year. In Bulgaria and Slovakia large domestic imbalances imply at best a year of stagnation or even another fall in output. In the states of the former Yugoslavia, other than Slovenia, the fall in output is likely to continue, although in Croatia, at least, at a lower rate than in 1993. Altogether, aggregate output in eastern Europe might rise in 1994, perhaps by a modest 1 per cent, but it would be the first year of growth since the collapse of the old system.

There seems to be little chance of the decline in output in Russia and most of the other CIS countries coming to an end in 1994. In Russia, the key question is whether the paralysis in macroeconomic policy, which has characterized most of the past year, can be overcome in order to provide some chance of meeting the targets, recently agreed with the IMF, for reducing inflation and the federal government's budget deficit. If the deficit target is met, the probable reduction in subsidies to state-owned enterprises might lead to a much larger cut in output than the 8-10 per cent currently envisaged by the government. If the deficit target is *not* met, the chances of a significant fall in the inflation rate are reduced and the continued supply of IMF funding placed at risk. In Ukraine and Belarus there seems little prospect at present of any effective programmes of macroeconomic stabilization being put into place and neither the fall in output nor the extremely high rates of inflation – which were moving across the threshold of hyperinflation in the last quarter of 1993 – are likely to be halted in the near future.

In eastern Europe the economic recovery in a small group of countries is a great relief to policy makers, but it must also be recognized that it is still very fragile, and given the depth of the recession, also very modest. Inflation rates and budget deficits remain high and government policies are still constrained by the need to reduce them. Moreover, the recovery of domestic demand has led to a rapid deterioration in the external accounts of many countries. There are a number of reasons for this, including in some cases an overvalued exchange rate. But it also seems likely that in the early stages of recovery a transition economy will have a high propensity to import both capital and consumer goods, because of the limitations of domestic production capacity. At the moment the countries most affected do not appear to be facing immediate difficulties in financing their current account deficits, but this is typically a situation that can change very quickly.

As far as the external economic environment is concerned, there should be some improvement in 1994. In western Europe economic growth is expected to pick up to some 1.5 per cent after falling by 0.1 per cent in 1993. Although there is quite a wide range of forecasts for Germany, GDP growth in this all-important market for eastern economies is likely to be some 0.5-1 per cent this year, a modest but distinct improvement on the 1.3 per cent fall last year. Although the recovery in the western market economies is exceptionally slow compared with previous upturns, there should nevertheless be a recovery in import demand; also, inflationary pressures are expected to remain weak and, together with continuing intense competition in world markets, this should help to keep the dollar prices of machinery and other imports into the transition countries fairly stable. Economic recovery in the west may also help to weaken the forces demanding protection from eastern imports – or help to stiffen the resistance of the authorities to such demands.

A major improvement in the external economic environment was the successful completion in December 1993 of the Uruguay Round of multilateral trade negotiations.[39] Its major achievements are the creation of the World Trade Organization (WTO), which finally provides the third pillar of the international institutional framework envisaged by Maynard Keynes at Bretton Woods in 1944; and the extension of GATT rules and disciplines into new or previously exempt areas. The GATT's coverage is now much more extensive, both in the coverage of trade and of trading countries.

The transition economies will benefit from the strengthening of GATT rules and authority, especially if this leads to much stricter control of anti-dumping procedures and other forms of contingent protection.

Previous issues of this *Survey* and the *Economic Bulletin for Europe* have repeatedly expressed the view

---

[39] For a review of the negotiations and an analysis of the Draft Final Act, see United Nations Economic Commission for Europe, *Economic Bulletin for Europe*, Vol.45 (1993), New York and Geneva, 1994, chapter 6, pp.3-5.

that both the volume and the coordination of international assistance for the transition economies has not been commensurate with the scale and complexity of the problems to be overcome. Those views are now shared by a growing number of observers, many of whom have expressed increasing concern over the past year at the rapid deterioration of the economic situation in a number of transition economies, especially among the former members of the Soviet Union, and the associated risks of social and political instability. However, these outbursts of anxiety often lead to hasty promises of action and assistance which either fail to materialize or fall considerably short of expectations. The perception of a growing gap between the rhetoric of assistance and its reality is a source of disillusion for much of the population in many of the eastern countries and provides useful ammunition to the various groups opposed to the transition process itself.

A recent proposal which addresses some of the concerns expressed by the ECE secretariat was made by the Director General of the GATT. Emphasizing the need for a new, high-level framework to coordinate communication and cooperation on economic matters, he stated the problem by posing the question: "Why should the problems of Russia, for instance, be discussed simultaneously but in comparative isolation from each other in the G7, the OECD, the GATT, the World Bank, the IMF, the EBRD, and so on? ... It might be reasonable if it were particularly effective – but, especially on the trade side, I do not think these discussions have done much to answer even Russia's problems".[40]

Another indication of increasing concern about the inadequacy of existing arrangements and policies is that the Commission of the EU is currently engaged in a fundamental reassessment of its policies towards central and eastern Europe. Among the proposals being discussed, apparently, is one to channel more aid into infrastructure projects and, another, to reduce or eliminate subsidies on EU exports of foodstuffs to transition economy markets.[41]

However, it is vitally important that improved mechanisms for international coordination address not only the question of avoiding duplication among the many sources of international assistance but also the more fundamental issues of coordinating short-term stabilization with long-term structural adjustment programmes and of targeting aid within coherent national programmes for economic reconstruction and development. Such programmes are needed not only to demonstrate coherence in a government's various policies for effecting the transition, which is inevitably a long-term operation, but also to generate a better understanding of the aims of the transition process on the part of national electorates whose support is essential for success. It is also vital to follow the wisdom of the Marshall Plan administrators, in the late 1940s, in insisting that such programmes for economic transformation are the primary responsibility of the countries themselves. This not only acknowledges that national administrators are usually better informed about local economic conditions than outsiders, but also the fact that such programmes are political and social programmes reflecting national preferences for one set of social and institutional arrangements over another. To regard the transition process as simply an economic problem which can be left to technical experts is to risk the loss of popular support for the entire process of reform. Nevertheless, to obtain international assistance, national programmes will need to be seen to be coherent and have a good chance of success. Such evaluation should be transparent and carried out in an international framework, such as that noted above, and along the lines of the peer-group examination of the post-war west European programmes that took place within the OEEC.

Another advantage of an improved international structure to coordinate the efforts of all the actors, both national and international, in the transition process, would be to promote a more rapid adjustment of assistance in order to confront key problems and bottlenecks as they arise. A number of problems have already been mentioned which require urgent attention. These include the inter-related issues of enterprise indebtedness, the solvency of the banks and the restructuring of large industrial enterprises, as well as the need to improve the physical infrastructure. Not all of these were anticipated four years ago and it is reasonable to assume that unforeseen obstacles to the transition will continue to arise. A framework in which an annual review of progress in the national transition programmes can be conducted in an open and rigorous manner would not only help to improve coordination but also to increase the flexibility and speed of response to the changing needs of the transition countries.

It would be unwise to assume that these proposals are now unnecessary for those countries where a recovery of output is under way. As is stressed in this *Survey*, the problems of structural change and macroeconomic stability are still considerable in these economies, and the fragility of the recovery could soon be tested by the increasing resistance of the labour force to further reductions in real wages. It would be more prudent to assume that new problems will arise rather than that they have all been overcome.

The signs of a serious reappraisal of the policies of international assistance for the transition economies are well-timed and very welcome: if they lead to concrete action to deal with the broader issues of coordination raised in this *Survey* over the past four years, they will help to consolidate the fragile recovery of the leading transition group of countries and improve the chances of the others eventually joining it.

---

[40] "Global Trade – The Next Challenge", address by Peter D. Sutherland to the World Economic Forum, Davos, 28 January 1994. The text is published in GATT, *News of the Uruguay Round*, NUR 082, Geneva, 28 January 1994.

[41] As reported in the *Financial Times*, 7 March 1994. Of course, in some eastern countries where agricultural supply has been constrained consumers will have benefited in the short-run from EU export subsidies.

Chapter 2

THE MARKET ECONOMIES

2.1 Expectations, policies, outcomes

(i) Overview of developments in 1993

Recession in western Europe and Japan ...

For the past year western Europe has been in one of the severest recessions of the post-war period. Indeed, for several countries the depth of the cyclical downturn has been unprecedented in their post-war economic history. Nevertheless, for the west European countries combined real GDP fell, only slightly, by 0.1 per cent compared with 1992 (table 2.1.1). This was the first absolute decline in output since 1975, when there was a fall of 0.4 per cent. But the aggregate figure conceals sizeable falls in output in a number of individual countries.

The recession has persisted in Japan against a backdrop of severe imbalances in the business sector. The potential stimulus provided by the three fiscal packages introduced between August 1992 and September 1993 has apparently only partially offset the forces restraining private sector demand. In addition, exports were affected by the strong appreciation of the yen and the recession in western Europe.

... but recovery gains momentum in North America

In North America, the recovery gained strength in the second half of 1993 led by strong consumer and investment demand, both of which responded to very low interest rates. There was a striking surge of activity in the United States in the final quarter of 1993 which appears to have continued in the first quarter of 1994. For 1993 as a whole, real GDP rose by 3 per cent (table 2.1.1).

For the industrialized countries combined, real GDP rose by only 1.2 per cent in 1993, declining output in western Europe and stagnation in Japan being more than offset by the favourable economic developments in North America.

Disinflation continues ...

Against a background of falling prices in international commodity markets, inflationary pressures remained subdued in the western market economies in 1993. Weak domestic demand, high margins of idle production capacity, and moderate wage increases due to the deterioration in the labour markets were the main factors behind the slow-down in the average rate of inflation in western Europe to 3.3 per cent in 1993 (table 2.1.1). Year-on-year increases in consumer prices in the final months of 1993 were the smallest for about thirty years. Within the overall inflation rate, price increases in services continued to run above average. In many countries increases in public administered prices, partly a reflection of efforts to consolidate public sector finances, were a major source of upward pressure on the overall price level.

In the United States inflationary pressures remained rather low in 1993, mainly a reflection of falling world market prices for energy and raw materials and strong productivity gains in manufacturing industry, which were only partly offset by increases in labour costs. In the event, the annual inflation rate was 3 per cent, unchanged from 1992 (table 2.1.1). With output set to continue growing faster than the expansion of capacity, more of the slack in the economy will disappear in 1994, suggesting that the process of disinflation probably bottomed out in 1993.

... and labour market problems get worse in western Europe

The sharp cyclical downswing has led to a considerable deterioration in the labour market in western Europe, where total employment fell by about 1.5 per cent in 1993. The loss of jobs was concentrated in industry, but a noteworthy feature is that the services sector is no longer offsetting, as it has done in the past, all or part of the decline in industrial employment. Indeed, employment in services has also started to fall against a background of weak demand and a perceived need for restructuring in order to reduce cost pressures. Against this background the number of persons unemployed in western Europe rose by some 2 million to an average of nearly 19.5 million in 1993. The average unemployment rate was 10.3 per cent compared with 8.9 per cent in 1992 (table 2.1.1).

In the United States employment growth picked up in 1993, a reflection not only of the strengthening of output growth in the course of the year but also of the usual lag between changes in output and the demand for labour over the growth cycle. The unemployment rate fell to 6.7 per cent in 1993.

The unemployment problem has taken on worrisome dimensions. Of particular concern is the incidence of long-term and youth unemployment. About ten million, or one third, of all persons recorded as unemployed in the western market economies in the ECE region are less than 25 years of age. Data for the four major west European economies suggest that at least some 25-30 per cent of the unemployed have been out of work for at least one year, with a low probability of finding a new job.

TABLE 2.1.1

Macroeconomic indicators for western Europe and the United States, 1991-1994
(Percentage change over previous year)

	1991	1992	1993	1994
Western Europe				
Real GDP	1.2	1.1	-0.1	1.5
Inflation [a]	4.9	4.0	3.3	..
Employment [b]	0.1	-0.6	-1.6	-0.5
Unemployment [c]	8.1	8.9	10.3	11
General government financial balance [d]	-4.3	-5.2	-6.9	-6.5
Current account balance [d]	-0.8	-0.8	-0.2	..
United States				
Real GDP	-0.7	2.6	3.0	3.5
Inflation [a]	4.2	3.0	3.0	..
Employment [b]	-1.1	0.2	1.5	1.8
Unemployment [c]	6.6	7.3	6.7	6.3
General government financial balance [d]	-3.4	-4.5	-3.6	-2.5
Current account balance [d]	-0.1	-1.1	-1.7	..

Source: ECE/DEAP based on national and international statistics.

[a] As measured by the consumer price index.
[b] Employment based on national accounts statistics.
[c] As a percentage of total labour force.
[d] As a percentage of GDP.

The bulk of job losses in industry over the last decade or so has fallen on male workers employed in sectors which are characterized by below average skill- and technology-intensity. Also many of the young persons entering the labour force fail to find a job because of lack of proper education and training which matches the requirements of the business sector (see section 2.4).

International trade slows down

The recession in western Europe was reflected in a sharp fall in import demand in 1993 which, given the importance of intraregional trade, was also reflected in falling exports. Weak import demand in western Europe, in turn, has been a major factor in a further slow-down in the volume growth of world trade. International trade was supported, however, by continuing strong import demand in North America and the developing countries. The volume of world trade is estimated to have grown by some 2.5 per cent in 1993 following an increase of 4.5 per cent in 1992. But this estimate is surrounded by an unusually large margin of uncertainty because of the problems encountered by member states of the European Union with the introduction of a new trade reporting system (Intrastat) at the beginning of 1993, which is believed to have led to a general underestimation of trade flows (see section 2.5).

Against a background of recession, there have been favourable changes in the current accounts of most west European countries, with either deficits falling or surpluses increasing. For western Europe as a whole the current account was in broad balance in 1993 (table 2.1.1).

In the United States the surge in the demand for foreign goods was the main factor behind a sharp rise in the current account deficit to some $110 billion corresponding to 1.7 per cent of GDP in 1993.

A changing policy mix

The stance of monetary policy in western Europe has become more relaxed in the wake of the crisis in the ERM in September 1992. Short-term interest rates started to fall and long-term rates fell further. But short-term rates fell more than long-term rates and this has gradually led to a flattening of the yield curve which, nevertheless, remained inverse in many countries until the end of 1993. For countries within the ERM the pace of interest rate reduction was restrained, however, by the cautious policy of the Bundesbank. Tensions in the ERM continued in the first half of 1993, possibly reflecting financial market perceptions that exchange rate targets were incompatible with domestic economic conditions. These tensions culminated in heavy speculative pressures on several currencies at the end of July and led governments to widen the fluctuation margins within the ERM from 2 August 1993.

Although this decision increased the autonomy of monetary policy in the individual member countries of the ERM, the increased scope for lowering interest rates relative to German rates was hardly used: the objective of keeping exchange rates in the vicinity of their previous central bilateral parities remained unchanged. In any case, tensions in the foreign exchange markets receded in the second half of the year.

In the United States the relaxed stance of monetary policy was maintained and short-term interest rates hardly changed in the course of 1993. But against a background of buoyant economic activity the Federal Reserve increased the federal funds rate in early February 1994 in order to signal its determination to prevent a rekindling of inflationary pressures.

Fiscal policies in western Europe were mainly directed at restraining a further rise in already large government budget deficits, but this proved to be difficult in a recession. There was a general rise in government budget deficits in western Europe to an average of about 7 per cent of GDP in 1993, largely a consequence of the operation of the built-in stabilizers, which supported domestic demand. In the United States fiscal policy continued to be restrictive, a reflection of the overriding objective of curbing the structural budget deficit.

(ii) Factors in recent economic performance

A major feature of the current economic situation is the striking desynchronization of the international business cycle, with much of western Europe struggling to get out of recession while recovery has already gained considerable momentum in North America.

Forecasts prepared in late 1992 had actually projected a modest pick-up in the business cycle in western Europe in 1993 and a further strengthening of economic growth in the United States. In the event, western Europe slipped into recession, while the recovery in the United States was stronger than expected.

CHART 2.1.1

Consumer and business confidence in the European Community and the United States, January 1991-January 1994

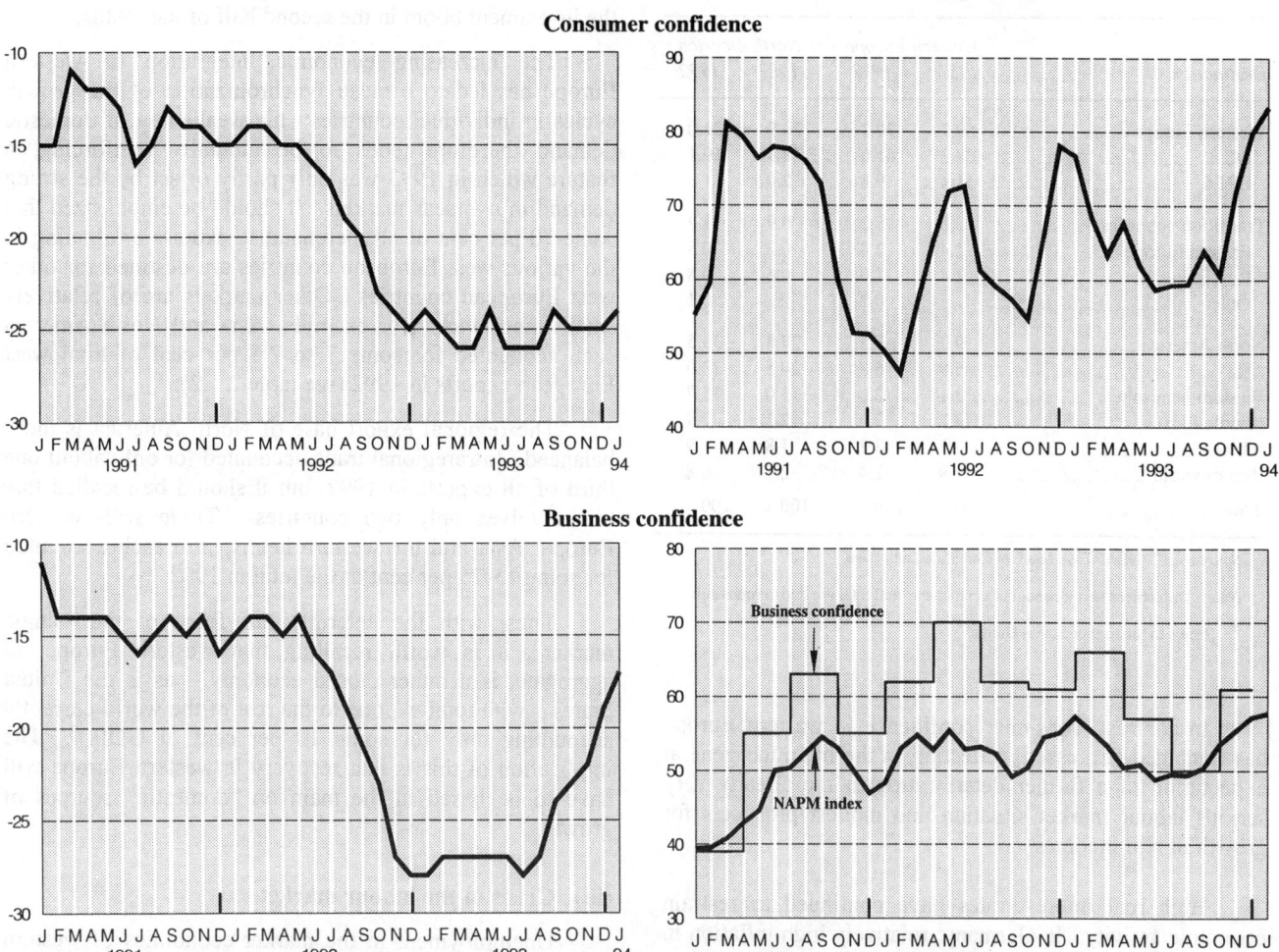

Sources: Data for the EC are from Commission of the European Communities, European Economy, Supplement B, monthly; United States: Consumer confidence index complied from United States Department of Commerce, Survey of Current Business, monthly; Business confidence: direct communications from the Conference Board, New York; NAPM index: direct communication from the National Association of Purchasing Management, Arizona.

Note: EC data show net balances between respondents giving positive and negative answers to specific questions. Data for business confidence refer to industry. For details see any edition of the source. United States: Consumer and business confidence according to the Conference Board. Consumer confidence is measured in index form with base year 1985=100. Business confidence is complied on the basis of answers to specific questions, with the following scale applying: 100 = substantially good; 75 = moderately good +; 50 = moderately good —; 25 = moderately bad; 0 = bad. The National Association of Purchasing Management (NAPM) Index pertains to the business situation in manufacturing industry. An index value above (below) 50 indicates that manufacturing industry is generally expanding (contracting). The data are seasonally adjusted.

In the *United States* the favourable economic performance in 1993 was mainly due to the stimulus which a very relaxed monetary policy provided to interest-sensitive components of demand, namely business fixed investment, housing and consumer durables. The policy of low interest rates was also instrumental in providing a conducive environment for balance sheet restructuring in the private sector. There has been considerable progress in this respect in the corporate and financial sectors. The average debt-income ratio is still very high in the private household sector but low interest rates – notably on mortgages – have greatly eased the debt service burden. Against the backdrop of a marked strengthening of the recovery in the second half of 1993, business climate in industry and consumer confidence rose in January 1994 to their highest levels of the past three years and this will continue to support domestic demand (chart 2.1.1).

In *western Europe* the disappointing performance reflects the interplay of several factors.

The sharp cyclical downswing was associated with steep falls in business and consumer confidence in western Europe in the second half of 1992. In fact, consumer confidence was more depressed than in the previous cyclical trough in 1981-1983, although industrial confidence remained slightly above its previous low point. In the second half of 1993, however, business confidence began to recover (chart 2.1.1): the decline in output had bottomed out, inventories had been adjusted to more comfortable levels, and there was a gradual improvement of export prospects. Also the fact that the recovery was gaining momentum in the United States may have strengthened the assessment that the trough of the cycle had been crossed in the first half of the year.

TABLE 2.1.2

Geographical structure of merchandise exports of western Europe and North America, 1987 and 1992

(Percentage share)

Destination	Western Europe 1987	Western Europe 1992	North America 1987	North America 1992
Western Europe	69.7	70.7	20.9	21.0
EC	58.3	61.0	18.9	19.1
EFTA	11.4	9.8	2.0	1.9
Transition countries	2.8	3.2	0.9	1.2
Eastern Europe	1.4	2.0	0.3	0.3
Russia	1.4 [a]	1.0	0.6 [a]	0.8
Other	..	0.2	..	0.1
North America	9.7	7.3	37.8	33.5
Asia	5.9	6.8	20.5	23.0
Western hemisphere	3.1	3.0	13.0	15.7
Middle East	3.2	3.4	2.3	2.9
Africa	3.7	3.2	1.8	1.9
Rest of world	1.9	2.4	2.7	0.8
Total	100	100	100	100

Source: ECE/DEAP based on UN Comtrade Data Base.

Note: Differences between sum of components and total are due to roundings.

[a] Refers to the former Soviet Union.

In contrast, consumer confidence in western Europe has remained depressed, reflecting in the main the general expectation of a further deterioration in the already very serious labour market situation and modest prospects for growth in real incomes.

High real interest rates have continued to restrain economic activity. In Germany, relatively high inflation in the wake of the unification boom and growth in money supply far above the Bundesbank's target range had led to a significant tightening of monetary policy until summer 1992. The ensuing rise in interest rates was propagated to the rest of western Europe via the ERM and intensified the recession.

Recovery from the recession has subsequently been protracted by the cautious policy of interest rate reductions pursued by the Bundesbank since September 1992, a caution which was not anticipated by the other west European countries. One reason for the disappointing outcome in western Europe in 1993 was the unexpected severity of the recession in west Germany, the weakness of domestic demand being reinforced by the faltering of demand from abroad.

Although the process of balance sheet adjustment, triggered in several countries by asset price deflation against a background of high debt-income ratios, has made progress, this nevertheless continued to restrain both consumers' demand and bank lending. Moreover, high and rising unemployment in conjunction with low earnings growth depressed real disposable incomes and this was reflected in very low consumer confidence. Households have increased savings against a background of increasing uncertainty about future incomes.

Finally, the business sector responded to high real interest rates and the faltering of demand by cutting investment, although the sharp downturn of fixed investment should also be seen against the background of the investment boom in the second half of the 1980s.

The increasing economic integration of western Europe has led to a close synchronization of the growth cycles in individual countries: the weakening of domestic demand therefore tends to be mutually reinforcing, a feature which in 1993 was only partly offset by the strong demand in overseas markets. It should be emphasized that some 70 per cent of all merchandise exports originating in the various west European countries are destined for other west European countries. Other markets are of relatively small importance: for example, Asia and North America each accounted for some 7 to 7.5 per cent of total west European exports in 1992 (see table 2.1.2).

The regional export base of North America is more balanced. Intraregional trade accounted for only about one third of all exports in 1992, but it should be recalled that this involves only two countries. Trade with western Europe, Asia and the western hemisphere each accounted for some 15-25 per cent of the total in 1992.

Thus, with the entering into force of the "single market", it is worth recalling that western Europe, in aggregate, is a rather closed economy – as is the United States – with total exports to the rest of the world currently accounting only for some 10 per cent of GDP.[42] The implication of this is that recovery in western Europe will have to be based in the main on "domestic" sources of growth.

(iii) **Crisis in the labour market**

Unemployment in the market economies of western Europe and North America is now approaching a total of 30 million people. With the recovery having gained considerable momentum, the situation in the North American labour market started to improve in 1993 and this is set to continue in 1994. In contrast, with only very modest growth prospects, the problem is bound to deteriorate further in western Europe in 1994. Indeed, there are fears that the crisis in the labour market could prove intractable even in the medium term. It is therefore not surprising that the target of full employment is being given much greater attention than it has received in the past decade or so from policy makers.

The dismal state of the west European labour markets reflects the combined effect of cyclical and structural factors, the relative importance of which varies from country to country.

---

[42] The share of exports of goods and services in GDP in 1992 was about 28.5 per cent for all west European countries combined. Based on the above figures, it can be assumed that some 65-70 per cent of these exports are intraregional trade flows, giving a share of 8.5-10 per cent of GDP for exports to the rest of the world. For the United States the corresponding share of exports in nominal GDP was about 10.5 per cent in 1992.

Clearly, part of the recent fall in employment will be offset in the next recovery but it is also probable that the level of structural unemployment will increase further.

Much of the structural unemployment seems to be accounted for by unskilled male workers, the demand for which has fallen relative to the demand for skilled workers. A factor in this adverse trend appears to be labour costs outpacing productivity which led to capital-labour substitution, a feature which was accentuated by technological progress. Another factor is the increasing competition from developing countries and, more recently, from the transition countries in the field of low-skilled, standardized tradeable goods. Given the sizeable wage differentials, there is hardly any possibility of western Europe defending its competitiveness in this area. Nor is it in the longer-term interest of the western industrialized countries to erect protectionist barriers against these changes in the pattern of relative comparative advantage.

The currently high profile of labour market problems was underlined when the EU heads of government met in December 1993 to consider the White Paper on employment, competitiveness and growth issued by the European Commission in spring 1993[43] and, more recently, by a special G-7 meeting of ministers on employment problems, which was held in Detroit in March 1994. These discussions have tended, however, to focus mainly on the structural component of unemployment, a reflection of the very narrow scope seen for a more expansionary policy in western Europe. Accordingly, policy prescriptions have stressed the need for more effective education and training and some mix of labour market reforms. But evidently the problem of how to regain full employment touches on a much wider range of issues such as international competitiveness, the role of public investment, and the perceived need to preserve established standards of social security and welfare.

The striking differences in labour market performance between western Europe and North America cannot in any case be reduced to the issue of output growth alone. In fact, over the period 1970-1993 the average annual rate of economic growth has been identical (at 2.5 per cent), temporary cyclical deviations being offset over the whole period (chart 2.1.2). But over the same period employment rose at an average annual rate of 1.7 per cent in the United States and about 0.5 per cent in western Europe.

The mirror image of this differential employment growth is the much better productivity performance in western Europe with its attendant benefit of rising real incomes (chart 2.1.2). Roughly 80 per cent of the output gains in western Europe over the period 1970-1993 are accounted for by increased labour productivity, which compares with a figure of about 30 per cent for the United States. In other words, an additional percentage point increase in west European output is generated with a significantly smaller growth in demand for labour than in the United States.

CHART 2.1.2

Output, employment and unemployment in western Europe and the United States, 1970-1993

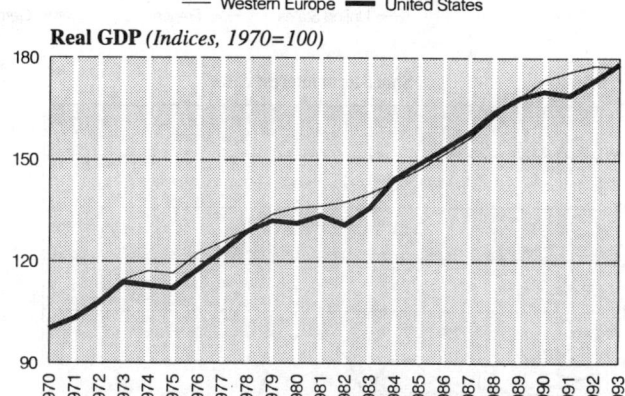
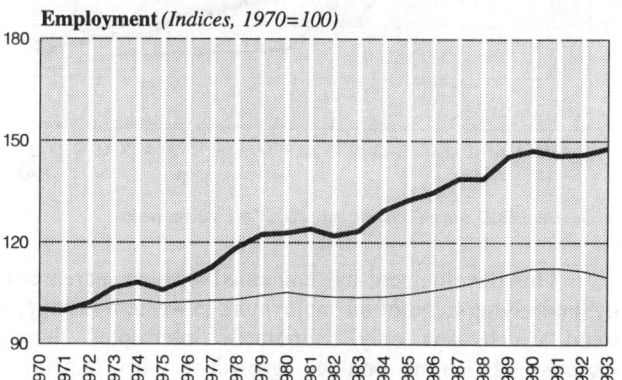
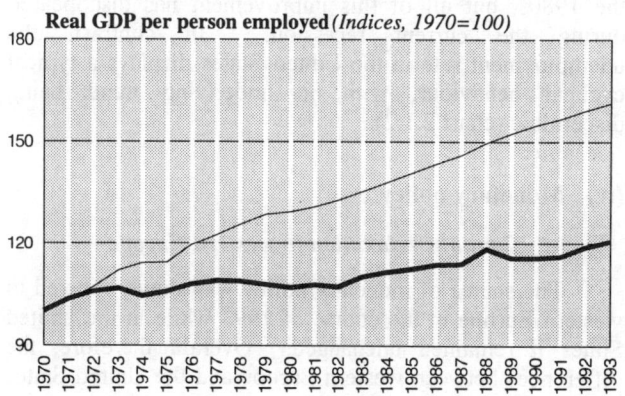

Source: ECE/DEAP based on national and international statistical publications.

---

[43] See section 2.4 below.

CHART 2.1.3
Nominal short-term and long-term interest rates in western Europe and the United States,
January 1992-January 1994
(Per cent)

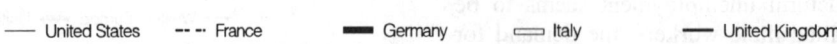

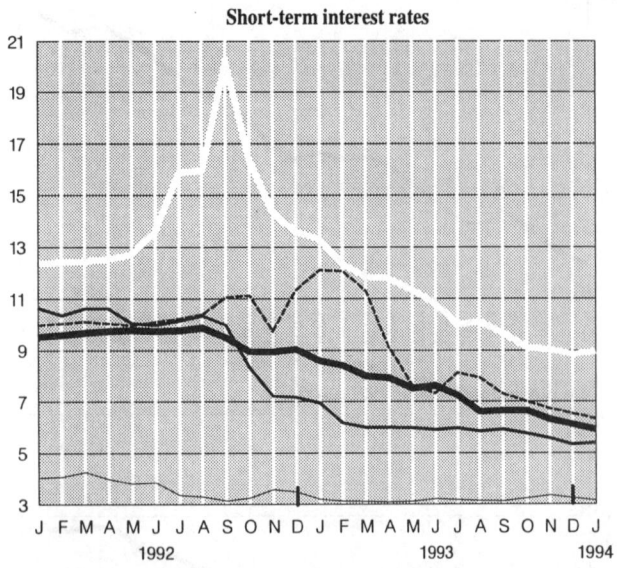
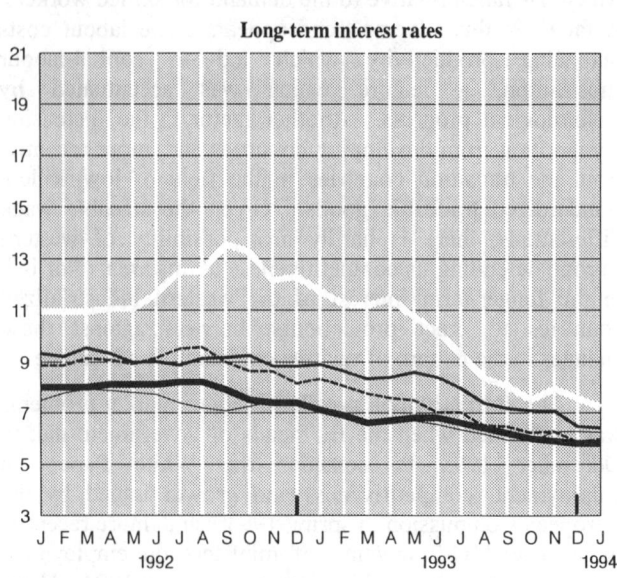

Source: OECD, Main Economic Indicators, Paris, various issues.

This development has coincided with an increase in the underlying trend of unemployment in western Europe, a trend which was only temporarily interrupted during periods of strong output growth. In fact, the unemployment rate fell significantly in the second half of the 1980s, but all of this improvement has disappeared during the current recession. In contrast, the unemployment rate in the United States displays a typical cyclical behaviour, with no underlying trend being discernible (chart 2.1.2).

(iv) Monetary policy

Cautious relaxation in western Europe

The stance of monetary policy was slowly relaxed in western Europe in the course of 1993 while in the United States it remained unchanged. Overall, therefore, the differences between western Europe and the United States narrowed in the course of 1993.

The Bundesbank cut the discount rate, which provides a floor to short-term money market rates, in five consecutive steps from 8 per cent in February 1993 to 5.75 per cent in October 1993. In February 1994 there was a further cut, taking the rate to 5.25 per cent. Compared to previous recessions, however, the stance of monetary policy is still rather tight. During the recession of 1975 the discount rate was cut to 3.5 per cent. The easing of German monetary policy is reflected in the decline in short-term interest rates from 8.6 per cent in January 1993 to 5.9 per cent in January 1994.

Short-term interest rates have also fallen in the other west European countries where, given the exchange rate constraint, official interest rates are lowered more or less in tandem with those in Germany.

In the United Kingdom, monetary policy was substantially eased in autumn 1992 following the suspension of membership in the ERM, a policy which was accompanied by a significant depreciation of sterling. The official base rate was reduced from 8 per cent in November 1992 to 6 per cent in January 1993 but remained at that level for the rest of the year. Only in February 1994 did the authorities decide on a further, albeit very small, cut to 5.75 per cent. The economic significance of the latter is rather small and should probably be seen as a stimulus to consumer confidence given the expected contractionary impact on disposable incomes of the tax increases to be enacted in April 1994.

Short-term rates in the United Kingdom, which had been significantly below German rates at the beginning of 1993, did not decline significantly in the course of the year and at the beginning of 1994 were only 0.5 percentage points lower than German rates, compared with 1.6 percentage points a year earlier.

The convergence of short-term rates in western Europe towards German rates is illustrated in chart 2.1.3. At the beginning of 1994 nominal short-term rates were below German rates in a number of countries (Finland, the Netherlands, the United Kingdom and Switzerland). Nevertheless, short-term rates are still quite high in real terms in a number of countries, amounting to more than 4 per cent in France and Italy in early 1994 compared with some 2.5 per cent in Germany. Among the west European countries they fell below German rates only in Switzerland.

Nominal long-term rates, which cannot be directly influenced by the monetary authorities, have also fallen in western Europe against a background of recession and reduced inflationary expectations (chart 2.1.3). The latter were probably influenced by widespread plans – under way

CHART 2.1.4

Approximate term structure of interest rates in the four major west European economies and the United States, January 1992-January 1994: Long-term rates less short-term rates
(Percentage points)

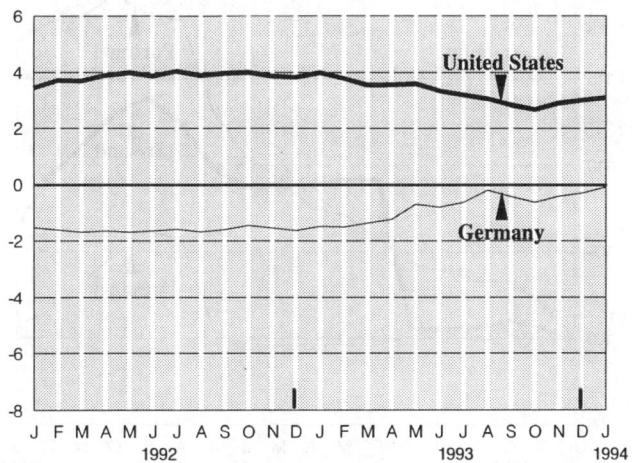
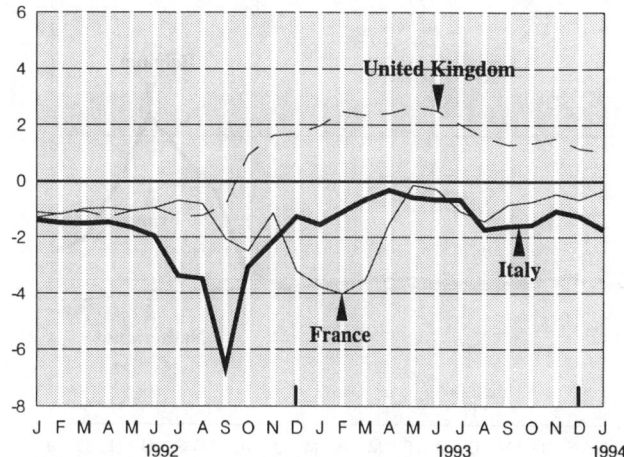

Source: ECE/DEAP based on OECD, *Main Economic Indicators*, Paris, various issues.

or announced – to curb large budget deficits and high levels of public sector debt. Nominal long-term rates fell below 6 per cent in late 1993 in France and Germany, but given the inflation differential real rates were still close to 4 per cent in France, but only slightly above 2 per cent in Germany.

Against a background of tight monetary policy the *term structure of interest rates* has been inverted over the last three years in Germany, with short-term rates exceeding long-term rates. This structure is usually perceived as favouring business investment in short-term financial assets rather than fixed capital formation. The yield curve has flattened out in the course of 1993 and at the beginning of 1994 the negative gap between long-term and short-term rates was virtually closed. The extent of the inversion of the yield curve has differed considerably among the west European countries, partly a reflection of the extent to which exchange rate pressures required increases in short-term rates to defend existing parities (chart 2.1.4).

US monetary policy

In the United States short-term interest rates hovered around 3.1 to 3.2 per cent in the course of 1993; in real terms they were negative during the first six months of the year and were only 0.5 per cent in January 1994. But the monetary authorities have been careful to forestall any rekindling of inflationary pressures and, against a background of strong output growth and a marked rise in industrial capacity utilization, the Federal Reserve increased the federal funds rate by 0.25 percentage points at the beginning of February 1994.

The decline in long-term rates continued during the first three quarters of 1993, a development which was influenced by the budget consolidation programme of the new administration. But the decline appears to have bottomed out in October 1993 when rates rose above 6 per cent. The backdrop to this was the pronounced strengthening of economic growth in the second half of the year which probably raised expectations of gradually rising inflationary pressures (chart 2.1.3).

Short-term rates continued to be significantly below long-term rates in 1993, a reflection of the accommodating stance of monetary policy in conjunction with subdued inflationary pressures (chart 2.1.4).

Given the relative changes in interest rates in the United States and Germany, the gap in favour of German short-term financial assets has sizeably narrowed, while for long-term rates the difference is now in favour of US assets. These changes have been reflected in the bilateral exchange rate: the US dollar tended to appreciate in the course of 1993 (chart 2.1.5), a tendency which is generally expected to continue in 1994, given that US interest rates are expected to continue to edge upwards.

CHART 2.1.5

Average monthly bilateral exchange rates between Germany, Japan and the United States, January 1992-January 1994
(Indices, August 1992=100)

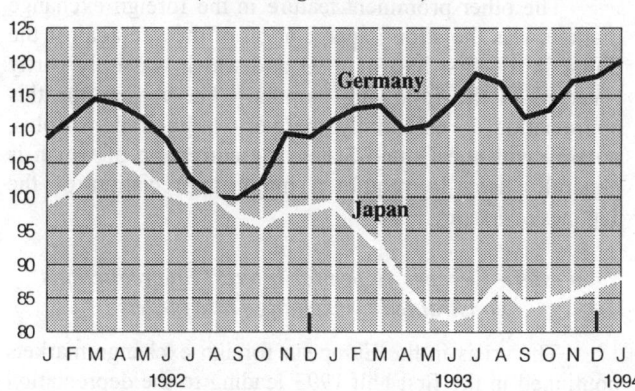

Source: Deutsche Bundesbank.

Note: National currency units per US dollar.

CHART 2.1.6

Average monthly bilateral exchange rates in western Europe, August 1992-January 1994 [a]

(Indices, August 1992=100)

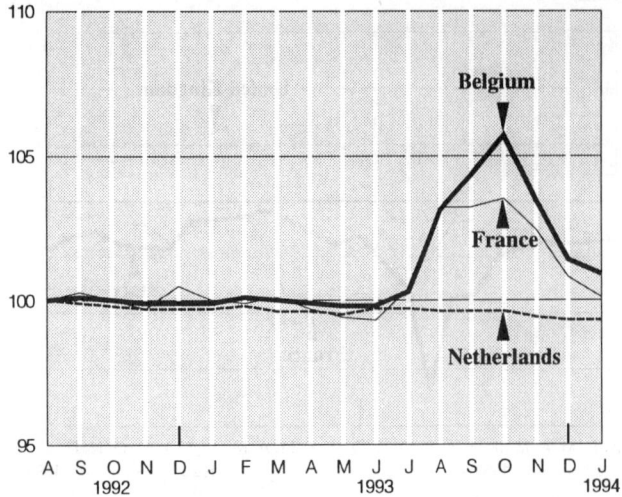
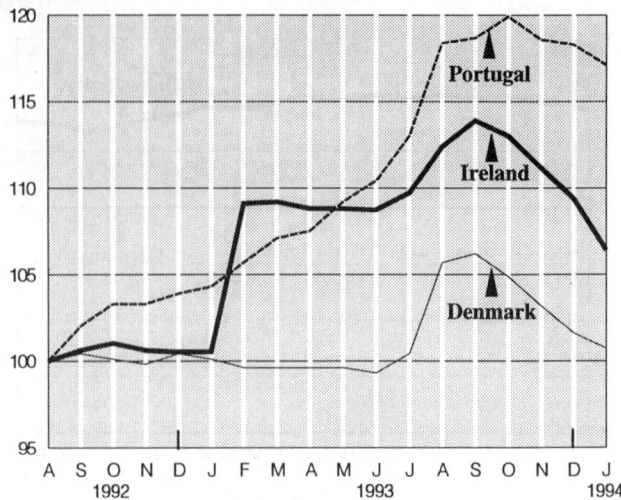
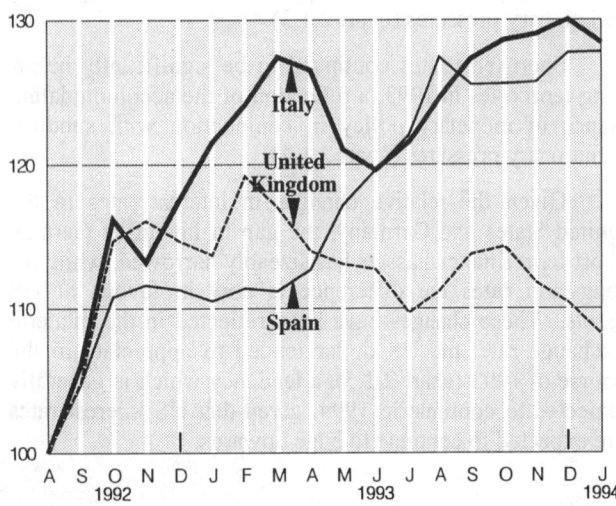
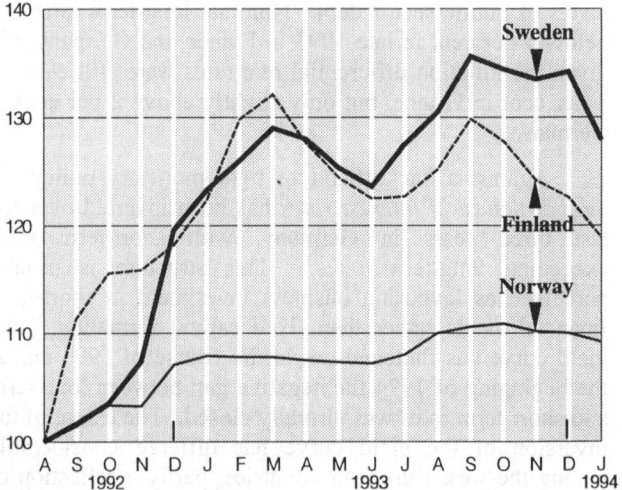

Source: Deutsche Bundesbank.

[a] Units of national currency per deutsche mark.

The other prominent feature in the foreign exchange markets was the strong appreciation of the yen against the dollar in the first half of 1993 and which was only partly reversed in the following months. The reason for this appreciation is essentially the very large trade surplus, notably with the United States, the correction of which is generally seen to require a major appreciation of the Japanese currency.

Western Europe: Scope for interest rate reductions constrained by exchange rate targets

The crisis in the European foreign exchange markets continued in the first half 1993 leading to the depreciation of the Irish pound in January and of the Portuguese escudo and the peseta in May 1993. But tensions remained because of perceptions that the cautious reduction of interest rates in Germany, at the given exchange rate structure, was entailing inappropriately high interest rates in other countries given the prevalence of high unemployment. There was also an increasing hesitancy on the side of the Bundesbank to provide short-term financing facilities for supporting currencies which had come under heavy selling pressure, given their distortionary effects on the German money supply.

To this has to be added the unwillingness of certain countries to consider realignment, a reflection of their concerns about the future credibility of their monetary policies.

Against a background of heavy speculative selling pressures against the Belgian franc, the Danish krone, the French franc and the Portuguese escudo the decision was taken on 2 August to widen the existing permissible fluctuation margins from ±2.25 per cent and ±6 per cent to

±15 per cent around central bilateral parities, which remained unchanged. The only exception is the exchange rate between the deutsche mark and the Netherlands guilder which, in a separate bilateral agreement between the two governments, will be maintained within the old narrow band of ±2.25 per cent.

The enlargement of the fluctuation margins was announced as a temporary measure only, but it is tantamount to a *de facto* demise of the old ERM. When and how a return to the old system will be possible is not clear. More generally, the crisis in the ERM has led to questioning the timetable for introducing a common European currency by 1999.

With the widening of the fluctuation margins the tensions in the European currency markets receded. Expectations that countries which had been constrained by the policy of the Bundesbank would now use the opportunity to lower significantly their interest rates were disappointed. There were also fears that countries might embark on a process of competitive devaluations, but that too did not occur.

Instead most west European countries pursued a cautious interest rate policy aimed at limiting the deviations from the central parities. Thus the overall stance of monetary policy continued to be relaxed more or less in tandem with moves by the Bundesbank. In the immediate wake of the enlargement of the fluctuation margins there was a general tendency for the deutsche mark to appreciate against the major west European currencies. This appreciation, however, was largely reversed later on. Also, the pound sterling and other currencies outside the ERM appreciated against the deutsche mark in the final months of 1993. In fact, the average level of the pound sterling in January 1994 was close to that in September 1992, when it was withdrawn from the ERM (chart 2.1.6).

(v) Fiscal policy

There was a further large deterioration in the financial balances of the government sector in *western Europe* in 1993. The general government budget deficit is estimated to have increased, on average, to some 7 per cent of GDP which compares with 5.2 per cent in 1992. However, the continuing rise in budget deficits in 1993 did not so much reflect an underlying change in the stance of fiscal policy as the working of the automatic stabilizers: declines in sales and incomes were reflected in lower tax revenues, while the deterioration in the labour market led to higher transfer payments, notably unemployment benefits. Given that the cyclical downturn was much stronger than projected in the budgets adopted in late 1992, actual deficits were sometimes considerably larger than planned. Chart 2.1.7 illustrates the evolution of the general government deficits since 1980, notably the marked deterioration in public finances since 1989.

Given the size of budget deficits, the scope for fiscal policy to support economic activity beyond the working of the automatic stabilizers is narrowly circumscribed since the larger part of the actual budget deficits is of a structural rather than a cyclical nature. Although estimates of

CHART 2.1.7

General government financial balances in western Europe and the United States, 1980-1993
(Per cent of GDP)

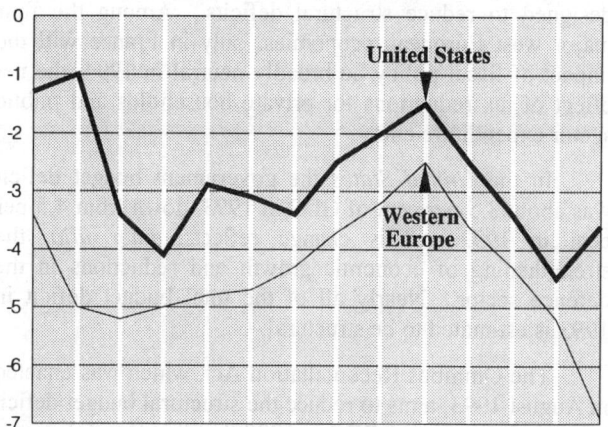

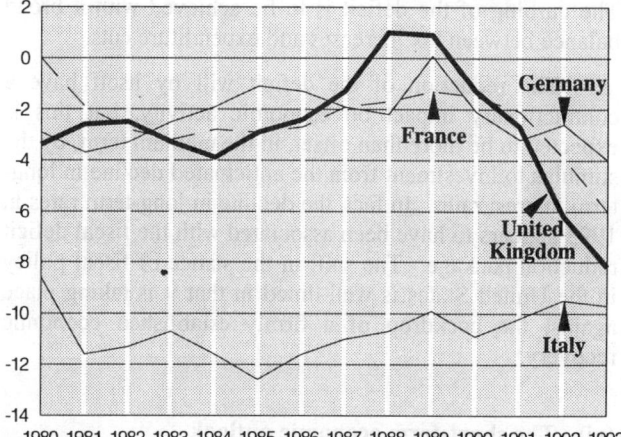

Source: OECD, *Economic Outlook*, December 1993, Paris.

structural deficits are surrounded with a relatively large margin of error, the magnitudes suggest that even after a return to high activity levels the problem of fiscal consolidation will remain acute.[44] The need to reduce deficits has also been increased by attempts to meet the Maastricht convergence criteria. It is against this backdrop that fiscal policy has failed to perform an active anti-cyclical policy in western Europe in 1993.

Nevertheless, in some countries fiscal policy was expansionary in 1993, the result of earlier measures designed to support output and employment. This was true of Denmark, Norway and the United Kingdom. In France the new government adopted a number of measures to restrain the rise in unemployment, but the net effect is likely to be small, given the more or less simultaneous introduction of other measures designed to raise government revenue.

---

[44] According to OECD estimates the structural component of the general government budget deficits corresponded, on average, to some 5 per cent of GDP in 1993. See OECD, *Economic Outlook*, No.54, Paris, December 1993, p.152, table A 27.

The prospect for 1994 is for a general tightening of fiscal policy in western Europe with a concomitant contractionary effect on output. Most of the restrictive measures to be implemented are part of medium-term plans designed to reduce structural deficits. Among the four major west European economies, only in France will the impact of fiscal policy be broadly neutral in 1994, the net effect of tax reductions for private households and public sector expenditure cuts.

In the *United States* the government budget deficit was about 3.5 per cent of GDP in 1993, down from 4.5 per cent in 1992. This change reflects, *inter alia,* the strengthening of economic growth and reductions in the defence sector. Nearly all of the total budget deficit in 1993 is estimated to be structural.

The Omnibus Reconciliation Act, which was enacted in August 1993, aims to reduce the structural budget deficit to some 2 per cent of GDP in 1998, but this target does not take account of the planned reform of the health service.[45] The curbing of the deficit is to be achieved with a broad balance between tax increases and expenditure cuts.

The reduction of the deficit will by itself have a contractionary impact on economic activity, but this is expected to be more than offset, in the medium term, by the stimulus to investment from the anticipated decline in long-term interest rates. In fact, the decline in long-term rates in 1993 appears to have been associated with the fiscal deficit reduction package. The shift in the stance of fiscal policy in the United States is well-timed in that it is taking place against the backdrop of a firmly established economic recovery.

(vi) The short-term economic outlook

The short-term outlook is for a modest cyclical recovery of output in *western Europe,* with all the major components of domestic demand remaining sluggish. Private consumption will continue to be held back by moderate or zero growth in real incomes against a background of falling employment and considerable wage restraint. In many countries hopes for a strengthening of household demand are therefore based on the assumption that the impact of weak income growth on purchasing power will be offset by a fall in savings. But this is very uncertain given the depressed state of consumer confidence and the expectation of a further deterioration in the labour market. No support is likely to come from public consumption given the tightening of fiscal policy. Fixed investment will remain weak against a background of large margins of excess capacity. The downturn of the inventory cycle has apparently bottomed out, and with a moderate improvement in the overall economic environment, there might be some increase in stockbuilding. As has so often been the case in the past, hopes for a recovery from recession are largely pinned on a gradual, but sustained, strengthening of net exports in 1994.

The demand for foreign goods within western Europe, however, is unlikely to strengthen significantly, given the pervasive weakness of domestic demand. In contrast, export demand from overseas markets should remain robust, a reflection of the continuing rapid economic growth in developing countries and strong import demand from the United States. Some support to domestic activity levels could also derive from the gains in European price competitiveness as a result of the expected appreciation of the US dollar in the course of 1994: the demand for dollar-denominated assets is set to increase given the favourable economic performance relative to western Europe and the increase in US short-term interest rates resulting from the expected tightening of monetary policy.

Real GDP in western Europe is expected to rise on average by some 1.5 per cent in 1994, a rate of increase which is too low to prevent a further fall in employment. Unemployment will therefore increase to record levels in 1994. Inflationary pressures are likely to remain subdued against a background of weak domestic demand and moderate growth in labour costs.

Economic policy will have an ambivalent impact on activity levels in western Europe in 1994. Fiscal policy will act as a drag on domestic demand given the widespread efforts to curb structural budget deficits. In contrast, the stance of monetary policy is expected to ease further. This shift in policy mix, however, is not without risks.

Against a background of high budget deficits it is evident that the scope for fiscal policy has been virtually exhausted and the need for fiscal consolidation over the medium term cannot be questioned. But the overall economic situation in western Europe is still very fragile and the significant fiscal tightening envisaged at the present stage in the cycle might well be counterproductive by restraining the forces making for a gradual recovery.[46] In this respect, the timing of the tightening of US fiscal policy is more appropriate in that it is occurring when the recovery is already well under way.

It remains to be seen to what degree these procyclical and contractionary fiscal effects will be offset by the indirect stimulus from lower long-term interest rates.

The balance of risks is also influenced by the speed at which short-term interest rates will continue to fall and, given existing exchange rate targets, this is largely determined by the Bundesbank. Inflationary pressures have been subsiding in Germany against a background of recession and the moderate outcome of the recent wage negotiations will accentuate these favourable trends. But the money supply target may be more difficult to meet. Also the underlying tendency of the dollar to appreciate against the deutsche mark could restrain the downward tendency of German short-term interest rates, given that a too rapid depreciation would risk an outflow of international capital and a rise in import prices.

---

[45] See *Economic Report of the President*, transmitted to the Congress February 1994, Washington, 1994, p.37.

[46] See also United Nations Economic Commission for Europe, *Economic Bulletin for Europe*, Vol.45 (1993), New York and Geneva, 1994, pp.35-36.

Nevertheless, the larger fluctuation margins within the ERM now provide countries with greater room for manoeuvre to decouple from German monetary policy by lowering their interest rates below German rates. Thus, if the Bundesbank continues – as is likely – with its cautious approach to lowering interest rates, the conflict between exchange rate targets and the policies appropriate for domestic economic conditions could become more acute.

In the *United States* the cyclical upswing will continue: real GDP is likely to increase by some 3.5 per cent in 1994, supported mainly by private consumption and business fixed investment. Fiscal policy will be tight and monetary policy has started to move from a relaxed to a more neutral stance. The slight upward pressure on short-term interest rates will probably be accentuated in the course of 1994 given that the expansion of output can be expected to lead to a significant reduction in spare capacity.

In *Japan* the recession appears to be gradually bottoming out, but only very weak growth can be expected in 1994.

Thus, for the western industrialized countries as a whole, real GDP growth this year is likely to be only slightly above 2 per cent.

2.2 Output and the components of demand

(i) Output

The pronounced contraction in economic activity, which started in *western Europe* in the second half of 1992, bottomed out in the spring of 1993. The end of the cyclical downturn, however, was not tantamount to the beginning of recovery: instead, there was a general tendency for economic activity to stagnate during the rest of the year.

Quarter-to-quarter changes in *real GDP* in France, Germany and Italy illustrate the fragile state of the west European economies in the second half of 1993 (table 2.2.1). After brief periods of modest output growth, partly reflecting temporary and involuntary stock accumulation, there were disappointing setbacks: real GDP fell again in Italy in the third quarter and in Germany in the final quarter of 1993. In France output growth slowed down to virtual stagnation in the last months of the year.

In contrast, in the United Kingdom, which has been out of phase with the general west European business cycle since the second half of 1990, the recovery continued in 1993 and strengthened in the course of the year. However, the upturn has been rather moderate so far: real GDP in the final quarter of 1993 was still 0.5 per cent below its cyclical peak in the second quarter of 1990.

In the *United States* the recovery gained considerable momentum in the second half of 1993 (table 2.2.1). Growth in real GDP accelerated between the third and final quarters to 1.7 per cent, equivalent to an annual rate of 7 per cent.[47]

In Canada, economic conditions improved markedly, reflecting, in the main, strong growth of exports to the US market and increased business investment.

Hopes that the recession had come to an end in *Japan* in the first quarter of 1993 were disappointed by a renewed downturn in the second quarter. Domestic demand continues to be restrained by the slow-down in income growth and balance sheet adjustments in the corporate and financial sectors. Export growth has fallen sharply because of the strong appreciation of the yen and weak demand in western Europe.

The degree of cyclical desynchronization among the major seven industrialized economies was thus accentuated in the course of 1993, with the recovery gaining momentum in North America and the United Kingdom and the other four economies struggling to get out of recession (chart 2.2.1).

Real GDP in western Europe in 1993 is currently estimated to have fallen slightly, by 0.1 per cent, after two years of output growth at just over 1 per cent (table 2.2.2). The performance in 1993 was the worst since 1975, when total output fell on average by 0.4 per cent against the background of the first oil price shock. In the United States real GDP rose by 3 per cent in 1993, the highest growth rate since 1988. Overall economic activity levels stagnated in Japan in 1993 compared with the preceding year, thus ending a period of 18 years of uninterrupted economic growth, which began after the recession of 1974, when real GDP fell by 0.6 per cent.

For the western industrialized countries taken together annual GDP growth slowed down to 1.2 per cent in 1993, falling output in western Europe and Japan being more than offset by growth in North America.[48]

For western Europe this was the third consecutive year when growth in actual output was significantly below the increase in potential output, which is probably around 3 per cent.[49] The degree of slack in the west European economy has thus increased considerably and this is mirrored in the labour market statistics, which show large falls in employment and sharp increases in unemployment.

The recession is widespread. Real GDP fell in 10 out of 17 west European countries in 1993 (table 2.2.2). Among the four largest economies, real GDP rose only in the United Kingdom. The largest falls were in Finland and Sweden, where total output fell by more than 2 per cent. The major drag on economic activity in western Europe stemmed from the deep recession in west Germany: real GDP declined by nearly 2 per cent though this was partly offset by the continuing recovery of output (an increase of 6.5 per cent) in the eastern part of the country. The share of east Germany in GDP of the whole German economy is still very small, however, amounting to some 7.5 per cent in 1993,[50] which compares with an employment share of about 17.5 per cent. Real GDP in the whole German economy therefore still fell by a considerable 1.3 per cent.

In contrast, the recession was much milder in France and Italy, where real GDP declined by less than 1 per cent. However, the sharp cyclical downswing in west Germany has to be seen in the perspective of the post-unification boom which led to a cumulative increase of 10.5 per cent in real GDP in 1990-1991.

---

[47] The presentation of quarterly changes in GDP in terms of annual rates is of long standing in the United States, but there tends, on occasion, to be confusion about the meaning of such figures. Real GDP in the final quarter of 1993 was 3.1 per cent higher than in the same quarter of 1992. The annual rate of 7 per cent is obtained by extrapolating the simple quarter-to-quarter percentage change over the next four consecutive quarters at a compound rate. This means that if the economy continues to grow at the same rate (1.7 per cent) as in the final quarter of 1993 then real GDP in the final quarter of 1994 would be 7 per cent higher than in the equivalent period of 1993. Given that the base period is the third quarter, this implies at the same time that output levels in the second half of 1994 would have increased by the same proportion over the equivalent period of 1993. The transformation of quarterly changes into annual rates is intended to facilitate comparison with standard year-to-year growth rates.

[48] Growth rates of regional aggregates are calculated on the basis of country weights derived from 1990 GDP data expressed in purchasing power parities (see box 2.2.1).

[49] Broadly speaking, potential output is defined as the output level that can be attained when the available capital stock is fully utilized. This implicitly assumes normal intensity of factor use to avoid excessive inflationary pressures.

[50] The aggregate change in west European output in 1992 and 1993 is therefore not very sensitive to the inclusion or exclusion of east Germany. Thus, real GDP in western Europe fell by 0.2 per cent, instead of 0.1 per cent, in 1993 if east Germany is excluded.

TABLE 2.2.1

Quarterly changes in real GDP,[a] 1992-1993
(Percentage change over preceding period)

	1992				1993			
	QI	QII	QIII	QIV	QI	QII	QIII	QIV
France	0.8	-0.1	0.1	-0.3	-0.7	0.1	0.4	0.2
Germany [b]	1.4	-	-0.4	-1.0	-1.8	0.7	1.0	-0.7
Italy	0.5	0.3	-0.5	-0.5	-0.2	0.7	-0.5	..
United Kingdom	-0.9	0.2	0.4	0.3	0.6	0.7	0.7	0.8
4 countries above	0.6	0.1	-0.1	-0.4	-0.7	0.5	0.5	..
United States	0.9	0.7	0.8	1.4	0.2	0.5	0.7	1.7
Canada	-	-	0.1	0.7	0.7	0.8	0.5	0.9
Japan	0.5	-0.5	-0.1	-0.3	0.9	-0.5	0.3	-0.6
7 countries	0.7	0.3	0.4	0.6	0.1	0.3	0.6	..

Source: National statistics.

[a] At market prices, data are seasonally adjusted.
[b] West Germany.

CHART 2.2.1

Real GDP in the seven major industrialized economies, 1990-1993
(Percentage change over the same quarter of previous year)

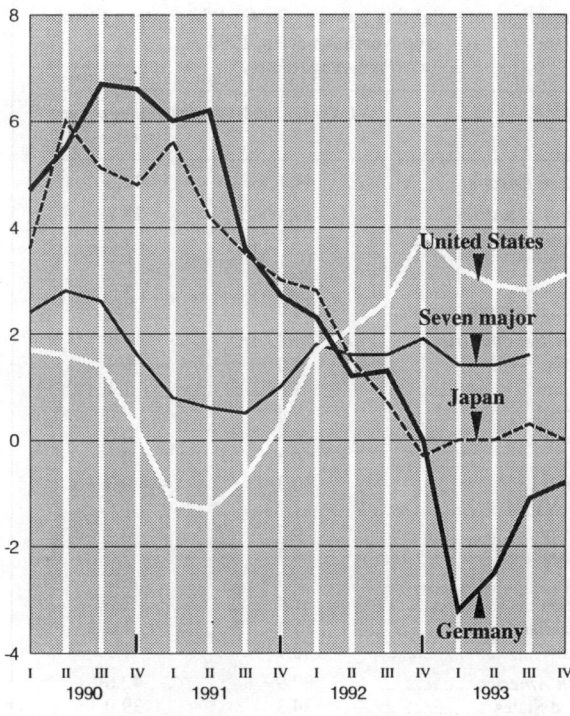
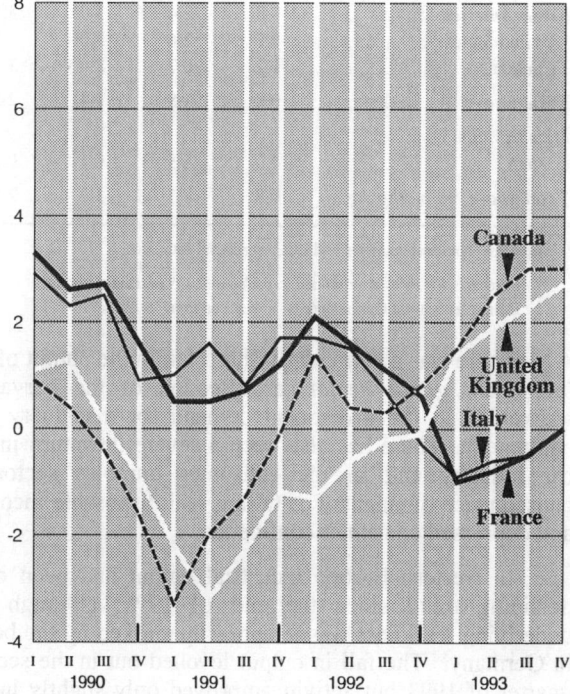

Source: National statistics.

Note: Data for Germany pertain to west Germany.

For Finland and Sweden the recession has already lasted for three years and has taken a heavy toll of the economy. In Finland real GDP in 1993 was 13 per cent lower than in 1990, the deepest recession experienced by this country in this century. In Sweden GDP declined by 5 per cent over the same period, much less than in Finland, but still the worst Swedish economic crisis since the Second World War. But in both countries the economic downturn appears to have finally bottomed out in the course of 1993.

Industrial output and capacity utilization

Industrial output[51] fell by 2.5 per cent in *western Europe* in 1993, the third consecutive year of decline (table 2.2.3).

Industrial exporters found some offset to weak domestic demand in western Europe in more buoyant overseas markets, notably those in South-East Asia, China and North America, but in general it was not sufficient to prevent a fall in total output.

---

[51] Industry excluding construction.

TABLE 2.2.2

Real GDP in western Europe and North America, 1991-1994
(Percentage change over previous year)

	1991	1992	1993	1994 [a]
Western Europe	1.2	1.1	-0.1	1.5
4 major countries	1.3	1.1	-0.3	1.0
France	0.7	1.4	-0.7	1.0
Germany [b]	4.5	2.1	-1.3	0.5
Italy	1.3	0.9	-0.7	1.0
United Kingdom	-2.2	-0.5	2.1	2.5
13 smaller countries	1.2	1.2	0.2	2.0
Austria	3.0	1.6	-0.5	1.5
Belgium	1.9	1.4	-1.2	1.0
Denmark	1.0	1.2	0.2	3.0
Finland	-7.1	-3.8	-2.6	1.0
Greece	3.3	0.9	0.5	1.0
Ireland	2.6	4.6	2.2	4.0
Netherlands	2.1	1.4	0.2	1.0
Norway	1.9	3.3	2.5	3.0
Portugal	2.1	1.6	-0.4	2.0
Spain	2.2	0.8	-0.8	1.5
Sweden	-1.1	-1.9	-2.1	2.0
Switzerland	-	-0.1	-0.6	1.0
Turkey	0.3	5.9	7.0	5.0
North America	-0.8	2.4	3.0	3.5
United States	-0.7	2.6	3.0	3.5
Canada	-1.7	0.7	2.4	3.5
Total above	0.2	1.8	1.4	2.5
Memorandum item:				
Japan	4.0	1.3	0.1	0.5
Total above, including Japan	0.8	1.7	1.2	2.0

Sources: National statistics and ECE secretariat estimates.

[a] Forecasts for 1994 are rounded to the nearest 0.5 percentage point.
[b] Data refer to total Germany (east + west) as from 1992.

There was a particularly sharp fall in the output of the *investment goods sector*, a reflection of the pervasive weakening in the investment demand for machinery and equipment. There has also been a severe downturn in the car industry and in the consumer durables sector, a consequence of stagnant or falling real disposable incomes and depressed consumer confidence.

In western Europe industrial output had been on a declining trend since the end of 1990, although the underlying weakness was temporarily masked by the boom in Germany. The fall in output levelled out in the second quarter of 1993 but activity improved only slightly in the second half of the year (see chart 2.2.2).

Industrial output fell in the majority of west European countries in 1993, but there were large differences in the annual growth rates (table 2.2.3). By far the largest decline in output (about 7.5 per cent) was in west Germany, a reflection of its strong specialization in investment goods. In contrast to the general picture, industrial activity was relatively buoyant in Finland, Ireland and Turkey in 1993. In Finland this was due to exports, which were boosted by strong gains in price competitiveness on account of the depreciation and wage moderation. Ireland continued to benefit from its strong specialization in high-tech goods, for which demand remained buoyant; and a consumption boom was the main factor behind the surge in output in Turkey.

BOX 2.2.1

Growth rates of GDP in this section have been calculated as weighted averages of the relative changes in the individual countries. The weights used for aggregating these growth rates have been derived from 1990 GDP data converted from national currency units into US dollars using purchasing power parities. Growth rates for the major components of demand were derived in a similar fashion, using their 1990 values as weights. Purchasing power parities are preferred to the use of nominal exchange rates in calculating regional aggregates because they provide a better approximation to international differences in price levels. The table below compares 1990 GDP weights based on exchange rates with those based on purchasing power parities and illustrates the impact on regional growth rates for recent years. It can be seen that the recession in western Europe in 1993 is somewhat more pronounced (a decline in real GDP by 0.3 per cent) if weights are derived on the basis on exchange rates rather than purchasing power parities (a decline of 0.1 per cent).

Comparison of weighting patterns for GDP in western Europe and North America, 1990
(Percentage share)

	Exchange rates	Purchasing power parities
Western Europe	44.1	42.0
4 major countries	30.3	28.7
France	7.4	6.9
Germany [a]	10.1	8.9
Italy	6.8	6.5
United Kingdom	6.0	6.4
13 smaller countries	13.8	13.3
Austria	1.0	0.9
Belgium	1.2	1.1
Denmark	0.8	0.6
Finland	0.8	0.6
Greece	0.4	0.5
Ireland	0.3	0.3
Netherlands	1.7	1.7
Norway	0.7	0.5
Portugal	0.4	0.6
Spain	3.0	3.2
Sweden	1.4	1.0
Switzerland	1.4	1.0
Turkey	0.7	1.3
North America	37.9	42.6
United States	34.3	39.0
Canada	3.6	3.6
Japan	18.1	15.3
Total above	100.0	100.0
Annual growth rates of real GDP		
Western Europe		
1991	1.3	1.2
1992	1.0	1.1
1993	-0.3	-0.1
Total above		
1991	1.0	0.8
1992	1.5	1.7
1993	0.8	1.1

Source: ECE/DEAP based on national statistics and OECD, *Main Economic Indicators*, Paris, various issues.

[a] Total east and west Germany.

CHART 2.2.2

Quarterly index numbers of industrial output in western Europe and the United States, 1989-1993
(1985=100)

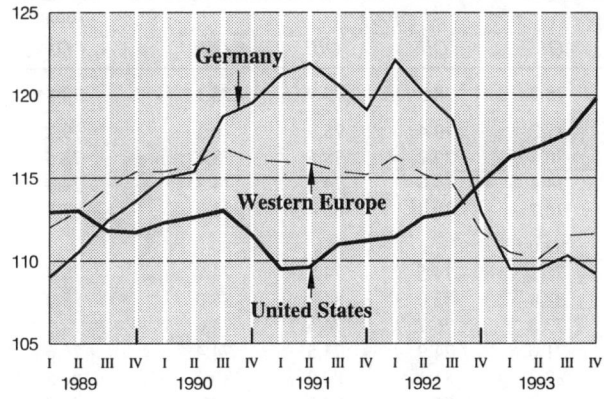
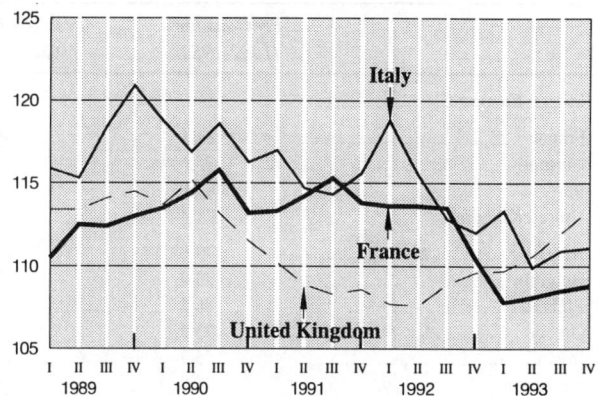

Sources: ECE/DEAP based on national statistics and OECD, *Main Economic Indicators*, Paris, various issues.

Note: Data for Germany pertain to west Germany.

TABLE 2.2.3

Industrial output in western Europe and North America, 1991-1993
(Percentage change over previous year)

	1991	1992	1993 [a]
Western Europe	-0.3	-0.9	-2.5
4 major countries	-0.4	-1.3	-3.0
France	-0.1	-1.1	-3.5
Germany [b]	2.9	-1.9	-7.5
Italy	-2.1	-1.6	-2.5
United Kingdom	-4.0	-0.5	2.5
13 smaller countries	-0.1	-	-0.5
Austria	1.6	-1.1	-2.0
Belgium	-2.0	-0.1	-5.5
Denmark	..	..	..
Finland	-9.8	2.5	5.0
Greece	-1.4	-1.2	-2.0
Ireland	3.2	9.3	5.5
Netherlands	3.9	0.2	-1.0
Norway	2.1	6.4	4.0
Portugal	0.1	-2.4	-5.0
Spain	-0.7	-2.9	-4.5
Sweden	-5.6	-4.0	2.0
Switzerland	0.5	-0.5	-
Turkey	1.8	4.2	8.0
North America	-2.0	2.2	4.5
United States	-1.9	2.4	4.5
Canada	-3.7	0.4	5.0
Total above	-1.2	0.6	1.0
Memorandum item:			
Japan	1.8	-5.7	-4.5
Total above, including Japan	-0.6	-0.6	-

Sources: National statistics; OECD, *Main Economic Indicators*, Paris, various issues and ECE secretariat estimates.

[a] Preliminary estimates rounded to the nearest 0.5 percentage point.
[b] West Germany.

The industrial recession is mirrored in a considerable fall in *capacity utilization rates* in western Europe. But the cyclical trough was apparently reached in summer 1993, when the average utilization rate was some nine percentage points lower than its previous cyclical peak (table 2.2.4).

In the *United States* industrial output rose by 4.5 per cent in 1993, buoyant demand for investment goods (including motor cars) and consumer durables being the main factors behind the acceleration. In manufacturing industry, actual output rose more or less in tandem with capacity output for most of the year. But utilization rates rose markedly in the final quarter of 1993 as a result of a surprisingly strong acceleration in output growth (table 2.2.4).

(ii) **The components of demand**

Viewed from the demand side the recession in *western Europe* reflects above all the weakening of domestic demand against a background of relatively tight fiscal and monetary policies.

Given the high degree of economic integration of the west European countries, weaker domestic demand spilled across the borders to other countries in the region. In fact, the rather close synchronization of growth cycles is the logical implication of an intensified division of labour within an increasingly unified market. The reverse mechanism can be observed during a cyclical upswing.

An important factor in the current downturn was the sharp decline in *import demand* in west Germany, which restrained economic activity not only in those smaller west European countries for which the German market has traditionally taken a large share of their total exports (e.g., Austria, Belgium, Denmark, the Netherlands and Switzerland), but also in France, Italy and the United Kingdom.

TABLE 2.2.4

Capacity utilization rates in manufacturing industry in western Europe and North America, 1982-1994 QI

(Per cent)

	Previous low (1982-1983)	Previous high (1988-1990)	1993 [a]				1994 [a]
			QI	QII	QIII	QIV	QI
Western Europe	..	87.2	78.7	78.5	77.9	78.1	78.8*
France	81.1	86.8	81.2	79.4	78.9	79.1	79.2
Germany	75.6	89.5	80.5	79.2	78.5	78.1	78.5
Italy	69.0	80.0	74.4	74.6	74.3	74.3	74.4
United Kingdom	71.4	94.8	76.7	80.8	80.4	81.7	83.5
Austria [b]	79.0	85.0	82.0 [c]	..	..	80.0	..
Belgium	73.8	82.2	75.3	74.5	74.5	74.9	76.4
Finland [d]	86.5	88.0	82.0	82.0	84.0	84.0	85.0
Greece	73.5	78.9	77.8	76.7	74.4	74.6	74.1
Ireland	55.7	78.7	71.6	74.9	73.5	74.4	76.6
Netherlands	75.8	86.2	82.2	81.1	80.3	80.5	80.5
Portugal	..	84.4	75.2	75.0	72.9	72.6	74.8
Spain	..	81.7	73.9	73.9	71.1	72.1	75.7
Sweden	79.7	89.0	81.4	82.2	82.3	82.7*	83*
Switzerland	80.1	88.5	79.4	79.5	80.0	80.3	80.5*
North America							
United States	70.0	85.1	80.1	80.1	80.3	81.5	82.5*
Canada	65.2	84.8	78.5	78.4	78.6	78.8*	79*

Sources: Belgium, France, Germany, Greece, Ireland, Italy, Netherlands, Portugal, Spain, United Kingdom: Commission of the European Communities, *European Economy, Supplement B*, February 1994, Table 1 (data refer to January, April, July and October); Sweden: *Allman Manadsstatistik*, No.2, 1994; Canada and the United States: OECD, *Main Economic Indicators*, No.2, 1994, Paris; Austria: *Oesterreichisches Institut für Wirtschaftsforschung, Monatsberichte No.1*, 1994, and previous issues; Switzerland: *Bundesamt für Statistik, La vie économique*, No.02, 1994, and previous issues; Finland: *Bank of Finland Monthly Bulletin No.1*, 1994.

[a] Quarterly rates are seasonally adjusted (Sweden: unadjusted).
[b] Data refer to November of each year.
[c] Data refer to November 1992.
[d] Only semi-annual data are available.

The sizeable exchange rate changes which have occurred in western Europe since summer 1992 have had an ambivalent economic impact on the region as a whole: in countries with depreciating currencies they supported net export growth to other west European countries and to markets outside the region, while the reverse holds for the others. The size and sign of the net effect on total west European output, however, is uncertain.

In the event, total domestic demand in western Europe fell by 1 per cent in 1993. This was almost entirely due to the sharp decline in *fixed investment*, which was accentuated by the continuing downturn in the inventory cycle, which started in 1991. There was little offset to these adverse changes from private consumption or from government consumption, which in general was neutral in its effect on output growth. The fall in domestic demand, however, was to a large degree offset by changes in the real foreign balance with imports falling in absolute terms by much more than exports. The net outcome was that real GDP fell by only 0.1 per cent in 1993 (table 2.2.5).

In the *United States* domestic demand responded to the very low interest rates brought about by the expansionary stance in monetary policy: the components of demand such as consumer durables, business and residential investment, which are sensitive to interest rates, were the main sources of higher economic growth in 1993. Government purchases, as in 1992, had a mildly depressing effect on domestic activity levels. Given the differential strength of domestic and foreign demand, the deficit in the real foreign balance rose significantly in 1993 and this subtracted about 1 percentage point from the growth of nearly 4 per cent in domestic demand (table 2.2.5).

Private consumption

Against a background of mounting unemployment and depressed consumer confidence, private households' spending on consumer goods was very subdued in *western Europe*: it rose by only 0.5 per cent in 1993, the smallest increase since 1982. The average, however, masks significant cut-backs in real expenditures in a number of countries (table 2.2.6). The main factor behind the sluggish consumer demand was a pronounced slow-down in the growth of nominal incomes, the combined effect of falling employment levels and moderate wage increases. In some countries (notably France, Germany and Italy) policy measures designed to restrain the growth of the public sector budget also curbed the growth in net incomes. The built-in stabilizers, in the form of rising unemployment benefits, provided a partial offset to these adverse factors.

The continuing disinflation tempered the impact of the deceleration in the growth of nominal disposable incomes on the real purchasing power of households. Nevertheless, aggregate real disposable incomes in western Europe were broadly unchanged in 1993 as compared with 1992, when there had been an increase of some 1.5 per cent. Among the four major economies real disposable incomes did, in fact, decline in Germany and Italy. Among the smaller economies they fell in Finland (by 6 per cent), Sweden and Switzerland.

TABLE 2.2.5

Contribution of domestic demand and the net foreign balance to annual changes of real GDP, 1992-1993
(Percentage points)

	Domestic demand		Net foreign balance		GDP	
	1992	1993	1992	1993	1992	1993
Western Europe	1.3	-1.0	-0.1	0.9	1.1	-0.1
4 major countries	1.3	-1.4	-0.2	1.1	1.1	-0.3
France	0.5	-1.0	0.9	0.3	1.4	-0.7
Germany	2.7	-1.4	-0.6	0.1	2.1	-1.3
Italy	1.0	-4.9	-0.1	4.1	0.9	-0.7
United Kingdom	0.3	1.2	-0.9	0.5	-0.5	1.7
13 smaller countries	1.2	-0.2	0.1	0.5	1.3	0.2
Austria	1.6	-0.1	-	-0.4	1.6	-0.5
Belgium	2.5	-2.2	-1.1	1.0	1.4	-1.2
Denmark	-0.6	0.7	1.9	-0.5	1.2	0.2
Finland	-5.8	-7.1	2.1	4.5	3.8	-2.6
Greece	1.0	0.8	-	-0.3	0.9	0.5
Ireland	-1.4	1.1	6.0	1.1	4.6	2.2
Netherlands	1.3	0.3	0.1	-	1.4	0.2
Norway	0.5	2.7	2.8	-0.2	3.3	2.5
Portugal	4.9	1.6	-3.3	-2.0	1.6	-0.4
Spain	1.2	-3.9	-0.4	2.9	0.8	-1.0
Sweden	-2.2	-5.0	0.3	2.9	-1.9	-2.1
Switzerland	-3.1	-1.6	2.9	0.8	-0.1	-0.6
Turkey	8.4	12.9	-2.5	-5.9	5.9	7.0
North America	2.6	3.7	-0.2	-0.7	2.4	3.0
United States	2.9	3.9	-0.3	-0.9	2.6	3.0
Canada	-	1.8	0.8	0.5	0.7	2.4
Total above	1.9	1.3	-0.2	0.1	1.8	1.4
Memorandum item:						
Japan	0.6	0.4	0.7	-0.3	1.3	0.1
Total above, including Japan	1.7	1.2	-0.1	-	1.7	1.2

Source: National statistics.

Note: Differences between total changes in GDP and sum of components are due to rounding.

TABLE 2.2.6

Real private consumption expenditures in western Europe and North America, 1991-1993
(Percentage change over previous year)

	1991	1992	1993
Western Europe	1.8	1.8	0.5
4 major countries	1.7	1.5	0.2
France	1.4	1.7	0.9
Germany [a]	4.5	2.3	-0.1
Italy	2.3	1.8	-2.3
United Kingdom	-2.2	-0.1	2.5
13 smaller countries	2.3	2.3	1.1
Austria	2.4	1.8	1.0
Belgium	3.1	2.9	-1.5
Denmark	1.4	0.7	1.5
Finland	-3.6	-5.1	-4.7
Greece	2.2	1.7	0.9
Ireland	1.6	2.9	2.0
Netherlands	3.0	2.1	1.0
Norway	-0.3	1.8	1.7
Portugal	5.2	4.4	1.5
Spain	2.9	2.1	-2.3
Sweden	1.1	-1.9	-3.8
Switzerland	1.5	-0.2	-0.8
Turkey	2.1	8.9	14.0
North America	-0.5	2.4	3.2
United States	-0.4	2.6	3.3
Canada	-2.0	1.1	1.6
Total above	0.5	2.1	1.9
Memorandum item:			
Japan	2.2	1.7	1.1
Total above, including Japan	0.8	2.1	1.8

Source: National statistics.

[a] Data refer to total Germany (east + west) as from 1992.

The favourable developments in the stock and bond markets in 1993 have improved the *net financial asset position* of households, but the impact on consumption behaviour, although difficult to gauge, has probably been rather small. It is also likely that changes in net wealth tend to affect spending behaviour only with a fairly long lag.

Heavy borrowing against a background of rising asset prices during the second half of the 1980s had led to a high level of household debt relative to incomes in a number of countries (notably Finland, Norway, Sweden and the United Kingdom) which became unsustainable when policies were tightened and asset prices started to fall. Large debt servicing burdens have been an important constraint on household expenditure in these countries in the last few years. But the decline in interest rates and the levelling out in the course of 1993 of the steep fall in housing prices has provided a more favourable environment for the required restructuring of balance sheets. Nevertheless, although debt servicing burdens have been reduced, they are still heavy enough to exercise a continuing restraint on consumption expenditures.

Against a background of high unemployment and rising uncertainty about future income levels, households have increased their precautionary *savings* in the majority of countries and this has accentuated the dampening impact on demand of low real income growth. Although interest rates fell, they were, none the less, still relatively high in real terms and this may have also stimulated savings. The reduced propensity to spend may have also been influenced by announced or expected measures to improve government finances. In only a few countries (Austria, Finland, Germany and the United Kingdom) did households offset the slow-down or fall in incomes by reducing savings in order to maintain consumption or to limit the decline in spending otherwise required because of falling real disposable incomes (see table 2.2.7).

In the *United States* consumer confidence improved markedly in the second half of 1993, and there was a pronounced rise in personal consumption. For the year as whole, personal consumption rose by more than 3 per cent (compared with 2.6 per cent in 1992).

Low interest rates stimulated borrowing for the purchase of consumer durables. The fall in interest rates to very low levels also led to a marked fall in debt service payments and this has also tended to support consumption. The high levels of debt which were built up in the second

TABLE 2.2.7

Savings ratios of private households in western Europe and North America, 1990-1993
(Percentage of disposable income)

	1990	1991	1992	1993
Western Europe	12.9	13.3	13.4	13.4
4 major countries	13.4	13.9	14.2	13.8
France	12.2	12.9	12.7	12.8
Germany [a]	13.9	13.5	12.8	11.9
Italy	18.4	18.6	18.7	18.9
United Kingdom	8.6	10.1	12.5	11.5
12 smaller countries	11.6	12.0	11.6	12.5
Austria	13.7	13.4	12.0	11.3
Belgium	18.1	19.8	20.0	21.7
Denmark	14.7	15.9	15.1	16.0
Finland	3.8	8.2	9.6	8.5
Greece	20.3	18.5	15.6	15.2
Ireland	9.6	11.7	12.2	12.6
Netherlands	16.3	13.2	13.1	13.2
Norway	0.9	2.6	5.0	5.9
Portugal	22.4	23.3	22.3	23.2
Spain	6.1	6.7	4.8	7.1
Sweden	-0.6	3.4	7.4	9.4
Switzerland	12.2	13.0	13.1	13.3
North America	4.8	5.2	5.7	4.6
United States	4.3	4.8	5.3	4.0
Canada	9.7	10.1	10.6	11.0
Total above	8.5	9.0	9.3	8.7

Sources: National statistics and OECD, *Economic Outlook*, Paris, December 1993.

[a] West Germany.

TABLE 2.2.8

Real public consumption expenditures in western Europe and North America, 1991-1993
(Percentage change over previous year)

	1991	1992	1993
Western Europe	2.1	2.1	0.4
4 major countries	1.6	2.2	0.1
France	2.5	2.7	1.1
Germany [a]	0.3	3.8	-0.7
Italy	1.5	1.1	0.2
United Kingdom	2.5	0.7	-0.1
13 smaller countries	3.0	2.1	1.1
Austria	2.6	2.4	2.0
Belgium	1.8	1.3	1.3
Denmark	-	0.7	2.4
Finland	2.5	-2.0	-5.8
Greece	3.5	-	0.7
Ireland	2.4	2.2	2.0
Netherlands	1.3	1.3	0.7
Norway	2.3	4.6	2.2
Portugal	3.0	1.4	0.8
Spain	6.9	3.8	1.6
Sweden	3.2	-0.6	-0.7
Switzerland	1.5	0.5	-0.4
Turkey	1.0	6.4	7.6
North America	1.5	-0.1	-0.6
United States	1.5	-0.1	-0.7
Canada	2.1	0.2	-0.1
Total above	1.8	1.0	-0.1
Memorandum item:			
Japan	1.7	2.4	3.2
Total above, including Japan	1.8	1.1	0.1

Source: National statistics.

[a] Data refer to total Germany (east + west) as from 1992.

half of the 1980s have been reduced and the ratio of debt to disposable incomes has fallen since 1990. Nevertheless, the ratio is still at a relatively high level suggesting a need for further balance sheet adjustment. This appears to be reflected in the very small rise in total outstanding credit in 1993. As in western Europe the net financial asset position of households was strengthened by rising share and bond prices.

The savings ratio had increased steadily from 4 per cent in 1989 to 5.3 per cent in 1992, a reflection of balance sheet adjustments and lingering uncertainties about future income prospects created by the hesitant and uneven recovery. But in 1993 the savings ratio fell back to its level in 1989 and was one of the main factors behind the stronger growth in private consumption.

Public consumption

There was also a marked slow-down in the growth of public consumption in the western market economies in 1993, largely a reflection of efforts to reduce the structural component of government budget deficits. In *western Europe*, public consumption rose on average by a mere 0.4 per cent in 1993 (table 2.2.8), with expenditures actually falling in Finland, Germany, Sweden and Switzerland. In marked contrast, the Danish government introduced various measures to stimulate economic growth and these are reflected in a higher growth rate of public consumption in 1993 compared with the preceding year.

In the *United States* government spending fell by 0.7 per cent in 1993, largely a reflection of reductions in the defence budget.[52]

Fixed investment

Against a background of weak demand and falling capacity utilization rates in the business sector, as well as tight public sector budgets, there was a sharp fall of 4.5 per cent in gross fixed capital formation in *western Europe* in 1993 (table 2.2.9). Business expenditures on machinery and equipment investment fell by some 7 per cent. Construction investment fell by some 2.5 per cent. Demand for industrial buildings and housing was weak and public investment was restrained by efforts to cut high government budget deficits.

Fixed investments were also held back by high real rates of interest. Although long-term rates fell in the course of 1993, their potential stimulus will be felt only with a lag. In countries where the corporate sector had been in severe financial imbalance over the last year or so, the process of balance sheet restructuring continued: companies preferred to use any increase in available funds to repay debt or invest in financial assets rather than undertake fixed investment. This was notably the case in Finland, France, Sweden and the United Kingdom.

---

[52] Note that the figures for public consumption in the United States include public investment expenditures.

TABLE 2.2.9

Real gross fixed capital formation in western Europe and North America, 1991-1993
(Percentage change over previous year)

	1991	1992	1993
Western Europe	-0.9	-0.5	-4.5
4 major countries	-0.6	0.3	-4.3
France	-1.5	-2.0	-5.4
Germany [a]	6.1	4.2	-3.3
Italy	0.6	-1.4	-8.1
United Kingdom	-9.8	-1.6	0.4
13 smaller countries	-1.5	-2.1	-4.9
Austria	4.9	2.7	-2.6
Belgium	-1.7	1.0	-7.1
Denmark	-5.4	-8.2	-1.1
Finland	-20.3	-17.3	-18.2
Greece	-4.4	1.2	3.2
Ireland	-7.3	-1.9	0.5
Netherlands	0.4	1.1	-3.8
Norway	1.0	3.5	17.6
Portugal	2.4	5.7	1.0
Spain	1.6	-3.9	-10.3
Sweden	-8.4	-11.0	-16.2
Switzerland	-2.5	-5.0	-4.3
Turkey	-0.5	3.7	5.1
North America	-7.0	5.3	9.7
United States	-7.7	6.2	11.0
Canada	-2.0	-1.3	0.7
Total above	-3.4	1.8	1.4
Memorandum item:			
Japan	3.0	-1.0	0.2
Total above, including Japan	-1.9	1.1	1.1

Source: National statistics.

[a] Data refer to total Germany (east + west) as from 1992.

The inverted yield curve may have also deterred fixed investment in favour of putting funds into short-term financial assets. Also, the high real rates at the short end of the maturity spectrum have not been conducive for fixed capital formation.

Given the uncertain economic environment, high margins of excess capacity and increasing international competitive pressures, the main objective of investment appears to have shifted from capacity augmentation to the rationalization and modernization of the production process, the overall aim being to cut costs and introduce new products to strengthen competitiveness.

For western Europe, 1993 was the third year of falling investment, entailing a cumulative fall of about 6 per cent since 1990. As can be seen from table 2.2.9, the cumulative downturn has been particularly severe in Finland and Sweden, where the volume of fixed investment fell by some 45 per cent and 30 per cent, respectively.

There were pronounced falls in fixed investment in France, Germany and Italy in 1993. In France this continued a downturn which began in 1991. The aggregate decline in Germany reflects a much larger fall, by about 7 per cent, in the western part of the country, which was partly offset by the continuing strong growth in the east of public infrastructure investment and investment spending by the business sector, in the main by west German firms.

A striking feature is the weakness of investment in 1993 in the United Kingdom, where the recovery, albeit moderate, has now been under way for nearly two years. The small increase in 1993 masks higher investment in the newly-privatized public utilities and public housing, which was offset by weakening expenditures in the trade and services sector. Manufacturing investment remained broadly unchanged compared with 1992. Despite the availability of temporarily higher capital allowances until October, business confidence and investment intentions were affected for most of the year by the uncertainties surrounding the steadiness of the recovery.

In the *United States* business fixed investment was stimulated by low interest rates and favourable changes in profits. Expenditures on new machinery and equipment rose in real terms by about 16 per cent in 1993, reflecting mainly the continuing buoyancy of demand for EDP equipment. There has, indeed, been an extraordinary surge in demand for information processing equipment during the past few years, a trend which can be explained by the productivity gains associated with this equipment and the considerable absolute and relative decline in the price of computers (see chart 2.2.3). As a result, the share of EDP equipment in total real expenditure on machinery and equipment rose from 31 per cent in 1985 to 44 per cent in 1993. However, since prices of EDP equipment fell by 25 per cent over this period while the prices of other investment goods continued to rise, the share of EDP in nominal outlays on equipment remained broadly unchanged at 34 per cent.

US business investment in structures rose slightly in 1993, following two years of sharp decline. Spending continues to be depressed by the prevailing glut in office space. Residential investment continued to be encouraged by very low mortgage rates and rose by some 8.5 per cent in 1993 following an increase of 16 per cent in 1992. Taken together, private non-residential and residential investment rose by 11 per cent in 1993 (table 2.2.9).

Trends in investment-output ratios

Fixed investment is the principal carrier of technical change. A high share of investment in total GDP is generally regarded as a necessary condition for increasing, in the long term, productive efficiency, the number of new jobs and raising the real incomes of the population.

Chart 2.2.4 provides a longer-term perspective of fixed capital formation by tracing the development of nominal and real investment-output ratios in western Europe and the United States since 1970. The divergence between the nominal and the real investment-output ratio reflects changes in the relative price of investment goods. Note that the data for the two regions are not directly comparable because the US investment data cover only the private sector, i.e., they exclude public sector investment.

CHART 2.2.3

Outlays on EDP equipment and total machinery and equipment by the US business sector, 1980-1993

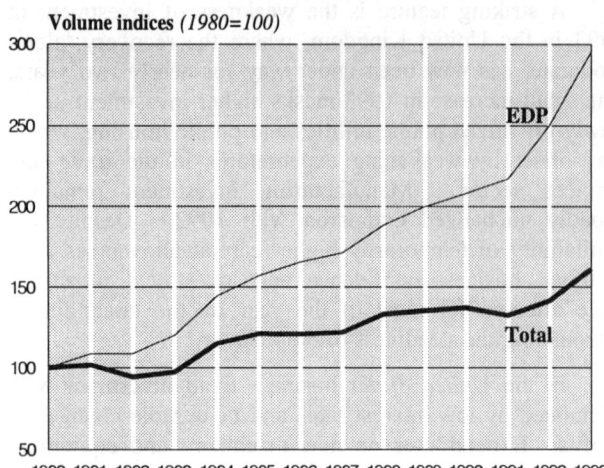
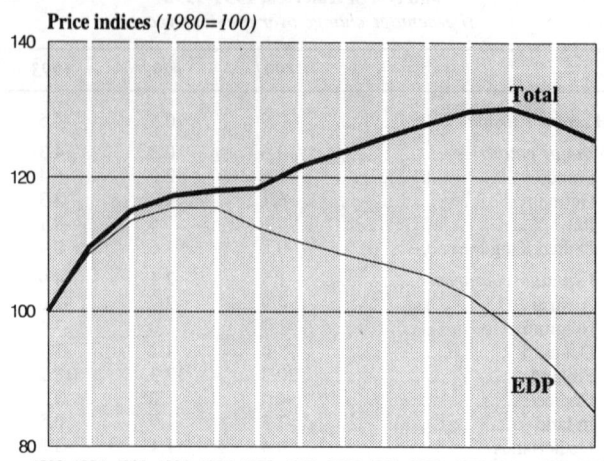

Source: ECE/DEAP based on US national accounts statistics.

Note: Volume indices derived from expenditures at 1987 prices; price indices are implicit deflators from national accounts.

TABLE 2.2.10

Volume of trade in goods and services in western Europe and North America, 1990-1993
(Percentage change over previous year)

	Exports			Imports		
	1991	1992	1993	1991	1992	1993
Western Europe	5.3	3.7	0.1	3.5	3.8	-2.7
4 major countries	5.9	3.4	-1.5	3.7	3.9	-5.6
France	3.9	7.0	-2.3	2.9	3.1	-3.2
Germany [a]	13.7	0.1	-11.1	12.1	2.6	-11.3
Italy	0.3	5.0	7.5	2.9	4.6	-8.1
United Kingdom	-0.9	2.6	4.0	-5.4	5.7	2.0
13 smaller countries	4.4	4.1	2.2	3.3	3.7	1.0
Austria	8.2	2.8	0.2	8.9	2.8	1.0
Belgium	2.5	1.6	-3.4	2.4	2.7	-4.4
Denmark	7.7	3.7	-5.0	4.9	-0.5	-4.8
Finland	-6.6	10.0	17.0	-11.7	1.1	0.1
Greece	16.4	8.0	4.8	13.2	5.8	4.1
Ireland	5.2	12.9	4.2	1.3	5.4	3.5
Netherlands	5.5	2.4	-	4.6	2.6	-
Norway	6.3	6.1	1.9	1.3	2.2	3.6
Portugal	1.1	6.8	2.6	4.9	9.7	4.5
Spain	7.9	6.7	8.8	9.1	6.6	-3.2
Sweden	-2.4	2.2	7.2	-5.0	1.3	-3.2
Switzerland	-0.7	3.4	0.8	-1.7	-3.8	-1.2
Turkey	7.5	3.3	7.3	-1.6	10.1	22.4
North America	5.4	6.7	4.7	0.1	7.9	9.8
United States	6.4	6.4	3.5	-0.5	8.7	10.3
Canada	0.8	7.9	9.6	2.7	4.9	7.6
Total above [a]	5.3	4.6	1.5	2.4	5.0	1.0
Memorandum item:						
Japan	4.9	4.9	1.0	-4.5	-	3.2
Total above, including Japan	5.3	4.4	1.5	1.8	4.6	1.2

Source: National statistics.

[a] Data refer to total Germany (east + west) as from 1992.

In the United States the investment-output ratio was on a declining trend in the second half of the 1980s. But whereas the fall in the real ratio has been to a large degree offset in the current recovery, there was only a moderate rise in the nominal ratio – a reflection of the fall in the price of investment goods relative to the prices of all other goods and services produced in the economy. Since 1979 there has been a clear long-term decline in the nominal investment-output ratio, which is much less obvious when price changes are eliminated.

In contrast, in western Europe the investment-output ratio has been declining in both nominal and real terms since the mid-1970s. The marked strengthening of investment activity in the second half of the 1980s, which was reflecting a pent-up need for restructuring, partly in anticipation of the forthcoming "single market", has been almost entirely reversed in the recent downswing. Among the four major west European economies, the trend in the real investment-output ratio has not shown a tendency to fall in Germany and the United Kingdom since the mid-1970s, a pattern which contrasts with developments in France and Italy. It is noteworthy, however, that the share of fixed investment in total output in the United Kingdom was lower than in the other three major west European economies in 1993, in spite of the differences in cyclical position.

Real foreign balance

Changes in the real foreign balance in *western Europe* in 1993 were largely influenced by the pervasive weakness in domestic demand and the differential changes in west European exchange rates since the summer of 1992 (see below, section 2.5).

The volume of imports of goods and services fell by about 3 per cent in western Europe in 1993. In contrast real exports virtually stagnated (a small increase of 0.1 per cent), which partly reflects the stronger demand in a number of overseas markets.

CHART 2.2.4

Investment-output ratios[a] in western Europe and the United States, 1970-1993
(Percentages)

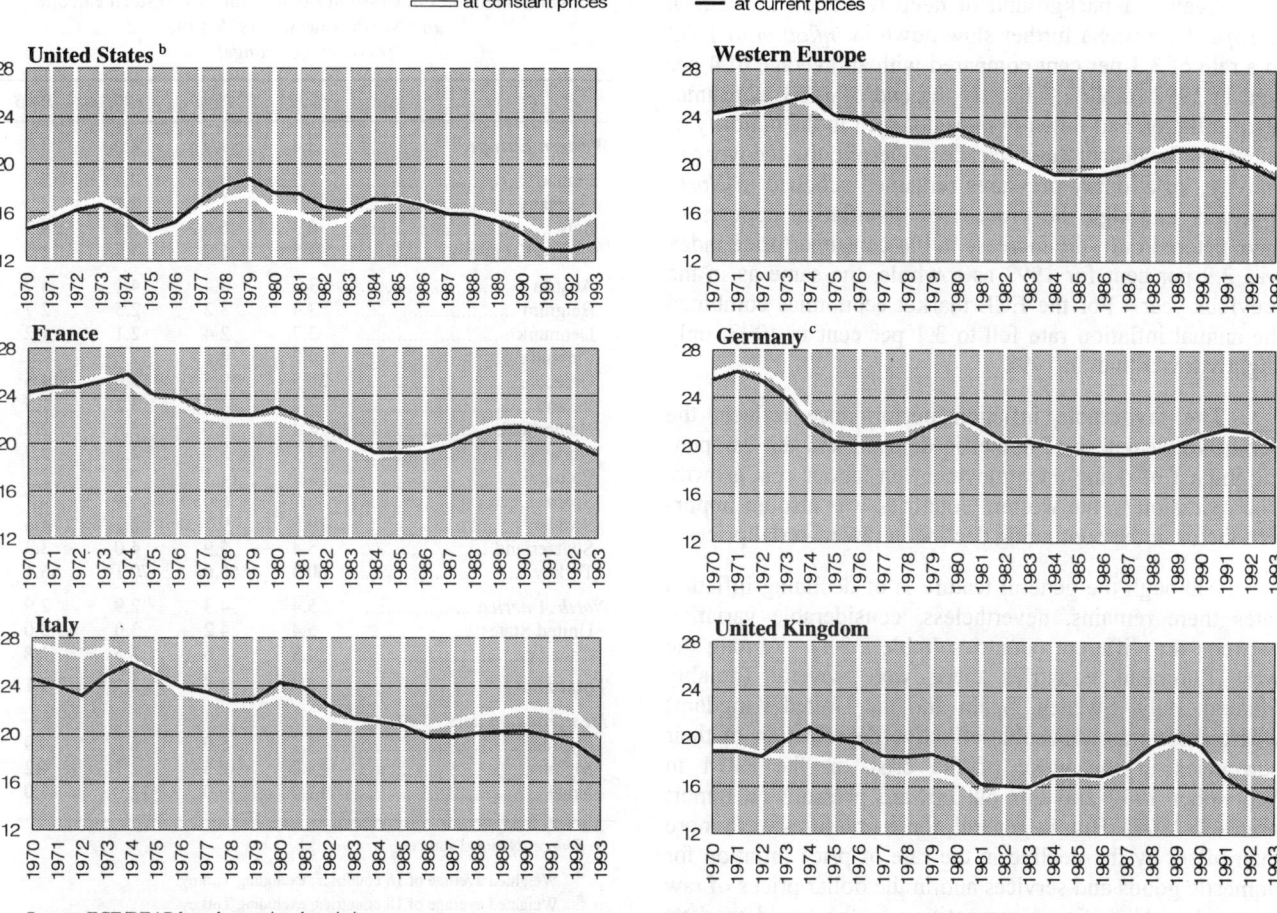

Source: ECE/DEAP based on national statistics.

[a] Gross fixed capital formation as a percentage of GDP.
[b] Investment data for the United States cover only private sector expenditures.
[c] West Germany.

Changes in the real foreign balance tended to support economic activity in western Europe in 1993 (table 2.2.5). In several countries (Finland, Italy, Spain and Sweden) the effects of the slump in domestic demand on activity were to a very large degree offset by a combination of rising exports and declining imports. In others (notably France and Germany) the positive contribution reflected a larger absolute fall in imports than for exports.

In the *United States* real export growth of goods and services slowed down to 3.5 per cent compared with 6.4 per cent in 1992. Important factors behind this performance, the weakest since 1985, were the recession in continental western Europe and Japan and the appreciation of the dollar against the major west European currencies since the second half of 1992. In contrast, import growth accelerated further in 1993, to an annual growth rate of 10.3 per cent (table 2.2.10), a consequence of the pronounced strengthening in domestic demand, notably for capital goods. The deficit in the real foreign balance rose to about $76.5 billion in 1993 compared with only $33.6 billion in 1992, a development which acted as a substantial drag on domestic activity levels (table 2.2.5).

2.3 Costs and prices

(i) Recent changes in consumer prices

Against a background of deep recession in *western Europe* there was a further slow-down in *inflation* in 1993 to a rate of 3.3 per cent compared with an average of 4 per cent in 1992 (table 2.3.1). By the end of 1993, consumer price inflation had fallen to rates not seen in the majority of countries for nearly three decades. Despite the recovery in activity, inflationary pressures remained subdued in *North America*, although the process of disinflation appears to have petered out: the increase in the consumer price index was 2.9 per cent for 1993 as a whole, the same as in the previous year. For the ECE market economies combined the annual inflation rate fell to 3.1 per cent in 1993, only slightly lower than in 1992.

The favourable inflation performance reflects the pervasive weakness of domestic demand and the dampening impact of rising unemployment on labour cost growth. The recession in the western countries was also an important factor in the continuing decline in raw material prices.

Although the general feature is of declining inflation rates there remains, nevertheless, considerable variation between the different countries (table 2.3.1). Among the west European countries there were several (notably Finland, Italy, Sweden, Spain and the United Kingdom) where there was a sizeable effective depreciation of their currencies in the wake of the crisis in the ERM in September 1992 and this put upward pressure on import prices in 1993. But, in general, these pressures were more than offset by the decline in the rate of price inflation for domestic goods and services and in the dollar prices of raw materials. Also, fierce competition in the world markets for tradable goods, against a background of sluggish international demand, has limited the ability of exporters to raise prices and profit margins. It is noteworthy that only in Sweden was there a significant acceleration in the annual inflation rate in 1993 and this was largely due to higher import prices and increases in indirect taxes. Of the other countries, only in Belgium and Canada was there a deterioration, albeit slight, in the inflation performance between 1992 and 1993.

In the United States the annual inflation rate was 3 per cent in 1993, the same as in the previous year. Inflation picked up in the early months of 1993 but this was a temporary feature only. Despite a pronounced strengthening of economic activity in the second half of 1993 consumer price inflation remained relatively subdued, partly a reflection of strong productivity growth in manufacturing industry and a fall in world energy prices, which spilled over to the retail level. However, the slack in the economy has been steadily taken up in the course of 1993 as exemplified by the increase in manufacturing capacity utilization rates in the final quarter. Given the forecast of continuing robust output growth in 1994, and the firming of prices of intermediate goods, a further deceleration of inflation is unlikely.

TABLE 2.3.1

Annual changes in consumer price index of western Europe and North America, 1990-1993
(Percentage change)

	1990	1991	1992	1993
Western Europe [a]	5.4	4.9	4.0	3.3
France	3.3	3.1	2.4	2.1
Germany	2.7	3.5	4.1	4.1
Italy	6.3	6.5	5.4	4.3
United Kingdom	9.5	5.9	3.8	1.6
Austria	3.2	3.4	4.1	3.7
Belgium	3.4	3.2	2.5	2.7
Denmark	2.7	2.4	2.1	1.2
Finland	6.2	4.1	2.6	2.1
Greece	20.5	19.5	15.9	14.6
Ireland	3.4	3.1	3.2	1.5
Netherlands	2.4	4.0	3.6	2.2
Norway	4.1	3.4	2.3	2.3
Portugal	13.5	11.3	9.2	7.1
Spain	6.7	6.0	5.9	4.7
Sweden	10.5	9.3	2.2	4.6
Switzerland	5.4	5.9	4.0	3.3
Turkey	60.3	66.0	70.1	66.1
North America	5.4	4.3	2.9	2.9
United States	5.4	4.2	3.0	3.0
Canada	4.8	5.6	1.5	1.8
Total above [b]	5.4	4.5	3.3	3.1
Memorandum item:				
Cyprus	4.5	5.0	6.5	4.9
Malta	3.0	2.5	2.7	4.2
Israel	17.2	19.0	12.0	11.0

Source: National sources.

[a] Weighted average of 16 countries, excluding Turkey.
[b] Weighted average of 18 countries, excluding Turkey.

In west Germany the annual inflation remained quite high in 1993: for the year as a whole the increase was 4.1 per cent, the same as in 1992. This compares with the Bundesbank's target of an annual inflation rate of 2 per cent. The outcome for 1993 was the worst performance since 1983, when consumer prices rose by 5.3 per cent. The high rate in 1993 reflects large increases in the prices of services and strong demand for housing which put upward pressure on rents. A major factor behind the rise in service prices (by more than 6 per cent) in 1993 was the increase in administered prices. The price level was also raised by the increase in VAT at the beginning of 1993. But the average annual inflation rate hides a weakening of inflationary pressures in the second half of 1993.

Disinflation continued in France and the annual inflation rate fell to 2.1 per cent in 1993, the lowest rate since 1956, and a reflection of the pervasive dampening of cost and price pressures in all major sectors of the economy. In fact, the annual inflation rate would have probably fallen below 2 per cent had it not been for the introduction of higher indirect taxes (notably on tobacco and alcoholic beverages) as part of the attempt to contain the rise in the government budget deficit. In any case, the inflation performance in France was one of the best in western Europe in 1993.

CHART 2.3.1

Quarterly changes in the consumer price index of western Europe and North America, 1990-1993
(Percentage change over corresponding quarter of the previous year)

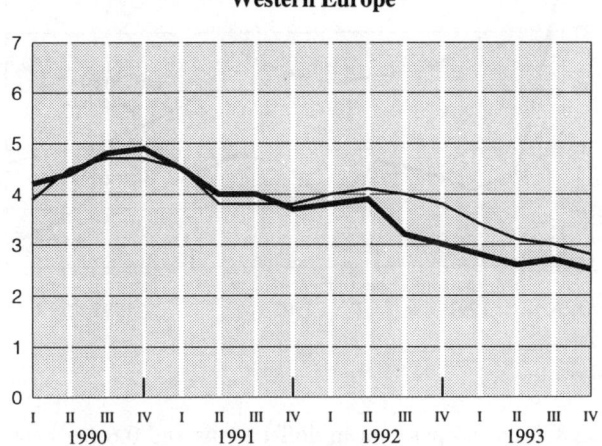
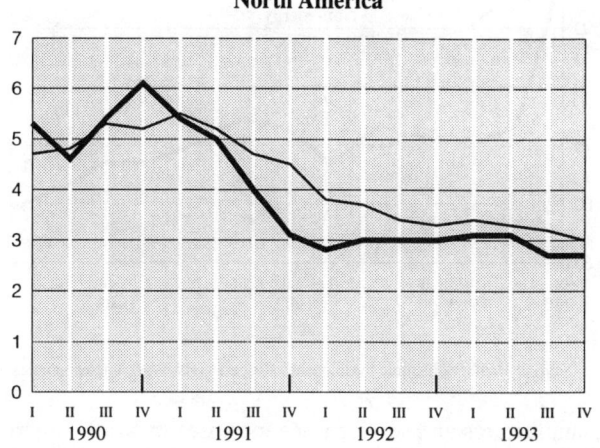

Source: National statistics.

[a] Weighted average of 10 countries, excluding Italy, Finland, Sweden and four south European countries.

Inflation remained above the west European average in Italy in 1993, but the gap was smaller than in 1992. The fall in the inflation rate was supported by smaller price increases for services and food, which more than offset the higher prices of imported consumer durables stemming from the sizeable depreciation of the lira.

There was a marked decline in the annual inflation rate in the United Kingdom, from 3.8 per cent in 1992 to 1.6 per cent in 1993. However, this fall was strongly influenced by the fall in mortgage interest rates since autumn 1992.[53]

Among the smaller economies, inflation remained relatively high in 1993 in Greece, Portugal and Turkey. In the first two countries, however, noteworthy progress has been made in slowing down the rate of price increase. In contrast, in Turkey, where lax monetary policy was an important factor in the persistent buoyancy of consumer demand, inflation was 66 per cent in 1993, hardly a significant improvement on the 70 per cent in 1992.

After sticking at around 4 per cent between mid-1991 and late 1992, the "underlying" west European rate of inflation[54] slowed down considerably during 1993 (chart 2.3.1). After falling steadily over the year, it fell to 2.7 per cent in the last quarter of 1993, compared with 3.8 per cent a year earlier. Also in North America the "underlying" inflation rate fell steadily in 1993, however, less sharply than in the previous two years, reaching 3 per cent in the fourth quarter of 1993 (compared with 3.3 per cent in the same quarter of 1992). This relative stickiness in the North American "underlying" rate may be explained to a large extent by the increasing strength of consumer demand in the United States which allowed US companies to raise profit margins. The very moderate decline in the "underlying" rate in 1993 suggests that the process of disinflation may have bottomed out in North America.

Among the major components of the consumer price index, prices of *manufactured goods* rose on average by only some 2 per cent in western Europe[55] in 1993, reflecting *inter alia* the strong international competition for market shares against a background of recession. Prices of *services* rose significantly more, by some 5 per cent, but this masks a marked slow-down to a year-on-year increase of 4 per cent in the final quarter of 1993, largely because of weakening demand for services. As a result, the difference between price increases for manufactured goods and services narrowed from 3.5 to some 2 percentage points between the fourth quarters of 1992 and 1993.[56] In North America the increase in manufactured goods prices in 1993 fell sharply to below 1 per cent in the closing months of 1993 compared with just below 3 per cent at the beginning of the year. On the other hand, the rise in service prices remained broadly stable at between 3.5 and 4 per cent in the course of 1993. Thus the difference between

---

[53] In contrast with most of the other western industrialized countries, the retail price index for the United Kingdom includes mortgage interest payments. The annual inflation rate excluding changes in mortgage interest rates was 3 per cent in 1993 compared with 4.7 per cent in 1992.

[54] Consumer prices excluding food and energy prices, which are more volatile than other items in the basket.

[55] Weighted average of six countries, i.e., France, west Germany, Belgium, Denmark, Norway and Switzerland.

[56] Given the limited sample of six countries, the west European weighted average in this part of the analysis is particularly influenced by the large weight of west Germany, where service price inflation averaged more than 6 per cent for the year as a whole, well above the weighted average of the six countries (4.6 per cent). In 1993, however, west German consumer price inflation for manufactures was 2.8 per cent, less than a percentage point above the weighted average of the six countries. Thus, excluding west Germany, the difference between the rates of change in the prices of manufactures and services was considerably narrower for the remaining five countries during 1993.

CHART 2.3.2
World market prices of raw materials in US dollars, 1990-1993
(1990 Q IV=100)

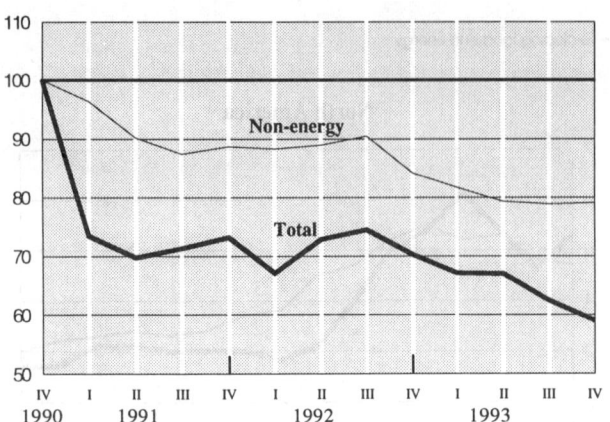
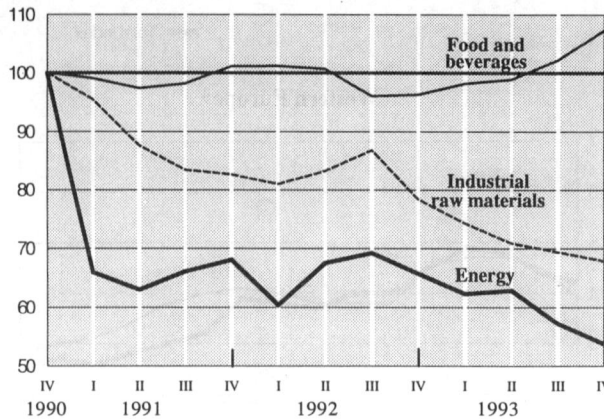

Source: Hamburg Institute for Economic Research (HWWA), Intereconomics, Hamburg (bi-monthly).

manufactures and service price increases in North America widened to nearly 3 percentage points at the end of 1993 compared with less than 1 percentage point at the beginning of the year.

(ii) World commodity prices

The protracted recession in the industrialized countries has put considerable downward pressure on world market prices of oil and most non-energy products which, in 1993, fell more than in 1992 (chart 2.3.2). One factor in the fall in non-energy prices was the increased supply of metals from eastern Europe and the former Soviet Union. *World commodity prices,* measured by the HWWA commodity index,[57] fell by 16.5 per cent in US dollar terms in the 12 months to December 1993. Allowing for the appreciation of the US dollar, the fall was still a considerable 8.4 per cent on an ECU basis. Most commodity prices fell except those for food, which increased by 12.9 per cent in dollar terms and nearly 24 per cent in ECUs over the 12 months to December 1993. Grain prices rose sharply during the last two quarters of 1993 due to heavy flooding in the United States. Crude oil prices plunged during the second half of 1993, reaching some $13.5 per barrel (for Brent crude) in December, its lowest value for five years and nearly one quarter below its price in March. The decline in crude oil prices reflects the weakness of demand and ample supply, with OPEC members competing for market shares and production in the North Sea reaching record levels. Consequently world energy prices[58] at the end of 1993 were 22.5 per cent lower in dollar terms and 15 per cent in ECUs than a year earlier. Over the same 12-month period industrial raw materials prices fell by 9.4 per cent in dollar terms and 0.6 per cent in ECUs.[59]

(iii) Input and output prices in manufacturing industry

Against the general background of a significant deterioration in labour markets and relatively tight monetary policies, the rate of increase in *average hourly earnings* in manufacturing industry continued to fall strongly during 1993 in all the west European countries[60] (table 2.3.2). The average annual rate of change fell from 6.7 per cent in 1991 (its most recent cyclical peak) to 5.6 per cent in 1992 and 4.2 per cent during the first three quarters of 1993. The rate of change remained broadly unchanged in the United States (2.6 per cent), however, at a rate much below the west European average. Although the slow-down in the growth of hourly earnings was pervasive in western Europe in 1993, year-on-year increases nevertheless remained quite high in a number of countries (west Germany, Austria and the United Kingdom).

Different rates of change in earnings and output prices are reflected in *real product wages,*[61] which were still rising strongly in the third quarter of 1993 compared with a year earlier: notably in Germany (5.9 per cent), Austria (4.8 per cent), and Belgium (4.1 per cent). In contrast, they were stable in the United Kingdom and fell in Ireland (4.8 per cent), Sweden (3.5 per cent) and Finland

---

[57] Produced by the HWWA (Institute for Economic Research), Hamburg, this index weights world market prices (in dollars) by the relevant commodity shares in total imports of western industrialized countries in 1974-1976.

[58] The weight of oil in the total energy component of the HWWA index is 91.3 per cent, and the weight of energy component in the total is 63.3 per cent.

[59] For example, according to the European Aluminium Association, aluminium exports from the CIS countries into western Europe more than quadrupled between 1990 and 1992, and continued to grow significantly in 1993. At the same time aluminium consumption in western Europe has been falling. Against this background, at a meeting held in Brussels in January 1994 the government representatives of Australia, Canada, Norway, Russia, the United States and the European Union reached an agreement on cutting world aluminium output by 10 per cent or some 1.5 to 2 million tons over the next two years. See *Financial Times,* 20 January 1994 and 15 February 1994.

[60] Excluding four south European countries.

[61] The change in nominal average hourly earnings deflated by the change in output prices in manufacturing.

TABLE 2.3.2

Producer prices and average hourly earnings in manufacturing industries of western Europe and North America, 1992-1993
(Annual percentage change)

	Output prices		Input prices		Average hourly earnings	
	1992	1993	1992	1993	1992	1993[a]
France	1.8	1.4	-1.7	-3.0	3.6	2.8
Germany	1.6	0.1	-1.3	-2.0	6.9	5.8
Italy	..	..	..	..	5.4	3.3
United Kingdom	3.6	4.0	0.5	4.5	6.6	4.7
Austria	-0.2	-0.4	-0.2	-1.3	5.8	4.9
Belgium	0.3	-1.2	-1.9	-1.5	4.7	2.5
Denmark	-0.8	-0.5	6.1	1.9	3.3	2.3
Finland	2.4	3.8	2.2	4.2	2.2	1.4
Ireland	1.7	4.6	1.9	2.8	4.8	1.0
Netherlands	2.6	0.7	-3.3	-3.4	4.1	3.3
Norway	0.2	-0.3	-3.4	-2.9	3.2	2.6
Sweden	-0.9	5.5	-9.2	4.6	4.6	3.3
Switzerland	0.8	..	-0.4	..	4.1	2.6
Western Europe	1.8[b]	1.4[b]	-1.2[b]	-0.5[b]	5.6	4.2
United States	1.2	1.2	-0.2	0.8	2.4	2.6
Canada	0.5	3.3	1.0	5.8	3.6	2.3

Source: National statistics.

[a] January-September 1993 over January-September 1992.

[b] Weighted average excludes Italy, Switzerland and four south European countries.

(2.1 per cent). For the 13 west European countries combined, real product wages increased nearly 3 per cent during the first three quarters of 1993, compared with an increase of just below 4 per cent during the same period of 1992. In the United States real product wages increased by 1 per cent during the first three quarters of 1993 compared to 1.4 per cent during the same period of 1992. The quite strong increase in real product wages in several west European countries suggests that, unlike the economy as a whole, profit margins in the manufacturing sector were still falling or stagnating in 1993 mainly due to very weak output prices, a reflection of intensive competition in the world market for tradable goods.

Given the fall in industrial raw material prices and the significantly increased competition in intermediate product markets, west European manufacturing industry's *material input prices* in 1993 continued the fall which had started in mid-1990 (table 2.3.2). Average input prices for 11 countries fell by 0.5 per cent in 1993 compared with 1.2 per cent in the previous year.[62] However, as was the case with output prices, there were large differences among countries. In the United Kingdom, Finland, Sweden and, to a lesser extent, in Ireland, the rise in input prices was due to the depreciation of their currencies. In the United States, input prices in 1993 continued their moderate upward trend which started in mid-1992.

Against this background of depressed demand and continued moderation in the growth of labour and material costs of production in most countries, the rate of change in west European *manufacturing industry's output prices*

---

[62] West European average excludes Italy, Switzerland and the four south European countries.

continued the downward trend which had started in mid-1991. For the year as a whole, the average increase was 1.4 per cent in 1993 compared with 1.8 per cent in 1992 and 4 per cent in 1989, the most recent cyclical peak. However, the differences among countries were large: output prices stagnated in west Germany; fell in Belgium and, to a lesser extent, in Austria, Denmark and Norway; and rose strongly in Sweden, Ireland, Finland and in the United Kingdom. The latter increases reflected mainly the pass-through of higher material input prices combined with improved profit margins mainly in the export industries where there was more scope for price increases because of currency depreciation. Manufacturing output prices continued to rise only moderately in the United States in 1993 (1.2 per cent for the year as a whole), a reflection of large gains in labour productivity, low wage growth, depressed prices for raw materials and intermediate goods, and relatively large margins of spare capacity throughout the year.

(iv) **Labour and non-labour unit costs in total economy**

Wage and non-wage *labour costs per employee* (i.e., total compensation per person employed) in *western Europe* increased by 3.3 per cent in 1993 compared with 5.1 per cent in 1992 and 7.2 per cent in 1990, its most recent cyclical peak (table 2.3.3). In *North America*, the deceleration in 1993 was even stronger than in western Europe. In the United States the rate of change fell to 2.9 per cent in 1993 from 5.1 per cent in 1992. In Canada labour costs per employee actually fell by 1 per cent. Among the west European countries the strongest deceleration in 1993 was in France, west Germany, the United Kingdom, the Netherlands and Switzerland.

The general moderation in labour costs per employee in 1993 was accompanied by a widespread slow-down in the growth of *labour productivity* (output per person employed in the total economy). The slow-down – or, in some cases, fall – in productivity growth reflects the well-known lagged adjustment of employment to changes in output in the downward phase of the business cycle. The main exceptions to this were the United Kingdom, Finland and Sweden. In Ireland, Norway, Switzerland, and the United States, productivity growth nevertheless remained quite strong (between 2 and 3 per cent) in 1993, but it stagnated in France and the Netherlands and fell slightly in Austria and west Germany.

However, the slow-down in labour productivity growth was more than offset by moderation in the growth of wage costs. The average rate of increase in west European *unit labour costs* continued to slow down: from 5.4 per cent in 1991 to 3.6 per cent in 1992 and 2.3 per cent in 1993. They accelerated only in Ireland and, albeit only slightly, in France.

For western Europe as a whole the rate of change in *unit profits* (the ratio of gross operating surplus to gross value added) in 1993 continued the uptrend which had started in 1992. Unit profits increased by 4.1 per cent in 1993 compared with 3.6 per cent in 1992. However, while they increased everywhere (except in Austria where they stagnated) the rate of change varied significantly between countries. Mainly as a result of currency depreciation, which provided scope for higher margins in the export

TABLE 2.3.3

Labour costs and profits in western Europe and North America, 1992-1993
(Annual percentage change)

	Labour costs per employee [a]		Labour productivity [b]		Unit labour costs [c]		Unit profits [d]	
	1992	1993	1992	1993	1992	1993	1992	1993
Western Europe [e]	5.1	3.3	1.5	0.9	3.6	2.3	3.6	4.1
France	4.0	2.4	1.9	-	2.1	2.4	3.6	2.3
Germany	5.4	2.9	0.7	-0.2	4.7	3.1	3.0	2.8
Italy	6.1	4.5	1.8	1.2	4.2	3.2	5.1	5.0
United Kingdom [f]	6.4	3.8	1.8	3.0	4.6	0.7	4.6	7.8
Austria	5.3	4.7	-	-0.7	5.4	5.4	2.8	-
Belgium	5.0	4.7	1.3	0.9	3.7	3.7	2.5	2.3
Denmark	2.9	2.4	1.3	0.9	1.6	1.5	4.3	1.5
Finland	1.4	1.8	3.4	3.8	-2.0	-1.9	6.7	9.4
Ireland	6.0	5.9	4.9	2.9	1.0	2.9	-1.2	4.5
Netherlands	4.6	3.0	0.6	0.3	4.1	2.7	-2.4	1.4
Norway [f]	3.8	2.9	3.6	2.5	0.2	0.4	-3.8	2.9
Sweden	2.3	2.6	1.6	2.0	0.6	0.5	11.5	11.5
Switzerland	5.7	3.2	2.2	1.9	3.4	1.3	2.0	4.1
North America	5.0	2.6	2.3	1.9	2.6	0.7	2.9	5.1
United States	5.1	2.9	2.4	2.0	2.6	0.9	3.4	5.0
Canada [f]	3.9	-1.0	1.5	1.1	2.3	-2.0	-2.0	6.2
Total above	5.0	2.9	1.9	1.4	3.1	1.5	3.3	4.6

Source: National accounts.

[a] Compensation of employees divided by total employment.
[b] Real gross value added divided by total employment.
[c] Compensation of employees per unit of real gross value added.
[d] Operating surplus including capital consumption per unit of real gross value added.
[e] Weighted average of 13 countries.
[f] Based on data for three quarters.

industries,[63] unit profits rose strongly in Italy, the United Kingdom, Finland, Ireland and Sweden. Also in both Canada and the United States unit profits rose sharply, due to the combined effect of significantly stronger domestic demand and weaker growth in unit labour costs.

(v) The sources of inflation

The GDP deflator (the ratio of nominal GDP to real GDP) is a very broad measure of inflation as it involves calculating the price changes of all goods and services (i.e., gross valued added) produced in an economy between a given year and a base year. This measure thus provides a different perspective on the (dis)inflation process. The rate of change in the GDP deflator decelerated both in western Europe and North America in 1993 (table 2.3.4). In western Europe, the average price increase for domestic value added in 1993 fell to 3 per cent compared with 3.5 per cent in 1992. In North America, despite significantly stronger demand and a marked disinflation over the last three years, the implicit GDP deflator rose by 2.2 per cent in 1993 down from 2.7 per cent in 1992. In 1993 the rate accelerated only in a few small west European economies with a high share of exports in GDP, namely, Finland, Ireland, Norway and Sweden. Nevertheless, in these countries it was still increasing at rates below the average rate for the region as a whole.

Viewed from the factor cost side, this favourable price performance in 1993 was mainly due to a significant moderation in the growth of unit labour costs which largely offset the rise in unit profits. In western Europe as a whole only two fifths of the change in the GDP deflator in 1993 was due to the increase in unit labour costs compared with more than half in 1992. In North America the proportion was even smaller, less than one fifth. Most of the rise in the GDP deflator in North America was due to the large increase in unit profits. Net indirect taxes also contributed significantly to price changes in some west European countries in 1993, namely in west Germany (nearly one fifth), Austria, Norway (about one third in both), and Finland (nearly one quarter).

The change in the domestic demand deflator, which takes into account the terms of trade effect on the overall rate of inflation in the economy, decelerated for the second consecutive year in most of western Europe and North America (table 2.3.4). Despite the significant moderation in domestic cost pressures (measured by the change in the GDP deflator excluding exports), the disinflation measured by the domestic demand deflator was much more modest. This mainly reflects the increased pressure from import prices in 1993 in those countries where there was effective exchange rate depreciation, namely, Italy, the United Kingdom, Finland, Ireland, Sweden and, to a lesser extent, Norway. In those west European countries where the monetary authorities had more or less closely followed the policy of the Bundesbank, import prices actually exerted a downward pressure on the domestic price level. This was the case for Austria, Denmark, France, the Netherlands and Switzerland (table 2.3.4). The net result was that nearly one quarter of the average west European inflation rate in 1993 was due to the depreciation of effective exchange rates. Also in Canada, higher import prices, due to the weaker effective exchange rate of the Canadian dollar, put pressure on the overall price level in 1993, but in the United States, a stronger US dollar more than offset a small increase in foreign suppliers prices.

---

[63] The rate of change in export prices, measured by the rate of change in national accounts export deflators, increased between 9 and 10 per cent in Italy, the United Kingdom and Sweden, 7.5 per cent in Finland and nearly 4 per cent in Ireland.

TABLE 2.3.4

Contribution to the changes in the GDP and domestic demand deflators in western Europe and North America, 1992-1993

(Percentages)

	Changes in GDP deflator [a]	of which due to:					Changes in domestic demand deflator	of which due to:			
		Unit labour costs			Unit profits [c]	Unit indirect taxes net of subsidies		Changes in GDP deflator excluding exports [d]	Import prices		
		Total	Compensation per employee [b]	Labour productivity					Total	Exchange rates [e]	Export prices of suppliers [f]
Western Europe [g]											
1992	3.5	1.9	2.7	-0.8	1.2	0.3	3.3	3.6	-0.2	-0.2	-0.1
1993	3.0	1.2	1.7	-0.6	1.4	0.4	3.1	2.5	0.7	0.7	-0.1
France											
1992	2.3	1.1	2.1	-1.0	1.3	-0.1	2.2	2.7	-0.5	-0.7	0.2
1993	2.4	1.3	1.3	-	0.8	0.3	2.1	2.8	-0.7	-0.5	-0.2
Germany											
1992	4.4	2.6	2.9	-0.4	1.0	0.8	3.9	4.3	-0.5	-0.8	0.3
1993	3.3	1.7	1.6	0.1	1.0	0.7	3.1	3.3	-0.2	-0.8	0.6
Italy											
1992	4.7	1.9	2.8	-0.8	2.3	0.5	4.5	4.2	0.2	0.6	-0.4
1993	4.1	1.5	2.0	-0.6	2.3	0.4	5.5	3.3	2.2	3.7	-1.5
United Kingdom [h]											
1992	4.4	2.6	3.7	-1.0	1.3	0.4	3.9	3.9	0.1	0.9	-0.9
1993	3.0	0.4	2.2	-1.7	2.3	0.3	3.1	0.8	2.3	2.5	-0.3
Austria											
1992	4.4	2.9	2.8	-	1.0	0.5	3.5	3.6	-0.2	-0.8	0.6
1993	4.3	2.9	2.5	0.4	-	1.4	3.6	4.7	-1.1	-1.0	-0.1
Belgium											
1992	3.8	2.0	2.7	-0.7	0.9	0.9	2.7	3.7	-0.1	-1.4	0.4
1993	3.2	2.0	2.5	-0.5	0.8	0.4	3.0	2.3	0.7	-0.4	1.0
Denmark											
1992	1.9	0.8	1.6	-0.7	1.3	-0.2	2.6	3.0	-0.4	-0.8	0.4
1993	1.5	0.8	1.3	-0.5	0.5	0.2	1.7	1.8	-0.1	-1.2	1.1
Finland											
1992	0.7	-1.2	0.8	-2.0	2.0	-0.1	1.1	-0.5	1.6	3.4	-1.7
1993	2.5	-1.1	1.0	-2.2	2.9	0.7	3.8	1.1	2.7	3.6	-0.9
Ireland											
1992	1.1	0.5	3.0	-2.5	-0.5	1.0	3.3	3.9	-0.6	-2.0	1.3
1993	2.9	1.5	2.9	-1.4	1.8	-0.3	2.9	0.8	2.1	3.0	-0.9
Netherlands											
1992	2.2	2.1	2.4	-0.3	-0.9	1.0	2.8	3.5	-0.7	-1.1	0.4
1993	1.8	1.4	1.6	-0.2	0.5	-0.1	2.1	2.3	-0.2	-1.3	1.1
Norway											
1992	-1.1	0.1	2.0	-1.9	-1.4	0.2	3.2	3.3	-0.1	-0.5	0.3
1993	2.0	0.2	1.5	-1.3	1.1	0.7	1.6	0.6	1.0	0.8	0.2
Sweden											
1992	1.4	0.4	1.4	-1.0	2.9	-1.9	1.6	2.3	-0.7	-0.3	-0.4
1993	2.7	0.3	1.6	-1.2	3.2	-0.9	4.2	0.9	3.3	6.2	-2.9
Switzerland [h]											
1992	2.6	2.1	3.5	-1.4	0.7	-0.2	3.4	2.7	0.7	0.6	0.1
1993	2.4	0.8	2.0	-1.2	1.4	0.2	2.1	2.4	-0.4	-1.0	0.6
North America											
1992	2.7	1.5	2.9	-1.4	0.9	0.2	2.6	2.6	-	0.4	0.4
1993	2.2	0.4	1.5	-1.1	1.7	0.1	2.0	2.0	-	-0.4	0.4
United States											
1992	2.9	1.6	3.0	-1.4	1.1	0.2	2.7	2.8	-0.1	0.3	-0.4
1993	2.3	0.6	1.7	-1.2	1.6	0.1	2.1	2.3	-0.2	-0.5	0.3
Canada [h]											
1992	1.1	1.3	2.2	-0.9	-0.6	0.5	1.4	0.7	0.7	1.6	-0.9
1993	1.0	-1.2	-0.5	-0.6	1.9	0.2	1.2	-0.1	1.4	1.4	-0.1
Total above											
1992	3.1	1.7	2.8	-1.1	1.1	0.3	3.0	3.1	-0.1	0.2	-0.3
1993	2.6	0.8	1.6	-0.8	1.5	0.3	2.6	2.3	0.3	0.1	0.2

Sources: National accounts and IMF, *International Financial Statistics*, Washington, D.C., various issues.

Note: Small discrepancies are due to rounding.

[a] GDP at market prices.
[b] Wage and non-wage labour costs per person employed.
[c] Includes capital consumption.
[d] Calculated as the residual of the change in the domestic deflator minus the contribution of the change in import prices.
[e] Based on nominal effective exchange rates.
[f] Prices of imports in terms of the national currency of the country of origin.
[g] Weighted average of 13 countries.
[h] Based on data for three quarters.

2.4 Labour markets

The recession in *western Europe* has brought a further significant deterioration in the labour markets in most countries in 1993, with additional job losses forecast for 1994. Whilst the cyclical downturn of output appears to have reached its turning point in some countries, an immediate improvement in the labour markets is not expected since employment growth tends to lag output growth over the business cycle, and output will have to rise more strongly than is currently expected before hiring starts again. Moreover, some part of the current high level of unemployment in western Europe stems from long-term changes in industrial structure, and from the labour market regulation which has increased the relative costs of hiring labour, and which is an important aspect of the current debate about the decline in competitiveness of western Europe *vis-à-vis* other regions of the world. With this scenario, the hoped for sustained economic growth is unlikely to reduce unemployment to acceptable levels, unless accompanied by measures to improve competitiveness, including comprehensive labour market reforms. In contrast, labour market indicators have performed well in *North America* in 1993, in part because the region is more advanced in the current cycle, but also because its labour markets, being less constrained by regulation, are more responsive in terms of relative wage costs at each phase of the cycle.

(i) Recent changes in the demand for labour

The demand for labour in *western Europe* fell in 1993 for the second successive year, with a decrease in *employment* in nearly every country. Some 2.8 million jobs were lost in total, a year-on-year decrease of nearly 2 per cent, and more than double the fall in employment experienced in 1992 (table 2.4.1). The rate at which jobs were lost accelerated in France and Italy between 1992 and 1993, while in western Germany employment fell 1.7 per cent, the first decrease since 1983. The United Kingdom, cyclically desynchronized with the other western European economies, began shedding labour in 1991, but the year-on-year rate of job loss decelerated for the second successive year in 1993, markedly so in the third quarter. Between the first and third quarters of 1993, some 124,000 net new jobs were created,[64] and some patchy evidence of skill shortages has been reported in various parts of manufacturing industry. Preliminary estimates show that employment fell in nearly all the smaller western European economies in 1993; it remained stable in Austria and Norway, and rose only in Turkey, where output growth continues to be very high. The Netherlands experienced the first decline in its employment total (man-years) since 1984, while the rate of job loss accelerated markedly in Belgium, Denmark, Portugal, Spain and Sweden between 1992 and 1993. In contrast, the demand for labour in *North America* was relatively strong in 1993 for the second successive year: employment rose by some 1.8 million people, an increase of 1.4 per cent over 1992, and employment growth is expected to continue at a little under 2 per cent in 1994.

While the currently divergent patterns in the demand for labour reflect cyclical desynchronization between most of western Europe and the United States, it is interesting to look at longer-term trends in the broad *sectoral structure* of employment (table 2.4.2). In the ten years to 1992, the share of agriculture in total employment has fallen in every country, as has that of industry (with the exception of Denmark and Turkey), while the share of services has risen, a reflection of above average employment growth. Much change has also occurred within the sectors: for example, a falling share in services sector employment of personal services and a rising share of financial services.

The year-on-year rate of employment growth in the *services sector* has slowed markedly in western Europe in the current recession,[65] from 2.4 per cent in 1990 to 0.6 per cent in 1992, and provisional figures show that services sector employment actually fell in 1993 (table 2.4.3). This slow-down in services sector employment growth, which was discussed in a previous edition of the *Survey*,[66] is possibly rooted in structural as well as cyclical causes, including rising labour productivity emanating from widespread investment in information technology.[67] It may also reflect some deceleration to a more sustainable rate of growth after the exceptionally rapid expansion of employment in financial services which followed the deregulation of financial markets in the 1980s.[68] In North America, service sector employment fell very slightly in 1991, but growth resumed in 1992, and provisional figures for 1993 show that there was a net increase of over 2 million jobs. With so many indicators confirming the strength of the recovery in the United States, steady growth in services sector employment is projected for 1994.

Slower employment growth in the services sector during the downturn of the early 1990s has temporarily weakened its cushioning effect on the long-term decline in *industrial employment* (table 2.4.2), which continued in 1992 in all the western countries of the ECE region (except Turkey), with a net loss of some 1.7 million jobs (table 2.4.3). Divergent cyclical patterns are also evident: the decline in industrial employment reached a trough in 1991 in North America and has since moderated, but the decline has accelerated in western Europe in the same period. Preliminary figures for 1993 show a further decrease of over 2.5 million industrial jobs, more than 80 per cent of which have been lost in western Europe.

---

[64] Department of Employment, *Press Notice*, 16 February 1994.

[65] In the recession of the early 1980s, year-on-year services sector employment growth in western Europe (same country coverage as table 2.4.3) did not fall below 1 per cent, although the rate slowed briefly in 1983. The growth rates were 1.4, 1.0 and 1.7 per cent for 1982, 1983 and 1984 respectively. In North America, the slow-down in this sector was a little more marked: growth rates of 1.8, 0.3 and 2.1 per cent for 1981, 1982 and 1983 respectively.

[66] United Nations Economic Commission for Europe, *Economic Survey of Europe in 1992-1993*, New York, 1993, pp.46 and 48.

[67] For example, in Italy, "employment in services fell by 0.6 per cent in the first six months of the year (1993) ... reflecting the restructuring under way in some parts of the sector as well as the impact of the cyclical slow-down; productivity in market services is in fact rising at a historically rapid pace". Banca d'Italia, *Economic Bulletin*, No.17, October 1993, p.24.

[68] Extensive and rapid financial deregulation took place in the United Kingdom, Finland, Sweden and the United States, while Switzerland was under competitive pressure from the rest of Europe and the "single market".

TABLE 2.4.1

Labour market changes in western Europe and North America, 1989-1993
(Annual average change: thousands and per cent)

	Western Europe [a]			North America		
	Labour force	Employment [b]	Unemployment [c]	Labour force	Employment [b]	Unemployment [d]
Annual average change *(thousands)*						
1989	1 279.9	2 315	-1 035.1	2 193	2 379	-186
1990	1 875.2	2 202	-326.8	1 922	1 485	437
1991	1 264	117	1 147	414	-1447	1 861
1992	125.8	-1 171	1 296.8	1 216	123	1 093
1993	-748.5	-2 823	2 074.5	1 219	1 804	-585
Memorandum item:						
Average level in 1993	165 795.9	146 550	19 245.9	138 486	128 134	10 352
Annual average growth rate *(per cent)*						
1989	0.8	1.6	-6.4	1.7	1.9	-2.4
1990	1.1	1.5	-2.2	1.4	1.2	5.8
1991	0.8	0.1	7.8	0.3	-1.1	23.3
1992	0.1	-0.8	8.2	0.9	0.1	11.1
1993	-0.4	-1.9	12.1	0.9	1.4	-5.3

Sources: National statistics, OECD and ECE secretariat estimates.

[a] Sixteen countries; excluding east Germany and Turkey.
[b] National accounts statistics, where available; otherwise labour force surveys.
[c] Unemployed persons registered in labour offices; not seasonally adjusted.
[d] Unemployed persons according to labour surveys; seasonally adjusted.

TABLE 2.4.2

Employment by sector, 1982 and 1992
(Per cent of total)

	Agriculture		Industry		Services	
	1982	1992	1982	1992	1982	1992
Western Europe	12.3	9.9	33.6	29.6	54.1	60.5
4 major countries	6.7	4.7	36.2	30.8	57.1	64.5
France	7.9	5.1	33.6	27.9	58.8	67.0
Germany [a]	5.0	3.1	41.9	38.5	53.1	58.4
Italy	12.1	9.2	34.2	28.7	53.7	62.1
United Kingdom	2.6	2.2	34.2	26.2	63.2	71.6
11 smaller countries	22.4	18.6	28.8	27.5	48.8	53.9
Austria	8.7	5.8	37.3	33.0	54.0	61.2
Belgium	3.1	2.6	31.8	27.5	65.1	69.9
Denmark	7.6	5.5	26.6	26.6	65.8	67.9
Finland	13.1	9.0	33.4	28.2	53.5	62.8
Ireland	16.8	13.3	31.0	28.1	52.2	58.6
Netherlands	5.6 [b]	4.9	28.7 [b]	26.3	65.7 [b]	68.8
Norway	7.8	5.8	28.0	23.0	64.2	71.2
Spain	18.6	10.1	34.1	32.4	47.3	57.5
Sweden	5.2	3.5	30.1	27.1	64.7	69.4
Switzerland	6.0 [c]	5.6	38.0 [c]	33.9	56.0 [c]	60.5
Turkey	54.1	44.1	19.2	23.1	26.7	32.8
North America	3.6	2.8	26.7	22.4	69.7	74.8
United States	3.4	2.6	26.7	22.3	69.9	75.1
Canada	5.3	4.3	26.5	22.7	68.2	73.0
Memorandum item:						
Japan	9.7	6.4	34.9	34.6	55.4	59.0

Sources: National accounts, labour force surveys and ECE secretariat estimates.

[a] West Germany.
[b] Estimated man-years.
[c] Estimate.

The long-term loss of industrial jobs has been accompanied by changes in the structure of industrial employment, and hence in the relative shares of industrial sectors, with steadily declining opportunities in low-skill, low-wage and low-technology industries (notably textiles and basic metals), where international competitive pressures may be increasing sharply. The share of the textiles, footwear and leather industries in manufacturing employment fell sharply in France, West Germany, the Netherlands and the Nordic countries between 1970 and the end of the 1980s, but was broadly maintained in Italy; in the basic metals industries it fell most in Sweden, the United Kingdom and the United States in the same time period.[69] It should be noted, however, that the variance of factor intensity within broad industry categories is likely to be fairly high: for example, some proportion of jobs in the Italian textile industry are, in fact, in high-skill, high-wage fashion design. Nevertheless, the loss of low-skill, low-wage jobs in industries which may be facing mounting competitive pressure from the newly industrializing countries of Asia and the transition economies of eastern Europe and the CIS, particularly in the post-Uruguay Round trading environment, undoubtedly risks adding to long-term structural unemployment in the western industrialized countries.

Notwithstanding longer-term changes in the structure of industrial employment in the western region of the ECE area, there have been recent job losses in some industries which had hitherto demonstrated strong international competitive advantage. Although these losses can be largely attributed to the current downturn and jobs could be expected to reappear as the recovery gains ground, the rate of employment creation during the next upswing will also depend on the extent to which countries are able to

---

[69] For a more detailed discussion, see OECD, *Industrial Policy in OECD Countries, Annual Review 1993*, Paris, 1993, pp.84, 87-110 and table A.12.

TABLE 2.4.3

Changes in employment by sector, 1990-1993
(Annual average change, thousands and per cent)

	(Thousands)				(Per cent)			
	1990	1991	1992	1993 [a]	1990	1991	1992	1993 [a]
Western Europe [b]								
Agriculture	-279	-285	-330	-318	-3.5	-3.7	-4.4	-4.4
Industry	577	-632	-1 073	-2 188	1.4	-1.5	-2.5	-5.3
Services	1 946	1 050	550	-182	2.4	1.3	0.6	-0.2
North America								
Agriculture	1	38	-114	-105	-	1.1	-3.2	-3.0
Industry	-377	-1 425	-664	-429	-1.2	-4.7	-2.3	-1.5
Services	1 860	-59	901	2 188	2.0	-0.1	1.0	2.3

Sources: National accounts, labour force surveys and ECE secretariat estimates.

[a] Provisional.
[b] West Germany; excluding Belgium, Greece, Portugal and Turkey.

maintain international competitiveness, which is linked to labour market practices. For example, Germany has experienced an unprecedented fall in engineering production in 1993, partly as a result of the decline in domestic demand, but also because of a sharp fall in exports, reflecting in particular the downturn of the international investment cycle. To some extent this is also attributable to the effective appreciation of the deutsche mark. However, wage restraint is seen as an important element in redressing the situation in the labour markets, and in maintaining international competitiveness.

(ii) **Recent changes in the supply of labour**

The *labour force* in *western Europe* grew steadily at an annual average rate of a little less than 1 per cent in the three years to 1991, adding 4.4 million potential workers, but growth slowed in 1992 and the labour force actually fell in 1993 by 0.4 per cent (table 2.4.1). Whilst annual labour force growth rates have been stronger in *North America* in 1989-1990, the rate slowed to 0.3 per cent in 1991, coinciding with a slight decrease in the labour force participation rate in the United States, and with the cyclical downturn in that country. Nevertheless, labour force growth picked up again in 1992, and a total of around 7 million potential workers have been added to the labour force in North America in the five years to 1993.

The growth in the labour force in the western ECE region is partly attributable to a rise in labour force *participation rates* in some countries (table 2.4.4). This rise has been most sustained in North America between 1973 and 1992; among the west European countries, the United Kingdom and especially the Netherlands showed notable increases between 1982 and 1992. Disaggregation by sex shows much greater participation by women in the workforce, with female participation rates rising between 1982 and 1992 in nearly every country for which data is available, substantially so in the Netherlands, Spain and Canada, while male participation rates are falling in every country except the Netherlands.

Further disaggregation by age shows that the major growth in *female* participation rates has been in the 25-54 age group: all the countries listed in table 2.4.4 experienced significant increases, with an average rise of more than 20 percentage points between 1973 and 1992. By 1992, rates ranged from 47 per cent in Ireland to 89 per cent in Sweden. This growth is in line with women's changing expectations of paid work outside the home, and is further explained by family economic imperatives and the expansion of part-time opportunities for women, notably in the services sector. It also reflects a longer-run demand pressure: given stagnant growth in the population of working age, higher female participation rates will be the main source of growth in the labour force. In contrast, *male* participation rates in the 25-54 age group have dropped slightly since 1973, by an average of 2.5 percentage points in all countries considered, albeit from very high starting levels around 95 per cent. This may be attributable to the discouraged-worker effect, as prime age male workers made redundant from declining manufacturing industries have been unable to find work to match their skills and have subsequently dropped out of the labour force.

A pervasive feature has been the notable reduction in participation rates among younger and older men: i.e., in the 15-24 and 55-64 age groups. Whilst lower participation rates in the younger age group can be explained in part by extended full-time education, rising male youth unemployment rates and the high proportion of young male long-term unemployed suggest that part of the lower participation may be attributable to young men dropping out of the labour force. The discouraged-worker effect in both the young and the prime age groups represents a serious market failure, and the social implications cannot be ignored by policy makers. In the younger age group, female participation rates have also fallen in many countries, though the decrease is much less than that for young men. While young women have been likewise staying longer in full-time education, they have also found more job opportunities than their male counterparts, largely in the services sector. In the 55-64 age group, the discouraged-worker effect is probably a driving force in lower male participation rates, but there may also be a willingness to substitute leisure for income, against a background of generous early retirement benefits. However, in the same age group, female participation rates rose in many countries.

TABLE 2.4.4

Labour force participation rates in western Europe and North America: 1973, 1982 and 1992
(Per cent)

	1973	1982			1992		
	All	All	Male	Female	All	Male	Female
France	68.6	68.2	80.6	55.9	66.8	75.1	58.5
Germany [a]	69.4	68.0	83.3	52.9	69.1	80.8	57.0
Italy	53.6	59.2	77.5	40.5	59.9	75.4	44.6
United Kingdom	75.2	75.0	89.3	60.8	78.0	87.6	68.3
Finland	75.2	77.5	82.8	72.2	74.7	78.7	70.7
Ireland [b]	63.3	62.6	88.7	35.8	62.4	80.7	43.4
Netherlands	57.8	58.8	77.7	39.4	68.4	80.8	55.5
Norway	69.5	77.4	89.3	65.2	78.2	84.2	71.9
Portugal	72.4 [c]	70.7	88.4	55.1	71.4	83.5	60.3
Spain	63.2	59.6	85.8	33.9	60.5	77.7	43.6
Sweden	77.1	83.0	88.2	77.6	82.7	85.2	80.0
United States	70.6	75.4	88.1	63.1	78.6	87.2	70.2
Canada	66.0	72.8	86.2	59.6	76.3	84.2	68.4

Sources: OECD, *Labour Force Statistics 1971-1991*, Paris, September 1993.

Note: The participation rate is the ratio of the total labour force to the total population aged 15-64. Data on participation rates are not standardized and may not be comparable between countries.

[a] West Germany, 1990.
[b] 1975, 1981 and 1991.
[c] 1974.

(iii) Unemployment

In *western Europe*, unemployment rose in 1993 for the third successive year, both in absolute terms, and as a proportion of the labour force. The growth in unemployment, which averaged 8 per cent each year in 1991-1992, rose to some 12 per cent in 1993, and over 2 million people were added to the registered jobless total in 1993 (table 2.4.1). There is little to indicate that the overall situation will ease in 1994. In *North America*, growth in unemployment peaked in 1991, with an annual average increase of some 23 per cent. Labour force surveys show an average decrease of nearly 600,000 in the jobless total in 1993, with most of this attributable to an unexpectedly sharp fall in November in the United States. The contrasting experiences of the different regions within the western ECE area can be seen in table 2.4.1: the United States entered the upswing of the cycle ahead of western Europe, and has displayed greater volatility in its annual average unemployment growth, which supports the view that its labour markets are less constrained by structural impediments.

The weighted annual average *unemployment rate* in western Europe has risen, with increasing momentum each year, from a previous cyclical trough of 7.8 per cent in 1990 to 10.3 per cent in 1993 (table 2.4.5). However, there are wide disparities, both between countries and between regions within countries. In western Germany, the annual average unemployment rate rose from 4.6 per cent in 1992 to 5.8 per cent in 1993. The unemployment rate has risen in every quarter since the fourth quarter of 1991, reaching 6.3 per cent by the final quarter of 1993. It is projected to rise further in 1994 as more redundancies are expected, particularly among short-time workers.[70] In both France and Italy, the rise in the annual average unemployment rate in 1993 was similar to western Germany, but from a 1992 rate which was already much higher at 10.3 per cent in each country. In France, the rate rose nearly every month to reach 12.1 per cent by December 1993, giving an annual average rate of 11.5 per cent. Whilst there are some indications that France may be moving towards moderate recovery in 1994, improvements in the labour markets will be weak at best, and unlikely to prevent a further rise in unemployment. Indeed, based on the experience of the previous upturn, significant reductions in unemployment are unlikely: after several years of strong growth, the unemployment rate stood at 9.4 per cent in 1989, suggesting deep-seated structural problems in the labour markets. In Italy, the unemployment rate has remained above 10 per cent in nearly every year since 1985, and has risen in every quarter since the third quarter of 1991, reaching 11.3 per cent by the final quarter of 1993, yielding an annual average rate of 11.1 per cent. In common with other countries, the debate in Italy has focused increasingly on active labour market policies, designed primarily to reduce the overall cost of labour compensation, but also to improve the quality of labour through better training. Unemployment rates have increased in all 13 of the smaller western European countries between 1992 and 1993, with the weighted average rate for the group rising from 9.4 to 11.4 per cent, and major increases in Finland, Spain, Sweden and Switzerland.

---

[70] In 1990, short-time workers in western Germany numbered only some 56,000. The level began to increase sharply towards the end of 1992, peaking in March 1993 at a little over 1 million, but declining thereafter to some 560,000 by December 1993 (with an additional 125,000 in the eastern *Länder*).

TABLE 2.4.5

Standardized unemployment rates in western Europe and North America, 1990-1993
(Per cent of labour force)

	1990	1991	1992	1993
Western Europe	7.8	8.1	8.9	10.3
4 major countries	7.5	7.9	8.6	9.5
France	8.9	9.4	10.3	11.5
Germany [a]	4.8	4.2	4.6	5.8
Italy	10.3	9.9	10.3	11.1
United Kingdom	6.8	8.7	9.9	10.3
13 smaller countries	8.2	8.4	9.4	11.4
Austria	3.2	3.5	3.6	4.3
Belgium	7.2	7.2	7.9	9.1
Denmark	9.5	10.4	11.2	12.3
Finland	3.4	7.5	13.0	17.8
Greece	7.6	7.6	9.2	10.0
Ireland	13.4	14.9	16.1	16.8
Netherlands	7.5	7.0	6.8	8.5
Norway	5.2	5.5	5.9	6.1
Portugal	4.6	4.1	4.1	5.5
Spain	15.9	16.0	18.1	22.4
Sweden	1.5	2.7	4.8	8.3
Switzerland	0.5	1.1	2.5	4.6
Turkey	8.0	7.7	7.9	8.6
North America	5.7	6.9	7.7	7.1
United States	5.4	6.6	7.3	6.7
Canada	8.1	10.2	11.2	11.1
Total above	6.9	7.6	8.4	8.9

Sources: OECD, *Quarterly Labour Force Statistics*, No.4, 1993, Paris; *Main Economic Indicators*, No.1, 1994, Paris; UN, *Monthly Bulletin of Statistics*, December 1993, New York and ECE secretariat estimates.

[a] West Germany.

Against a background of steady, albeit moderate, recovery, the United Kingdom alone among the major European economies has seen a decline in its unemployment rate during 1993: from a peak of 10.5 per cent in the first quarter of 1993, it fell to 10 per cent in the final quarter, dipping to 9.9 per cent in December 1993. These favourable changes contrast with previous recoveries when decreases in unemployment and increases in employment lagged much further behind the upturn in GDP growth.[71] The United States also experienced a declining unemployment rate in 1993: from a peak of 7.4 per cent in the second quarter of 1992 it declined to 6.5 per cent by the fourth quarter of 1993, with the annual average rate falling from 7.3 to 6.7 per cent between the two years.

The number of women registered as unemployed in western Europe has risen by more than 700,000 between 1992 and 1993, while the number fell by over 100,000 in North America, a reflection of the divergence of cyclical positions. However, estimates of *female unemployment* based on registration are likely to understate the actual total, since many women work in part-time or temporary occupations with no benefits entitlement and may have little incentive to register when unemployed. Preliminary estimates for 1993 of the level of female unemployment and its share in total unemployment are shown in table 2.4.6. It is notable that the United Kingdom has a much lower share of women in total unemployment (some 23 per cent) than any other country in the region, which may be partly attributable to the high incidence of part-time work,[72] and the related non-registration of unemployment. Female unemployment rates exceed or roughly match male rates in the majority of countries in the western ECE region, with the exception of Finland, Sweden and the United Kingdom, where female rates are significantly lower. The disparity between male and female unemployment rates is greater in western Europe than in North America: in the European Community, the seasonally adjusted unemployment rate for men increased from 8.8 to 9.7 per cent in the year to December 1993, while that for women increased from 11.7 to 12.6 per cent in the same period; in the United States, the male rate fell from 7.1 to 6.4 per cent, and the female rate from 7.5 to 6.7 per cent between the third quarters of 1992 and 1993.[73]

One of the most serious and pressing problems facing countries in the western ECE region is the high and rising level of *youth unemployment*. With almost 6.5 million jobless young people in western Europe, and a further 3.3 million in North America (table 2.4.6), something in the order of one third of all those unemployed in the western ECE region in 1993 are less than 25 years of age, with the share of youth unemployment in total unemployment approaching 50 per cent in Italy, and above 30 per cent in Norway, Portugal, Spain and the United States. Although youth unemployment rates are still below the levels reached in the previous recession of the early 1980s, they have been rising since 1990, and the seasonally adjusted rate for the EC reached 21 per cent by December 1993. There is however a very wide range: from 5.2 per cent in western Germany to 39 per cent in Spain. The economic cost of this unused human capital in terms of foregone output is enormous, but the social costs, though difficult to quantify, are potentially much more serious. The regulation of labour markets, which sets minimum levels of compensation and offers employment protection to workers, along with weak standards of education and training, are often cited as the root causes of youth unemployment. Active labour market policies tend to focus on raising the levels of skill and experience of young people whilst temporarily subsidizing their employment costs, but the efforts have been piecemeal in many countries, and the results often disappointing.[74]

---

[71] See for example *Bank of England Quarterly Bulletin*, November 1993, pp.431-434. The early cyclical rise in employment may be attributable to the responsiveness of more flexible labour markets; to a correction of the overreaction by employers towards the end of 1992, following the exit of the pound sterling from the ERM; and to a higher activity level than that shown by official data.

[72] In 1992, some 45 per cent of employed women were working part-time in the United Kingdom (only Norway was higher), while women's share in part-time employment was some 85 per cent (the highest). OECD, *Employment Outlook*, July 1993, p.188, table D.

[73] EUROSTAT, *Unemployment*, 2 February 1994, Luxembourg; OECD, *Quarterly Labour Force Statistics*, No.4, 1993, Paris.

[74] For example, in the United Kingdom, between April and October 1992, one quarter of young people leaving the government's Youth Training Scheme became unemployed, only one third gained qualifications, while 52 per cent of those who started the scheme quit early. *Financial Times*, 13 December 1993.

TABLE 2.4.6

Unemployment by sex, age and duration in western Europe and North America, 1993 [a]

(Thousands and share in total unemployment, per cent)

	Female [b]		Young people [c]		Long term [d]	
	Thousands	Per cent	Thousands	Per cent	Thousands	Per cent
France	1 567.6	49.4	722.0	22.8	968.8	30.6
Germany [e]	1 000.5	43.7	315.5 [f]	14.3	579 [g]	25.3
Italy	2 573.0	53.1	2 799.0 [h]	47.2	..	..
United Kingdom	683.1	23.4	842.5	28.6	1 064.4	36.1
Austria	95.6	43.0	41.6	18.7	37.9	17.0
Belgium	312.7	56.9	..	..	..	..
Denmark	177.0	51.6	60.9	17.4	..	..
Finland	199.5	40.7	99.3	22.5	82.4	18.7
Greece	88.0	50.0	..	..	..	..
Ireland	100.5	34.1	86.6	29.4	..	..
Netherlands	136.5	32.9	93.0	25.0	172.0	46.0
Norway	46.5 [i]	39.3	43.0	34.0	30.0	24.1
Portugal	206.5	59.5	89.6 [j]	37.7	68.1	28.6
Spain	1 344.9	53.0	1 171.9	35.0	1 244.0	35.3
Sweden	156.6	41.0	98.0	27.4	..	..
Switzerland	66.6	45.9	32.2 [k]	19.8	30.9 [l]	18.5
United States	3 877.3 [j]	44.0	2 835.7 [j]	32.1	..	..
Canada	665.9	42.7	428.8 [k]	27.3	211.7 [k]	13.5

Sources: OECD, *Quarterly Labour Force Statistics*, No.4, 1993, Paris; national statistics and ECE secretariat estimates.

[a] Annual average, some figures are preliminary.
[b] Registered at labour offices, may understate total.
[c] Less than 25 years of age.
[d] Unemployed for one year or more.
[e] West Germany.
[f] First half average.
[g] End of August.
[h] 1992.
[i] Average of first eight months.
[j] Average of first three quarters.
[k] Average of nine months.
[l] Average of last ten months.

Since the beginning of the 1970s, unemployment in many countries in western Europe has tended to ratchet upwards with each cycle (chart 2.4.1), a trend which has gone hand-in-hand with a rise in both the average duration of unemployment and the incidence of *long-term unemployment* (the proportion of the jobless total who have been unemployed for one year or more). Whilst data are not available for all countries, it is clear that long-term unemployment is a major problem in the larger economies of the western ECE region: over 30 per cent of total unemployment in France and the United Kingdom in 1993 and some 25 per cent in western Germany, a total of some 2.6 million people (table 2.4.6). The root causes of this problem include changes in industrial structure and technological innovation, which have made traditional skills obsolete; labour market rigidities, which have kept labour costs above market-clearing levels; and generous benefits provision, which may discourage some of the unemployed from accepting work. The remedy is widely seen to lie in a mixture of closely targeted vocational training and retraining, wage restraint and wide-ranging labour market reforms, underpinned by sustained economic growth.

The concurrence of rising long-term structural unemployment and the lengthening duration of unemployment is sometimes cited as evidence of a deterioration in the competitive position of the economies of western Europe. As discussed above, there has been a long-term decline in manufacturing employment, accompanied by a change in the relative shares of different industrial sectors, and much current debate concerns the possible causal relationship between these trends and changing patterns of international trade. Studies tend to show, however, that trade has had an impact mainly on the structure of industrial employment rather than its overall level, where its effect appears to have been minimal.[75]

(iv) Labour market policy

The re-emergence of unemployment as a central focus of concern among economic policy makers has prompted debate about the appropriateness of different labour market policy instruments to address the problem. Whilst there is agreement that cyclical unemployment is likely to moderate as countries emerge from recession and move progressively into recovery, the strength of any increase in the demand for labour will depend crucially on whether there is *sustained* growth in output, and on the outcome of collective bargaining rounds, particularly in

---

[75] An early study of the decomposition of employment growth found that imports displaced less jobs than were gained by exports in France (1977-1985) and Germany (1978-1986), while the reverse was true for the United Kingdom (1968-1984), and in the United States (1972-1985) the net effect was zero. Factors other than trade were more important, with domestic demand the main positive influence and higher labour productivity the main negative influence on overall employment growth. At the industrial sector level the pattern which emerges is of import substitution causing employment losses in low-technology industries, while export expansion is a factor in job creation in the high-technology sector, a pattern which is repeated in a later study of 13 countries using more recent data (1980-1989). OECD, *Industrial Policy in OECD Countries*, op.cit., pp.106-108.

respect of wage restraint. Furthermore, there is a lack of consensus on the policy mix required to tackle the hard core of structural unemployment, with the argument split along broadly ideological lines. On the one hand, there is support for a strategy of more deregulated labour markets, which could involve a less generous social security net and possibly more decentralized wage bargaining procedures. This approach is exemplified by the labour market reforms introduced in the United Kingdom in the 1980s,[76] and is characteristic of labour markets in the United States. On the other hand, there is the more consensual approach of social partnership which has evolved in continental western Europe since the Second World War, and which is embodied in the Social Chapter of the Maastricht Treaty of the European Community. A recent example of the consensual approach is the agreement of July 1993 between the employers, trade unions and Government of Italy on a range of instruments for intervention in the labour market,[77] the stage for which was set by the termination of automatic wage indexation (scala mobile) in July 1992.

The tension between the two approaches was evident in the discussion on the prepublication drafts of the European Commission White Paper on growth, competitiveness and employment,[78] which was eventually endorsed at the summit meeting of the twelve heads of government in Brussels in December 1993. Recommending that the EU should adopt a target of creating at least 15 million new jobs by the year 2000, it is argued in the White Paper that this can be achieved by increasing the rate of sustainable economic growth to at least 3 per cent, and by increasing the employment content of that growth.[79] A growth strategy is set out, based on "three inseparable elements": a macroeconomic framework which supports market forces; action to improve the competitiveness of European industry; and active policies and structural changes in the labour markets.

To increase the rate of economic growth in the EU to 3 per cent, and to sustain it at that level in coming years, requires an increase in productive capacity, which in turn will depend on a significant increase in the investment-output ratio. A major role is assigned to investment in trans-European telecommunications, transport and energy networks, for their potential impact on both international competitiveness and job creation.

Whilst it is proposed to implement a combination of macroeconomic and structural policies in pursuit of sustained economic growth, the role envisaged for macroeconomic policy is essentially limited. It is argued that budgetary policy and wage behaviour must adapt to an inflation target of 2 to 3 per cent before interest rates can fall. In addition, budgetary policy will be restrained both by the convergence criterion of the Maastricht Treaty (budget deficits of less than 3 per cent of GDP), and by the need to increase national saving through higher public saving. Although there are occasional hints in the White Paper of the need for a boost in demand, the proposals leave little scope for expansionary fiscal policy, and there are no remedies to raise employment in the short term.

With macroeconomic policy limited to providing a "stable framework" role, greater weight is given to structural policy changes: a range of non-binding options is identified which can be adapted to the needs of each member state, with the EU playing a supporting role. A review of measures to enhance employment creation emphasizes the importance of adapting education and vocational training systems, and of mitigating factors which impede the transformation of growth into jobs, particularly the effects of statutory charges on labour.

It is acknowledged in the White Paper that there are no quick miracle cures to the immediate and pressing problem of mass unemployment in western Europe. However, whilst presenting a comprehensive analysis of the causes of the current levels of unemployment, the policy prescriptions focus mainly on the classical component of unemployment and largely ignore the Keynesian deficient demand component and the mechanism by which the latter may be transformed into the former. Yet tight macroeconomic policy is currently holding back output and employment growth in western Europe, and it is difficult to see how sustained output growth of at least 3 per cent a year can be achieved under the present policy regime. Given international interdependencies, a joint, coordinated macroeconomic initiative by the G-7 countries would make national policies more effective.[80]

---

[76] Reforms designed to increase work incentives included, *inter alia*, the reduction of the replacement ratio for unemployment benefits, the elimination of benefits for young people and mandatory six-monthly job-search interviews for all unemployed. Reforms to weaken union power, particularly in respect of the strike weapon, were embodied in four Employment Acts. In addition, the Wages Councils were abolished, measures were introduced to enhance self-employment, and there were new training initiatives. See D. Blanchflower and R. Freeman, "Did the Thatcher Reforms Change British Labour Market Performance?", Centre for Economic Performance, *Discussion Paper*, No.168, August 1993, p.21, table 2. The conclusions of this paper are that the "reforms succeeded in reducing union power and increasing the incentive to work – and may have increased the responsiveness of wages and employment at the micro-level. But they did not improve the response of real wages to unemployment nor the transition for men out of unemployment, and were accompanied by rising wage inequalities ...". (p.18).

[77] Banca d'Italia, *Economic Bulletin*, No.17, October 1993, pp.25-27. The agreement deals principally with incomes policy (two rounds of formal consultations each year), collective bargaining procedures (national industry-wide agreement setting contractual minimum wages, with decentralized agreements at company or local level, as in the past, but wage negotiations conducted more frequently) and labour market policy (rationalization of the regulatory framework).

[78] Commission of the European Communities, "Growth, Competitiveness, Employment: The Challenges and Ways Forward into the 21st Century", White Paper, *Bulletin of the European Communities*, Supplement 6/93, Luxembourg, 1993.

[79] It estimates that the target could be reached if, from 1995, the EU could sustain a rate of growth of at least 3 per cent a year, and an increase in the employment intensity of growth of between 0.5 and 1 percentage point (that is, a gap between output growth and employment growth of 1 to 1.5 percentage points). Evidently, for a given rate of output growth this implies a fall in total productivity growth. Op.cit., p.46.

[80] For a fuller discussion see G.D.N. Worswick, "The scope for macroeconomic policy to alleviate unemployment in western Europe", United Nations Economic Commission for Europe, *Discussion Papers*, Vol.2(1992), No.3, New York, 1992.

CHART 2.4.1

Standardized unemployment rates in western Europe and North America, 1973-1993
(Per cent of labour force; seasonally adjusted)

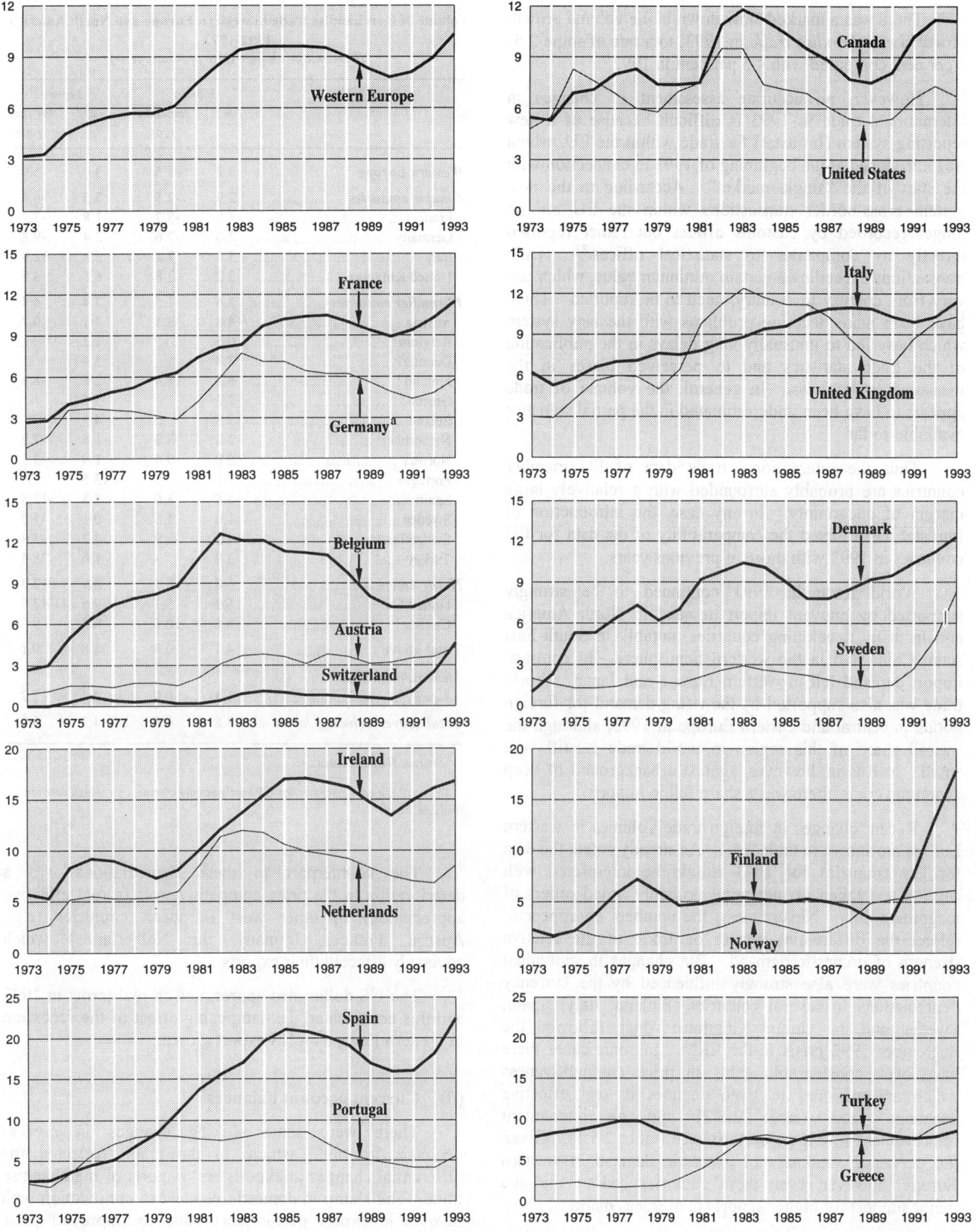

Sources: OECD, *Quarterly Labour Force Statistics*, No.3, Paris, 1993; *Economic Outlook*, No.53, June 1993, Paris; national statistics and ECE secretariat estimates.

[a] West Germany.

2.5 Foreign trade and payments

(i) Trade volumes

There was a marked slow-down in the volume growth of *world merchandise trade* in 1993, to a rate of some 2.5-3 per cent compared with 4.5 per cent in 1992.

However, an accurate assessment of changes in international trade in 1993 is difficult because of a new reporting system (Intrastat) for trade within the EU, which was introduced at the beginning of 1993 in connection with the start of the "single market". According to the new system cross-border transactions within the EU are no longer recorded by customs offices but rather reported directly by companies to statistical offices.[81] Only transactions exceeding a certain minimum value, which can vary from country to country, need to be reported. There have been many teething problems with the new system which have led to unusually long delays in the publication of the trade statistics and to perceived biases in the measured trade flows. In general, the volume of trade appears to have been underestimated in the partial statistics available so far.

Thus the international trade data of EU member countries are probably surrounded with a relatively large margin of uncertainty. In any case, the introduction of Intrastat has affected the comparability of the data for EU countries in 1993 with those of previous years.

World trade in 1993 continued to be strongly supported by buoyant import demand in North America and in many developing countries, notably in South-East Asia, China and in the western hemisphere. In contrast, import demand fell in western Europe and Japan. World trade was also supported by the rising demand for foreign goods in central and eastern Europe in 1993, although the overall share of this region in world trade is still very small. In Russia, however, against a background of deep economic crisis, there was a sharp fall in imports.

Recent changes in foreign trade volumes in western Europe are shown in table 2.5.1. As already noted, the data for EU countries for 1993 should be interpreted with caution and taken as indicating probably broad orders of magnitude only. Nevertheless, the numbers do appear to reflect the differential impact on trade of the relative strength of domestic demand. But changes in individual countries were also strongly influenced by the currency depreciations in several countries (Finland, Italy, Spain, Sweden and the United Kingdom) which followed the September 1992 crisis in the ERM. In some cases there have been considerable gains in price competitiveness which are mirrored in large declines in real effective exchange rates (table 2.5.2) and a concomitant improvement in export performance (table 2.5.1). Given the pervasive weakness of domestic demand in western Europe, however, even these countries had to find the major support for higher exports in overseas markets.

TABLE 2.5.1

Volume of merchandise trade in western Europe and North America, 1992-1993
(Percentage change over previous year)

	Exports		Imports	
	1992	Jan.-June 1993	1992	Jan.-June 1993
Western Europe	3.2	-1.5	3.0	-5.9
4 major countries	2.9	-2.5	3.5	-6.6
France	4.8	-5.7	1.8	-7.7
Germany	2.0	-7.6	2.4	-9.8
Italy	3.5	7.2	3.3	-12.9
United Kingdom	2.2	3.8	6.5	3.5
13 smaller countries	3.6	1.5	2.4	-4.4
Austria	4.8	-3.1	4.7	-0.7
Belgium	0.5	..	1.3	..
Denmark	3.8	..	3.4	..
Finland	8.2	14.4	-2.6	-8.3
Greece	7.2	..	5.6	..
Ireland	13.8	..	4.9	..
Netherlands	2.2	-3.3	1.5	-7.2
Norway	5.0	-0.4	1.9	-2.3
Portugal	7.1	..	13.5	..
Spain	5.5	8.0	8.8	-12.8
Sweden	1.0	1.5	0.1	-1.0
Switzerland	4.3	-1.9	-4.3	-5.3
Turkey	3.0	-	1.6	38.4
North America	6.8	6.4	8.9	12.3
United States	6.2	5.1	9.5	13.0
Canada	8.6	10.6	6.4	9.4
Total above	4.1	0.8	4.8	0.1
Memorandum item:				
Japan	1.5	0.9	-0.4	1.2
***Total above*, including Japan**	3.8	0.8	4.3	0.2

Source: National statistics.

Note: Regional aggregates for 1993 include only countries for which data are available.

The counterpart to these depreciations was a deterioration in the price competitiveness (a real effective appreciation) of other west European countries (e.g., Austria, France, Germany, the Netherlands) which adversely affected their exports.

The US dollar also appreciated in real terms in 1993 and this accentuated the dampening effect of the recession in western Europe on US export growth.

(ii) Current account balances

There were some striking changes in *current accounts* in 1993, which, in the main, reflected the differential changes in exports and imports of merchandise trade. The slump in domestic demand in conjunction with favourable export performance, due to improved price competitiveness, led to a swing from deficit to surplus in the current account of Italy and to markedly lower deficits in Finland, Spain and Sweden (table 2.5.3). In France, an

---

[81] Trade with countries outside the EU continues to be recorded by customs.

TABLE 2.5.2

Real effective exchange rates, 1988-1993
(Indices, 1987=100))

	1988	1989	1990	1991	1992	1993
France	97.6	95.2	97.5	93.4	94.6	97.1
Germany [a]	100.5	98.3	104.1	102.6	106.1	112.5
Italy	97.8	102.3	109.0	109.8	108.0	88.6
United Kingdom	105.7	110.0	105.4	109.2	106.7	96.9
Austria	95.3	92.4	92.5	90.3	91.8	95.4
Belgium	97.4	96.1	100.5	100.2	101.3	101.2
Denmark	99.6	97.3	103.0	100.0	100.4	103.9
Finland	103.4	107.9	112.5	104.8	85.5	75.7
Ireland	94.7	86.8	88.4	82.7	81.4	76.0
Netherlands	97.3	91.9	93.2	92.7	96.4	101.0
Norway	101.8	99.3	98.8	95.5	94.8	92.6
Spain	105.0	113.2	122.3	126.5	128.9	117.0
Sweden	103.7	110.4	111.2	110.7	111.2	84.8
Switzerland	99.2	92.3	98.2	97.7	96.2	..
North America						
United States	94.6	97.5	90.9	89.6	87.1	91.7
Canada	109.2	118.4	121.0	124.6	116.8	108.2
Memorandum item:						
Japan	105.8	100.1	88.9	95.5	99.4	121.4

Source: IMF, *International Financial Statistics*, various issues.

Note: Data refer to period averages. A fall in the index is equivalent to an increase in price competitiveness.

[a] Data refer to total Germany (east + west) as from 1992.

TABLE 2.5.3

Current account balances in western Europe and North America, 1991-1993
(Billion US dollars and per cent of GDP)

	1991	1992	1993	Per cent of GDP 1992	Per cent of GDP 1993
Western Europe	-60.9	-61.8	14.4	-0.8	0.2
4 major countries	-62.9	-67.0	-20.1	-1.2	-0.4
France	-6.1	3.6	10.5*	0.3	0.8
Germany	-19.9	-25.3	-21.9	-1.7	-1.3
Italy	-23.3	-27.9	7.2	-2.3	0.9
United Kingdom	-13.5	-17.5	-16.0	-1.7	-1.7
13 smaller countries	2.0	5.2	34.6	0.2	1.6
Austria	0.1	-0.1	-0.9	-0.1	-0.5
Belgium	4.6	6.2	10.9	2.8	5.3
Denmark	2.1	4.8	5.3	3.4	4.0
Finland	-6.6	-4.9	-1.0	-4.6	-1.2
Greece	-1.5	-2.1	-1.4	-2.7	-1.9
Ireland	1.5	2.6	2.5	5.2	5.5
Netherlands	7.8	7.5	9.4	2.3	3.1
Norway	5.1	2.9	2.5	2.5	2.4
Portugal	-0.7	-0.1	-0.4	-0.1	-0.5
Spain	-16.7	-18.9	-5.0	-3.3	-1.0
Sweden	-4.4	-6.6	-0.4	-2.7	-0.2
Switzerland	10.6	15.1	18.7	6.2	8.0
Turkey	0.3	-0.9	-5.8	-0.8	-5.0
North America	-29.0	-89.3	-128.8	-1.4	-1.9
United States	-3.7	-66.4	-109.2	-1.1	-1.7
Canada	-25.3	-22.9	-19.6	-4.0	-3.6
Total above	-89.9	-151.1	-114.4	-1.0	-0.7
Memorandum item:					
Japan	72.9	117.6	131.3	3.2	3.1
Total above, including Japan	-17.0	-33.5	17.0	-0.2	0.1

Sources: National statistics; IMF, *International Financial Statistics*, Washington, D.C., various issues; OECD, *Main Economic Indicators*, Paris, various issues.

absolute decline in imports of goods outstripped the decline in exports and this was the major factor behind the marked rise in the current account surplus, which corresponded to nearly 1 per cent of GDP in 1993. Relative to GDP, the current account deficit remained broadly unchanged in Germany and the United Kingdom.

In the United States the current account deficit increased to some $109 billion or about 1.7 per cent of GDP in 1993, which compares with 1.1 per cent in 1992. In Japan the current account surplus rose in US dollar terms in 1993 because of the strong appreciation of the yen; when measured in yen, the surplus actually fell, albeit only slightly. For the west European countries combined there was a swing from deficit into a small surplus in the current account in 1993. This, together with the considerable surplus in Japan, however, was virtually fully offset by the deficit in North America, thus yielding a broadly balanced current account for the western industrialized countries as a group (table 2.5.3).

Chapter 3

THE TRANSITION ECONOMIES

3.1 Expectations and outcomes for 1993

The process of transforming the previously centrally planned economies of eastern Europe and the former Soviet Union into viable market economies entered a critical stage in 1993.[82] Important progress has been achieved in liberalizing economic activity, scrapping old bureaucratic institutions and establishing foundations of a market system, and output recovery has gained momentum in some countries. Nevertheless, the process of adjustment to the new environment is slow, confirming the view that large-scale structural change is much more difficult to achieve with market instruments alone than envisaged. After four years of reforms and stabilization efforts, symptoms of "reform fatigue" are spreading across the region, and early hopes for rapid and painless transition have given way to more sober and increasingly pessimistic expectations. The prolonged economic recession, sharply reduced job security and greater income differentiation have all contributed to political polarization and mounting social tensions in most of the transition countries. The signs of growing discontent observed in more advanced transition countries contrast with their improved macroeconomic performance in 1993, which demonstrates that market reforms begin eventually to deliver results. However, recent political developments in some transition countries, including election out-turns in Slovakia, Lithuania, Poland and – most recently – Russia, have shown that, at the popular consciousness level, these results are commonly regarded as limited, inadequate, and coming late.

The overall economic and social situation of transition countries remains rather complex, and does not lend itself to easy generalizations. While statistical data for 1993 offer many signs of improving macroeconomic performance in a number of countries, they also point to emerging new problems and constraints. Moreover, there are growing differences between the countries in the region: while some of them are now fairly advanced in transition and demonstrate rather strong growth potential, many others are still in the midst of deep recession with few prospects for an upturn in the near future. The picture is further blurred by lack of some important statistics, generally low reliability of officially published data, and substantial delays in their release by national statistical services. Those available in early 1994 point to varying mixtures of positive and negative developments.

(i) Overview of developments in 1993

Signs of a fragile recovery in eastern Europe

Recession continued in *eastern Europe* as a whole in 1993, but the situation improved significantly relative to 1992. In several transition countries the output decline has been stopped, and in some of them even reversed, while in most of other countries it has strongly decelerated. *Eastern Europe* as a whole still registered a GDP fall of some 3 per cent in 1993, which thus becomes the fourth year of contraction for the region (see table 3.1.1). Only Albania and Poland showed relatively significant growth of *gross domestic product* in 1993, by 11 and 4 per cent, respectively, while in Romania and Slovenia the decline of output was reversed. In the Czech Republic and Hungary GDP fell by another 1-2 per cent, but an upturn of industrial output in Hungary and a steady increase of domestic absorption in the Czech Republic since the beginning of the last year suggest that the contraction has bottomed out. In the remaining east European countries, however, output contraction continued quite strongly and without significant let-up as the year progressed, although the rates of fall have been much smaller than in 1992. GDP levels have fallen by 5-8 per cent in Bulgaria, Croatia and Slovakia, by 15 per cent in the FYR of Macedonia and by 37 per cent in FR Yugoslavia.

Industrial output grew strongly in Poland (by 7 per cent) and also, albeit by somewhat smaller margins, in Hungary, Romania and perhaps Albania. In the Czech and Slovak Republics, where industrial output appeared ready to turn up in the last quarter of 1992, thus prompting hopes of quick recovery, a new downturn came in the first half of 1993 which reflected largely the impact of the separation of the two countries. A further decline of industrial output was also registered in Bulgaria (by 9 per cent) and in the states which emerged from former Yugoslavia. As a whole, eastern Europe recorded a further decline of (gross) industrial output by about 4 per cent in 1993 relative to

---

[82] *Eastern Europe* here refers to the formerly centrally planned economies of Albania, Bulgaria, Hungary, Poland and Romania, and the successor states of Czechoslovakia and of the Socialist Federal Republic of Yugoslavia. Statistical aggregates for eastern Europe may be based, for reasons of data availability, on information from a smaller number of countries only. Among the newly-independent countries formerly republics of the *Soviet Union*, distinction is made between the *Baltic states* (Estonia, Latvia and Lithuania), and the majority of the remaining republics which cooperate in the institutions of the Commonwealth of Independent States (CIS) the *CIS countries*. Reference to the *European transition countries* comprises all of the above. Developments in the eastern *Länder* of Germany, the former German Democratic Republic, as a *sui generis* transition economy, are noted in the tables for reference.

TABLE 3.1.1

European transition countries: Economic activity, 1990-1993
(Percentage change over same period of preceding year)

	NMP or GDP [a]					Gross industrial output			1993				
	1990	1991	1992	1993	1994 forecast	1990	1991	1992	Jan.-March	Jan.-June	Jan.-Sept.	Jan.-Dec.	1994 forecast
Albania	-13.1	-29.4	-6.0	11*	8	-7.5	-30.0	..	..	..	..	-1 [b]	..
Bulgaria [b]	-9.1	-11.7	-7.7	-6*	..	-17.2	-22.2	-16.2	-10.9	-8.2	-8.5	-9.3*	..
Bosnia-Herzegovina	1.6	..	..	..	..	0.9	-10.5	-25	..	..	..	..	..
Croatia [c]	-8.5	-29	-8	-8*	-	-11	-28.5	-14.6	-1.1	-1.5	-3.7	-6.0*	..
Czech Republic [b]	-1.2	-14.2	-7.1	-0.5	1.5-2.5	-3.3	-24.4	-10.6	-7.3 [d]	-6.7 [d]	-7.4	-7.1* [d]	-(0-2)
Hungary [b]	-3.3	-11.9	-5.0	-2*	..	-4.5	-19.1	-9.8	0.1	2.4	4.2	3.8*	..
Poland [b]	-11.6	-7.6	1.5	4.0	4.5	-24.2	-11.9	4.2	7.1	9.3	8.3	7.4	..
Romania [b]	-8.2	-13.7	-15.4	1	1.5	-19.0	-18.7	-22.1	-16.0	-6.7	-1.2	1.3	2.0
Slovakia [b]	-2.5	-14.5	-7.0	-4.7	..	-4.0	-25.4	-12.9	-26.2	-18.2	-14.7	-15.4	..
Slovenia [b]	-4.7	-9.3	-6.0	1	1	-10.5	-12.4	-13.2	-7.4	-6.7	-4.8	-2.8	-2
The FYR of Macedonia [c]	-10.2	-12.1	-13.4	-15.0*	-8	-11.0	-17.4	-15.8	-2.3	-7.5	-12.4	-15.0*	-12
Yugoslavia (FR) [c]	-8.4	-11.2	-26.1	-30.3	-10	-11.7	-17.6	-22.4	-39.8	-41.1	-38.7	-37.4	..
Eastern Europe	-7.9	-12.3	-7.4	-3	1*	-15.1	-18.1	-10.0	-7.6	-4.6	-3.6	-4*	..
CETE-4	-7.5	-10.2	-2.2	1	3*	-15.3	-16.8	-2.4	0.2	2.2	2.1	2*	..
SETE-8	-8.6	-15.0	-14.5	-8	-2*	-15.0	-19.6	-19.2	-16.7	-12.9	-10.5	-10*	..
Armenia	-8.2	-11.4	-46.0	-9.9	..	-7.5	-7.7	-52.5	-58.4	-51.4	-39.9	-11.1	..
Azerbaijan	-11.3	-0.4	-28.1	-13.3	..	-6.3	4.7	-24.0	-20.4	-12.4	-11.6	-6.8	..
Belarus	-3.2	-1.9	-10.6	-10	..	2.1	-1.0	-9.4	-16.5	-16.3	-14.9	-10.9	..
Georgia	-4.3	..	-43.4	-35	..	-5.7	..	-45.8	..	..	..	-26.6	..
Kazakhstan	-0.9	-10.3	-14.2	-12.8	..	-0.8	-0.9	-14.8	-11.3	-10.7	-11.8	-16.1	..
Kyrgyzstan	4.8	-5.2	-19.0	-17.4	..	-0.6	-0.3	-26.8	-22.4	-24.6	-26.0	-24.2	..
Moldova	-1.5	-18.0	-21.3	-4	..	3.2	-11.1	-21.7	0.2	0.9	7.0	-10 [e]	..
Russia	-4.0	-14.3	-22.0	-13	..	-0.1	-8.0	-18.0	-19.3	-18.0	-16.7	-16.2	-12
Russia [b]	-2.0	-12.9	-18.5	-12	-(8-10)	..	..	..	..	..	..	..	..
Tajikistan	0.2	-8.4	-31.0	-21	..	1.2	-3.6	-24.3	-28.2	-30.5	-24.5	-19.5	..
Turkmenistan	1.8	-4.7	..	7.8	..	3.2	4.8	-16.7	5.1	16.9	15.9	5.3	..
Ukraine	-3.6	-11.2	-16	-16	..	-0.1	-4.8	-9.0	-15.0 [e]	-18.0 [e]	-18.0 [e]	-22.4 [e]	..
Uzbekistan	4.3	-2.4	-12.9	-3.5	..	1.8	1.5	-6.2	-3.5	-1.9	4.7	-7 [e]	..
CIS	-3.4	-12.2	-19.9	-13	-10*	-1.1	-7.	-18.2	-17.5	-16.1	-14.9	-14.6	..
Estonia [b]	-8.1	-10.0	-14.4	-2*	..	-5.6	-9.0	-38.9	-39.8	-34.9	-31.8	-26.6	..
Latvia [b]	2.7	-8.3	-33.8	-19.9	..	-0.2	-0.6	-35.1	-41.9	-40.9	-38.4	-34.6	..
Lithuania [b]	-6.9	-13.1	-37.7	-17*	..	-2.8	-4.9	-51.6	-52.0	-51.9	-48.5	-46.0	..
Baltic states	-3.9	-10.8	-31.5	-14.8*	-2*	-2.5	-4.2	-43.3	-45.2*	-44.7	-41.7	-38.2	..
Total transition economies	-4.8	-12.3	-16.9	-10.0	-6*	-3.6	-8.8	-15.7	-16.3	-15.0	-13.8	-13.8	..
Ex-GDR *Länder* [b]	-15.5	-29.1	9.7	7.0	6-7	-27.3	-49.1	-6.2	-2.3	2.2	4.4	5.5*	..

Sources: National statistical publications and statistical office communications to ECE; IMF estimates for Albania; non-governmental forecasts. Aggregates for eastern Europe, the Baltic states and total transition economies are ECE secretariat computations based on 1992 weights and some estimates for missing components. Forecasts for 1994 are generally end-1993 forecasts of national conjunctural institutes.

Note: Aggregates are: *Eastern Europe* (the 12 countries above that line), with sub-aggregates *CETE-4* ("central European transition economies": Czech Republic, Hungary, Poland, Slovakia) and *SETE-8* ("south European transition economies": Albania, Bulgaria, Romania, and the 5 Yugoslav successor states); *CIS* (12 member countries of the Commonwealth of Independent States); *Baltic states* (Estonia, Latvia, Lithuania), and *total transition countries*.

[a] Net material product (produced) unless otherwise noted.
[b] Gross domestic product.
[c] Gross material product (value added of the material sphere including depreciation).
[d] Enterprises with 25 or more employees.
[e] Sample of physical output indicators. Since March 1993, the Ukrainian Ministry of Statistics publishes two industrial output indicators: one based on deflated gross output value analogous to those shown for other CIS countries, and one based on an aggregation of physical indicators. The former shows much more moderate rates of output contraction in 1993 (5 per cent for January-June, 8 per cent for January-September, 7.4 per cent for January-December), but may be affected by inadequate deflation procedures during a period of rapidly accelerating inflation. Similar physical indicator measures of industrial output for the full year 1993 were also published for Moldova (-10 per cent, vs. 4.2 per cent growth in deflated output value) and Uzbekistan (-7 per cent, vs. 4.1 per cent growth). The physical indicator values are recorded in the table.

1992 (see table 3.1.1). With few exceptions (Romania, Poland, Albania), *agricultural production* also decreased in transition countries due to poor weather conditions and structural reforms. By contrast, the *service sector* continued to expand rapidly in all countries.

The output results in 1993 are generally *below expectations*: earlier official forecasts for GDP figures proved over-optimistic for Hungary, the Czech Republic, Slovakia, Bulgaria, and the successor states of the former SFR Yugoslavia. In contrast, in Albania, Poland, and Romania GDP grew faster then predicted. The sluggishness of recovery in eastern Europe has been a result of a confluence of unfavourable external and internal factors, such as recession in western Europe, tight macroeconomic policies pursued in many countries, sanctions imposed on FR Yugoslavia which also affected neighbouring countries, the split of the Czechoslovak federation, and the continued economic and political instability in most CIS countries. The lack of vigorous expansion is also probably linked to the slow pace of restructuring and privatization, and to the traditional behaviour of managers of state-owned enterprises. The impact of all these factors could only partly be offset by some positive developments, such as improved access to west European markets for certain categories of goods (mostly manufactures), low international interest rates and falling energy prices.

Symptoms of economic *recovery* observed in some transition countries have been widely publicized. Poland's case is the least controversial, because the upturn in that country is well documented by output and demand indicators showing a continuous and quite strong growth of production and domestic absorption during the last eighteen months. Signs of emerging recovery in Albania, the Czech Republic, Hungary, Romania and Slovenia are also clearly visible though generally less impressive. However, the underlying mechanism and the driving forces of the recovery in most cases offer a less reassuring picture and may give rise to some concern. This is because the changes in the structure of final demand in these countries in 1993 suggest that in nearly all cases the expansion has been fuelled mainly by rapidly growing *consumer expenditures*.

Although the data on national accounts are still incomplete, the available figures show a further decline of overall *investments* in 1993 by 10 per cent in real terms in the Czech Republic, and stagnation or a modest increase in Hungary and Poland; only in Slovenia there was a strong upturn in investment expenditures (by 11 per cent). Except for the Czech Republic, imports rose faster than exports in these countries (in Hungary, exports actually declined sharply), and government consumption increased. Indirect evidence on the consumption "boom" in Poland, the Czech Republic and Slovenia can be obtained from statistics on retail trade which show an increase in real terms of 11, 3 and 5 per cent, respectively. This observation is consistent with the recent data on rapidly growing personal incomes and a fall of the rate of savings in all the countries concerned.

Such *consumption-led recovery* may not, however, be sustainable in the medium-term perspective, because typically it translates into higher imports and reduces domestic financial resources available for capital investments. In fact, the *current account deficits* registered in east European countries in 1993 strongly supported domestic absorption, as they correspond to inflows of resources from abroad. But the deficits of such a magnitude probably cannot be financed on a sustained basis. Given their precarious external balance situation, the countries concerned risk running up against balance-of-payments constraints rather soon, which would force them to impose restrictions on domestic absorption and thus slow down economic growth. The danger may be headed off if exports are vigorously encouraged to expand, but to make this option feasible in the longer run, new investments are needed in the existing and new export sectors.

No end to contraction in the CIS countries and Baltic states

In the former republics of the Soviet Union contraction of output continued in 1993 at an average rate of some 13 per cent. Though the drop was less than in 1992, prospects for immediate recovery remain bleak. However, macroeconomic performance differed widely across countries. The fall of GDP has been particularly deep in several Asian *CIS* republics (exceeding 20 per cent), where ethnic conflicts disrupted the economies, and also in the *Baltic states* where drastic stabilization measures as well as the sudden break of the trade links with the former Soviet Union produced more severe recession than in other republics. At the other end of the spectrum was Turkmenistan where an increase of GDP by 8 per cent was officially reported; the fall of output was also relatively moderate in Moldova and Uzbekistan (4 per cent).

In the *Russian Federation*, during 1993 the GDP is estimated to have fallen 12 per cent below its 1992 level, a certain improvement over the staggering 19 per cent fall in 1992, but still an enormous setback for a peacetime economy. *Industrial output* dropped generally by a somewhat larger margin than GDP: by 16 per cent in Russia, by 15 per cent for the CIS as a whole, and by almost 40 per cent in the Baltic states.

Macroeconomic performance in Russia, Ukraine and most other CIS states in 1993 turned out to be generally worse than initially expected. At the beginning of the year the Russian government aimed at slowing down the output decline to 5 per cent, and stabilization at that level was predicted for 1994. But continued controversies between the executive and legislative branches over the required course of macroeconomic policies, and lack of control over credit policy and public finances, contributed to a deeper than expected contraction of output.

(ii) **Scourges of transition: Inflation and unemployment**

Inflation proves harder to control than expected

Inflation decelerated to 20-40 per cent in a number of *east European* transition economies in the course of 1993, but showed a tendency to accelerate again towards the end of the year. Notable exceptions to this pattern were Croatia and Romania, where the annual inflation rates nearly doubled in 1993, and especially FR Yugoslavia, where unrestricted money emission has resulted in an explosion of hyperinflation since the end of 1992. Although slowing, inflation remained dangerously high also in Bulgaria. Inflation was lower than in 1992 in the Czech Republic, Hungary and Poland, but in no country has it come down to single-digit annual rates. The persistence of inflation in most transition countries seems to be chiefly associated with structural rigidities such as those observed on the labour market, with policy decisions such as frequent changes in the tax and customs regimes, with continuous devaluations and, in some cases, with large budget deficits. With rates of 1-2 per cent per month in the second half of

1993, the Czech Republic, Hungary, Slovakia and Slovenia registered the lowest inflation in the region.

In the area of the former Soviet Union, inflation subsided sharply only in the *Baltic states* in the wake of the shift to national currencies and disciplined monetary and fiscal policies. In *Russia* and most other *CIS states* inflation continued at an average monthly rate of 20 per cent for most of 1993 but, contrary to earlier predictions and fears, it has not so far developed into hyperinflation, and in some countries (Russia) it even slowed down towards the end of 1993. However, prospects for 1994 are uncertain, with the new economic policy course in Russia still to be clarified after the December 1993 parliamentary elections. Much higher inflation rates – ranging between 50 and 80 per cent per month – were observed in *Georgia, Belarus* and *Ukraine*.

The fight against inflation figures prominently on the list of policy priorities of governments in transition countries, but the task appears to be much more difficult than expected. While most east European countries were indeed able to bring down inflation from rates in some cases dangerously close to hyperinflation, they seem to face many more difficulties in reducing it further to single-digit rates. In some countries financial and budgetary policies have become too permissive, in others structural rigidities, cost pressures and depreciating exchange rates continue to push prices up.

Where an easing of inflationary tendencies was observed in the east European countries, it has not only come as a result of the painful medicine of restrictive financial policies, but has reflected also the dwindling impact of repercussions from the initial price liberalization steps implemented in 1990 and 1991. In some countries the fall of inflation rates was strongly enhanced by the introduction of *new national currencies* accompanied by determined efforts to strengthen monetary and credit discipline and backed by international support programmes. The examples of successful monetary reforms in Estonia and Latvia highlight the crucial role of a stable currency in the fight against inflation. However, the change of currency, if not accompanied by monetary and fiscal restraint, is not in itself sufficient to fight inflation, as demonstrated by the recent experience of some CIS states, such as Georgia or Ukraine.

Unemployment rises steadily in most countries

Entering the fourth year of reforms, the transition countries of *eastern Europe* are increasingly confronted by macroeconomic problems of a somewhat different nature to those which dominated the initial stage of transformation. Perhaps the most important is the issue of *unemployment*, which is becoming a serious threat to social stability in those countries where tough financial policies have forced ailing state enterprises to lay off workers on a massive scale. Unemployment rates of 15-16 per cent, currently registered in Bulgaria, Poland and Slovenia, may not look particularly high by international standards. However, these rates have grown very rapidly in recent years, and are difficult to tolerate in societies which had hoped for better, but got worse in many respects. In fact, real unemployment is most likely even higher: as demonstrated by labour market surveys in some countries, many unemployed do not register because they have either lost their unemployment compensation benefits or have never been entitled to receive them.

The slow-down in output decline has not led to any marked improvement on the *labour markets*. During 1993, *employment* continued to fall and *unemployment* continued to rise in nearly all transition countries, albeit at a much slower pace than in 1992. In *eastern Europe*, total unemployment increased from 6.4 million at the end of 1992 to 7 million (more than 14 per cent of the total work force in the region) at end-1993. However, rates of unemployment differed widely across countries. The highest rates were reported in FR Yugoslavia and the FYR of Macedonia (some 25-30 per cent), while in most other transition countries unemployment rates varied between 12 and 17 per cent. The exception to this pattern is the Czech Republic where the unemployment rate remained exceptionally low, at about 3.5 per cent, despite the substantial fall in GDP of more than 20 per cent over the last three years. This suggests continued labour hoarding and perhaps also different labour market policies as compared with other transition countries.

Unemployment has been increasing also in the *former Soviet republics*, although it still remains at relatively low levels when compared with the contraction of output. This anomaly not only reflects deficiencies in the official statistics (which certainly underestimate the actual unemployment) and weak incentives for the unemployed to register, but also specific policies of extensive subsidies and lax credit, aimed at shoring up state enterprises in some countries.

Unemployment is a relatively novel experience for transition countries, and this may be one of the reasons for the low efficiency of policy measures aimed at stimulating employment and opening new job opportunities for persons laid off by state enterprises. Another reason may be the reluctance of the new governments committed to liberal, free-market policies to re-install some of the instruments of direct intervention on the labour market. Conceptual weakness and ideological prejudices, but increasingly also budgetary constraints, have so far prevented transition countries from undertaking large-scale remedial programmes (with possibilities ranging from retraining of workers to public works activities).

(iii) External imbalances

In all transition economies of *eastern Europe* a sharp deterioration of *trade balances* has been observed in 1993. Trade deficits have widened (or surpluses shrunk) particularly rapidly in those economies where domestic demand has shown signs of recovery (Hungary, Poland). The trade balance of eastern Europe (excluding FR Yugoslavia, where trade was affected by rather special circumstances) shifted from a small surplus in 1992 to a massive deficit of $8-9 billion in the first three quarters of 1993, and is not likely to have improved towards the end of the year. The emergence or growth of trade deficits has in most cases been the result of rising imports and falling exports; only in the Czech Republic, Poland and Romania did overall exports rise, though (except for the Czech Republic) at a slower rate than overall imports. The highest export growth was reported by the Czech Republic (by some 15 per cent in dollar terms compared with 1992), but this has been to some extent caused by the diversion of exports away from Slovakia to other markets. The uneven performance of east European export sectors is somewhat disappointing in view of earlier hopes which arose from various policy measures aimed at improving access to western markets, in particular those linked to the Association Agreements with the European Union and EFTA. While the data are still incomplete, it is clear that eastern Europe's trade balance with the European Union deteriorated significantly in 1993.

According to official data, both exports and imports of the *Baltic states* increased substantially in 1993. However, the reported figures should be treated with caution, as they may not be fully comparable with 1992 data because of the shift to new currencies and to new systems of reporting. By contrast, *Russia and other CIS states* posted large trade surpluses in 1993, which in most cases reflected predominantly cuts in imports, rather than expansion of exports. According to official data, Russian exports to countries other than former Soviet republics ("dal'nee zarubezh'e") in 1993 increased by 1 per cent and imports declined by 27 per cent in current dollar value terms, and the trade surplus for the whole year reached $16 billion.

Factors behind the slow-down of exports of transition countries can be classified into two categories. Among the *external factors*, three are commonly cited: economic recession in industrialized countries, restricted access to western (particularly EU) markets and sanctions against FR Yugoslavia. The fall of *western import demand* was substantial in 1993, and east European exports may have been particularly badly affected because of their specific commodity structure, concentrated in intermediate products and lower-quality finished goods. The second explanation links the poor export performance of transition countries with *protectionist policies* of the EU; but it is not easy to support this hypothesis with hard evidence. Tariffs on imports of most industrial goods from those transition countries which acquired association status with the EU have been lifted and, according to many studies, remaining quantitative limits are as a rule not fully taken up.[83] Access to EU markets was probably more restricted in 1990 and 1991 than in 1992, and yet many transition countries posted large increases of exports to the EU in those years. In fact, neither recession nor market restrictions prevented Czech and Polish exporters from increasing sales on EU markets by 15-20 per cent in dollar terms in 1993.

On the other hand, it may also be argued that the very existence of quotas and of other safeguard provisions is sufficiently effective in restricting the expansion of exports from transition countries to western markets. These provisions do not have to be actually triggered off to have an intimidating effect.[84] Also, the impact of QRs may be felt more strongly at the level of particular products, an effect which is not always captured by the analysis of aggregate trade data. The imposition of restrictions on steel exports from the Czech Republic is one example of how constraining such limits may be, and the 1993 ban on exports of meat and live animals from eastern Europe is another.

The impact of the UN Security Council's *trade embargo* on FR Yugoslavia has been particularly disastrous for Bulgaria and the FYR of Macedonia. Both countries suffered not only from cuts in direct trade links with the republics of FR Yugoslavia (Serbia and Montenegro), but also from disruption of traditional transit routes linking them with western Europe. According to a recently released report by the Bulgarian government, total direct and indirect losses incurred by that country due to the sanctions against FR Yugoslavia may amount to $3 billion.[85] Substantial trade and income losses have also been incurred by Albania, Hungary and Romania.

Apart from external causes, there are also other reasons for the sluggish export expansion of transition countries. The first is stabilization-oriented *economic policies* followed in most of them. In the previous edition of this publication, the ECE secretariat drew attention to the continuous real appreciation of some east European currencies, especially the Hungarian forint and the Polish zloty, and warned that this could lead to dampened exports because of its impact on the competitiveness of producers.[86] These currencies came under pressure already in 1992, but governments and central banks resisted devaluations, fearing unwanted effects on domestic inflation and overall business confidence. Poland eventually devalued the zloty in August 1993, when the cumulative trade deficit since the beginning of year had reached almost $1.5 billion (according to balance of payments statistics). Similarly, Hungary decided to accelerate its micro-devaluations only after the current-year trade gap exceeded $2 billion. These decisions were probably long overdue.

But devaluation is a short-term measure and its impact will be limited if there are *structural constraints* in export sectors. The slow-down of export growth observed in 1992-1993 in transition countries may actually be a result of a lack of strong export capacities within the existing economic structures. Once initial reserves have been exhausted in response to trade liberalization, the transition countries face increasing problems in

---

[83] See U. Möbius, D. Schumacher, "Community trade barriers facing Central and Eastern European countries. Impact of the Europe Agreements", mimeo, Deutsches Institut für Wirtschaftsforschung, Berlin, November 1992, and P. Messerlin, "The Trade Relations of the Central and East European Countries", paper presented at the XVth Workshop on European Economic Interaction and Integration, *The Vienna Institute for Comparative Economic Studies*, Vienna, November 1993. The impact of quantitative restrictions on east European exports to the EU is extensively discussed in UN Economic Commission for Europe, *Economic Bulletin for Europe*, Vol.45 (1993), New York and Geneva, 1994, chapter 3.2.

[84] This point is stressed by many commentators; see e.g., J. Rollo, A. Smith, "The political economy of Eastern European trade with the European Community: Why so sensitive?", *Economic Policy*, No.16, April 1993, p.166.

[85] *Balkan News International*, 2 January 1994.

[86] United Nations Economic Commission for Europe, *Economic Survey of Europe in 1992-1993*, New York, 1993, pp.153-154.

establishing and developing new, competitive export sectors. It is unlikely that these sectors can expand under recessionary conditions and without significant inflow of domestic and foreign investments. The structural constraints have been exacerbated by a lack of comprehensive export promotion schemes, including such standard measures of export support as export credits, export insurance and guarantees, market information and promotion.

(iv) Fiscal constraints

Another problem which raises growing concern among policy makers in transition countries is the precarious position of their *fiscal budgets*. Deficits of the central budgets have been essentially the result of budget revenues falling much below planned levels. Particularly large revenue gaps were registered in Bulgaria and the Baltic states, although in some countries (FR Yugoslavia, Croatia, Ukraine, Moldova) the impact of the fall in revenues was compounded by higher than planned government expenditures. Such outcomes were inevitable, even though not anticipated, in the light of the far too optimistic assumptions concerning expected economic performance which as a rule underlaid the draft budgets for the last two fiscal years. Officially reported budget deficits in 1993 varied in a very wide range from 1-2 per cent of GDP in Romania, Poland and Slovenia, and 6-8 per cent in Hungary and Slovakia, to 10-11 per cent in Bulgaria and Russia, and even to 30-40 per cent in FR Yugoslavia and Ukraine. Again, an exception to this pattern was the Czech Republic where a small fiscal surplus (of some 0.1 per cent of GDP) was posted in 1993.

The deterioration of fiscal balances observed in some transition countries is commonly associated with the deep recession and the ensuing fall of tax revenues and increase of social transfer payments, chiefly unemployment benefits. But the widening budget deficits have also to a large extent been engendered by the structural deficiencies of traditional fiscal systems and tax evasion on a massive scale. The collapse of tax revenues in some countries forced the governments to step up borrowing on the domestic money markets. It may have also had recessionary implications, because under conditions of generally restrictive credit limits, in many cases agreed upon with the IMF, increased government borrowing is bound to crowd business investors out of the credit market.

Nevertheless, there are also symptoms of some improvement in public finances, especially in those countries where a recent recovery of output and shifts to VAT systems and personal income taxation yielded higher than expected budget revenues in the final months of 1993. In Poland and Romania, the actual deficits for 1993 were ultimately only half of those planned, chiefly because of increased tax proceeds. In Hungary, the actual budget deficit, although the highest among central European countries, was somewhat smaller than initially anticipated.

Continued deficits have resulted in a rapid accumulation of public debt, raising serious concerns about the risks of falling into a *fiscal trap*. The ratio of (total) public debt to GDP has already reached worrying proportions in Bulgaria, Hungary and Poland (between 60 and 80 per cent of GDP), and the burden of servicing the debt is likely to grow in the near future because of high interest rates. Hungary's position appears to be particularly difficult in this respect.

Efforts to regain fiscal balance are proving not only difficult but heavily loaded with important social implications. Attempts to cut expenditures meet with growing resistance from various social groups, as in many countries the level of public financing directed to such areas as education, health care, communal housing, or research and development has been reduced to below acceptable levels.

(v) Transformation: The new sectors

The lingering reform in banking

The backwardness of the financial system and the generally poor condition of the banking sector is considered one of the stumbling blocks on the road to the recovery of output and investment.[87] Commercial banks in transition countries are financially weak, over-burdened with a large stock of uncollectible loans and other non-performing assets, and suffer from an acute shortage of professional and experienced staff. Compared to the pre-reform period, when not more than 5 to 10 large state-owned banks operated in each centrally planned economy, the number of banks in transition countries has increased dramatically over the last several years; between 50 and 80 banks are now registered in each of the central European countries, and more than 1,900 in Russia alone. The boom was made possible by hastily liberalized banking laws and generally very lenient criteria of entry into the sector; but most new banks are small private institutions with a very weak capital base and no experience in financial services. In consequence, bank bankruptcies have been numerous, especially in Hungary, Poland, and the Baltic states.

The fragile position of the banks has direct implications for the financial health of the enterprise sector: credit, especially for investment projects, is scarce, expensive and rather difficult to obtain. Several countries in the region have initiated large-scale programmes for the restructuring of commercial banks, aimed at their recapitalization, the consolidation and cleansing of their balance sheets, and the subjection of commercial bank operations to international audit and prudential standards. But progress has been limited, hampered by insufficient financial means allocated to the programmes and complicated legislative procedures *vis-à-vis* insolvent debtors.

The private sector continues to expand

Efforts to regain macroeconomic control have been accompanied in all transition countries by the continuation of *institutional and structural reforms*. Privatization remained the central focus, but progress has been constrained by the slow pace of legislative procedures, administrative delays, the poor financial condition of state enterprises, and controversies over the social and political

---

[87] See M.D. Nuti, R. Portes, "Central Europe: the way forward", in R. Portes, (ed.), *Economic Transformation in Central Europe. A Progress Report*, CEPR-European Communities, Luxembourg, 1993, pp.1-20, and "Twin Challenges Confront Economies in Transition in Eastern Europe", *IMF Survey*, 31 May 1993, pp.168-171.

implications of privatization decisions. As a result, the actual transfer of state property into private hands has been below expectations in most countries. Progress has been relatively fast in the Czech Republic and, more recently, in Russia, where mass voucher schemes were implemented. However, even in the more advanced countries, privatization has been mostly limited to formal changes of ownership, and has not yet led to the establishment of effective control over enterprises by the new owners. As a result, improvement in managerial and economic performance of privatized companies due to the new structure of property rights has been slow.

Nevertheless, the share of the *private sector* in output and employment of the transition countries has been increasing steadily, chiefly as a result of the mushrooming of new private companies. The growth of the private sector is generally seen as the main driving force behind the emerging recovery, and even in those countries where overall output has continued to fall, production from the private sector has generally increased. Any attempt to gauge the true scope of the private sector's activities is a rather difficult task, because a large part of the private sector operates in the so-called "grey" or "shadow" economy and is thus not fully reflected in official statistics. None the less, available estimates point to a further substantial increase of the share of the private sector in output and employment of transition countries in 1993, which now varies between 12-13 per cent in Bulgaria, 20 per cent in the CIS states, and 50 per cent in Poland.

Emerging capital markets are booming

One of the most spectacular developments in transition countries in 1993 was the rapid rise of stock exchange markets. Established first in Budapest in 1990, and next in Warsaw, Prague, Bratislava and other east European capital cities, stock exchanges were initially regarded as somewhat superfluous and largely marginal institutions of no real significance to the economy – because of the very limited number of joint stock companies officially listed, rather modest domestic capital resources, and lack of a tradition of stock trading. However, after a sluggish start, most of the new markets took off vigorously, with stock prices rising at astounding speed in the course of 1993.

The largest market is the Prague Stock Exchange which, apart from a few fully listed shares, also has a large over-the-counter segment trading in the shares of nearly 1,000 companies. Two weekly trading sessions have a turnover of $75-90 million each, and the HN-Wood 30 Index ended the year up 137 per cent in dollar terms. Even faster growth was registered last year on the Warsaw Stock Exchange, where the weighted average price of 22 listed companies increased by 875 per cent in dollar terms between January and December 1993. The Budapest stock market, after a fall in 1992, also registered a strong growth towards the end of 1993, although investors there were less enthusiastic than in Warsaw or Prague.

One of the initial triggers for the surge of stock prices and trading volumes was the inflow of foreign portfolio investments, mainly from the depressed capital markets in the United States and western Europe in early 1993; but when stock prices went up responding to this new demand, domestic investors rushed to join. The factor which partly explains the phenomenal speed with which prices have been rising is of course the very slowly growing supply of new stocks, especially in Hungary and Poland. As a result, most east European stock markets may now be considered as substantially over-valued (average price/earning ratios are well above 20, and in Poland even above 50). Even if one admits that risks are now high and that investors should be cautious, it is reassuring that so many east Europeans have engaged in this market game with so much enthusiasm. If the financial investments translate into expansion of production and export capacities, the stock market boom may contribute strongly to economic recovery in the region.

(vi) Growing political instability

Prolonged recession, massive unemployment and the falling living standards of large segments of the population have contributed to further polarization of the *political scene* in transition countries. A strengthening of leftist political movements and growing opposition to orthodox liberal economic policies could be observed in Bulgaria, Lithuania, Romania, Slovakia and, most recently, in Poland and Russia. Unconditional and sometimes enthusiastic support for free market reforms, so overwhelming in 1989-1990, faded away when liberal programmes failed to deliver on many of their promises, whether these had been explicitly formulated by democratic governments or implicitly assumed by east European populations.

Growing yearning for social protection and job security may be expected to shift the balance of political power towards parties which favour a more active involvement of the state in the economy. An abandonment of the path to the market system is unlikely, but tendencies to follow a more gradual approach to reform have gained in strength in some countries. While such policy changes may indeed alleviate immediate political tensions through measures such as trade protection or increased budget support for state enterprises, they are also likely to lead to an easing of some of the monetary and fiscal restraints. If not carefully balanced, such policies may result in accelerating inflation, weakening of domestic currencies and worsening external balances. Such a course of events would obviously be undesirable because it would build up inflationary expectations, reduce business confidence, slow down the inflow of foreign investments and, eventually, bring the structural adjustment to a stalemate. For those countries which are either heavily indebted or have relied on large foreign capital inflows, an excessive policy shift towards more direct intervention would also complicate relations with the IMF and, consequently, with external creditors.

3.2 Output and demand

(i) Overview

Output and demand developments in the transition countries in 1993 followed a much more diversified pattern than in 1992. A general declining trend observed during the last several years in nearly all countries of the region has now been replaced by diverging tendencies with rates of change differing widely between individual countries and sectors (table 3.2.1). Although output and demand of the transition region as a whole still continued to fall, the rate of decline not only diminished significantly relative to 1992, but in some countries the downturn has been stopped and even reversed.

The fall of GDP by 3 per cent in *eastern Europe* as a whole can be regarded as a signal of relative improvement as compared with the three preceding years, when GDP for the region declined by 8, 12 and 7 per cent, respectively. Nevertheless, 1993 was another year of recession, bringing the cumulative fall of GDP/NMP in eastern Europe between 1989 and 1993 to nearly 29 per cent below its pre-transition level. Even though the overall reliability and accuracy of macroeconomic statistics may legitimately be questioned because of difficulties connected with measuring changes in real output and demand levels under conditions of high inflation and rapidly growing unregistered private sector activities, it is very unlikely that even much more elaborate and accurate estimates would yield a fundamentally different picture of the macroeconomic performance of transition countries.

Behind the aggregate figure for the GDP fall in eastern Europe in 1993 were important differences in the performance of individual countries (see table 3.1.1). While the contraction of output continued unabated in most former Yugoslav republics, it has slowed down somewhat in Bulgaria, Hungary and Slovakia, almost halted in the Czech Republic, and reversed in Romania and Slovenia. Poland, and probably also Albania, showed relatively strong growth of output in 1993, which in the case of the former country was a continuation of a recovery from 1992.

In the *former republics of the Soviet Union*, output developments were generally much worse. The CIS-wide NMP level in 1993 fell to 13 per cent below the corresponding 1992 figure and there was an even larger GDP fall for the Baltic states. These declines were smaller than those registered in 1992, when NMP in the CIS grouping fell by 20 per cent, and GDP in the Baltic republics by around 30 per cent. The CIS-wide figure for 1993 reflected a 13 per cent drop in *Russia* and a contraction higher than this in Ukraine (16 per cent). The decline was reportedly smaller in Moldova, but there are good reasons to suspect that it may be considerably understated.[88] The picture was very mixed in the five central Asian countries; this region contains the only CIS country (Turkmenistan) to have claimed a rise in overall output, as well as two others where the output fall was higher than the CIS average.

The *cumulative* loss of output in the countries of the former Soviet Union over the last four years has even been larger than in eastern Europe, and can be estimated at 44 per cent below the 1989 level in Russia for NMP (39 per cent for GDP), 41 per cent for NMP in the CIS as a whole, and a staggering 49 per cent for GDP in the Baltic states. Even if the caveat noted earlier applies to the quality of official statistics, the magnitude of the output fall in the territory of the former Soviet Union is unprecedented.

Differences in the macroeconomic performance of individual countries reflected the varying degree of advance of market reforms and various developments on the side of supply and demand factors. The relatively better situation in eastern Europe has basically been the result of a certain recovery of *domestic demand*, fuelled chiefly by rapidly growing private sector activities in individual countries, but output levels in the south European transition countries and in the successor republics of former Czechoslovakia have also been adversely affected by the disruption of trade and production links in the wake of the disintegration of the former federal states, as well as the economic and political ramifications of the military conflict in Bosnia-Herzegovina. In the former Soviet republics, the revival of domestic absorption was much weaker than in central Europe. The protracted recession was primarily caused by continued macroeconomic instability and the slow progress of institutional reforms which disrupted demand patterns while the lagged repercussions of the abrupt economic disintegration arising from the collapse of the Soviet Union in early 1992 also gave rise to severe supply-side constraints.

(ii) Sectoral output developments

Available data on changes in *sectoral contributions* to GDP point to two different patterns of structural adjustment in transition economies. In most *east European* countries, data based on current-price values show that the share of industry and agriculture in GDP has been decreasing steadily over the last three years, while the share of the service sector has gone up. The shift is especially evident in Bulgaria, the Czech Republic, Poland and Slovakia, where the share of *industry* in GDP has fallen by 5-7 percentage points in each country since 1990 (table 3.2.1). Nevertheless, the industrial sector generally remains the main contributor to GDP, and its share in nearly all transition countries substantially exceeded the

---

[88] Moldova and Ukraine now report two industrial production indices; the first, based on enterprise returns in constant price terms, shows a 1993 industrial output *increase* of 4 per cent for Moldova and a 6 per cent *decline* for Ukraine, while the second, calculated on the basis of physical indicators by the statistical authorities in the two countries, shows a 10 per cent and an over 22 per cent decline, respectively. It is not clear whether the second, probably more realistic, figures (shown for Ukraine in chart 3.2.2) are incorporated into the two countries' GDP estimates.

Output and demand 59

TABLE 3.2.1

GDP by major sectors, 1990-1992
(Percentage shares)

	Agriculture	Industry	Construction	Services	Other and residual	Total
Bulgaria [a]						
1990	17.7	51.3	..	31.0	..	100.0
1991	15.4	48.0	..	36.7	..	100.0
1992	10.4	46.6	..	43.1	..	100.0
Czech Republic						
1990	7.2	50.0	8.3	32.0	2.5	100.0
1991	5.6	54.9	6.3	30.8	2.4	100.0
1992	..	..	..	..	..	..
Hungary						
1990	12.6	26.8	5.6	41.0	14.1	100.0
1991	8.7	28.0	5.0	46.8	11.5	100.0
1992	7.4	27.6	5.3	47.0	12.6	100.0
Poland						
1990	8.4	44.9	9.2	35.9	1.6	100.0
1991	6.9	40.2	10.2	40.7	2.0	100.0
1992	7.4	38.0	8.6	43.9	2.1	100.0
Romania [a]						
1990	18.0	48.3	5.7	28.1	..	100.0
1991	18.5	43.6	5.0	32.9	..	100.0
1992	18.9	44.7	4.3	32.1	..	100.0
Slovakia						
1990	7.4	50.3	9.3	31.0	2.0	100.0
1991	..	..	..	..	..	..
1992	..	..	..	..	..	..
Slovenia						
1990	4.7	33.4	4.4	56.3	1.2	100.0
1991	4.9	37.1	3.7	52.2	2.1	100.0
1992	5.0	33.7	4.1	56.5	0.7	100.0
Belarus [a,b]						
1990	27.8	41.7	11.2	19.3	..	100.0
1991	24.8	46.3	10.1	18.8	..	100.0
1992	23.8	46.7	12.0	17.5	..	100.0
Russia [a,c]						
1990	13.7	29.1	8.7	48.5	..	100.0
1991	11.2	34.7	8.6	45.5	..	100.0
1992	7.8	41.9	6.8	43.5	..	100.0
Ukraine [a,b]						
1990	30.3	41.3	9.7	18.6	..	100.0
1991	30.2	42.4	10.9	16.5	..	100.0
1992	22.5	50.7	14.7	12.1	..	100.0
Ex-GDR Länder						
1990	..	..	..	..	..	100.0
1991	1.4	38.3	..	41.6	18.7	100.0
1992	1.5	36.5	..	41.5	20.4	100.0

Source: Annual statistical yearbooks and direct communication from governments. World Bank, *Trends in Developing Economies 1992*, Washington, D.C., 1992, p.462.

Note: Sectoral shares were calculated on the basis of current prices. Services include producer services (trade, transport and communications) and consumer services. However, there are some differences in coverage of sectors between countries. Thus, construction is included in industry for Bulgaria and the ex-GDR *Länder*.

[a] Services include other and residual.
[b] Percentage shares in NMP.
[c] NMP components as percentage of total GDP.

OECD average of 34-35 per cent.[89] Of the transition countries, only Hungarian and Slovenian industry contributed a lower share of output in 1992 (28 and 34 per cent) and in both services contributed a correspondingly high share of (47 and 57 per cent). In other east European countries, industry accounted for around 40-55 per cent and services for between approximately a quarter and a third. Along with industry, *agriculture* has borne the brunt of recession and adverse relative price changes, with its share in GDP falling sharply in most transition countries.

Data on sectoral contributions to GDP in the *CIS countries* are incomplete and difficult to interpret. Current-price data are available only up to 1992 for Belarus, Russia

---

[89] The share of industry in GDP in OECD countries varied from 25 per cent in Denmark and Greece to 40 per cent in Germany.

and Ukraine and from these it appears, that the pattern of structural change in 1991-1992 was different from that in most east European countries.

Industry's share of material sphere production and of GDP in Russia increased sharply in current value terms during the period 1990-1992 (table 3.2.1). If gross output is any guide, the increase was only slightly less in constant prices but the most recent figures on gross output might suggest that the rise in industry's share halted in 1993. The share of *agricultural output* in NMP and GDP virtually halved in 1990-1992 in current price terms. Gross output data show a much smaller decrease than for industry in volume terms, but the price changes of the most recent years – particularly petrochemical based inputs (fuel and nitrogenous fertilizers) – have almost certainly reduced the value added by the farm sector. Changes in prices paid for farm products may also have been unfavourable compared with those paid to other sectors due to the relatively weak bargaining power of farm producers *vis-à-vis* the powerful monopsonistic government-procurement and wholesale trade networks still left over from central planning. Changes in the sectoral shares of GDP in Russia and Belarus, the only European CIS countries for which 1993 GDP data are available, have also been affected by performance in the *service sector*. Differences between the levels of, and changes in, GDP and material production suggest that the share of services rose in Russia and Belarus in 1990-1993 in constant prices, though it fell somewhat in current prices.

Given the low share of services at the outset of transition, a decline of the share of industry in GDP and an improvement in the relative position of services should generally be considered as a tendency likely to continue for some time in all the transition countries. Developments in eastern Europe so far contrast with those in the CIS countries, where the relative importance of the industrial sector increased. But this probably reflects the recent fundamental changes in relative prices favouring industry in general and the fuel and energy branches in particular. These account for a very large share of industrial output, especially in Russia. The influence of this once for all phenomenon on output structures will not be present on the same scale in the future.

Changes in industrial production were probably the most important single component of the changes in GDP in 1993, but little information is available on the changes in industrial *value added* which would be the relevant indicator. *Gross industrial output* generally grew at a higher rate than GDP in the economies which were expanding, and it fell faster in those countries where recession continued. In *eastern Europe*, the rate of growth of gross industrial output in 1993 fluctuated between 2 and 6 per cent in Hungary, Poland and Albania, exceeding the corresponding GDP growth rates by 2-3 percentage points. In the other countries, gross industrial production contracted by several percentage points more than GDP: between 5-6 per cent in the Czech Republic, 10 per cent in Bulgaria and 13 per cent in Slovakia. *Monthly data* in 1993 do not show any significant reversal of medium-term tendencies if seasonal changes are ignored (chart 3.2.1); only in Romania and Hungary was there an upturn of industrial production in the second and third quarters, probably signalling a more permanent recovery in industrial output.[90]

Unlike previous years since the transition process began, in almost all of the *CIS countries* gross industrial output showed a rather bigger decline than total material sphere net value added in 1993. Industrial production fell by almost 2 percentage points more than NMP in the CIS and by over 3 percentage points more in Russia (in 1992 gross industrial output fell by 2 and 4 percentage points respectively *less* than NMP). This difference largely reflects relatively better agricultural performance though it may also reflect changes in entrepreneurial behaviour especially in the large industrial enterprises which dominate output in the region.

As in the case of GDP, the industrial output series for most countries give no sign of a production upturn in 1993 (chart 3.2.2). Indeed, monthly data show that a modest month-on-month upturn in Russia earlier in the year was reversed in the second half; in Belarus and Ukraine, the brief upswings seen from August almost certainly reflect seasonal factors rather than the start of a recovery.

Industrial output suffered another big decline in the *Baltic states*, with falls of 27 per cent in Estonia, 35 per cent in Latvia, and 46 per cent in Lithuania, as compared with 1992. Even if these statistics probably do not capture a large part of private sector activities, the scope of *de-industrialization* in the Baltic countries seems still to be unmatched by any other transition country: industrial output in Estonia, Latvia and Lithuania in 1993 fell to between 25 and 40 per cent of their 1989 levels.

Developments in the *agricultural sector* in 1993 were generally below expectations. In *eastern Europe*, after the severe drought in 1992, a fall of livestock production was expected in 1993 as a consequence of higher grain and fodder prices; however, the climatic conditions in 1993 were not much better than in 1992, keeping crop production at a relatively low level in most countries in the region. Only in *Albania* and *Romania* was a strong recovery of agricultural output registered in 1993, by 15 and 12 per cent, respectively, while in *Poland* an increase in crop production by 15 per cent was probably largely offset by a drop in meat production – despite a 12 per cent fall recorded in herd sizes. These developments yielded a modest increase in aggregate output of 2.2 per cent for the whole farming sector. In all other countries of eastern Europe agricultural production declined in 1993, with the rates of fall ranging between 0.8 per cent in the *Czech Republic*, 12-13 per cent in *Slovakia* and 20-25 per cent in *Bulgaria* and *Hungary* (table 3.2.2). The sharp fall of farm output in the latter country was a combined effect of poor weather conditions and of a reduced area sown, which in turn was the result of uncertainty surrounding the on-going privatization of collective farms.[91]

---

[90] In Romania, however, the slow-down manifested by the monthly percentage changes over the same month of the preceding year was to some extent a purely statistical effect of the sharp deterioration of industrial performance in mid-1992. Nevertheless, industrial expansion has continued since then.

[91] According to official reports, the grain harvest in Hungary in 1993 was 13 per cent smaller, production of cereals 19 per cent smaller, and production of potatoes 22 per cent smaller than in 1992. *MTI News Agency*, 20 January 1994, quoted from BBC, *Summary of World Broadcasts*, EEW/0317, 27 January 1994.

Output and demand

CHART 3.2.1

East European countries: Monthly indices of gross industrial output, 1992-1993
(January 1992=100)

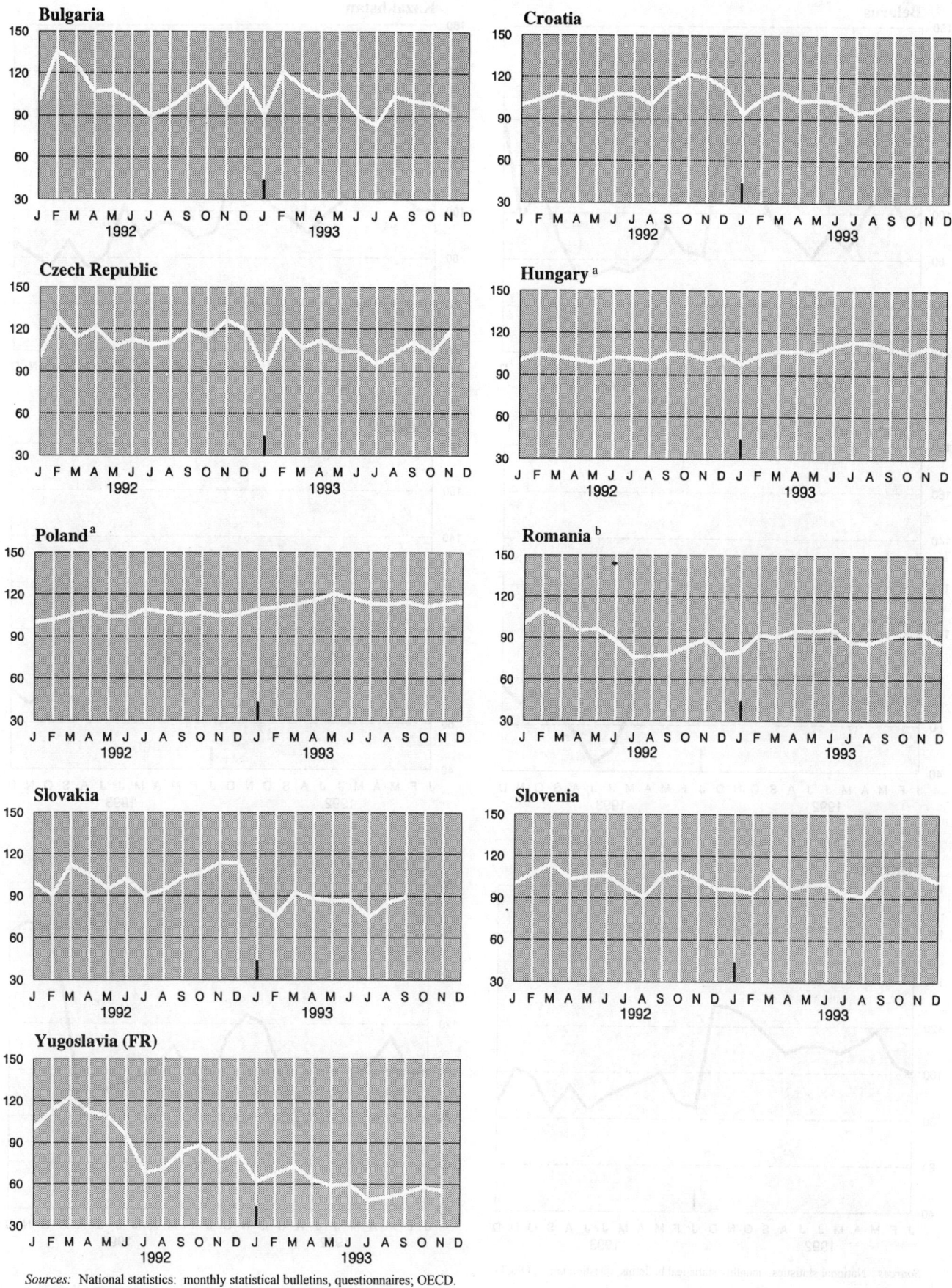

Sources: National statistics: monthly statistical bulletins, questionnaires; OECD.

[a] Seasonally adjusted.
[b] Adjusted for variation in the number of working days.

CHART 3.2.2

CIS countries: Monthly indices of gross industrial output, 1992-1993
(January 1992=100)

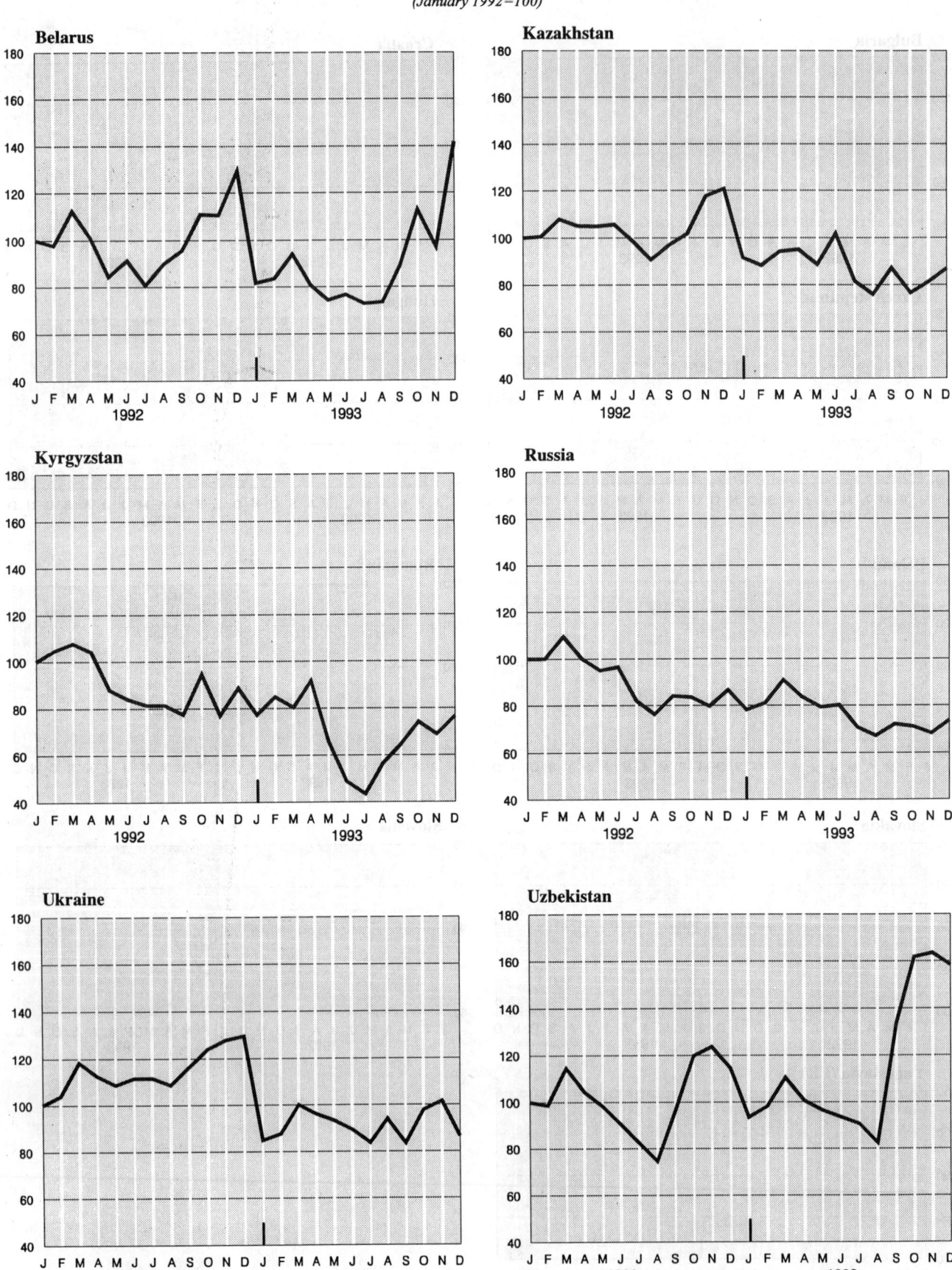

Sources: National statistics: monthly statistical bulletins, questionnaires; OECD.

TABLE 3.2.2

European transition countries: Gross agricultural production, 1990-1993
(Percentage change over same period of preceding year)

	1990	1991	1992	1993
Albania	-6.9	-24	..	15.0
Bulgaria	-6.0	-6.4	-12.5	-20.1
Bosnia-Herzegovina				
Croatia	-3.2	-7.0	-13.0	..
Czech Republic	-2.3	-8.9	-12.8	-0.8
Hungary	-3.8	-5	-22.7	-25.0*
Poland	-2.2	-2.0	-11.9	2.2
Romania	-2.9	1.2	-13.2	12.2
Slovakia	-7.2	-7.4	-13.9	-12.5*
Slovenia	1.7	-3.3	-10.0	-3.5
The FYR of Macedonia [a]	-10.2	17.6	0.4	-20.0
Yugoslavia (FR)	-7.0	9.7	-17.8	-7.2
Eastern Europe	-3.5	-2.1	-14.1	-1.9*
CETC-4	-2.9	-3.9	-14.1	-4.8*
SETC-8	-4.4	0.3	-14.2	1.7*
Armenia	-11.4	11.0	-13	-5
Azerbaijan	-0.1	-	-25	-17
Belarus	-8.7	-4.9	-9	2
Georgia	6.9	..	-17	-54
Kazakhstan	6.8	-8.0	1	-3
Kyrgyzstan	1.3	-8.0	-5	-8
Moldova	-12.8	-11.0	-16	3
Russia	-3.6	-4.5	-9	-4
Tajikistan	2.8	-10.0	-27	-2
Turkmenistan	7.0	-2.0	-9	9
Ukraine	-3.7	-13.2	-8	-1
Uzbekistan	6.3	-5.0	-6	-
CIS	-2.6	-6.9	-9	-2
Estonia	-13.1	-20.7	-21.1	-16.8
Latvia	-10.2	-3.5	-13.8	-11.5
Lithuania	-9.0	-4.6	-23.6	-6.7
Baltic states	-10.1	-7.3	-20.1	-10.1
Total transition economies	-3.0	-5.4	-10.7	-2.9

Sources: ECE secretariat Common Data Base, national publications and direct communications. Aggregations use 1991 weights.

[a] Value added.

In the *CIS countries*, where agricultural output had fallen by a reported 9 per cent in 1992, it dropped by a further 2 per cent in 1993, but by 4 per cent in Russia alone. Belarus and Moldova recorded small increases and Ukraine a 1 per cent decline only (table 3.2.2). The total CIS grain harvest in 1993 was roughly the same as the 1986-1990 average and fell only marginally compared with 1992. In Russia the drop of grain production was more pronounced – by 7 per cent – but other European CIS countries taken together recorded substantial increases. Other main food crops, with few exceptions in either the European or in the other CIS countries, continued to decline steeply, with staple potato, vegetable and sugar beet crops falling 30-35 per cent below 1986-1990 levels. Cotton output rose in all four of the central Asian producing states but other industrial crops remained depressed throughout the region. These generally modest results of arable farming may partly reflect the halving of fertilizer production between 1989 and 1993. Livestock output in the CIS also continued to be depressed due to shortages of fodder and also of fuel for the winter maintenance of herds. By 1 December 1993, overall livestock numbers in Russia, for example, had fallen by 5-10 per cent compared with the previous year, despite 5-10 per cent rises in the private sector. Meat output in the CIS countries and in Russia in 1993 were respectively about one quarter and one fifth below their 1986-1990 averages, and for milk the drops were 15 and 13 per cent. The contractions in Ukraine and Belarus were nearly twice as high, and in Moldova twice to three times as high, as in Russia.

Losses in agricultural production were also large in the *Baltic states*. Having developed in the past large export potentials to supply other republics of the former Soviet Union, especially in meat and dairy production, the farming sector in the Baltics has been very hard hit by the shift to convertible currency prices and settlements in trade with the CIS countries. Under the new, market trade regime, and especially in view of highly appreciated Baltic currencies *vis-à-vis* the Russian rouble, agricultural production became uncompetitive almost overnight. On the other hand, the acute lack of financial resources did not permit small, individual farms in the Baltic states to restructure. As a result, even if good harvests in 1993 allowed the maintenance or even an increase (in Lithuania) in arable sector output, the production of meat and poultry fell by between 17 (Lithuania) and 36 per cent (Estonia), and the output of milk and dairy products declined by 13 and 25 per cent, respectively.

The volume of *construction activities* generally fell in 1993 by larger margins than industrial output in most *east European* countries. Poland was the only country where a strong increase of construction output (by 13 per cent) was registered. This was most probably concentrated in the production sphere, because housing construction fell by some 5 per cent. Also, preliminary estimates point to a small upturn in Romania (by 1 per cent). In other countries, the drop of construction activities varied from 4 per cent in the Czech Republic to 23 per cent in Slovakia.

For the *CIS countries*, indicators published so far relate only to residential construction (including a roughly 1 per cent recovery in housing completions in Russia), and construction of educational and medical facilities; they show patchy performance but there is certainly no sign of a sustained recovery in any CIS country. The continued decline in investment (see below), which had decelerated up to the middle of the year, gathered pace again in the last half of 1993 and contributed strongly to the slump in construction activity.

Recession in the construction sector continued in the *Baltic states*. Partial data for 1993 show a fall in activity of 52 per cent in Latvia and of 38 per cent in Lithuania. These losses are even larger than the very substantial declines registered in 1992, when the volume of construction output fell in the two countries by 51 and 26 per cent, respectively.

In the general absence of gross output data for any sector other than industry and agriculture, only tentative assessments can be made as to the developments in other

TABLE 3.2.3

Transition economies: Index of industrial output, by branch
(1989 = 100)

Branch	Bulgaria 1992	Bulgaria 1993 [b]	Czech Republic 1992	Czech Republic 1993 [c]	Hungary 1992	Hungary 1993 [d]	Poland [a] 1992	Poland [a] 1993	Romania 1992	Romania 1993 [b]
Coal mining	71.6	79.8	..	..	61.0	54.8	63.6	61.4	65.7	68.1
Fuels	69.4	112.2	..	..	..	..	75.7	78.8	43.6	41.6
Energy	76.1	73.8	91.3	..	81.6	..	80.0	78.2	59.1	58.7
Iron and steel	29.6 [e]	32.1 [e]	59.3	..	34.2	41.5 [f]	61.1	61.6	40.4 [g]	40.0 [g]
Non-ferrous metal	48.4	61.1	36.0	..	56.8	..	57.2	56.0	..	..
Metal products	..	..	60.5	..	..	..	70.8	79.9	41.8	38.8
Mechanical engineering	44.6 [h]	34.9	52.1	..	49.7	48.0	60.5	63.4	52.5	56.1
Electrical engineering	26.8	23.3	39.9	..	47.4	48.7	76.1	89.2	54.5	56.0
Transport means	.. [i]	.. [i]	..	..	26.0	34.9	62.2	74.7	46.1 [j]	56.3 [j]
Telecommunications	.. [k]	.. [k]	..	..	44.5	51.3	..	..	44.5	44.0
Precision instruments	..	..	..	..	22.8	22.9	87.6	103.2	37.8	27.8 [l]
Chemicals	46.3	47.3	64.9	..	54.8	55.2	70.2	76.9	45.2	48.8
Building materials	39.6	35.3	60.2	..	55.0	61.8	74.0	79.8	39.6	40.4
Glass, ceramics	63.2	63.5	68.1	..	..	..	73.0*	78.5*	..	..
Wood products	61.8	55.1	58.0	..	66.0	69.8	82.6	90.9	51.2	48.2
Pulp and paper	57.6	55.3	78.3	..	71.3	62.6	82.2	85.2	37.0	34.5
Printing	95.5	121.6	64.7	..	61.7	77.9	111.3	131.8*	..	..
Textiles	59.9	48.3	56.6	..	42.5	43.4	50.9	56.7	51.9	50.7
Clothing	78.4	53.3	46.8	..	71.0	74.5	87.2	101.8	52.7	47.6
Leather, footwear	64.6	50.9	56.0	..	46.6	47.4	59.9	59.2	55.3	53.1
Food processing	56.0	44.6	75.1	..	78.2	74.1	75.5	83.4	59.9	51.5
Total industry	53.2	48.7	63.2	..	69.7	72.4*	69.4	74.5	51.5	51.8

Source: National statistics.

[a] Industrial output sold.
[b] January-September 1993 over January-September 1992.
[c] Indices for 1993 not fully comparable with 1992 because of change in industrial classification.
[d] January-November 1993 over January-November 1992.
[e] Including metal ores extraction.
[f] Including aluminium.
[g] Including non-ferrous metallurgy.
[h] Including metal products.
[i] Included in mechanical engineering.
[j] Road vehicles only.
[k] Included in electrical engineering.
[l] Computers and office equipment.

sectors. The overall picture for the *transport* sector reflects the contraction in other sectors, with reported substantial declines in railway and road freight, generally by 5-15 per cent in most east European countries. Poland and Romania were again the only exceptions, recording slight increases in the volume of transport services. In the CIS countries taken together, freight transport in 1993 dropped by over one fifth. As in previous years, this is substantially more than the contraction of output as a whole, reflecting probably a further decline in long-haul traffic associated with still falling intra-CIS trade.

Data on the recent performance of other sectors are scanty at the moment, but there is some fairly solid evidence on rapidly developing *domestic trade* and *telecommunications* sectors and on further expansion of *banking and financial* services.

(iii) Structural change in industry

The large falls of industrial output in transition countries since the beginning of transformation have not been uniform across all branches. Available data demonstrate that important structural changes have been under way, with some industries improving their relative position and some others declining rapidly. It is interesting to note that the pattern of structural change within the industrial sector has been broadly similar in many transition countries, as shown in tables 3.2.3 and 3.2.4. The data on the cumulative change in the volume of output in individual branches in selected countries show both the unprecedented scale of industrial contraction, as well as the intensity of the underlying structural shifts.

The total, *cumulative fall* of industrial output between 1989 and 1993 reached truly staggering proportions, especially in Bulgaria and Romania: these two countries have lost nearly half of their industrial production since 1989. Less dramatic, but still very large, were the losses in former Czechoslovakia. Even in Poland, where recovery has been going on for the second year running, the level of industrial output (sold) still remains more than a quarter below the 1989 peak.

The "*losers*", that is the branches which have been hardest hit by recession, are broadly the same in all east European countries: they include iron and steel production, mechanical engineering, textiles and some high-tech branches, such as telecommunications. Non-ferrous metallurgy, electrical engineering and building materials (except in Poland) have also been seriously affected. In some extreme cases, industrial branches

TABLE 3.2.4

European CIS countries: Industrial growth by branch, 1991-1993
(Indices, 1990=100)

	Belarus			Russia			Ukraine [a]		
	1991	1992	1993 [b]	1991	1992	1993 [b]	1991	1992	1993
Fuel	95	54	31	94	87	82 [c]	89	76	58
Energy	101	98	91	100	96		96	90	73
Ferrous metals	113	97	87	93	78	68	88	80	63
Non-ferrous metals	101	72	..	92	68	61	..	..	..
Engineering, metal working	105	96	91	90	77	65	104	101	105
Chemicals, oil refining	93	80	65	94	73	58	93	81	62
Timber, wood paper	107	100	95	91	77	58	102	104	101
Building materials	105	91	80	97	78	65	101	98	79
Light industry	101	104	91	91	64	46	97	103	87
Food	91	75	66	91	76	67	87	75	68
Total	99	90	76	92	75	63	95	89	82

Sources: National statistical yearbooks and current reporting.

[a] Data based on enterprise returns in constant prices. These show a much smaller output decline than official estimates based on physical units produced: for instance, a 22 per cent decline in total industrial output in 1993 compared with only 6 per cent reported by enterprises. See text.
[b] Estimates from official sources.
[c] Fuel and energy.

produced in 1993 barely a quarter of what they used to produce only four to five years earlier: this is, for instance, the case of electrical equipment and electronics in Bulgaria, and precision instruments and data processing in both Hungary and Romania. What is indeed worrying about this pattern is that among the main victims of transformation appear to be more advanced industries, very often the islands of high technology and intensive technical progress.

Turning to the *"winners"*, the relatively expanding branches include such industries as printing and publishing, energy production and, to a lesser extent, clothing and food processing. But, except for printing and publishing (and precision instruments and clothing in Poland), their position improved only in relative terms – that is, because their output fell at a slower pace than that of other branches. Thus, the observed restructuring is mainly the outcome of a general contraction going on at an uneven pace in particular branches. The slower-than-average decline of output in the energy branch may appear somewhat inconsistent with the efforts of all countries to reduce the excessive energy-intensity of overall production. Possible explanations for the increase of the share of fuels and energy in total output can be looked for in the expansion of exports of fuels and energy and growing energy consumption in the rapidly expanding service sector.

Generally, the larger-than-average fall in the output of the engineering and metallurgy branches suggests that there is some shift away from capital goods which dominated industrial output of socialist countries in the past, and towards consumer goods, although the precise picture of this change cannot be obtained from available data. For instance, pulp and paper and food processing performed relatively well in Poland and the Czech Republic, but much less so in Bulgaria and Hungary. Similarly, clothing production declined less than total industrial output in Bulgaria, Hungary and Poland, but contraction in the textile branch was generally much deeper. If foreign trade commodity statistics are mapped on the figures on industrial restructuring, it can also be observed that the (relative) expansion of some branches has clearly been driven by increase of exports: this was certainly the case for the clothing and food processing industries.

Structural changes in industrial output since 1990 have been also considerable in *Russia* (table 3.2.4), but most of the change resulted from the fact that the production decline in the fuel and energy branches was less than half the contraction in industry overall. No recent estimates of branch shares are available from regular official publications but, according to some estimates, these two branches accounted for about 11 per cent of total industrial output in 1993 (compared with about 8 per cent in the late 1980s);[92] the same source notes that the high energy intensity of industrial production did not diminish in 1993. In the CIS countries as a whole, output of oil, natural gas and coal in that year was down by 12, 2 and 10 per cent, and in Russia by 12, 3 and 9 per cent respectively. The share of extractive industries as a whole in total Russian industrial output rose by nearly 3 percentage points (to 18 per cent) between 1990 and 1993.[93] The fall in the share of manufacturing output in Russia was spearheaded by the light industry (textiles, clothing and footwear), chemicals, timber and non-ferrous metals branches; in all of them output declined noticeably faster than the industrial average. Food, engineering, ferrous

---

[92] Government Centre for Conjunctural Economics of the Russian Federation, *Russia 1993*, No.4, p.152.

[93] RF Goskomstat, the Ministry of Economics and the Government Centre for Conjunctural Economics, with the participation of other ministries and organs, of the Russian Federation, *Polozhenie Rossiiskoi ekonomiki v 1993 godu i perspektivy ee razvitiya na 1994 god* (The situation of the Russian Economy in 1993 and Development Prospects for 1994), Moscow, 1994, p.8.

metals and building materials were the only manufacturing branches to have held their share more or less unchanged.

Output of the fuels and food branches in Belarus and Ukraine, in contrast with Russia, declined faster than the industrial average in 1990-1993. In the case of fuels, this added further pressure on industrial inputs already severely restricted by the breakdown in intra-CIS trade, as did the faster-than-average fall in chemicals and non-ferrous metals in Belarus and chemicals and metals as a whole in Ukraine. Output of coal, the major domestically produced Ukrainian fuel, fell by a quarter over 1990-1993. In contrast with Russia, light industrial output and, as in Russia, engineering production both declined at slower-than-average rates in both of these countries.

In 1993, aggregate *consumer goods output* as a whole declined by less than the all-industry average in the CIS as a whole and in most individual CIS countries, the main exceptions being Moldova and Ukraine. Non-food goods, and in particular consumer durables, generally performed slightly better than the rest of industry; their aggregate decline was limited to 10 and 7 per cent, respectively, in the CIS as a whole, and to 11 and 7 per cent in Russia (compared with all-industry contractions of 15 and 16 per cent, respectively). Output of the Russian *defence branches* (which are also responsible for a considerable amount of consumer durable output) in the first nine months of 1993 fell by somewhat less than total industrial output; but while production of military hardware dropped by almost one third, the defence sector's output of goods for civilian uses fell by 9 per cent only.[94]

(iv) Factors behind the output changes

Changes in the level of output in most *east European countries* were generally determined by recovery of *internal demand* (see section (v) below). Growth of domestic consumption, fuelled by increasing wages and falling savings, as well as growing revenues of the private sector, explains a large part of the upturn in output in the Visegrad countries and Slovenia, where private consumption was the fastest growing component of aggregate demand. The output response of enterprises may have been hindered by financial constraints and growing interenterprise arrears. No systematic evidence is available on the importance of supply-side constraints, but it seems that, except for restricted access to credits, neither shortage of production inputs nor trade restrictions played a role in limiting the growth of output.

By contrast, among the main factors behind the fall of output in Bulgaria is the economic embargo imposed by the UN Security Council on FR Yugoslavia in May 1992 and, according to enterprise surveys, the high interest rates on short-term credits and high level of interenterprise indebtedness.[95] On the other hand, the massive fall of output in the successor republics of the former Yugoslav Federation (except Slovenia) has been chiefly the outcome of the continuous political and military confrontation in the region, as well as the trade embargo, which, although it primarily affected the economy of FR Yugoslavia, entailed very substantial losses also to the FYR of Macedonia.

The proximate causes of the production slump in *Russia and other CIS states* seem to be more complex and should be sought in a devastating combination of weak, distorted, or non-existent market institutions, and continued macroeconomic instability. Slack contractual discipline in fulfilling orders and making due payments disrupts output plans and the lack of adequate banking mechanisms for prompt settlement of accounts reduces incentives for firms seeking to expand their activities. Massive non-payments[96] and the acute shortage of financial resources, along with insufficient effective demand, are commonly cited by enterprises as the main constraints on output.[97]

This poses particular problems in the context of cross-border deliveries and settlements between CIS countries and is a major factor in the continuing decline in intra-CIS trade, as discussed in earlier editions of this publication.[98] Reduced supplies of fuels from Russia to other CIS states may be the single most important factor behind output decline in the latter countries.[99] But similar problems arise from the high degree of specialization and large size of manufacturing production units in the former Soviet Union. The source of many vital manufactured production inputs is a sole or majority supplier now cut off from its clients by an international border.[100]

Another major contributor to the production decline has been the greatly depreciated rouble exchange rate which makes imports of many production inputs prohibitively expensive. Excessive depreciation of the Russian currency in 1992 and the first half of 1993 was not only inflationary, given the "informal" indexation of many

---

[94] Government Centre for Conjunctural Economics of the Russian Federation, *Russia 1993*, No.4, p.198.

[95] See National Statistical Institute, *Current Economic Business*, Sofia, December 1993, p.18.

[96] According to a statement by the Russian Finance Minister S. Dubinin, the total value of non-payments in the economy amounted to R15-16 trillion in December 1993, around 9 per cent of annual GDP. *RFE/RL Report*, 7 February 1994; see also RF Goskomstat, *Sotsial'no-ekonomicheskoe polozhenie Rossii 1993 g.* (The Socio-Economic Situation of Russia in 1993), Moscow, 1993, p.137.

[97] RF Goskomstat et al., op.cit., p.8.

[98] United Nations Economic Commission for Europe, *Economic Survey of Europe in 1992-1993*, New York, 1993, p.139.

[99] Despite declining output of the major fuel products, Russia sharply increased its shipments of oil and gas to non-CIS countries in 1993, and plans for shipments from Russia to the other CIS countries in 1993 were underfulfilled by 25 and 21 per cent for Ukraine, 30 and 45 per cent for Kazakhstan, and 23 per cent for oil deliveries to Belarus. Quantities shipped to CIS partners have thus fallen steeply in recent years, from 75.5 million tons of crude oil and 106.5 billion cu m of natural gas in 1992 to 48 million tons and 78.6 billion cu m respectively, in 1993 alone. *CIS Statistical Committee Bulletin*, No.4, February 1994, p.16.

[100] The inputs concerned include potassium fertilizers, polyesters, supplied almost exclusively from a plant in Belarus, oil extraction equipment and sulfanol for detergents from Azerbaijan, chloroprene rubber from Armenia, multi-bucket excavators for coal mining from Estonia, titanium, magnesium, chrome ore and carbide from Kazakhstan, gas-pumping, geo-exploration pipes and metal-smelting kiln linings from Ukraine, etc. See T. Snyder, "Soviet Monopoly" in J. Williamson (ed.), *Economic Consequences of Soviet Disintegration*, Institute for International Economics, Washington, D.C., 1993.

prices on the exchange rate, but also contractionary, because of the low flexibility of supply structures with respect to the increases of key input prices, and "cost-plus" pricing. The high rate of the dollar of course primarily reflects lack of confidence in the rouble but is supported by the specific foreign exchange regime which requires Russian exporters to surrender most of their foreign exchange earnings to the Central Bank. Only one third of the total is being made available for offers on the currency exchange auctions – much of which is used as an inflation hedge by the banks. The supply of foreign currencies on interbank auctions is further reduced because Russian exporters tend to keep large amounts of export proceeds abroad to avoid the compulsory surrender.[101]

Thirdly, tighter credit superimposed upon the heavy interenterprise indebtedness which built up in 1992 and the consequent shortage of working capital has, in any case, limited the power of enterprises to respond to rises in demand; the small recovery of Russian consumer demand in 1993 (see below) appears to have been held back by the failure to raise production of consumer goods, and may therefore have translated into a further round of inflationary pressure.

Finally, continued high inflation and the inability of the government to persevere with strong anti-inflationary policies, together with the lack of clear perspectives from governments on the future of market reform, are prolonging the investment slump. As a result, a progressive deterioration of the production base is now under way which is having serious effects on current, as well as future, production potential.

The *Baltic states* still struggle to contain the damage done by the abrupt separation from the former Soviet Union and the rouble zone. Frequent stoppages in the supplies of vital production inputs from the CIS countries, especially of gas and oil from Russia, and the inability to shift immediately to alternative markets, depressed the level of industrial activities. This supply-side shock was further exacerbated by efforts of the governments to curb inflation and stabilize domestic currencies. Restrictive monetary policies, especially in Estonia and Latvia, as well as strong appreciation of the domestic currencies against the Russian rouble, have also strongly contributed to the fall of output in 1992-1993.

(v) Changes in domestic absorption

Developments in domestic absorption of the transition economies can only be approximately estimated because the official data on the main components of final expenditures on GDP are extremely scanty. At the time of writing, only the Czech Republic, Romania and Slovenia had published preliminary statistics on changes in domestic demand for 1993, and few countries have given quarterly data. Among the reasons for the slow release of the relevant data are the underdeveloped national-accounting statistical systems which are still at an early stage of formation in most transition countries, as well as technical and statistical problems arising from the efforts to gauge the real changes in macroeconomic variables under conditions of high inflation, changing currencies, and mushrooming, often under-recorded, private sector activities. For the same reasons, indirect and partial estimates of real changes in the main components of final demand are also extremely difficult. Therefore, the analysis below provides only a very tentative assessment of developments in final demand in the transition countries.

From the point of view of year-to-year changes in *domestic absorption* in 1993, transition countries fall into two broad categories. Domestic aggregate demand certainly increased in Albania which benefited from massive transfers financed by external assistance programmes; in Poland where output recovery and expanding activities of the private sector resulted in rapidly growing household incomes and expenditures; and in Hungary where domestic absorption was additionally boosted by large inflows of foreign capital. Aggregate demand probably grew in the Czech Republic and Slovenia, but growth there was rather limited (unlikely to exceed 1-2 per cent). There may have been some improvement in Romania and Estonia also, although its scale in these countries is very uncertain because of some conflicting data. The second group of countries, where a further fall of domestic absorption was observed, includes Bulgaria, Slovakia, all former Yugoslav republics except Slovenia, and most of the former respublics of the Soviet Union, including the two other Baltic countries.

For *eastern Europe*, two main tendencies can be identified in nearly all countries. First, GDP used was generally higher than GDP produced. The difference was made up by the negative balance on trade in goods and services, which varied in individual countries from less than 1 per cent (Slovenia) to more than 8 per cent of GDP (Hungary). The Czech Republic, with a current account surplus of about 1.5 per cent of GDP in 1993, was the only exception to this pattern. The second general tendency, which was observed also in 1992, is that consumption increased more, or decreased less, than the overall GDP and investments (see table 3.2.5). This is, of course, a different pattern of consumption/investment behaviour than in developed market economies where fluctuations of investment activities across the business cycle tend to be considerably wider than fluctuations of consumption. There are several possible reasons for this continuous, though relative, improvement of consumption performance. First, investments in most transition countries have been continuously depressed by restrictive monetary policies and overall uncertainty surrounding business activities. Second, after having fallen sharply at the beginning of stabilization, consumption standards may be more resistant to further reduction – especially if they are already close to, or below, the minimum subsistence levels for large segments of the population.

---

[101] The magnitude of capital flight in 1993 for Russia has recently been estimated at $10 billion. *ITAR-TASS News Agency*, Moscow, 11 February 1994, quoted from BBC, *Summary of World Broadcasts*, SU/1921, 14 February 1994.

TABLE 3.2.5

European transition countries: Domestic production and absorption, 1990-1993
(Annual percentage change)

Country and period	GDP (1)	Final domestic demand (2)	Consumption Total (3)	Consumption Personal (4)	Consumption Social (5)	Investment Total (6)	Investment Fixed capital formation (7)	Investment Changes in stocks [a] (8)	Memorandum items Retail trade turnover (9)	Memorandum items Real income per capita (10)
Bulgaria										
1990	-9.1	-7.6	0.6	-16.1	14.1	-25.1	-18.5	9.1	-8.7	4.1
1991	-11.7	-10.5	-8.3	-8.4	-7.8	-15.6	-19.9	9.0	-47.2	-37.4
1992	-7.7	-13.1	-7.7	-7.4	-9.0	-27.9	-1.5	3.1	-9.2	..
1993	-6	..	..	-12*	..	..	-8	..	-3*	-4
Croatia	[c]						[d]			[b]
1990	-8.5				..		-23		-7.4	-16.2
1991	-29				-18.1		-40		-26.5	-25
1992	-8				-11.4		-55		-37.5	-43.5
1993	-8*				-15.6		-32		-28.1	-4.1
Czech Republic										
1990	-1.2	2.8	2.4	3.2	0.9	5.4	6.5	7.9	1.9	-1.2
1991	-14.2	-22.4	-7.2	-23.4	-4.6	-53.7	-26.8	5.7	-33.5	-24.3
1992	-7.1	-4.9	-	11.1	-22.9	-15.7	3.8 [d]	-6.7	16.3	5.8
1993	-0.5	-3.2	2.2	1.9	2.9	..	-10.5 [d]	-8.4	1.0	..
Hungary										
1990	-3.3	-4.3	-3.5	-3.6	-2.6	-7.0	-7.1	0.3	-7.6	-1.8
1991	-11.9	-9.1	-5.3	-5.8	-2.7	-11.5	-11.6	0.4	-9.9	-1.7
1992	-5.0	-6.2	-2.0	-2.2	-1.1	-21.4	-6.4	-3.1	-5.6	-4.3
1993	-2.0	0-3*	0-2	..	..	0-5	0-5	..	-0.6	-3.0
Poland										
1990	-11.6	-11.4	-11.7	-15.3	0.5	-24.8	-10.6	4.3	-17.4	-15.1
1991	-7.6	-1.3	3.3	7.4	-6.5	-14.2	-4.5	1.9	3.7	5.5
1992	1.5	3.2	5.0	5.2	4.5	-2.5	2.8	0.7	7.9	3.2
1993	4.0	..	..	10	-	..	1	..	11	-3.0 [b]
Romania										[b]
1990	-8.2	4.1	9.0	8.0	14.0	-7.2	-35.6	10.5	17.2	5.6
1991	-13.7	-11.4	-11.6	-15.7	10.0	-10.8	-26	13.7	-13.0 [e]	-17.2
1992	-15.4	-12.0	-8.5	-11.2	2.3	-21.6	-2.1	16.2	-28.0 [e]	-13.0
1993	1.0	0.5	1.1	-1.3	10.8	-1.0	-0.8	14.1	-39.0 [e]	-14.9
Slovakia							[d]			
1990	-2.5	..	..	..	..	..	5.2	..	0.5	-3.5
1991	-14.5	..	..	..	..	..	-28.1	..	..	28.4
1992	-7.0	..	..	..	..	..	1	..	13.5	4.3
1993	-4.7	..	..	-8.9	..	..	-21	..	0.8	14.3*
Slovenia							[d]			[b]
1990	-4.7	..	..	..	..	..	-9.8	..	-17.6	-26.5
1991	-9.3	..	..	..	..	..	-14.8	..	-1.2	-15.1
1992	-6.0	..	..	..	..	..	-14.5	0.4	-11.8	-2.8
1993	1.0	8*	8*	10*	3*	6*	3*	1*	3.5 [f]	16
Yugoslavia (FR)	[c]									[b]
1990	-8.4	..	2.5	4	-4.3	..	-20.1	..	-	-4.7
1991	-11.2	..	-5.1	-7	-0.6	..	-13.9	..	-2	-5.8
1992	-26.1	..	-26.9*	-26	-30.7*	..	-28	..	-40	-48.7
1993	-30.3*	..	..	-32*	..	..	-39*	..	-57	-61
Belarus		[g]							[h]	[i]
1990	-1.9	0.2	..	..	..	..	9	..	14.7	12.0
1991	-1.2	3.1	..	..	..	..	4	..	-8.2	-2.0
1992	-10.6	-9.0	..	..	..	..	-15	..	-26.3	-29.3
1993	-11.0	..	..	..	..	..	-13	..	-21.9	-21.9
Moldova	[j]	[g]							[h]	[i]
1990	-1.5	-6.8	..	..	..	..	0.5	..	..	9.0
1991	-18.0	7.2	..	..	..	..	-9	..	-16.5	-18.2
1992	-21.3	-27.0	..	..	..	..	-48	..	-59.3	-49.3
1993	-4.0	..	..	..	..	..	..	..	-29.2	-33.6
Russia		[g]					[d]		[h]	[i]
1990	-2.0	-4.2	..	..	..	..	0.1	1.4	10.0	9.0
1991	-12.9	-16.6	..	..	..	..	-15.5	13.6	-8.4	-10.5
1992	-18.5	-21.8	..	..	..	..	-39.7	11.3	-31.4	-46.5
1993	-12	..	..	..	..	..	-15	4.7	-1.5	9.0
Ukraine							[d]		[h]	[i]
1990	-2.6	-2.7	..	..	..	..	1.9	..	11.5	11
1991	-10.0	-4.7	..	..	..	..	7.1	..	-10.9	-3.8
1992	-14.0	-19.8	..	..	..	..	-36.9	..	-23.1	-38.5
1993	-15	..	..	..	..	..	-22	..	-34.5	..

Sources: ECE secretariat Common Data Base, based on national statistical publications or direct communications to the ECE secretariat.

[a] Expressed as percentage of GDP (Bulgaria, Romania and Russia current prices).
[b] For Croatia, Slovenia and Yugoslvaia (FR), real wages; for Poland, real wages and social transfers only; for Romania, real earnings.
[c] Gross material product.
[d] Refers to gross fixed investment prepared according to the material product system.
[e] Revised series.
[f] January-September.
[g] Net material product used for consumption and accumulation.
[h] Retail trade in goods and services.
[i] Total money incomes deflated by the consumer price index.
[j] Net material product produced.

The lack of quarterly national accounts data is still a serious obstacle in addressing policy outcomes on domestic absorption in the *CIS countries*. For 1992, as pointed out in the last issue of this publication, very large reported decreases in real incomes, gross fixed investment and public expenditure and a deteriorating balance on external trade in all CIS countries were considerably larger in total than the NMP and GDP declines. In Russia's case they could only be reconciled on the assumption of large increases in stocks and in the Russian balance of trade surplus with other CIS countries.[102] For 1993 the apparent discrepancies are smaller; an apparent bottoming out in partial indicators of private consumption in Russia and a slower rate of decline in the other CIS countries, and a smaller investment contraction than in 1992, even though partially offset by falling stocks, are not inconsistent with the decelerating GDP declines noted earlier. In the CIS countries other than Russia, information gaps remain with regard to changes in intra-CIS trade balances. But steep increases in foreign trade surpluses with the outside world and, in Russia, in its surplus on trade with other CIS countries, suggest that domestic absorption declined faster than GDP in the CIS countries as a whole. Investment cuts, lower public expenditure and destocking appear to have spearheaded the decline in Russia – where partial data indicate a small recovery in private consumption. But the continued weakness of private consumption still played the major role in depressing demand in the other CIS countries.

As noted above, full year data on changes in *private consumption* are not available for most east European countries. Available figures indicate a small decline of individual consumption in Romania (by 1 per cent), a bottoming out or a modest increase in the Czech Republic and perhaps Hungary (by 0-2 per cent), and a large increase in Poland and Slovenia (by 10 per cent). A steep fall was reported for Bulgaria (12 per cent). For other countries, indirect estimates made on the basis of the changes in the volume of retail trade confirm a substantial increase of individual consumption in Poland (where the volume of retail sales rose by 11 per cent in 1993) and, to a lesser extent, in Slovenia (growth of retail sales of about 3 per cent), and a modest increase in the Czech Republic. They also suggest much larger falls of individual consumption in Croatia, Romania and FR Yugoslavia. In the Baltic region, Latvia and Lithuania also report large falls in retail trade volumes.

Data on real changes in *retail sales* are almost certain to underestimate the true level of individual consumption for two reasons. First, these data are collected from reports by officially registered retail establishments, while a considerable share in domestic retail trade is taken by private shops and "street" sellers which either under-report their turnover, or are not officially registered at all. The margin of this "shadow" trade seems to be particularly important in the countries of the former Soviet Union. Second, there are also growing imports of consumer goods by individuals, especially in such areas as electronics or clothing. Unfortunately, estimates of the magnitude of these two effects are not yet available from national statistical services.

Two additional indicators which might be helpful in estimating the real changes in the level of private consumption, at least in some countries, are the changes in real money incomes and savings of the population. Availability of relevant data is not much better than in the case of national accounts data, but for those countries for which some figures have been published, they generally confirm the earlier observations (see table 3.2.5). Registered *household incomes* in real terms (nominal incomes deflated by CPI or retail price index) increased sharply in Slovenia (by 16 per cent), and also in the Czech Republic (by 6 per cent in January-November 1993), but they fell by some 3-4 per cent in Bulgaria and Hungary. Polish statistics show a decline of real wage incomes by 3-4 per cent and an unchanged level of social transfers, but if other sources of individual incomes are taken into account, such as foreign transfers, revenues from private sector activities, and farmers' incomes, a substantial increase is expected to be reported for 1993. Data on real money receipts per household member in the Baltic states indicate a modest increase of real incomes in Estonia and Latvia (by some 6 per cent), and a large fall of 35 per cent in Lithuania.

Personal *saving* is estimated to have decreased in proportion to current incomes in the Czech Republic, Hungary, Poland and Slovenia, that is in all four countries where the signs of recovery are relatively strong. In *Hungary*, the growth of individual savings in the first 11 months of 1993 was much smaller than in 1992: Ft 209 billion against Ft 261 billion, or 29 per cent and 18 per cent, respectively. Since nominal incomes for the same period increased from Ft 1,543 billion in 1992 to Ft 1,818 billion in 1993, the *savings ratio* fell sharply from 17 per cent to 11 per cent. A very similar tendency was observed in *Slovenia*, where an increase in nominal incomes of 58 per cent was accompanied by a much smaller increase in nominal savings of 22 per cent, which resulted in the fall of the savings ratio from 17.7 per cent in 1992 to 13.7 per cent in 1993. Preliminary estimates for *Poland* also suggest a decline in households' propensity to save: the increase of savings in 1993 was only 6 per cent higher in nominal terms than in 1992, whereas consumer price inflation was 35 per cent, and the increase of nominal incomes is expected to have exceeded the inflation level.

Developments in private consumption in 1993 were bolstered in *Russia* by an increase in households' money incomes (11 times), which outstripped the inflation rate (10.1 times) for the first time since the transition process began, and hence by a rise in *per capita* real incomes of 9 per cent.[103] On the other hand, personal savings ratios more than doubled between 1990 and 1993 in the European CIS countries – to around 20-25 per cent of total money incomes, although the increased savings are not

---

[102] United Nations Economic Commission for Europe, *Economic Survey of Europe in 1992-1993*, New York, 1993, p.81.

[103] *Izvestiya*, 17 February 1994.

finding their way to the banking system.[104] Given the generally low level of living standards, this high growth of savings may suggest that part of it may have been "involuntary" savings, resulting from shortages which may still plague the consumer markets in the CIS countries.

In Russia, the foregoing developments contributed to a broadly unchanged level of retail sales of goods and services taken together – a 1.2 per cent rise in the first case and a 30 per cent fall in the second, for which price increases were much higher than for goods.[105] But rather substantial falls in retail sales of goods and services were evident in Belarus, Moldova and especially in Ukraine.

In all CIS countries but Russia, average wages grew faster than non-wage incomes. Russia seems to be one of the few CIS countries which has obtained results in protecting non-wage incomes (predominantly pensions and other social transfers). Even so, it is estimated that some 30 per cent of the Russian population received less than the minimum subsistence income in the last quarter of 1993, compared with 26 per cent at end-1992 and 12 per cent at end-1991. Pensions in Russia averaged 30 per cent of monthly wages in 1993, compared with about one quarter in other CIS countries.

Government consumption also increased in most *east European* transition countries in 1993, even in those where a fall of GDP was reported. Partial data show an increase of public consumption by 2 per cent in Slovakia during the first three quarters of 1993, and by 3 and 11 per cent in the Czech Republic and Romania for the full year. Available data on current expenditures from state budgets also offer indirect evidence of a growing share of government consumption in GDP for Bulgaria, Hungary, Slovenia, and a small relative decline for Poland. Government consumption in the Baltic states is estimated to have remained broadly unchanged in proportion to national GDP in 1993.

Public consumption in the *CIS countries* can only be estimated from the scanty data available on budgetary expenditure and outcomes. Falls in the volume of government expenditure can be assumed as the real resources available were cut by the output declines. Governments also budgeted to pull down expenditures relative to GDP in 1992, but an increase was foreseen in 1993 by Belarus and, in an April budget, in Ukraine but probably not in Russia. In fact, Russia did not succeed in this in either 1992 or in 1993; expenditures on the consolidated budget in fact rose to almost 40 per cent of GDP at current prices in the latter year. In Ukraine, this share fell very sharply in 1992, but first half year figures suggest that it probably rose again in 1993.

Among all principal components of aggregate demand, *fixed capital investments* seem to have been most adversely affected during transition. Although official data for 1993 are very incomplete, a tendency which emerges from partial data and some independent estimates is that officially reported investment expenditures declined by rather considerable margins in most of the south European transition countries, but held level or slightly increased in the central European transition countries (table 3.2.6). The fall in 1993 for eastern Europe as a whole is probably in the range of about 5 per cent, thus bringing the cumulative decline of fixed investments to nearly 40 per cent below the 1989 level. The largest falls in the volume of investment in 1993 were reported in FR Yugoslavia, Croatia, and the FYR of Macedonia (probably by between 15 and 40 per cent).[106] The current level of investments in these countries is now probably somewhere between one fourth and one third of the peak level registered in 1987-1988.

Fixed investments generally decreased in *eastern Europe*, except for Slovenia where official statistics show a remarkable increase of investment expenditures by 11 per cent in constant prices during January-November 1993.[107] Preliminary results for Hungary and Poland indicate that the level of investments in these countries in 1993 may have increased slightly or remained broadly unchanged in real terms as compared with 1992.[108] In Poland, however, investment other than housing is estimated to have increased by 5 per cent. Investment activities in Slovakia accelerated in the second half of 1993, especially in the service sector, but three quarters figures still show a decline of total investments by 2 per cent.

Investment probably held level or declined slightly in Romania, but fell much more in Bulgaria and the Czech Republic.

A closer look into the structure of investment outlays, to the extent made possible by available data, allows the identification of several tendencies which are common to most east European transition countries. *First*, investments in machinery and equipment grew faster, or declined slower, than investments in buildings and construction; this tendency is consistent with the reported growth of imports

---

[104] Comparison of the official figures on money revenues and expenditures of the population for the CIS countries for 1993 show that a very large proportion of incomes is not spent, but rather increases nominal money balances of population (the proportion of unspent revenues ranges from 13 per cent in Belarus and 23 per cent in Russia, to 55 per cent in Armenia and 68 per cent in Turkmenistan. On the other hand, the officially reported increase of savings deposits with the banking system in 1993 was in most countries only 3-5 per cent of total incomes (e.g., 3.1 per cent in Russia). One explanation for this discrepancy may be the negative real interest rates on deposits and increasing "dollarization" of money balances in the CIS countries. See CIS Statistical Committee, *Ekonomika stran sodruzhestva nezavisimykh gosudarstv v 1993 godu*, Moscow, January 1994, pp.35 and 38.

[105] Official estimates show that if "unregistered" retail trade (goods only) is included, the rise was 1.9 per cent.

[106] Croatia's official statistics show that the monthly levels of investment during January-October 1993 were only 12-24 per cent of the average monthly level in 1990. *Croatian Economic Trends*, No.8-10, August-October 1993. According to a report by an independent research institute, the level of investment in Croatia in 1993 dropped to about 80 per cent of the value of annual depreciation. Z. Rohatinski, *Hrvatska u 1993 godini. Izmedu hiperinflacije i stabilizacije*, Ekonomski institut, Zagreb, February 1994, direct communication to ECE.

[107] Centre for International Cooperation and Development – CICD, *Economic Developments in Slovenia in 1993*, Ljubljana, January 1994.

[108] See Ministry of Finance, *Economic Processes 1993*, Report No.9-10, Budapest, December 1993, pp.2-3; GUS, *Informacja o sytuacji społeczno-gospodarczej kraju in 1993*, Warsaw, January 1994, p.54.

TABLE 3.2.6

European transition countries: Gross fixed investment and construction sector activity, 1990-1993
(Percentage change over same period of preceding year)

	Gross fixed investment					Construction				
				1993					1993	
	1990	1991	1992	Jan.-June	Jan.-Dec.	1990	1991	1992	Jan.-June	Jan.-Dec.
Albania	-14.8	..	..	..	..	-13.9	..	..	..	..
Bulgaria	-18.5	-19.9	-1.5	..	-8	-19.1	-59.3	-11.4	..	-13.7
Croatia [a]	-23	-40	-55	..	-32	-34.9	-34.4	-39.6	-15	..
Czech Republic	6.5	-26.8	3.8	1.5	-10.5 [a]	-5.8 [b]	-32.4 [b]	21.5 [c]	10.5 [c]	-5.0 [b]
Hungary	-7.1	-11.6	-6.4	..	0-5	-15.6	-9.4	0.8	-10	..
Poland	-10.6	-4.5	2.8	-10.0	1	-14.4	8.9	5.7	12.7	13.3
Romania	-35.6	-26	-2.1	..	-0.8	-36.6	-23.0	-29.4	-7.5	..
Slovakia	5.2	-28.1	1	..	-2.4 [d]	-10.2 [b]	-33.1 [b]	14.0 [c]	-18.7 [c]	-25.3
Slovenia	-9.8	-14.8	-14.5	-4	11	-10.8	-16.6	-10	-15	-4
The FYR of Macedonia [a]	-15.2	-1.2	-29.1	..	-15	..	..	..	..	..
Yugoslavia (FR) [a]	-20.1	-13.9	-28	..	-39	-33.5	-7.3	-31.6	..	..
Eastern Europe	-11.9	-17.6	-5.9	..	-8	..	..	..	..	..
CETC-4	-4.0	-13.5	-1.5	..	-4	..	..	..	..	..
SETC-8	-20.6	-22.2	-14.2	..	-13	..	..	..	..	..
Armenia	-4.6	-35.2	..	..	..	..	..	..	..	..
Azerbaijan	-3.6	-14.3	..	..	..	..	..	..	..	..
Belarus	9	4	-15	..	-13	..	-9.0	..	-19.7	..
Georgia	14.4	..	..	..	..	..	..	..	..	..
Kazakhstan	-2.9	0.5	-43	..	..	..	..	..	..	..
Kyrgyzstan	11.3	-12.8	-35*	..	-69	..	..	..	..	..
Moldova	0.5	-9	-48	-41	..	..	..	..	..	..
Russia	0.1	-15.5	-39.7	-6	-15	..	..	..	..	..
Tajikistan	0.7	-14.6	-6.9	..	..	..	..	..	..	..
Turkmenistan	7.5	11.2	20*	..	..	..	..	..	..	..
Ukraine	1.9	-7.1	-36.9	..	-22	..	..	..	..	..
Uzbekistan	13	4.6	-35*	..	..	..	..	..	..	..
CIS	1	-11.7	-39	-7	-14	..	..	..	..	..
Estonia	2.7	-12	-39.8	..	..	..	-10.6	..	..	..
Latvia	-8.2	-36.3	-53	-45	-37	..	-40.5	-51.1	-69.5	-52.2
Lithuania	-10.3	-46	-34.3	-32.4	-35	-15	..	-26.3	-38.6	-39.0
Baltic states	-7.1	-36.1	-41.5	..	..	..	..	..	..	..
Total transition economies	-2.8	-13.9	-28.2	..	..	..	..	..	..	..
Ex-GDR *Länder* [a]	13.5	33.4	24.0	11.8	..	1.8	1.1	36.2	18.8	..

Sources: ECE secretariat Common Data Base, national publications and direct communications. Aggregations use 1991 weights.

[a] Gross fixed capital formation (GDP coverage).
[b] Enterprises with 100 and more employees.
[c] Enterprises with 25 and more employees.
[d] Three quarters.

of engineering goods, especially in the Visegrad countries (except Slovakia), and suggests that industrial restructuring may ultimately be gathering momentum in these countries. *Second*, the most dynamic growth of investment activities was observed in the service sector, mostly in trade and telecommunications, while it was relatively slow in industry and agriculture. In Slovakia, for instance, the volume of investments in retail and wholesale trade in January-September 1993 increased by 80 per cent and in transport and telecommunications by 22 per cent, as compared with the corresponding period of 1992. In Poland, investment outlays in tele-communications increased in January-November 1993 by 122 per cent in current prices, and in domestic trade by 39 per cent, while the growth of overall investment was only 18 per cent in nominal terms. *Third*, there was a distinct asymmetry of investment behaviour in the private sector and in the state sector in 1993: while in the former investments expanded rapidly, in the latter they continued to decline in most countries. Also, government investments have been falling systematically in all transition countries. *Fourth*, available evidence suggests that the share of foreign direct investment in total investment has been increasing rapidly, although except for Hungary and the Czech Republic, it still remains at a relatively low level.

Investment expenditures in the *CIS countries* taken together, which had fallen by nearly 40 per cent in 1992, declined by a further 14 per cent in 1993 (table 3.2.6). In Russia, investment is now equivalent to no more than 14 per cent of GDP compared with over one fifth in 1990. This leaves investment in 1993 at some 55 per cent of its

1990 peak and at about the same level as in 1970. Current investment levels are inadequate even to satisfy replacement needs; in the late 1980s, for instance, nearly half of total Soviet investment was already used for this purpose, a share which had doubled since the early 1970s as overall investment growth slowed down.[109] The ageing of the capital stock, which resulted from the lengthening of write-off periods in the final decade of the Soviet era, has thus been exacerbated in the first years of transition as resources for repair and replacement tailed off. Moreover, the declines considerably underestimate the effects on productive capacity. In the first place, investment for productive purposes fell rather faster than the average in 1993 and now accounts for 62 per cent of the total, compared with 64 per cent in 1992 and nearly 70 per cent in 1990. (In Russia, the corresponding figures were 60, 65 and 71 per cent.) Secondly, the investment fall understates the fall in the volume of new capacity being brought into operation; whereas in the past the value of uncompleted investment was equivalent to just over half of investment in Russia in 1990, it rose to *more* than twice the investment total in 1993. Third, the share of machinery and equipment installed, from which rapid production results can be expected, has declined sharply.[110]

All production sectors have been seriously affected by the heavy concentration of available resources on the fuel-energy complex, which apparently occurred in all CIS countries.[111] This already accounted for 52 per cent of all CIS industrial investment in 1992 and a fifth of investment overall. In Russia, the corresponding shares are estimated at nearly 60 per cent and one quarter by 1993,[112] respectively, compared with an already high 42 and 16 per cent in 1986-1990.

Changes in the structure of investment within industry can only be traced for Russia, where the steep rise in the share of the fuel-energy complex took place at the expense of engineering in particular, the latter's share in total industrial investment apparently having fallen by half or more between 1986-1990 and 1993. Although no data on investment by branch are available for other countries, the fall in industry's share of investment overall, coupled with the rise in the share of fuels noted above, suggests that the non-fuel branches may have been squeezed by as much as or more than in Russia.

Continued declines are also characteristic of the *investment* expenditure in the *Baltic states* – preliminary data indicate that in 1993 gross fixed investment fell by 37 per cent in Latvia and by 35 per cent in Lithuania, thus adding to the earlier massive falls in 1991-1992 by 70 per cent and 65 per cent, respectively.

Investments in *stocks* are difficult to assess because only a few countries have so far published the figures on change in inventories in the first half or three quarters of 1993 (table 3.2.5). However, some indirect evidence based, *inter alia*, on the behaviour of other components of aggregate demand, strongly suggests that there has been a sharp decline in the level of stocks in some *east European economies*, especially in the Czech Republic, Romania and Slovenia.[113] A similar process can be also observed in Slovenia and, probably, in Romania. By contrast, the level of stocks appears to have increased in Hungary, judging from the faster rate of growth of industrial output than that of industrial sales.[114]

Changes in inventory accumulation in *Russia*, which contributed no less than 11 per cent of the country's GDP in 1992, tailed off to less than 5 per cent in 1993 (in current prices). Although this seems high for an economy in steep recession, there was in fact clearly a large fall in volume terms, probably by about one quarter of 1992 levels.[115] This suggests that greater financial stringency could now be starting to change Russian industrial managers' behaviour by limiting their past tendency to produce and stockpile goods which cannot be sold at the prices set by them. No data on stocks are available for other CIS countries.

The level of stocks was decreasing in all three *Baltic countries* in 1993. Apart from the overall fall of output which reduced working capital requirements, the strict monetary and credit policies after the introduction of national currencies were also responsible for the fall of inventories.

(vi) Foreign sector impact

The impact of the foreign sector on the level of domestic output and income works through two main channels. Changes in the volume of *net exports* (exports minus imports) of goods and services show to what extent foreign demand contributes to the employment of domestic resources. An increase of net exports indicates that foreign demand helped to raise output above the level which would otherwise be achieved. Changes in *terms of trade*, for a given volume of trade, show the impact of export and import price changes on a country's national income. Improving terms of trade allow the country to spend less on a given volume of imports, and thus increase national income.

The impact of the foreign sector on transition economies in 1993 can be only tentatively examined because of the lack of necessary information. The full-year figures on the volume of trade in goods and services are not yet available for most of transition countries (see table 3.2.7), and data on price changes are very scanty. Available statistics on merchandise trade and current account, which in most cases cover only three quarters or eleven months of 1993, show a deterioration of net foreign balances for nearly all *east European* countries. The current account balance in *current dollars* (excluding transfers) declined broadly by $1 billion in Bulgaria, and by $2 billion in Hungary and Poland; it also deteriorated,

---

[109] ECE secretariat Common Data Base.

[110] In Russia this mainly reflects the large rises in the share devoted to geological survey work.

[111] CIS Statistical Committee, *Statisticheskii byulleten'*, No.18, September 1993, p.147.

[112] RF Goskomstat et al., op.cit., p.216, table VI.23.

[113] According to preliminary data for the first three quarters of 1993, the fall in stocks in the Czech Republic was equivalent to some 7 per cent of GDP, compared to less than 1 per cent of GDP in the corresponding period of 1992.

[114] In Hungary, industrial output produced increased in 1993 by 4.5 per cent while industrial output sold, by 3.3 per cent.

[115] RF Goskomstat et al., op.cit., p.16, table II.5.

TABLE 3.2.7

European transition countries: Volume of foreign trade, 1990-1993
(Percentage change over same period of preceding year)

	Exports					Imports				
				1993					1993	
	1990	1991	1992	Jan.-Sept.	Jan.-Dec.	1990	1991	1992	Jan.-Sept.	Jan.-Dec.
Bulgaria	-23.4	-30.1	1.6 [a]	-13.4 [a]	..	-23.3	-17.1	-27.5 [a]	0.2 [a]	..
Czech Republic [b]	-3.0	-8.4	8.3 [c]	9.1 [c]	8.0 [c]	7.9	-41.2	12.0 [c]	9.4 [c]	4.1 [c]
Hungary	-4.3	-4.9	2.0	-19.0	-13.1	3.4	5.5	-8.1	12.7	20.9
Poland [c]	15.1	-1.7	1.4	6.9 [a]	..	-10.2	31.6	9.2	24.9 [a]	..
Romania	-41.5	-4.8	8.0 [c]	..	0.3 [c]	15.1	28.6	11.4 [c]	..	-4.0 [c]
Slovakia [e]	-8.3	19.5	6.3	-9.4 [c,d]	..	17.5	-8.7	0.4	-4.2 [c,d]	..

Sources: ECE secretariat Common Data Base, national publications and direct communications.

[a] Change in value at current dollar prices rather than volume.
[b] 1990-1991 (and also 1992 data for Slovakia) are estimates based on data in current crowns deflated by export and import price indices for former Czechoslovakia.
[c] National accounting methodology including services.
[d] January-June.

albeit to a lesser extent, in Slovakia and Slovenia. This suggests that the volume of *net exports* of goods and services fell considerably in 1993, and thus the stimulating impact of foreign demand on domestic output diminished as compared with 1992. This confirms the earlier observation on the dominant role of domestic private consumption in improved output performance of the majority of east European countries in 1993. The Czech Republic and Romania were exceptions to this pattern, posting substantial increases in the net exports of goods and services as compared with 1992.

The impact of *terms of trade* changes is more difficult to examine, given that by the end of February 1994, only three countries had reported foreign trade price statistics for the preceding year: the Czech Republic, Hungary and Slovenia. The published figures are not strictly comparable (see section 3.5 for details), but the overall pattern of their trade price changes is consistent: all three countries experienced a *decline in the dollar price* of their exports and their imports; moreover, in every case, the fall was slightly stronger on the side of import prices. As a result, each of the countries experienced a mild *improvement in the terms of trade* (by 1.1, 2.2 and 3.1 per cent in Hungary, Slovenia and the Czech Republic, respectively). Although no direct evidence is available on foreign price changes in the other east European countries, given the broad similarity in their commodity and territorial trade structure, there is no reason to assume that the *ratio* of the change in export and import prices was significantly different in the other economies. Thus, the observation of *slightly improving terms of trade* in 1993 is likely to hold for the region as a whole.

For the *CIS countries*, no volume data are available but the dollar figures point to a sharp increase in *net exports* in 1993 in Russia. The large dollar surplus in Russia's non-CIS trade, seems to indicate that a big and growing share of a Russia's declining GDP is being taken up by net exports. However, given that the experience in other transition countries has shown that statistical under-reporting tends to affect imports more than exports, the true size of the trade surplus may be smaller than that shown in officially reported trade flows. These figures point to a strong positive impact of foreign demand on Russia's output.

This favourable *volume* effect has probably been to a large extent offset by the negative *price* effect. It is virtually certain that in Russia the terms of trade *deteriorated*, chiefly because of falling energy prices, though only a crude estimate of the actual magnitude of the change can be provided. For Russian exports, direct price information which is available on roughly half of foreign sales (oil, gas and other energy products, metals) shows an average fall in dollar export prices of over 20 per cent. Assuming that for the other half of exports the decline in prices was not much larger than in the reporting east European countries (4-5 per cent), the average decline in Russian export unit values can be estimated to be around 12-13 per cent. In imports, a slight decline in the price of grain (3 per cent) and a comparable decrease of prices of imported machines suggest that the overall level of import prices is not likely to have fallen by more than 3-5 per cent. Thus, the *deterioration of terms of trade* in Russia can be estimated to be in the order of 8-10 per cent, which implies a substantial loss to national income.

As far as intra-CIS trade is concerned, only Russia had reported some statistics at the time of writing. The previously published volume data, showing the fall of overall trade (exports plus imports) by half between 1991 and 1992,[116] imply another cut of around 25 per cent between 1992 and 1993.[117] The 1992 Russian trade surplus with other CIS countries of 1.6 per cent of GDP doubled in 1993 (at current prices) but in volume terms (1992 prices), it appears to have scarcely changed. The nominal increase reflects Russia's terms of trade gains as the export price of Russian fuels were adjusted upwards.

---

[116] RF Goskomstat, *Sotsial'no-ekonomicheskoe polozhenie ...*, op cit.

[117] A direct communication by RF Goskomstat to the ECE secretariat shows falls of 37 and 30 per cent in volume terms for exports and imports respectively, between 1991 and 1992. RF Goskomstat also estimates a fall of 50 per cent in the volume of total turnover (exports plus imports) of trade with CIS states between 1991 and 1993. See RF Goskomstat, *Sotsial'no-ekonomicheskoe polozhenie ...*, op.cit., pp.89-90.

3.3 Cost and prices

(i) Overview

The fight against inflation remained high on the list of policy priorities of governments in transition countries in 1993, but the task appears to be much more difficult than expected. While most *east European* countries managed to bring down inflation from rates in some cases dangerously close to hyperinflation, they seem to face much more difficulty in reducing it further to single-digit annual rates. In general terms, inflation *decelerated* in the transition region in 1993, but the picture is very different when the developments in individual countries are compared. Inflation was relatively low and falling in central European transition countries and the Baltic states, but high in the CIS and most of the Balkan region. Measured by the annual change in the *consumer price index* (CPI), inflation abated in 1993 in Albania, Bulgaria, the FYR of Macedonia, Poland, Slovenia and the Baltic states, and remained broadly unchanged in Hungary. Year-on-year price increases in 1993 were somewhat higher than in 1992 in the Czech Republic and Slovakia, but this was chiefly a result of certain one-off policy changes at the beginning of 1993, and a clear deceleration was observed throughout the rest of the year. In contrast, inflation was on the rise for most of the year in Croatia and Romania, and especially in FR Yugoslavia, which entered a full-speed hyperinflation[118] spiral in 1993. Inflation accelerated also throughout the *CIS region,* with highest rates registered in Armenia, Tajikistan, and especially Georgia and Ukraine, where the hyperinflation barrier was breached. Only in Russia was some slow-down of inflation observed, with a tenfold increase in the CPI in 1993, compared to a fifteenfold increase in 1992.

Despite the general downward tendency observed in east European countries, the gains on the inflation front have been rather meagre. Even the lowest inflation rates in the region (between 20 and 23 per cent per annum), observed in the Czech Republic, Hungary and Slovakia are still relatively high compared to international standards. They suggest that the *underlying* inflation rates,[119] fluctuating probably around 1-1.5 per cent a month, are also well above those prevailing in western Europe and North America, are not likely to change much in the near future.

Causes of inflation varied throughout the region, and included factors that worked on the demand and supply side of the economy. On the *demand side,* lax monetary (cheap credits) and/or fiscal (budget deficits) policies contributed to demand-pull inflation in Bulgaria, Romania, Croatia, FR Yugoslavia and in some CIS states. The impact of the demand factors was further exacerbated by various cost pressures such as a switch in taxation or devaluation, and the effects of market imperfections (monopolies). In addition, the general decline in the region's output resulted in an increase in the average unit cost of production. The role of *supply-side* factors has been particularly important in low-inflation countries, such as the Czech Republic or Slovakia, where macroeconomic balance was brought under control. In all countries, but especially in the CIS and former Yugoslav republics, price increases were also boosted by inflationary expectations, fed by the lack of credible policy actions aimed at curbing inflation.

(ii) Consumer prices

In all reforming countries, transition from central planning to a market system was associated with strong initial acceleration of inflation, which came as a consequence of the liberalization of previously controlled prices, effected – though to a varying extent – in all transition countries at the outset of reforms. Control over inflation has therefore been a common economic policy goal in the transition countries since 1990, and this priority may be expected to remain high on the policy agenda also in 1994. However, the accomplishment of this objective varied across the region in 1993 because the causes and intensity of the problem, as well as the policies applied, differed among the countries concerned. In *eastern Europe*, figures for the average *year-on-year* inflation rates in 1993 (table 3.3.1) show a mixed picture, with inflation being only slightly lower than in 1992 in Bulgaria and Poland, but falling rapidly in Albania, Slovenia and the Baltic states where achievements in restoring price stability in 1993 were perhaps most remarkable, given the very high level of inflation in the previous year. On the other hand, no decisive anti-inflationary policy moves were made until the final months of 1993 in Croatia, Romania and FR Yugoslavia. Even more worrying were price developments in the *CIS states,* where the annual inflation rates varied between 500 per cent in Uzbekistan to almost 4,500 per cent in Ukraine and some 12,000 in Georgia, being generally well above the 1992 rates. In Russia and, to a lesser extent, in Uzbekistan the year-on-year inflation rates in 1993 decreased somewhat from 1992 levels, though they still remained in the range of several hundred per cent per annum.

Monthly data show considerable variations in within-year price movements. However, if adjusted to eliminate certain one-time price shocks, the monthly data confirm the declining tendency in consumer price inflation as indicated by the annual changes, at least in *east European* countries. It may be observed (table 3.3.2) that higher annual changes in 1993 were in most cases caused by certain one-time policy changes, producing "spikes" of inflation and shifting the price levels upwards. This was the case of the Czech and Slovak Republics, where the VAT reform in January 1993 produced an instant price jump of 8-9 per cent, after which inflation came down again to 0.4-2.4 per cent per

---

[118] Conventionally defined, hyperinflation starts when retail prices increase 50 per cent or more a month. A country is considered to be out of hyperinflation when the monthly rate of inflation is continuously below 50 per cent, for at least one year.

[119] The underlying inflation rate may be interpreted as a medium-term inflation rate reflecting structural constraints and inertial tendencies, but netted of the impact of one-time shocks, such as policy shifts of changes in weather conditions.

TABLE 3.3.1

Transition countries: Changes in consumer price indices, 1991-1993
(Percentage change over preceding year)

	1991	1992	1993 January-March	1993 January-June	1993 January-September	1993 January-December
Albania	104.0	266.0	196.2	159.2	117.0	..
Bosnia-Herzegovina	..	..	..	..	..	..
Bulgaria	254.3	79.4	82.8	79.5	76.0	72.9
Croatia	223.0	765.5	1 280.3	1 479.9	1 649.4	1 537.5
Czech Republic	56.7	11.1	21.7	21.7	21.6	20.8
Hungary	35.0	23.0	24.8	23.3	23.0	22.7
Poland	70.3	43.0	41.4	39.7	38.0	36.9
Romania	165.5	210.9	171.0	194.7	228.5	257.4
Slovakia	61.2	10.2	19.0	20.5	22.2	23.1
Slovenia	117.7	201.3	57.9	43.8	36.7	32.7
The FYR of Macedonia	..	..	1 353.3	602.9	442.8	349.8
Yugoslavia (FR)	120.0	8 990.9	82 705.9	423 663.4	64 422 464.5	..
Armenia	174.1	728.7	905.7	839.5	785.7	2 260.0
Azerbaijan	101.8	1 063.0	920.0	949.5	966.6	980.9
Belarus	94.1	1 016.4	666.4	823.5	1 042.1	1 682.1
Georgia	..	768.7	1 294.3	1 011.2*	1 929.2*	11 647.0
Kazakhstan	90.9	884.8	611.4	674.5	787.1	1 161.8
Kyrgyzstan	107.4	906.2	584.1	733.8	944.6	1 145.8
Moldova	98.1	941.0	554.0	589.8	908.4	1 576.3
Russia [a]	100.3	1 468.0	753.5	746.0	865.3	911.3
Tajikistan	84.8	913.0	411.0	759.6	1 218.1	2 350.9
Turkmenistan	88.5	710.0	269.2	381.5	525.0	1 761.1
Ukraine	83.5	1 240.0	1 326.4	1 570.8	2 029.9	4 474.0 [b]
Uzbekistan	106.0	598.5	389.1	345.4	397.6	532.5
Estonia	283.0	968.6	256.8	182.8	120.9	87.6
Latvia	172.2	949.7	362.9	249.6	166.6	109.1
Lithuania	216.4	1 020.0	652.0	694.2	572.6	410.2
Ex-GDR *Länder*	..	11.2	8.9	8.9	8.9	8.9

Source: National statistics. For CIS republics, Latvia and Slovenia: retail prices of goods and services.

[a] Consumer prices (goods and services).
[b] Goods only, in state and cooperative outlets.

month and remained low during the rest of the year. A similar reaction was observed in Hungary, where prices in January increased by 6.8 per cent, responding to the increase in the VAT rates and elimination of some subsidies previously given to selected services. Also in Romania, the decision to liberalize food prices in May 1993 resulted in an immediate price jump of 30 per cent, while the introduction of the VAT system in July 1993 produced another price increase of 13 per cent. Poland also introduced the VAT system in July 1993, but the inflation impact was probably postponed by 3-4 months because of temporary controls on consumer prices imposed by the government. However, producer prices reacted strongly in July (an increase by 6 per cent), with the lagged impact on consumer prices manifesting itself with higher monthly inflation rates towards the end of the year. In Latvia, an increase of turnover tax rates in November 1993 produced a jump in consumer prices by nearly 9 per cent in that month. Other important policy-induced shocks were in most cases associated with the removal of subsidies and/or administrative increases of energy prices, this happened in Poland, Romania and the Baltic states.

If these one-off shocks are put aside, the monthly data show relatively stable and moderate inflation levels in the four central European countries and Slovenia. Somewhat higher variability of inflation rates was observed in Albania, Bulgaria, Romania and the Baltic states, most notably in Lithuania. Much larger fluctuations were characteristic for the FYR of Macedonia and FR Yugoslavia. Apart from the policy-induced shocks, month-over-month variations in the inflation rates were chiefly caused by changes in food prices, which were either associated with seasonal production cycles (e.g., the temporary fall of prices of agricultural products in the FYR of Macedonia in June 1993), or reflected drops in production levels due to unfavourable climatic conditions (e.g., the increase of meat prices in Poland and the Baltic states in December 1993). Nevertheless, it is not entirely clear whether the acceleration of inflation registered towards the end of 1993 in countries such as Lithuania, Latvia or Poland was only a result of seasonal factors or reflected some more fundamental shifts in financial policies.

Towards the end of 1993 and the beginning of 1994 new efforts were undertaken by some of the countries suffering from high inflation to regain control over price increases with more comprehensive stabilization programmes. Croatia was the first, introducing a radical

TABLE 3.3.2

Transition countries: Monthly changes in consumer price indices, 1992-1993
(Percentage change over preceding month)

	1992 December	1993 January	February	March	April	May	June	July	August	September	October	November	December
Albania	1.3	6.8	4.3	0.9	-0.1	-0.5	0.1	7.8	1.3	4.3	1.9	0.6	0.3
Bosnia-Herzegovina	..	..	..	..	..	..	..	..	..	..	..	..	..
Bulgaria	4.6	6.9	4.7	5.6	3.9	5.3	4.1	1.0	2.6	3.8	4.2	4.6	3.9
Croatia	22.0	31.0	25.0	28.0	23.0	26.0	29.0	27.0	28.5	30.6	38.7	1.4	0.6
Czech Republic	0.6	8.5	1.3	0.6	0.6	0.4	0.4	0.7	0.7	1.4	1.1	0.5	0.8
Hungary	1.1	6.8	1.7	0.8	0.8	0.4	0.3	0.6	1.8	2.9	1.7	0.7	1.3
Poland	2.2	4.1	3.4	2.1	2.3	1.8	1.4	1.1	2.3	2.5	1.9	4.0	5.6
Romania	13.2	11.5	8.2	9.2	10.0	30.4	5.5	13.2	10.8	10.9	16.3	14.2	10.0
Slovakia	1.0	8.9	1.6	1.0	1.2	0.5	0.4	1.1	2.4	2.4	1.4	1.1	0.6
Slovenia	1.1	3.7	1.6	1.4	1.0	1.4	1.5	0.8	1.7	1.7	2.9	1.6	1.5
The FYR of Macedonia	15.8	16.9	32.5	8.3	2.1	16.1	-8.9	9.4	9.8	9.0	13.9	11.3	11.6
Yugoslavia (FR)	46.7	100.6	211.8	225.8	114.1	205.0	366.7	431.2	1 880.6	643.2	1 896.6	20 190.0	178 882.0
Armenia	32.2	28.7	42.2	19.9	7.0	9.6	17.7	4.7	10.3	9.6	39.9	500.4	76.3
Azerbaijan	94.5	42.4	14.7	1.4	4.6	18.8	10.1	17.4	8.8	13.7	16.8	49.0	58.9
Belarus	36.7	27.7	32.6	34.5	29.2	22.5	24.1	18.3	23.1	36.0	47.6	49.1	52.4
Georgia	25.0*	31.0*	16.0*	120.0*	35.0*	-25.0*	29.0*	57.0*	102.0*	95.0*	7.0*	335.0*	190.0*
Kazakhstan	21.0	29.8	29.0	27.8	21.5	16.3	17.3	15.1	25.8	39.0	35.8	52.0	38.5
Kyrgyzstan	22.9	35.9	39.2	23.0	16.0	24.6	16.6	15.8	25.2	36.1	32.3	21.6	16.8
Moldova	23.0	33.8	25.8	21.0	19.4	17.5	18.8	34.3	34.4	64.0	38.1 [a]	38.1	59.2 [a]
Russia [a]	24.9	26.0	25.0	20.0	23.0	19.0	20.0	22.0	26.0	23.0	19.3	16.0	13.0
Tajikistan	15.7	22.8	37.4	44.5	58.1	41.4	15.6	25.2	56.3	38.7	24.3	42.2	111.4
Turkmenistan	14.7	14.6	41.3	15.1	28.0	15.4	49.0	16.3	15.1	21.7	27.7	429.1	26.2
Ukraine	29.7	79.8	32.3	19.2	18.2	22.1	42.2	31.1	26.0	64.5	77.3	45.3	90.8
Uzbekistan	12.6	29.3	18.2	7.6	13.2	9.2	28.9	18.2	15.1	9.5	28.7	43.7	40.5
CIS	27.0	26.2	23.1	19.3	18.1	17.9	25.6	20.7	22.1	32.3	35.5	29.8	..
Estonia	3.3	3.4	1.7	3.6	2.3	1.7	1.3	0.3	0.7	3.0	2.6	4.0	4.1
Latvia	2.6	4.2	2.9	2.4	0.3	-0.3	2.3	0.8	-1.7	2.0	3.8	8.8	5.1
Lithuania	27.8	9.4	10.2	21.4	24.9	12.7	6.2	2.9	0.9	4.1	7.4	6.8	6.2
Ex-GDR *Länder*	0.2	6.7	0.5	0.2	0.4	0.1	0.4	0.0	-0.1	0.1	0.2	0.2	–

Source: National statistics.

Note: For CIS Republics, Latvia, Lithuania, Slovenia and FR Yugoslavia: retail prices. Percentage changes derived from indices.

[a] Consumer price indices (goods and services).

stabilization package in October 1993. Early results were rather encouraging, because inflation came down from the monthly rates of 23-39 per cent to less than 1.5 per cent a month in November and December 1993 and the foreign exchange rate stabilized.[120] Romania also seems to have decided to implement more radical anti-inflationary measures, based on the agreement signed with the IMF in November 1993; indeed, inflation has been falling gradually since December. In FR Yugoslavia, the hyperinflation spiral continued unabated in 1993, reaching an astronomic level of 180,000 per cent a month in December 1993. Only at the end of January 1994 did the country decide to stabilize prices with a programme based on a new, fully convertible dinar, backed by international reserves of the central bank. But it is uncertain whether the programme also includes the necessary cuts in budgetary expenditures which would be required to eliminate the underlying sources of inflationary pressures.

[120] The stabilization programme is based on extremely tight monetary policy and strict wage controls. For details, see *Central European*, February 1994, pp.35-38, and *Balkan News International*, 27 February 1994, p.14.

Short-term price developments in the *CIS countries* do not show any significant turnround in inflationary tendencies. The monthly changes in the retail price index indicate both a relatively high level and a considerable degree of variability of inflation rates across individual CIS countries. Inflation declines somewhat during 1993 only in Russia (and probably in Kyrgyzstan), but the sustainability of this downward tendency may legitimately be questioned given the large fiscal deficit planned for 1994 (see section 3.7(iii)); in all other CIS countries inflation remained very high and even accelerated towards the end of 1993, after a modest slow-down during the summer. The exceptionally large jumps registered in Armenia and Turkmenistan in November 1993 were connected with the liberalization of food prices in these countries.

The monthly increases in consumer prices in Russia averaged around 20 per cent during 1993 and, except for January, did not differ much from the inflation rates registered in 1992. A relative deceleration of the rate of inflation to 16 per cent in November and 13 per cent in December 1993 was an encouraging development; however, the deceleration may not be sustainable. First, there are certain concerns about the accuracy of the official

TABLE 3.3.3

Transition countries: Producer prices, 1993
(Percentage change over previous month)

	January	February	March	April	May	June	July	August	September	October	November	December
Bulgaria	2.0	1.5	2.7	0.5	2.6	2.1	-1.3	0.5	2.3	1.2	1.1	-0.7
Croatia	29.7	25.3	33.7	27.7	26.8	30.2	24.8	23.2	37.8	29.1	-4.6	-1.5
Czech Republic	3.7	3.7	0.6	0.5	0.3	0.2	0.8	0.2	0.5	0.6	-0.1	..
Hungary	3.0	0.3	0.1	0.7	0.3	0.3	0.0	1.0	1.3	2.2	-0.1	..
Poland	3.8	2.7	0.8	2.1	2.0	1.7	6.3	2.4	2.2	1.9	2.2	2.6
Romania	..	1.7	2.6	3.6	22.2	15.3	12.6	10.0	6.9	11.6	11.4	8.3
Slovakia	10.1	1.5	0.7	-0.2	0.3	-0.3	0.5	2.1	1.1	1.4	0.6	–
Slovenia	4.6	1.5	-0.2	-0.6	0.1	1.9	0.8	0.8	1.2	3.3	1.4	2.4
Yugoslavia (FR)	83.0	245.1	221.0	104.6	180.9	377.6	360.7	2 371.5	855.0	2 008.5	18 881	179 920
Russia	32.0	30.0	23.0	24.0	19.0	18.0	29.0	27.0	21.0	19.0	16.0	16.0
Estonia	2.7	6.4	1.2	3.9	1.4	2.1	1.2	3.6	1.0	1.1	4.4	3.1
Latvia	8.4	10.3	4.2	-0.7	0.0	-2.2	1.7	2.1	2.6	1.3	2.4	1.9
Lithuania	13.3	9.3	10.2	21.0	16.0	2.0	-1.3	2.2	2.6	4.6	3.2	5.6
Ex-GDR *Länder*	0.2	0.2	0.3	0.2	–	–	–	-0.2	–	–	0.2	–

Source: National statistics and current reporting.

data. Calculations by an independent institute reveal that the respective inflation rates were 23 and 25 per cent in those two months.[121] Second, the deceleration in inflation may have been temporary and "artificial", obtained by deferring the payment of obligations of the government to the defence industry and the agro-industrial complex, as well as postponing wage increases in the social service sector.[122] Those deferred payments, which represented around one third of the budget for the last quarter of 1993, have been passed on to the budget for the first quarter of 1994. Therefore, they can be expected to have a stimulating impact on the budget deficit and price increases in early 1994.

(iii) Producer prices and wages

Changes in the CPI may not be the best indicator of the impact on investment decisions or the international competitiveness of domestic goods. Another indicator, the *producer price index* (PPI), may be a superior measure in this context. There is a link between the two indices, but the relationship is not straightforward. The differences are chiefly in the coverage and the stage of the distribution at which the data are collected.[123]

None the less, changes in the PPI may send valuable signals to policy makers about possible developments in the CPI in the near future and indicate the need for policy action. Typically, the CPI increases faster than the PPI because the former included prices of services which tend to grow faster than prices of goods due to the slower pace of productivity growth in the service sector. If, however, the difference between the two indicators is very large, it may suggest that there is demand pressure in the economy so that restraint in expenditure may be a desirable policy course. Conversely, if the PPI accelerates faster relative to the CPI, that indicates a mounting cost pressure in the economy.

Monthly changes in the PPI in the transition countries in 1993 (table 3.3.3) reveal the sensitivity of the PPI to major shifts in economic policy. Normally, following price liberalization of changes in turnover tax rates, the PPI accelerates faster that the CPI because of the steep increase in prices of material inputs (chiefly energy); but as stabilization proceeds, the PPI has a tendency to lag behind the CPI. In 1993, producer price inflation was generally lower than consumer price inflation, with the difference between the *average monthly* changes in the CPI and PPI in the low-inflation transition countries around 1 percentage point. For instance, the average monthly rates for the CPI and PPI were 1.4 and 0.9 per cent in the Czech Republic, 1.9 and 0.8 per cent in Hungary, 2.7 and 2.5 per cent in Poland, and 1.9 and 1.5 per cent in Slovakia. The difference was higher in Bulgaria and Romania (4.2 and 1.2 per cent, and 12.4 and 9.6 per cent. respectively). In contrast, in Russia, producer prices grew faster than consumer prices (23 versus 21 per cent per month), indicating strong pressure from the cost side.

Each time there was an introduction of VAT or a change in it rate of coverage, producers' prices reacted to the policy change with a "spike" which typically was stronger and more short-lived than the reaction of

---

[121] See a report by the All-Union Research Institute for the Consumer Market and Marketing, in *Rossiiskaya gazeta*, 6 January 1994, p.2.

[122] It was also reported that the Russian Finance Ministry sold hard currency from government reserves to the Central Bank and, subsequently, attributed 6.8 trillion roubles from that sale as its income. *Rossiiskie vesti*, 2 February 1994.

[123] The CPI includes prices of home and imported *consumer* goods which contain (wide and flexible) retail margins and prices of services, with all taxes and subsidies; the PPI consists typically of prices of all domestically produced goods but excluding services. The prices of services in transition economies have been generally increasing faster than the prices of goods. That has happened because of lower productivity in services than in manufacturing, increases in the labour costs, non-tradability of services (lack of foreign competition), and relatively modest domestic infrastructure that could support the operation of a competitive service sector. As a result, increases of CPI have typically been bigger than increases of PPI.

TABLE 3.3.4

Transition countries: Average nominal monthly wages, 1993
(Percentage change over previous month)

	January	February	March	April	May	June	July	August	September	October	November	December
Albania	..	..	..	..	..	..	..	..	..	..	..	..
Bosnia-Herzegovina	..	..	..	..	..	..	..	..	..	..	..	..
Bulgaria	-16.5	3.3	22.0	-1.8	3.8	11.8	..	..	..	..	..	..
Croatia	26.1	22.7	44.3	27.8	37.8	32.8	34.0	28.7	34.0	9.0	4.4	5.2
Czech Republic	-8.0	-2.3	12.3	-0.8	6.8	4.4	-5.4	-4.3	0.5	7.9	13.7	..
Hungary	-26.7	2.3	14.1	2.9	4.9	2.9	-1.9	4.8	-3.6	3.4	10.7	14.4
Poland [a]	-14.2	7.3	10.4	-0.6	-2.7	2.4	1.6	1.1	2.7	2.8	6.6	14.8
Romania	-14.9	5.0	27.4	3.2	33.2	15.4	13.8	5.4	5.8	6.7	16.7	8.9
Slovakia	..	..	..	..	..	..	..	..	..	..	..	..
Slovenia	-0.9	8.9	-3.0	0.5	-0.8	2.7	3.5	1.4	3.4	2.5	4.8	..
The FYR of Macedonia	22.9	23.5	26.6	14.4	9.6	8.0	10.0	6.3	14.2	10.7	12.7	8.7
Yugoslavia (FR)	47.9	130.1	160.7	197.7	115.4	350.1	419.0	1 586.4	719.0	1 933.0	20 000.0	..
Armenia	8.9	21.5	28.2	14.3	30.7	17.8	44.4	10.1	17.2	50.7	12.4	9.4
Azerbaijan	18.5	5.0	12.8	1.0	8.9	13.1	29.1	6.4	16.0	3.6	20.2	46.7
Belarus	7.3	26.4	16.1	23.9	12.6	43.7	12.3	34.4	16.3	44.0	29.3	23.5
Georgia	..	..	..	..	..	..	..	..	..	..	..	..
Kazakhstan	-16.7	35.7	30.0	12.7	37.8	25.9	11.3	25.3	37.6	32.8	..	..
Kyrgyzstan	-20.4	31.0	17.1	11.7	12.9	14.8	13.2	21.8	27.0	13.0	11.1	19.5
Moldova	-29.7	13.5	30.4	7.7	16.3	39.5	54.4	14.2	18.3	10.6	..	..
Russia	-4.8	24.8	23.3	29.7	22.7	26.4	18.1	16.8	23.7	15.0	9.1	28.1
Tajikistan	-42.5	30.6	22.0	21.5	26.3	86.1	-0.9 [b]	7.5	9.0	43.9	18.3	21.7
Turkmenistan	..	..	..	..	..	..	..	..	..	..	..	..
Ukraine	-0.8	27.8	23.1	10.7	19.6	98.6	26.5	14.9	135.3	22.0	..	..
Uzbekistan	-13.1	12.7	20.9	15.6	9.2	120.4	44.9	13.6	17.0	10.2	14.3	44.0
Estonia [c]	..	4.2	11.6	20.7	-1.9	3.8	-13.7	..	..	..	..	..
Latvia	-9.6	9.2	8.6	-5.4	8.0	6.4	-0.9	-0.7	5.2	0.6	9.8	21.2
Lithuania [a]	10.0	27.3	12.5	10.8	7.3	11.8	6.7	2.5	5.8	8.9	10.7	16.3

Sources: National statistics and current reporting. *PlanEcon Report* (for the Slovak Republic). *Russian Economic Trends*, Vol.2, No.2, 1993 (for Russia). *CIS Statistical Bulletin*, various issues; questionnaire (for Belarus).

Note: For the CIS countries including material assistance and fringe benefits, except for Russia. State sector excluding collective farms.

[a] Net monthly earnings (wages and salaries in enterprise sector).
[b] This is not a mistake: see *CIS Statistical Bulletin*, 16(34) and 20(38).
[c] Country report data.

consumer prices. This was the case in the Czech Republic, Hungary and Slovakia in January 1993, as well as in Poland and Romania in July 1993.[124]

One of the key components of productions costs are manpower unit costs, which in turn depend on changes in the nominal wage and employment levels. Average *nominal* monthly wages continued to grow fast in 1993 in all transition economies, but the actual pace of growth differed across the region (table 3.3.4). The nominal growth was influenced to a large extent by accelerating inflation, various types of official and unofficial indexation schemes, and pressure from the labour unions. If compared on a monthly basis, nominal wages in most east European countries were rising in 1993 at rates close to the observed inflation rates, although variability of wage changes was generally higher. With few exceptions (e.g., the Czech Republic), the growth of wages lagged behind inflation. Strong acceleration of wage increases observed in many countries in December 1993 seems to be a normal cyclical development, reflecting some extra payments of end-year bonuses, and does not necessarily signal acceleration of inflation. Nevertheless, the growth of nominal wages may have contributed to producer price inflation through an increase of overall wage bills in those transition countries where employment held level despite the output fall while average wages increased (the Czech Republic, Slovenia, Estonia, Latvia).

In spite of relatively substantial increases in average nominal wages, average *real wages* in transition countries increased only slightly (Slovenia being a notable exception with an increase in average real wages of 16 per cent), or fell even further in 1993, adding to the substantial declines in the 1991-1992 period. In order to obtain a correct picture of changes in real wages, the increases in average nominal wages need to be adjusted by suitable deflators for wage-earners' consumption baskets. Since these deflators are generally not available for 1993, the CPI was used to deflate the nominal wages. The figures obtained show that in the majority of the transition countries consumer prices still outpaced the growth of wages in 1993 (table 3.3.5). Only in the Czech Republic, Slovenia and probably Estonia and Latvia were there some relatively considerable advances in real wages. According to the official data, the

---

[124] Although there was a relatively even development in the CPI in Poland in July after the introduction of the VAT because of the temporary price control, the PPI reacted to the change with a "spike" (6.3 per cent) in that month that was translated into the CPI in the following months.

fall of real wages in Russia has been rather small in 1993 (less than 2 per cent compared to 1992), but it remains to be seen whether the slow-down signals a turning point in the downward trend from 1991-1992 or is only a short-term fluctuation. Available data for the full year or for three quarters show that in 1993 the average real wages fell most sharply in Belarus, the FR Yugoslavia, the FYR of Macedonia, Lithuania, Moldova and Ukraine (by between 28 and 61 per cent).

TABLE 3.3.5

Transition countries: Real wages, [a] 1990-1993
(Percentage change over preceding year)

	1990	1991	1992	1993
Bulgaria	6.9	-39.4	19.2	-10.4 [b]
Croatia	-16.2	-25.0	-43.5	-0.5
Czech Republic	..	..	10.1	8.6 [c]
Hungary [d]	-3.7	-4.0*	-4.0*	-1.6*
Poland	-24.4	-0.3	-2.7	-1.8
Romania	5.5	-16.6	-13.2	-15.8
Slovakia	..	..	..	..
Slovenia	-26.5	-15.1	-2.8	16.0
The FYR of Macedonia	..	..	-32.9	-26.5*
Yugoslavia (FR)	-4.7	-5.8	-48.7	-61.0*
Belarus	10.1	2.0	-15.3	-27.9
Moldova	9.9	-15.3	-30.9	-34.0
Russia	8.7	-7.2	-29.8	-1.7
Ukraine	7.9	1.9	-18.2	-49.1*
Estonia	6.8	-43.1	-30.8	5.0 [e]
Latvia	5.3	-29.2	-22.7	6.7
Lithuania	6.3	-17.7	-14.0	-43.0

Sources: National statistics and current reporting. *Polish Statistical Yearbook, 1993*, p.202, table 5(309). CIS Statistical Committee, *Statisticheskii byulleten*, 24(42), p.23. Estonian Academy of Sciences, *On the Estonian economy at the end of 1993*, p.21.

[a] Nominal wage change deflated by consumer price index.
[b] January-June.
[c] January-July.
[d] Workers and employees.
[e] January-September.

If observed over the medium term, the developments in average real wages seem to go through several stages, corresponding to the stages of the transition process. In all countries where strong stabilization-cum-liberalization programmes were implemented, the first year of transition brought about a sharp fall in real wages, as a consequence of price liberalization coupled with wage/income controls. This initial reduction was relatively easy to implement because of the readiness of wage earners to accept substantial real wage cuts in the initial stage of transition. In the following year or two, resistance of wage earners to further cuts became stronger, and the fall of real wages was either curtailed or even reversed. It seems that this stage has already been reached by early reformers, such as the Czech Republic, Hungary or Poland. As time goes by, wage earners demand (real) increases in wages in order to recover the losses which they incurred during the initial shock that was brought about by the transition process. As the experience of east European countries shows, a fall by approximately one third of the real wage may be about the maximum concession that wage earners are ready to accept over the short or medium term as their one-time "contribution" to the transition process. Once this limit is reached, strong demands for increases in real wages are likely to reappear, aimed at making up for the sacrifice of the preceding period.

Even in the most successful reforming countries the cumulative fall in real average wages over 1990-1993 was substantial, varying from 12-15 per cent for Hungary and the Czech Republic, to around 30 per cent for Poland. The cumulative fall in real wages since 1990 has been much more dramatic in some other countries (e.g., in Moldova, Lithuania, the FYR of Macedonia, FR Yugoslavia – see table 3.3.5), where it was exacerbated by some adverse developments not directly related to the transition process, such as the consequences of the abrupt disintegration of the former federal countries or internal ethnic conflicts.

When interpreting the changes in real wages in transition countries, two important caveats should be kept in mind. First, the statistical offices in transition economies do not employ identical statistical methods to arrive at the officially reported rate of change in real wages. Some of them use cost-of-living indices for particular consumers categories, while others apply the CPI for the adjustment of nominal wages. In the latter case, the real wage index may give distorted information since the CPI deflates average nominal wages across the board; it does not take into account the variety of consumption patterns among different layers of wage earners, or shifts within the same layer due to changes in wages and/or prices. Second, the statistical fall in real wages (and, consequently, in the standard of living of wage earners) after price liberalization was to some extent "artificial" as it ignored improvements in the availability of goods due to the elimination of shortages. Nevertheless, even if those statistical and conceptual problems are solved, the general sharp decline in real wages in the first stage of transition cannot be questioned.

Chart 3.3.1 illustrates the developments in the CPI, the PPI and average nominal monthly wages[125] in the select group of transition countries for which a comparable set of data is available for 1992-1993. As can be seen, the prices of manufactured goods measured by the PPI accelerated at much higher rates than the CPI in Russia and the Baltic states since the end of 1991, suggesting the importance of cost-push inflation relative to demand-pull. It originated in price liberalization (most relevant for energy, raw materials and other inputs), falling productivity of labour and the monopolistic behaviour of suppliers. Such a tendency is common throughout the CIS region. As for the average nominal monthly wages, they fell in real terms, but due to extensive labour hoarding, overall manpower costs have probably increased, contributing to cost-push inflation in most of the former Soviet republics.

---

[125] Data in chart 3.3.1 refer to the average nominal monthly wages in the entire economy for all countries. Since they include wages in both the manufacturing and the service sectors, there is no one-to-one relation between wages and the PPI. The exception is the Czech Republic where only the wages in the manufacturing sector were included.

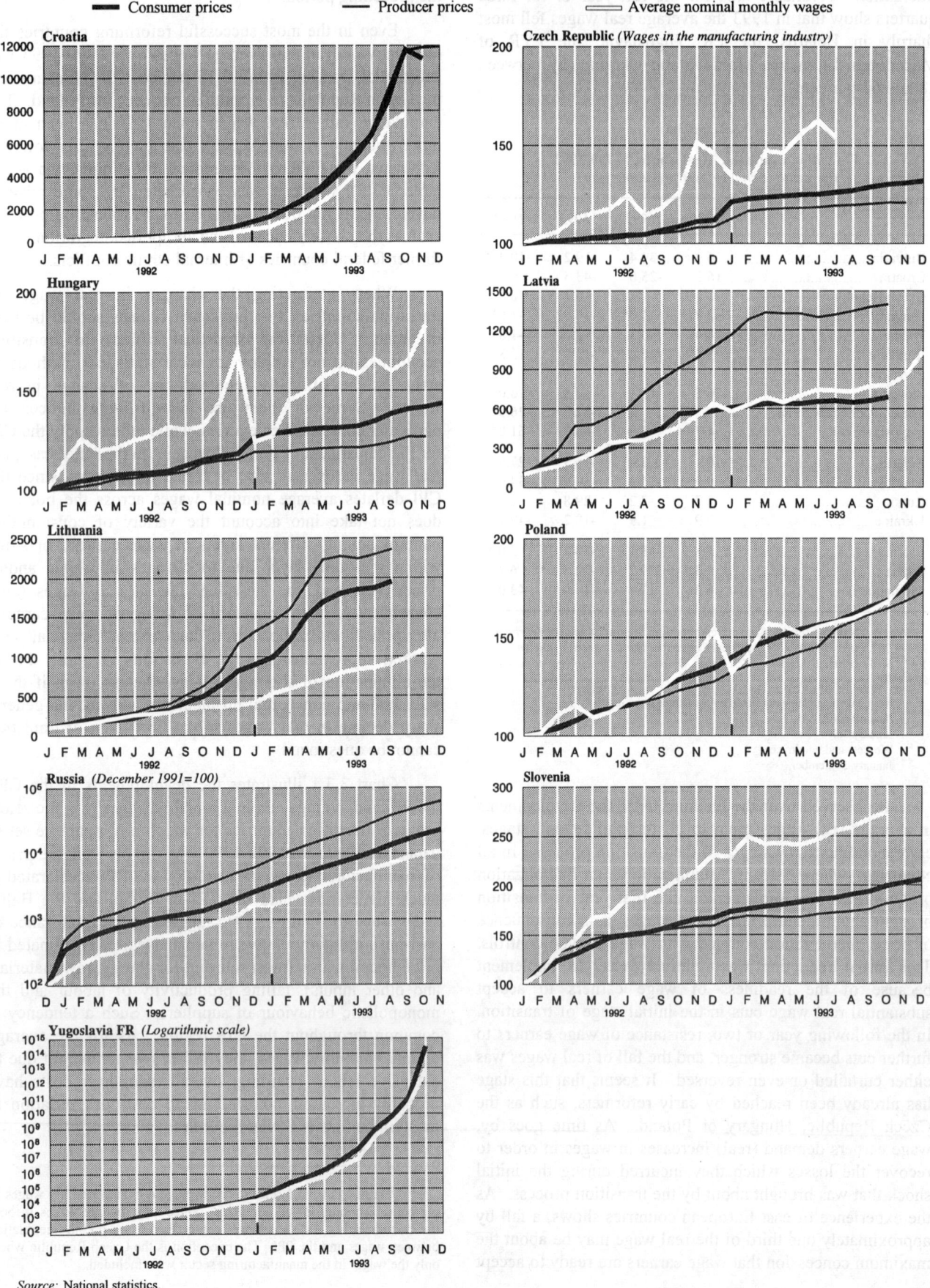

CHART 3.3.1

Consumer prices, producer prices and average nominal wages of transition countries, 1992-1993
(Monthly indices, January 1992=100)

Source: National statistics.

A different picture can be observed in the Czech Republic, Hungary and Slovenia, where a halt in output decline in 1993 has probably ignited strong upward pressure on wages, which were growing faster than consumer prices (chart 3.3.1). This pressure on costs of production has not yet converted strongly into inflation, but some potential for such a wage-push increase in prices will remain in the near future.[126] There were, however, some attempts to moderate age increases. In Slovenia, for example, wages were frozen in the period February-June 1993 in order to reduce wage costs and increase the international competitiveness of goods, but after that period they continued to increase. The Czech Republic, too, introduced wage controls for the second half of 1993 in order to moderate wage increases. Wage increases in Poland remained broadly in line with consumer price inflation, while elsewhere in the transition countries average wage rises were below the rate of inflation, indicating a fall in real terms in 1993.

(iv) Origins of inflation

Although transition countries have suffered from a variety of inflation sources, the relative importance of particular factors differed from country to country, depending on their initial macroeconomic balance, the degree of market distortion inherited from central planning, and the adopted course of economic policy and reforms during the first stage of transition. The first two factors jointly determine the magnitude of the initial price shock which comes as a consequence of price liberalization. In the next stage, inflation is expected to abate, provided that stabilization policies which follow the price decontrol are consistent and strong, and are supported by the necessary institutional measures.

In this context, two broad groups among the transition countries can be distinguished. In the *high inflation* countries, the main reasons behind high and accelerating price increases are to be found in *soft financial policies* in the period after the initial price liberalization, which tended to expand aggregate demand and strengthen inflationary expectations. In some of these countries (Romania, and most of the CIS states), a lack of firm control over money and credit emission resulted in a massive and indiscriminatory inflow of new resources (subsidies, credits) to the enterprise sector. The "soft" budget constraint in enterprises translated into higher wage payments affected across the board, even in bankrupt firms. Negative interest rates in some countries kept unprofitable businesses running artificially and hence prevented large-scale bankruptcies, unemployment and restructuring of the economy. Such a policy increased *expectations* about inflation in the future, which in turn accelerated the velocity of money in countries such as Ukraine, Russia or FR Yugoslavia.

In other countries, the main source of inflation was a massive *budget deficit*, which was largely financed by primary emission of the central bank. The conventional view on the inflationary impact of deficits leads to rather tough policy prescriptions: reduce or eliminate the budget deficit. But it is worth noting that the relationship between the deficit and inflation is not straightforward; it depends on how the deficit is financed and on whether or not an economy's resources are fully employed. If the deficit is financed with credit from the central bank, the money supply increases and, under constant velocity of circulation, there will be an inflationary impact on prices. But if the velocity decreased, as often happens during disinflation, the inflationary impact will be smaller. The second possibility is to finance the deficit by borrowing from commercial banks and/or from the general public. In this case, the money supply does not change; nevertheless, the inflationary impact can still work though two channels. First, it can arise from a shift of resources from groups with higher propensity to save to groups with lower propensity to save. Typically, this shift does indeed take place because of the specific composition of budgetary revenues and expenditures. Second, if the economy is near or at full employment, additional borrowing by the government can raise interest rates, and contribute to cost inflation.

Most *high-inflation* countries financed budget deficits, at least in large proportion, with credits issued by the central bank. The resulting increase in money supply ended up in the hands of low-propensity-to-save social groups. In addition, in those countries which registered trade surpluses (e.g., Russia) domestic money supply expanded to the extent net export earnings added to net international reserves of domestic banks. But since the *real money supply* actually decreased in most countries, the inflationary impact could only have materialized if the velocity of circulation increased. Although this is probably what happened Romania, Russia, Ukraine and some other CIS countries, as well as in FR Yugoslavia, it is unlikely that the increase in velocity alone would account for entire inflation. It may be assumed that other inflationary factors, mostly those working on the supply side, were also present in 1993.

The supply-side factors were probably much more important than the demand-side factors in the *low-inflation countries*. Material costs of production increased significantly due to the collapse of the intra-CMEA trade, price liberalization (increased cost of energy in particular[127]), devaluations of the national currencies, increases in interest rates, removal of subsidies and disintegration of the formerly composite countries like the

---

[126] An increase in average nominal monthly wages does not necessarily translate into a demand-pull inflation (e.g., if employment falls); it may be a cost-push source of inflation.

[127] In Slovenia, for example, the switch to the higher winter rates for electricity in January and October 1993 contributed to an acceleration of the monthly rates of inflation from around 1.5 per cent to 3.7 and 2.9 per cent, respectively. Similar seasonal price increases were made in the Baltic states.

USSR, Yugoslavia and Czechoslovakia. Supply-side constraints in the form of bottlenecks and shortages that prevented production even if demand existed interacted to generate unused production capacities. A change in the production technology that would adjust to the new circumstances can only take place in the medium or longer term. Therefore, the increased costs of production, as well as the need to make profits, were passed on to higher prices.

With falling manufacturing output, fixed costs of production were distributed on a smaller amount of output units which gave a cost-push acceleration to inflation (most evident in the case of the CIS countries). The rate of fall in output was significantly larger than the rate of fall in employment throughout the transition region, hence labour hoarding was common (for estimates of labour hoarding, see section 3.4). Initially, it was possible for firms to offset the increased cost of labour hoarding through lowering real wages; but in the medium term, pressures for real wage increases are likely to intensify, leading to a wage-push inflation. That wage-push source of inflation was present in 1993 in the Czech Republic and Slovenia, and it may be expected to gain importance also in other countries in the near future.

In the countries where monetary policy was tight (the Visegrad group and the Baltic states, for example), credits were relatively expensive so that the rates of interest were increasing costs of production for the firms that needed to resort to financial markets for funds.

Devaluation may also have an impact of the rate of inflation. The role of the foreign exchange rate in determining changes in the domestic price level depends on the size of an economy, its openness in terms of trade shares, and degree of "dollarization". From this point of view, all transition economies seem to be rather susceptible to changes in the foreign exchange rate. The currencies of most transition countries were devalued or have depreciated in relation to western currencies to a smaller or larger extent in 1993; hence in nominal terms these changes contributed to domestic inflation. On the other hand, currencies of nearly all transition countries were devalued by less than the difference between domestic and foreign inflation, and hence they appreciated in real terms (see sections 3.5 and 3.7(iii)). Thus the inflationary impact of devaluations was cushioned by the margin of real appreciation.

Indexation represents another source of inflationary pressure in transition countries like Belarus, Bulgaria, Croatia, Romania and, to some extent, Poland. That policy tool permits economic agents to increase their current and future incomes or prices of output in a predetermined way, to mitigate the income-reduction burden that comes from stabilization, and to reduce uncertainty. On the other hand, however, indexation introduced a strong, self-sustaining mechanism of price increases, and blunts incentives to fight inflation with radical means. As such, it creates expectations of future inflation.

TABLE 3.3.6

Introduction of the value-added tax in transition economies and rates in January 1994

Country [a]	Date	Rate in per cent		
		Special [b]	Preferential	Standard
Bulgaria	1 April 1994	-	..	22
Czech Republic	1 January 1993	..	5	23
Hungary	1 January 1988	10	15	20
Poland	5 July 1993	-	7	22
Romania	1 July 1993	..	..	18
Slovakia	1 January 1993	..	6	25
Belarus [c]	1 January 1992	..	..	20
Kazakhstan [c]	1 January 1992	..	..	28
Russia [c]	1 January 1992	-	10	20
Ukraine [c]	1 January 1992	..	..	20
Lithuania	22 June 1992 [d]	..	..	18

Source: National statistics.

[a] The countries of the former Yugoslavia intend to introduce the VAT during 1994.

[b] Applied to the basic foodstuffs and items for children.

[c] There is a statement of intent of the CIS countries to eliminate discrepancies in the VAT rates among the partner countries and to introduce a standard rate of around 20 per cent (*Ekonomika i zhizn'*, No.37, September 1992, p.1).

[d] Fully implemented only from April 1994.

Apart from the elimination of subsidies due to price liberalization and consequent increases in prices, the introduction of the *value-added-tax* (VAT) had its impact on the CPI (table 3.3.6). As the experience of 1993 shows, the implementation of VAT produced an instant and one-time monthly "spike" in the rate of inflation. Its impact in the Czech Republic and Slovenia has already been noted.[128] Hungary changed the rate at which VAT applied and dismantled subsidies previously given to certain services in January 1993 which jointly raised the rate of inflation for that month to 6.8 per cent.[129] Romania introduced VAT at a single rate of 18 per cent in July 1993. That step was coupled with the repeal of the limits on profit margins that was previously restricted to 30 per cent. The combined effect of those changes affected the monthly rate of inflation which accelerated from 5.5 per cent in June to 13.2 per cent in July. The introduction of VAT in Poland in July 1993 engendered a rise in producers' prices, which was, after a lag, transmitted into consumer prices.

[128] Slovakia slightly increased the rate at which the VAT applied in August, which accelerated inflation in that month.

[129] There was a small "spike" in the CPI in Hungary in September which was due to the extension of the coverage of the VAT to previously tax-free items and a devaluation of the forint of 4 per cent.

3.4 Labour markets

Against a background of continued recession in the majority of the transition countries, there was a further deterioration in labour markets in 1993, albeit at a slower pace in general than in 1992. Although signs of recovery recently emerged in several countries, given the traditionally lagged response of labour demand to changes in output, employment continued to fall everywhere in 1993 and unemployment reached new highs. By the end of 1993, the total number of unemployed reached 7.5 million in eastern Europe and 1.3 million in the former Soviet republics. Compared to December 1992, there were some 1.3 million (16.5 per cent) more unemployed persons in December 1993 in all transition countries taken together, two thirds of whom were in eastern Europe where the rate of unemployment reached 14 per cent. Although high and rising unemployment rates are a general feature, there remains considerable variation between the east European countries. Excluding the Czech Republic, where the unemployment rate remained low at 3.5 per cent, all east European countries recorded double-digit rates varying between 10 and 30 per cent at the end of 1993. Unemployment has been increasing also in the CIS countries, but official unemployment rates still remain very low (around 1 per cent) both in comparison with the east European countries and relative to the cumulative contraction of output. This implies, *inter alia*, a much higher degree of overmanning in these countries, where cheap loans and credits have kept otherwise insolvent state enterprises afloat in order to avoid, at least in the short run, the political consequences of mass unemployment in an environment where people have been used to decades of practically guaranteed employment and steady income. Policy approaches to transition-related labour market problems vary substantially between countries. Assessing the real magnitude of labour market developments in the transition economies over time and in a comparative perspective remains difficult because of the limited and often varying coverage of available statistics.[130] Despite these deficiencies, the general tendencies dominating the labour markets in the transition economies can be discerned.

(i) Employment

Among the major labour market indicators, perhaps the most difficult to measure is employment. Data on employment in the contracting state sector are relatively complete, but the coverage of the expanding private sector, particularly of the self-employed, is in general far from comprehensive. Furthermore, for many countries very little information is available on within-year changes. Nevertheless, the statistics, such as they are, indicate a large fall in employment in the transition economies in general during the early 1990s.

Three important features of the employment structure in eastern Europe have to be taken into account in considering labour market developments in the early 1990s.[131] First, economic restructuring is being targeted at a distorted industrial output and employment structure. In particular, the service sector is relatively small and inadequate for a modern economy and it is generally recognized that new jobs and skills will have to be developed in that part of the economy. Secondly, the size structure of enterprises is unbalanced, by developed market economy standards, with a large proportion of the workforce concentrated in large-scale enterprises with obsolescent technology. The third structural feature is, of course, the predominant role played by the state in the past and the overwhelming emphasis given to "privatization" as the means of economic regeneration. All this has contributed to shrinking employment, segmentation of labour markets and soaring structural unemployment.

(a) Changes in employment during 1985-1993

Data for 1985-1989 show the annual average growth of total employment at around 0.5 per cent in both eastern Europe and the former Soviet Union (table 3.4.1). Economic reforms, which accelerated in 1989 in eastern Europe, resulted in a contraction in employment. However, despite the considerable decrease in output, the overall decline in employment in 1990 was relatively modest. In 1991, the decline in employment began to accelerate and mass unemployment emerged in most of the economies of the region. In 1992, and again in 1993, the situation in the labour markets deteriorated further.

In eastern Europe the cumulative fall in employment over the three years 1990-1992 amounted to some 12 per cent. However, the rate of fall varied widely: between less than 5 per cent in Romania and nearly 30 per cent in Bulgaria. In the states of the former Soviet Union the decrease was much smaller – about 4 per cent in the CIS countries as a whole and slightly more than that in the Baltic states. In 1992, total employment in all the transition countries taken together was nearly 180 million, some 11 million (6 per cent) less than in 1989.

Preliminary estimates indicate that total employment continued to decline in most of the east European countries in 1993. In Poland, Slovakia, Romania and possibly Hungary, the decline is estimated to be at the 1992 rate or less. In the CIS countries, as a whole, employment fell by 1.3 per cent in 1993 compared with 3 per cent in 1992.[132] However, in two Asian republics (Kazakhstan and Turkmenistan) there was an increase in employment of nearly 2 per cent. Russia registered a slight decline of 1 per cent in 1993 compared with 2.5 per cent in 1992.

---

[130] For a detailed discussion of the methods of collecting labour market statistics in the transition economies see United Nations Economic Commission for Europe, *Economic Survey of Europe in 1992-1993*, New York, 1993, pp.90-91.

[131] G. Standing, *Structural Changes and the Labour Market Crisis in Eastern and Central Europe*, United Nations Economic Commission for Europe, EC.AD/R.71, 29 March 1993.

[132] CIS Statistical Committee, *Ekonomika stran sodruzhestva nezavisimykh gosudarstv v 1993 godu*, Moscow, 1994, p.30.

TABLE 3.4.1

Transition countries: Employment, 1985-1992
(Percentage change)

	1992 (Thousands)	1985-1989 [a]	1990	1991	1992	1990-1992 [b]
Albania	1 127	3.5	-0.7	-1.7	-19.7	-21.7
Bosnia-Herzegovina	..	..	..	..	..	..
Bulgaria	3 113	-0.5	-6.1	-13.0	-12.7	-28.7
Croatia	1 261	1.1	-3.1	-8.7	-11.9	-22.1
Czech Republic	4 927	0.6	-0.9	-5.5	-2.6	-8.8
Hungary	4 242	-0.5	-0.6	-2.6	-9.1	-12.1
Poland	14 974	-	-3.6	-5.5	-4.0	-12.6
Romania	10 458	0.8	-1.0	-0.5	-3.0	-4.5
Slovakia	2 160	0.9	-0.8	-7.9	-5.3	-13.5
Slovenia	697	0.3	-4.4	-8.1	-6.7	-18.1
The FYR of Macedonia	481	2.1	-1.5	-2.8	-5.3	-9.3
Yugoslavia (FR)	2 536	1.6	-3.0	-3.0	-3.4	-9.1
Eastern Europe	45 977	0.4	-2.4	-4.8	-5.5	-12.2
CETE-4	26 303	0.1	-2.4	-5.2	-4.7	-11.9
SETE-8	19 674	0.8	-2.5	-4.1	-6.6	-12.7
Armenia	1 578	0.8	1.9	2.6	-5.6	-1.4
Azerbaijan	2 743	1.7	-0.3	4.0	-5.4	-1.9
Belarus	4 887	0.4	-0.9	-2.5	-2.6	-6.0
Georgia	1 948	0.5	3.7	-10.1	-22.6	-27.8
Kazakhstan	7 356	1.1	1.3	-0.9	-1.8	-1.5
Kyrgyzstan	1 765	1.3	2.8	-1.0	2.0	3.8
Moldova	2 050	0.1	-1.0	-0.1	-1.0	-2.0
Russia	72 000	0.2	-0.4	-2.0	-2.5	-4.2
Tajikistan	1 908	2.8	3.1	1.7	-3.1	1.5
Turkmenistan	1 573	2.9	2.8	1.9	0.1	4.9
Ukraine	23 985	-0.2	-0.6	-1.2	-4.0	-5.6
Uzbekistan	8271	3.6	4.2	4.8	-0.6	8.5
CIS	130 065	0.5	0.1	-1.2	-3.0	-4.0
Estonia	750	0.1	-2.0	0.5	-6.3	-7.6
Latvia	1 345	0.2	0.1	-0.8	-3.7	-4.4
Lithuania	1 848	0.6	-2.6	2.4	-2.6	-2.9
Baltic states	3 943	0.3	-1.6	0.9	-3.7	-4.3
Total above	179 984	0.5	-0.6	-2.1	-3.7	-6.3

Source: National statistics. For definition of country groups, see the note to table 3.1.1.

[a] Average annual growth rate.
[b] Cumulative change over the period.

(b) Employment by broad sectors

In response to structural changes in production, all transition economies have experienced changes in the sectoral distribution of employment. Though there are substantial variations between countries, employment in the traditional "productive" sectors of agriculture, industry and construction has fallen the most (table 3.4.2). Among the east European countries reviewed, employment in agriculture increased only in Romania during the 1990-1992 period. This may reflect the fast privatization of small plots of farmland, which was nearly complete with more than four fifths of land in private ownership in Romania by mid-1993.[133]

On the other hand, one of the major labour market trends in transition countries is that employment in services has increased or fallen much less than in agriculture and industry since the beginning of the reforms. Employment in health, education and other social services, where privatization is less significant, has generally fallen less than overall employment. Furthermore, employment in distribution, catering and particularly financial services has increased, thanks to the growing number of small private business units.[134] Hence the share of services in total employment increased in all the east European countries

---

[133] European Communities, *European Economy*, August/September 1993, Luxembourg, pp.14-15.

[134] The growth of the private sector has been strong in many transition economies and it has provided most of the additional jobs created during the transition period. In eastern Europe, the share of private sector employment in total employment varied in 1990 from 5 per cent in Slovakia to 34 per cent in Poland. In 1992, it amounted to 12 per cent in Romania and some 45 per cent in Poland. See O. Blanchard, S. Commander, F. Coricelli, *Unemployment and Restructuring in Eastern Europe*, a paper presented to the Workshop on Economic Interaction and Integration, Session XV, Vienna, 21-25 November 1993, p.3. In Russia, the share of the private sector in total employment almost doubled from some 14 per cent to nearly 26 per cent over the same period. Russian Federation Statistical Committee, *Rossiiskaya Federatsiya v 1992 godu*, Yearbook, Moscow 1993, p.123.

TABLE 3.4.2

Selected transition countries: Changes in employment by broad sectors, 1989-1992

(Percentages)

| | Cumulative changes in employment 1990-1992 | | | | Share in total employment | | | | | |
| | | | | | Agriculture | | Industry | | Services | |
	Total	Agriculture	Industry	Services	1989	1992	1989	1992	1989	1992
Bulgaria	-28.7	-31.2	-37.1	-16.8	18.6	18.1	46.0	40.6	35.4	41.3
Czech Republic	-8.8	-29.5	-14.2	2.7	10.6	8.1	47.6	44.7	41.8	47.2
Hungary	-12.1	-34.3	-17.7	-0.5	17.9	13.5	36.8	34.8	45.3	51.7
Poland	-12.6	-13.3	-20.4	-5.7	27.8	27.6	36.3	33.0	35.9	39.4
Romania	-4.5	12.9	-21.4	5.8	27.9	33.0	45.1	37.1	27.0	29.9
Slovakia	-13.5	-27.5	-22.6	1.8	13.8	11.6	46.3	41.4	39.9	47.0
Russia	-4.2	-3.7	-6.9	-1.7	13.4	13.4	43.0	41.8	43.6	44.7

Source: National statistics and ECE data base.

Note: Agriculture includes forestry. Industry includes construction. Services was obtained as residual.

TABLE 3.4.3

Selected transition countries: Output-employment relationship, 1990-1992

(Annual change, per cent)

| | 1990 | | | 1991 | | | 1992 | | |
	GDP	Employment	Excess employment indicator [a]	GDP	Employment	Excess employment indicator [a]	GDP	Employment	Excess employment indicator [a]
Bulgaria	-9.1	-6.1	3.0	-11.7	-13.0	-1.3	-7.7	-12.7	-5.0
Poland	-11.6	-3.6	8.0	-7.6	-5.5	2.1	1.0	-4.0	-5.0
Hungary	-3.3	-0.6	2.7	-11.9	-2.6	9.3	-5.0	-9.1	-4.1
Slovakia	-2.5	-0.8	1.7	-11.2	-7.9	3.3	-7.0	-5.3	1.7
Czech Republic	-1.2	-0.9	0.3	-14.2	-5.5	8.7	-7.1	-2.6	4.5
Belarus	-1.9	-0.9	1.0	-1.2	-2.5	-1.3	-10.0	-2.6	7.4
Ukraine	-2.6	-0.6	2.0	-10.0	-1.2	8.8	-14.0	-4.0	10.0
Romania	-8.2	-1.0	7.2	-13.7	-0.5	13.2	-15.4	-3.0	12.4
Russia	-2.0	-0.4	1.6	-12.9	-2.0	10.9	-18.5	-2.5	16.0
Yugoslavia (FR) [b]	-8.4	-3.0	5.4	-11.1	-3.0	8.1	-26.1	-3.4	22.7

Source: Secretariat estimates based on national statistics.

Note: Countries are ranked according to the excess employment indicator in 1992.

[a] Change in the degree of "excess employment", as indicated by the difference between changes in employment and changes in GDP.
[b] Gross material product.

and Russia between 1989 and 1992. In the Czech Republic, Romania and Slovakia not only the share of the service sector, but also the absolute number employed in services, increased in the same period. The highest share of the service sector in total employment in 1992 was in Hungary, mainly reflecting the rapid growth of private financial and business services.

(c) Excess employment

Simultaneous examination of annual rates of change of output and employment during 1990-1992 shows that even though employment fell significantly in most of the transition economies, its rate of decline was generally much less than the rate of decline in output (table 3.4.3). Such a large differential suggests that there is a significant degree of excess employment (overmanning, disguised unemployment) in many of these countries. This phenomenon, which characterized these labour markets also under central planning, has several possible explanations including, *inter alia*, mismanagement, the slow implementation of bankruptcy provisions, and the strong position of labour unions. But perhaps the most important reason is that most governments are reluctant to countenance a sudden and large increase in open unemployment at a time when comprehensive social safety nets are lacking and when popular support for economic reforms is increasingly fragile.

While excess employment was a general feature of these countries at the start of the reform process, its scale and behaviour over time has varied widely among countries. In 1990 relatively small changes in the degree of excess employment could be observed in many countries, but there was a large rise in Poland, Romania and FR Yugoslavia.[135] After 1990, with the speeding up of privatization and restructuring, excess employment started to diminish and by the end of 1992 two distinct groups of countries emerged. The first group consisted of the early reforming countries where excess employment must have diminished significantly. In the second group, which

---

[135] The difference between the rates of change in employment and output can be used as a indicator of the *change* in the degree of excess employment.

TABLE 3.4.4

Transition countries: Unemployment, 1990-1993
(Thousands and per cent of labour force, end of period)

	Thousands				Per cent of labour force			
	1990	1991	1992	1993	1990	1991	1992	1993
Albania	150.7	139.8	394.3	301.3	9.8	9.4	26.7	25*
Bulgaria	72.2	419.1	576.9	626.1	1.8	11.5	15.6	16.4
Bosnia-Herzegovina	..	..	..	..	..	..	..	..
Croatia	195.5	283.3	261.0	243.1	8.0 a	14.1	17.8	16.9
Czech Republic	39.4	221.7	134.8	185.2	0.7	4.1	2.6	3.5
Hungary	81.4	406.1	663.0	632.1	1.7	7.4	12.3	12.1
Poland	1 126.1	2 155.6	2 509.3	2 889.6	6.1	11.8	13.6	15.7
Romania	150.0	337.5	929.0	1 170.0	1.3	3.1	8.2	10.1
Slovakia	39.6	302.0	260.3	368.1	1.6	11.8	10.4	14.4
Slovenia	55.4	91.2	118.2	137.1	5.3 a	10.1	13.3	15.4
The FYR of Macedonia	156.3	164.8	173.3	177.2	17.1 a	24.5	26.8	29.6
Yugoslavia (FR)	687.6	707.1	749.0	732.0	14.7 a	15.7	24.6	24.6
Eastern Europe	2 754.2	5 228.2	6 769.1	7 460.6	4.8	9.4	12.5	13.8
CETE-4	1 286.5	3 085.4	3 567.4	4 075.0	4.1	9.7	11.3	12.9
SETE-8	1 467.7	2 142.8	3 201.7	3 385.6	5.6	8.9	14.2	15.0
Armenia	..	..	56.3	102.6	..	..	3.5	6.2
Azerbaijan	..	3.8	6.4	19.5	..	0.1	0.2	0.7
Belarus	..	2.3	24.0	66.2	..	..	0.5	1.3
Georgia	..	1.7	18.9	39.6	..	..	1.0	2.0
Kazakhstan	..	4.1	33.7	40.5	..	..	0.5	0.6
Kyrgyzstan	..	0.1	1.8	2.9	..	..	0.1	0.2
Moldova	..	0.1	15.0	14.1	..	..	0.7	0.7
Russia	..	61.9	577.7	835.5	..	0.1	0.8	1.1
Tajikistan	..	..	6.8	21.5	..	..	0.3	1.1
Turkmenistan	..	..	..	..	..	..	..	..
Ukraine	..	6.8	70.5	83.9	..	..	0.3	0.4
Uzbekistan	..	..	8.8	13.3	..	..	0.1	0.2
CIS	..	..	819.9	1 200.0	..	..	0.6	1.0
Estonia	0.6	0.9	15.0	16.2	..	0.1	1.9	2.6
Latvia	..	1.9	31.3	76.7	..	..	2.1 b	5.8 b
Lithuania	..	4.6	20.7	30.5	..	0.3	1.0	1.6
Baltic states	..	7.4	67.0	123.4	..	..	1.5	3.2
Total above	..	..	7 656.0	8 784.0	..	..	4.1	4.8

Source: National statistics. For definition of country groups see note to table 3.1.1.

a Annual average.
c Percentage of working age population.

includes the CIS countries, FR Yugoslavia[136] and Romania, excess employment must have reached very significant proportions, a reflection of hesitance in the reform process in these countries. Preliminary estimates for 1993 indicate that in this second group of countries excess employment further intensified, since the downward trend in output continued to outpace the employment decline.

(ii) Unemployment

(a) Changes in unemployment during 1990-1992

One of the major costs of the reforms has been surging unemployment which did not exist, at least officially, under central planning, with the main exception of the former Yugoslavia. Available unemployment statistics for the region, which are generally based on the number of people registered at labour offices, suggest two different phases of unemployment growth in eastern Europe. In 1989 and 1990, the gradual rise in unemployment in most countries came from the combination of a slow decline in employment due to individual redundancies and the influx of new labour force entrants whilst recruitment was drying up. In December 1990, the total number of persons unemployed in eastern Europe was around 2.8 million and, with the exception of Albania, Poland and the former Yugoslavia, unemployment rates were still below 2 per cent of the labour force (table 3.4.4 and chart 3.4.1).

In most of the east European countries, this initial phase of gradually rising unemployment was soon replaced by a second phase characterized by mass lay-offs and plant closures. Open unemployment rose sharply in eastern Europe in 1991, nearly doubling compared with 1990, as stabilization programmes got under way, privatization began to spread, and market forces began to influence the behaviour of the "new" entrepreneurs. In 1992, all countries of the region, except the Czech Republic and Romania, recorded double-digit rates of unemployment, a situation for which they were ill-prepared, psychologically, financially or administratively. In Poland, there were 2.5

---

[136] According to some experts, in the FR Yugoslavia the present level of activity probably requires not more than some 600,000 employed (at 1979 productivity levels) compared with some 2.3 million currently employed. See Center for Economic Studies, *Economic Developments in FR Yugoslavia*, Belgrade, September 1993, p.9.

CHART 3.4.1
Selected transition countries: Unemployment rates, 1990-1993
(Per cent of labour force, end of period)

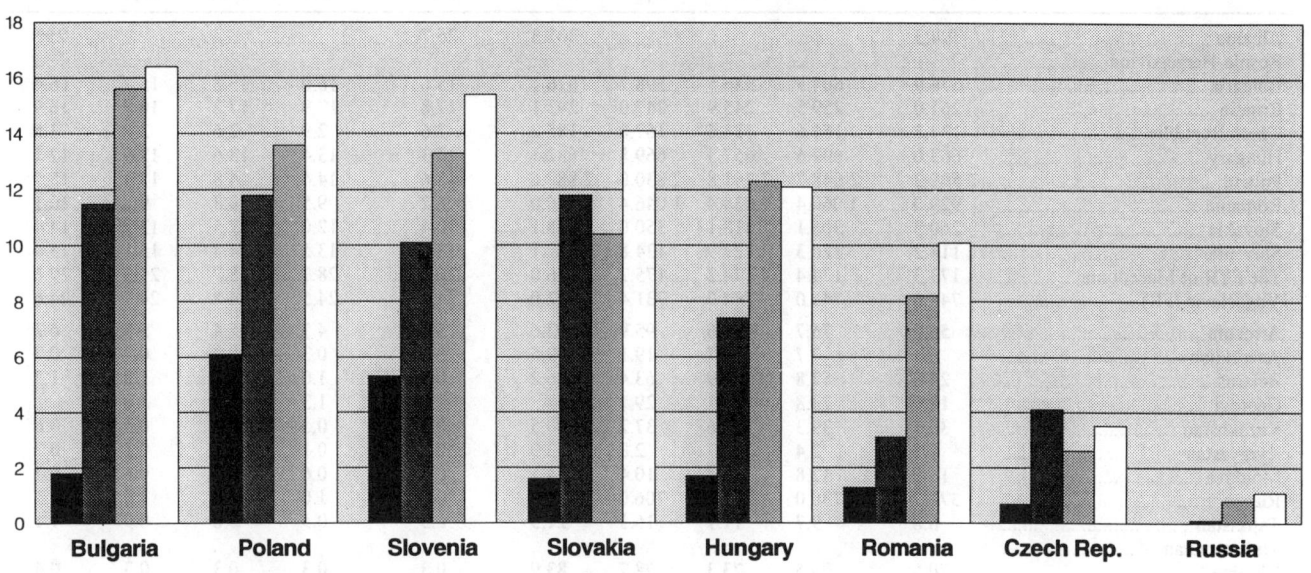

Sources: National statistics.

Note: Countries are ranked according to 1993 unemployment rates.

million registered unemployed by the end of 1992, representing 13.6 per cent of the economically active population, and more than 100 registrants for every job vacancy. During 1992, unemployment rates in Slovakia and Hungary rose towards the levels experienced in Poland.

In most of the former Soviet republics, unemployment statistics began to be collected only in the second half of 1991, after unemployment legislation became effective on 1 July 1991. Registered unemployment remained very low, particularly in the CIS countries, both in 1991 and 1992. There are ample reasons for believing that these official statistics chronically understate the real magnitude of joblessness.[137] Some are of a technical nature and simply reflect the general deficiencies of the official statistics including, *inter alia*, a rather complicated system of registration.[138] Furthermore, very low unemployment benefits in the CIS countries do not offer a strong incentive to register, and many jobless prefer to look for work independently.[139] However, probably the major reason for low levels of official unemployment in the CIS countries is the specific employment behaviour of enterprises, which is generally directed towards maintaining employment to the maximum possible extent and represents an attempt to reform the production structure in stages without cuts in personnel. This widespread approach is a consequence of the reluctance of governments to adopt or enforce bankruptcy laws.[140] In addition, in most of the CIS countries, soft budgets and easily obtainable credits allow loss-making firms to keep their workforce largely intact, even if a large proportion is underemployed.

(b) Changes in unemployment during 1993

In 1993, unemployment continued to increase in all countries of *eastern Europe*, except Hungary and Croatia, though slower than in 1992 (table 3.4.5). In the Czech

---

[137] G. Standing, Director of the Central and Eastern European Team of the ILO, has listed more than ten factors which distort real unemployment statistics in Russia. See interview in *Izvestiya*, 16 September 1993.

[138] In Russia, for example, this requires the submission of a set of documents, including a valid passport with a residence permit *(propiska)*. This discourages registration by the increasing number of migrants and refugees who are actually seeking jobs. Definitions also cause confusion since the Russian Federal Employment Service reports monthly data on the number of registered job seekers and the number of registered unemployed, but gives the number of registered unemployed as the official unemployment figure. In December 1993, there were 1.1 million registered job seekers (about 1.4 per cent of the labour force), but only 835,000 of them (some 70 per cent) obtained official status of being "unemployed", one of the preconditions for obtaining unemployment benefits. However, even the number of registered job seekers, which is probably closest to international definitions, is likely to underestimate real unemployment because those who are "out of employment" but do not register with the Federal Employment Service are not counted.

[139] See section (c) below on unemployment benefits.

[140] In Russia, for example, the bankruptcy law came into effect on 1 March 1993, but by the end of 1993 no official statistics on the implementation of the law had been published. According to Russian experts, with well-developed bankruptcy procedures and in the absence of state support, at least 20 per cent of industrial enterprises would have been considered possibly bankrupt at the end of 1993. *Finansovye Izvestiya*, 10-16 December 1993.

TABLE 3.4.5
Transition countries: Unemployment, 1992-1993
(Thousands and per cent of labour force, end-of-period)

	Unemployment (thousands)					Unemployment rate (per cent)				
	1992	1993				1992	1993			
	Dec.	Mar.	June	Sept.	Dec.	Dec.	Mar.	June	Sept.	Dec.
Albania	394.3	..	..	..	301.3	26.7	..	..	..	25*
Bosnia-Herzegovina	..	..	..	..	..	..	..	..	..	..
Bulgaria	576.9	604.5	586.5	598.7	626.1	15.6	16.0	15.5	15.7	16.4
Croatia	261.0	259.5	245.9	247.0	243.1	17.8	17.9	17.2	16.9	16.9
Czech Republic	134.8	151.6	138.6	167.0	185.2	2.6	2.9	2.6	3.2	3.5
Hungary	663.0	697.6	657.3	669.8	632.1	12.3	13.4	12.6	12.9	12.1
Poland	2 509.3	2 648.7	2 701.8	2 830.0	2 889.6	13.6	14.4	14.8	15.4	15.7
Romania	929.0	1 060.4	1 035.4	1 046.4	1 170.0	8.2	9.5	9.3	9.2	10.1
Slovakia	260.3	306.1	318.1	350.0	368.1	10.4	12.0	12.5	13.7	14.4
Slovenia	118.2	120.3	127.9	134.8	137.1	13.3	13.5	14.4	15.1	15.4
The FYR of Macedonia	173.3	174.4	174.2	175.2	176.0	26.8	28.7	28.7	29.3	29.6
Yugoslavia (FR)	749.0	741.0	744.0	731.4	732.0	24.6	24.5	24.8	24.7	24.6
Armenia	56.3	76.7	87.6	95.9	102.6	3.5	4.7	5.4	5.8	6.2
Azerbaijan	6.4	7.7	6.7	19.1	19.5	0.2	0.3	0.3	0.7	0.7
Belarus	24.0	52.8	54.9	63.4	66.2	0.5	1.0	1.1	1.3	1.3
Georgia	18.9	23.8	27.1	29.1	..	1.0	1.3	1.5	1.6	..
Kazakhstan	33.7	39.3	37.6	37.2	40.5	0.5	0.5	0.5	0.5	0.6
Kyrgyzstan	1.8	2.4	2.7	2.8	2.9	0.1	0.1	0.1	0.1	0.2
Moldova	15.0	12.8	9.8	10.4	14.1	0.7	0.6	0.5	0.6	0.7
Russia	577.7	730.0	717.1	706.0	835.5	0.8	1.0	1.0	1.0	1.1
Tajikistan	6.8	9.7	11.7	16.5	21.5	0.3	0.5	0.6	0.9	1.1
Turkmenistan	..	..	..	..	..	..	..	..	..	..
Ukraine	70.5	79.5	73.3	78.7	83.9	0.3	0.3	0.3	0.3	0.4
Uzbekistan	8.8	14.9	15.1	14.4	13.3	0.1	0.2	0.2	0.2	0.2
Estonia	15.0	21.3	19.2	15.3	16.2	1.9	2.8	2.7	2.4	2.6
Latvia [a]	31.3	49.6	64.6	72.8	76.7	2.1	3.7	4.8	5.4	5.8
Lithuania	20.7	29.2	32.2	32.1	30.5	1.0	1.6	1.7	1.7	1.6
Ex-GDR *Länder*	1 100.7	1 140.6	1 100.0	1 159.1	1 175.2	13.9	15.7	15.1	15.9	16.2

Sources: National statistical publications and direct communications to ECE.

[a] Percentage of working age population.

Republic, Poland, Slovenia, and Slovakia unemployment rose at the same pace or even more strongly than in 1992. The number of unemployed in eastern Europe reached nearly 7.6 million[141] by the end of December 1993 – 12 per cent higher than in December 1992 and equivalent to 14 per cent of the labour force.

Rates of unemployment in December 1993 varied widely, from 3.5 per cent in the Czech Republic[142] to some 30 per cent in the FYR of Macedonia. In the Czech Republic, a clear exception to the general experience, the unemployment rate remained remarkably low despite an increase of nearly one percentage point during the year. The rate was not only the lowest by far among the east European countries, but also very low given the considerable decline in output and employment. One reason for this might be the strict unemployment eligibility rules introduced in January 1992, clearly discouraging many jobless people from registering as unemployed. In addition, the gradual approach to restructuring and closing down bankrupt or obsolete enterprises might have limited labour shedding.

In the *CIS countries*, the rise in unemployment continued to be slow also in 1993 and by the end of December there were only some 1.2 million officially registered unemployed. Hence, rates of unemployment remained very low; for all CIS countries together the rate was 1 per cent at the end of 1993, up from 0.6 per cent a year earlier. Unemployment rates varied only slightly among countries (between 0.2 per cent and 2 per cent) except in Armenia where the rate reached some 6 per cent. In Russia, while the official unemployment total was only some 835,000 (1.1 per cent of the labour force) by the end of 1993, the total number of job seekers, short-time workers and persons taking involuntary unpaid leave[143] is estimated to have amounted to 7.8 million (10.4 per cent of the labour force). However, according to ILO definitions (those not working but available for work and actively seeking employment) the total number of unemployed would reach 3.8 million (5.1 per cent of the labour force) in Russia by the end of 1993.[144]

---

[141] Excluding Bosnia-Herzegovina due to lack of information.

[142] Registered job seekers reported by the Ministry of Labour. Note, however, that a Statistical Office sample survey of 23,000 households put the unemployment rate at 3.9 per cent at the end of the second quarter of 1993, compared with 2.8 per cent according to the Ministry of Labour. See BBC, *Summary of World Broadcasts*, EEW/0305, 28 October 1993.

[143] To prevent mass unemployment and to keep their pool of skilled personnel largely intact, enterprises can send workers on compulsory unpaid leave for up to one month. Beyond a month these workers receive wage compensation at the level of the official minimum wage which was R14,620 in December 1993, about one third of the subsistence minimum and some 10 per cent of the average wage. People on unpaid leave are still recorded in the employment figures.

[144] RF Goskomstat, *Sotsial'no-ekonomicheskoe polozhenie* ... op.cit., p.153.

TABLE 3.4.6

Selected transition countries: Unemployment rates by sex
(Per cent of labour force)

	September 1991			September 1992			September 1993		
	Total	Male	Female	Total	Male	Female	Total	Male	Female
Czech Republic	..	..	..	2.6	1.9	3.5	3.2	2.5	4.0
Hungary	6.1	6.6	5.5	11.4	12.9	9.8	12.9	15.1	10.5
Poland	10.7	9.4	12.2	13.6	11.7	15.9	15.4	13.5	17.8
Romania	2.4	1.8	3.2	7.2	5.3	9.5	9.2	6.3	13.0
Slovakia	..	..	..	10.6	12.3	9.3	13.7	11.7	16.8
Slovenia	8.1	8.4	7.8	12.2	12.8	11.4	15.3 [a]	16.1 [a]	14.3 [a]
Ex-GDR *Länder*	11.7	9.1	14.3	14.1	9.6	19.0	15.9	10.7	21.6

Sources: National statistics and ECE secretariat estimates.

[a] October.

In the *Baltic states* unemployment during 1993 continued to increase rapidly and at the end of the year numbers reached some 123,000, nearly double the level in December 1992. Among the three Baltic states, Latvia had the fastest increase: the number of unemployed more than doubled and the share of the unemployed in the working age population reached nearly 6 per cent, which implies a higher unemployment rate measured on a labour force basis. The unemployment rate would be further pushed up if people who are officially employed but have been sent on unpaid leave or work reduced hours are taken into account.[145]

In most countries for which statistics are available, the registered rate of unemployment for women was higher than that for men during 1991-1993, except in Hungary and Slovenia (table 3.4.6). In September 1993, the widest differences were in Slovakia and particularly Romania, where the rate of female unemployment was twice as high as that of males. No comprehensive data on unemployment rates by sex are published for Russia, but the high share of women in the total number of registered unemployed in Russia in 1993 (70 per cent) suggests that the unemployment rate for women exceeds that for men by a substantial margin.

(c) Unemployment benefits

When reform programmes were initiated, all governments stressed the importance of a comprehensive social safety net and agreed to protect vulnerable groups of the population by providing them with a minimum level of income. At the outset of the reform process unemployment was at negligible levels and most new governments introduced fairly generous unemployment benefit schemes with relatively easy eligibility. Now, when the reform process is well under way in the group of early reformers, and unemployment rates are above 10 per cent in most cases, maintaining a comprehensive safety net is proving extremely difficult. Public finances are under severe pressure everywhere due to the shrinking tax base whilst numbers in need of social protection continue to soar. Hence benefit regimes are tightening and the relative amount of benefits is diminishing. As chart 3.4.2 shows, the level of unemployment benefits relative to average wages fell considerably between 1991 and 1992. The benefit/wage ratio nearly halved in Bulgaria and Czechoslovakia, to 34 per cent and 25 per cent respectively in 1992. Also in Poland, entitlements were severely reduced by the Employment Act introduced in December 1991 which cut the level of benefits from some 50 per cent to 36 per cent of the average wage in the preceding quarter. Among the transition countries where data are available, the lowest benefit/wage ratio in December 1993 was in Russia with 10 per cent, which was equivalent to some 30 per cent of the minimum subsistence income. Clearly such low benefits are not only an ineffective tool of social protection but also provide little incentive for the jobless to register, which is believed to be one of the major reasons for very low rates of official unemployment in Russia and probably in most CIS countries. Not only were the benefit levels reduced in general but in many countries also the eligibility criteria were tightened significantly and the duration was shortened. In Czechoslovakia, for example, those eligible for benefits declined from four fifths of the total number registered as unemployed in 1991, to less than two fifths during 1992. Similar decreases were recorded also in Bulgaria, Hungary and Poland between 1991 and 1993. Among those countries where information is available, the proportion of registered unemployed receiving benefits in 1993 was lowest in the successor states of the former Yugoslavia, varying between 8 per cent in the Federal Republic of Yugoslavia to 30 per cent in Slovenia. Among the CIS countries, the share varied from 23 per cent in Azerbaijan to 66 per cent in Russia at the end of 1993.

(iii) Vacancies

The rise in the number of unfilled vacancies which occurred in a few east European countries during 1992 became more widespread in 1993. This may suggest that the process of economic restructuring is finally beginning to create new jobs, although it probably also reflects, at least in part, a shift from informal to formal channels of

---

[145] According to some estimates "real" unemployment in Latvia was about 8 per cent in 1993. See *The Baltic Independent*, 24-30 September 1993. Also in Estonia the official figures exclude those underemployed, on short-time working and on indefinite unpaid leave. Including these, the unemployment rate would be as much as 10-12 per cent. Economist Intelligence Unit, *Estonia Country Report*, 4th Quarter 1993, p.17.

CHART 3.4.2

Selected transition countries: Unemployment benefits/wage ratio [a] and share of unemployed receiving benefits, 1991-1993
(Percentage, end of period)

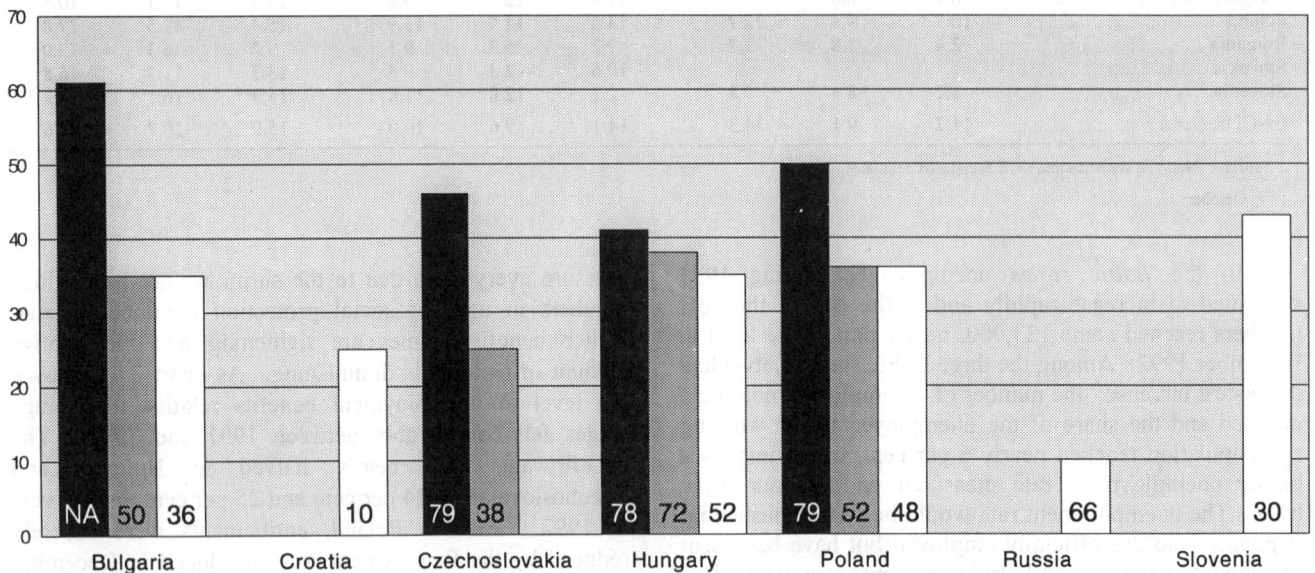

Sources: National statistics, EC, *Employment Observatory Central and Eastern Europe*, No.4, May, No.5, December 1993: OECD, *Short-term Economic Indicators, Transition Economics*, Paris, No.1, 1994.

Note: Numbers in the bars indicate share of registered unemployed receiving benefits.

[a] Unemployment benefits divided by average nominal wage.

vacancy notification.[146] Furthermore, the combination of falling employment, rising unemployment and increasing vacancies may indicate some structural mismatch in the labour markets.

In 1993, there was a clear tendency for the number of vacancies to grow in most of the east European countries. Only in Slovakia, where the number of vacancies more than halved, and to a much lesser extent the Czech Republic, was there a decline in the number of vacancies between December 1992 and 1993.[147] However, in most of the CIS countries, except Russia, Ukraine and Uzbekistan, the decline in the number of reported vacancies continued through 1993. Latvia and notably Lithuania recorded an increase in the number of vacancies in 1993.

The ratio of the unemployed to the number of unfilled vacancies (u/v ratio), which, in a market economy, is an indicator of structural mismatch in the labour markets, should be interpreted with caution in the case of the transition economies, where these ratios are currently influenced not only by economic factors, but also by a range of institutional changes which affect labour market statistics. However, the order of magnitude of u/v ratios may still provide additional insight into the size of the unemployment problem in these countries. That is, the higher the ratio, probably the worse the labour market situation.

The u/v ratio remained broadly stable or increased in most countries of the region between December 1992 and 1993, due in many cases to a rapid growth in the number of unemployed rather than to a decline in the number of vacancies (chart 3.4.3). However, the level of u/v ratios differed widely between countries. A visible decline in the u/v ratio during 1993 was registered only in Slovenia (a moderate growth of unemployment accompanied by a strong increase in the number of vacancies). In many other east European countries, the u/v ratio varied between some 20 to 50 unemployed per vacancy in December 1993. In Bulgaria, the ratio exceeded 80 persons per vacancy, while in Poland it reached a record level of some 130 persons per vacancy in December 1993. The CIS countries, excluding Moldova and particularly Armenia, had the lowest u/v ratios, with levels not exceeding five job-seekers per vacancy in December 1993. The Czech Republic was the only east European country with a ratio similar to this group.

---

[146] Statistics on unfilled vacancies are provided by labour offices and measure the number of unfilled vacancies reported to labour offices on a given date. The reliability of these figures obviously depends on the extent to which labour offices are consulted by enterprises to fill their vacancies. For a more detailed discussion on the subject see United Nations Economic Commission for Europe, *Economic Survey of Europe in 1992-1993*, New York, 1993, pp.90-91.

[147] At the time of writing, data on vacancies were not available for Romania and Estonia.

CHART 3.4.3

Selected transition countries: Unemployment vacancy ratio, 1991-1993

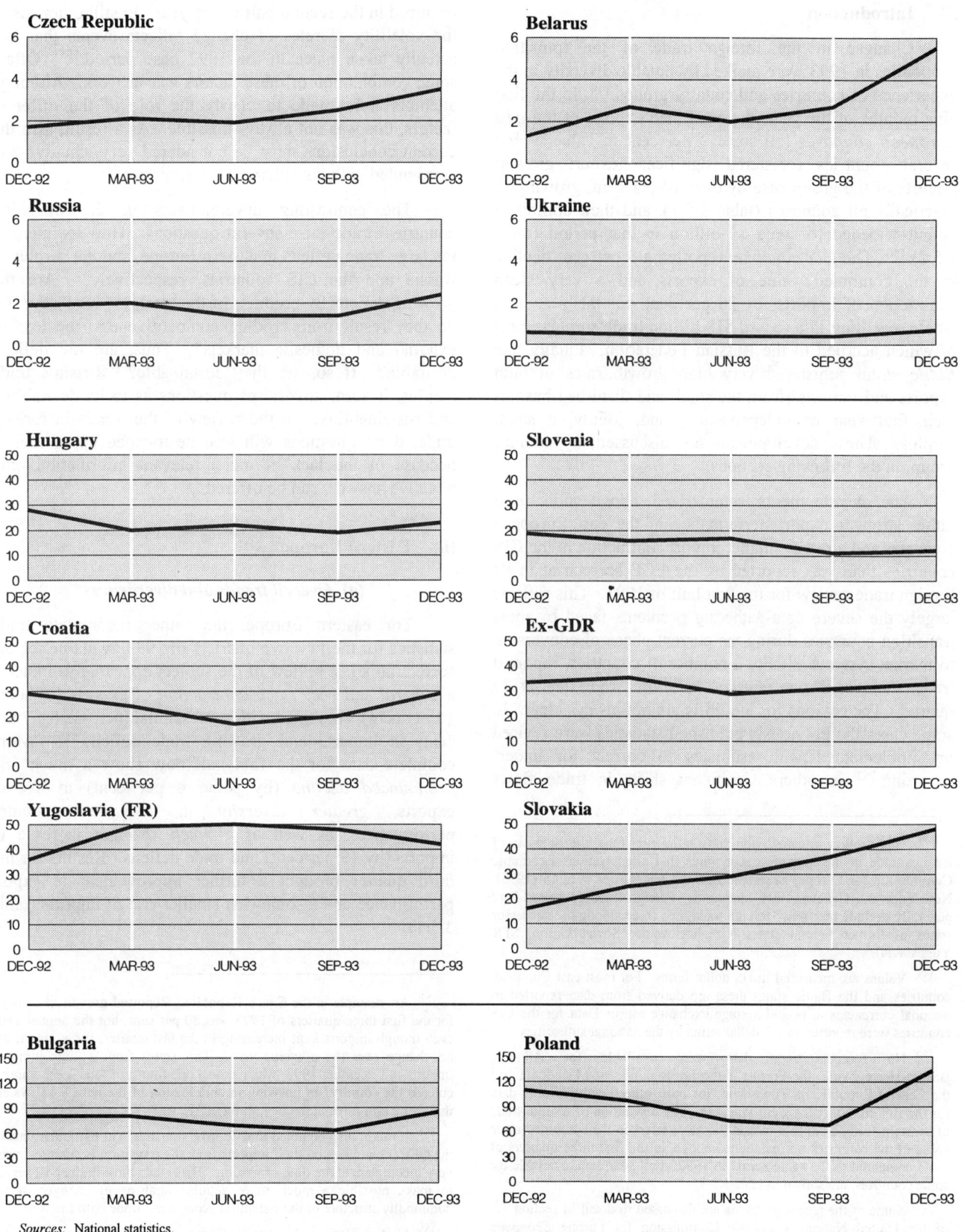

Sources: National statistics.

Note: Calculated as the ratio of officially registered unemployed to number of vacancies, end of period.

3.5 Foreign trade of the transition economies

(i) Introduction

Changes in the foreign trade of the transition economies in 1993 were marked by notable diversity in the experience of countries and country groups.[148] In the first nine months of the year, the combined exports of the *east European countries* fell some 2 per cent in value,[149] but several countries registered significant export growth; imports of the group rose by over 14 per cent, growing in practically all countries (table 3.5.1), and their combined deficit widened to some $9 billion in that period (table 3.5.2).[150] The *CIS countries* reported a 3 per cent decline in the combined value of exports and a very steep contraction of imports, by 26 per cent, for the year as a whole, resulting in a record $18 billion trade surplus, most of which accrued to the Russian Federation. Finally, the *Baltic states* registered very high growth rates in both exports and imports (from the small and disturbed base of their first year of independence) and, jointly, a small surplus. These developments are discussed, by country group, in the following sections.

The developments summarized above indicate a rather stronger export performance of the east European countries and a rather smaller import contraction in the CIS countries than was reported by the ECE secretariat in its foreign trade review for the first half of 1993. This reflects largely the severe data-gathering problems faced by most transition countries during the current phase of conversion to market systems.[151] For a number of countries, reported trade statistics show *unusual volatility* from quarter to quarter. The reasons for the shifts are not always clear. In some cases the previously published statistics were revised or supplemented with estimates to correct for under-reporting,[152] in others significant shifts in trade flows occurred in the second half of the year. In still other cases, the volatility of rates of change reflects events that had actually taken place in the 1992 base period.[153] Often, some combination of these factors was at work. Although attempts were made to clarify the role of the different factors, this was not always possible. As a result, also the current conclusions must be considered very tentative and surrounded with considerable uncertainties.[154]

The contrasting developments in the transition countries' trade raise several questions. How to interpret the large trade deficits in eastern Europe, and the surplus in Russia and the CIS countries, respectively? Are the growing deficits by-products of the emerging recovery? Or do they result from eroding competitiveness, the loss of external and domestic markets? Thus, are the deficits desirable? If so, are they sustainable? Russia's trade surplus, in turn, also raises questions as to its desirability and sustainability. In the review of the trends in foreign trade, these questions will also be touched upon, though because of the lack of much relevant information only tentative answers can be offered.

(ii) Eastern Europe

(a) Overall trends and divergences

For eastern Europe, the rather incomplete trade statistics for the first two quarters of 1993 available for the secretariat's last review of the subject appeared to indicate a *general* and *very steep contraction* of exports (of some 14 per cent), combined with a substantial increase (of 7 per cent) in imports and growing trade deficits.[155] More complete data for the first half now show a much *less pronounced decline* (by some 4 per cent) in overall exports, *greater diversity* in individual country performances, as well as a *much stronger* increase in imports (by 19 per cent) and trade deficits. Results for the third quarter brought a further improvement in export performance and a somewhat smaller rise of imports (table 3.5.1).

---

[148] This section updates, with substantial revisions, the analysis of foreign trade in the transition economies in United Nations Economic Commission for Europe, *Economic Bulletin for Europe*, Vol.45 (1993), New York and Geneva, 1994, chapter 3. Foreign trade data used here generally exclude the "new" foreign trade, i.e., trade among the successor states of former federal states (Czechoslovakia, Soviet Union, SFR Yugoslavia).

[149] Values are measured in US dollar terms. For most east European countries and the Baltic states these are derived from data reported in national currencies at period-average exchange rates. Data for the CIS countries were reported in US dollar terms by the national authorities.

[150] No foreign trade data were available for Albania, Bosnia-Herzegovina, the Former Yugoslav Republic of Macedonia and the Federal Republic of Yugoslavia; for most other countries only data for the first nine months were available. The discussion of foreign trade of "eastern Europe" in this section therefore refers to the combined trade value of the countries not mentioned above, in the first three quarters of 1993 compared to the same period in 1992. Full-year data, available for some countries, are shown in table 3.5.3.

[151] Some of the recent problems are discussed in detail in section 3.1 of the United Nations Economic Commission for Europe *Economic Bulletin for Europe*, Vol.45 (1993), New York and Geneva, 1994.

[152] This is notably the case in the Russian data, where the statistical authorities recently have begun to provide estimates of transactions – especially important on the import side – that have escaped border controls and therefore are missing from the customs service data.

[153] An example is the Czech Republic. Reported growth of imports for the first three quarters of 1993 was 20 per cent, but the annual data, even though imports kept increasing in the last quarter, show practically no change over the previous year. This stems from a huge jump of imports in December 1992, when almost one fourth of total 1992 imports entered the country, an upswing in anticipation of the new VAT system that came into force at the beginning of 1993.

[154] It might also be noted that "mirror statistics" (in particular data of the OECD countries on their imports from the transition economies) were very incomplete at the time of writing. These data have in the past served to make possible a much more detailed analysis of changes in the commodity structure of the transition economies' trade with the west.

[155] United Nations Economic Commission for Europe, *Economic Bulletin for Europe*, Vol.45 (1993), New York and Geneva, 1994, table 3.1.1. In particular, only payments data were at that time available for Poland, indicating a *fall* in export earnings. The customs statistics, published later, show an *increase* in Polish exports for the first half of 1993, which continued in the third quarter.

TABLE 3.5.1

European transition countries: Foreign trade, by direction, 1991-1993
(Value in billion US dollars; growth rates in percentages) [a]

Country or country group [b]	Exports Value 1992	Growth rates 1991	Growth rates 1992	Growth rates 1993 [c]	Imports Value 1992	Growth rates 1991	Growth rates 1992	Growth rates 1993 [c]
Eastern Europe, to or from:								
World	53.3	-6.9	-4.8	-2.1	60.6	-4.1	1.1	14.4
Transition economies	12.3	-24.6	-21.2	-8.0	15.2	-19.8	-3.2	-1.3
Soviet Union/successor states	5.4	-25.1	-31.7 [d]	-16.0 [d]	8.8	-9.3	-6.5 [d]	1.3 [d]
Eastern Europe [e]	3.0	-20.1	-9.7 [d]	-13.1 [d]	2.8	-25.8	-4.4 [d]	-10.5 [d]
Developed market economies	34.9	6.6	0.4	-2.2	39.6	7.8	9.2	20.7
Developing countries	6.1	-11.8	8.1	9.0	5.8	-9.2	-22.1	18.4
Russia/Soviet Union,[f] to or from:								
World	42.4	-24.6	-25.2	1.4	37.0	-35.9	-21.3	-27.1
Transition economies	13.0	-35.0	-25.8	-12.6	8.8	-43.4	-42.8	-14.7
Eastern Europe [e]	7.8	-40.8	-32.7 [g]	-7.9 [g]	5.5	-51.6	-49.7 [g]	-46.1 [g]
Developed market economies	24.6	-16.2	-20.3	4.6	23.1	-31.0	-13.0	-36.9
Developing countries	4.8	-29.0	-44.0	23.1	5.2	-35.8	-2.6	-4.5

Source: Secretariat of the United Nations Economic Commission for Europe, based on national statistical publications and direct communications to the ECE secretariat from national statistical offices.

Note: Data exclude "new" foreign trade (trade among successor states of former Czechoslovakia, Soviet Union and Yugoslavia).

[a] Growth rates are calculated on values expressed in US dollars. Trade with "transition" and east European countries in 1990 was revalued on the basis of an adjusted dollar measure reflecting consistent rouble/dollar crossrates. For details of the revaluation, see the note to table 2.1.3 and the discussion in box 2.1.1 and section 2.1(iii) in United Nations Economic Commission for Europe, *Economic Bulletin for Europe*, Vol.43 (1991), New York, 1991. All trade values for 1992 and 1993 were either originally reported in dollars or were converted to dollars at the appropriate national conversion coefficient.
[b] "Eastern Europe" refers to Albania, Bulgaria, Czechoslovakia (through 1992) or the Czech and Slovak Republics (for 1993), Hungary, Poland, Romania and Yugoslavia (SFR Yugoslavia for 1991; Croatia, Slovenia and FR Yugoslavia for 1992; Croatia and Slovenia only for 1993). The partner country grouping follows the practice until recently prevalent in the national statistical sources, which differs from the breakdown usually employed in United Nations publications. Thus, "transition economies", which covers the ex-socialist trade partners, in addition to the east European countries, the Soviet Union, and the Asian centrally planned economies, includes Yugoslavia and Cuba. "Developed market economies" differs from the aggregate used in section 3.6 below by the exclusion of Turkey and the inclusion of Australia, New Zealand and South Africa.
[c] January-September 1993 from January-September 1992 for eastern Europe, data for Russia refer to the full year 1993.
[d] Data from six reporting countries only (Bulgaria, Czech Republic, Hungary, Poland, Romania and Slovakia).
[e] Excluding former Yugoslavia.
[f] 1991 growth rates refer to the former Soviet Union.
[g] Trade with all former CMEA members (i.e., including Cuba, Mongolia, Vietnam).

TABLE 3.5.2

European transition countries: Trade balances, 1990-1993
(Billion US dollars)

Country group	1990	1991	1992	January-September 1992	January-September 1993	1993
Eastern Europe						
World	-1.9	-3.9	-7.2	-2.0	-8.8	..
Transition economies	0.6	-0.1	-2.9	-1.6	-2.2	..
Developed market economies	-0.9	-1.5	-4.7	-0.5	-6.6	..
Developing countries	-1.4	-1.8	0.3	0.3	-	..
Russia/Soviet Union [a]						
World	-5.9	1.3/6.4	5.4	2.1	11.0	16.0
Transition economies	-3.8	-0.3/1.2	4.3	2.5	..	3.9
Eastern Europe [b]	-3.9	0.5/0.7	2.7 [c]	..	..	4.6 [c]
Developed market economies	-5.1	0.0/2.9	1.5	-0.2	..	11.1
Developing countries	3.0	1.6/2.3	-0.4	-0.2	..	1.0

Source and country groups: As for table 3.5.1.

[a] 1990 data are for the former Soviet Union. For 1991, the first figure refers to the Soviet Union, the second to the Russian Federation. 1992-1993 data are for the Russian Federation.
[b] Excludes the former Yugoslavia.
[c] Russian Federation balance with all former CMEA members (i.e., including Cuba, Mongolia, Vietnam).

In terms of trade partner groups, east European exports to the *developed market economies* declined slightly in value (and may have merely stagnated in volume terms, as world market prices for east European exports generally appear to have fallen somewhat), while imports from that group increased very rapidly – by 21 per cent. Substantial increases in both exports and imports were registered in east European trade with the *developing countries*, although the share of these countries in east European trade still remains rather small, at 10-12 per cent (as against over 20 per cent in the trade of the OECD countries). By contrast, trade with other *transition economies* continued to contract in 1993. This concerns in particular *intraregional* trade,[156] where the fall not only continued, but accelerated somewhat, to 11-13 per cent, resulting in a further slide in the share of trade among the countries of the region (from some 8 per cent in 1992 to 5-6 per cent in 1993). Contrary to expectations, the "reserves" for trade reduction among the smaller former CMEA members thus do not yet seem to have been exhausted. The contraction of the region's exports to the successor states of the Soviet Union also continued, if at a slower pace than in 1992, while east European imports from that region increased somewhat.

Behind these overall changes lies an *increasing diversity* of individual country experiences within the region. This is illustrated by the fact that three countries reported impressive growth rates in total exports, two recorded a large fall and three experienced a moderate decline. Thus, general statements on the export performance of the region as a whole may easily miss the point that some countries have been surprisingly successful. If a common trend can be seen, it is in the general — and usually very rapid – rise in imports, and the common tendency of deteriorating trade balances and accumulation of deficits. The 14.5 per cent growth in the combined value of imports of eastern Europe was preceded by a 4 per cent decline in 1991, and a mere 1 per cent increase in 1992. Therefore, the rapid growth in 1993 was not necessarily an adverse development, in particular if related to an improvement (or even to the preliminary signs of a turn) in economic activity and an increase in the imports of capital goods for investment. The sharp deterioration of trade balances is another issue. This trend, even if desirable on grounds of contributing to the necessary structural changes in the transition economies, may turn out to be unsustainable. Here again, one should not expect general answers: the position of country groups and individual countries is likely to differ in terms of both the desirability and the sustainability of the growth in imports and trade deficits.[157]

(b) Trends in the growth and geographical pattern of trade: Review by country groups

The differences among east European economies in 1993 export and import performance cut across the standard groupings applied for the countries of the region. It is therefore more instructive to group the economies of the region according to their actual trade, more specifically, export, performance (see table 3.5.3).[158] Based on changes in exports in 1993, three broad categories can be identified. The *first* consists of the three countries where exports increased, although at different rates (the Czech Republic, Poland and Romania). The *second* group covers the countries where exports fell moderately. In two of these (Croatia and Slovenia) imports grew very rapidly; in Slovakia, the third in this group, import growth also was moderate. Finally, the *third* group includes the two countries displaying the combination of a significant decline in exports and a smaller (or no) growth in imports (Bulgaria, Hungary).[159]

As countries that are generally considered to have similar economic features fall into different groups, and countries within the same group above are at different stages in their economic reforms and, moreover, display large variations in macroeconomic performance, there are not likely to be any simple explanations for the diverse trade performances within the region. None the less, an attempt will be made in the review below to identify some regularities.

Export growth

The group displaying *export growth* includes Poland, where economic recovery is clearly on its way; the Czech Republic, where the fall in overall output was largely due to the impact of the country's recent separation from Slovakia; and Romania, whose industrial output shows signs of recovery in 1993. In Poland the growth of imports was also very rapid, while the preliminary Romanian data for the whole year indicate some fall in imports. The trade deficit contracted in the Czech Republic and Romania, but increased in Poland, the country with the highest output growth.

---

[156] Intraregional trade here refers to trade among six reporting eastern European countries (the four central European countries, Bulgaria and Romania).

[157] It may be assumed that where the increase of imports (and deficits) is accompanied by growth of exports, and the composition of imports changes towards capital goods from western countries, the import growth is desirable, even if accompanied by deterioration of the trade balance. If, on the other hand, the growth of the trade deficit results from falling exports and an increase of consumer goods imports, the deterioration of the trade balance may be undesirable. Furthermore, if a growing trade deficit is attributable to a decline in the country's competitiveness, the deficit is neither desirable nor sustainable. Whether or not a "desirable" trade deficit is sustainable depends on the country's balance of payments and foreign exchange position and, perhaps more importantly, on how foreign creditors of, and potential investors in, the country perceive the deficit: whether *they* consider it as desirable and sustainable. If they do not, even the most "desirable" deficit may turn out to be unsustainable. In any case, the notion that deficits in eastern Europe may be considered as *prima facie* evidence of economic recovery, and, therefore, as a positive symptom, has to be treated with care. This is the interpretation of several observers; see, e.g., L. Csaba, "Utelágazások Közép-Európában" (Crossroads in eastern Europe), *Figyelö*, 6 January 1994.

[158] In the case of countries that have recently separated (the Czech Republic, Slovakia, Croatia and Slovenia) the data in table 3.5.3 refer to the "old" foreign trade, excluding the trade which until recently was within common borders.

[159] According to full-year data, Hungary registered a 17 per cent decline in exports and a 13 per cent increase in imports; most of the rise in imports, however, came from a rather special one-time transaction (military equipment from Russia, in settlement of an old rouble debt); in the absence of this, the import rise would have been only 7 per cent.

TABLE 3.5.3

European transition countries: Change in foreign trade values and trade balances by partner region, 1991-1993
(Growth rates in percentages; trade balances in billion US dollars)

Country and trade partner groups [a]	Growth rates						Trade balance (billion US dollars)		
	Exports			Imports					
	1991	1992	1993 [b]	1991	1992	1993 [b]	1991	1992	1993 [b]
Bulgaria									
World	-34.2	1.6	-13.4	-51.5	27.5	0.2	0.7	-	-0.4
Transition economies	-27.8	-25.7	-12.2	-43.1	-4.3	18.3	0.6	0.2	-0.4
Developed market economies	-36.3	61.6	-17.2	-59.8	79.3	-11.7	-0.1	-0.3	-0.2
Developing countries	-47.6	14.2	-8.9	-54.4	26.7	-10.0	0.2	0.1	0.1
Croatia									
World	13.0	-5.0	-6.2	-13.5	-10.4	21.3	-0.5	-0.3	-0.8
Transition economies	..	-18.5	-15.5	..	1.4	3.6	-0.1	-0.2	-0.1
Developed market economies	..	6.3	-7.5	..	-5.6	52.3	-0.1	0.2	-0.5
Developing countries	..	-57.0	30.4	..	-34.7	3.8	-0.3	-0.3	-0.2
Czech Republic/Former Czechoslovakia [c]									
World	5.6	3.2	15.5	-7.2	14.6	0.5	0.4	-0.9	-0.1
Transition economies	6.8	-33.0	-0.6	0.3	-10.2	-14.2	-	-1.0	-0.2
Developed market economies	6.9	26.4	19.5	-13.7	39.6	5.2	0.3	-0.4	-0.4
Developing countries	-6.0	27.4	24.2	4.4	-20.4	6.5	0.1	0.5	0.5
Hungary									
World	5.1	4.1	-16.8	30.2	-3.2	13.2	-1.2	-0.4	-3.6
Transition economies	-26.8	3.2	-6.0	2.8	1.8	32.9	-0.3	-0.3	-1.4
Developed market economies	21.4	8.9	-21.0	44.3	-1.7	5.9	-0.9	-0.3	-2.1
Developing countries	21.8	-23.9	-8.0	29.0	-46.5	15.3	0.1	0.1	-0.1
Poland									
World	-18.5	-11.6	6.9	24.3	1.8	24.9	-0.7	-2.7	-3.3
Transition economies	-62.0	-18.9	-19.2	-42.8	-10.3	-20.0	-0.5	-0.7	-0.3
Developed market economies	13.7	-13.8	12.1	71.7	6.9	29.8	0.3	-2.0	-2.5
Developing countries	-15.5	26.8	13.9	151.0	-8.5	75.9	-0.5	-	-0.5
Romania									
World	-7.1	5.2	6.4	-17.6	8.2	6.1	-1.4	-1.7	-0.9
Transition economies	29.2	-16.3	-3.0	-8.9	-8.5	-0.9	-0.2	-0.3	-0.1
Developed market economies	-22.8	1.3	7.3	-9.4	40.3	15.6	-0.3	-1.2	-0.9
Developing countries	-11.9	55.4	14.4	-32.7	-17.2	-11.5	-0.9	-0.2	0.2
Slovakia									
World	..	6.5	-5.6	..	-1.1	2.3	..	-0.1	-0.4
Transition economies	..	..	-7.3	..	..	3.9	..	..	-0.4
Developed market economies	..	..	-8.3	..	..	16.3	..	..	-
Developing countries	..	..	6.1	..	..	-34.3	..	..	0.1
Slovenia									
World	-6.3	8.0	-3.4	-12.5	0.1	18.9	-0.3	-	-0.4
Transition economies	..	-14.7	37.8	..	4.9	6.9	-	-0.1	-
Developed market economies	..	13.4	-6.9	..	-0.9	16.9	-0.3	0.1	-0.3
Developing countries	..	-6.3	-10.3	..	3.1	71.3	-	-	-0.1
Russia/Soviet Union [d]									
World	-24.6	-25.2	1.4	-35.9	-21.3	-27.1	1.3	5.4	16.0
Transition economies	-35.1	-25.8	-12.6	-35.9	-42.8	-14.7	-0.3	4.3	3.9
Eastern Europe [e]	-40.8	-32.7 [f]	-7.9 [f]	-51.6	-49.7 [f]	-46.1 [f]	0.5	2.7 [f]	4.6 [f]
Developed market economies	-16.2	-20.3	4.6	-31.0	-13.0	-36.9	-	1.5	11.1
Developing countries	-29.0	-44.0	23.1	-35.8	-2.6	-4.5	1.6	-0.4	1.0

Source: Secretariat of the United Nations Economic Commission for Europe, based on national foreign trade statistics.

Note: Growth rates and trade balances are based on trade values in terms of US dollars. As an approximation to a consistent dollar valuation of rouble-denominated intra-group trade flows here, the pre-1991 national-currency data on trade with the market economies were revalued, in national currency terms, at a common rouble-dollar crossrate and reaggregated with the data on trade with the then centrally planned economies to obtain new trade totals (see box 2.1.1 and the discussion in section 2.1(iii) in United Nations Economic Commission for Europe, *Economic Bulletin for Europe*, Vol.43 (1991), New York, 1991). 1991-1993 trade flows were either originally reported in dollars or were converted to dollars with the relevant national conversion coefficient.

[a] The partner country grouping follows the past practice of the national statistical sources, which differed from the breakdown usually employed in United Nations publications. Thus, "transition economies" — the former "socialist countries" — includes former Yugoslavia and Cuba, in addition to the east European countries formerly CMEA members, the Soviet Union, and the Asian centrally planned economies.

[b] Full year data for Czech Republic, Hungary, and Russia; January-September 1993 relative to the same period in 1992 for Bulgaria, Poland, Romania, Slovakia, and Slovenia.

[c] Growth rates in 1991-1992 refer to former Czechoslovakia, and those for 1993 to the Czech Republic.

[d] 1991 data refer to trade of the former Soviet Union.

[e] Excluding Yugoslavia.

[f] Russian Federation trade with all former CMEA members (i.e., including Cuba, Mongolia and Vietnam).

The *Czech Republic* registered the best *export performance* in the region in 1993. The dollar value of total exports and of exports to the west increased by almost 16 and 20 per cent, respectively. Official *import* data show only a slight rise of total imports (and a 5 per cent increase of imports from the west) for the year as a whole, but this is rather deceptive, the result of an enormous import upswing in December 1992 to avoid the imposition of VAT which started on 1 January 1993. With a correction shifting an estimate of such anticipated flows into the first quarter of 1993 (when they would normally have occurred), the increase would be 26 per cent (36 per cent for imports from the west),[160] in keeping with the very rapid growth recorded in the first three quarters (20 and 32 per cent increases in overall and western imports, respectively).

The country's trade deficit narrowed substantially in 1993 (from $1.4 billion in 1992 to $0.1 billion in 1993). If Czech trade with Slovakia is included, the Czech Republic actually registered a small trade surplus in 1993, the only east European transition country to do so.

While there can be no doubt about the country's outstanding export performance, it is important to remember that the data referred to above exclude the Czech Republic's trade with Slovakia, its *"new"* foreign trade. Compared to the 1992 domestic trade between the two parts of Czechoslovakia, these flows contracted substantially: Czech exports to, and imports from, Slovakia are estimated to have fallen by 24 and over 26 per cent, respectively.[161] If the "new" foreign trade were to be included, therefore, the growth of the Czech Republic's exports and imports would be much lower than indicated above: some 5-7 per cent for exports and 8-10 per cent for imports (corrected for the end-1992 shifts). More to the point, the export performance of the country *vis-à-vis* its "old" foreign trade partners is likely to have been positively influenced by the emergence of the "new" foreign trade in two distinct ways. On the one hand, as happened after the collapse of eastern export markets in 1991, there may have been a substantial geographical restructuring towards other countries of former sales to Slovakia. On the other hand, some part of the former direct trade is likely to be conducted via other countries (which is, again, familiar from experiences following the demise of the CMEA), increasing the recorded value of the "old", while decreasing that of the "new" foreign trade.[162]

In *Romania*, both exports and imports expanded by over 6 per cent in the first three quarters of 1993, with somewhat faster growth, especially in the case of imports, in trade with the developed market economies (see table 3.5.3). The preliminary figures for the year as a whole (available, at the time of writing, only for overall exports and imports, but not for the geographical composition) indicate roughly the same growth in exports, but, instead of an increase, a slight fall in imports.[163] The country's favourable export performance coincided with an improvement in industrial output. The correspondence between the two appears to be close indeed. In the first two quarters, both exports and industrial production had still decreased; it was only from the third quarter that both showed strong growth.[164] Thus, Romania was the first country in the region to show certain signs of an export-led recovery; in fact, the trade deficit in the first three quarters was $0.9 billion, in the same order as in the corresponding period of the previous year. An important factor in the country's export growth seems to be the relatively high price of foreign exchange. In spite of the real appreciation of the leu in 1993, Romania still had the lowest level of wages (expressed in US dollars) among the east European countries, and the productivity differential apparently did not eliminate this advantage.

In *Poland*, the 7 per cent growth of exports in the first three quarters of 1993 followed two years of export decline. The country's rapid export growth towards the developed market economies and, in particular to the EU (18 per cent), was especially notable (table 3.5.3).[165] Here, in contrast with the Czech Republic (where exports to the EU rose almost at the same rate), there were no one-time factors contributing to the improvement in export performance. However, Poland stands out not only with its export growth, but also with the largest increase in imports (26 per cent in the January-September period), as well as the widest gap between exports and imports, among the countries of the region. The latter symptoms are almost certain to be related to the marked recovery of the Polish economy. Nevertheless, the sustainability of the trade deficit, approaching $3.5 billion in the first three quarters of 1993, remains an important question.

Moderately falling exports, growing imports

Two of the countries characterized by *moderate export decline*, Slovenia and Croatia, have in common that they both recorded *significant import growth* and both are

---

[160] Czech imports in December 1992 came to Kc 61.4 billion, as against average monthly imports of Kc 24.5 billion in the preceding 3 months. The rough adjustment mentioned in the text was made on the assumption that about one half (Kc 30 billion) of the December imports would under normal circumstances have occurred in the first quarter of 1993. The same procedure was used for imports from the developed market economies. These adjustments may in fact be on the low side (i.e., the result of understatement of the 1993 import growth).

[161] J. Krovak, "The disintegration of Czechoslovakia", paper prepared for the ECE, December 1993. The figures refer to the change in the first half of 1993 over the corresponding period of the previous year. See United Nations Economic Commission for Europe, *Economic Bulletin for Europe*, Vol.45 (1993), New York and Geneva, 1994, section 3.1 for a more detailed analysis of the new Czech-Slovak trade.

[162] See United Nations Economic Commission for Europe, *Economic Bulletin for Europe*, Vol.45 (1993), New York and Geneva, 1994.

[163] The reasons for the difference between the change of imports in the first three quarters and the whole year (over the corresponding period of the previous year) are that imports declined slightly in the last quarter of 1993 and, more importantly, that in the fourth quarter of the 1992 base period there had been an exceptionally large increase of imports: almost 40 per cent of the value of goods bought by the country in 1992 was imported in that quarter. The fall in imports in late 1993 appears to be related to the tightening of the supply of foreign exchange (see *Business Eastern Europe*, 21 February 1994).

[164] Although Romania's trade with the transition economies declined somewhat, this was chiefly the result of the large (40 per cent) fall in exports to the CIS (mainly Russia); exports to the other east European countries increased quite significantly.

[165] Full-year data for Poland were not yet available at the time of writing.

successor states of former Yugoslavia. Their economic record, especially their macroeconomic performance, was rather different, but the overall trends in foreign trade were quite similar. *Slovenian* exports fell moderately, while imports increased by almost 20 per cent. *Croatia's* imports grew at a slightly higher rate, and the decline in exports was more pronounced. There were substantial differences, however, in the regional composition of changes in their trade, in particular as regards the importance of transition economies, which declined in Croatia and rose strongly in Slovenia (see table 3.5.3). As successor states of a former federation, both have an important *"new"* foreign trade component (with other parts of former Yugoslavia) which contracted sharply. In Slovenia, "new" exports and imports both fell by almost 50 per cent; in Croatia, the share of this trade was higher, but the decline was less intensive: 36 and 28 per cent in exports and imports, respectively. Since both countries had a surplus of roughly $100 million in their "new" foreign trade, their overall deficits were smaller than those indicated by the balance of trade with the rest of the world.

Slovakia is another country where a distinction between the "old" and the "new" foreign trade is necessary. The mild fall in exports to the world outside former Czechoslovakia was relatively evenly spread among partner regions; the increase of imports was mainly due to the growth from the west European countries. As to the "new" foreign trade, some doubts surround its precise magnitude, since the data supplied by the Czech and Slovak Republics contradict each other. In Slovak exports (i.e., Czech imports), the difference between the two figures is not too large, but in imports from the Czech Republic the reported figures are rather confusing: Slovakia recorded $1.6 billion imports from, while the Czech side reported almost $2 billion exports to the other country in the first three quarters of 1993. Both countries reported a surplus with respect to the other. Without resolving this problem, it is safe to conclude that Slovakia experienced a strong decline in its "new" foreign trade. Moreover, since the weight of this trade is relatively large (almost 75 and 60 per cent of exports and imports in "old" foreign trade, respectively), the combined value of Slovakia's external trade is likely to have fallen quite significantly. One point is clear: Slovak foreign trade did not show signs of the powerful geographical trade reorientation which characterized the trade of the Czech Republic.

Sharply falling exports

In *Bulgaria* and *Hungary*, exports fell to the largest extent within the region;[166] besides, their imports increased relatively mildly. While in Bulgaria the transformation recession seems to be especially enduring, Hungary, at least in terms of industrial output, shows some signs of recovery. Both have been traditional exporters of agricultural and food products and have suffered serious declines in the production and exports of these products. Furthermore, both were rather strongly affected by the trade embargo on FR Yugoslavia. However, these circumstances do not appear to be sufficient to account for the similarities in the two countries' trade performance. Not only was the large magnitude of overall export decline a similar feature; so was its geographical composition. In both countries, exports to the west fell to a larger degree than those to the east, and in both imports from the east also grew. In consequence, the transition countries' share in their foreign trade rose. Exports to the developing region also declined in both countries.

In *Bulgaria*, the contraction of trade with the west was preceded by an exceptionally vigorous growth of both exports and imports in 1992 (by, respectively, 62 and 80 per cent). The fall in 1993 may reflect that, given the continuing overall contraction of the economy, the attained level of exports and imports turned out to be unsustainable. However, the line of causation may also be the opposite. Namely, if economic policies did not (or could not) induce further growth of exports, then economic growth may have been hindered, both directly and indirectly (through the balance-of-payments constraint).

Because of the large difference between the two countries in terms of foreign reserves, the balance-of-payments constraint is certain to have been more effective in the case of Bulgaria than in Hungary. In Bulgaria the trade deficit, following a year of balanced trade, was $0.4 billion, while in Hungary it reached $2.5 billion in the first three quarters of 1993 and increased by a further $1 billion in the last quarter. In fact, the argument that insufficient policy support for exports led to the export decline which, in turn, contributed to poorer than possible macroeconomic performance, is more likely to hold for Hungary – an issue which is treated below.[167]

While it has become clear that the overall characteristics of the groups displaying favourable and unfavourable performance do not offer simple explanations for the differences, certain regularities can be identified. All countries that recorded growth of both exports and imports achieved a larger increase in their western exports and imports than in their overall trade. By contrast, in those groups of countries where total exports fell, exports to the developed market economies fell even more; and, in most cases, the share of other transition economies increased in their total exports and/or imports. These trends reflect not only the fact that the western economies gained a decisive role in the foreign trade of eastern Europe, but also that, in general terms, "success" in exports is related to the performance in western trade. For the time being, no country that managed to improve its relative performance in its trade with the eastern partners could improve its overall trade performance.

---

[166] It is worth noting that it is mainly due to the large fall in Hungary's exports that the east European export aggregate shows a slight fall in the first three quarters of 1993. An aggregate excluding Hungary would show 3 per cent export growth (and 4.5 per cent for exports to developed market economies).

[167] This proposition is far from being universally accepted in Hungary. Some experts claim that the level of exports reached after the growth in 1991-1992 was unsustainable (a point mentioned above in the context of Bulgaria's export decline). Moreover, since that level included "inefficient" exports as well, policy efforts aimed at maintaining the former level would have been undesirable. See, e.g., K. Antalóczy, "A kivitel növelése illúzió" (The increase of exports is an illusion), *Népszabadság*, 21 December 1993.

Trade prices and volumes

To assess the region's trade performance, it is important to review the *volume changes* characterizing exports and imports of the east European countries. However, foreign trade *price indices* are not available for most countries. The exceptions are the Czech Republic, Hungary and Slovenia, whose price indices, even though not strictly comparable, depict similar movements: a 4-6 per cent decline in the US dollar prices of exports and a 6-7 per cent fall of import prices, respectively.[168] These figures suggest that, *in real terms*, the region's overall *exports are likely to have increased*, and that the increase of imports was even larger than the strong rise at current prices. Also, some economies have (or are likely to have) achieved internationally outstanding growth rates in the volume of their exports. This holds in particular for the western exports of the Czech Republic, Poland and Romania, where the volume of exports to the west may have increased in the range of 22-24, 16-18, and 8-12 per cent, respectively. The real growth of imports in the countries of the region is also likely to have been very strong. All in all, the east European region, with due consideration to its modest share in the total, had a positive impact on world trade.

The large diversity of country experiences in terms of export and import performance on the one hand, and the similarity regarding their growing trade deficits, on the other, raises some important questions. One concerns the reflection of the differences in trade performances in the commodity structure of trade. The other refers to the relative role of external and domestic factors in explaining the variations in trade performances.

(c) Diverging trade performances: Some characteristics of the commodity pattern and the importance of domestic policies

Commodity patterns

Since the information on the commodity pattern of trade from national foreign trade statistics is rather uneven and not directly comparable across countries, a comprehensive analysis of trends in the commodity structure of foreign trade is not feasible. Rather, the example of a few countries is offered to illustrate different experiences regarding changes in exports and imports. The questions to be addressed are the following: are high growth rates, and large falls, respectively, in exports associated with specific changes in the trade pattern? What type of changes accompany the significant growth of imports? Are certain changes in the commodity composition related to large and/or rapidly growing trade deficits?

In the *Czech Republic*, the high growth rate of exports and imports in 1993 was accompanied by favourable shifts in the commodity pattern of trade.[169] While total *exports* increased by 15 per cent, machinery exports (representing 28 per cent of total) grew by 34 per cent. In exports to the developed market economies, the shift towards highly-processed products was even more pronounced: whereas total exports to that region increased by 17.5 per cent, exports of machinery grew by almost 50 per cent. (The share of this group was roughly 24 per cent in exports to the western industrial countries.) By and large, similar trends can be in observed in *imports*. While overall imports and those from the developed market economies increased by 17 and 27 per cent, respectively, total machinery imports grew by 23 per cent, and those from the developed market economies increased by 24 per cent.[170]

Poland reports the commodity composition of foreign trade in a national classification, and for 1993 it has not as yet published data on the commodity pattern according to partner regions; hence the figures below are not fully comparable with those for other countries.[171] In Polish *exports*, the share of the group referred to as "electro-engineering", representing 23 per cent of total exports in 1992, increased its share to 26 per cent in 1993. This was due to a roughly 18 per cent growth in dollar value, which can be compared to the 7 per cent growth of total exports. In *imports*, the share of this commodity group did not change, but its value increased in line with total imports, i.e., by about 25 per cent in US dollars. This involves a very substantial growth in imports of capital goods, but for the time being neither information on the actual composition of these imports, nor on their geographical origins is available.[172]

In *Hungary*, *exports* of practically all commodity groups declined, with agricultural and food products (with a share of 21 per cent in total exports) showing the sharpest contraction (34 per cent).[173] Exports of industrial

---

[168] The Hungarian foreign trade price indices refer to the cumulative change in the period January-September 1993 over the corresponding period of the previous year (-6.1 and -7.1 in exports and imports, respectively). The Czech indices refer to the change between September 1993 and the same month of the previous year (-4.5 and -6.5 in exports and imports, respectively). Finally, the Slovenian figures are estimates for the change in 1993 over the previous year 1992 (-4 and -6 per cent in exports and imports, respectively). Hungarian Statistical Office; OECD, *Short-term Economic Indicators – Central and Eastern Europe*; Slovenia, Ministry of Economic Affairs and Development, *Slovenia: Economic trends in 1993*, November 1993.

[169] The commodity data cover January-October 1993; growth rates refer to changes in values in national currency over the same period of the previous year. Since the dollar exchange rate of the Czech currency changed only insignificantly over this period, the growth rates in national currency can be taken as rough approximations of the changes in US dollar values. *Statistické prehledy*, No.1, 1994.

[170] As international trade prices fell in this period, the rise in volumes is larger than those shown. The change in the price of imported western manufactures can be approximated by the change of the developed countries' export unit value index for manufactures. This was -2.1 and -2.9 for the OECD countries and the EEC, respectively, in the first three quarters of 1993 relative to the same period of 1992. United Nations, *Monthly Bulletin of Statistics*, XLVII-No.12, December 1993, p.256.

[171] The data refer to January-September 1993. *Biuletyn statystyczny*, January 1994.

[172] In both Poland and the Czech Republic, imports of consumer goods increased rapidly as well. However, the focus here is on whether the rapid growth of imports reflected expansion of machinery imports. In the case of these two countries the answer is clearly affirmative.

[173] The Hungarian trade figures refer to January-October, 1993; percentage changes reflect changes in the dollar value over the corresponding period of the previous year. National Bank of Hungary,

consumer goods and raw materials also fell steeply (by 31 and 19 per cent, respectively); the only important commodity group displaying a milder decline was machinery and capital goods (3.5 per cent). This reflected an 80 per cent increase of machinery (transport equipment) exports to the successor countries of the USSR, whereas exports of this product group to the industrial countries fell by 24 per cent. In exports to the developed market economies, the largest fall was recorded in industrial consumer goods (35 per cent). As for *imports*, compared to their 5 per cent overall average growth, the 17 per cent increase of machinery imports should be a favourable development, predicting an upturn in investments. However, much of the upswing was in transport equipment (including passenger cars), which in the Hungarian classification is included in this group. The 8.5 per cent increase of imports in this group from the developed market countries derives from the purchase of aircraft, which is an important investment, but not the kind that would indicate an upturn in overall investment activity. Moreover, an important element in the rise was a 210 per cent increase in imports from the successor countries of the former USSR.[174]

The changes in the commodity structure of foreign trade in *Romania* reveal yet another pattern.[175] Here, the growth of *exports* resulted from a sharp increase in the foreign sales of textiles, clothing and other products of light industry (up by 50 per cent) and metals and metal products (by 14 per cent), while machinery exports fell by 19 per cent (their share in total exports decreased by 2.5 percentage points, to 8.5 per cent). As for *imports*, the foreign purchase of machinery increased by almost 20 per cent; imports of food and some other consumer goods grew at a slower pace. The rapid growth in labour-intensive exports supports the view that the low level of wages (expressed in foreign currencies) is likely to have contributed significantly to the increase in foreign sales.

In spite of the limited scope of this analysis and the problems of comparison among countries, it may be concluded that in the economies reviewed differences in trade performances were associated with more or less characteristic changes in the commodity pattern of overall foreign trade, and (in the cases where the relevant information is available) in that of trade with the developed market economies. In our very narrow set of examples, a favourable overall export performance was associated with a relatively high growth rate of manufactured exports (in two cases of machinery and, where identifiable, towards the developed market economies). It was also associated with a rapid increase of imports, particularly those of capital goods. Poor export performance, in turn, seems to have been accompanied by the fall of manufactured (among others, machinery) exports towards western countries. In addition, a fall of overall exports was associated with a slow growth of imports, in particular those of capital goods originating from the industrial countries. These experiences, combined with the trends that emerged from the review of the regions' trade performance, as well as information on the western demand facing these economies, give grounds to some general remarks that apply to the other east European countries as well.

External environment

The proposition that exports of the transition economies to the western countries were constrained by the economic activity of the latter region might hold as a general statement, but does not necessarily apply to every exporting country and is altogether misleading as an explanation for *differences* in export performances. While western demand facing the transition countries as a whole fell by five per cent in 1993, the *"specific western demand"*[176] facing the two economies with the highest growth rate of exports to the OECD countries fell to a larger degree than the average (-5.5 per cent in the case of the Czech Republic and Poland); and by less (or not at all) in the case of the two countries where the decline in exports to the west was the most significant (-4.7 per cent and zero, for Hungary and Bulgaria, respectively; see chart 3.5.1).

Moreover, though the problems related to market access impose serious constraints for many countries and in the exports of several commodity groups, these do not seem to have hindered the export expansion of some countries in the region.[177]

Exchange rate policy and competitiveness

Thus, the roots of differences in export performance are more likely to be found in the domestic conditions and policies of the respective countries. As emphasized in recent ECE publications,[178] relative price and cost competitiveness, as well as shifts in the latter, indicated by *real exchange rate changes*, may be especially important factors explaining the diversity of country experiences. In the period 1990-1991, most east European countries had devalued their currencies sharply, which resulted in significant real depreciations. This was followed by a

---

Monthly Report, 1993, No.11-12. Full-year statistics are not yet available in a commodity and geographical breakdown.

[174] Including (for the first ten months) $59 million of military equipment from Russia (in settlement of a Soviet rouble debt). In the last two months of 1993 these special imports increased by an additional $650 million.

[175] The figures refer to January-September 1993; growth rates reflect changes in US dollar values over the corresponding period of the previous year. The commodity structure of foreign trade is not available in geographical breakdown. *Informatii statistice operative*, No.4, Bucharest, December 1993.

[176] Import demand change in western countries aggregated with the shares of individual western countries in the exports of a given transition economy as weights.

[177] In addition, though the international trade embargo imposed on FR Yugoslavia has certainly caused serious losses to many neighbouring countries (in terms of foregone exports), this factor cannot account for the disappointing export performance of some countries, the less so, since Romania, also closely affected by these sanctions, recorded increasing exports.

[178] See United Nations Economic Commission for Europe, *Economic Survey of Europe in 1992-1993*, New York, 1993, section 3.3, and United Nations Economic Commission for Europe, *Economic Bulletin for Europe*, Vol.45 (1993), New York and Geneva, 1994, chapter 3.

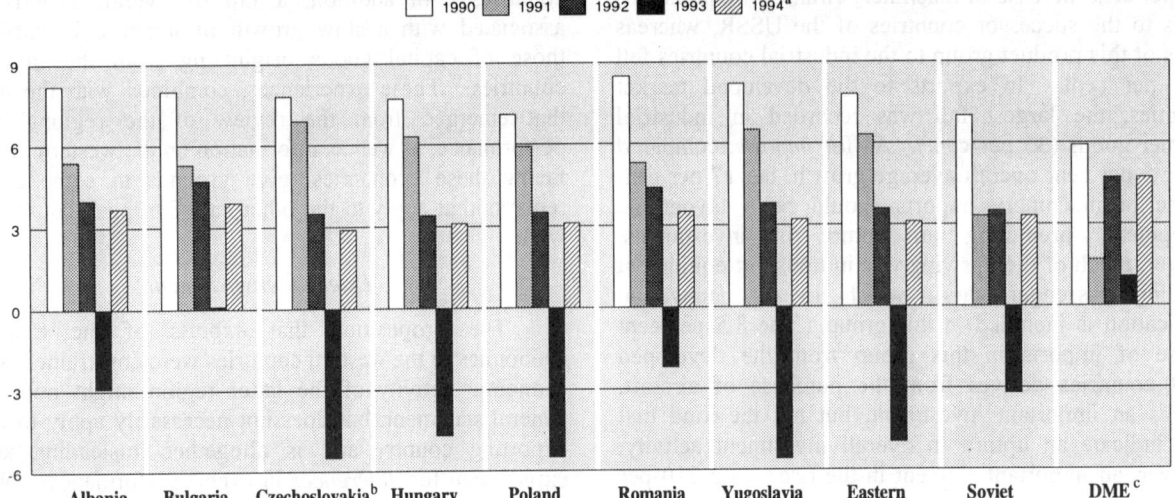

CHART 3.5.1

Specific western import demand facing eastern Europe and the former Soviet Union, 1990-1994
(Annual percentage change in volume terms)

Sources: ECE secretariat computations: aggregation of observed import volume growth of individual western countries weighted with its share in the exports of each eastern country. Import data cover goods and services.

[a] Forecast.
[b] For 1993 and 1994 the average for the Czech Republic and Slovakia.
[c] Growth of total import into the developed market economies.

TABLE 3.5.4

Eastern Europe: Average monthly US dollar wages, 1991-1993
(Levels in US dollars, change in per cent)

	Levels			Change [a]	
	1991	1992	1993 [b]	1992	1993
Bulgaria	58	70	122	21	110
Czechoslovakia	128	163	235 [c]	27	84 [c]
Hungary	240	278	320	16	33
Poland	166	214	220	29	32
Romania	98	66	85	-33	-13

Source: National statistics.
[a] Change from 1991.
[b] June.
[c] Czech Republic.

period of real appreciation for the majority of the countries of the region.

At the same time, the relative position of individual countries in terms of the *levels* of *costs and prices* differed substantially. By taking one significant element of production costs, wages, a rough idea can be given as to the magnitude of the differences as well as the direction of the changes (see table 3.5.4). Average monthly wages converted at the ruling exchange rates in eastern Europe varied from $58 (Bulgaria) to $240 (Hungary) in 1991; from $66-70 (Romania and Bulgaria, respectively) to $280 (Hungary) in 1992; and from $85 (Romania) to $320 (Hungary) in mid-1993. As compared to 1991, wages converted to US dollars increased substantially in all countries except Romania, with Poland recording the smallest and Bulgaria the largest rise. Even if the *increase* in the *Czech Republic* was more significant than in Hungary, in the latter country the *level* of wages in foreign currency was still considerably higher (by almost 40 per cent).

To be sure, wages expressed in foreign currency are but one component of external cost competitiveness.[179] Nevertheless, the observed pattern across countries is, by and large, consistent with developments in exports. In fact it may help to explain some of the differences unaccounted for as yet. In particular, the marked difference between the export performances of *Bulgaria* and *Romania* is likely to be related to the fact that in Bulgaria wage costs in foreign currency have not only increased much more rapidly, but also have reached a significantly higher level than in Romania. In addition, the favourable export performance of *Poland* may at least in part be explained by the fact that in 1993 it had registered the smallest increase among east European countries in the US dollar wage levels.

On the other hand, *Hungary's* unfavourable experiences also become understandable. According to several indicators (including those in table 3.5.4), the real appreciation was more prolonged and started from a significantly higher cost and price level (expressed in foreign currency) in Hungary than in the other economies,

---

[179] Actually, what matters from the point of view of international cost-competitiveness (or its change) is the level of (the changes in) *unit labour costs* expressed in foreign currency, as determined jointly by the level of (changes in) nominal wages, exchange rates and productivity. As consistent data are not available on productivity, wage levels expressed in foreign currency may be applied as *partial* indicators of external competitiveness.

where there had been large "initial" devaluations.[180] In the absence of the large initial "buffer" to absorb the effects of real appreciation available in other countries of the region, this exchange rate policy turned out to be detrimental for the price- and cost-competitiveness of the Hungarian exporting sectors.[181] It is likely to have undermined the competitiveness of sectors facing import competition as well. Hence the poor export performance in Hungary may, to a large part, be attributed to the exchange rate policy pursued.[182] The initial strict application of the harsh bankruptcy laws also contributed to the demise of several significant exporting companies.

The message of the Hungarian experience for the east European and other transition economies is straightforward. The continuation of the real appreciation may turn out to be destructive for exports (and for domestic producers competing with imports).[183] Broader measures to support the foreign trade sector of the economy are also required, especially in the infrastructure field (financing facilities, trade credit insurance and the like). In addition, companies in financial distress, but having hopes of restructuring and significantly contributing to exports, may need government assistance for reshaping their activities.

Belatedly, in the autumn of 1993, the Hungarian government decided to implement a programme for export-promotion, involving, among other things, the establishment of an export-guarantee agency and facilities for financing and promoting both exports and investments contributing to exports. Other countries have taken similar steps, which indicates that policy makers in eastern Europe have begun to realize that the one-time surge in exports to the west at the early stage of the transition is far from being self-sustaining; in the absence of measures to facilitate export financing and to maintain and enlarge export capacities, the export growth may be reversed, just as it happened in Hungary.

---

[180] For statistical evidence and the elaboration of these points, see OECD, *Economic Surveys: Hungary*, Paris, 1993, pp.59-66; G. Oblath, "Exchange rate policy and real exchange rate changes in economic transition" in J. Gács and G. Winckler (eds.), *International trade and restructuring in eastern Europe*, Physica Verlag, Heidelberg, 1994.

[181] Of course, even Hungary's relatively high US dollar wage level is very low in comparison with the west European countries, but the east European economies apparently have to compensate not only for the productivity differential but also for a number of other factors that seriously hinder their non-price competitiveness. See P. Havlik, "The influence of exchange rates and wages on export competitiveness in Hungary, Poland and former Czechoslovakia", *WIIW Mitgliederinformation*, 1993/1, pp.3-12, and S. Richter, "East-west trade under growing western protectionism", *WIIW Forschungsberichte*, No.198, June 1993.

[182] Other factors were at work as well. The drought, coupled with the uncertainties surrounding privatization and property rights in agriculture, has certainly had an unfavourable effect on the supply side of food exports. The embargo on supplies to the neighbouring FR Yugoslavia has also resulted in foregone exports; the losses are estimated by the Hungarian Ministry for Foreign Economic Relations at around $700-800 million in 1993 (press release, Budapest, 17 February 1994).

[183] Hungarian economic policy makers seem to have realized that the process of real appreciation is not sustainable: in the second half of 1993, a slow depreciation in real terms was set into motion, which continued in early 1994 with devaluations by 1 per cent and 2.6 per cent in January and February.

(iii) The Commonwealth of Independent States

Any assessment of foreign trade developments in the CIS countries in 1993 can only be very tentative at this time, given the very large revisions in successive official reports, especially on the foreign trade of the Russian Federation, its dominant component.[184] This data instability reflects the difficulties faced by the state authorities in obtaining information necessary for the conduct of economic policy. The revisions are consecutive attempts to cope with the data-gathering problems stemming from the existence of new frontiers, the inexperience of the customs service with its new data-collection functions, and probably widespread evasion of frontier controls of trade transactions which in part underlies the reported massive capital flight. This review is based on the latest statistical reports, but the fundamental uncertainties surrounding the reliability of these data have to be kept in mind.

(a) CIS foreign trade

The 3 per cent fall in the value of aggregate exports of the CIS countries to the "far abroad"[185] and the 26 per cent contraction of imports in 1993 were shaped, of course, by the developments in Russian foreign trade (to be discussed below), and thus not "typical" of the experience of the other republics. In the other CIS countries, *exports* on average *fell much more sharply*, by some 16 per cent in aggregate. Export growth was registered only in Kyrgyzstan, Moldova, Tajikistan and Turkmenistan, but only in the last was this rise, based on natural gas and cotton exports, quantitatively at all significant (see table 3.5.5). *Imports*, on the other hand, *increased* on average in the non-Russian CIS republics, by some 12 per cent in aggregate, and *trade balances worsened* in all of them.

Very substantial *deficits* relative to export earnings were registered in Armenia, Tajikistan and Uzbekistan. These were financed by external support, including western collateralized facilities, bilateral credits (Uzbekistan-Turkey), and some Russian support in the case of Tajikistan. Enormous *surpluses* (multiples of total imports) were recorded in Kazakhstan and Turkmenistan, both fuel exporters, and reported surpluses were substantial also in Azerbaijan and Ukraine. It may be doubted, however, whether these trade balance results correlate to any degree with changes in the convertible-currency current account positions of these countries. For one thing, transactions other than those in convertible currencies still constituted a very large (although declining) part of the export operations of many republics (e.g., 48 per cent in Belarus, 27 per cent in Kazakhstan, 28 per cent in Russia); for another, barter operations remained significant (in the

---

[184] In United Nations Economic Commission for Europe, *Economic Bulletin for Europe*, Vol.45 (1993), New York and Geneva, 1994, p.63, doubts were expressed concerning the reliability of the official statistics then available; these statistics have now been revised in several steps.

[185] For developments in the "new foreign trade" among the CIS countries, or trade with the "near abroad", see section (c) below.

TABLE 3.5.5

Foreign trade of Commonwealth of Independent States with non-CIS countries, 1993

(Million current dollars, percentage change)

Country	Exports	Imports	Change from 1992 (per cent) Exports	Change from 1992 (per cent) Imports
Armenia	31.0*	87.0*	..	..
Azerbaijan	355.3*	239.7*	-53	-28
Belarus	710.1	743	-33	-1
Kazakhstan	1 270.6	358.3	-15	-24
Kyrgyzstan	100.4	105.8	31	50
Moldova	163.9*	181.7*	5	7
Russia	42 970.7	27 031.9	1	-27
Tajikistan	263.2	370.6	138	180
Turkmenistan	1 157.0*	490.0*	27	1 550
Ukraine	3 001.0	2 181.0	-20	-2
Uzbekistan	706.5	947.3	-19	2
Total	50 729.7	32 736.3	-3	-26

Source: CIS Statistical Committee, *Statisticheskii Byulleten*, No.2, February 1994, p.8. Starred entries are estimates by the CIS authorities.

same three countries, 39 per cent, 28 per cent and 10 per cent, respectively, of all foreign trade operations).[186]

The economic weight of foreign trade remained rather small in all CIS republics. In the absence of meaningful GDP data, this can be illustrated by *per capita* levels of exports and imports (based on the data in table 3.5.5). Only Russia and Turkmenistan had per capita exports in the vicinity of $300 in 1993 (Russia $289, Turkmenistan $311). In the other republics, per capita exports ranged from $9 (Armenia) through $76 (Kazakhstan), with an average of $52. Even the more industrialized western republics, Belarus and Ukraine, exported only $60-$70 per capita. A similar picture emerges for imports, with per capita levels of $130 and $180 in Turkmenistan and Russia, and an average of $42 for all other republics (with a range from $26 in Armenia to $70 in Belarus).[187] Apart from the general economic crisis, this reflects the lack of established foreign trade relations in most republics and the difficulties of setting up new institutions and policies after the break with the centralized Soviet foreign trade system.

(b) Russian Federation

With its share of more than 80 per cent in the external trade of the CIS countries, Russia's trade was the dominant component. On the estimates available at the time of writing, *exports* of the Russian Federation increased slightly in value in 1993 (just over 1 per cent) while *imports* contracted by 27 per cent (table 3.5.1). Earlier data for the same period had reported much stronger export growth as well as, alternatively, much smaller and much larger falls of imports.[188] The uncertainty seems to be particularly large as regards the development of imports, where important flows apparently go unregistered and can be estimated only with large error margins.[189] Hence the data available now are unlikely to constitute the last word. All estimates, however, agree on a very substantial increase in the Russian *trade surplus* in 1993 (to some $16 billion, from $5 billion in 1992), more than half of which arose in trade with the developed market economies.

The shrinking internal demand and the further depreciation of the rouble must have curtailed import demand. Import barriers also rose in 1993, as tariffs were raised, new excise duties introduced and VAT imposed on imported goods.[190] But these measures were not the only reasons for the import decline. In fact, the bulk of the fall (some $8 billion of the $10 billion contraction) appears to have occurred in the so-called "*centralized critical imports*" purchased by the government and distributed internally at highly subsidized prices.[191] By contrast, imports through commercial channels, which, in principle, should be very sensitive to such trade policy measures, are reported to have contracted in the first half but increased significantly during the second half of 1993. The import contraction thus mainly reflected the budgetary constraint on government import purchases, the attendant reduction of import subsidization (at unsubsidized prices, the quantities demanded must have been sharply lower),[192] and the

---

[186] As reported in the CIS Statistical Committee, "Ekonomika stran Sodruzhestva nezavisimykh gosudarstv v 1993 godu" (The economy of the CIS countries in 1993), *Statisticheskii byulleten*, No.2, February 1993, p.9. Presumably barter operations are included in the non-convertible currency totals.

[187] For comparison, per capita exports of the 12 EU countries stood at some $4,000 in 1991 ($1,500 if mutual trade is excluded). East European exports per capita averaged some $450 in 1993, with a range from $200 in Romania, some $350 in Bulgaria and Poland, to about $1,000 in the Czech Republic and $2,000 in Slovenia.

[188] The present review follows RF Goskomstat, *Sotsial'no-ekonomicheskoe polozhenie ...*, op. cit. Estimates published only a few days earlier showed a rise in exports of 13 per cent and a 12 per cent fall in imports, but RF Goskomstat data released as late as December 1993 saw imports falling by more than 40 per cent.

[189] There is also some uncertainty whether the data on commodity flows in 1992 and 1993 include or exclude deliveries of "humanitarian aid", worth some $2.2 billion in 1993. If these are included in the 1992 data, but not in 1993 (as shown in some analyses: e.g., Mikhail Sarafanov, "Paradoksy platezhnogo balansa" (Paradoxes of the balance of payments), *Finansovye Izvestiya*, 27 January-2 February 1994), the import fall would be only 21 per cent.

[190] Import duties were raised in 1993. Under a new import tariff schedule in force since April 1993, *ad-valorem* rates on "most favoured nations" (MFN) imports vary between 5 to 150 per cent; rates double for non-MFN imports. On other trade barriers, see United Nations Economic Commission for Europe, *Economic Bulletin for Europe*, Vol.45 (1993), New York and Geneva, 1994, pp.72-73. A number of further tariff increases, which had been under discussion since late 1993, were put into force in mid-March 1994 (*Izvestiya*, 16 March 1994). These will in particular offer substantial new protection to Russian agricultural and consumer goods producers.

[191] The "centralized critical imports" accounted for almost $20 billion, or 54 per cent of total imports in 1992 and for under $12 billion or 44 per cent in 1993 (M. Sarafanov, loc.cit.); in terms of commodities, they provided for grain and other agricultural supplies, pharmaceuticals, and certain industrial inputs.

[192] The subsidization of centralized imports takes the form of "preferential coefficients" (*l"gotnye koeffitsienty*) applied to the exchange rate (which apparently are financed through extra-budgetary accounts). Reduction of the "preferential coefficients" has repeatedly been stated as a policy aim (see, e.g., "Plan deistvii Soveta Ministrov – Pravitel'stva

resulting change in the structure of imports. At the same time, there probably also were external financing constraints: in 1992, 35 per cent of total imports had been financed through government-guaranteed medium- and long-term external loans ($12.8 billion); this proportion fell to 20 per cent ($5.5 billion) in 1993.[193]

Directions of trade

Russian exports to the *developed market economies* grew almost 5 per cent whereas imports from these countries decreased steeply (37 per cent). Even with lower levels of their Russian trade, Germany and Italy kept their leading positions, receiving respectively $6 and $3 billion of Russian exports and contributing $7 and $1 billion on the import side.[194] The developed market economies to which Russian exports increased significantly include Japan (30 per cent growth), United States (167 per cent), Austria and Switzerland (110 and 68 per cent growth, respectively). Imports from these countries, except for Switzerland, decreased (by 11 and 48 per cent in the case of Japan and the United States, respectively).

A surplus arose also in Russia's trade with the *developing countries*, where exports grew especially strongly while imports fell.

Among the *transition economy* trade partners, the share of the *former CMEA countries* and the *Baltic states* in Russia's foreign trade continued to fall in 1993 (to 18 per cent in Russian exports and to 11 per cent in Russian imports). Russian imports from China, however, expanded very significantly.[195]

Measures taken by the Russian government in April 1993 with the aim of facilitating trade with the former CMEA members – such as the permission to make payments in national currencies and exemption from the compulsory resale of hard currency earnings from exports to these countries – did not have the expected effect. In 1993, Russian exports to these countries fell by some 8 per cent and imports from them by 46 per cent. The further contraction of trade with the ex-CMEA and Baltic countries was mainly the result of the continuing geographical reorientation of foreign trade in most of these economies towards western markets; the disruption of former intra-industry relations, accompanying the economic changes under way in these countries; reasons related to political attitudes and sentiments may also have played a role.

Commodity composition of trade

The *commodity composition* of Russian *exports* continued on the previous patterns. Exports of mineral products, oil, gas and other raw materials accounted for almost 80 per cent of total exports; their physical volumes increased in spite of various restrictions.[196] Oil exports, of 80 million tons, were up by 20 per cent on 1992, gas exports were up to 96 billion cu m (up by 9 per cent) and exports of oil products went up by 36 per cent, to 34.5 million tons. Even with sharply falling world market prices for fuels, the share of energy products still accounted for 48 per cent of Russian export revenues in 1993 (against 53 per cent in 1992).[197] Most other categories of Russian exports declined, aside from metals and some chemicals;[198] the value of exports of machinery and equipment was down by 23 per cent (the share of the group was about 6.5 per cent in 1993).

The fall in Russian *manufactures exports* reflects both the further contraction of supply (industrial output) and the loss of former markets for these goods. Formerly, non-consumer manufactured goods predominated in this part of Russian exports. The developing countries used to be the major importers of these products. However, unable to get further soft credits for purchases of machinery and equipment, they decreased their imports from Russia substantially. Nevertheless, they remained importers of spare parts and technologically necessary semi-manufactures. The CMEA countries cut back on their imports of these goods from Russia as well. Only some categories of Russian non-food consumer goods were still in demand; however they did not reach even 1 per cent of total exports.

On the *import* side, virtually all categories of goods were in decline, in particular, agricultural products and some manufactured consumer goods. Meat and grain

---

Rossiiskoi Federatsii po realizatsii ekonomicheskoi reformy v 1993 godu" (Plan of action of the Council of Ministers – Government of the Russian Federation for the implementation of economic reform in 1993), *Rossiiskie vesti*, 2 March 1993), but appears exceedingly difficult to implement. Thus, at the end of 1992 a reduction of the coefficient for grain imports from 95 per cent to 50 per cent was proposed, but rejected by the government (Minister of Economic Affairs A. Nechaev, as cited in *Izvestiya*, 14 December 1992). With a coefficient of this order of magnitude, the freeing of the import price of grain (abolition of the subsidy) might have produced an even larger reduction in grain imports than that which was implemented within the centralized import programme (by 62 per cent).

[193] M. Sarafanov, loc.cit.

[194] According to the Russian data, exports to Italy fell by 7 per cent and imports contracted by 66 per cent in 1993. This contrasts with an Italian report on the "substantial" growth of trade between Italy and Russia (BBC, *Summary of World Broadcasts*, SUW/0314 WC/5, 7 January 1994). The discrepancy in the mirror data might be a reflection of the processes used for capital flight from Russia.

[195] The doubling of imports from China, to $4 billion (15 per cent of total Russian imports), made that country the second largest trade partner after Germany.

---

[196] In 1993, the export of "strategic" goods (fuels, metals, timber, etc.) was still restricted by various administrative instruments (licensing, quotas and export tariffs). The system of centralized exports was also re-established, in part to improve the state's access to foreign currency. See United Nations Economic Commission for Europe, *Economic Bulletin for Europe*, Vol.45 (1993), New York and Geneva, 1994, pp.72-73.

[197] In 1993, the export price of Russian crude oil fell by 20 per cent against the 1992 average, those of oil products, natural gas and coal by 39, 11 and 21 per cent, respectively (RF Goskomstat, *Sotsialno-ekonomicheskoe polozhenie* ..., op. cit., p.85). The fall of energy prices lowered Russian export earnings by some $5.3 billion from what the same volume would have brought in 1992.

[198] Russian metal exports to the west had already surged in 1992. The sharpest rise in 1993 occurred in aluminium: the volume of exports increased by another 62 per cent in 1993, but in the face of a 29 per cent fall in world prices, export revenues rose only by 16 per cent. See United Nations Economic Commission for Europe *Economic Bulletin for Europe*, Vol.45 (1993), New York and Geneva, 1994, pp.109-110, and section 4.2(iii) below on the trade and production constraints imposed by the international community in response to this export rise.

TABLE 3.5.6

Russia's trade with CIS countries, 1992-1993
(Levels in billion roubles at current prices; growth rates in per cent)

	Levels				Growth rate [a]	
	1992		1993			
	Exports	Imports	Exports	Imports	Exports	Imports
Armenia	26.1	9.8	69	17	-67.8	-50.7
Azerbaijan	54.5	38.7	167	181	-72.0	-81.5
Belarus	329.6	133.2	2 205	1 966	-29.5	-55.5
Georgia [b]	26.1	6.2	42	26	-83.2	-56.0
Kazakhstan	569.1	243.3	2 386	1 414	-55.8	-38.8
Kyrgyzstan	42.7	18.4	208	112	-48.6	-35.8
Moldova	66.4	31.5	402	112	-36.2	-62.5
Tajikistan	28.5	8.7	97	34	-64.1	-58.2
Turkmenistan	49.8	26.0	194	86	-58.9	-65.1
Ukraine	913.0	515.8	7 365	3 647	-15.0	-25.5
Uzbekistan	175.5	43.1	735	1 026	-55.9	150.9
Total	2 281.3	1 074.7	13 870	8 621	-35.9	-15.5

Sources: RF Goskomstat, direct communication to ECE.

[a] Growth rates calculated from notional US dollar values obtained by converting rouble values at the "purchasing power parity" (PPP) conversion rates of R41/$ for 1992 and R389/$ for 1993 (RF Goskomstat communication to ECE and ECE extrapolation). These PPP conversion rates were estimated on the basis of prices in intra-Russian transactions, and hence will not properly reflect prices in intra-CIS trade.

[b] Georgia joined the CIS in 1993.

imports fell by 73 and 62 per cent, respectively. Medicine imports contracted by 73 per cent, footwear and knitwear imports decreased by 51 and 49 per cent, respectively. The share of machinery and equipment imports fell to 26.5 per cent (from 36.8 per cent in 1992) in total imports.

(c) Intra-CIS trade

Information on intra-CIS trade is so scanty that no comprehensive assessment of the development of trade relations among the former Soviet republics in 1993 can be offered at this point. In particular, as data are available only for the intra-CIS trade of *Russia*, almost nothing is known about the *mutual trade of the other CIS republics*, which in the period just before the break-up of the Soviet Union accounted for some 60-65 per cent of Soviet inter-republican trade.

Table 3.5.6 shows Russia's trade with the CIS countries in 1992 and 1993 at current rouble prices. The data provide a rough notion of the geographical directions of Russian trade, in particular the large role of *Ukraine* as a partner (53 per cent of Russian exports and 42 per cent of imports in 1993), followed by *Belarus* and *Kazakhstan* (16-17 per cent of exports, 23 and 16 per cent of imports) and, at some distance, *Turkmenistan* (5 per cent of exports, but 12 per cent of imports – mainly cotton). The data also indicate the *imbalance* in these trade relations: the large Russian trade surpluses (deficits of the other CIS countries), amounting to over 50 per cent of Russian exports in 1992 and 38 per cent in 1993, and to even more in a number of bilateral relations.

The large increase of the *rouble value* of Russian trade with the CIS countries, however, conceals a significant *real* contraction. Rouble prices not only rose very rapidly in general (as discussed in section 3.3 above), but also rose faster in transactions with the "near abroad" than in intra-Russian trade, and probably faster in Russian exports than in imports because of the dominance of fuels in the former. Fuel prices had been most out of line (relative to world market prices) in the Soviet price system, and therefore rose faster than the average as relative prices began to be adjusted towards world market levels; this movement, in turn, was more pronounced in trade with the CIS countries than in the Russian domestic price system.[199] Moreover, as intra-CIS trade prices are largely determined in bilateral inter-state negotiations, there is no reason to assume that the impact was the same in Russian trade with individual CIS partners. All this goes to say that in the data shown in table 3.5.6 one rouble does not equal another, not only between years, but also between exports and imports or between transactions with different partner countries in the same year.

In order to indicate at least the *direction* of change in Russian intra-CIS trade, the second panel of table 3.5.6 shows rates of change for 1993 in terms of "notional" dollar equivalents at purchasing power parity conversion rates. It follows from the above observations that these rates can at best be very rough approximations of the 1993 change, but their *sign* is likely to be right.[200] That these

---

[199] For instance, the price for Russian natural gas sold to Ukraine under intergovernmental agreements appears to have risen more than twentyfold in rouble terms in the course of 1993, but was still below the world market level at the end of the year; world market prices are to be charged in 1994. Similar trends prevailed in oil prices. See United Nations Economic Commission for Europe, *Economic Bulletin for Europe*, Vol.45 (1993), New York and Geneva, 1994., p.75; also E. Whitlock, "Ukrainian-Russian trade: the economics of dependency", *RFE/RL Research Report*, 29 November 1993.

[200] The "purchasing power parity" conversion coefficients were probably defined on a comparison of average intra-Russian and world market trade prices; hence they would not take account of the faster rise of rouble prices in intra-CIS trade, especially on the side of Russian exports dominated by fuels. In consequence, the fall in the "notional" dollar equivalent of Russian intra-CIS trade – especially Russian exports – would be understated by this measure.

TABLE 3.5.7

Russian exports of oil to CIS countries, 1991-1993
(Million tons; per cent)

Country	1991	1992	1993 [a]	Per cent of quotas 1993 [b]
Azerbaijan	2.5	0.9	0.24	34
Belarus	33.1	19.7	10.8	68
Kazakhstan	12.1	11.5	8.1	67
Turkmenistan	2.2	1.1	0.12	14
Uzbekistan	5.6	4.1	3.8	94
Ukraine	49.3	33.5	15.6	69

Sources: CIS Statistical Committee, *Statisticheskii Byulleten*, No.24(42), December 1993 and *Ekonomika i zhizn'*, No.28, July 1993.

[a] January-November 1993.
[b] Fulfilment of export quotas fixed in bilateral agreements.

trade flows continued to *contract* substantially *in real terms* in 1993 is confirmed by all available data. According to RF Goskomstat, 1993 turnover (exports plus imports) in Russian trade with the "near abroad" was 50 per cent in volume terms below the *1991* level; what is not known is how this fall was distributed between the two years (1992 and 1993) or between exports and imports. Data on physical quantities of certain commodities which in general are Russian exports suggest that the volume of Russian exports contracted more sharply than that of imports (see table 3.5.7 for oil exports).[201] The halving of intraregional trade over the two-year period exceeds the 30 per cent decline in the NMP of the CIS countries and was both a causal factor in the regional recession and evidence of continued regional disintegration.

Before the dissolution of the Soviet Union at the end of 1991, the later CIS republics were very tightly interdependent, owing not only to geographical proximity but, more importantly, to the long-term impact of Soviet development policy with its stress on economies of scale, and the resulting high degree of regional specialization.[202] This was reflected in very high NMP-trade ratios.[203] Inter-republican trade imbalances at domestic prices were small in the case of Russia, in some other republics substantial in terms of NMP, but did not matter much as long as trade was inside the same payment sphere and financing was automatic. Their magnitude at world market prices was hidden by distorted relative prices.

Once internal trade became external trade (albeit initially only "quasi-external" under the special trade regime for the "near abroad"), and prices started to be adjusted to world market ratios, these immanent imbalances emerged in the recorded trade imbalances, which were worsened by the lack of institutional solutions to manage *payments* and *financing* issues during the transition.[204]

Since 1991, intra-CIS trade volumes fell sharply, as noted above. The full magnitude of this contraction is impossible to quantify because of the absence of data for important components of the trade network (in particular, for trade outside the central relation between Russia and the other CIS republics), as well as a lack of information on price movements (and especially relative price movements). In consequence, the degree of regional integration, as measured by the ratio of nominal trade value to nominal GDP, declined steeply.

At the same time, imbalances in intraregional trade rose sharply as relative prices, especially energy prices, were adjusted. The rise of these imbalances accelerated substantially in 1993, not only in rouble value but, more importantly, in relation to national product: the Russian surplus in intra-CIS trade can be estimated to have been some 7 per cent of Russia's NMP in 1992 and 4 per cent in 1993. These proportions are much more important in other CIS countries: the deficit of the Ukraine in trade with Russia alone in both years probably came to 11-12 per cent of Ukraine's NMP.[205]

In the absence of financial reserves, the trade deficits led to large payments arrears of the CIS republics *vis-à-vis* Russia. Negotiations for their settlement brought forth, in 1993, various proposals of *debt for equity swaps*. Thus, it was proposed that the Russian natural gas export firm Gazprom acquire pipelines and storage facilities in Ukraine and Belarus in settlement of arrears. In the environment of newly-acquired political independence, these proposals touched on very sensitive issues, evoking fears of a loss of

---

[201] In 1993, Russian deliveries to CIS countries of crude oil, natural gas, gasoline and metals were lower than in 1991 by 60, 8, 60 and 64 per cent, respectively. Owing to the adjustment of prices towards world market levels, however, the *share* of energy products in the value of Russian exports to the CIS countries has risen sharply, accounting for 88 per cent of total Russian deliveries "for production purposes" in 1993, against 51 per cent in 1992 (RF Goskomstat, *Sotsial'no-ekonomicheskoe polozhenie ...*, op.cit., pp.90-92).

[202] On inter-republican specialization and interdependence in the Soviet Union, see A. Granberg, "The economic interdependence of the former Soviet republics", and A. Vavilov and O. Vyugin, "Trade patterns after integration into the world economy", both in John Williamson (ed.), *Economic Consequences of Soviet Disintegration*, Washington, D.C., 1993.

[203] In 1990, inter-republican trade of the CIS republics relative to total NMP was close to 25 per cent on average, with large differences among republics: the ratio was the highest in the smallest republic, Moldova – 62 and 53 per cent for export and imports, respectively – and the lowest in Russia at 17 and 15 per cent of Russian NMP. United Nations Economic Commission for Europe, *Economic Bulletin for Europe*, Vol.44 (1992), New York, 1993, table 2.4.1, p.85. On the basis of the values in table 3.5.6 and estimated nominal NMP of 120 trillion roubles, the ratios for Russia have now fallen to 12 per cent for exports and 7 per cent for imports.

[204] For a very clear exposition of the evolution of settlement and financing issues in the post-Soviet period now, see Thomas Wolf et al., *Financial Relations Among Countries of the Former Soviet Union*, IMF Economic Reviews, 1994, No.1, (Washington, D.C., February 1994), a study received too late to be fully taken into account in the present *Survey*. See also United Nations Economic Commission for Europe, *Economic Bulletin for Europe*, Vol.44 (1992), New York, 1993, pp.38-45.

[205] In the last years of the 1980s, *Ukraine* had been in surplus of 1-4 per cent of NMP with all Soviet republics. In 1993, in addition to the deficit with Russia, it was also in deficit with other energy-supplying CIS republics, and there were probably few offsets in its intra-CIS trade relations. *Belarus* tended to register large surpluses at Soviet domestic prices, 12-16 per cent of NMP in 1988-1990; its deficits with Russia alone was 25 per cent of NMP in 1992, but seems to have fallen to 4 per cent in 1993.

economic sovereignty. Delivery stoppages were resorted to when payments did not materialize or negotiations failed during 1993 and again in early 1994, and few of the outstanding issues are settled at the time of writing.

The outlook for intra-CIS economic relations is on the whole rather bleak. The problems are *structural*, the inheritance of past development policy which built up energy-intensive manufacturing and agriculture in the non-Russian republics dependent on energy supplies from Russia (and some other republics). Adjustment to structural problems of such magnitude is inherently difficult and possible only over longer time spans. What worsens the outlook is that there seems to be the least movement towards adjustment precisely in those republics where the problem is the greatest (e.g., Ukraine and Belarus).

(iv) **The Baltic states**

The radical changes in the foreign trade of the Baltic states, stemming from their final separation from the rouble area in 1992, continued during 1993. All three countries had to absorb very significant changes in their terms of trade in consequence of their exit from the rouble price system, almost certainly negative, but unquantifiable on the basis of available data. Considerable efforts were made to reorient trade to western markets. The bilateral free trade agreements signed with several western countries and the General System of Preferences applied by the EU facilitated the expansion of exports. For imports, the continuing decline of domestic demand was more important. The introduction and stabilization of their own currencies in 1992-1993, and the introduction of partial currency convertibility have had an impact as well.

The US dollar value of the foreign trade of all three Baltic states increased substantially in 1993 (see table 3.5.8), but the significance of these value *changes* is very uncertain, owing to the difficulty of measuring the dollar value of trade in 1992.[206] For the large proportion of the Baltic countries' trade conducted with the CIS countries, and therefore also for total trade, the data for 1992 and 1993 are not really comparable; however, no such stricture applies to the data for trade with the market economies. Trade with western countries clearly rose rapidly in Estonia and Lithuania in 1993 as the dependency on the former Soviet partners weakened, but the growth was much weaker in Latvia.

Export and import *volume* appears to have risen considerably in Estonia.[207] Scattered commodity data for the other two countries indicate that export volume may also have increased in 1993, but imports are more likely to have remained at the level of 1992 or fallen.[208]

Latvia and Lithuania ran trade surpluses in 1993 ($80 and $117 million, respectively). In Estonia, by contrast, the foreign trade balance turned negative in that year ($91 million).[209]

The trade levels in all three Baltic countries are now quite high relative to national product: exports came to two thirds of GDP in Estonia and Latvia and to 40 per cent in Lithuania (first three quarters of 1993). These high ratios reflect a substantial rise in the volume of re-exports (see below).

In all three Baltic countries, import growth from the west was to some extent supported by direct foreign investment which took the form of deliveries of equipment, machinery, etc. Lithuania also received some western support to finance imports from Russia and other CIS countries (Norwegian government credit, IMF and World Bank credits to cover payments to Russia for natural gas and fuel).[210]

Change in the geographical structure of trade was most rapid in *Estonia*, where already in 1992 the share of trade with CIS countries had dropped by 49 points in exports and by 33 points in imports. In 1993, the CIS partners accounted for 29 per cent of Estonian exports and 22 per cent of imports (and Russia for 23 and 17 per cent, respectively). Among commodities imported from Russia, nearly two thirds were mineral products (basically fuels); on the export side, agricultural produce and foodstuffs amounted to 31 per cent and motor vehicles another 30 per cent.

The switch in Estonian foreign trade was made towards Finland, Sweden and Germany. In January to November 1993, those three countries accounted for nearly 40 per cent of Estonian exports and for more than 47 per cent of imports. On the import side, western investors were

---

[206] Dollar values were obtained, using official exchange rates, from reported data expressed in the new national currencies introduced in the course of 1992. The national-currency data for 1992 reflect, for at least part of the year (i.e., the period prior to the introduction of world market prices, generally at about mid-year), the conversion by the national authorities of the rouble-denominated values of trade with the CIS countries at internal Soviet prices. Very little is known about the methods used for this conversion; it probably differed from country to country, but almost certainly does not reflect a revaluation of the CIS trade flows at world market prices. It can be hoped that eventually the national authorities will provide estimates of trade *volume* changes across the transition gap.

[207] According to Estonian officials, the volume of exports and imports in the first half of 1993 was roughly equal to the total volume of 1992 (*Eesti Pank Quarterly Review*, 1993:3, p.37).

[208] For Latvia, this judgement is based on a comparison of selected commodity flows in 1993 and the second half of 1992 (State Committee for Statistics of Latvia, communication to ECE). In the case of Lithuania, the very large falls in the volume of imports of natural gas, heavy oils (*mazut*) and ferrous metals in the first six months (by 46, 37 and 52 per cent, respectively) lead to this conclusion (Statistical Department of Lithuania, *Lietuvos ekonominé ir socialiné raida*, Vilnius, 1993, p.45).

[209] In Estonia, humanitarian aid received from western countries (pharmaceuticals, medical equipment, etc.) is included in the import data. According to Eesti Pank, during the first half of 1993 such imports totalled 141 million kroons or approximately $11 million, compared with the deficit of $12 million registered during the same period.

[210] After the switch, in mid-1992, to convertible currency payments and world market prices in trade with Russia, the Baltic countries ran up substantial payments arrears for oil and natural gas, which in turn prompted Russian fuel supply cuts or stoppages in mid-1993 until the debt was paid. In addition to foreign exchange shortage, disputes about unsettled mutual debts were involved.

TABLE 3.5.8

Baltic states: Foreign trade by direction, 1992-1993
(Value in million US dollars, growth rates in percentages)

	Exports Value 1992	Exports Value 1993 [a]	Exports Growth 1993	Imports Value 1992	Imports Value 1993 [a]	Imports Growth 1993	Balance 1992	Balance 1993 [a]
Estonia, *to or from:*								
World	444.2	806.8	81.6	410.5	898.2	118.8	33.7	-91.4
Transition economies	226.0	349.4	54.6	192.6	262.8	36.4	33.4	86.6
CIS [b]	154.9	234.1	51.1	164.6	195.8	19.0	-9.7	38.3
Baltic states	53.8	94.0	74.7	21.9	54.1	147.0	31.9	39.9
Eastern Europe	17.3	21.3	23.1	5.2	12.9	148.7	12.1	8.4
Developed market economies	205.7	433.4	110.7	208.9	610.3	192.1	-3.2	-176.9
Developing countries	12.5	24.0	92.7	9.0	25.1	178.9	3.5	-1.1
Latvia, *to or from:*								
World	843.1	1 039.4	23.3	794.1	959.2	20.8	49.0	80.2
Transition economies	456.2	587.4	28.8	401.2	509.4	27.0	55.0	78.0
CIS [b]	376.7	476.4	26.5	297.7	362.1	21.6	79.0	114.3
Baltic states	41.3	62.1	50.4	75.6	128.1	69.4	-34.3	-66.0
Eastern Europe	38.2	48.9	28.0	27.9	19.2	-31.2	10.3	29.7
Developed market economies	348.0	355.4	2.1	275.2	284.0	3.2	72.8	71.4
Developing countries [c]	38.9	96.6	148.3	117.7	165.8	40.9	-78.8	-69.2
Lithuania, *to or from:*								
World	852.3	1 171.1	37.4	601.9	1 054.4	75.2	250.4	116.7
Transition economies	659.7	936.6	42.0	502.6	914.2	81.9	157.1	22.4
CIS [b]	559.1	734.9	31.4	476.1	887.0	86.3	83.0	-152.1
Baltic states	50.3	149.7	197.6	17.5	15.9	-9.1	32.8	133.8
Eastern Europe	50.3	52.0	3.4	9.0	11.3	25.6	41.3	40.7
Developed market economies	180.6	221.5	22.6	92.7	123.0	32.7	116.9	98.5
Developing countries	12.0	13.0	8.3	6.6	17.2	160.6	-23.6	-4.2
Baltic states, *to or from:*								
World	2 139.6	3 017.3	41.0	1 806.5	2 911.8	61.2	333.1	105.5
Transition economies	1 341.9	1 873.4	39.6	1 096.4	1 686.4	53.8	245.5	187.0
CIS [b]	1 090.6	1 445.5	32.5	938.4	1 444.8	54.0	152.2	0.7
Baltic states	145.4	305.8	110.3	115.0	198.2	72.3	30.4	107.6
Eastern Europe	105.8	122.2	15.5	42.1	43.4	3.1	63.7	78.8
Developed market economies	734.3	1 010.3	37.6	576.8	1 017.3	76.4	157.5	-7.0
Developing countries	63.4	133.6	110.7	133.3	208.1	56.1	-69.9	-74.5

Sources: National statistics and direct communications to ECE.

[a] Preliminary data for Estonia and Lithuania.
[b] Including Georgia.
[c] Including non-allocated transactions.

important.[211] Large inflows of new technology and raw materials resulted from these activities – about $78 million according to the Estonian customs data. Roughly half of all imports from the three western trade partners in the first half of 1993 consisted of machinery, equipment, vehicles, mineral products and chemicals. The improved technology and higher quality of inputs, as well as the market access and marketing knowledge acquired through joint ventures, created the possibility to expand western exports as well. While the metals and metal products that in the first half of 1993 accounted for almost a quarter of the exports to these three countries (12 per cent of total export and up by 1 point compared with 1992) were mainly *re-export* items, the other two leading export commodities were timber and timber products (18 per cent of exports to the west and 9 per cent of total exports) and textile and textile products (17 per cent of western and 12 per cent of total exports). These products originate in Estonia, and were traditionally exported along with agricultural products. For this reason Estonia has proposed to negotiate a separate protocol on textiles and processed foods, now under discussion as an addendum to its free trade agreement with the EU.

Similar changes, but at a lower level, characterized the foreign trade of *Latvia*. In 1993, the share of CIS countries decreased to 46 and 38 per cent of exports and imports, respectively. Russia's share was about 28 per cent in both exports and imports. Mineral products made up 52 per cent of imports, and here the CIS countries were the main contributors. In the structure of Latvian exports to the CIS countries, machinery, equipment and vehicles

---

[211] The number of registered joint ventures and the amount of foreign investments in Estonia were the highest among the Baltic states. As of end-June 1993, there were 4,052 joint ventures in operation in Estonia (as against 2,700 and 2,638 in Latvia and Lithuania, respectively) and foreign direct investment in Estonia during the first half of 1993 reached $78 per capita (only $22 in Lithuania).

accounted for 38 per cent, agriculture products and foodstuffs for 20 per cent, and textile and textile products for 16 per cent.

In western trade, EU and EFTA countries were the main partners – altogether they received 33 per cent of total Latvian exports and contributed 28 per cent on the import side. Germany was the most important trade partner, followed by Sweden and the Netherlands. The first two had a pre-war tradition of trading with Latvia and now have established sea-ferry connections with Riga and Ventspils. Germany also became the main foreign investor in Latvia.[212] As in the case of Estonia, about 60 per cent of Latvia's imports from western Europe consisted of machinery, vehicles, mineral products and chemicals. In exports, crude oil and petroleum products dominated (53 per cent of exports to the west and 22 per cent of total exports). This reflects *re-export* of Russian oil, mainly through the Ventspils terminal, as Latvia neither produces oil nor refines it. Timber and timber products were the second most important commodity group in exports to western Europe, and textiles and textile products the third. The last two groups of goods had been also, as in Estonia, traditional exports during the pre-war period.

Lithuania's situation was somewhat different. The CIS share in exports dropped to 63 per cent, but in imports the country is still fully dependent on fuel, gas and other raw material supplies from Russia, Kazakhstan and Ukraine. The trade deficit with Russia reached $275 million in 1993, and the CIS still accounted for 84 per cent of total imports. More than 83 per cent of Lithuania's imports from the CIS countries (and about 73 per cent of total imports) consisted of crude petroleum and some petroleum products. These high petroleum imports were not just for internal use: Lithuania has one of the biggest oil refineries in post-Soviet countries and still refines and exports back to Russia considerable amounts of oil products (about 40 per cent of exports to Russia). The oil products are also important in exports to Latvia and Belarus.

In exports to the west, the share of fuels, mineral products and metals has doubled in 1993, but accounted for only 9 per cent. Since the Soviet period, western countries bought from Lithuania mainly chemical products (basically fertilizers), which accounted for 20 per cent of exports in the first half of 1993,[213] and foodstuffs, 18 per cent of export to the west (31 per cent in 1992). In contrast witht Estonia, which has Finland as a close neighbour (both in a geographical and cultural sense), Lithuania lacked interest for foreign investors and trading companies up to 1993. The steep economic contraction, high inflation rate, and unstable government (six governments since independence) made it the least attractive among the three Baltic states. Foreign direct investment amounted to only $50 million (13 dollars per capita) in 1992, almost half of which was from the CIS countries and Poland. In 1993 foreign investment doubled, the main contributions coming from the United States, Great Britain and Germany.[214] That again caused an increase in the share of manufactured goods in imports from the west (machinery, vehicles, chemicals up to 51 per cent) and also gave a push to exports, consisting of 70 per cent of manufactured goods (chemical products, building materials, timber and timber products, textiles).

The *mutual trade* of the Baltic countries was some $200-$300 million in 1993, 7-10 per cent of total trade.[215] Historically, intra-Baltic trade has never exceeded 10 per cent of these countries' total trade. With rather similar industrial structures, formerly highly integrated with the Soviet economy, and a specialization in meat and dairy products, the Baltic countries see each other more as competitors in foreign trade than as trading partners. Even in the pre-war period there was very little cooperation among them. Nevertheless, in the face of the regional approach of the EU and the concern of western companies that their individual markets are too small (and too closed) to be of interest, they finally considered the importance of facilitating mutual trade. Thus, a Free Trade Agreement was concluded on 13 September 1993 and will come into force on 1 April 1994, after ratification by all three parliaments. The unification of custom procedures and the lifting of visa requirements have started as well. However, the Free Trade Agreement does not apply to agricultural produce, and some tariffs and quotas still remain. The economic significance of the agreement might be limited in the beginning, but it is a good start of economic cooperation and further economic integration for the three small countries.

The systemic and policy decisions taken by the Baltic countries in 1992 and at the beginning of 1993, such as initial devaluations, currency convertibility and trade liberalization, were the basis for export growth in 1993. However, as the experience of some other reforming countries show, this impact could be short-term. Only serious structural changes will support further growth of foreign trade. Restructuring of industry, less energy-consuming technologies, increased productivity and better marketing skills must provide the basis to increase the competitiveness of the Baltic producers and exporters and to keep exports growing.[216]

---

[212] By October 1993, German investors accounted for more than $27 million, or about 28 per cent of total foreign investment (*Estonia, Latvia, Lithuania – EIU Country Report*, 4th Quarter 1993, p.28).

[213] The UK Fertilizer Manufacturers Association and France (controlling 86 per cent of the west European ammonium nitrate market) recently tried unsuccessfully to impose anti-dumping duties on Lithuanian exports of fertilizers (*East European Report*, 23 January 1994). If this points to some weight of Lithuanian fertilizers in the west European market, it also threatens further export growth.

[214] During 1993, 457 joint ventures with EU countries were established in Lithuania. Up to 1991, foreign investments came to about $50 million, another $50 million was invested in 1992, and $100 million in 1993. Major countries were the United States ($38 million), Great Britain ($33 million), Germany ($22 million). See *Lietuvos Aidas*, 26 January 1994.

[215] The range stems from the discrepancy between export and import levels in table 3.5.8, which of course in this closed triangle should be identical.

[216] The significant real appreciation of the Baltic currencies, after steep initial devaluations, may turn out to be unsustainable in the longer run.

(v) Trade imbalances and trade policies: Some tentative conclusions

Most of the transition economies recorded significant shifts in their trade which resulted in large imbalances in 1993. In eastern Europe, a marked growth of trade deficits was the characteristic feature; in Russia and some other CIS countries, large trade surpluses arose. These opposite trends raise questions concerning both their desirability and sustainability.

In eastern Europe, quite different trends in exports and imports contributed to the growth of trade deficits. In some economies it was mainly a decline of exports that produced the deficits, while in others import growth outpaced that of exports.

In the latter group, which includes Poland and the Czech Republic, shifts in the composition of imports towards capital goods could be observed, implying that the imbalances are by and large desirable as contributions to the restructuring of the economies concerned. In some other countries in the region, it is not simply the fall of exports but also the lack of a clear shift towards imports for investments that may raise doubts concerning the economic "justification" of the deficits.

However, even with increasing exports and favourable changes in the structure of imports, the trade deficits may be unsustainable. This holds for Poland, and perhaps yet more strongly for Hungary (with its export decline) and those other east European countries where exports fell and there were no clear signs of economic restructuring (growth of investment goods imports). Still, the countries with increasing exports and imports of capital goods should have better prospects than others for sustaining their trade imbalances. If this were not the case, the emerging recovery in these economies would be blocked, involving extremely discouraging prospects for the transition process in the whole region.

The trade *surplus* of Russia and several CIS countries raises similar questions. Taking due account of the statistical uncertainties, it is clear that the surplus in foreign trade in these countries results from the decline of imports, which is neither desirable nor sustainable in the longer run. The less so, since sooner or later it is likely to lead to the contraction of exports as well. This reversal is already visible in a number of CIS countries, and it may also reach Russia, if the fall of production and imports continues.

In almost all transition economies, irrespective of the sign and magnitude of their trade imbalance, some steps have recently been taken to increase the protection of domestic activities from foreign competition. In some countries tariffs have been raised or duties were introduced on imported goods, while in others quality requirements for imported products have been tightened. These measures may indicate some reversal of the liberal trade policies which prevailed in most transition countries. However, their new trade and tariff regimes have in some cases initially indeed been extremely liberal, perhaps unseasonably so at the early stages of the transition process. In fact, the exceptionally strong (system-inherent) protection provided to industries under central planning was removed very abruptly; and perhaps the overall macroeconomic conditions of the transition economies justify some protection for domestic activities that have a hope for survival. At the same time, however, it must also be noted that in some instances undesirable protectionist impulses are on the rise, which can threaten the health of the transformation process.

3.6 Balance of payments, reserves and debt

(i) Overview

The external financial positions of the transition economies tended to weaken in 1993.[217] Export performance flagged while import growth was generally strong and, as a result, balance-of-payments current accounts deteriorated and foreign debt increased. Although official reserves generally strengthened, those of many countries remained inadequate, in part because of their failure to qualify for official financing (see section 4.1). Aside from the significant improvement in its current account, Russia shared in these developments.

Through the first three quarters of 1992, the external sector had been the bright spot for several economies in transition. The former Czechoslovakia, Hungary, and Poland had experienced sustained export booms (although the export growth of the latter two countries was slowing), current accounts were in surplus and external reserves were increasing. Hungary repaid some of its foreign debt, while Poland benefited from the debt reduction scheme agreed with the Paris Club. Export growth was expected to further reduce debt burdens.

While the external performance of the Czech Republic remained good, for other countries the picture changed in 1993, with possible implications for future growth and financing. Already in late 1992, there was a general deterioration in the current-account balances of the transition countries, which continued in 1993 and left many in deficit (table 3.6.1).[218] For eastern Europe as a whole, the current account moved from near balance in 1992 to a deficit of almost $8 billion in 1993, mainly because of movements in the accounts of Hungary, Poland and Slovenia. The results were worse than had been expected in early 1993, when the authorities of these countries had projected deficits of only $200 and $600 million and a surplus of $700 million, respectively. In general, the worsening of current account positions was due to weakening trade balances, the result of stagnant or contracting exports receipts and rising imports.[219]

The situation in Russia also developed differently than had been anticipated, although in this case the current account moved from deficit to a large surplus, due largely to a significant increase in the trade surplus. In Estonia and Lithuania, the only other republics of the former USSR for which data were available for 1993, current account surpluses declined.

The external indebtedness of most eastern countries increased in 1993 (table 3.6.2). However, the impact of new borrowing and, in certain cases, the accumulation of arrears was partially offset by the valuation effect due to the appreciation of the US dollar (which tends to reduce the dollar value of the debt).[220]

In 1993, the policies of the transition economies aimed to further strengthen foreign currency positions (table 3.6.3). At the turn of the decade most of these countries had embarked on economic reform with depleted reserves and some progress was made in the following years. In general, foreign currency reserves continued to increase in 1993, due to borrowing, spontaneous capital inflows and, in some instances new payments arrears. However, in many cases reserves remained below expectations and, also, below the recommended three months' coverage imports of goods and services (i.e., a reserves-imports ratio of 25 per cent; table 3.6.4). The unfavourable development of current account balances and failure of some countries to conclude agreements with the IMF were contributing factors (see section 4.1).

(ii) Results by country

The external financial positions of the transition economies continued to show considerable diversity in 1993, although on the whole they remained relatively weak. In the following discussion, these countries have been grouped according to standard financial indicators and the recent performance of their external sectors. These groupings do not necessarily reflect the financial markets' perceptions of eastern countries' current creditworthiness (see section 4.1).

The Czech Republic is alone in a first group as the only country whose financial position, already favourable at the outset of 1993, improved markedly during the course of the year.[221] Continuing strong export growth led to an unexpectedly large current account surplus (a surplus of

---

[217] Although the availability of external financial statistics of the transition economies has improved, adequate coverage remains a problem in many countries, particularly in the CIS. Publication of data by some countries is irregular at best. Methodologies applied in balance of payments statistics and definitions of debt continue to vary from country to country and sometimes are changed in successive reporting periods without explanation. The problems of customs trade statistics, which some countries use in their balance of payments accounts, are discussed in section 3.5.

[218] The adverse impact of the UN Security Council economic sanctions against the FR Yugoslavia on the trade of several transition countries has already been noted in section 3.5. In addition the sanctions have been blamed for losses of revenues from transport, tourism and other services and higher transport costs. The repercussions appear to have the greatest for the financially weak countries in the region. National estimates of the losses due to sanctions, which often run into billions of US dollars, were presented in United Nations Economic Commission for Europe, *Economic Bulletin for Europe*, Vol.45 (1993), Geneva and New York, 1994.

[219] It should be recalled that this section is based on balance of payments statistics, for which merchandise trade data are generally collected on a cash basis. They may differ significantly from the customs data used in section 3.5. This is strikingly so in Poland, where cash flow data show a *decline* in export receipts, while customs data indicate a continuing *rise* in export deliveries.

[220] The valuation effect stems from the fact that a large share of eastern debt is denominated in non-dollar currencies, while total debt is measured in a common currency, the US dollar.

[221] The uncertainty surrounding the dissolution of Czechoslovakia had led to a substantial loss of reserves in late 1992, which continued to adversely affect the new Czech and Slovak Republics in early 1993. In both countries this tendency was subsequently reversed.

TABLE 3.6.1

Convertible currency current account balances of transition countries, 1990-1993

(Million US dollars)

	1990	1991	1992	January-September 1992	January-September 1993	1993	Projections 1994
Albania [a]	-95	-167	-49	-30*	-50*	-92 [b]	-105
Excluding official transfers	-97	-250	-439	..	..	-440 [b]	-380
Bulgaria [a]	-1 152	-887	-297	-181*	-575* [c]	-800* [c]	..
Cash basis [d]	..	-77	451	381	62 [c]	..	..
Croatia [a]	-500*	-589	329	331	-76	-100*	..
Czech Republic	492	1 143	53	30*	556	637 [e]	300-450
Hungary	127	267	324	853	-2 484	-3 455	..
Poland	716	-1 359	-269	279	-2 330	-2 329	..
Romania	-1 650	-1 369	-1 460	-770	-810 [a]	-1 526	-780 [a]
Slovakia	-612	-786	172	130*	60	–	..
Slovenia [a]	680 [f]	315 [f]	932	857	-9	-17 [e]	150
The FYR of Macedonia [a]	-400	-262	-11	-10	-50	-71 [b]	-44
Yugoslavia (FR)	..	-35	-1 284	..	..	..	-616
Eastern Europe [f]	-3 498	-3 694	-276	1 489	-5 768	-7 753	..
Belarus	..	..	372	..	..	..	..
Moldova	..	-476	-22	..	..	..	..
Russia [a,g]	-4 500	3 500	-2 700	-4 400	..	15 100	..
Ukraine	..	..	..	..	..	..	..
Estonia [a]	..	..	153	129	84	125	..
Latvia [a]	..	..	50	..	..	..	..
Lithuania [a]	..	..	322	260	167	..	..
Former Soviet Union [g]							
All currencies	-21 000	-3 300	-7 600 [b]	..	..	..	..
Convertible currencies	-4 800	-800	..	..	..	..	..

Sources: National statistics; IMF, Russian Federation, *Economic Review*, April 1992 and *International Financial Statistics*, Supplement on countries of the former Soviet Union, Supplement Series No.16, 1993; World Bank, *Russian Economic Reform*, September 1992; ECE estimates.

[a] All currencies.
[b] Projection.
[c] For 1993 merchandise trade is also on a cash basis; see text.
[d] Includes only interest paid.
[e] January-November.
[f] Excluding transactions with Yugoslavia (FR).
[g] Including gold sales (but excluding gold swaps and grants). Excludes inter-republican trade.

$200 million had been forecast),[222] which, together with inflows of equity capital (see section 4.1) and modest foreign borrowing boosted foreign currency reserves to nearly five months' import coverage). Although gross debt increased, the low debt burden[223] (table 3.6.4) declined even further.

All other east European countries experienced a deterioration of their current account balances.

A second group includes countries with low debt burdens and, in general, insufficient, although generally improving, reserves positions. It can be divided according to export performance.

In Estonia and Lithuania receipts from goods and services increased rapidly in 1993, nearly doubling in the former. However, since expenditures increased even faster (doubling in both), their current account surpluses declined. These surpluses and net inflows of capital allowed the authorities to raise foreign currency reserves, which exceed their low external debts. However, only Estonia has reserves which cover more than three months' expenditure on goods and services.[224]

Romania, Slovakia, and three republics of the former Yugoslavia, Croatia, Slovenia and the Former Yugoslav Republic of Macedonia, experienced stagnant or declining export receipts and increased expenditures on imports. As a result their current account deficits grew or their surpluses were eliminated. In most cases reserves increased, which contributed to the decline of the debt burden of Croatia, Slovakia and Slovenia. In 1993 Romania incurred the fourth consecutive annual current account deficit of some $1.5 billion. It was financed chiefly by guaranteed credits and short-term borrowing.[225]

---

[222] The Czech Republic's current account surplus in 1993 (table 3.6.1) is even larger if transactions with Slovakia are included. These show a surplus of some $200 million (excluding official transfers). The Czech Republic experienced a large deficit on official transfers (nearly $600 million) which reflects an exceptional once and for all adjustment of property claims between the two countries.

[223] The debt burden is measured by the ratio of net debt to exports of goods and services (table 3.6.4).

[224] The Baltic states' debts are entirely recent, as on regaining independence their new governments refused to assume responsibility for the debts contracted by the former Soviet Union.

[225] In 1990 and part of 1991, the current account deficits had been financed by reserve reduction.

TABLE 3.6.2

External debt in convertible currencies of the transition countries, 1990-1993
(Billion US dollars, end-of-period)

	Gross debt				Net debt			
	1990	1991	1992	1993	1990	1991	1992	1993
Albania	0.3	0.5	0.7	0.8 [a]	0.1	0.4	0.6	0.7 [a]
Bulgaria	10.4	11.9	13.0	13.2*	10.4	11.5	12.1	12.5
Croatia [b]	2.5	2.7	2.5	2.5 [c]	2.4	2.5	2.0	1.8 [c]
Czech Republic	4.4	7.5	7.5	8.7	3.5	5.0	4.0	2.7
Hungary	21.3	22.7	21.4	24.6	20.2	18.7	17.1	17.9
Poland	48.5	48.4	47.1	46.8 [d]	44.0	44.8	43.1	43.0 [d]
Romania	0.2	1.1	2.4	3.3	-0.1	0.7	1.5	2.3
Slovakia	1.5	1.8	2.3	2.9	1.3	1.3	1.6	1.2
Slovenia [b]	1.9	1.9	1.7	1.9	1.5	1.5	0.6	0.3
The FYR of Macedonia [b,e]	0.5	0.4	0.7	0.9	0.5	0.4	0.7	0.9
Eastern Europe	91.5	98.9	99.3	105.6	83.8	86.9	83.3	83.3
Moldova	..	..	..	0.2	..	..	..	..
Russia [f]	61.1	65.3	80.8 [g]	85*	59.5	64.3	78.8	79*
Estonia	..	..	-	0.1	..	..	-	-0.3
Lithuania	..	..	-	0.1	..	..	-0.1	-0.2

Sources: National statistics; ECE secretariat estimates and table 3.6.3 for foreign exchange.

Note: Net debt equals gross debt less total foreign currency reserves, or if the latter are not available, reserves held by the central bank.

[a] Projection.
[b] Allocated medium- and long-term debt only (see text). Comparable debt of Bosnia-Herzegovina and the FR Yugoslavia in 1962 was $1.5 billion and $5.3 billion, respectively.
[c] September.
[d] November.
[e] Since reserves are not available, net debt equals gross debt.
[f] Prior to 1991, debt of former Soviet Union.
[g] Excluding US Lend Lease debt (about $800 million).

Foreign currency reserves held by the national bank amounted to only $41 million at the end of the year. Despite the deterioration of Slovakia's current account, it none the less developed better than had been expected at the beginning of the year.[226] The current account surplus actually increased during the first six months and narrowed thereafter, due to the widening of the trade deficit, but was still slightly in surplus for January-September. This, and various inflows of capital and some borrowing from the IMF, enabled the authorities to boost reserves to nearly five months' import coverage (end-September).

Attention is drawn to the fact that the official external debt figures for Croatia, Slovenia and the FYR of Macedonia presented in table 3.6.2 reflect only part of the debt for which these countries are liable, i.e., only the "attributable" component of the medium-and long-term debt.[227] Adjusting the debts of these three countries to take into account the "unallocated" debt of the former SFR Yugoslavia would not raise them (and estimates of debt-export ratios) by much. Although the debt burdens of Croatia and the FYR of Macedonia are relatively low, both countries are in arrears on servicing their debts. This allowed them to increase their reserves in 1993.[228]

A third group consists of Bulgaria, Hungary and Poland, moderate to highly indebted countries, which experienced stagnant or declining receipts from goods and services, increasing expenditures and comparatively large current account deficits in 1993. The reserve positions of Bulgaria and Poland weakened.

Hungary's creditworthiness (see section 4.1) allowed the authorities to borrow record amounts in 1993, which, together with inflows of equity capital, financed the current account deficit and a large increase in reserves (to over five months' import coverage).[229] However, the external debt and the debt-export ratio rebounded, the latter also due to the decline in exports of goods and services. In the two preceding years Hungary had made substantial progress in reducing its debt burden, by repaying debt and, especially, by increasing convertible currency export receipts. The

---

[226] It is not known whether the current account data for Slovakia include transactions with the Czech Republic.

[227] The problem stems from the fact that the repartition of the external liabilities of the former Socialist Federal Republic of Yugoslavia remains to be agreed by the successor states. According to data which had been provided by the National Bank of SFR Yugoslavia, the medium- and long-term debt of the former SFR Yugoslavia was $15 billion at the end of 1991. Of this amount, $12 billion was directly attributable to legal entities based on the territories of the individual republics and autonomous provinces (so-called allocated debt). The remaining $3.1 billion was incurred for use by the federation without ascertainable beneficiaries (unallocated debt). Centre for International Cooperation and Development, *Economic Developments in Slovenia in 1993*, Ljubljana, September 1993, p.13.

[228] The FYR of Macedonia has not published data on the level of its reserves. However, a build-up of reserves is shown in its balance of payments statistics.

[229] Hungary's reserves increased by around $600 million in December 1993, due to a single $875 million equity investment (see section 4.1). This increase in reserves had the effect of holding down the country's net debt, since there was no corresponding increase in liabilities.

TABLE 3.6.3

Foreign currency reserves (FCR) and BIS deposits of transition countries, 1989-1993

(Billion US dollars, end-of-period)

	1989	1990	1991	1992	1993 [a]
Albania					
FCR	0.42	0.22	0.09	0.08	..
BIS	0.31	0.22	0.03	0.07	0.10
Bulgaria					
FCR [b]	..	–	0.31	0.86	0.70 [c]
BIS	1.18	0.58	1.03	1.40	1.32
Croatia					
FCR	..	..	0.20	0.50	0.75
FCR [b]	..	..	–	0.17	0.48
Czech Republic					
FCR	..	..	..	3.46	6.00 [c]
FCR [b]	..	..	..	0.73	3.70 [c]
Hungary					
FCR	1.25	1.07	3.94	4.35	6.69 [c]
BIS	1.18	1.78	3.74	2.84	2.32
Poland					
FCR [b]	2.31	4.49	3.62	4.10	3.54 [d]
BIS	3.95	7.82	5.14	7.51	6.64
Romania					
FCR	1.76	0.37	0.37	0.82	1.00 [c]
FCR [b]	..	..	..	..	0.04 [c]
BIS	1.84	0.58	0.58	0.74	0.90
Slovakia					
FCR	..	..	..	0.72	1.67
FCR [b]	..	..	..	0.34	0.42
Slovenia					
FCR	..	0.27	0.37	1.16	1.57
FCR [b]	–	–	0.11	0.72	0.80 [c]
The FYR of Macedonia					
FCR	..	..	..	0.04	0.13
Former Czechoslovakia					
FCR	2.16	1.10	3.05	4.18	..
FCR [b]	..	..	1.54 [e]	1.08	..
BIS	2.20	1.35	2.80	3.82	4.33
Former Yugoslavia					
FCR	4.14	5.46	2.68	1.48 [a]	..
BIS	7.07	7.98	5.05	4.66	3.87
Estonia [f]					
FCR	..	..	..	0.21	0.38 [c]
Lithuania					
FCR	..	..	..	0.17	0.27
Former Soviet Union					
FCR	..	..	–	2	6-7
BIS	14.70	8.63	8.87	14.21	17.70

Sources: National statistics; BIS, *International Banking and Financial Market Developments*, Basle, February 1994; IMF, *International Financial Statistics*, Washington, D.C., February 1994.

Note: BIS: Deposits held with BIS reporting banks.

[a] September.
[b] Holdings of the national bank only.
[c] December.
[d] November.
[e] February 1991.
[f] Total reserves and holdings of national bank, including gold.

---

adjusted to utilize merchandise trade statistics reported on a cash basis (i.e., on the basis of payments made through banks), to maintain comparability with preceding years.[230] These trade data result in a more favourable current account performance than is shown in the National Bank's primary presentation does. The other departure from that presentation in table 3.6.1 involves the inclusion of all interest due, which yields a higher current account deficit.[231] In 1993 the deficit was financed primarily by arrears on interest payments and, to a lesser extent, by reserves and official credits. In consequence the debt of Bulgaria continued to increase and foreign currency reserves, which were to have been strengthened with the help of an IMF standby credit that eventually was not finalized (see section 4.1), remain inadequate.

Poland's export receipts declined marginally in 1993 while imports continued to rise.[232] The devaluation of the zloty in August 1993 appears to have only temporarily stemmed the growth of the current account deficit, which was financed through an accumulation of interest arrears on commercial debt, inflows of equity capital, some repatriation of assets from abroad and a further rundown of reserves (reduced to less than three months' import coverage). In 1992, a write-off of principal (on Paris Club obligations) reduced Poland's convertible currency debt; the small further decline in 1993 is a valuation effect (estimated at some $1.6 billion) reflecting the appreciation of the US dollar. It offset the impact on debt of the capitalization of interest arrears on commercial obligations and the use of some new credits.

Russia's financial position can be discussed only in broad terms due to incomplete information and uncertainty surrounding the official statistics. After registering a deficit of nearly $3 billion in 1992, the current account of Russia swung into surplus in 1993, apparently of the order of $15 billion.[233] This resulted primarily from the increase in the trade surplus from $4.2 billion to $13.8 billion,[234]

small devaluations of the forint in the latter part of 1993 did not stem the growth of the current account deficit which exceeded $3 billion for the whole year.

It should be noted that the official data on Bulgaria's current account balance for 1993 (table 3.6.1) were

---

[230] Through 1992 the National Bank of Bulgaria provided balance of payments statistics which included merchandise trade reported on a *cash* basis. In 1993, however, current account data provided by the Bank include merchandise trade statistics from *customs* sources (exports $2,503 million, imports $2,903 million and a trade *deficit* of $400 million in the first three quarters of 1993). An explanation for this change in reporting is not given. In a note to the balance of payments statement, the Bank also provides trade data on a cash flow basis (exports, $3,132 million; imports $2,914 million, and a trade *surplus* of $219 million), and these have been incorporated in table 3.6.1.

[231] The adjustment reflecting interest due was made in conformity with IMF recommendations. The National Bank of Bulgaria reports only interest paid (i.e., on a cash settlements basis).

[232] As noted above, customs statistics show a further rise in Poland's exports, by some 7 per cent in dollar terms in the first three quarters of 1993 (also see section 3.5).

[233] RF Goskomstat, *Sotsialno-ekonomicheskoe polozhenie* ..., op. cit.

[234] The trade data used in the balance of payments statement are: for 1992, exports $41.1 billion, imports $36.9 billion, and trade balance $4.2 billion; for 1993, exports $43 billion, imports $29.2 billion and trade balance $13.8 billion. In 1992 exports contain sales of gold, which is presumably also the case in 1993. In 1993, imports contain $2.2 billion of humanitarian and technical assistance, which is also presumably the case in 1992. As discussed in section 3.5, Russia's trade statistics are at best preliminary estimates of somewhat uncertain coverage.

TABLE 3.6.4

Net debt-exports and reserves-imports ratios of transition countries, 1990-1993
(Per cent)

	Net debt-export ratio				Foreign currency reserves-import ratio			
	1990	1991	1992	1993*	1990	1991	1992	1993*
Albania	36	495	742	887	45	26	12	12
Bulgaria	311	275	202	206	-	7	15	12
Croatia [a]	53	55	44	37	2	4	11	13
Czech Republic	50	61	36	19	16	36	30	45
Hungary	227	157	124	151	11	31	30	43
Poland	361	312	265	269	44	26	25	21
Romania	-4	17	31	45	7	7	13	15
Slovakia	48	40	35	29	5	13	17	38
Slovenia [a]	20	19	7	4	6	5	16	21
The FYR of Macedonia [a,b]	42	33	56	78	..	..	..	..
Eastern Europe	162	145	118	118	15	20	22	28
Russia [c]	72	121	214	158	2	2	6	16
Estonia [d]	..	..	6	-22	..	..	36	32
Lithuania	..	..	-14	-11	..	..	25	20

Sources: ECE secretariat estimates based on national sources; tables 3.6.2 and 3.6.3.

Note: Net debt equals gross debt less total foreign currency reserves. Exports and imports include convertible currency merchandise trade and services.

[a] Allocated medium- and long-term debt only (see text).
[b] Gross debt-export ratio.
[c] Prior to 1992, debt of former Soviet Union. Except for 1993 exports and imports reflect only merchandise.
[d] Reflects foreign currency reserves including gold.

and, to a lesser extent, to smaller net payments for services and investments.[235]

Official data on Russia's foreign currency reserves and convertible currency debt in 1993 do not appear to have been published. By the end of 1992, the convertible currency debt of the Russian Federation (now responsible for the entire debt of the former Soviet Union) is reported to have risen to $80.8 billion,[236] although lower figures have also been cited.[237] A further increase in 1993 is probable, perhaps to the $85 billion reported in the western press.[238] This would be due to the capitalization of interest arrears, new medium-term borrowing, and drawing of the $1.5 billion tranche of the IMF Systemic Transformation Facility (STF) in 1993, partially offset by valuation effects (due to the appreciation of the US dollar) and some repayment of debt. The *total* debt of Russia is reported to have reached around $90 billion, of which over $80 billion appears to be due to the west and the remaining $10 billion (which presumably includes obligations originally contracted in convertible currencies) to the east European countries.[239]

Balance of payments data indicate that the official net reserves of Russia increased by $3.3 billion in 1993. Since this includes the $1.5 billion tranche of the IMF STF, gross foreign currency reserves increased by an estimated $4.8 billion, perhaps to a level of some $6-7 billion.[240] This was made possible by the current account surplus, recourse to some new credits, and the low level of debt service payments.

A continuation of significant capital flight is suggested by the balance of payments figures for 1993. The $7.6 billion "errors and omissions" item is reported to include exports of capital.[241] Because of its very nature, capital flight is difficult to measure.[242] Estimates of such

---

[235] Russia's deficit on services declined from $4 billion in 1992 to $0.5 billion in 1993, while the deficit on (net) investment income diminished from $4.5 billion to $1.6 billion. The latter improvement presumably results from the accrual (but not necessarily cash receipts) of higher interest income in 1993 from Russia's large foreign assets. As with the trade figures, the year-to-year comparability of these elements of Russia's balance of payments is uncertain.

[236] This figure excludes outstanding balances on clearing accounts in convertible currencies, barter operations, lend-lease debt and external debt to the countries of eastern Europe, including the former GDR. GATT, "Accession of the Russian Federation", Memorandum on the Foreign Trade Regime (from the Ministry of Foreign Affairs of the Russian Federation), L/7410, 1 March 1994.

[237] For example, a convertible currency debt of $77.7 billion (end 1992) has been estimaited. See article by J. Mikhailov in *Rossiiskaya Gazeta*, 5 June 1993.

[238] Among other sources, the $85 billion debt figure was cited in *International Herald Tribune*, 17 January 1994. In September 1993, the Russian authorities provided financial information to western creditors which included a debt estimate of around $80 billion. *Financial Times*, 24 September 1993. Other important details were made available. Presumably the figure excludes lend-lease obligations to the United States.

[239] *Rossiiskie Vesti*, 23 March 1994. The $80 billion includes most of the debt of the former USSR and $10 billion contracted by the Russian Federation during 1993-1994.

[240] The Russian Federation's currency reserves are reported to have increased to $5-6 billion by early September 1993. (Former Russian Minister of Finance B. Fyodorov, quoted in *Wall Street Journal*, 7 September 1993.?

[241] RF Goskomstat, *Sotsialno-ekonomicheskoe polozhenie* ..., op. cit., p.89.

[242] It should be noted that capital flight as measured by "errors and omissions" reflects the accuracy of the individual elements of the balance of payments, including that of merchandise trade. Thus, for example, if

outflows from Russia vary significantly, but are generally higher than the figure given above. For example the Russian Federal State Customs Committee estimates that the country was losing more than $10 billion annually because export receipts were not being remitted to Russia.[243] These funds are believed to enter accounts which are often beyond the control of the Russian monetary authorities. Such outflows are partially reflected in the build-up of BIS bank liabilities *vis-à-vis* the former USSR (i.e., the deposits in western banks of citizens, enterprises and banks domiciled in the successor states and of their monetary authorities).[244] These deposits rose rapidly in 1992, mostly in the second half of the year when the rouble depreciated steeply, increasing the incentive to transfer funds abroad, and further in 1993, reaching nearly $18 billion by the end of June 1993 (table 3.6.3).[245]

Capital flight had important implications for the Russian economy in 1993, contributing to an outflow of resources (see section 4.1) and a decrease in domestic absorption. It is likely that the authorities' inability to access these funds partially explains the decision to cut back so-called "centralized critical imports" (see section 3.5). While the reduction of these imports may have been desirable, the economized funds could have been used to increase foreign currency reserves which remain relatively low.

(iii) Concluding observations

With some exceptions, the external financial positions of the eastern countries weakened in 1993. Some worsening of current account balances had been foreseen, in reflection *inter alia* of exchange rate policies which tended to produce a further appreciation of real exchange rates and, in certain countries, of economic recovery. However, cessation of export growth in a number of countries had not been anticipated and import expansion appears to have surpassed expectations. In most cases, the deterioration of current accounts was due to additional expenditures on the import of goods and services.

Yet imports provide essential support for the transition and economic recovery where it occurred. In many cases, further current account deficits will only be sustainable if the authorities promote policies to revive export growth, including utilization of borrowed funds for the creation of debt servicing capacity. A number of countries took limited policy measures in 1993, e.g., small real devaluations of the currencies, but they may not have been sufficient.

Policies to strengthen export capacity should also help the transition countries to exploit their borrowing potential and help them attract foreign investment. The analysis presented above shows that the debt burdens of several countries are low (two of the Baltic states are net creditors). However, potential creditors look at other indicators, especially commitment to outward looking economic policies and export prospects (see section 4.1).[246] Most countries need to strengthen foreign currency reserves.

The existing debt burdens and recent relatively large current account deficits of Bulgaria, Hungary and Poland are likely to make the implementation of external adjustment policies more pressing. Bulgaria and Poland are or will be benefiting from debt reduction schemes which are intended to help them become creditworthy and access new finance. However, they will only be successful in this regard if their export performance eventually improves in parallel with the build-up of new debt.

In the near term, it appears that a number of countries will need to finance current account deficits. Needless to say, it would be undesirable if financial constraints were to choke off their economic recovery. Without detailed economic projections it is difficult to generalize about financing prospects in the region. However, it appears that Hungary should be able to finance another current account deficit (although probably not on the scale registered in 1993)[247] and make scheduled repayments in 1994. These needs could be met by its high reserves, the $1.1 billion of financing arranged in late 1993 for drawing in 1994 (see section 4.1), and further inflows of equity capital. The availability of these resources may even reduce the demand for new borrowing, which may explain Hungary's absence from the financial markets in early 1994. Bulgaria and Poland may be able to attract more private capital now that they have reached agreement on the reduction of their London Club debt. In 1993 a number of countries faced external financial constraints due to their failure to conclude an agreement with the IMF. Success in this regard in 1994 would give access to the resources of that institution and of others which link their lending to the implementation of IMF programmes.

The financial position of Russia has also developed somewhat differently than expected, with a large current account surplus created chiefly by a sharp fall in imports. An improvement in the current account is normally looked upon favourably. However, the contraction of imports is likely to have adversely affected domestic output. Moreover, the potential benefits of the large current-account surplus (i.e., increasing reserves or lowering of debt) have been foreclosed by massive capital flight.

---

for whatever reason imports are under-reported by customs, as was apparently the case in earlier estimates released by the Russian Federation, capital flight appears correspondingly larger than it actually is. The balance of payments methodology underestimates capital flight if exporters undervalue shipments for customs purposes or if customs totally fail to record export shipments.

[243] Mr. Anatolyi Kruglov, chairman of the Russian Federal State Customs Committee, as reported by ITAR-TASS (BBC, *Summary of World Broadcasts*, SUW/0322 WA/2, 4 March 1994).

[244] The BIS data do not yet distinguish between the republics of the former USSR.

[245] There was, however, no further increase in these deposits in the third quarter of 1993. BIS, *International Banking and Financial Market Developments*, Basle, February, 1994. These data also include the funding of successor states banks' foreign affiliates and the working balances of successor states' enterprises.

[246] Aside from economic considerations, political uncertainty in the region continues to be a deterrent to the involvement of private capital in certain eastern countries.

[247] Even before the full scope of the deterioration in Hungary's current account balance in 1993 was known, some observers opined that raising funds would be more difficult in 1994. See, for example, Mr. W. Riecke, head of the monetary department of the National Bank of Hungary, *Financial Times*, 17 November 1993.

3.7 Macroeconomic policies

(i) Overview of central policy issues

Macroeconomic policies in the transition countries have not changed much in 1993; most countries followed up priorities and targets established in 1991 or 1992. *Price stabilization* remained the key objective for most east European governments, although both the instruments of anti-inflation policy and its efficiency differed between countries. Other objectives put to the forefront by the governments typically included strengthening of domestic currencies, keeping state budgets under control, and reducing unemployment. By contrast, policies aimed at restoring and consolidating external balance seem to have received relatively less attention.

Efforts to clamp down on *inflation* continued to dominate macroeconomic policies in Albania, Bulgaria, the Czech and Slovak Republics, Hungary, Poland, Slovenia, and all three Baltic states, and necessarily implied application of restrictive monetary and fiscal measures. In all these countries inflation receded in 1993, although in most of them it has still remained high by international standards (especially in Bulgaria).

On the other hand, financial policies continued to be more permissive in the CIS states, as well as in FR Yugoslavia, Croatia and Romania, although in the latter two countries new efforts were made towards the end of 1993 to tighten the money supply and bring inflation under control. Even though combatting inflation featured as an important objective in official policy statements of all these countries, it appears also that protection of *employment and output* in ailing state enterprises has been implicitly given at least the same priority. This, however, involved excessive flows of credits and government subsidies to those sectors which were most strongly hit by recession, such as heavy metallurgy, engineering and agriculture. Lack of consistency in macroeconomic policy translated into higher inflation and larger imbalance in public finances, while open unemployment has been kept at relatively low levels.

Anti-inflationary policies in transition countries have been dominated by the "orthodox" measures: restrictions on *money and credit supply* remained the main instrument, while direct price or incomes controls were used only occasionally. However, the efforts to achieve price stabilization have not been very successful: in no country in the region has inflation come down to single-digit annual rates, and progress relative to 1992 was in most cases very modest. That inflation proved to be more persistent than expected was partly a result of much more permissive *budgetary policies* in most transition countries (particularly in Russia, other CIS states, and FR Yugoslavia), and partly reflected pressures coming from cost-side factors, such as increases of regulated energy prices, devaluation of domestic currencies, upward shifts in tax and customs tariff rates. Generally, the inflationary record of transition countries in 1993 seems to suggest that monetary policies alone are of limited use in combatting inflation, and need to be coordinated with other measures, especially in the domain of public finance. A combination of large budget deficits which are bound to be financed mainly from domestic sources, along with reduced real money supply, probably resulted in further contraction of output and compromised efforts to bring inflation under control in countries such as Russia, Ukraine, or Bulgaria.

The issue of *unemployment* received a lot of attention in public discussions, but in no country has the problem of unemployment been addressed with a comprehensive policy package, including such measures as investment incentives or public works programmes.[248] Apart from the all too obvious scarcity of budgetary funds which certainly precludes the undertaking of immediate public works programmes on a larger scale in many countries, the lack of serious actions aimed at reducing the scope of unemployment may have also been caused by controversies over the overall concept and desired degree of government intervention on the labour market.

(ii) Macroeconomic policies in eastern Europe and the Baltic states

(a) Monetary policy

In all transition countries (except FR Yugoslavia) for which monetary statistics are available, monetary policy in 1993 seems to have been rather restrictive if assessed by changes in money stock in real terms (nominal money stock deflated by the CPI). This policy orientation was chiefly dictated by continued efforts to bring inflation under control. None the less, progress on the inflation front in 1993 was rather meagre, which suggests that restrictive monetary policy is not a very efficient anti-inflation tool if budget deficits are large and structural constraints prevent the production sector from adjusting quickly.

The nominal growth of *money supply* has been much lower than the growth of consumer prices and, as a result, the *real* money supply continued to fall in nearly all *east European countries* (table 3.7.1). It is interesting to observe that the monetary contraction in real terms was particularly strong in Romania and Bulgaria, where inflation was highest. The failure to slow inflation in these countries despite the sharp decrease in the real money supply indicates that cost pressures persist, while, in addition, inflationary expectations have still been strong enough to increase the velocity of money circulation.

Both the conduct and the actual results of monetary policies were quite different across the countries concerned. The differences were perhaps most pronounced in the area of interest rate policy and credit allocation. Lax credit policy in Romania and Croatia in 1992 and until

---

[248] Public works programmes were undertaken on a relatively larger scale only in the Czech Republic. As for the other transition countries, the apparent lack of deliberate policy response to unemployment is indeed surprising in the context of the rapidly deteriorating situation on the labour market and growing social discontent.

TABLE 3.7.1

Transition countries: Indices of monetary aggregates in December 1993
(December 1992=100)

	Cash plus demand deposits (M1)	Broad money (M2) [a]	Net domestic assets	Interest rates [b]		
				December 1992	June 1993	December 1993
Albania	..	..	..	..	..	..
Bulgaria	127.3	153.1	147.4	47.7	57.3	63.0
Bosnia-Herzegovina	..	..	..	..	..	..
Croatia	988.8	837.4	903.1	28.3 [c]	25.0 [c]	2.5 [c]
Czech Republic	102.7 [d]	116.7	103.8 [d]	9.5	8.0	8.0
Hungary	110.7 [d]	110.3 [d]	117.6 [d]	21.0	19.0	23.0
Poland	128.2	135.0	132.2	38.0	35.0	35.0
Romania	201.2 [e]	200.5 [e]	194.5 [e]	70.0	70.0	70.0 [e]
Slovakia	..	..	..	..	..	..
Slovenia	130.7 [e]	153.2 [e]	212.8 [e]	25.0	18.0	18.0
The FYR of Macedonia	..	..	..	..	..	..
Yugoslavia (FR)	21 700 [f]	..	7 600.0 [f,g]	..	..	..
Belarus	..	..	..	..	240.0	..
Moldova	..	..	..	..	..	..
Russia	219.9	249.4	254.8	70.0	140.0	210.0
Ukraine	365.5	362.9	335.6	70.8	211.0	240.0 [f]
Estonia	..	..	..	..	..	..
Latvia	..	..	..	120.0	..	27.0
Lithuania	249.3 [h]	191.8 [h]	175.3 [h]	80.0	130.0	74.0 [d]

Source: National statistics.

[a] Broad money (M2) = (M1) plus time deposits and foreign exchange deposits.
[b] Central bank rates.
[c] Monthly rates.
[d] September 1993.
[e] End-November 1993.
[f] January-June 1993.
[g] Domestic credit.
[h] January-September 1993.

November 1993 obviously had different causes, but subordination of monetary authorities to executive branch and political bodies was a characteristic of both countries.[249] Practically unrestricted monetary accommodation in FR Yugoslavia has thrown the country into full speed hyperinflation in 1993, a phenomenon not seen in Europe since the Hungarian hyperinflation in 1946. The stabilization programme of January 1994, based on the new and fully convertible dinar, cannot be expected to succeed unless it directly addresses the underlying causes of inflation (excessive budget spending in the first place).

Interest rates remained consistently positive in real terms in most other central European transition countries. With commercial credit rates much higher than the central bank rates, the real interest rates on commercial credits reached very high levels in some cases, from 10 per cent in Hungary to more than 20 per cent in Poland. Restrictive interest rate policies were implemented also in Slovenia, Estonia, and especially Latvia, where the real interest rates in the first several months of 1993 exceeded 50 per cent per annum. Real interest rates remained negative in Bulgaria for most of 1993, and the central bank had to resort to bank-specific credit limits in its efforts to curb the money supply. High and accelerating inflation forced the Bulgarian National Bank to increase the interest rates sharply at the end of 1993.

Comparing inflationary trends in two groups of transition economies – those with negative and those with positive real interest rates – there seems to be no doubt that inflation cannot be effectively brought down unless the interest rates are raised to levels which the general public considers as matching the expected inflation rates. Credit rationing or credit ceilings alone are not sufficient; not only can they not dampen the soaring demand for credits, but they are also unable to reverse inflationary expectations. High interest rates were one of the key measures behind the successful stabilization of prices in Poland in 1990, and in the Baltic states in 1992-1993. It is symptomatic that inflation in Russia cannot be brought under control, even though total credits have been significantly reduced (in real terms) and the real money supply fell by nearly 70 per cent since the beginning of 1992. In Latvia, by contrast, not only has the real money supply been drastically cut in conjunction with the introduction of the new currency, but also interest rates were raised from 25 per cent in May 1992 to more than 120 per cent in October 1992. As a result, inflation rates fell from 700-800 per cent per annum in mid-1992 to less than 15 per cent in the second quarter of 1993.

---

[249] See State Institute for Macroeconomic Analysis and Forecasting, *Croatian Economic Trends*, No.5-7, 1993, and National Bank of Romania, *Monetary Policy during the Transition Period*, November 1992.

TABLE 3.7.2

Minimum obligatory reserve requirements, selected countries, 1992 and 1993
(Per cent) [a]

	December 1992	June 1993
Transition economies		
Bulgaria	7.0	..
Croatia	11.0	23.5
Czech Republic	9.0	12.0
Hungary	16.0	14.0
Poland	25.0	23.0
Romania	10.0	..
Slovakia	9.0	..
Russia	8.0	20.0
Estonia	..	10.0
Latvia	20.0	..
Lithuania	10.0	12.0
Market economies		
Austria	4.5-9.0	..
Canada	1.0-10.0	..
France	1.0	..
Germany	6.6-12.1	..
Greece	9.0	..
Japan	0.05-1.3	..
Netherlands	0-2.4	..
Spain	3.0	..
Switzerland	2.5	..
United States	3.0-10.0	..

Source: OECD, *Main Economic Indicators*, various issues and national statistics.

[a] For demand deposits.

Given the well-known weaknesses of capital and money markets in transition countries, structural budget deficits, and the apparent reluctance to resort to more direct measures of government intervention, the main burden of reducing inflationary tendencies has fallen on credit and money restrictions, that is, on maintaining high interest rates and credit limits. As shown by the experience of some countries, this approach is a costly one as it entails significant losses in terms of output and investment. After a moderate relaxation of monetary policy stances in several transition countries in mid-1992, a new tightening was observed in early 1993. Acceleration of inflation in Bulgaria in the end of 1992 prompted the central bank to raise the base interest rate again from 49 per cent to 58 per cent. As a result, recession deepened but no major breakthrough is in sight on the inflation front. In the Czech Republic, interest rates were raised in January 1993 in anticipation of the inflationary shock connected with the shift to VAT; but a marked deceleration of inflation in mid-1993 allowed for a cautious relaxation of credit conditions. A steady decline of inflation in Poland and Hungary also opened some room for a lowering of central bank rates in the first half of 1993, but in Hungary another tightening was made in September to offset potential inflationary effects arising from the devaluation of the *forint*.

An important instrument of monetary policy which has been used to fight inflation in transition countries is the *reserve requirement ratio*. In fact, in most transition countries official reserve requirements are already at relatively high levels. Table 3.7.2 compares reserve requirements in selected transition economies and market economies. Very high minimum reserve requirements applied in Poland and the Baltic states may indeed be one of the factors behind the wide differentials between the central bank rates and lending rates of commercial banks in these countries. In these countries, a *reduction* of reserve requirement ratios would be a preferable policy action aimed at expanding credits available to the production sector.

(b) Fiscal policies

Fiscal policies in east European transition countries have been marked by constant and in most cases unsuccessful efforts to regain control over rapidly growing budget deficits and to reduce the share of government expenditures in total domestic demand. Fiscal positions continued to be particularly difficult in Bulgaria, Hungary and Slovakia, where budget deficits in 1993 reached 11, 7 and 6 per cent of GDP, respectively; it was even worse in Croatia and FR Yugoslavia, where rapidly growing budget expenditures exceeded revenues by large margins (15 and 28 per cent of GDP, respectively). The Czech Republic was the only transition country to register a small budget surplus in 1993 (see table 3.7.3).

The key reason behind the fragile budget position in many transition countries was the continuous *fall of revenues*, especially of profit taxes and turnover taxes, which in turn was caused by contraction of sales by enterprises, lower profits of banks, and weak tax collection discipline. As a result, first half-year 1993 figures for budget revenues were again below targets in almost all countries. In *Bulgaria*, total revenues for the first semester, amounting to lev 21.9 billion, were only 31 per cent of the level projected by the 1993 State Budget Law. Since the annual deficit target was overshot already in October, the Bulgarian parliament amended the budget law to provide for lower revenues and a larger deficit. Final out-turns for the year show revenues of lev 54.2 billion, still 24 per cent below the amount projected in the amended November budget. Tax receipts were one quarter below target, and payments from the banks were barely 14 per cent of the planned amount for the year.[250]

According to some sources, the main reason for the yawning budget deficit in *Hungary* was lower-than-expected revenues from privatization;[251] but this explanation can at best account for only a small part of the deficit. Revenues were lagging behind planned targets by a substantial margin: for the first half of 1993 they amounted only to 42.3 per cent of the annual figure.[252] However, the situation improved quite considerably in the second half of

---

[250] See Bulgarian National Bank, *News Bulletin*, No.13, 1-15 July 1993, pp.29-31; *Balkan News International*, 2 January, 1994.

[251] See *Business Update: Hungary*, No.153, Vol.2, 27 August 1993, and BBC, *Summary of World Broadcasts*, EEW/0301, 30 September 1993.

[252] The Hungarian budget was revised upwards in July 1993, with new targets for revenues increased from Ft 960 billion to 1,075 billion, and for expenditures from Ft 1,145 billion to 1,325 billion.

TABLE 3.7.3

Transition countries: Budget accounts, current prices, 1992-1993
(National currency and per cent of GDP)

	1992				1993			
	Revenues	Expenditures	Balance	Per cent of GDP	Revenues	Expenditures	Balance	Per cent of GDP
Albania	..	..	..	-17.0	..	..	..	-6.0 [a]
Bulgaria	39.6	51.3	-11.7	-7.1	54.19	86.41	-32.22	-12.3
Croatia	957	1 033	-76	-3.1	4 806	4 956	-150	..
Czech Republic	251.9	253.6	-1.7 [b]	..	358.0	356.9	1.4	0.1
Hungary	793.3	990.4	-197.1	-7.0	939.6	1 139.3	-199.7	-6.0
Poland	312.8	381.9	-69.1	-6.1	458.9	502.7	-43.8	-2.8
Romania	1 364	1 627	-263	-4.8	3 792	4 127	-334.9	-1.6
Slovakia	..	..	-7.9 [b]	-2.8	65.2	80.0	-22.6	-5.5
Slovenia [c]	466.8	463.6	3.2	0.2	646.3	658.0	-11.7	-0.9
The FYR of Macedonia	..	..	..	..	..	..	..	..
Yugoslavia (FR)	..	..	..	..	..	..	..	-28.0 [d]
Belarus	..	..	..	..	..	..	..	-5.8*
Moldova	..	..	..	..	..	..	..	..
Russia [e]	..	..	..	..	29 400	41 800	-12 400 [f]	-7.6 [f]
Russia [g]	5 314	5 969	-655	-4.7	53 000	64 000	11 000	-6.8
Ukraine	..	..	..	-32.0	3 026	5 319	-2 293	-10.7
Estonia	..	..	..	..	1.77	1.75	0.02	0.2
Latvia	55.5	58.1	-2.6	-1.4	172.7	191.3	-18.6	-3.2
Lithuania	86.0	81.1	4.8	1.6	..	..	0.07	0.2

Source: National statistics.

Note: Trillions of domestic currency for Poland and Croatia; billions of Latvian roubles for 1992 and millions of lats in 1993 for Latvia; billions of domestic currency for other countries. Central budget figures, unless otherwise stated.

[a] First half of 1993.
[b] Only republican budget, excluding federal budget deficit on Kcs 4.1 billion.
[c] General government.
[d] In per cent of gross social product.
[e] Federal budget.
[f] On a cash basis. On a commitment basis, the deficit was R17 trillion or 10.5 per cent of GDP.
[g] Consolidated budget.

1993: gradual recovery in industrial sales and in domestic consumption, together with an increase of VAT tax rates in July 1993, all boosted indirect tax receipts, while rapidly growing imports yielded much higher customs revenues than planned. As a result, the final budget deficit for 1993 remained practically unchanged in nominal terms as compared with 1992 (Ft 199.7 billion against Ft 199.1 billion), less than the original target of Ft 213 billion and considerably below the amended figure of Ft 230 billion. This positive development came about because annual revenues had been Ft 30 billion bigger than expected, chiefly due to high corporate and VAT tax payments in the last month of the year.[253]

In *Slovakia*, a balanced budget was planned for 1993; however, revenues for January to June 1993 amounted to only 41 per cent of the annual budget, while expenditures exceeded 50 per cent. Unrealistic assumptions for economic growth and inefficient tax collection were the main causes behind these large discrepancies.[254] Tax payment arrears by enterprises and individuals, as well as unpaid contributions to the social security funds (estimated at Sk 13 billion, nearly the amount of the first-half deficit) obviously played an important role. As in other transition countries, the government made efforts in the second half of 1993 to curb expenditures and improve tax collection, but the results seem to have been limited, as the budget deficit for the country in 1993 is estimated to have exceeded Sk 22 billion (more than $650 million, or some 6 per cent of GDP).

In *Poland*, economic recovery and the introduction of the VAT system in mid-1993 helped to boost tax revenues above the limits established in the annual budget. On the other hand, expenditures were also slightly below those planned, mainly because of continuous lack of finance arising from the lower-than-planned sales of short-term government bills which were to finance the originally envisaged deficit of Zl 81 trillion. Difficulties in borrowing on the domestic money market and higher tax revenues helped to trim the final deficit for 1993 to Zl 44 trillion (about 2.7 per cent of GDP). The VAT reform and the upturn in domestic output were also the principal causes behind the relatively good fiscal performance in *Romania*, where the rapidly growing shortfall in the first half was reduced by the end of 1993 to lei 335 billion, or 1.6 per cent of GDP.

Attempts to narrow the gap between dwindling revenues and planned expenditures have taken various

---

[253] *Magyar Hirlap*, 26 January 1994; BBC, *Summary of World Broadcasts*, EEW/0318, 3 February 1994; *Balkan News International*, 30 January 1994, p.24.

[254] "Hospodarsky vyvoj Slovenska v prvnim pololeti 1993" (Economic development of Slovakia in the first half of 1993), *Hospodárské Noviny*, 4 October 1993, p.4; *Balkan News International*, 23 January 1994.

forms. The most frequently used method was to raise taxes and duties, delay payments due from the budget, especially for wage increases in the budgetary sphere and, eventually, to push for revision of budget figures in the legislative bodies. After a battle in the Parliament, the Hungarian government won crucial political approval to increase VAT rates on foodstuffs and other staples from 6 per cent to 10 per cent.[255] Also in Slovakia the base VAT rate has been increased to 25 per cent, and the budget was amended in July 1993, in a move which takes into account more sluggish production trends in the Slovak economy.[256] In addition, the Slovak government imposed a 20 per cent surcharge on imported consumer goods in July 1993. The relatively better budget position in Poland and Romania, as noted, was buttressed by the introduction of VAT systems in July 1993. The VAT reform probably led to some increase in the overall taxation level and pushed up inflation (especially in Romania), but at the same time it greatly improved tax collection discipline.

The *budget deficits* were financed by various combinations of primary emission and internal borrowing, with external commercial financing playing a role only in the case of the Czech Republic and Hungary.[257] Government borrowing on the domestic money markets faced a number of obstacles, ranging from underdeveloped institutions of financial intermediation, such as the lack of a secondary market and the limited number of players, to lack of demand on the part of commercial banks to buy more securities, which in turn was linked to the low level of domestic savings. The demand barrier has been particularly strong in 1993 in Poland and Bulgaria, where the banks were unwilling to purchase more securities from the government. On the other hand, long-term bonds have been used on a very limited scale: they were issued and sold to the general public only in the central European transition countries and, starting from February 1993, also in Russia.[258]

Technically, *deficits* can only materialize if they are financed. In this context, the government may essentially choose from four possibilities: selling bonds to the non-bank public, selling bonds to commercial banks, borrowing from the central bank and borrowing from external sources. A fifth possibility, which should be particularly relevant for transition countries, involves selling state assets (privatization); this has so far been exploited only to a rather limited extent. With external sources of funds very limited because of the low creditworthiness of most transition countries (with the exception of the Czech Republic and Hungary) and their generally high levels of foreign indebtedness, the choice among domestic sources of finance depends largely on the degree of development of financial markets.

Transition countries have used all types of deficit financing, but the role of financing provided by the central bank has been typically more important in the less advanced countries where the commercial banking system and money markets are still underdeveloped. To strike the right balance between borrowing from various sources poses an important policy dilemma which so far has not been solved satisfactorily. Since both recession and inflation are continuously present in transition economies, the main difficulty is to estimate correctly the implications of various ways of deficit financing in terms of their contribution to macroeconomic imbalance.

Although borrowing on domestic money markets is a relatively new policy instrument in the transition countries (with the exception of Hungary), its very dynamic expansion since 1989 resulted in rapidly growing levels of domestic public debt. The level of *internal debt* increased sharply in Bulgaria, from nearly zero to 20.6 per cent of GDP at end-1992, and is estimated to have grown further to 28.1 per cent at the end of 1993. The proportion of internal debt to GDP has been somewhat smaller in Poland (23 per cent in 1993, up from 21.3 per cent one year earlier and from 15 per cent in the end of 1991), and in the Czech Republic (18.3 per cent of GDP in 1993).[259] In Hungary, the official figure for the level of internal debt (77 per cent of GDP) is overstated, because the figure includes the debts of the government to the central bank.[260] A relatively high level of internal debt is also reported in Croatia (100 per cent of GDP).[261] These levels of overall indebtedness cannot be raised much if the countries concerned want to avoid falling into a *debt trap*. Given the high inflation and interest rates in some countries, the cost of servicing the debt is already substantial. The situation is rather precarious in Bulgaria, where the share of domestic interest payments in 1993 amounted to 28 per cent of all budget expenditures, and to 8 per cent of GDP.[262] The high level of domestic debt is also inflationary, because the government, faced with the problem of servicing the debt, may be more inclined to tolerate higher inflation with the aim of reducing the real value of the debt, and/or may

---

[255] Also, a 10 per cent VAT rate was charged on household electricity consumption, which had been earlier exempted from VAT (*National Bank of Hungary*, Monthly Report, No.4, 1993, p.20).

[256] Slovak Radio, Bratislava, quoted in BBC, *Summary of World Broadcasts*, EE/1738, 12 July 1993.

[257] Formally, the Hungarian government does not directly borrow abroad, but only on the domestic money market. External borrowing is done by the National Bank of Hungary.

[258] The Romanian government also plans to issue state securities to partly finance the budget deficit in 1994 (*Romania Economic Newsletter*, January-March 1994, vol.3, No.4, p.5).

[259] See an interview with Czech Minister of Finance I.Kocarnik, in *Ekonom*, No.40, 1993, pp.15-17.

[260] The major part of the government debt to the central bank reflects the foreign debt contracted by the central bank and used to refinance the borrowing needs of the government sector. Thus, the 77 per cent figure actually refers to the share of total (external plus internal) public debt in Hungary. If the debt to the central bank is excluded, internal debt amounted to some 13 per cent of GDP in 1992. It should be noted that the Hungarian government has not so far paid interest on the large proportion of domestic debt to the central bank which accrued as a result of foreign exchange rate changes. Out of the total debt of Ft 2.033 trillion which the government owes to the National Bank of Hungary (as of 30 June 1993), Ft 1.052 trillion, or 51.7 per cent, has accumulated because of devaluations of the forint.

[261] See *Vjesnik*, 29 April 1993, p.2.

[262] "Bulgaria: The Economic Situation and Outlook. The Status of the Reform Process", a study prepared by the Agency for Economic Coordination and Development, Ministry of Finance, Ministry of Trade and Bulgarian National Bank, Sofia, May 1993, mimeo.

resort to finance the debt obligations with primary emission.

(c) Price and incomes policies

Price and incomes policies have also been used in transition countries to better control inflationary pressures, but in most cases their effects are ambiguous. The gradual approach adopted in *Romania* for price liberalization has not proven its superiority over the "cold turkey" operation applied in some other countries. While avoiding the initial jump in prices, Romania entered a long period of persistent inflation with repeated shocks associated with the subsequent stages of price decontrols. Most of the remaining restrictions on price formation referring to foodstuffs, utilities and transport tariffs were removed on 1 May 1993 – but in spite of the earlier preparatory steps and corrective price increases made in accordance with the logic of gradual liberalization, the ensuing jump of prices was rather substantial, which also reflects higher inflationary expectations.[263] When the new wave of inflation came after the introduction of a VAT on 1 July (prices increased by 13 per cent in July and 11 per cent in August), the Romanian government decided to reinstall administrative limits on price hikes in October.[264]

It should be emphasized here that the policy of periodical changes in the controlled prices of energy, basic consumer goods or production inputs and transport tariffs is likely to strengthen the inflationary spiral unless it is checked with strong monetary and credit restrictions. Under generally inflexible production structures, the restrictions are in turn likely to have an adverse impact on output levels. The persistence of inflation-cum-recession in many transition countries is to a considerable extent the effect of periodical increases of prices of some key production inputs such as electricity, gas and transport tariffs, under generally austere monetary and credit policies.[265]

Rapid increases of nominal *wages* in the Czech Republic, Slovakia and Bulgaria led to substantial wage increases in real terms, which clearly added to already existing inflationary pressures. The growth of wages was particularly strong in the Czech Republic: the average wage grew by 27.8 per cent in the first half of 1993, while total incomes of the population were up by 25.8 per cent as compared with the first half of 1992. Given that at the same time the savings ratio was falling, the increase of effective demand was even higher (by 29 per cent). The Czech government responded quickly to this potentially destabilizing development by introducing a system of wage controls based on progressive taxation of excessive wage increases.[266] The system, which broadly resembles the regulations existing in Poland (although the Czech version is somewhat less restrictive), had been initially established for six months, but was recently extended for 1994. Meanwhile, in Poland, the government decided to scrap the current excess-wage tax system by the end of the first quarter of 1994 and to replace it with several optional wage-control regimes for state enterprises, linking the penalty-free wage hikes to company-specific profit rates, rather than to any macroeconomic indicator.[267] In Bulgaria, wage controls have become tighter after the new principles for wage indexation and increased taxation were introduced in March 1993. Also in Croatia wages are linked to price inflation via an indexation mechanism. In Slovenia, in contrast, the rapid growth in nominal wages in the last quarter of 1992 prompted the government to impose a temporary freeze on wages from February to June 1993.

(d) Exchange rate policies

An important role in the process of macroeconomic stabilization and structural reforms in transition countries has been played by *foreign exchange policies*. The exchange rate has been used in most countries as an anti-inflation device, rather than as an instrument for the control of the external balance. This was quite evident in the countries with fixed exchange rate regimes, but even in others where a floating rate regime was in operation, efforts were made by the central banks to reduce the pace of devaluation and to keep it below inflation rates.

While all countries achieved some degree of convertibility of domestic currencies, this was essentially limited to current account transactions. Perhaps the most liberal systems exist now in Latvia and Lithuania where, in addition to current account operations, capital account transactions have also been largely decontrolled. In other east European countries convertibility for residents is still restricted in one way or another (except in Poland and Slovenia), but payments for trade transactions are generally liberalized. Currency convertibility of a much narrower scope is now in place in Albania, Croatia, Romania, and FR Yugoslavia: in these countries the foreign exchange market operates mainly through auctions accessible only to a limited number of licensed banks.

Transition countries differ also with respect to foreign exchange regimes they follow: these range from a fixed-rate system in Estonia and the Czech Republic to an adjustable peg in Hungary, Slovakia and Lithuania, a "crawling" peg in Poland, and a managed float in Bulgaria, Romania and Slovenia. The power to regulate the exchange rate is in most countries entrusted to the central banks, but there are exceptions: for instance, in Hungary,

---

[263] For instance, prices for bread rose fourfold within a few days, electricity fivefold, butter sevenfold, etc. (*International Labour Review*, No.3, 1993, pp.285-286). As a result, the consumer price index increased in May alone by more than 30 per cent.

[264] *Neue Zürcher Zeitung*, 25 October 1993. None the less, prices still rose by more than 10 per cent a month through the end of the year.

[265] It is estimated that the direct inflationary impact of the fuel, electricity and central heating price rises in Bulgaria amounted to 2.2 percentage points of inflation, thus accounting for 12 per cent of inflation in the first quarter of 1993 ("Bulgaria. The economic situation and outlook ... ", op.cit., p.9).

[266] The regulation, which entered into force on 1 July 1993, stipulates that wage increases of the range between 15 and 30 per cent per quarter are penalized with a "fine" of 100 per cent paid out of profits, and wage increases exceeding 30 per cent are charged with 200 per cent "fine". For wage increases below 15 per cent no tax is paid (BBC, *Summary of World Broadcasts*, EE/1731, 3 July 1993; *Hospodárské Noviny*, 2 September 1993).

[267] *Rzeczpospolita*, 26 January 1994.

TABLE 3.7.4

Official exchange rates, transition countries, end-December 1993

	US dollars		Deutsche mark	
	A	B	A	B
Albania	99	82.5	..	..
Bulgaria	32.71	133.5	18.92	125.1
Croatia	6 562	822.1	3 802	768.0
Czech Republic	30.12	106.5	17.28	96.8
Hungary	100.70	121.2	58.06	111.7
Poland	21 079	136.4	12 611	113.0
Romania	1 274	277.0	..	..
Slovakia	32.88	114.1	..	..
Slovenia	131.82	133.6	76.37	124.9
The FYR of Macedonia .	..	..	..	..
Yugoslavia (FR)	..	..	..	..
Belarus	6 990	351.7	..	..
Georgia	98 819	2 410.2	..	..
Moldova	3.64	..	..	..
Russia	1 247	304.1	..	..
Ukraine	12 610	1 967.2	415.1	..
Estonia	13.60	104.4	8.0	100.0
Latvia	0.59	..	..	..
Lithuania	3.90	..	..	..

Source: National statistics.

Note: A = In units of domestic currency per one unit of foreign currency; B = Index, December 1992=100.

changes in the official exchange rate in excess of plus or minus 4 per cent are decided by the government.

In nearly all transition countries, foreign exchange rates appreciated in real terms in 1992 and this tendency continued through 1993, as may be seen from table 3.7.4. To reduce pressures on domestic currencies and to maintain export competitiveness, some countries devalued their currencies repeatedly in discrete steps or by allowing a faster slide of the floating rates. A noticeable policy shift could be observed in Hungary, where the government, faced by a sharp deterioration of trade balance in 1993, seems to be ready to abandon the policy of a "strong" forint followed for several years. During the first half of 1993 the *forint* was devalued six times, by 1.6-2.9 per cent each time, and then by an additional 3 per cent on 9 July and 4.5 per cent at the end of September. This brought the cumulative devaluation of the *forint* in 1993 to 14.6 per cent, i.e., still below the current inflation rate as measured by the CPI (some 17 per cent over the same period).[268] Also the Polish National Bank decided, apparently after coming under strong pressures from the government, to devalue the *zloty* by 8 per cent on 26 August, but at the same time it reduced the rate of the "crawl" from 1.8 per cent to 1.6 per cent per month. The move broadly compensated Polish exporters for the earlier loss in competitiveness connected with the steady increase of producer prices (by 23.9 per cent over January-August).

The Czech Republic has not changed the *koruna* rate since the beginning of the stabilization programme in 1991; given the high and growing level of international reserves, this fact suggests that the country enjoys the most stable currency in eastern Europe. Even if the koruna appreciated in real terms by some 20 per cent in the course of 1993, its initial depreciation had probably been large enough to safely absorb the recent loss in competitiveness. According to some sources, the Czech currency is still one of the most undervalued among all east European currencies; this seems plausible in the light of the relatively good trade out-turns in 1993. By contrast, Slovakia devalued its currency on 10 July 1993 by 10 per cent against convertible currencies, a move which followed an earlier devaluation against the Czech koruna within the system of bilateral clearing, and which was largely seen as necessary to make the exchange rate consistent with the country's more fragile external balance situation after the split of Czechoslovakia earlier in 1993.

Exchange rate developments varied also in countries where floating exchange rate regimes have been in operation. In Bulgaria, the *lev* depreciated only by a fraction of the inflation rate, but, as in the case of the Czech Republic, it still remains substantially undervalued. However, continuous economic recession and larger than expected losses from the economic sanctions on FR Yugoslavia put the Bulgarian currency under strong speculative pressures in the last quarter of 1993. The central bank tried to intervene but, given the very limited foreign reserves, the action met with only little success, and the *lev* fell sharply against convertible currencies, from lev 29/$ at end-October 1993 to lev 39/$ at end-January 1994. The fall during these two months was significantly larger than the depreciation over the whole period since the outset of reforms in February 1991.

The pace of devaluation was faster in Romania, but it still lagged behind the current price increases. The *leu* weakened substantially against convertible currencies in the final months of 1993 and in the beginning of 1994, in reaction to partial liberalization of foreign exchange transactions and consolidation of the foreign exchange market.[269] Only in Slovenia did the currency depreciate slightly more than the inflation rate.

The real appreciation of domestic currencies in transition countries may have lessened inflationary pressures, especially in the Czech Republic and the Baltic states, but on the other hand it wiped out substantial margins of export competitiveness. Combined with the slackening demand in the west, the exchange rate appreciation has most likely contributed to the sharp deterioration of the external balance observed in most transition countries in 1993.

(iii) Macroeconomic policies in Russia and Ukraine

As in 1992, macroeconomic policies in Russia and other CIS states in 1993 suffered from internal inconsistencies and lack of effective instruments of

---

[268] In order to counter the inflationary effects of the last devaluation in September, the Hungarian National Bank increased its base interest rate from 19 to 20 per cent.

[269] *Balkan News International*, 23 January 1994.

financial control. Except for Ukraine, macroeconomic policies of the CIS countries followed rather closely the example of Russia; this was reflected in rather close similarity of inflation rates, rates of output decline and developments on labour markets in individual CIS republics.

Although macroeconomic stabilization was the principal policy objective of the Russian government throughout 1993, the actual policies applied have gone through three distinct stages. The change of the government in December 1992 was followed by a period of relative relaxation of macroeconomic stance between December 1992 and April 1993, especially in the field of monetary policies. Money and credit emission was increasing fast, even though output was falling continuously. After the April referendum, however, the position of radical reformers in the Russian government was strengthened and macroeconomic policies became more restrictive. Interest rates began to rise, credit emission was tightened, and inflation, after a lag, started to decline. This policy course came under heavy criticism after the December 1993 parliamentary elections, and seems now to have been modified.

(a) Russia: Conflicting policies in early 1993

After the change of government in December 1992 many observers feared that market reform would slow down in *Russia*, as the results of the stabilization programme in 1992 had not been at all encouraging.[270] The first decisions of the new government seemed to confirm this perception: the new Prime Minister started with opening a new tranche of low-interest credits of R200 billion for the mining sector and signed a regulation on direct price controls in the beginning of January 1993.[271] Later events demonstrated, however, that these early decisions did not signal the beginning of an anti-reform course. Price controls were revoked only two weeks later,[272] and a new ambitious economic programme of combatting inflation was soon announced.

The programme remained broadly within the framework of the reform strategy formulated by the previous government, but it drew some lessons from the mistakes made in 1992. The main thrust of the programme was to fight inflation and stabilize public finances: the two central targets were to lower the budget deficit to 5 per cent of GDP and the inflation rate to 5 per cent per month by the end of 1993. These goals were to be achieved through a combination of "orthodox" monetary and fiscal measures, including sharp rises in interest rates, a shift to non-inflationary ways of deficit financing, and restrictions on credit emission, which would slow down the growth of money and credit to 7-10 per cent per month.[273] The programme was warmly received by the representatives of international financial institutions, but many observers were sceptical about the political chances for its implementation.[274]

Indeed, the declared intention to restrain *credit emission* met with strong opposition from the central bank and representatives of the industrial sector. The government request to the central bank to increase the refinancing interest rate from 80 to 100 per cent in March and 140 per cent in April was rejected by the central bank, even though inflation was running at that time at 20-25 per cent per month, or 1,000-1,500 per cent per annum. The polemics which followed revealed fundamental differences on the general concept of reforms and policy approaches between the government and the central bank.[275] Eventually, as the balance of political power gradually shifted in favour of reformers, the bank gave in to government pressures. The interest rate was raised to 100 per cent on 30 March, and credit ceilings were set for central bank credits to commercial banks, limiting credit expansion to 30 per cent (or R2.8-3 trillion) in the second quarter 1993.[276] The joint statement on economic policy, issued by the government and the central bank, confirmed the 10 per cent inflation target and specified that the central bank rate would not be lower by more than 7 percentage points than the interest rate prevailing on the interbank market.[277]

(b) Gradual stabilization since April 1993

The results of the April 1993 referendum strengthened the position of the reformers in shaping economic policy, and interest rates were raised further in May and June. Even though interest rates still remained strongly negative in real terms, it was certainly reassuring to note the apparent shift in the Russian central bank's policy with respect to credit emission.

Adherence to the policy of strongly negative interest rates by the Central Bank of Russia (followed also by the central banks in other CIS states) left no choice but to resort to direct credit rationing as the key instrument in regulating the supply of credits. Even though total credit in Russia increased 2.5 times in the first semester of 1993, the rate of expansion was still much below the rate of price

---

[270] See E. Whitlock "New Russian Government to Continue Economic Reforms?", *RFE/RL Research Report*, Vol.2, No.3, January 15, 1993. For an overview of the Russian stabilization programme in 1992, see United Nations Economic Commission for Europe, *Economic Survey of Europe in 1992-1993*, New York, 1993, pp.160-169.

[271] See *Finansovye Izvestiya*, 14 January 1993.

[272] Prime Minister Chernomyrdin was even quoted to the effect that these regulations "... should not have been issued at all" (BBC, *Summary of World Broadcasts*, SU/1582, 9 January 1993).

[273] See "O finansovo-ekonomicheskoi politike Rossii", *Izvestiya*, 26 January 1993.

[274] See L. Boulton, "The plan is perfect. But does anyone believe it?", *Financial Times*, 28 January 1993.

[275] Central Bank Governor V. Gerashchenko accused Finance Minister B. Fedorov of "mechanical transposition of the principles of formulating and implementing monetary policy in countries with developed market relations", while he himself was accused by President Yeltsin of "adventurism". See *Financial Times*, 5 February 1993; *Rossiiskaya gazeta*, 2 April 1993, and *Argumenty i fakty*, No.13, April 1993. The debate was joined also by foreign advisors (see e.g., the interview with J. Sachs in *Finansovye Izvestiya*, 11-17 February 1993).

[276] Immediately after signing the agreement with the government on credit restrictions, Mr. Gerashchenko expressed his strong scepticism as to the possibility of enforcing the agreed limits (*Financial Times*, 19 April 1993).

[277] *Ekonomika i zhizn'*, No.21, May 1993, p.6.

TABLE 3.7.5

Russian Central Bank's interest rates, 1991-1993
(Per cent)

Date	Interest rates
1991	8.0
1992	
1 January	20.0
7 April	50.0
23 May	80.0
1993	
30 March	100.0
2 June	110.0
22 June	120.0
29 June	140.0
15 July	170.0
1 October	200.0
15 October	210.0

Source: Ekonomika i zhizn', various issues.

inflation; but in the absence of sound efficiency criteria in credit allocation this restrictive policy could not support structural adjustment on any significant scale. A series of increases in central bank rates effected in the second half of 1993 (table 3.7.5) suggest that the Russian government had succeeded in forcing the central bank to soften its commitment to low nominal interest rates, which had dictated the course of monetary policy in 1992 and which resulted in the unsaturated demand for credits from state enterprises.

Despite high inflation, *budget accounts* in Russia have not deteriorated further in 1993; they even showed some signs of improvement towards the end of the year. A major breakdown in revenues was avoided because the government introduced indexation and frequent collection (twice a month) of tax liabilities; also, VAT was extended to imports. Furthermore, the government imposed an additional levy on enterprise profits of 7 per cent and increased excise taxes on natural gas and oil (from 18 to 30 per cent) from 1 July. At the same time, coal prices were liberalized and subsidies to coal mines cut substantially. All these measures helped to keep the budget deficit within limits agreed upon with the IMF. But it should not be overlooked that the foundations of this modest success are very fragile because the bulk of government revenues still comes in the form of profit tax from enterprises, which is a rather uncertain tax base. On the other hand, the relatively high tax revenues collected from Russian enterprises suggests that their financial position may not be as bad as in some other transition economies, or as one might judge from the overall condition of the Russian economy.

In May 1993, the government for the first time issued government bonds to finance the budget deficit and cover internal debt. Initially, 3-month bonds were floated and their value was planned to reach R600-650 billion for 1993.[278] But the actual results of the first flotations were disappointing: between May and August less than R13 billion were placed, much below initial plans.[279] Lack of tradition, high uncertainty and relatively low premiums have been behind these very low out-turns. Later in the year the market for government securities gradually increased, and more than R200 billion of bonds were in circulation at the end of 1993.[280] The move marked the beginning of a departure from the most inflationary method of deficit financing based on primary emission and direct credits from the central bank.

Monetary and price developments in Russia in 1992 and 1993 present an interesting case of an economy balancing on the brink of *hyperinflation* without going over it. There seem to be several reasons for this escape.

Data on the changes in monetary and credit aggregates presented in table 3.7.6 show that the high dynamics of consumer prices did not translate into an increase in the velocity of money circulation, which is a typical development in an economy with high inflation. This was partly caused by massive non-payments and delayed payments, which in turn were linked to the contraction of the real money supply. After having diminished sharply in January 1992, the money stock did not recover in real terms to previous levels throughout the rest of 1992 and 1993. In December 1992 the level of real supply of domestic money (deflated by the CPI) was 66 per cent (M1) and 70 per cent (M2) lower than in December 1991. In June 1993 the real money supply was only 22 per cent (M1) and 19 per cent (M2) of the level registered at end-1991.

Obviously, the money stock in Russia has been supplemented with various rouble surrogates, chiefly by foreign exchange; but their share in total money stock is unknown. Hence, the true degree of real money contraction has probably been smaller than that indicated by the statistics on domestic money developments.

There were, however, some other explanations for the escape from hyperinflation. The first is that the growth of wages systematically lagged behind the growth of prices – a phenomenon which eventually resulted in a drop of the statistical average real wage by some 32 per cent between December 1991 and June 1993. This moderation of nominal wage increases was linked to a number of factors; but one of the most relevant was probably the insufficient flow of credits from commercial banks to enterprises. As can be seen from table 3.7.6, between December 1991 and December 1992 total credit to enterprises increased 11.6 times, while consumer prices rose 26 times and producer prices by more than 60 times. Real credit contraction continued in 1993: between end-1992 and end-June 1993, credit to enterprises rose much less than consumer prices (2.5 times and 3.4 times, respectively).

---

[278] *Finansovye Izvestiya*, 30 April-7 May 1993.

[279] *Izvestiya*, 12 August 1993.

[280] *Finansovye Izvestiya*, 24-30 December, 1993.

TABLE 3.7.6
Changes in monetary aggregates and consumer prices in Russia, 1992-1993
(Previous month=100)

	Cash in circulation	Cash plus demand deposits (M1)	Broad money (M2) [a]	Cash plus deposits of commercial banks [b]	Central Bank of Russia credits	Credits to enterprises	Consumer price inflation
1992							
January	110.8	115.7	112.7	101.3	120.1	117.8	345.3
February	113.9	113.9	112.1	115.0	139.5	134.8	138.0
March	118.3	117.6	114.1	130.6	149.2	131.7	129.9
April	128.2	112.5	110.4	120.4	141.6	111.7	121.7
May	115.1	110.6	109.2	119.4	121.3	101.7	111.9
June	124.5	131.2	128.0	167.7	163.1	133.7	119.1
July	141.2	127.6	125.5	114.0	147.8	133.5	110.6
August	125.1	132.9	130.9	198.1	155.1	115.8	108.6
September	118.1	133.0	131.5	93.1	124.1	133.7	111.5
October	120.6	127.9	127.0	117.3	106.1	129.6	122.9
November	120.4	105.4	105.2	123.3	109.9	120.3	126.1
December	124.4	120.7	120.4	118.1	153.0	113.7	124.9
December [c]	1 033.5	883.5	773.0	1 317.2	3 244.3	1 162.2	2 602.6
1993							
January	113.4	119.2	118.3	105.4	109.8	121.1	126.5
February	119.3	110.0	110.0	113.0	112.0	115.6	125.7
March	112.0	115.9	117.0	121.0	124.1	122.3	121.4
April	128.5	122.9	122.9	114.0	113.7	122.5	124.7
May	120.9	118.6	119.0	115.0	106.3	107.0*	119.0
June	127.0	101.4	116.1	114.0	111.6	112.0*	120.0
June [c]	3 089.7	1 984.5	1 998.4	2 837.0	6 677.8	2 920.7*	8 946.4
July	122.2	137.3	119.3	..	114.2	113.0	122.0
August	118.8	113.6	113.7	..	111.3	..	126.0
September	115.2	103.0	103.3	..	111.7	..	121.0
October	116.4	110.4	110.6	..	108.9	..	120.0
November	111.6	..	108.3	..	108.7	..	116.0
December	119.7	..	121.5	..	..	..	113.0

Sources: Compiled from *Russian Economic Trends*, 1993, 1994; Central Bank of Russia, *Tekushchiye tendentsii v denezhno-kreditnoy sfere*, vypusk 3, Moscow, May 1993 and national statistics.

[a] Broad money (M2) = (M1) plus time deposits.
[b] High powered money.
[c] December 1991=100.

The relatively sluggish transfer of new credit resources from banks to enterprises is another factor that may explain why inflation in Russia did not explode into hyperinflation in 1992. It can be seen from table 3.7.6 that credits issued by the CBR grew much faster than commercial bank credits to enterprises. If the ratio of all credits outstanding to enterprises to total CBR credits in December 1991 was 2.3, the multiplier fell to 0.7 in December 1992; similarly, the proportion of all credits to enterprises to CBR credits issued to commercial banks diminished from 3.3 to 1.9. Massive injections of CBR credits into the banking sector were not fully transmitted to the enterprise sector,[281] because the banks preferred to increase their investments in other assets, primarily in foreign exchange holdings.[282] These "leakages" reduced sharply the funds available for enterprises and thus hampered possibilities of restructuring in the production sector. Paradoxically, the backwardness of the Russian banking sector and the lack of sophisticated financial intermediation may have been helpful in avoiding hyperinflation in Russia.

But this situation started to change in early 1993. More credits found their way through to the enterprise sector, and eventually to wages. The ratio of all credits to enterprises to total CBR credits, and the ratio of all credits to enterprises to CBR credits to commercial banks increased to 1.1 and to 3.1, respectively, by the end of June 1993, which implied an increase in the money multiplier. The growth of nominal wages in March-June 1993 surpassed the consumer price index. Velocity of circulation seems to have accelerated as well, and thus inflationary pressures intensified, even though credit

---

[281] Between end-1991 and end-1992, CBR credits outstanding to commercial banks increased from R134 billion to R2.624 trillion, i.e, nearly 20 times, while total credits to enterprises increased from R439 billion to R5.102 trillion, i.e., less than 12 times.

[282] The average annual interest rate on commercial banks' deposits kept with the central bank in 1992 was about 70 per cent (with a tendency to increase towards the end of the year to some 120 per cent), but the dollar appreciated over January-December 1992 by 180 per cent in nominal terms. This differential in nominal rates of return on liquid assets diminished considerably in the first half of 1993, mostly due to the increase of interest rates on the inter-bank money market to 140-160 per cent per annum.

emission by the CBR had slowed down in the first half of 1993. The recent series of interest rate increases, otherwise long overdue, may therefore have had a mitigating impact on credit expansion.

At the end of May 1993, the government and the CBR concluded an agreement with the IMF imposing strict limits on the growth of monetary, credit and budgetary flows, which opened the way for release of the first tranche of credits within the so-called Systemic Transformation Facility (STF) of $3 billion. Half of this amount was granted immediately after the agreement had been signed, while the second tranche was to be disbursed only after first results of the new policy were known. The targets specified in the agreement foresaw a deceleration of central bank credit emission from 20 per cent of GDP in the last quarter of 1992 to 19 per cent in the first half of 1993, 15.9 per cent for the first three quarters, and to 13.8 per cent of GDP for the whole of 1993. The government budget was to be reduced (on a cash basis, i.e., excluding foreign debt payments arrears) to 8.9 per cent of GDP in the first half of 1993, and to 8.3 per cent for the whole year. As a result of these measures, inflation was expected to come down to one-digit monthly rates at the end of the year.

These restrictive measures met with immediate opposition from the Russian parliament. It may be noted that Russia's budget for 1993 had not been formally approved: the draft budget prepared by the government after negotiations with the IMF was rejected by the parliament, which postulated an increase of the planned deficit from 10.4 to more than 20 per cent of GDP. This proposal was vetoed by President Yeltsin, but the parliament overruled the president's veto by qualified majority voting. The dissolution of the Russian parliament in September left the country with no formally approved budget for 1993, but the government was quick to declare that it would adhere to the targets specified in its agreement with the IMF.[283]

The government's perseverance with strict austerity measures started to bring some encouraging results in the third and fourth quarters of 1993. The rouble exchange rate practically stabilized, fluctuating around R1,000-1,100/$ between June and November, and the inflation rate eventually came down from 20-25 per cent in January-September 1993 to 16 per cent in November and to 13 per cent in December. Although this may indeed have reflected the impact of monetary tightening, working with a standard 3-4 months lag, there are reasons to suspect that the easing of inflation was achieved, at least partly, in a somewhat "artificial" way, through non-implementation of certain budgetary obligations.

(c) The policy shift at the end of 1993

The situation changed in the aftermath of the December 1993 parliamentary elections, which demonstrated that political support for the parties favouring fast and radical approach to market reforms in Russia has weakened substantially. The political shift is likely to be reflected in the government's policies; this is most readily evident from some of the recent declarations of the Russian Prime Minister.[284]

The new policy course is rather difficult to interpret; the government has still to find a balance between maintaining the necessary financial discipline on the one hand and avoiding social crisis on the other hand. Apart from many general declarations on the need to soften the monetary restrictions and to stimulate production, no comprehensive programme has been presented so far. But two tendencies appear to be rather clear. First, the government tends now to disassociate itself from the policies based on monetary restrictions which, according to many observers, have proved ineffective in fighting inflation while inhibiting production and consumption.[285] This criticism has recently been supported by reports showing that a part of the widely publicized slow-down in inflation in November-December 1993 may have been achieved through the non-implementation of obligated government expenditures in the last quarter of 1993. For instance, the government, trying to keep the cash flow budget deficit within the agreed target of 8.3 per cent of GDP, deliberately postponed payments of higher wages to the budgetary sector, due from 1 December, and deferred payments for grain purchases by the state. The payments arrears of the budget, estimated at R7.5 trillion, will have to be paid out in January-February 1994, adding to the already high budget deficit of R10 trillion planned for the first quarter, and with obvious consequences for inflation.[286]

This criticism may not be fully justified. While the improvement in the 1993 budget was indeed achieved "artificially", the slow-down in inflation appears to have been real enough. The impact of the reduction of budget expenditures in December 1993 on inflation would normally materialize with a lag in the first quarter of 1994. Furthermore, some other indicators, such as the relative stability of the rouble exchange rate, also confirm the easing of inflationary pressures in the second half of 1993.

The second tendency, which is evident from the budget projections for 1994, is more worrying. The government has come under very strong pressure to release large amounts of funds to the ailing sectors of the economy, chiefly to the agro-industrial and military-industrial complexes. Official reports speak about new

---

[283] *Rossiiskie vesti*, 27 August 1993. Most recent declarations speak of about 10 per cent of GDP as the target for the budget deficit in 1993 (*Rossiiskie vesti*, 3 November 1993).

[284] Prime Minister Chernomyrdin was quoted as saying at a press conference on 20 January 1994: "The period of market romanticism has ended ... Economic policies will be corrected to make people's lives easier" (*RFE/RL Daily Report*, No.14, 21 January 1994).

[285] According to CBR President V. Gerashchenko, the monetary contraction was excessive (the real money supply fell by 70 per cent between December 1991 and December 1993), and thus the recent reduction in inflation was "artificially achieved" (*Rossiiskie vesti*, 9 February 1994).

[286] See the interview with Prime Minister V. Chernomyrdin, *Ekonomika i zhizn'*, No.4, January 1994, and the statement by the deputy governor of the Central Bank of Russia, A. Khandruyev in *Rossiiskie vesti*, 2 February 1994.

subsidies granted to agriculture of R14 trillion,[287] but other sources put the full figure of financial assistance to the sector at R35 trillion.[288] The new draft budget provides for R121 trillion of revenues and R182 trillion of expenditures, with a deficit of R61 trillion for 1994, or 10.2 per cent of forecasted GDP, and envisages continued borrowing from the central bank to cover the planned shortfall of revenues. Some of the central bank credits will be charged with a interest at a symbolic rate of 10 per cent per annum.[289]

The government believes inflation can be kept within planned limits despite the massive budgetary spending. Official forecasts speak about 15-18 per cent inflation in the first quarter, to be gradually reduced to 7-9 per cent by the end of 1994,[290] but this slow-down may not be achievable in the face of the expected fiscal expansion.[291] A strong inflationary impulse is likely to come from another fall in the rouble exchange rate, which depreciated strongly in January 1994 in reaction to the announced changes in economic policy stances. Moreover, it is not clear what precisely will be the anti-inflationary policies of the government if "non-monetary" measures are to be used instead of monetary, credit and budget restraint.[292] On the other hand, while criticizing the policies formerly used, the government seems also to be reluctant to espouse alternative approaches, based on direct controls over prices and wages and massive interventionism, along the lines of certain proposals recently prepared by some Russian experts.[293]

The prospects for macroeconomic stabilization in Russia seem to be rather uncertain at present. If the government programme is not comprehensive and credible enough, strong pressures to increase financial support to various industrial sectors may greatly increase the risk that the Russian economy will drift again towards higher inflation.[294] While the output decline may be halted and even reversed in some sectors, it is unlikely that a vigorous restructuring can take place in a high-inflation environment.

(d) Lack of macroeconomic controls in Ukraine

Macroeconomic policy in *Ukraine* has been even less disciplined than in Russia. The highest (implicit) priorities of the two successive governments in 1993 seem to have been avoiding massive bankruptcies and unemployment through a policy of constantly increasing subsidies, concessionary credits, wage indexation, and foreign trade controls. As a result, inflation has been substantially higher than in other CIS countries, but the true explosion came in June 1993, when inflation reached the psychological barrier of 50 per cent per month and the growth of wages was even higher (84 per cent). At the same time, the state budget remained in deep deficit; its proportion to GDP, although high by all standards, was still much lower in the first half of 1993 than it was in 1992 (10.8 per cent compared to 32 per cent).[295] Prolonged political crisis, which led to the fall of two governments in the course of 1993, has also resulted in further weakening of macroeconomic discipline.[296]

Sharp rises of food prices in June 1993 provoked panic on the market and a steep fall of the rate of the *karbovanets* against the dollar (table 3.7.7). In addition, also in June the National Bank was instructed by the parliament to issue large new credits at an interest rate of 30 per cent per annum, to agriculture, coal mining and metallurgy, in response to wage hike demands and a wave of strikes in these sectors. As a result, monetary policy accommodated the price increases with additional money issuance, and inflation accelerated in the summer. In July and August alone the cash circulation increased from karbovanets 1,710 billion to 2,625 billion, i.e., by 54 per cent, but despite this massive emission frequent shortages of cash were reported by the banks.[297] Another shock to the Ukrainian economy came in September, when prices for energy and some foodstuffs were raised again and partly liberalized.[298] At the same time, the rate of the karbovanets on the interbank exchange collapsed from 8,000 per dollar to 20,000 per dollar, and the monthly inflation rate jumped to 80 per cent.

Macroeconomic statistics on the Ukrainian economy are scarce, but it can easily be observed that the lack of restraint on credit emission and continuous fiscal imbalance pushed inflation into three-digit monthly rates.[299] State expenditures exceeded state revenues by more than one third, i.e., karbovanets 6.2 trillion in January-November 1993, with the shortfall covered by primary emission. Even though the central bank rediscount rate was raised to 240 per cent in the second half of 1993, the decision was purely formal because the whole amount of refinancing credits was earmarked for implementation of the "state conversion programme" and charged at an annual rate of 28 per cent only. On the other hand, commercial banks were lending at higher rates,

---

[287] According to the statement by Deputy Prime Minister A. Zaveryukha (*Izvestiya*, 3 February 1994).

[288] *Izvestiya*, 9 February 1994.

[289] *Segodnya*, 10 February 1994; *Rossiiskie vesti*, 4 March 1994.

[290] See the interview with V. Chernomyrdin, *Ekonomika i Zhizn'*, op.cit.

[291] Some experts predict much higher inflation (30 per cent per month) already in the first quarter of 1994 (G. Yavlinski, quoted after BBC, *Summary of World Broadcasts*, SU/1913, 4 February 1994).

[292] *Financial Times*, 24 January 1994.

[293] For a discussion of an alternative stabilization programme prepared by L. Abalkin, N. Petrakov and S. Shatalin, see *Izvestiya*, 29 January 1994.

[294] For a discussion of necessary components of a stabilization programme in Russia, see United Nations Economic Commission for Europe, *Economic Survey of Europe in 1992-1993*, New York, 1993, pp.160-169.

[295] *Ukraine in Numbers*, Monthly Economic Bulletin, No.8, August 1993.

[296] See S. Johnson, O. Ustenko, "Ukraine Slips into Hyperinflation", *RFE/RL Research Report*, Vol.2, No.26, 25 June 1993.

[297] UNIAN News Agency, Kiev, 17 September 1993, as quoted in BBC, *Summary of World Broadcasts*, SUW/0301, 1 October 1993.

[298] E.g., the price of bread and flour went up by 10 times (*Izvestiya*, 29 September 1993).

[299] 80 per cent in September, 66 per cent in October, 45 per cent in November and nearly 100 per cent in December 1993 (*Uryadovy kuryer*, 1 February 1994).

TABLE 3.7.7

Ukraine: Key financial indicators, 1993
(Previous month=100)

Month	Cash plus demand deposits (M1)	Broad money (M2) [a]	Central Bank credits	Commercial Bank credits	Retail price index	Central bank dollar rate [b]
1993						
January	128.4	132.5	..	135.8	179.8	123.5
February	113.7	110.5	..	125.1	132.3	124.9
March	138.4	140.1	..	137.5	119.2	224.2
April	106.3	109.3	106.1	111.2	119.0	137.6
May	105.4	104.8	103.5	111.0	121.3	100.0
June	154.6	154.2	165.9	128.7	149.8	132.7
June [c]	350.0	362.2	..	371.1	613.1	631.2
December [c]	1 800.0	2 500.0	..	..	11 000.0	2 001.6

Source: *Ukraine in Numbers*, Monthly Economic Bulletin, No.8, August 1993 and national sources.

[a] Broad money (M2) = (M1) plus time deposits and foreign exchange deposits.
[b] Central bank rates, end of month.
[c] December 1992=100.

hand, commercial banks were lending at higher rates, averaging 280 per cent by end-1993, but still much below the level of inflation.

Unless serious stabilization measures are taken soon, the Ukrainian economy may experience an accelerating hyperinflation spiral in 1994. The country does not have any stabilization policy at the moment, because controversies over the required strategy of reforms have developed into a deep political crisis.[300] The coexistence of the official exchange rate of the karbovanets of 12,600/$ and an interbank rate of more than karbovanets 30,000/$ (end-December 1993) discourages official exports and invites speculation. Decisions by the Ukrainian authorities in 1993 to tighten direct administrative supervision over key sectors of the economy suggest that centralized controls, rather than radical market-oriented measures, are regarded as the appropriate policy to cope with the present economic crisis.[301]

---

[300] For an extensive discussion of policy dilemmas in Ukraine, see H. Clement et al., "Verschärfte Wirtschaftskrise in der Ukraine", *Ost-Europa Institute,* Working Papers, No.161, Munich, September 1993.

[301] Viz. the Presidential decree on maintaining the state ordering system into 1994 (*Financial Times*, 3 November 1993).

3.8 Short-term outlook

The year 1994 is likely to bring some improvement in the output performance of most transition economies; in fact, it may turn out to be the first year since the beginning of transition towards a market economy when overall output grows in eastern Europe. The improvement, however, means different things for different countries. In the economies where growth had already started (Albania, Poland, Romania, Slovenia), it is expected to continue, and where the fall was moderate in 1993 (the Czech Republic, Hungary, and, among the Baltic countries, Estonia) a slight upward change can be foreseen. In the rest of the transition economies – a group with a much larger weight, as it includes practically all CIS countries, most successor states of SFR Yugoslavia, Bulgaria, Slovakia, and the other two Baltic states – the fall in output is likely to continue, though at a lower rate than in 1993.

However, even in those countries where economic decline seems to be ending or has reversed, the emerging recovery is expected to be slow and hesitant, and it cannot be taken for granted that a fundamental breakthrough in underlying economic trends is taking place. Although the official government forecasts as well as reports by international organizations predict considerable improvement in economic performance in 1994,[302] this optimism should not neglect the fact that most of these countries are going to face rather serious macroeconomic constraints. Thus, the end of the "transformational recession"[303] does not yet imply the beginning of a sustained "transformational expansion" in these countries. Just as the factors contributing to the contraction of output during the last four years have been quite different from those associated with the cyclical weakening of economic activity in developed market economies, the recovery is also likely to show distinct and atypical features.

This is partly due to the still difficult macroeconomic conditions and probable course of economic policies, but also to the fragility of both the real economy and the financial sector in these countries. The serious financial difficulties of the business sector, the heavy indebtedness of even viable companies, the huge stock of interenterprise arrears (unpaid bills), the large share of bad loans in the portfolio of commercial banks these are just a few examples which indicate that even in the countries with the best relative position in the region, the condition of the business and banking sector appears to be too fragile and uncertain to permit expectations of an untroubled and sustained recovery.

(i) Constraints on emerging recovery in eastern Europe

The implications of domestic imbalances, the role of the external sector, and structural constraints are likely to be the most important factors determining the speed and sustainability of the economic recovery in *eastern Europe*. With the exception of the Czech Republic, *domestic imbalances* (large budget deficits and high rates of inflation) do not leave much room for either fiscal or monetary policies to give a sizeable stimulus to economic activity although, in most countries, both the public sector deficit and the high rate of inflation are partly the reflection of the output contraction.[304] Indeed, the significant decline in the budget deficit-to-GDP ratio in Poland (from 6 per cent in 1992 to 2.8 per cent in 1993) is a clear indication that economic recovery has a powerful and positive influence on the state of public finances. Gains on inflation have also been more significant in the economies displaying better output performance. Still, these achievements have generally resulted not from an expansionary stance of overall macroeconomic policies, but rather from certain improvements in microeconomic conditions (in particular, the growth in the private sector) on the one hand, and more or less autonomous increases in domestic demand (mainly individual consumption). Restrictive macroeconomic policies can be expected to continue during 1994 in the low-inflation countries of central Europe; moreover, more austerity is also likely to be seen in the high-inflation countries of southern Europe.

As for the *external sector*, it is likely to exert an ambiguous influence on the recovery in the transition economies. On the one hand, it is not only the large budget deficits and high rates of inflation that limit the scope of expansionary economic policies; so do the increasing external imbalances of most transition economies. (In contrast with eastern Europe, in Russia and the CIS countries "external imbalance" means a massive trade surplus, which also indicates serious, although certainly different, problems.) On the other hand, the overall external environment (i.e., economic activity in the developed market economies) is likely to be more supportive of the *growth of exports* from the transition economies than it was in 1993. While "specific western import demand" facing eastern Europe fell by 5 per cent in 1993, it is projected to *increase* by roughly 3 per cent in 1994.[305]

However, regarding economic policies, growing trade and current-account deficits are likely to impose serious constraints on most governments in the region. These constraints may enjoin some further tightening of monetary policies, the need to implement restrictive fiscal measures, and/or the tightening of import regimes (higher tariffs) in order to reduce the deficits. The worrying aspect is that the deterioration of the external balances appeared at a very early stage of economic recovery; in several cases even before the recovery actually got under way. Thus,

---

[302] See, e.g., "Progress in the Economies in Transition in Central and Eastern Europe: The Role of Policies and External Assistance", address by M. Camdessus, *IMF Survey*, 1994, No.2, International Monetary Fund, Washington, D.C., 14 February 1994; "Economic Recovery in the East", *PlanEcon Report*, Vol.IX, No.49-52, 10 February 1994.

[303] See J. Kornai, "Transformational Recession. A General Phenomenon Examined through the Example of Hungary's Development", Collegium Budapest, Institute for Advanced Studies, *Discussion Papers No.1*, June 1993.

[304] The fall of output increases unit costs, and thus contributes to the rise in prices; it also results in the contraction of the tax base and the growth of public expenditures related to increasing unemployment.

[305] See chart 3.5.1 and the related discussion in section 3.5.

corrective macroeconomic policy measures may have to be implemented even before the countries are able to reach sustained economic growth. This, in turn, would have strongly negative effects on the transformation process.

One of the key reasons behind the fragility of recovery in transition countries is that it has been fuelled mainly by expansion of consumer expenditures, while *capital investment* has been falling since 1989 and now remains at a very depressed level (see section 3.2). And yet, no sustained growth can be reasonably foreseen without a strong upturn in investments, which is badly needed to modernize and restructure production capacities in transition economies. But immediate prospects for expansion of investment activities are mixed at best. First, the low level of *savings* in most transition countries (except Hungary) limits the availability of financial resources for capital accumulation. Second, relatively high inflation and large budget deficits can be expected to keep *interest rates* at high levels, thus discouraging investment decisions. Attempts to reduce fiscal imbalances from the expenditure side in order to ease the upward pressure on interest rates are likely to meet with strong resistance from wage-earners, farmers and social groups depending on fiscal transfers. Even if some relief for the strained budget can probably come from better tax collection and consolidation of the tax base through the VAT reform, the overall budget position is likely to remain difficult in the medium-term perspective in most transition countries.

Investment possibilities are further hindered by the generally high level of indebtedness of state enterprises and considerable accumulation of non-performing loans in the banking sector – two problems which have to be addressed jointly because they are in fact two facets of the same non-payment issue.[306] Attempts have been undertaken by some governments in transition countries to tackle the twin problem of *restructuring state enterprises* and *commercial banks*, using varying combinations of debt write-offs, debt-for-equity conversion, privatization, and recapitalization of banks, but progress has been slow and results can be expected only in the medium-term perspective. Nevertheless, the launching in 1993 of various restructuring programmes in countries such as Hungary, Poland or Romania is a reassuring development. By contrast, in less advanced transition countries, such as most CIS states, the restructuring and reform of the financial sector has not even reached the stage of the preparation of comprehensive and operational plans.

In consequence, the prospects for a *sustained* recovery appear to be better in countries with smaller internal and external imbalances, and with advanced structural reforms. In particular, the *Czech Republic* and *Slovenia*, where the external constraint is weakest and inflation among the lowest in the region, are likely to display the strongest recovery in 1994. Beside the relatively favourable external payments position, Slovenia is likely to benefit also from the strong upturn in investment activity registered in 1993. The recovery in the Czech Republic may, however, clash with the exigencies of a more vigorous restructuring of privatized enterprises which could result in additional unemployment and a temporary fall in output.

Hungary is in a special situation, as the sharp deterioration in its current account in 1993 was accompanied by a strong improvement of its foreign exchange position, with international reserves reaching historically high levels due to heavy foreign borrowing by the central bank in 1993. As a consequence, the country has somewhat greater room for manoeuvre than is suggested by the huge deficit in its current account, and the difficult measures for redressing the external balance may well be postponed, to be left to the new government that will take office after the elections in May 1994. But interest rates remain high because of continued inflationary pressures and the large budget deficit; in consequence, the fledgling economic recovery under way might easily turn out to be short-lived, losing steam in the second half of the year. Also in *Romania*, where the upturn in industrial production has been the result not only of increasing exports but also of an acceleration of credit expansion, the sustainability of the emerging economic growth appears to be under a question mark. In fact, stagnating output is the most likely development in 1994, given the generally restrictive course of fiscal and monetary policies which has been made a precondition for the agreement with the IMF signed in November 1993.

In *Poland*, the first country to come out of the recession, economic growth is likely to continue at about 4 per cent, as in 1993. This may be expected in spite of the tensions due to the growing trade and payments deficits, because the country managed to conclude its agreement with the international commercial banks in March 1994 and can count on additional inflows of foreign capital. Moreover, the trade imbalance in Poland has so far been accompanied by a relatively strong growth of exports, which makes the deficit more acceptable than, e.g., in Hungary, where the fall of exports is at the root of the large increase in the trade deficit.

As for prospective developments in *employment* in the east European transition countries, in the short run no positive impact of economic growth on the level of unemployment can be expected. Unemployment is likely to rise significantly (although still to a relatively low level) in the Czech Republic, and to remain high or even increase in most other transition countries. An improvement on the labour markets can only come in the medium term, when new investments should gradually bring about new job opportunities, but probably not earlier than in 1995 in the central European countries and even later in others.

In all these countries, further gains on the *inflation* front are likely to be modest; in Hungary, even some acceleration of inflation is possible. Among possible exceptions are Croatia and FR Yugoslavia, where year-over-year inflation may decelerate if the two countries persevere with the recently introduced stabilization programmes. The main reasons for the persistence of inflation are to be found in large fiscal deficits, increases of tax rates and customs tariffs, upward drift of controlled energy prices, and depreciation of domestic currencies. In the countries where the foreign trade and payments balances have been strongly deteriorating, it is no longer feasible to use the exchange rate (via currency appreciation in real terms) as an anti-inflationary device; to redress the external accounts, real depreciations appear to be inevitable.

---

[306] See S. van Wijnbergen, "Enterprise reform in eastern Europe", Centre for Economic Policy Research, *Discussion Paper Series*, No.738, November 1992.

In the remaining countries of eastern Europe where GDP fell rather sharply in 1993, a further, though somewhat milder, *decline* can be expected in 1994. Some of them seem not to be very far from a bottoming out of the recession (Slovakia, Bulgaria), while in others significant further declines are likely (FR Yugoslavia, the FYR of Macedonia). In *Slovakia*, the government expects zero growth, but current trends in the economy point rather towards some further decline in output with significantly increasing unemployment. The prospects are similar in *Bulgaria*. Here too, even though government forecasts envisage mild economic growth, GDP is more likely to drop slightly; internal imbalances (the large budget deficit and an inflation rate still over 50 per cent) and external payments difficulties both constrain the recovery.

(ii) Uncertain prospects for the CIS economies

The economic outlook for the CIS economies is extremely uncertain. What may be forecast with confidence is that output in most these countries will continue to decline, although the rate of fall is expected to be much smaller than in 1993. The main problem faced by *Russia* and other *CIS states* is the lack of firm macroeconomic control over the economy which could slow down inflation and establish foundations for growth. Macroeconomic instability results chiefly from excessive budgetary expenditures in support of loss-making enterprises and from deficient credit policy which has been unable to allocate financial resources according to efficiency criteria. Low discipline of contract enforcement, accumulating payments arrears, frequent changes in economic legislation and constant controversies over necessary policy measures contribute to inflation by increasing transaction costs and adding to general business uncertainty.

Official government forecasts in *Russia* are cautiously optimistic: the rate of output decline is expected to fall from 12 per cent to 8-10 per cent and monthly inflation is to slow down to less than 10 per cent by the end of 1994. At the same time, the budget deficit is to be kept at 7-7.5 per cent of GDP.[307] Nevertheless, serious doubts remain as to whether these ambitious targets are feasible. As noted by some commentators, the deficit may actually be higher because expected tax revenues appear to reflect overly optimistic assumptions,[308] and the planned expenditures limits are likely to run into parliamentary resistance. Besides the ability of the government to cope with inflation (which, in turn, depends on its capacity to control public finances and primary money emission aimed at assisting companies and sectors facing difficulties), the prospects for Russia's external economic performance also raise serious questions. In particular, the huge trade surplus of 1993, which was based on a sharp decline of imports and the stagnation of exports, has not benefited the liquidity of the state because of capital flight on a considerable scale. On the other hand, the surplus is not likely to be sustainable if the decline of output is to be eventually halted; thus, the trade balance may deteriorate in 1994.

The outlook for the *Ukrainian* economy is on most counts (i.e., regarding output, inflation, public finance, external accounts), even worse than that of other CIS countries. The chances for stabilization depend on whether a comprehensive austerity programme can be implemented; but no prospects for such a programme can be seen at the moment. The government, divided over various concepts of reform, seems unable to break the inflationary spiral and to enforce a hard budget constraint on the large state sector. The most likely outcome is a further significant deterioration of macroeconomic performance in Ukraine in 1994.

(iii) End of recession in the Baltic states?

Among the Baltic states, *Estonia* has the best prospects for moderate growth in 1994. The output fall seems to have bottomed in the last quarter of 1993, and both the fiscal balance and foreign balance appear to be less of constraint on recovery than in other countries. However, growth is not likely to be significant, as gross fixed capital formation still is contracting. Government forecasts envisage 2 per cent or slightly higher real growth of GDP in 1994 and an inflation of 19-20 per cent. These targets seem realistic, given the broadly balanced fiscal position in 1993, and the balanced state budget planned for 1994. Restrictive monetary policy is not likely to give too much room for a strong pick-up of domestic demand; the recovery can be expected to be generated chiefly by growth of exports.

Although the government of *Latvia* also expects that the economy will start to grow in 1994, the prospects are less optimistic because of the continuing steep fall of output in 1993 and the very high interest rates. With investments still on the decline, and almost two thirds of the state budget assigned for social needs, a more vigorous stimulus for economic recovery can only come from foreign direct investment and external assistance. However, even if the inflow of foreign investments accelerated strongly in 1993, there is no evidence that this tendency will continue at a similar speed in 1994.

Doubts are even stronger about the prospects of the *Lithuanian* economy. The government forecasts speak of 1 per cent growth of GDP and 4-5 per cent growth of industrial output in 1994, but these figures seem highly optimistic, given the steep 17 per cent decrease of GDP and 46 per cent fall of industrial sales in 1993. Moreover, there is no sign as yet of any reversal in the downward course of investments. While the contraction of output can be expected to slow down rather significantly in 1994, it is rather unlikely to be stopped or reversed before 1995.

The Baltic states have suffered enormous economic losses since the beginning of transformation, chiefly because of the abrupt severance of economic links with Russia and other republics of the former Soviet Union. Given the limited domestic resources and the small size of these economies, as well as structural imbalances inherited from the Soviet era, prospects for recovery depend crucially on inflows of *foreign direct investments and western financial support*.

---

[307] RF Goskomstat et al., op.cit., p.127; *BIKI*, No.26, 5 March 1994.

[308] Reports on the recent negotiations between the Russian government and the IMF over the release of the second tranche of the Systemic Transformation facility of $1.5 billion suggest that important differences of opinions remain as to the possibility of reaching the established macroeconomic targets in 1994. *Financial Times*, 23 March 1994.

Chapter 4

EXTERNAL SUPPORT FOR THE TRANSITION ECONOMIES

4.1 Financial flows and commitments of financial assistance

(i) Overview

The transition economies continued to make progress, albeit limited, in gaining access to international finance in 1993. The increase in their access to private foreign capital was modest but, significantly, included countries which only recently gained their independence and thus were new to creditors and investors. However, the growing inflow of borrowed private funds and equity investment into the region remained concentrated in Hungary and the new Czech Republic. Hungary is well established in the international funds markets and the Czech Republic inherited the good credit rating of Czechoslovakia. Only these two countries were able to further diversify their sources of private funds. Enterprises in a number of countries managed to borrow directly from abroad, in some cases as part of co-financing operations with the international financial institutions. However, the use of purely commercial bank credits remained limited, due primarily to banks' perception of political and economic risks in the region.

These small improvements in access to alternative sources of funds occurred against the background of a general deterioration in current account balances (except in the case of the Czech Republic and Russia – see section 3.6). Although the resulting deficits appear to have been readily financed, the weakening of exports in 1993 raises questions about the capacity of these countries to generate sufficient foreign exchange in the future. Insufficient information is currently available to determine whether the recent growth of imports into eastern Europe has strengthened export capacity. The rising dependence of some countries on spontaneous capital inflows – however welcome it is at the moment – may also increase their vulnerability to sudden shifts in investor preferences.

In general, the transition economies made little use of officially-backed export credits. Domestic investment remained depressed while insurance coverage for the east European countries tends to be limited (in various degrees). For Russia and several other republics of the former USSR, it has been constrained to projects where raw material outputs can serve as collateral. In 1993, the conditions applying to insurance coverage generally tightened.

An increasing number of transition economies gained access to the resources of the international financial institutions in 1993. Those concluding arrangements with the IMF rose to almost one half of the IMF's eastern country membership. However, only seven countries finalized full standby agreements while the remaining six gained access to the new systemic transformation facility. IMF disbursements to eastern Europe declined and rose to the CIS (but the amount released to Russia was considerably less than had been envisaged). Financial commitments of the development institutions (EIB, EBRD, and the World Bank group) to the transition countries increased rapidly, faster than their disbursements.

During 1990-1993, loan commitments[309] by the development institutions were concentrated in the three countries (Hungary, Czech Republic, and Poland) which also accounted for the bulk of the eastern region's international borrowings and equity investment reflects *inter alia* the advanced stage of their reforms, their relatively greater commitment to IMF-approved macroeconomic policies and, in some cases, their creditworthiness. However, a number of transition economies had arranged only little or no funding at all by the end of 1993. This distribution of resources, which might be modified by including projects in the pipeline, runs counter to the notion that the transition economies have broadly similar requirements and that multilateral funds should be used to compensate for the inability of most of them to attract private capital. Loan commitments of the development banks for infrastructure projects (transport, telecommunications, etc.), essential for transition economies trying to integrate into the world economy, do not appear to be very large and also appear to be concentrated in the most advanced countries. Overall, the results suggest a large gap between the requirements of the transition economies and the multilateral resources allocated so far.

A problem shared by many of the transition economies has been their inability to meet the conditionality requirements of the international financial institutions. Most have failed to adopt an economic programme approved by the IMF; or to meet periodic performance criteria for the release of scheduled tranches; or to satisfy other conditions agreed with the development banks. In consequence, the disbursement of funds by these institutions was lower than the transition countries would

---

[309] Loans and equity investments approved by their governing boards.

have been qualified to receive and also lower than outstanding commitments would have permitted. It is not certain, however, whether the inability of these countries to obtain access to these funds contributed to their inadequate economic performance and, thus, also to their failure to meet the conditions set by the financial institutions.

In 1993 most east European countries received a net transfer of resources from abroad. These inflows supported domestic absorption, although their relative contribution to consumption and investment cannot easily be determined given the information available at this time. In contrast, eastern Europe transferred resources to the rest of the world in 1992, chiefly through the build-up of foreign currency reserves, while consumption and investment declined. The position of Russia has developed differently, shifting from virtually no net transfers in 1992 to a massive outflow of resources in 1993. The latter was due in part to capital flight and had large negative consequences for domestic absorption.

(ii) Private capital flows

(a) The importance of access to foreign capital

The transition economies will require large capital investments to modernize and restructure their industries. Foreign capital, in the form of funds as well as technology, management skills, know-how, etc., can help to meet these needs. Hence, an inflow of private foreign capital is essential, especially since narrow domestic capital markets are often a constraint on investment. Several considerations are involved in attracting private foreign funds: foremost among these are the country's perceived creditworthiness and political factors. Second, potential creditors are likely to regard a strong commitment to sound stabilization and structural adjustment policies (to improve the supply responsiveness of the economy, particularly of the export sector) as strengthening performance and medium-term growth prospects. Such policies should benefit from appropriate official financial support. Third, once a country has successfully raised funds in the international capital markets, it is in a better position to attract FDI and repatriate flight capital.

For those countries which have failed to service their debts, refinancing and rescheduling of obligations *vis-à-vis* London and Paris Club creditors are essential steps towards regaining creditworthiness. In extreme cases this may require the cancellation of some obligations. Experience in Latin America suggests that debt reduction combined with appropriate economic policies has reduced potential creditors' concerns about debt overhang effects.

Aside from actual entry into the funds markets, diversification of sources of capital (i.e., bonds, equity flows, bank loans and, in some cases, capital repatriation) can provide benefits in the form of more stable access to funds and more flexible financing options. An important step towards diversification is getting bonds rated as investment grade by a credit rating agency so that they become eligible for the portfolios of pension funds and other fiduciary institutions. Such wider access to funds is reflected in improved borrowing terms, for example, in lower coupons on bonds and in longer maturities.

(b) Funds raised in international markets

Total funds raised by the eastern countries in the *international markets* rose sharply in 1993 (table 4.1.1), exceeding the previous peak (in 1989-1990) when the Soviet Union was a major borrower. Hungary and the new Czech Republic, the only two transition economies which enjoy significant access to these markets, accounted for the bulk of the borrowing. In terms of instruments, the structure parallels that of creditworthy developing countries, i.e., chiefly bond issues emitted by relatively few borrowers.[310]

According to the OECD, *Hungary* obtained $5.1 billion in 1993, including three DM 1 billion emissions, to finance an unexpectedly large current account deficit (see section 3.6), maturing debt, and an increase of foreign currency reserves. A part of the funds was also intended to meet anticipated needs in 1994.[311] The first issues by the new *Czech Republic* consisted of a $375 million Eurodollar bond (in March) and a yen 35 billion ($328 million) offering (in July). Although the Czech Republic inherited the former Czechoslovakia's international credit rating, there were initial doubts about the market's receptivity to the first issue after a bout of capital flight precipitated by the latter's dissolution. However, these fears proved unfounded and the subsequent evolution of the country's financial situation facilitated the second emission. The first bonds of the *Slovak Republic* were issued in September through an international private placement. In January 1994, Calex launched a three-year $21 million Eurobond, the first for a Slovak corporation.[312]

Hungary and the Czech Republic consolidated their access to the markets in 1993. The Czech Republic was assigned investment grade *credit ratings* by Moody's Investment Services and Standard and Poor's.[313] In January 1994, Prague became the first east European city to obtain an (investment grade) international credit rating.[314] For some time, Moody's has assigned a Ba1 rating to Hungary, one notch below investment grade. Both countries managed to diversify the *currency structure*

---

[310] UNCTAD, *Trade and Development Report*, New York, 1993, pp.49-50. The observation concerning the developing countries was made on the basis of data for 1991. This pattern appears to have carried over into 1992 and 1993. See OECD, *Financial Statistics Monthly*, Paris, September 1993.

[311] The National Bank of Hungary reports that $5.4 billion was raised in 1993 of which $4.4 billion was drawn. The remaining $1 billion was to be drawn in the first half of 1994. National Bank of Hungary, *Monthly Report*, 11-12/1993.

[312] World Bank, *Financial Flows and the Developing Countries*, Washington, D.C., February 1994. The bond carried a spread of 325 basis (percentage) points over US Treasury bills.

[313] Moody's Investment Services and Standard and Poor's assigned the Czech Republic a Baa3 and a BBB rating, respectively, the latter being two notches above investment grade.

[314] Prague received a BBB rating from Standard and Poor's. *Hospodarske Noviny*, 20 January 1994. The rating was obtained in conjunction with the city of Prague's plan to emit a bond issue, valued at least at $150 million.

TABLE 4.1.1
Medium- and long-term funds raised on the international financial markets by transition countries, 1988-1993
(Million US dollars)

	1988	1989	1990	1991	1992	1993	International bond issues: amounts outstanding [a]
Bulgaria	194	580	–	–	–	–	200
Czech Republic	..	..	..	..	..	903	–
Hungary	1 016	1 708	987	1 378	1 446	5 071	10 400
Poland	–	163	–	5	9	–	–
Romania	–	–	–	–	–	–	–
Slovakia	..	..	..	..	..	240	–
Slovenia	..	..	..	..	..	100	..
Former Czechoslovakia	330	334	438	278	40	..	1 400
Eastern Europe	1 540	2 785	1 425	1 661	1 494	6 150	11 900
Georgia	..	..	..	..	–	20	–
Russia	..	..	..	..	–	8	–
Former Soviet Union	2 679	1 858	3 250	–	..	..	1 600
CMEA Banks	75	75	–	–	–	–	–
Transition economies	4 294	4 718	4 675	1 661	1 494	6 341	13 500
of which:							
Bank loans [b]	1 050	2 047	2 993	86	235	590	
Foreign bank loans [c]	1 652	358	–	60	9	–	..
Other [d]	232	75	–	–	–	–	..
Bonds	1 360	2 239	1 682	1 516	1 250	5 751	..

Sources: OECD, *Financial Statistics Monthly*, Part I, February 1994 and previous issues; BIS, *International Banking and Financial Market Developments*, Basle, February 1994.

[a] End-September 1993.
[b] International bank loans in Eurocurrencies, excluding officially guaranteed loans and rescheduled debt.
[c] In domestic currency of lending countries, excluding guaranteed loans.
[d] Other bank facilities, including bankers' acceptances.

of their borrowings. For the first time Hungary borrowed in pound sterling and Austrian schillings, and the Czech Republic in yen, among other currencies. The *terms* of Hungary's bond issues have also improved. For example, the third DM 1 billion issue carried a margin of 1 percentage point, below the 2½-3 points which Hungary had to pay in 1992. Much of this decline, however, appears to have been due to changing market conditions which benefited borrowers in general and investors searching for relatively high yield securities as interest rates continued to fall.

(c) Equity investment

The flow of *foreign direct investment* into eastern Europe rose modestly in 1993 reaching $3.5 billion (table 4.1.2). Overall, however, the levels of FDI are below the expectations of several years ago and, in general, the amounts are still small. (It should be borne in mind that the FDI statistics presented here derive from balance of payments accounts. They provide a narrow measure of foreign investment since they cover only cash inflows and thus exclude investment goods and other contributions in kind as well as reinvestment of profits by foreign partners.)

As in the past few years, FDI was highly concentrated. Hungary received a net inflow of some $2.2 billion, of which $875 million involved a single investment in MATAV telecommunications. Without this deal FDI in Hungary would have declined slightly in 1993. It fell even more steeply in the Czech Republic, the other leading destination for FDI in the area. The doubling of the flow of FDI into Estonia is noteworthy. Per capita FDI flows, too, suggest that after a slow start Estonia (and Slovenia) have been relatively successful in attracting foreign investment (table 4.1.2).

The factors determining foreign investment are complex. So far, Hungary and the Czech Republic, the countries perceived by the international capital markets as being the most creditworthy, have also received the largest amounts of FDI. The stage reached in privatization also seems to affect investor activity. It has been suggested that the decline in FDI experienced by the Czech Republic was due to the absence of large foreign acquisitions and anticipation of the second wave of privatization in the spring of 1994. Increased foreign investment in Poland in 1992 and 1993 has in part been attributed to the passage of legislation dealing with privatization.

A new phenomenon was the flow of funds into the emerging stock markets in eastern Europe. Poland led the global stock market boom with a price gain of nearly 800 per cent in 1993. In the last four months of 1993 the stock market index for the Czech Republic rose by 138 per cent, while Hungary's stock market gained 44 per cent in the second half of 1993.[315] So far, however, the coverage of

---
[315] PlanEcon, *Czech Economic Monitor and Review of 1993 Stock Market Performance*, 14 January 1994.

TABLE 4.1.2

Joint ventures and foreign direct investment in transition countries, 1990-1993
(Number of projects, million US dollars)

	Joint ventures [a]		Net flows of FDI					
	1992	1993	1990	1991	1992	Jan.-Sept 1993	1993	Per capita [b]
Albania	..	..	–	–	19	25*	30 [c]	9
Bulgaria	1 200*	2 300*	4	56	42	36	48*	5
Croatia	..	..	–	–	-1	56	75*	16
Czech Republic	3 120*	5 000	135	510	983	399	409 [d, e]	43
Hungary [f]	17 182	21 500	311	1 459	1 471	822	2 328	226
Poland [f]	5 740	6 800	88	117	284	346	380 [d]	11
Romania	20 684	29 115	-18	37	73	35	48	2
Slovakia [f]	2 875	4 350*	53	82	71	100*	120*	28
Slovenia	2 815*	3 300*	-2	41	113	94	110	55
Eastern Europe	53 616	72 365	573	2 302	3 055	1 917	3 548	33
Belarus	714	1 250*	..	..	..	..	..	..
Russia	3 252	7 989	..	100	800	..	400	3
Ukraine	2 000	2 800*	..	..	..	..	..	..
Estonia [f]	2 662	4 150*	..	..	58	106	140*	89
Latvia	2 621	2 850*	..	..	..	..	..	..
Lithuania	2 000*	3 000*	..	..	..	..	..	..
Total	13 249	22 039	..	..	..	..	..	..

Sources: United Nations Economic Commission for Europe joint venture database; national balance of payments statistics.

[a] Number of foreign direct investment projects registered, end of period.
[b] FDI in US dollars per capita in 1993.
[c] Projected.
[d] January-November.
[e] Excludes $942 million in portfolio investment.
[f] Joint venture figures refer to the number of operational enterprises.

portfolio investment in the official statistics of the transition economies is very limited. The Czech National Bank reported a net inflow from abroad of $962 million in the first 11 months of 1993, while the Russian Federation registered a net inflow of $100 million ($400 million gross) for the whole year. Flows into Hungary and Poland are uncertain since portfolio investment is not reported separately from direct investments.

(d) Bank lending

International bank lending to the eastern countries continued sluggishly in 1993, reflecting creditors' generally negative perception of the area. *Publicized medium- and long-term bank loans* amounted to some $430 million (table 4.1.1), accounted for chiefly by Hungary, the Czech Republic and Slovenia. For Hungary this was the first internationally syndicated credit since 1989, and for the other two countries, their first as independent states.[316]

BIS data, which are more comprehensive in several respects, show a similar picture of relatively low commercial bank lending to the transition economies during the first three quarters of 1993 (table 4.1.3). Adjusted for exchange rate movements, commercial bank claims[317] generally declined indicating that the value of new loans was smaller than repayments.[318] Access to world capital markets has enabled the Czech Republic and, especially, Hungary to diversify out of bank credits through an expanding variety of financial instruments, as noted above.[319] In 1992, there had been signs that western banks' direct lending to private enterprises in the former Czechoslovakia, Hungary and Poland had risen (in contrast with the reduction of their exposure to the official sector in these countries).[320] However, this tendency did not continue in the first half of 1993. Overall, the 9.6 per cent share of the non-bank private sector in the total claims of BIS banks on the eastern countries is still far below the 34 per cent average for the developing countries. However,

---

[316] Slovenia has obtained two syndicated loans, the first for $100 million and the second for $15 million, the latter increased from $10 million due to oversubscription. World Bank, op.cit.

[317] Excluding loans covered by government guarantees, except in the third quarter of 1993 when guaranteed credits are included (see table 4.1.3).

[318] BIS/OECD, *Statistics on External Indebtedness*, Basle and Paris, January 1994. Reporting banks' commercial claims on Bulgaria, Poland and the former Soviet Union declined in the first half of 1993. Presumably this reflects the decisions of banks to write-down, write-off or sell (at a discount) debt of these countries whose debt servicing is in arrears. The value of these operations exceeds the accumulation of interest arrears.

[319] BIS, *The Maturity and Sectoral Distribution of International Bank Lending, First Half 1993*, Basle, January 1994.

[320] BIS, *The Maturity and Sectoral Distribution of International Bank Lending, Second Half 1992*, Basle, July 1993.

TABLE 4.1.3

Bank and non-bank debt of transition economies *vis-à-vis* BIS and OECD reporting institutions, 1990-1993
(Billion US dollars, exchange rate adjusted changes)

	1990	1991	1992	1993 QI-II	1993 QIII
Bulgaria					
Total bank debt	-0.5	-0.70	-0.5	-0.4	-0.1
Commercial debt	-0.2	-0.7	-0.4	-0.4	..
Guaranteed debt	-0.3	-	-0.1	-	..
Non-bank debt	-	0.3	-	-	..
Total guaranteed debt [a]	-0.3	0.3	-0.1	-	..
Former Czechoslovakia					
Total bank debt	-0.4	-0.8	-0.1	-0.2	-0.1
Commercial debt	-0.2	-0.8	-0.4	-	..
Guaranteed debt	-0.3	-	0.3	-0.3	..
Non-bank debt	-	0.2	0.3	-0.5	..
Total guaranteed debt [a]	-0.3	0.2	0.6	-0.8	..
Hungary					
Total bank debt	-1.9	-1.5	-1.5	0.1	-1.1
Commercial debt	-1.7	-1.2	-1.7	-	..
Guaranteed debt	-0.1	-0.2	0.2	0.1	..
Non-bank debt	0.1	0.3	-	-	..
Total guaranteed debt [a]	-0.1	0.1	0.2	0.1	..
Poland					
Total bank debt	-	-	0.1	-0.5	-0.2
Commercial debt	0.2	0.3	-0.4	-0.6	..
Guaranteed debt	-0.2	-0.3	0.5	0.1	..
Non-bank debt	0.8	-0.3	0.3	-0.2	..
Total guaranteed debt [a]	0.6	-0.6	0.8	-0.2	..
Romania					
Total bank debt	-	0.6	-	0.1	0.1
Commercial debt	-	0.1	-	-0.1	..
Guaranteed debt	-	0.5	-	0.2	..
Non-bank debt	-	-	0.1	0.2	..
Total guaranteed debt [a]	-	0.5	0.1	0.4	..
Total above					
Total bank debt	-2.7	-2.3	-2.0	-0.9	-1.4
Commercial debt	-1.8	-2.4	-2.9	-1.1	..
Guaranteed debt	-0.9	0.1	0.9	0.1	..
Non-bank debt	0.8	0.4	0.6	-0.5	..
Total guaranteed debt [a]	-0.1	0.5	1.7	-0.4	..
Former Soviet Union					
Total bank debt	-6.2	2.0	5.5	0.4	-
Commercial debt	-10.7	-5.2	-1.9	-0.3	..
Guaranteed debt	4.6	7.2	7.5	0.7	..
Non-bank debt	0.1	0.4	0.5	2.8	..
Total guaranteed debt [a]	4.7	7.6	8.0	3.5	..

Sources: BIS, *International Banking and Financial Market Developments*, Basle, February 1994; BIS/OECD, *Statistics on External Indebtedness*, Basle and Paris, January 1994 and previous issues.

[a] Guaranteed bank and non-bank debt.

the proportion reported for the former Czechoslovakia, 31 per cent, is not far behind.[321]

(iii) Official credits

Given the transition economies' generally restricted access to private capital, official funding will continue to be a key element of support for years to come. Within the context of the international assistance effort on their behalf, individual western countries and the EU have made large financial commitments to the east, in the form of export credits, guarantees, and so on.[322] Virtually all of the transition economies have become members of the IMF, the World Bank and the EBRD (the latter having been established specifically to support the transition), thus gaining access to these institutions' considerable resources.

(a) Bilateral credits

Eastern Europe's use of western guaranteed credit facilities[323] remained weak in the first half of 1993 (table 4.1.3), presumably because of the persistence of low domestic investment and the high cost and restrictive conditions applying to credit insurance offered by western institutions. The virtual lack of change in western guaranteed claims (at constant exchange rates) on these countries implies that new credits only equalled repayments.[324] However, western claims on Romania and the former Soviet Union did rise, by $3.5 billion on the latter. In addition to new lending,[325] this large increase reflects the build-up of interest arrears and the virtual absence of debt repayments.

At the beginning of 1993, only Hermes of Germany had made credit insurance available for most transition economies.[326] ECGD limits cover to the Czech Republic, Hungary, (as does NCM in both cases),[327] Russia[328] and, as of July 1993, to Poland.[329] NCM also provides cover for Romania and Slovakia. More recently, there are signs that the conditions for western coverage are being tightened due to both growing perceptions of risk in the eastern region and mounting pressures in the west against guarantees because of their budgetary implications.[330] Various degrees of short-term coverage are available for most east

---

[321] BIS, op.cit., January 1994.

[322] See United Nations Economic Commission for Europe, *Economic Survey for Europe in 1992-1993*, New York, 1993, pp.239-241.

[323] These loans comprise guaranteed bank credits, facilities extended by official credit agencies, and guaranteed non-bank short-term trade credits. The data represent changes in the claims of western institutions on the transition economies, adjusted for exchange rate movements.

[324] In the former Czechoslovakia, which has access to alternative sources of finance, repayments substantially exceeded new credits.

[325] Officially guaranteed lending reflects the increased exposure of banks in Germany and a new debt deferral agreement in March 1993. BIS, *International Banking and Financial Market Developments*, Basle, August 1993, p.9.

[326] UNCTAD, *Trade and Development Report*, 1993, op.cit., p.64.

[327] Ibid., p.68. NCM is the Nederlandsche Credietverzekering Maatschappi and the ECGD is the Export Credits Guarantee Department of the United Kingdom.

[328] In April, the ECGD announced that it was doubling the upper limit (to $1 billion) to the cover it would provide for the republics of the former USSR, $800 million of which was earmarked for Russia. At present only Russia has met the conditions for cover, although the agency's position on Kazakhstan, Estonia, Latvia and Lithuania is under review. *East European Finance*, 28 July 1993, p.13.

[329] In July, the ECGD resumed medium-term cover for Poland, which was withdrawn in 1982 after Poland ceased servicing official debt. Cover has been restored because of the country's agreement with the Paris Club and the IMF's satisfaction with its economic performance. EIU, *Poland, Country Report*, 3rd Quarter, 1993.

[330] *Business Eastern Europe*, 14 February 1994.

TABLE 4.1.4

IMF arrangements in force in transition economies in 1992-1994
(Million SDRs)

	Duration		Arrangement		STF [a]	Total
	Commencement	Expiration	Type	Amount		
Albania	26 Aug. 1992	25 Aug. 1993	Standby	20.0	–	20.0
	14 July 1993	13 July 1996	ESAF [b]	42.4	–	42.4
Bulgaria [c]	17 Apr. 1992	16 Apr. 1993	Standby	155.0	–	155.0
Czech Republic	17 Mar. 1993	16 Mar. 1994	Standby	177.0	–	177.0
Hungary	20 Feb. 1991	19 Feb. 1994	Extended [c]	1 114.0	–	1 114.0
	15 Sept. 1993	14 Dec. 1994	Standby	340.0	–	340.0
Poland	18 Apr. 1991	17 Apr. 1994	Extended [d]	1 224.0	–	1 224.0
	8 Mar. 1993	7 Mar. 1994	Standby	476.0	–	476.0
Romania	29 May 1992	28 Mar. 1993	Standby	314.0	–	314.0
	Dec. 1993 [e]		Standby	131.0	375.0	506.0
Slovak Republic	27 July 1993	–	–	–	64.5	64.5
CSFR	3 Apr. 1992	2 Apr. 1993	Standby [f]	236.0	–	..
Eastern Europe			Total: 1992	725.0 [g]	–	725.0 [g]
			Total: 1993	993.0 [g]	64.5	1 057.5 [g]
Belarus	28 July 1993	–	–	–	70.1	70.1
Kazakhstan	23 July 1993	..	–	–	61.9	61.9
	2 Jan. 1994	1 April 1995	Standby	123.8	61.9	185.7
Kyrgyzstan	12 May 1993	11 April 1994	Standby	27.1	16.1	43.2
	21 Sept. 1993	–	–	–	16.1	16.1
Moldova	3 Feb. 1993	–	–	–	13.5 [h]	13.5
	1 July 1993	30 June 1994	–	–	22.5	22.5
	17 Dec. 1993	16 Mar. 1995	Standby	51.8	22.5	74.3
Russia	5 Aug. 1992	4 Jan. 1993	Standby [i]	719.0	–	719.0
	30 June 1993				1 078.3	1 078.3
Estonia	16 Sept. 1992	15 Sept. 1993	Standby	27.9	–	27.9
	27 Oct. 1993	26 Mar 1995	Standby	11.6	11.6	23.2
Latvia	14 Sept. 1992	13 Sept. 1993	Standby	54.9	–	54.9
	15 Dec. 1993	14 Mar. 1995	Standby	22.9	22.9	45.8
Lithuania	21 Oct. 1992	20 Oct. 1993	Standby	56.9	–	56.9
	22 Oct. 1993	21 Mar. 1995	Standby	25.9	25.9	51.8
Former Soviet Union			Total: 1992	858.7	–	858.7
			Total: 1993	139.3	1 309.3	1 478.2

Sources: IMF, *International Financial Statistics*, Washington, D.C., various issues and press releases.

[a] Systemic tranformation facility (the two equal tranches are listed separately).
[b] Enhanced structural adjustment facility.
[c] Superseded by standby arrangement of September 1993.
[d] Superseded by arrangement of March 1993.
[e] Letter of credit signed.
[f] Lapsed upon the dissolution of the CSFR.
[g] Excludes extended arrangements for Hungary and Poland originally extending through 1994.
[h] Compensatory and contingency financing facility.
[i] First credit tranche.

European countries, but short- and medium-term coverage are generally difficult to come by for the CIS.[331]

(b) Multilateral financing

The activities of the international financial institutions in the transition countries gathered pace in 1993. The number of transition countries reaching agreement on programmes with these institutions has grown, as has the range of projects and facilities. This is reflected in the marked increase in financial *commitments* in 1993, chiefly because of higher lending by the development banks (tables 4.1.4 and 4.1.5). *Disbursements*, however, increased only modestly and remained below the level of 1991 (table 4.1.6). Several transition economies have yet to qualify for the resources of these institutions.

The slow pace of disbursement by some development institutions prompted a lot of criticism during 1992 and early 1993. Much of the criticism does not appear to be justified, but it led some of them to raise their targets for lending. As discussed below, the results so far appear to be mixed. The reasons for slow disbursement are complex, varying from case to case and involving factors on the side

---

[331] Ibid. Short term coverage is available for the following countries (in ascending order of perceived risk): the Czech Republic, Hungary and Poland; Romania, Slovenia and Slovakia (medium-risk category); Bulgaria (extremely limited coverage). For the CIS, coverage is virtually limited to Russia and Kazakhstan, for projects from which earnings are guaranteed by collateral in raw materials, fuels and gold.

TABLE 4.1.5

Financial commitments of the development institutions to transition economies, 1990-1993
(Million US dollars)

	Eastern Europe [a]					CIS/Baltics		
	1990	1991	1992	1993	Cumulative [b]	1992	1993	Cumulative [b]
IBRD	1 597	2 587	1 567	1 991	7 742	895	1 162	2 057
EBRD	-	400	840	1 120 [c]	2 360	304	697 [c]	1 005
EIB	273	354	414	1 031	2 072	-	6	6
IFC [d]	84	111	132	238	565	-	87	87
Total	1 954	3 452	2 953	4 380	12 739	1 199	1 952	3 155

Sources: Annual Reports; direct communication to the ECE secretariat.

[a] Excludes former Yugoslavia; includes all regional funds.
[b] 1990-1993.
[c] 1 January-21 December.
[d] Fiscal year 1 July to 1 July.

of both donors and recipients. Access to IMF funds requires a country to demonstrate its commitment to an economic programme approved by the IMF (for a standby credit) or progress towards the formulation of such a programme (for a systemic transformation facility (STF)).[332] Such a stamp of approval is also often required for the release of certain funds by the World Bank, which adds its own conditions as well. Even if a country has a programme in place, further disbursements may be denied if it misses agreed performance targets. These and other factors hindering access to multilateral funds have been discussed in past issues of this *Survey* and the *Economic Bulletin for Europe*.[333]

IMF arrangements

During 1993, 13 out of a total of 27 European transition economies reached some kind of arrangement with the IMF (table 4.1.4).[334] Nine of them – Albania,[335] the Czech Republic, Estonia, Hungary, Latvia, Lithuania, Moldova,[336] Poland and Kyrgyzstan – concluded full standby agreements. However, Belarus, Kazakhstan, Russia and Slovakia could qualify only for the new STF, for which conditionality is somewhat less demanding than for a standby credit. A STF may also be attached to a standby agreement, a combination obtained by the Baltic states, Kyrgyzstan and Moldova (the first tranche of a STF is available immediately).[337] The other transition economies, which have not made any kind of arrangement with the IMF, have failed to do so for lack of sufficient progress in formulating their economic programmes, in some cases because of armed conflict on their territories. The exception is Slovenia, which apparently found IMF resources unnecessary at the time.

In total, the IMF made commitments of SDR 2,536 million in 1993 (table 4.1.4). Over one half was accounted for by the new STF, extended chiefly to the republics of the former Soviet Union, and the balance by standby credits. Disbursements in 1993 (in some cases from facilities arranged in 1992) amounted to $2.3 billion (SDR 2 billion), the same as in 1992 (table 4.1.6).

Gross disbursements to *eastern Europe* amounted to only $300 million and even less on a net basis, since repayments began on the first loans received by these countries. The small drawings reflect the inability of several countries to meet IMF conditions or, in certain instances, the lack of any need for IMF resources. *Bulgaria* and *Romania* had completed upper tranche arrangements in 1992, but they had difficulties in obtaining IMF approval for their economic programmes in 1993. Romania finally signed a letter of credit at the end of the year. Parliament voted on the arrangement in February

---

[332] The STF is a new temporary IMF financing facility designed to provide assistance to member countries facing balance of payments difficulties arising from severe disruptions of their trade and payments arrangements due to a shift from significant reliance on trading at non-market prices, such as prevailed among members of the CMEA, to multilateral, market-based trade. The conditions attached to the facility allow the IMF to make loans to countries which are moving toward policies that could be supported under an upper credit tranche standby agreement. The STF loan is disbursed in two tranches, half at the outset and the remainder in about six months (but not more than twelve) after the first drawing, provided that satisfactory progress is made towards meeting agreed economic targets. The new facility was announced in April 1993. IMF, *Press Release*, No.93/17, 23 April 1993.

[333] Several other key reasons may be mentioned here: all western and international institutions have been faced with starting up operations in an area where they had limited or no experience; it takes time for projects to move from the planning to the implementation stage; the recipient countries may be slow in deciding on and carrying out those things under their responsibility and control; recipients may be concerned about initiating projects that will increase external debt; and so on.

[334] All of the eastern transition economies with the exception of the Federal Republic of Yugoslavia (Serbia/Montenegro) and Bosnia-Herzegovina are members of the *International Monetary Fund* (IMF). Early in 1993 the IMF decided that the republics of Croatia and Slovenia (January) and the FYR of Macedonia (April) had fulfilled the necessary conditions for membership. Tajikistan was the last of the former USSR republics to gain membership (April 1993).

[335] *Albania's* second arrangement with the IMF is an enhanced structural adjustment facility (ESAF). Albania is the only transition economy which has qualified for the ESAF, which makes available concessional loans to low-income members undertaking structural adjustment programmes and requiring balance of payments support. The loans carry a rate of interest of 0.5 per cent and are repayable over ten years with a grace period of five and a half years.

[336] Moldova reached agreement with the IMF only towards the end of December 1993. For much of the year, its access to IMF funds was limited to the cereal component of the compensatory and contingency financing facility (CCFF) and then to a STF. Access to the CCFF was granted because of a major failure of the cereal crop due to drought followed by heavy rains, which necessitated a large increase in imports.

[337] Kazahkstan reached a similar arrangement in early 1994.

TABLE 4.1.6

Gross disbursements by international financial institutions to the transition economies, 1991-1993
(Million US dollars)

	1991	1992	1993
To eastern Europe by:			
Development institutions:			
IBRD	1 274	1 148	894
EIB	30	143	..
EBRD	–	166	489 [a]
Total	1 304	1 457	1 383 [b]
IMF	3 716	1 266	314
Total above	5 020	2 723	1 697 [b]
To former USSR by:			
IMF	–	1 061	1 985
IBRD	–	3	506
Total	–	1 064	2 491 [b]
Grand total	5 020	3 787	4 188 [b]
of which:			
IMF	3 716	2 327	2 300
Development institutions	1 304	1 460	1 889 [b]
Memorandum item:			
G-24	1 166	838	40

Sources: IMF, *International Financial Statistics*, Washington, D.C., various issues and annual reports.

[a] Includes disbursements to republics of former USSR.
[b] Total of partial data.

1994, paving the way for approval by the IMF board. Bulgaria is reported to be close to agreement on a standby arrangement, a condition for finalizing a restructuring of its Paris Club debt (scheduled for April). Due to budgetary problems, neither *Hungary* nor *Poland* were able to draw significantly on the funds attached to their three-year extended arrangements (which were to run through 1994).[338] Negotiations on new standby arrangements began in 1992, but they were finalized only in March and September 1993, respectively.[339] With the favourable development of its external financial situation, the *Czech Republic* drew only the first, SDR 70 million, tranche of its standby credit and repaid it several months later. The loan had been intended to rebuild reserves and strengthen confidence in domestic policies in the wake of the dissolution of the former CSFR. Poland passed up the first tranche of its standby loan (available on 15 May) because at that time the authorities considered foreign currency reserves ample.[340]

IMF lending to *Russia* fell well short of that envisaged in the two financial packages proposed by the G-7 in early 1992 and 1993.[341] In both cases access to a $4 billion standby credit and a $6 billion currency stabilization loan had been envisaged, but neither arrangement was finalized because of shortcomings in the implementation of the country's economic programme. In 1993 only a SDR 1.1 billion STF was released (in June).[342] A second equal disbursement was envisaged for September 1993, but it was not authorized. Persistent uncertainty concerning the future course of economic reform in Russia has led to repeated postponement of the second tranche.

Development institutions

The lending activity of the international development banks quickened in 1993, commitments rising to $6.3 billion from $4.2 billion in the previous year (table 4.1.5). Disbursements also rose, but by much less (table 4.1.6).

The value of new projects approved by the *European Bank for Reconstruction and Development* (EBRD) increased by nearly one half and disbursements rose to almost $500 million (from a low base reflecting the start-up of operations). Although the pace picked up in the second half of the year, the EBRD appears to have fallen short of its internal lending targets for the year as a whole.[343] The EBRD started lending to the transition economies in 1991. By the end of 1993 it had approved projects worth about $3.3 billion in 20 transition economies.

Aside from Latvia and Lithuania, the *European Investment Bank* (EIB) has authorized funding for projects in all of the transition countries within its lending mandate.[344] New commitments increased by $1 billion in 1993, enabling the bank to meet its cumulative lending target of ECU 1,700 million for the end of 1993 (outstanding commitments stood at ECU 920 million at end-1992). In the process the combined ceiling of ECU 700 million for Bulgaria, the Czech Republic, Romania and Slovakia was reached, while the ECU 1,000 million limit set for Hungary and Poland was nearly exhausted. However, a new ECU 3 billion three-year facility will enable the EIB to further increase its lending to these countries.[345] Priority will be given to infrastructure

---

[338] Due to these budgetary problems, Hungary voluntarily refrained from drawing the second (and subsequent) instalment of funds available for 1992, and Poland was able to draw only $321 million before further disbursements were suspended in mid-1991.

[339] Lack of formal approval of the agreement through September did not appear to hinder Hungary's ability to borrow substantial sums on the international capital markets in 1993. A "gentlemen's agreement" had already been reached between Hungary and the IMF in May 1993.

[340] *East European Finance*, 29 September 1993. The (second) tranche, of 15 August, is reported to have been frozen while the IMF board considers a new letter of intent covering performance criteria for the second half of 1993.

[341] See the United Nations Economic Commission for Europe, *Economic Bulletin for Europe*, vol.45(1993), New York and Geneva, 1994, table 4.1.7.

[342] *Russia* had been able to make a drawing in the *first tranche* in August 1992.

[343] In 1993 the value of approved and signed projects rose to ECU 1,516 million (compared to ECU 881 million in 1992) while disbursements amounted to ECU 450 million. It has been reported that the EBRD's targets for new commitments and disbursement in 1993 were ECU 2-2.6 billion and ECU 694 million, respectively. *Eastern Europe Finance*, 23 June 1993 and *Wall Street Journal*, 15 July 1993.

[344] The EIB had been authorized to lend up to ECU 2,050 million to eastern Europe: ECU 1,000 million to Hungary and Poland (decided 1989); ECU 700 million to Bulgaria, the Czech and Slovak Republics and Romania (1990); ECU 200 million to the three Baltic states (July 1993); and ECU 150 million for Slovenia's road and rail network (July 1993).

[345] The new facility awaits approval by the EIB Board of Governors. See EIB, *Financing in Central and Eastern European Countries*, October 1993. Lending will be allowed to Albania (which presently does

TABLE 4.1.7

Gross financial flows to eastern Europe and the former Soviet Union/Russia, 1990-1993
(Thousand US dollars)

	Eastern Europe				Former Soviet Union/Russia			
	1990	1991	1992	1993	1990	1991	1992	1993*
Private flows								
Capital markets	1 425	1 661	1 494	6 341	3 250	–	–	28
FDI (net)	573	2 302	3 055	3 548	–	200	858 [b]	540 [b]
Portfolio (net)	–	–	–	962	–	–	–	100 [a]
Total	1 998	3 963	4 549	10 851	3 250	200	858	668
Official flows								
Grants	1 200	1 700	1 500	1 500*	–	2 200	3 735	3 500*
Bilateral and guaranteed credits	500 [c]	1 000 [c]	800 [c]	800*	7 650 [d]	12 000	12 500 [a]	5 100 [a]
Multilateral credits	1 774	6 186	3 561	1 734	–	–	1 000	2 491
Total	3 474	8 895	5 861	4 034	7 650	14 200	17 235	11 091
New finance	5 472	12 858	10 410	14 885	10 900	14 400	18 093	11 759
Special finance	10 417	9 628	7 396	5 644	4 500	-500	13 900	18 200
Grand total	15 889	22 486	17 806	20 529	15 400	13 900	31 993	29 959

Sources: OECD, *Financial Statistics Monthly*, Part I, February 1994 and previous issues; BIS, *International Banking and Financial Market Developments*, Basle, various issues. *Flows to Central and Eastern Europe in 1990*, Paris, October 1991, and *Aid and Other Resource Flows to the Central and Eastern European Countries and the New Independent States of the Former Soviet Union in 1991 and 1992*, Paris, 1994. Russian/Soviet balance of payments statistics. Secretariat estimates.

[a] Russia only.
[b] Russia and Estonia.
[c] Concessionary credits.
[d] Estimate, includes commercial bank credits.

projects intended to facilitate the development of trade (especially through the development of Trans-European Networks (TENS)) and the restructuring of the industrial sector in the transition economies. The EC is to allocate more PHARE (EC aid programme for the central and east European countries) grants to finance feasibility studies and provide technical assistance in conjunction with these projects. This should help offset the burden of these projects on domestic financing.[346]

The *World Bank (IBRD)*, the development institution with the longest engagement in eastern Europe, remained the largest provider of development funding to the transition economies. Its new commitments rose from $2.5 billion in 1992 to over $3 billion in 1993 (table 4.1.5). Russia obtained the largest individual loan ($610 million) which is intended to help stem the rapid decline in domestic oil production.[347] Due chiefly to the $360 million disbursed to Russia, funds released to the republics of the former USSR rose to $500 million in 1993 (they obtained virtually no funds in 1992).[348] However, disbursements to eastern Europe declined. Overall, drawings were made chiefly on structural adjustment and other loans which could be quickly disbursed (see section (v)). By end-1993, the IBRD had approved loans to 18 transition economies, including those extended by the International Development Association to Albania and Kyrgyzstan.

The decline in the disbursement of World Bank funds to eastern Europe in 1993 appears mainly due to the failure of certain countries to meet the conditions set by the IMF (see above) and the World Bank itself.[349] In the case of Russia, disbursements from the $600 million rehabilitation loan (arranged in 1992) were suspended after the release of the second tranche of the IMF STF was delayed in September. No funds from the above-mentioned oil loan have been forthcoming.

(iv) **Resource flows into the transition economies**

Gross annual flows of finance into the transition economies from the west have been considerable in the last few years, ranging from some $16 to $22 billion and from $14 to $32 billion into eastern Europe and the former

---

not qualify for EIB funds), Bulgaria, the Czech Republic, Hungary, Poland, Romania and Slovakia, and Estonia, Latvia and Lithuania.

[346] In general, the financial implications for the recipient countries are likely to be small since these funds depend on the budget allocation for PHARE. For 1994 this amounts to ECU 990 million (including ECU 150 million reserved for improvement of border crossings), and, of course, is also used to fund numerous other activities.

[347] The project is co-financed by the EBRD to the extent of $250 million. The funding and support for the design of policy reforms are intended to make the oil sector more attractive to foreign investment. The plan calls for reforming energy prices and taxes, drafting an acceptable legislative framework for the oil sector, clearing up jurisdictions between government institutions responsible for the oil sector, and streamlining investment procedures.

[348] In the context of official financial assistance for Russia in 1993, the G-7 had foreseen combined disbursements by the EBRD and World Bank of $5 billion, according to Mr. M. Camdessus, Managing Director of the IMF. IMF, *Survey*, 7 February 1994, p.45.

[349] Release of the following was reported to have been delayed: second tranche of structural adjustment loans for Bulgaria; $200-300 million earmarked for the recapitalization of Hungary's commercial banks; projects worth some $1 billion in Poland. The failure of Romania to reach an agreement with the IMF in July is reported to have led to the postponement of the release of some $3 billion, including credits offered by the EC and G-24 governments. *Eastern Europe Finance*, 13 October 1993.

TABLE 4.1.8

Two measures of net transfer of resources into the transition countries and changes in reserves, 1991-1993
(Million US dollars)

	Bulgaria			Czech Republic		Hungary		
	1991	1992	1993 [a]	1992	1993 [b]	1991	1992	1993 [b]
Net transfer of resources [c]								
Capital inflows less income payments	87	-108	-	-	2 256	1 122	-780	3 784
Trade balance plus non-capital services	49	-528	207	-47	-591	-1 598	-1 541	1 935
Reserves net change [d]	45	400	-179	-80	2 687	2 720	760	1 949
of which:								
IMF (net) [e]	386	217	43	283	-3	905	-7	30

	Poland			Romania			Slovenia		
	1991	1992	1993 [b]	1991	1992	1993	1991	1992	1993 [a]
Net transfer of resources [c]									
Capital inflows less income payments	-902	-664	705	639	1 504	1 322	-273	-105	65
Trade balance plus non-capital services [c]	-637	-300	1 726	1 364	1 369	1 358	-499	-1 024	-47
Reserves net change [d]	-1 188	720	-447	-693	128	168	83	603	42
of which:									
IMF (net) [e]	322	-33	-138	772	261	-	-	-	-14

	Russia [f]			Estonia [a]		Lithuania [a]	
	1991	1992	1993	1992	1993	1992	1993
Net transfer of resources							
Capital inflows less income payments [g]	-4.9	-0.9	-13.4	-28	156	130	190
Trade balance plus non-capital services	-3.5	0.2	-13.5	-153	-84	-320	-160
Reserves net change [d]	-0.6	1.3	3.3	67	148	320	200
of which:							
IMF (net) [e]	-	1.0	1.5	11	48	24	100

Source: ECE estimates based on national statistics.

[a] January-September.
[b] January-November.
[c] A positive sign indicates an inflow of resources.
[d] A positive sign indicates an increase in reserves.
[e] A positive sign indicates net borrowing from the IMF.
[f] Billion US dollars.
[g] Reflects estimated capital flight (assumed equivalent to "errors and omissions" in the balance of payments) of $1.4 billion, $6.4 billion and $7.6 billion in the three years 1991-1993, respectively.

USSR, respectively (table 4.1.7).[350] Much of this is special finance,[351] the importance of which has increased in the former USSR and diminished in eastern Europe. In eastern Europe, special finance has been the principal source of external financing for Bulgaria and Poland.[352] The increasing importance of private capital in eastern Europe is noteworthy, but it is still minor in the former USSR.

On a *net* basis financial flows are, of course, considerably less and were actually negative for Russia in 1993. In 1993, there was a net inflow of resources into the east European countries, in contrast to an outflow in 1992 (table 4.1.8). The *net transfer of financial resources* is measured here by two indicators:[353]

- *capital account flows less (net) income payments*,[354] which reflects external resources available for increasing domestic absorption (i.e., consumption and investment), assuming that foreign reserves and/or external debt remain unchanged; and

- *trade balance plus non-capital services and private transfers* (i.e., the current account excluding (net) investment income payments and official transfers), which measures the combined change in domestic absorption and foreign reserves.

---

[350] Note should be taken of gaps in the data, particularly for 1993. Information on new commercial bank loans (except for syndicated credits) is not available, which is also the case for guaranteed bilateral credits for eastern Europe (data in table 4.1.3 suggest that all types of bank loans to eastern Europe were small in the first three quarters of 1993). Reliable estimates of grants are lacking for 1993.

[351] Special finance relates to deferrals and rescheduling of payments of interest and principal, and cancellation of debt.

[352] Bulgaria has benefited from special financing of $2-$3 billion annually in 1990-1992; for Poland the figures are almost $8 billion per annum in 1990-1991, falling to about $4-5 billion in 1992-1993.

[353] Mathematical expressions for the two measures of net financial transfers in terms of standard SNA variables were derived in *World Economic Survey 1986*, United Nations publication, Sales No.E.86.II.C.1, pp.163-164.

[354] Income payments made by the transition economies still consist chiefly of (net) interest payments on debt.

According to the first measure, virtually all the east European countries received positive financial transfers in 1993. However, the inflows, which were largest in the case of Hungary and the Czech Republic, were put to different uses. In *Hungary*, *Poland* and *Romania*, they supported domestic absorption, although Hungary used about one half of its inflow to boost foreign reserves (an increase in reserves is equivalent to an outflow of funds).[355, 356] The situation was similar in Romania, although the increase in its reserves was smaller. In contrast, the inflow into the *Czech Republic* and *Slovenia* went fully into reserves. Moreover, the second measure of resource transfer indicates that in these two cases external flows had a negative impact on domestic absorption.

The situation in 1993 represents a marked change from the previous two years when financial resources left eastern Europe and consumption and investment there fell. This was reflected in current account surpluses posted in 1991-1992, which most countries used to strengthen reserves.

Romania has been unique among the east European countries in that it has received a positive transfer of resources in four consecutive years. Inflows of capital have enabled the country to run current account deficits (and thus raise absorption beyond what it otherwise would have been), but at the cost of growing foreign debt.

The large (net) resource transfer from *Russia* in 1993 (table 4.1.8) stands in marked contrast to the $30 billion gross inflow of finance. The difference is, of course, due to the fact that a large (accounting) inflow of funds in the form of arrears, deferred and rescheduled payments is offset by scheduled debt repayments (not actually made – see below). Moreover, the first measure of resource transfer reflects significant capital flight, estimated at nearly $8 billion (also see below and section 3.6). The second measure reflects Russia's large current account surplus (net of interest payments), which had a large negative impact on domestic absorption.

In recent years, most transition economies experienced some *capital flight*, depriving them of the use of badly needed foreign currency. The most serious and persistent case has occurred in the *former USSR* (also see section 3.6). The outflows are reported to have increased considerably following the December elections in Russia, but this is not easy to verify.[357] Early in 1994, the Russian authorities began to implement a system of foreign exchange controls intended to stem capital flight.[358] Modelled on control systems formerly used in France and Italy, the scheme is designed to ensure that Russian exporters repatriate all of their convertible currency earnings.[359] Currently it applies only to exporters of strategic commodities but at the beginning of March it will be extended to all goods. Aside from the reasons already cited, efforts to stem capital flight are important since it tends to discourage creditors from extending new funding, especially if it is not tied to specific projects. With appropriate economic policies and a general increase in confidence, eastern governments may be able to stem, or even reverse, the outflow – as some Latin American countries have been able to do.

(v) **Relations with the London and Paris Clubs**

For some time Albania, Bulgaria, Poland and Russia have been unable to fully service their external debts. The debt burdens of Bulgaria and Poland became so large that the possibility of them resuming payments of all interest and principal falling due was very small. Creditors therefore agreed to reduce the debt and debt service obligations of both. In contrast, due to its vast natural resource base and longer-term economic potential, Russia has obtained more conventional restructuring of its financial obligations.

Such debt operations are intended to provide financial relief and time for debtor countries to achieve macroeconomic stability and restructure their economies, which in turn should help create the means to fully service their obligations, regain access to credit markets and attract foreign investment. A key issue is how much debt relief a country requires to achieve these objectives, given the current consumption needs of the population, the scale of economic transformation required, and the longer-term needs for economic development.

In April 1991, Paris Club creditors agreed to reduce the net present value of *Poland's* $33 billion official debt by 50 per cent.[360] The second stage of the reduction, involving the remaining 20 per cent of the debt, can go ahead once the Polish parliament passes the budget for 1994 and a new standby arrangement is formally approved by the IMF. Under the Paris Club agreement, Poland was obligated to seek – as indeed it is in its interest to – an equivalent reduction in private sector debt (over $13 billion). Negotiations with London Club bank creditors resulted in an agreement in March 1994, according to which Poland will obtain a 42.5 to 45 per cent reduction in the net present value of outstanding commercial loans and unpaid interest.[361] The exact amount of the reduction will depend on the mix of repayment methods chosen by creditor banks from the options established by the agreement.

In *Bulgaria* the bulk of outstanding debt is held by commercial creditors. After protracted negotiations, the two parties concluded a comprehensive agreement in

---

[355] In Poland domestic absorption was also buoyed by a rundown of foreign currency reserves in the first eleven months of 1993.

[356] It should be noted that changes in reserves include net borrowing from the IMF.

[357] According to news reports citing international bankers and businessmen dealing with Russia, the flight of capital rose to some $1 billion per month and possibly as high as $2 billion. *International Herald Tribune*, 14 January 1994.

[358] Mr. Y. Ivanov, of the National Bank of Russia, *International Herald Tribune*, 20 January 1994.

[359] *Financial Times*, 16-17 October 1993. The system attempts to avoid fraud by relying upon separate reporting by exporters, banks and customs.

[360] For details, see UNCTAD, *Trade and Development Report, 1992*, New York, 1992, p.50.

[361] *Financial Times*, 12-13 March 1994.

November 1993 to reduce the country's debt and debt service obligations by about 50 per cent. Some $8.8-8.9 billion is subject to reduction ($7 billion in principal and $1.7-1.8 billion in interest arrears).[362] The arrangement is subject to approval by the Bulgarian parliament and a downpayment of $865 million to creditor banks. Further annual payments of not less than $300 million (on average) are to be made in the first seven years of the agreement. The deal, which is expected to be signed by 30 June 1994, sets out a menu of options for achieving the reductions.[363] In August 1992 Bulgaria resumed limited debt servicing to commercial banks, but in July 1993 the government stopped further payments of interest until September, citing the country's losses arising from United Nations' sanctions on Yugoslavia (FR) in justification (see section 3.2).[364]

Bulgaria has completed two rescheduling arrangements with Paris Club members, which hold only a small fraction of the country's obligations. A meeting is scheduled for April 1994, by which time negotiations on a third agreement should be far advanced. At issue will be the restructuring of debt which has come due since the end of April 1993. Bulgaria concluded its second agreement with its official creditors on 14 December 1992, covering debt falling due in the five months December to April 1993 (the termination date of the IMF agreement then in effect).[365]

Poland's current, and Bulgaria's prospective, agreements with the IMF and World Bank contain financial set-asides, which are intended to help finance the reduction of commercial debt.[366]

Russia has formally accepted responsibility for the debt incurred by the former Soviet Union.[367] The former USSR fell behind on debt repayments at the end of 1991. After several deferrals of the official debt service obligations, the Russian authorities and the *Paris Club* reached a restructuring agreement in April 1993 involving $15 billion coming due in 1993.[368] The first meeting dealing with $10 billion of interest and principal falling due in 1994 (of an official debt of $54 billion) was held in January.[369] Apparently, western officials were to begin exploring whether a more comprehensive debt relief plan for Russia is required to replace the current short-term approach.[370] Last year attention was drawn to the potential benefits of a multi-year rescheduling of Russian debt, modelled on Paris Club accords with certain Latin American debtors.[371] In accordance with Paris Club procedures, Russia must first reach agreement with the IMF before a formal rescheduling can be concluded.

In early October 1993, Russia and the commercial banks (*London Club*) commenced negotiations on a long-term debt rescheduling agreement. For some two years, banks have rolled-over principal falling due in 90-day periods (the latest expired at the end of December). Russia's commercial debt has risen to some $27.5 billion, of which more than $3 billion is arrears on interest payments.[372] London Club creditors are reported to have offered a 15-year rescheduling arrangement, involving a five-year grace period.[373] If confirmed, these terms would be more favourable than those obtained earlier in the year from the Paris Club. One issue to be resolved centres on the banks' insistence that Russia waive its "sovereign immunity", which would give them unlimited claims on state-owned assets. The Russian authorities, however, were prepared to grant only a more limited government guarantee for debt repayment.[374] Rejection of this guarantee by London Club members resulted in the cancellation of an earlier agreement under which Russia would have repaid $500 million by the end of 1993.[375]

Albania has also failed to service its debt (nearly $700 million at the end of 1992), most of which is owed to western commercial banks. Acting on the advice of the IMF and the World Bank, these obligations, contracted by Albanian banks operating under the former regime, have been accepted by the Albanian state as a formal responsibility. Thus once a negotiator is appointed for the Albanian side, it will be possible to begin negotiations with creditor banks.[376]

---

[362] According to Mr. Stoyan Aleksandrov, Bulgarian Minister of Finance, BBC, *Summary of World Broadcasts*, EE/1857 B/2, 27 November 1993 and *Financial Times*, 26 November 1993. In the latter source, the debt subject to reduction is given as $9.3 billion.

[363] The reported options include: a debt buy-back option allowing the country to repurchase its debt quoting its own price; a front-loaded interest reduction bond (FIRB) of 18 years (an 8-year grace period) with a fixed interest rate starting at 2 per cent for the first eight years and a floating coupon of LIBOR plus 13/16 per cent for the remainder; a collateralized discount bond of 30 years to be exchanged for existing debt at a 50 per cent discount at LIBOR plus 13/16 per cent and full principle and 12 months' interest collateral. Ibid.

[364] BBC, *Summary of World Broadcasts*, EE/W0289, 8 July 1993.

[365] Principal and interest due during this period was rescheduled for a period of 10 years, with a six-year grace period (instead of the normal five years). Bulgaria was to resume interest payments at the beginning of April 1993. World Bank, *Financial Flows to Developing Countries, Quarterly Review*, Washington, D.C., January 1993, p.16.

[366] One quarter of Poland's current IMF standby credit is earmarked for eventual debt reduction operations. The IMF and World Bank will make some $300-400 million available to Bulgaria for this purpose.

[367] The development of Russia's acceptance of this responsibility has been discussed in recent volumes of this *Survey* and the *Economic Bulletin for Europe*. Although the distribution of the debt (and assets of the former Soviet Union) between Russia and the Ukraine, which holds 16 per cent of the total, does not appear to have been definitely resolved, the 1993 Paris Club agreement contains a new legal framework under which Russia assumes all of the debt.

[368] See UNCTAD, *Trade and Development Report, 1993*, New York, 1993, p.192, and *Economic Bulletin for Europe*, Vol.45(1993), New York and Geneva, 1994.

[369] *International Herald Tribune*, 17 January 1994.

[370] Ibid. Reschedulings have applied to debt falling due in the current year (and outstanding arrears). In the case that a formal rescheduling is delayed, obligations coming due are deferred for three months.

[371] See UNCTAD, *Trade and Development Report, 1993*, op. cit.

[372] *Financial Times*, 24 September 1993.

[373] *Financial Times*, 8 October 1993.

[374] According to Mr. A Shokhin, Vice-Premier. *Financial Times*, 12 October 1993.

[375] Russia insists on a repayment guarantee scheme similar to that accepted by the Paris Club; overdue debts will remain unpaid until the issue is resolved. According to Vice-Premier A. Shokhin, quoted in *Business Update Russia*, 9 November 1993.

[376] Information provided by the Albanian delegation to the EFTA Third Parliamentary Colloquium, Geneva, 18-19 October 1993.

(vi) Development bank sectoral lending

This section briefly reviews the sectoral lending of the EBRD, EIB, and the World Bank Group (IBRD, IDA and IFC)[377] to the individual eastern economies during 1990-1993. Among other things, these organizations are expected to help create institutions, modernize business infrastructure, restructure industry, provide technical assistance, etc., so as to establish the framework for a functioning market system. Such changes should help to attract the private capital which will be essential for achieving sustained economic growth. As discussed above, the development institutions and the IMF often constitute the only significant sources of external finance for the tasks at hand.

In general, these institutions provide funds at much better terms than private sources (if these are accessible at all). Typically they lend at cost (i.e., at favourable market rates reflecting their excellent credit ratings) plus a small margin to cover operating expenses,[378] and offer long maturities. In comparison, Hungary, for example, had to pay a sizeable premium of 2 to 3 percentage points above benchmark rates until recently (now down to some 1 percentage point) on bonds with a maturity of 10 years. Thus lending by the development banks includes a substantial implicit subsidy.[379] Concessional loans are available to the transition economies through the IDA, the World Bank's soft loan window, but only Albania and Kyrgyzstan have qualified to date. The funds provided by the development banks are debt creating, except for equity investments made by EBRD and IFC.

(a) Data and sectoral classification

The data presented in tables 4.1.9 and 4.1.10 reflect the funding commitments[380] for projects approved by the boards of the various institutions.[381] Individual loans and investments were classified according to ten selected International Standard Industrial Classification (ISIC) divisions, on the basis of descriptions accompanying the announcements.[382] A subtotal reflects projects and lending for roads. Roads are not included in ISIC, but they were added here because they constitute a key element of business infrastructure (see below).

Several sectors or loan categories have been added in the tables to accommodate loans which do not fit into any ISIC sector. The content of these sectors is described below in the terminology used by the creditor institutions:

- Labour market loans: include funding for *social safety nets* and *retraining of workers*.
- Global loans: include EIB *global loans*/EBRD *multi-sector loans*/IFC *Apex loans* which are temporary credit lines to eastern banks for on-lending, generally to small and medium-sized private industrial and tourism projects, small-scale energy projects, and environmental protection schemes. Also included are IFC and EBRD investments in *private equity funds*, established to furnish equity capital for the privatization of existing enterprises and the formation of new private

However, by end-December 1993, some ECU 400 million of those projects still had not reached the signing stage. The latter are thus not reflected in the tables.

TABLE 4.1.9

Financial commitments of the development institutions to the transition economies, by industrial sector, 1990-1993
(Million US dollars)

	EBRD	EIB	IBRD	IFC	Total
Sector:					
Agriculture (1)	171	15	866	18	1 070
Extraction (2)	436	-	610	72	1 117
Manufacturing (3)	440	117	-	341	898
Energy (4)	458	304	929	-	1 691
Tourism (63)	40	-	-	46	86
Transport (71)	144	468	291	-	902
Telecommunications (72)	652	409	435	15	1 511
Roads	368	265	240	-	872
Financial services (81)	65	-	266	63	394
Other services (8-81)	21	-	415	12	447
Social and personal services (9)	121	-	868	-	989
Total ISIC division	2 916	1 578	4 920	567	9 977
Type of loan:					
Labour market development	-	-	183	-	183
Global loans	452	501	-	87	1 041
Structural adjustment loans	-	-	3 306	-	3 306
Restructuring loans	-	-	1 316	-	1 316
Emergency assistance	-	-	26	-	26
Environment	-	-	48	-	48
Total non-ISIC division	452	501	4 879	87	5 920
Total	3 366	2 079	9 800	653	15 898

Sources: Annual reports of the EBRD, EIB, IBRD and IFC; press releases; direct communications to ECE secretariat.

Note: ISIC divisions in parenthesises.

---

[377] International Bank for Reconstruction and Development, International Development Agency, and International Finance Corporation.

[378] For example, the margin applied by the EIB is 0.15 per cent while the World Bank collects a commitment fee of 0.25 per cent on the part of the loan which has not been drawn. Maturities of 15-20 years with a five-year grace period are available from the World Bank. Maturities available from the EBRD are shorter (generally 5-10 years, exceptionally 15 years for public sector infrastructure projects) with variable margins. A front-end fee is charged at signing and an annual commitment fee is charged on undisbursed loans.

[379] Even with the advantageous terms offered by the development banks, several eastern countries were discouraged from borrowing by the high interest rates prevailing several years ago. The recent large reduction in international interest rates has made all borrowing more attractive.

[380] The sources are press releases, annual reports and direct communications to the ECE secretariat. Commitments in ECU, the accounting unit of the EBRD and EIB, were converted to US dollars at the exchange rate prevailing in the month in which the project was approved. No distinction is made between loans, which account for the bulk of the commitments, and equity investment made by the EBRD and IFC. Technical cooperation funds are not included.

[381] The considerable number of projects known to be in the pipeline are not taken into account. Data for the EBRD includes only projects approved and signed, implying that some funds have been released already at the time of announcement. In 1992 projects valued at ECU 1.2 billion were approved (see EBRD, *Annual Report 1993*, London, 1993).

[382] The institutions themselves generally do not classify new projects according to a standard, or even consistent, classification scheme.

TABLE 4.1.10

Total financial commitments of the development institutions to the transition economies, by industrial sector, 1990-1993
(Million US dollars)

	Albania	Bulgaria	CSFR	Czech Republic	Slovakia	Hungary	Poland	Romania	Slovenia	The FYR of Macedonia	Eastern Europe	Armenia	Belarus
Sector:													
Agriculture (1)	20	-	-	3	-	174	694	179	-	-	1 070	-	-
Extraction (2)	-	-	-	-	-	-	-	30	-	-	30	-	-
Manufacturing (3)	3	-	38	289	-	218	309	41	-	-	898	-	-
Energy (4)	-	201	246	-	65	86	701	31	91	28	1 448	59	47
Tourism (63)	12	-	-	20	-	44	9	-	-	-	86	-	-
Transport (71)	18	34	-	30	-	98	478	147	55	-	861	-	-
Telecommunications (72)	10	165	-	257	169	404	251	185	-	-	1 441	-	44
Roads	-	68	-	-	30	411	202	161	-	-	872	-	-
Financial services (81)	-	4	7	9	5	103	246	9	-	-	383	-	-
Other services (8-81)	-	55	-	-	-	107	279	-	-	-	441	-	7
Social and personal services (9)	15	-	-	-	-	373	406	150	-	-	944	-	-
Total ISIC divisions	*78*	*527*	*291*	*608*	*269*	*2 018*	*3 575*	*933*	*146*	*28*	*8 474*	*59*	*98*
Type of loan:													
Labour market development	13	-	-	-	-	-	100	-	-	-	113	-	-
Global loans	-	34	-	74	36	185	272	39	-	-	639	-	-
Structural adjustment loans	41	250	450	-	80	450	300	580	-	-	2 151	-	120
Restructuring loans	4	17	-	-	-	229	790	-	80	-	1 120	12	8
Emergency assistance	-	-	-	-	-	-	-	-	-	-	-	-	-
Environment	-	-	-	-	-	-	18	-	-	-	18	-	-
Total non-ISIC	*58*	*301*	*450*	*74*	*116*	*864*	*1 480*	*619*	*80*	*-*	*4 041*	*12*	*128*
Total	**136**	**828**	**741**	**682**	**385**	**2 882**	**5 055**	**1 552**	**226**	**28**	**12 515**	**71**	**226**

Sources: Annual reports of the EBRD, EIB, IBRD and IFC; press releases; direct communication to the ECE secretariat.

Note: ISIC divisions in parenthesises.

corporations. Since local banks, or equity funds, decide on which business to invest in, the sectoral destination of these resources is only known *ex post*.

- Structural adjustment loans: include World Bank *structural adjustment loans* (SAL) and *rehabilitation loans*, which are intended to promote structural transformation of the economy.[383] They may be used to import essential goods and services and thus complement standard balance of payments financing.

- Restructuring loans: include *institution building loans, privatization loans* and *technical assistance*, intended to promote microeconomic restructuring of the economy and lay the groundwork for a market economy. In those cases where a loan is earmarked for restructuring in a particular sector (e.g., loans for restructuring agriculture are common), the commitment is classified under that sector.

Since the nature of these instruments prevents a full accounting of the financial resources received by ISIC sectors, the sectoral distributions in the tables should be considered as preliminary. Some refinements are possible, but they would require additional detailed information.

(b) The structure of development bank lending

In 1990-1993 the development banks committed some $16 billion to the transition economies, of which nearly $13 billion went to eastern Europe and the balance to the republics of the former Soviet Union (table 4.1.10). Of this total, some $10 billion can be classified by ISIC sector. The remainder is composed of SALs, global/multi-sector loans and restructuring loans, which either cannot be allocated to a specific sector or are used to finance reform activities in general. The World Bank was the largest lender committing almost $10 billion, followed by the EBRD and the EIB with commitments of around $2-3 billion each (table 4.1.9).

Inter-institutional differences in funding reflect their resources, membership (or geographical lending mandate), and the type of lending prescribed by their statutes. The World Bank has operated in eastern Europe since the 1970s, although its activities were limited to Hungary, the former Yugoslavia and Romania (which was inactive in the 1980s). In contrast the EBRD is a new institution which began lending only in September 1991. Since 1990 the EIB's lending mandate has included eastern Europe and the Baltic States (see above).[384] The EIB and the World Bank are heavily engaged in infrastructure projects. The EBRD can participate in these as well, but its statutes limit its lending to the state sector to 40 per cent of its exposure to any single country. The larger part of the EBRD's activity has to be directed towards the private sector, a requirement which has proved difficult to meet in the early stages of the transition because of a dearth of attractive investment possibilities. The IFC's activities are restricted to the private sector.

---

[383] The Bank's approval of a SAL is conditional upon the recipient country adopting a programme of economic transformation (formally set out in a Letter of Development Policy, similar to a letter of intent agreed with the IMF).

[384] The EIB's lending mandate had included the former Yugoslavia, but now includes only Slovenia among the successor states.

TABLE 4.1.10 (continued)
Total financial commitments of the development institutions to the transition economies, by industrial sector, 1990-1993
(Million US dollars)

Kazakh-stan	Kyrgyz-stan	Moldova	Russia	Ukraine	Uzbeki-stan	CIS	Estonia	Latvia	Lithuania	Baltic states	Regional	Total	Sector:
-	-	-	-	-	-	-	-	-	-	-	-	1 070	.... Agriculture (1)
-	-	-	1 034	-	54	1 087	-	-	-	-	-	1 117	.... Extraction (2)
-	-	-	-	-	-	-	-	-	-	-	-	898	.... Manufacturing (3)
-	-	-	-	-	-	105	50	40	48	138	-	1 691	.... Energy (4)
-	-	-	-	-	-	-	-	-	-	-	-	86	.... Tourism (63)
-	-	-	-	5	-	5	23	12	-	36	-	902	.... Transport (71)
-	-	-	9	1	-	54	-	-	-	-	16	1 511	.... Telecommunications (72)
-	-	-	-	-	-	-	-	-	-	-	-	872	.... Roads
-	-	-	4	-	-	4	-	-	-	-	7	394	.... Financial services (81)
-	-	-	-	-	-	7	-	-	-	-	-	447	.... Other services (8-81)
-	-	-	45	-	-	45	-	-	-	-	-	989	Social and personal services (9)
-	-	-	*1 092*	*6*	*54*	*1 307*	*73*	*52*	*48*	*174*	*23*	*9 977*	.... *Total ISIC divisions*
													Type of loan:
-	-	-	70	-	-	70	-	-	-	-	-	183	..... Labour market development
115	-	-	40	4	62	220	6	-	-	6	175	1 041	.... Global loans
180	60	60	600	-	-	1 020	30	45	60	135	-	3 306	.... Structural adjustment loans
38	-	-	90	27	21	196	-	-	-	-	-	1 316	.... Restructuring loans
-	-	26	-	-	-	26	-	-	-	-	-	26	.... Emergency assistance
-	-	-	-	-	-	-	-	-	-	-	30	48	.... Environment
333	*60*	*86*	*800*	*31*	*83*	*1 532*	*36*	*45*	*60*	*141*	*205*	*5 920*	.... *Total non-ISIC*
333	60	86	1 892	37	136	2 840	110	98	108	315	228	15 898	.... **Total**

Almost two thirds of the development banks' commitments in 1992-1993 were to Poland ($5 billion), Hungary ($2.9 billion), and the former Czechoslovakia ($1.8 billion) (table 4.1.10). These three also received the largest commitments on a per capita basis. In contrast, seven other countries, including several republics of the former USSR and Yugoslavia, have obtained no funds at all.[385] Other countries have received only SALs and perhaps one sectoral loan. There are complex reasons for this outcome, some of which have been mentioned above. Internal factors are often important – the recipient countries' commitment to reform, progress in meeting various economic performance criteria, official interest in the institutions' involvement, implications for the budget, political stability, and so on.

Despite the considerable differences among the transition countries, they do have broadly similar requirements for certain types of external assistance[386] – especially that provided by the development banks. So far, however, lending has been concentrated in the three eastern countries which have the highest per capita incomes and are the most advanced in their reforms. Yet less well-off countries would seem to have equal, if not more pressing, needs. Projects which are in the pipeline, and thus not yet reflected in the data, may eventually reduce these intercountry differences.

Table 4.1.10 shows considerable intercountry differences in the sectoral distribution of financial commitments. In Poland and Hungary virtually all of the sectors have received funds. In contrast, many other countries have received only one or two loans, one of them a SAL. For the reasons mentioned above, a fairly large degree of similarity in the sectoral structure of financing might have been expected.

One of the major challenges of the reform is the upgrading of infrastructure which is essential for the smooth functioning of a market economy, for creating links with foreign markets and attracting FDI. *Telecommunications* has in fact received the second largest single amount of financing ($1.5 billion), chiefly from the EBRD. *Roads* and other *transportation* facilities (including railways, airports and air traffic control systems) have each received commitments of about $900 million. Much of the $3 billion in infrastructure lending, too, is concentrated in just a few east European countries; in many transition countries no project at all had reached the approval stage.

The actual *disbursement* of funds for infrastructure projects is likely to have been far smaller than the above-mentioned commitments. Although sectoral data are not generally available, it may by noted that the development banks released a *total* of some $4.6 billion during 1990-1993 to the whole eastern area, of which $1.9 billion was in 1993 (table 4.1.6).[387] The amount accounted for by

---

[385] Eleven of the fifteen successor states of the USSR, including the three Baltic states, have obtained commitments.

[386] See "Economic reform in the east: A framework for western support", United Nations Economic Commission for Europe, *Economic Survey of Europe in 1992-1993*, New York, 1993.

[387] Measures taken recently by bilateral and multilateral creditors/donors to increase the pace of lending to the transition

infrastructure projects would, of course, be considerably less.

It may be noted that one potential constraint on the expansion of infrastructure projects is the burden on the national budget of the recipient country. Although multilateral development banks generally fund as much as 50-60 per cent of the total investment cost of infrastructure projects, the balance must be met from domestic resources. Such programmes can therefore conflict with policies to curb budget deficits and, thus, with short-term macroeconomic stabilization goals. Most eastern governments are facing serious difficulties in holding down their budget deficits, but their attempts to do so run the risk of compromising the much-needed programmes of public infrastructure investment. Where this is the case the public sector ought to be considered an appropriate target for foreign assistance.[388]

Reconstruction of the *banking* sector is also a crucial ingredient for systemic reform and economic restructuring, but progress has been disappointing (see section 3.1). Virtually all of the transition economies require external funding for technical assistance and the recapitalization of existing banks. So far the *financial services* sector, which includes non-bank financial services, has been promised some $400 million.[389]

The *manufacturing* sector requires huge injections of funds for restructuring and modernization. The bulk of these funds will have to come from domestic sources supplemented by the foreign private sector. Lending and investment by the EBRD, IFC, and EIB to manufacturing enterprises are intended to act as a catalyst to attract private funds. Projects clearly identified as being in the manufacturing sector have been promised $900 million. However, part of the $1 billion in EIB and EBRD global/multisectoral loans is also for on-lending to manufacturing enterprises. The manufacturing sector represents the largest share of the IFC's portfolio and ranks third in that of the EBRD. Lending to this sector has been constrained by the relatively small number of feasible investment projects.

The international institutions, of course, are not the sole sources of finance for the transition economies. As a rule they are allowed to finance only a share of the total value of a project or investment. Although the situation varies from case to case, funding for a particular project may also be made available from the national budget, other development banks,[390] officially-backed trade credits and private capital. Indeed a key responsibility of the institutions is to act as a catalyst for funds from other sources. Technical assistance (in general, not reflected in the data discussed here) may be financed through PHARE, TACIS (Technical Assistance to the CIS) and other bilateral grants and other funds.

Information on the country and sectoral distribution of private foreign investment and lending in the east are not available or, at least, not in a form easily comparable to the data provided here. However, the distribution of total FDI among the eastern countries (see table 4.1.2) is similar to that of lending by the international institutions (i.e., both are concentrated in Hungary, the Czech Republic and Poland). Thus, so far, FDI and commitments from the financial institutions have developed in parallel, reinforcing rather than narrowing differences in the flows of foreign capital received by individual eastern countries.

It is difficult to assess the appropriateness of the sectoral allocation of development bank funds without a framework of what needs to be accomplished to create the conditions for a functioning market economy and sustained economic growth. Estimates of the capital required to bring key sectors such as telecommunications, transport, etc., up to minimal western standards run into the hundreds of billions of dollars. From this viewpoint the commitments made by the institutions are comparatively small and, as noted above, some countries do not have any projects at all in these key areas. However, in the most advanced transition economies, at least, the foreign private sector is becoming heavily involved and domestic resources have been mobilized as well.

In attempting to assess the adequacy of foreign commitments, one possible basis of comparison involves EIB financing for the new German *Länder* (the former GDR), which amounted to ECU 2,073 million between October 1990 and September 1993[391] (some $150 per capita). This compares with loans to eastern Europe of $12 billion, or $100 per capita, approved by all four development institutions.[392] The new *Länder* have also obtained huge investments in infrastructure, etc., from the rest of Germany and EU regional funds. The comparisons are even less favourable if the CIS countries are included. Overall, these figures suggest a large gap between the requirements of the transition countries and the actual allocation of multilateral resources.

---

economies have been discussed in the United Nations Economic Commission for Europe, *Economic Bulletin for Europe*, Vol.45(1993), New York and Geneva, 1994.

[388] See United Nations Economic Commission for Europe, *Economic Survey of Europe in 1992-1993*, New York, 1993, p.17.

[389] Included in that $400 million are World Bank funds earmarked for reducing Poland's external debt.

[390] As part of their catalytic function, it is not unusual for the EIB, EBRD and World Bank to co-finance projects. This practice is encouraged by limits on the share of total project costs which they are allowed to finance. According to some critics, the institutions also have a propensity to get involved in similar prestige projects with high visibility.

[391] EIB, *EIB Information*, Brussels, November 1993.

[392] The former GDR does not have access to the resources of EBRD and the World Bank Group.

4.2 East-west cooperation agreements and market access

(i) Introduction

The external support which greater and more secure access to western markets can provide for the economies in transition has been extensively discussed. The removal of or reductions in western barriers should help these countries to increase export earnings, restructure their economies, and integrate into the world economy. Indeed the liberalization measures taken by the west since 1989 facilitated the subsequent boom in western imports (i.e., in 1990-1992) from a number of transition economies. This strengthening of trade ties with the west has partially offset the loss of trade with their former CMEA partners. More accessible western markets can also act as a powerful stimulant to FDI seeking an eastern base for exporting.

Although access to markets is undoubtedly an essential element of a country's ability to generate foreign currency receipts, supply factors can be, and in the case of the transition economies generally have been, more important.[393] This has been particularly true of some key eastern exports, e.g., raw materials and fuels from Russia, which do not face high tariffs or restrictive quotas in the west (although certain goods have become subject to anti-dumping actions).

While the policies of virtually all the transition countries have given precedence to the development of trade with the west, the promotion of intra-eastern trade, including the removal of barriers, has received less attention. Despite the major domestic economic repercussions of the collapse of the CMEA and, especially, intra-CIS trade, few steps appear to have been taken to promote these trade links.[394] This is reflected, for example, in the very limited preferential trade arrangements which have emerged among former CMEA partners in conjunction with the reform of their trade and payments regimes.[395]

Nevertheless, there are powerful economic arguments for promoting the development of intra-eastern trade, or at least placing it on an equal footing with exchanges with the west. Economic reforms have created the preconditions for new trade patterns in the east based on comparative advantage reflecting world prices of traded goods, enterprises operating according to commercial principles, outward looking trade policies, and so on (i.e., all the economic conditions which were absent under the old system).[396] The new domestic conditions need to be complemented by a reduction in external barriers affecting their intra-trade and an upgrading of the business-supporting infrastructure. Such policies would also foster the development of intra-industry trade, an important aspect of economic growth in the west, but underdeveloped in the former CMEA.

All of the above points apply to the republics of the former USSR as well. The rejuvenation of trade between the new republics takes on special importance in that context. The high degree of specialization built into the production system of the former USSR resulted in a strong interdependence among the successor republics. As a result, the disintegration of these trade links contributed to the massive fall in output throughout most of the area. Overcoming these difficulties will require an improvement in the current inter-republic payments system, alleviating convertible currency shortages of the republics running large trade deficits with Russia, and the adoption of effective structural and macroeconomic policies throughout the area.

The next section briefly reviews the progress achieved in the elimination of discriminatory trade measures and the extension of preferential trade arrangements in the east-west context; it brings up to date the secretariat's earlier and more extensive discussion.[397] Section (iii) presents a review of recent contingent protection actions affecting eastern exports. It offers some suggestions as to why such actions against east European products may have subsided, although new ones continued to be taken against selected goods from several republics of the former USSR. Section (iv) summarizes the reduction in western trade barriers and the current state of EU-EFTA-based preferential agreements in Europe. It ends with a discussion of the implications of these agreements for the CIS, which according to the current timetable will not benefit from preferential agreements for some time.

(ii) The transformation of east-west commercial relations

Since the economic reforms in eastern Europe and the former Soviet Union got under way, east-west trade

---

[393] The dominant role of developments in the eastern area – the decline in domestic demand, distress sales, the collapse of the CMEA, reforms of the trade system, and so on – in shaping eastern exports to the west have been discussed in recent volumes of the United Nations Economic Commission for Europe *Economic Survey of Europe* and *Economic Bulletin for Europe*, and section 3.5 above. It is noteworthy that in 1993 a number of eastern countries were able to increase exports to the west despite a substantial drop in western import demand.

[394] Arguments against concerted actions to strengthen intra-eastern trade centred on the risks of recreating the CMEA under a different guise, although this attitude now appears to be changing. Eastern Europe, however, has retained its interest in the republics of the former USSR as major markets for its manufactured goods (now limited by shortages of convertible currency) and as a source of raw materials.

[395] The CEFTA agreement came about primarily to correct the incongruity that arose after the Czech and Slovak Republics, Hungary and Poland signed Association Agreements with the EU and free trade agreements with EFTA. Without CEFTA, goods traded between any two of these eastern countries would have met less favourable tariff conditions than goods traded between one of them and the EU or EFTA.

[396] With respect to intra-eastern trade, the new comparative advantages of the transition countries are likely to better reflect cost advantages due to their geographical proximity and a greater exploitation of scale economies. Better use of the latter can result from producing (similar) goods for export to all markets. Under the former system, costs were often high because products were tailored for particular markets.

[397] United Nations Economic Commission for Europe, *Economic Bulletin for Europe*, Vol.45(1993), New York and Geneva, 1994, chapter 4.2.

relations have been transformed. The transformation has involved major progress toward the *normalization* of trade relations and, to a more limited extent, the creation of *preferential arrangements*. Both lines of action are intended to support the east's reforms and to facilitate the area's integration into the world economy. In general, the degree of western liberalization has been linked to the eastern partner's progress toward a market-based system.

(a) Normalization of trade relations

The process of normalizing trade relations between east and west essentially involves the elimination of specific inherited discriminatory practices. The latter had arisen in part from the interaction of two fundamentally different economic systems, market economies on the one hand and centrally planned economies (CPEs) on the other.[398] The centrally planned system provided for a large measure of trade discrimination (actually applied for political purposes in the form of strong CMEA preferences) and for the arbitrary pricing of exports. Western trade policies *vis-à-vis* the east contained a political element as well, but they were also designed to offset the particular consequences of the administered trade systems of the east and to meet security concerns. These policies involved specific (i.e., discriminatory) quantitative restrictions applied by the EC exclusively to certain imports from state trading countries; denial by the United States of MFN treatment to some eastern countries; special procedures for anti-dumping investigations; and controls on the exports of militarily useful technologies.

Although western trade barriers had already been somewhat reduced in the 1970s,[399] further steps were taken in the late 1980s with the conclusion of Trade and Cooperation Agreements between the EC and Hungary (1988) and Poland (1989). These were non-preferential agreements which aimed at promoting mutual trade through MFN treatment, the removal on the EC side of certain specific quantitative restrictions over a period of several years, and a framework which provided for further trade concessions. Similar agreements were subsequently concluded with Czechoslovakia (1990), Romania (1991) and the Soviet Union (1990).

The decision of the new eastern governments to transform their economies from centrally planned to market-based systems paved the way for the full normalization of east-west trade relations.[400] In July 1989, the G-7 responded to the reform initiatives of Hungary and Poland by pledging easier access to G-7 markets. This policy, which was later extended to other eastern countries, was intended to provide external support for the transition and complement measures of financial assistance. Henceforth, reforming eastern countries were to be treated increasingly as market rather than centrally planned or state trading economies. Four actions taken by the western countries merit special attention:

- In 1989-1990, the EC temporarily suspended all specific quantitative restrictions affecting east European exports (which under the trade and cooperation agreements were to have been phased out over several years).[401] In 1992, after the breakup of the USSR and Yugoslavia, the EC concluded trade and cooperation agreements with the three Baltic states, Slovenia and Albania. Meanwhile, the members of the CIS accepted the obligations of the original trade and cooperation agreement concluded with Russia. All of these agreements stipulate the eventual removal of specific quantitative restrictions.[402, 403]

- Over a period of several years, the United States extended MFN status to all eastern countries, including all the republics of the former Soviet Union,[404] but excluding the FR Yugoslavia.[405] Prior to 1989, only Hungary, Poland, Romania[406] and Yugoslavia had benefited. All west European countries and Canada had previously accorded MFN status to their eastern trade partners and extended it to most of the new states as well. In consequence, MFN tariff treatment is now almost universally applied throughout the ECE region.

- Some western countries have modified their legislation governing relations with the eastern countries. For example, the EC has removed several of its eastern partners from the "state trading (or non-market) category".[407] Among other things, the reclassification has potential implications for the way in which anti-dumping investigations are carried out.[408]

---

[398] A summary of recent unilateral measures and agreements between the developed market and transition economies and the dates of their entry into force are given in the United Nations Economic Commission for Europe, *Economic Survey of Europe in 1992-1993*, New York, 1993, table 4.2.1, pp.254-255.

[399] This included the conclusion of a preferential trade arrangement between the EC and Yugoslavia in 1980 (see below).

[400] Structural reforms of the external sector in most countries involved the replacement of the administered system of trade and payments by economic instruments compatible with decentralized decision making: foreign trade rights for enterprises, tariffs and explicit quotas in the trade sphere, and internal convertibility of the domestic currency in the payments sphere.

[401] The specific quantitative restrictions were removed permanently under the provisions of the Association Agreements concluded with a number of transition economies at a later date.

[402] Under the provisions of the trade and cooperation agreement, the EC undertook *inter alia* to abolish or suspend various quantitative restrictions on a range of products according to a set timetable (excluding steel and textiles which are subject to separate agreements). *Official Journal*, No.L 48/3, 15 March 1990.

[403] Slovenia benefited from the removal of specific quantitative restrictions on goods from Yugoslavia in October 1990.

[404] Uzbekistan was the last member of the former Soviet Union to be granted MFN by the USA. BBC, *Monitoring Service*, 13 November 1993.

[405] For reasons having to do with the recognition of the new states, other western countries have also denied MFN to FR Yugoslavia, and, in certain cases, to other successor states of SFR Yugoslavia.

[406] The United States suspended MFN for Romania in November 1987, after the then Romanian government unilaterally renounced these privileges. Legislation restoring MFN for Romania was signed by President Clinton in November 1993.

[407] By end-1993, the EC had made this change with respect to Bulgaria, the Czech and Slovak Republics, Hungary, Poland and Romania.

[408] These issues are discussed in more detail in the United Nations Economic Commission for Europe, *Economic Bulletin for Europe*, Vol.45(1993), New York and Geneva, 1994, box 4.2.1.

- The decision taken in November 1993 to terminate COCOM (Coordinating Committee on Multilateral Export Controls)[409] is perhaps the most symbolic of all the changes in east-west commercial relations. Established in 1950 during the Cold War, the 17-member organization (consisting of NATO members plus Japan) was intended to prevent the transfer of western technology to eastern Europe and the former Soviet Union. COCOM lists of proscribed exports included not only military goods but also civilian technologies with potential military applications (so-called dual-use technologies). In its concern to restrain the build-up of the east's military capacity, COCOM also hindered the eastern area's efforts to modernize the civilian sector (although the controls were not the major reason for its technical backwardness). The lifting of the controls should facilitate the technical improvement of certain sectors. Western national export control regimes will remain in place. They are currently undergoing review, with the aim of relaxing restrictions.

As part of the normalization process, virtually all of the eastern economies have begun to modify their relations with the *GATT*. Previously, several eastern countries had failed to apply for GATT membership for economic and/or political reasons. Most of those which had become members – Hungary, Poland and Romania – had been obliged to accept special terms which reflected the administered nature of their economies. They are now renegotiating their terms of accession to reflect their ongoing market-oriented reforms. Those countries which are seeking membership for the first time (e.g., Bulgaria) will be required to show their commitment to market principles, as will also be the case for others which are only at the stage of applying for observer status.

(b) Preferential arrangements

Preferential arrangements in east-west trade date from the cooperation agreement concluded between the EC and Yugoslavia in 1980. In 1991, the EC made available trade preferences equivalent to those under this agreement to Bosnia-Herzegovina, Croatia, Slovenia, and the former Yugoslav Republic of Macedonia.[410] A trade and cooperation agreement concluded between the EC and Slovenia in November 1992 placed these trade arrangements on a contractual basis.[411]

The next move toward preferential market access occurred in 1989 when the G-24 extended *GSP* privileges, first to Hungary and Poland, and subsequently to other transition countries.[412] These were unilateral concessions granted by the western partners, implementing the decisions of the G-7 (Paris) summit in July 1989.

Subsequent trade liberalization has been achieved through bilateral and multilateral economic agreements which aim at free trade in industrial products over a period of several years. In negotiating these agreements (and, to a much lesser extent, in granting GSP privileges) the western countries have generally sought to differentiate between the transition economies, linking the degree of access to progress by the latter in reforming their economies.

This graduated approach is reflected in the fact that the most liberal arrangements – the EC *Association Agreements* (Europe Agreements) and the EFTA *free trade agreements* – were concluded in 1991 with countries furthest advanced in their reforms, i.e., with the Czech and Slovak Republics (then Czechoslovakia), Hungary and Poland, and then with Bulgaria and Romania in 1992. The goals of these agreements are the eventual elimination of all import duties and non-tariff barriers affecting industrial goods[413] and improvement of access for agricultural products.[414] The trade provisions are asymmetric in the sense that the EC and EFTA grant their east European partners immediate duty free access upon entry into force of the agreements, with the exception of sensitive goods on which tariffs are to be reduced according to separate timetables. In contrast, the eastern partners have transition periods of up to ten years before having to grant full reciprocity. The aim of the agreements is to gradually link the economies of the EC and EFTA member states and those of their east European partners so as to prepare for the latter's eventual membership of the Community. As noted above, the trade and cooperation agreements in force between the EC and other transition economies contain provisions for a much more modest reduction in trade barriers.

As regards the actual implementation of these accords, the *interim (trade) agreements* of the Association Agreements with the former Czechoslovakia, Hungary, and Poland came into force on 1 March 1992, resulting in immediate improvements in access to the EC market.[415] Subsequently, these countries (the Czech and Slovak Republics separately) benefited from the scheduled second

---

[409] According to the original announcement, the Committee is to be dissolved no later than 31 March 1994. COCOM is to be replaced by a new, expanded organization which would include Russia, other eastern countries and industrialized western countries not currently members of COCOM. Its basic objective will be to control exports of technology for producing atomic, bacteriological and chemical weapons. *Bulletin of the United States Mission (Geneva)*, 18 November 1993. *Financial Times*, London, 16 November 1993.

[410] In view of the civil war in Yugoslavia, the EC Council of Ministers decided in November 1991 to denounce the application of the agreement. In the following December it made available equivalent trade preferences to these four successor republics. EC Commission, *Overview, EC-East Europe*, Brussels, 29 January 1993.

[411] Under these arrangements, almost all industrial products originating in Slovenia will eventually enter the EC duty-free and almost one third of its agricultural exports will receive preferential access. Ibid.

A separate protocol deals with textile and ECSC products (i.e., steel and coal).

[412] Romania had already received limited GSP privileges from the EC in the 1970s, chiefly for political reasons.

[413] The timetables for the reduction of tariffs and dismantling of quotas contained in the agreements with the former Czechoslovakia, Hungary and Poland can be found in United Nations Economic Commission for Europe, *Economic Survey of Europe in 1991-1992*, New York, 1992, pp.187-188.

[414] Unlike the provisions of the EC Association Agreements, trade in agricultural products between EFTA members and their eastern partners is subject to bilateral arrangements.

[415] The full Association Agreements with Hungary and Poland have been ratified and entered into force 1 February 1994.

round of liberalization on 1 January 1993 (although the reduction in barriers was smaller than the first round), and from the third round on 1 January 1994. For Romania, the first and second stages of trade liberalization began on 1 May 1993 and 1 January 1994, respectively. The interim agreement with Bulgaria was to have gone into force on 1 July 1993, but implementation was delayed until 31 December 1993 because of differences among the member states of the EC over safeguard agreements.[416] This delay is reported to have caused large losses for Bulgarian business.[417]

The calendar for implementation of the *free trade agreements* between EFTA and the same six eastern partners has been more complex since the dates relevant to each accord have been arranged bilaterally. The agreements with the Czech and Slovak Republics came into force in the second half of 1992, and those with Bulgaria, Hungary, Poland and Romania in 1993. Implementation of FTA's has lagged behind that of the Association agreements.

Five of the eastern signatories of the Association Agreements (except Bulgaria) have also benefited from the EC decision to accelerate the scheduled reduction of EC customs duties[418] on certain imports of *sensitive basic industrial products*[419] on which tariffs were abolished at the end of the second year after the entry into force of the Agreement (instead of at the end of the fourth year); *industrial products affected by the consolidation of GSP*,[420] for which quotas and ceilings were increased by 30 per cent (for Poland, the Czech and Slovak Republics, Bulgaria and Romania) and 25 per cent (Hungary) per year, starting from the second half of the second year after the entry into force of the Agreement (instead of by 20 and 15 per cent, respectively). In addition, levies/duties on *agricultural products* subject to quotas were reduced by 60 per cent six months earlier than foreseen in the Agreements. The 10 per cent increase in the quotas, foreseen from the third year onwards, has been applied six months earlier than scheduled. Finally, *outward processing operations* have been exempted from customs duties as from the beginning of 1994.[421]

After the unification of Germany, the *EC* granted duty-free treatment to certain imports from Bulgaria, Czechoslovakia, Hungary, Poland, Romania, the former USSR and Yugoslavia, to the limits foreseen in trade agreements entered into by the former German Democratic Republic. These preferences, which are important to the transition economies since the former German Democratic Republic was one of their major markets, were authorized in 1990 by a waiver of GATT rules on transitional trade measures taken in connection with the unification of Germany.[422] In 1993 the EC requested another year's extension of the waiver.

In general, EFTA has followed the lead of the EC in reshaping its economic relations with the east, taking into account constraints imposed by the European Economic Area (EEA) and aiming at a certain compatibility between the EC's agreements with the individual eastern countries. However, in their economic relations with the *Baltic states*, *Finland*,[423] *Norway*, *Sweden* and *Switzerland* have set the pace by concluding a network of bilateral FTAs. All of these accords have been in force since May 1993 or earlier.

(c) Negotiations in progress

As noted above, *Albania, Estonia, Latvia, Lithuania and Slovenia* currently conduct their trade with the *EU* within the framework of trade and cooperation agreements (which in the case of Slovenia already provide for some preferential access, as noted). For most of these countries, negotiations are under way or are planned to conclude new accords which would lead to greater, preferential access to the EU market. A mandate is under preparation within the EU which will allow negotiations on a full Association Agreement with *Slovenia* to begin. The prospective accord could enter into force in early 1995. In the current discussions between the EU and the *Baltic states*, consideration is being given to accords which are at least comparable to free trade agreements but not as comprehensive as full Association Agreements.[424] Such an outcome would provide greater access to the EU market than exists at present and would be compatible with the bilateral free trade agreements already in force between the Baltic states and the Nordic countries. The issue of compatibility between future arrangements is of concern to the EU because, under the current accords, goods originating in the Baltic states could circumvent EU tariffs by entering the EU via the Nordic countries. Ultimately, Estonia, Latvia and Lithuania hope to conclude full Association Agreements. This is also the objective of the Community "as soon as the necessary conditions have been met [by the Baltic states]".[425]

---

[416] *Agence Europe*, 6 October 1993 and 4 December 1993.

[417] *Agence Europe*, 20 July 1993, according to Bulgarian foreign minister, Stanislav Daskalov.

[418] The decision to accelerate the schedule for trade liberalization contained in the Association Agreements was taken at the Copenhagen Summit in June 1993. See *Agence Europe*, Documents Nos.1844/45, 24 June 1993, p.6.

[419] Those contained in Annex IIb of the Interim Agreements, which is concerned with certain metal base products.

[420] This refers to the annual Community tariff quotas or ceilings which are raised progressively. The products concerned are contained in Annex III which covers certain sensitive products such as textiles (not MFA products), footwear, iron and steel (not ECSC products), glassware, motor vehicles and furniture.

[421] In other sectors, the rate of tariff reductions is somewhat lower: regarding *industrial products* subject to consolidation of GSP, tariffs are to be abolished at the end of the third year (instead of at the end of the fifth year); on *textile products* tariffs will be eliminated at the end of five years instead of six years; on *ECSC steel products* tariffs are to be abolished, at the latest, by the end of the fourth year instead of at the end of the fifth year, subject to compliance with specific decisions relating to trade in steel products.

[422] GATT, *Focus*, No.99, May/June 1993. The original waiver from GATT rules, for a period of two years, was sought by the EC at the end of 1990. GATT, *Circular* L/6730, 1990.

[423] Finland's long-standing free trade agreement with the former Soviet Union was extended to the Baltic Republics.

[424] *Agence Europe*, 2 and 22 December 1993.

[425] European Council of Copenhagen, 21-22 June 1993, *Agence Europe*, Documents Nos.1844/45, 24 June 1993.

As regard initiatives involving *EFTA*, preparations are underway for opening negotiations with *Slovenia*, which would proceed in parallel with the EU-Slovenia talks. Currently, trade between EFTA members and Slovenia is conducted on an MFN basis, except for Slovene products which receive GSP treatment.

Trade relations between the *CIS* and the *EU* also continue within the framework of trade and cooperation agreements (originally concluded with the former Soviet Union). The maintenance of this arrangement reflects, *inter alia*, the EU's reservations about the degree to which these economies are functioning according to market principles. In the near future, EU-CIS economic relations are to be governed by non-preferential *Partnership and Cooperation Agreements*. Among other things, they are to include MFN treatment for trade in goods[426] (except for products qualifying for GSP, which is granted separately). It appears that separate sectoral agreements are to cover agriculture, ECSC goods (steel and coal), and, possibly, uranium and aluminium. Quotas in these sectors are to be set periodically, probably annually, in bilateral negotiations.[427] Until these are decided, it will not be possible to determine the extent of any additional access to the EU market that these countries will receive.

In the case of *Russia*, the European Commission's original mandate for negotiating a Partnership Agreement was broadened on a number of occasions in 1993 in order to strengthen support for Russia's economic reforms. Although the agreement was not completely finalized by the end of 1993, a "Joint Political Declaration" was signed in December 1993 which contains most of the main principles envisaged for the Partnership Agreement.[428] In the economic sphere these include:

- improved market access on the basis of mutual MFN treatment and reductions in quantitative restrictions;
- recognition that Russia is no longer a state trading country, but an economy in transition;
- creation of more stable and predictable trade conditions. *Inter alia*, the agreement will include references to safeguard and anti-dumping procedures and to the establishment of conditions for fair competition;
- agreement to examine the possibility of creating a free trade area between the EU and the Russian Federation[429] and a promise to work together for the gradual liberalization of services and capital movements.

The terms of the prospective agreement reflect the progressive enlargement of the EC's mandate during the negotiations. Initially, the EC had resisted Russia's demand to be treated like a GATT member and to incorporate in the agreement the objective of the free movement of goods, services, capital (with some restrictions) and persons. The EC argued that Russia did not yet comply with market economy rules, notably with respect to the relationship between costs and prices of goods.[430] Instead, the EC had insisted on a special safeguard clause which would remain operational until Russia complied fully with GATT rules. This clause would permit the EC to block imports it considered were being "dumped" on its market, especially in "sensitive sectors" such as aluminium, steel and textiles.[431] According to the prospective agreement, Russia will be removed from the EC's list of state trading countries and be treated like GATT members in the application of the safeguard clause, anti-dumping and anti-subsidy regimes, etc. Conclusion of the full Partnership Agreement has been delayed beyond the end-March 1994 target date.[432]

By early 1994, the EC and *Ukraine*, *Belarus* and *Kyrgyzstan* had concluded their third, second and first rounds of negotiations, respectively, towards partnership and cooperation agreements.[433] Discussions also started with a number of other countries. Ukraine and Belarus have sought reference in their agreements to the creation of a free trade agreement as a future goal. A new broader negotiating mandate taking these requests into account is under consideration in the EC. Ukraine is also seeking an explicit reference to its possible association with the EC.

(iii) The rise of contingent protection: A trend or a blip?

The transition economies' gains in access to western markets have been partially offset by new restrictions on certain eastern exports. Against a background of deepening recession in 1992 and the first half of 1993, there was a steady stream of complaints against imports of certain eastern goods which eventually culminated in a number of import restrictions. Thus, while standard measures of protection (tariffs and quotas) affecting the east diminished, contingent protection measures (anti-dumping and safeguard actions) were used more frequently, including by the EC against those countries with which it had Association Agreements. Thus, one of the earliest concerns voiced about the Association Agreements – the large scope they allowed for the application of contingent protection – appears to have been justified.

The ECE secretariat has compiled an inventory of some of the measures taken against eastern exports during

---

[426] Statement by the representative of the European Commission on behalf of the EU to the ECE Committee on the Development of Trade, Geneva, 1-3 March 1994.

[427] These new agreements would appear to replace sectoral accords between the EC and the USSR which were extended to the new republics. EC quotas on imports from the USSR contained in these agreements are allocated to the individual successor republics.

[428] Unresolved issues relating to restrictions on the operations of foreign banks in Russia, maritime transport, and EU demands for safeguards in connection with imports of Russian uranium are reported to have prevented full agreement. *Agence Europe*, 10 December 1993 and 19 January 1994.

[429] It appears that the timetable for discussions on a free trade area will not be decided until 1998. *Agence Europe*, 10 November 1993.

[430] *Agence Europe*, 10 June 1993.

[431] Ibid.

[432] *Europe*, 19 January 1994.

[433] Statement of representative of the European Commission, op.cit.

TABLE 4.2.1

Restrictive actions taken by western countries against products from transition economies
(Number of actions) [a]

Products from:	Eastern Europe	Republics of former Soviet Union
August-December 1992	2	1
January-July 1993	11	4
August 1993-January 1994	1	4

Source: United Nations Economic Commission for Europe, *Economic Bulletin for Europe*, Vol.45 (1993), New York and Geneva, 1994, section 4.2.

[a] An "action" is defined in the text.

the course of 1992-1993.[434] Twenty actions were noted during the period, most of which were taken in the first seven months of 1993 and affected mainly east European products (table 4.2.1).[435] The bulk of the restrictions was imposed by the EC. In many of these cases, imports from the eastern partner(s) had risen substantially, often by between 100 and 500 per cent, over periods ranging from one to three years. Their market shares rose rapidly, but rarely exceeded 10 per cent (although in two cases it rose to about 30 per cent). Overall, however, the transition countries still account for only a small share of the western market: in 1992 eastern Europe and the former Soviet Union accounted for only 1.5 per cent and 1.1 per cent of total western imports, respectively. Even in the sensitive iron and steel sector, EC imports from the transition economies (some 4 million tons in 1992) represented less than 3 per cent of the EC's apparent consumption.

The inventory also shows that all of the restrictions affect the sensitive sectors (agriculture, steel, certain metals (including aluminium from the former Soviet Union) and bulk chemicals) in which the transition countries are considered to be most competitive and where much of their exports are concentrated. The latter two product groups have traditionally been the subject of western anti-dumping or safeguard actions. It is difficult to gauge the loss of export revenues since, among other things, shipments may have been diverted to other markets.

An incomplete list of new actions initiated by the western countries against eastern goods in the six-month period to end-January 1994 suggests a lull in new measures (table 4.2.1). Only one action appears to have been taken against an east European country, but new measures against Russia and other Soviet successor states continued. They include:

- initiation by the EU of anti-dumping proceedings concerning imports of *unwrought magnesium* originating in Russia, Ukraine and Kazakhstan following a complaint lodged by Euro Alliages on behalf of Pechiney (since 1992, the sole producer in the EU).[436] The complaint states that the Community producer was injured due to rapidly rising imports[437] during a period of stable consumption and that these producers undercut prices by some 30 per cent;

- introduction by the EU of provisional anti-dumping duties (in principle valid for four months) on imports of *hematite pig iron* from Russia, Ukraine, Poland and Brazil.[438] The combined imports from these four countries had increased from 242,000 tons in 1987 to 414,000 tons during the investigation period (presumably 1992 or 1993), but the market shares of Poland, and Russia and Ukraine (together) rose to only 5.3 per cent and 8 per cent, respectively (compared with 37 per cent for Brazil).[439]

The third case pertains to *aluminium* exports from the former Soviet Union. Against the background of the western recession and a sharp decline in the world price of aluminium – it fell by some 40-50 per cent – Russian exports are reported to have quadrupled from 1990 to about 1 million tons in 1992 (and probably further in 1993).[440] In response to this surge, the EC restricted imports of unwrought aluminium from the successor states of the former Soviet Union (primarily from Russia) to 60,000 tons for the period 7 August to 30 November 1993.[441] The quota was extended from 1 December 1993 to 28 February 1994 and set at a level of 45,000 tons.[442] However, a multilateral initiative by major aluminium producing countries has sought to stabilize world market prices by cutting production capacity by 1.5-2 million tons. Under an EU plan announced at the end of January, Russia is reported to have offered to cut output by 500,000 tons in return for financial assistance to restructure its aluminium industry.[443] A key issue from the point of competition is how this multilateral agreement can be implemented without extending a global cartel. The agreement

---

[434] United Nations Economic Commission for Europe, *Economic Bulletin for Europe*, Vol.45(1993), New York and Geneva, 1994, section 4.2.

[435] In table 4.2.1, a single action generally involves several eastern countries (and often other countries as well) and several products. For example, one action was directed against imports of livestock, meat and dairy products from 18 eastern countries. Cases involving extension of the time limits on a restriction and separate preliminary and final determinations of dumping and injury to domestic industry are treated as single actions. The numbers presented in table 4.2.1 for 1992 are incomplete.

[436] *Europe*, 17-18 January 1994.

[437] Imports from these countries "rose from 2,300 tons in 1991 to more than 8,000 tons in 1992 and even more in 1993". Ibid.

[438] *Europe*, 17-18 January 1994. In the case of Russia and Ukraine, a dumping margin of 104.51 per cent was determined. For Poland the estimated margin range was 31.53 to 50.2 per cent, depending on the exporter.

[439] Ibid.

[440] *Financial Times*, 27 January 1994.

[441] Commission Regulation (EEC) No.2227/93, *Official Journal*, No.L 198, 7 August 1993, p.21.

[442] Commission Regulation (EEC), *Official Journal*, No.L 321, 23 December 1993. A second tranche of 6,750 tons was intended to act as a reserve for the EC and was to be subject to a later distribution among member states by 1 February 1994.

[443] Russia is to cut its output by 300,000 tons during February-April and by a further 200,000 tons during May-July. Although details of the financial assistance are not specified in the agreement, western governments are understood to have promised to help restructure Russia's aluminium industry, the EU through the TACIS. *International Herald Tribune*, 31 January 1994 and *Financial Times*, 1 February 1994.

represents another step towards managed trade, which, as a matter of principle, the transition countries are being urged to avoid as they dismantle their state trading systems, and from which the western market economies were expected to retreat after the completion of the Uruguay Round.

What explains the apparent decline in the frequency of new measures taken against east European exports since mid-1993? A number of possible reasons may be suggested. The competent western authorities may have been more successful in resisting demands for additional protection, especially after earlier actions had provoked criticism and raised questions about the strength and consistency of western support for the transition process. Second, the pressure from east European exports has diminished. The east European export boom of 1991-1992,[444] which is likely to have contributed to some of the western actions in the first place, largely petered out in 1993 (see section 3.5). Third, eastern exporters may have become more cautious as a result of the active western anti-dumping policy during the previous two years. Although these actions were generally taken against narrowly defined products, contingent protection is known to have a far broader impact on "vulnerable" foreign exporters. At the very least, they may "voluntarily" curtail the growth of their sales to reduce the probability of a formal complaint being lodged against them.[445] Even if the frequency of new actions subsides, the restraining effect of the threat of contingent protection may remain unchanged.[446]

Unlike eastern Europe, economic activity in the CIS continued to decline sharply in 1993. In consequence, further quantities of certain products became available for export (including metals and some chemicals from Russia – see section 3.5) increases of which could have contributed to the western decisions to take the new measures mentioned above (table 4.2.1). The CIS may be particularly susceptible to anti-dumping actions since many western governments still regard them as state trading countries, due to their lagging reform programmes.

In two recent cases against Russian exports, the determination or complaint that the exporter had engaged in dumping was based on comparisons with prices in third (so-called surrogate) countries. In one case, prices in the Japanese market were used by Euro Alliages for comparison, while in the second the price in the Brazilian market was used. It appears that under the provisions of the prospective Partnership Agreement between the EU and Russia, the latter would be treated as a GATT member in the application of the anti-dumping clause. In principle, the EU would look at the price of the good in question in the Russian market to determine a possible dumping margin (i.e., as opposed to taking the price of a similar product in a surrogate country). It is difficult to determine the implications for Russia – indeed for all transition economies entitled to GATT treatment – of this and other prospective changes in anti-dumping procedures. It has been pointed out that classification of a country as a market economy (instead of a state trading economy) does not necessarily imply that it will be subject to fewer actions.[447] The new GATT anti-dumping code is likely to offer the transition countries some additional protection. Positive results may also come about from the introduction of a greater degree of transparency in the EU's new anti-dumping procedures, but the net impact of the overall streamlining of these procedures remains to be seen.

(iv) **Summary of trade liberalization measures and prospects**

The easing of standard measures of protection (i.e., tariffs and quotas) in the west has improved the east's access to western markets.[448] Trade between the transition countries and the western market economies is now on a MFN basis and the transition countries generally enjoy GSP privileges.

In other respects, progress towards the removal of barriers has and will continue to be uneven. The most significant steps taken so far involve the preferential agreements (i.e., Association and free trade agreements) concluded by the EU and EFTA with six east European countries and between individual EFTA countries and the Baltic states. Even in the case of these agreements, however, trade barriers remain in place. While some restrictions were lifted at the time of their entry into force, in the "sensitive" manufactures sectors (e.g., textiles) tariffs and quotas will be eliminated completely only over a number of years. Most assessments are that improvements in market access in the agricultural sector have not been – and will not be – large, although this sector is of current or potential importance to several transition economies. At the same time, western subsidization of agricultural exports has hindered eastern Europe's ability to compete, including in traditional eastern markets, and harmed the agricultural sector in the transition countries.[449]

Reduction of trade barriers in the EU facing other transition economies – those with which trade is conducted within the framework of non-preferential, trade and cooperation agreements – has proceeded more slowly. However, accords currently under negotiation (or planned)

---

[444] The rapid growth of east European exports to the west in 1991-1992 is explained in part by the collapse of domestic demand (including the metals-intensive military sector) and of the CMEA trading system, which prompted eastern exporters to channel goods to the west. The weakening of east European exports in 1993 may reflect the stabilization of economic activity in this area.

[445] The literature stresses the high cost of legal proceedings and the possibility of a permanent loss of market share.

[446] While some eastern exporters may have "voluntarily" held back sales to the west, it is doubtful that the spate of contingency protection measures can explain the downturn in the exports of several east European countries in 1993. The exports of the Czech Republic, among the most affected by contingency protection measures, continued to rise. See above, section 3.5.

[447] See B. Hindley, "Helping transition through trade? EC and US policy toward exports from eastern and central Europe", EBRD, *Working Paper*, No.4, March 1993.

[448] See United Nations Economic Commission for Europe, *Economic Bulletin for Europe*, Vol.45(1993), New York and Geneva, 1994.

[449] See, for example, the comments of east European speakers, referring mainly to EU exports, at the Agra Europe conference in Budapest. *Financial Times*, 8 March 1994.

will extend the EU-EFTA-centred[450] preferential zone eastward over the next decade. EFTA-EU agreements with Slovenia may be ready for implementation in early 1995 and the EU-Baltics FTAs probably somewhat later. In the case of Russia and probably Ukraine (the most advanced of the CIS in their negotiations with the EU), however, discussions on a FTA are not to begin before 1998. The willingness of the EU to conclude preferential agreements has depended on its perception of the partner's degree of commitment to market principles, and this is likely to be the case in the future as well.

This timetable, together with the (typical) six-year transition period for the elimination of EU tariffs and quotas on eastern industrial products, implies that the transition economies will receive unequal treatment into the next century. By 1997 the industrial products exports of the first group of east European countries[451] to have concluded Association/FTAs will enjoy free access to the EU and EFTA markets. In that year, the Baltic states and Slovenia will be about half way through their transition period and will have reaped most of the benefits of trade liberalization.[452] However, Russia, Ukraine and presumably other CIS republics will still be subject to MFN tariffs (except for GSP products) and face sectoral quotas (although the degree of restrictiveness cannot be determined at this time).

Clearly, the front runners in this process will derive the greatest benefits, and the CIS will be at a disadvantage through at least the remainder of the decade.[453] However, the value of tariff preferences will be reduced due to the one third cut in MFN tariffs agreed under the Uruguay Round accord (which will be implemented over a period of years).

So far only a limited number of transition economies have taken steps to liberalize *eastern intra-trade*.[454] The Czech and Slovak Republics, Hungary and Poland have created the Central European Free Trade Agreement (CEFTA)[455] and they are now in the process of concluding bilateral FTA's with Slovenia. The Baltic Free Trade Agreement has been ratified by the governments of Estonia, Latvia and Lithuania and it was to come into force on 1 April 1994. Trade between Russia and the CIS republics is carried out within the framework of bilateral free trade agreements, most of which date from 1992.[456] However, exchanges of many products are subject to quantitative restraints, implemented through a system of indicative and obligatory lists, and Russian exports of a broad range of goods are subject to export taxes.[457] A CIS summit on 24 September 1993 agreed in principle to set up a CIS Economic Union. The preliminary agreement on the Union posited the gradual reduction and eventual elimination of all customs duties and other trade barriers. However, no further action appears to have been taken.

An aspect of the preferential schemes discussed above which generally receives little attention is their *rules of origin*.[458] Application of these rules can restrict market access and hinder integration of the transition countries not only with the west but among themselves as well. The free trade zones created by, for example, the EU-east European countries, EFTA-east European countries, etc., are essentially bilateral arrangements which are not linked to each other.[459] Material originating in one free trade area is regarded as third country material when exported for processing to another free trade area. If such imported material exceeds certain limits, it fails to qualify for trade preferences offered in another trade area.

In order for certain products exported from a transition country to qualify for trade preferences (i.e., lower or zero tariffs) granted in a particular trade area (e.g., EU and EFTA) those products must be produced from inputs which are either wholly obtained in the exporting country; imported from the country or group of countries granting the preferences; or obtained from a third country (or trade area), but only within limits set out in the trade accord between the contractual parties. In practice little use of material coming from the outside is allowed. Material inputs which exceed specified limits have to undergo sufficient domestic working or processing for the final product to qualify for area treatment.

The implication is that exports from any one transition economy must be produced chiefly from domestic inputs or from materials originating in the respective free trade zone (EU or EFTA, but not both taken

---

[450] EFTA member countries which are to join the EU will presumably adopt its external policy towards the transition countries, although no specific provisions or timetable for this currently exist (except in the EFTA countries' bilateral FTAs with the Baltic states).

[451] Tariffs and quotas facing Bulgaria and Romania will be phased out somewhat later, since their interim agreements came into force after those of the Czech and Slovak Republics, Hungary and Poland.

[452] The terms of these agreements provide for the removal of a large share of the western partners' trade obstacles in the early years of the accord.

[453] The importance of these differential gains is difficult to assess due to the complexity of the schedules for tariff and quota liberalization in the Association Agreements and EFTA FTAs and, also, the large differences in the commodity structures of the transition economies' exports. Moreover, whether a country benefits or not depends on its capacity to supply additional goods to the relevant market.

[454] The following agreements are discussed in "Establishing Conditions Conducive to Expanding Trade among Economies in Transition", Economic Commission for Europe, TRADE/R.603, 20 December 1993.

[455] The CEFTA agreement, which went into effect on 1 March 1993, originally provided for an eight-year transition period to free trade in industrial products. Subsequently, the target date for the removal of trade barriers was brought forward to 1 January 1998 and its scope was enlarged to include agricultural produce and services. The declaration of principle covering these changes was signed 4 February 1994. BBC, *Summary of World Broadcasts*, EEW/0319 WA/1, 10 February 1994.

[456] GATT, *Accession of the Russian Federation*, Memorandum on the Foreign Trade Regime (from the Ministry of Foreign Affairs of the Russian Federation), L/7410, 1 March 1994.

[457] RF Goskomstat, *Sotsial'no-ekonomicheskoe polozhenie Rossii 1993 g.* (The socio-economic situation of Russia in 1993), Moscow, 1993.

[458] Rules of origin contained in the east-west preferential agreements and their implications are discussed more extensively in United Nations Economic Commission for Europe, *Economic Bulletin for Europe*, Vol.45(1993), New York and Geneva, 1994, pp.106-107.

[459] These are often described as wheel-spoke arrangements in which the EU and EFTA are the hubs.

together) to qualify for preferences in either of them. Basically, no material originating in other transition economies can be used. The exception to this otherwise restrictive system is that materials from any of the four CEFTA countries (the Czech and Slovak Republics, Hungary and Poland) cumulate (bilaterally) for export to the EU or EFTA.[460]

In order to allow the parties to these agreements to benefit fully from the lower trade barriers, EFTA and others have made proposals to link the free trade zones through a coherent pan-European system of cumulation of origin rules. The EU Commission is conducting an analysis of rules of origin prior to submitting proposals for their harmonization for all products from associated countries in central and eastern Europe and EFTA.[461]

Under the EU Association and EFTA FTA agreements, eastern partners are benefiting from a slower reduction of trade restrictions on their industrial imports than their western partners do (i.e., the asymmetrical reduction provision). Meanwhile, the increasing demand for protection in the east has caused some concern. No one factor appears to explain the reasons for the measures taken so far, but they appear to include[462] adjustment of trade instruments to better meet current needs of the transition,[463]

domestic pressures arising from the deep and persistent recession, reinforced by the appreciation of east European currencies (in real terms), balance of payments considerations (see section 3.6), and demands from sectoral interests, including foreign investors pressing for greater protection of their products. The eastern authorities often point to restrictive western policies, but it is uncertain whether any of the eastern actions have been taken specifically for this reason.

Although the restrictive moves may be justified, the danger remains that the policies will become entrenched, as they have in the west. In their attempts to attract foreign direct investors, eastern governments have on occasion granted exclusive marketing rights to western manufacturers. Since these investments are generally made in oligopolistic markets an important element of potential competition may be sacrificed.

In addition to lowering standard trade barriers, western countries have taken other measures to facilitate the transition economies' access to their markets. These include, *inter alia*, assistance through the PHARE-TACIS programmes (arranged bilaterally) to help eastern exporters adapt to EU technical and other standards; setting up customs systems and improving border crossings; and upgrading telecommunications and transport infrastructure (see section 4.1).[464] To help the eastern countries promote their exports, the west has provided some assistance for setting up export credit facilities, lack of which has especially hindered exports of engineering goods. But a great deal still remains to be done in this area, including funding the schemes.

---

[460] This special arrangement excludes Bulgaria and Romania, which individually are able to use only domestic materials or materials from the EU and EFTA (but not from each other) for exports to either of these groups of countries. Also, cumulation between the CEFTA countries is bilateral under the provisions of the CEFTA Agreement, i.e., only domestic material and material originating in the country of destination qualify for cumulation purposes.

[461] *Agence Europe*, 10 June 1993.

[462] A partial inventory of these measures was presented in the United Nations Economic Commission for Europe, *Economic Bulletin for Europe*, Vol.45(1993), New York and Geneva, 1994, pp.111-112.

[463] There are grounds for believing that in certain cases the reforms resulted in excessively open systems which prematurely exposed domestic industries to foreign competition.

[464] Loans for the development of transport infrastructure in the east are available through the multilateral development institutions, including EIB loans for TENS (see section 4.1).

Chapter 5

RESTRUCTURING OF STATE-OWNED ENTERPRISES IN EASTERN EUROPE

5.1 The experience of enterprise restructuring in transition economies

(i) Key issues and comparative perspectives

There is only one former centrally planned economy where the transformation of large state-owned enterprises into capitalist firms has taken place on a large scale. This is the former German Democratic Republic, where most state-owned enterprises have been privatized and the great majority of privatized enterprises in terms of employment are in the hands of a western – usually a west German – company, family or individual. In the ex-German Democratic Republic there is thus an effective owner, usually private, able to exert control over the management of the enterprise. The rapidity with which this could be achieved in Germany has been due to the extent of *enterprise restructuring prior* to privatization by the Treuhand (the German privatization agency) and the *availability of financial resources* to dampen the opposition of the "losers" to employment shedding. In both respects, of course, the choices available in Germany have been much larger than those open to other countries in transition.

By restructuring usually is meant both efficiency- and competition-oriented measures to enhance productive and allocative efficiency. Concretely this includes the breaking up of large enterprises and the separation out of the core businesses, hiving off of social assets, employment shedding, closure of unviable activities and restructuring of balance sheet to deal with the problem of enterprise debts. Restructuring should be distinguished from other measures undertaken by enterprises to protect them from the market environment.[465] However (as confirmed by the German examples in section 5.3(iv) below) it is not always possible to judge *ex ante* whether a particular adjustment strategy is market-conforming or not.

Foreign direct investment and restructuring

Parallels can be drawn between the large-scale involvement of west German investors in the process of privatization in east Germany and the role of foreign direct investment (FDI) elsewhere in eastern Europe in creating a specific type of capitalist firm (a subsidiary) through the acquisition of former state-owned enterprises (SOEs). Consistent with the pattern in east Germany, foreign acquisitions in eastern Europe have typically required substantial restructuring of the SOE, including labour shedding, before a deal was possible.[466] Cases where this has not been true have often involved the purchase by the foreign company of a monopoly, where from the perspective of the buyer the race to win access to monopoly profits offsets the requirement for restructuring prior to privatization.

Relative to expectations, the volume of foreign direct investment in eastern Europe has been disappointing. Moreover, from a welfare perspective its structure has been suboptimal, showing a bias in the direction of the "purchase of monopoly power". One recent study shows, for example, that the two largest foreign direct investments in the Czech Republic in 1992 (accounting for one third of FDI that year) were the sale of domestic monopolies.[467]

Privatization and the establishment of effective owners

Outside east Germany, rapid privatization of large SOEs has only occurred on any scale in the former CSFR. One reason for the failure to find *foreign* buyers on a large scale has been given above. Slow progress in achieving transfer of ownership to *domestic* agents in a number of countries can be explained by the concern of policy makers to create through the privatization process *effective* owners of firms. This concern has deterred others from following the Czech example of privatization through vouchers. As is well-known, somewhat ironically, the CSFR voucher method has not produced "popular capitalism" (dispersed ownership) but ownership concentrated in financial institutions. How close this places the Czechs to achieving effective control over the management of enterprises is not yet clear.[468]

Managerial incentives and the role of organizational structures

Studies of enterprises in the transition countries reveal that even in the absence of privatization, managerial passivity has been far from universal. The contrast between Russian case studies, where market-oriented

---

[465] See Ickes and Ryterman (1993) for a discussion of the "survival-oriented-enterprise". (Bibliographical references are shown at the end of this chapter.)

[466] Business International/Creditanstalt (1992).
[467] See section 5.2 below, and Charap and Zemplinerova (1993c).
[468] Takla (1993).

adjustment by management even of *privatized* firms was generally very limited,[469] and studies of east European firms is striking.[470] There appears to be an emerging common finding that a *hardening of the enterprise budget constraint* promotes manager-initiated restructuring. As will be argued below (section 5.1(ii)), this is likely to be a necessary but not sufficient condition for market-oriented adjustment which promotes efficiency. The results of the case study of Russian firms already mentioned can be used to highlight the role of labour market conditions in complementing the budget hardness effect. If job prospects outside the enterprise are very poor (e.g., as in Russia compared with the Czech Republic), then the option of lowering wages exists as a way of avoiding adjustment.

A simple model developed by Aghion, Blanchard and Burgess tries to explain why a *hardening of the budget constraint* can lead to adjustment – including the closure of units and labour shedding – before privatization and in the absence of high-powered managerial compensation schemes.[471] The hardening of the budget constraint raises the prospect of the non-survival of the enterprise if the status quo is maintained. Even if there is no clear prospect that the manager will have a stake in the ownership of the privatized firm, the perception that success in restructuring may enable managers to enhance their career prospects in the enterprise or elsewhere can be a powerful motivation.

However, career incentives for managers may be inadequate to promote restructuring in the face of opposition from the potential losers within the enterprise. Indeed, it seems that the *organizational structure* of state-owned enterprises as well as the distribution of viable and non-viable activities can have an important effect on the ability of both managers and employees to block efficiency-oriented restructuring.

Two organizational characteristics could have a particular bearing: (i) the case in which top management of the enterprise becomes irrelevant after unbundling and will therefore oppose the breaking up of the enterprise; and (ii) the case in which there are a large number of non-performing units in the enterprise and hence the influence of losers dominates. If restructuring is socially optimal, then it is possible for the gainers to compensate the losers. This "suggests a role for the government in easing the restructuring process while enforcing hard budget constraints upon firms that do not restructure. Financial support from the government might include credit for severance payments and debt write-downs or debt reallocations" (for firms which undertake restructuring).[472]

(ii) Macroeconomic environment and enterprise restructuring

The resilience of reforms in the transition economies appears to rest on a complex interaction between macroeconomic and microeconomic measures. The tough macroeconomic policy stance which has been sustained for several years in the former Czechoslovakia, Hungary and Poland, appears to have had positive effects on enterprise behaviour. Evidence has been gathered to show that state-owned enterprise management has felt the pressure of the hard budget constraint and has initiated efficiency-oriented restructuring measures.[473]

However, the impact of the hard budget constraint in inducing microeconomic adjustment requires qualification. The fundamental problem concerns loss-making enterprises. The persistence over many years of a harsh macroeconomic environment runs the risk of tipping the balance in the economy from a situation in which the majority of enterprise managers perceive a reasonable likelihood of viability in the market economy to a situation in which viability appears improbable. If the enterprise is thought to have "no chance" under market conditions, management and employees will be prone to seek survival strategies for the "enterprise community" which may not be market-conforming. As long as the balance in the economy remains in favour of potential viability (for at least some core business activities of the bulk of enterprises), then reform remains on track in the sense that enterprise managers will generally be more engaged in seeking paths to adjustment than in seeking ways to circumvent the changeover to a hard budget constraint regime.

If loss-making becomes prevalent there is a danger that the incentive for managers to push forward with restructuring is dulled. Widespread loss-making has the additional effect of undermining the incentives for the banks to use appropriate credit-worthiness criteria when assessing loan requests from enterprises. Whilst macroeconomic toughness appears necessary to promote the process of manager-initiated restructuring in SOEs, it runs the risk of undermining the credibility of a hard budget constraint by raising the weight in the economy of loss-making enterprises. Section 5.4 relating to the *Hungarian* experience underlines this danger in the transition economy with the most sophisticated financial system and with a substantial private sector.

There is a second important interaction between the stance of macroeconomic policy and prospects for enterprise restructuring. This relates to the choice of the *exchange rate*. *East Germany* is an extreme case where, at the outset of the transition (given the initial poor quality of the capital stock and the collapse of the CMEA trading system), a large revaluation compounded by subsequent wage increases rendered virtually the entire SOE enterprise sector loss-making. This extreme situation in part accounts for the procedures undertaken by the Treuhand to identify which of these loss-making enterprises should be closed down. As pointed out in section 5.3, even in east Germany it was immediately apparent that the ready-made west German bankruptcy law was quite inappropriate for the circumstances of transition.

Elsewhere in the transition economies, sharp depreciations of the exchange rate were incorporated in the macroeconomic stabilization programmes. One rationale

---

[469] Hare (1993).

[470] Estrin et al. (1993) and Pinto et al. (1993).

[471] Aghion et al. (1993).

[472] Aghion et al. (1993), p.21.

[473] See, e.g., Pinto et al. (1993).

for this was to provide a boost to competitiveness as trade was radically liberalized.

However, in *Czechoslovakia,* the substantial real devaluation, due to the absence of an effective policy for demonopolizing sheltered industries, has distorted the incentives for enterprise restructuring through its effects on the relative profitability of different sectors. In spite of a clear trend towards deconcentration in the aggregate data (section 5.2), a recent study shows that it is the most highly concentrated branches of industry which have increased their share of industrial sales and profits from 1989 to 1992.[474] The exchange rate policy thus appears to have strengthened the position of heavy, energy-intensive industry in the Czech Republic.[475] Such branches were able to benefit doubly from price and trade liberalization-cum-devaluation: in the domestic economy, their monopoly power (given the absence of effective regulation) and inelastic demand allowed the widening of profits, whilst the devaluation afforded them protection against import competition.

The distorted distribution of profits across industries interferes with the desired effects of tight macroeconomic policy by selectively softening the budget constraint. This could be expected to slow down adjustment in the "favoured" sectors and may sufficiently weaken profitability elsewhere as to raise the possibility of the case sketched above of a general undermining of the hard budget constraint.

(iii) Privatization and enterprise restructuring

Hungarian experience over the past three years (section 5.4) highlights vividly the difficulty of attempting to identify *ex ante* whether actions taken by enterprise managers should be classified as efficiency-oriented restructuring or not. In the process misleadingly known as spontaneous privatization, SOE managers engaged in a process of enterprise reorganization which entailed the creation of many legally independent units. A hard enterprise budget constraint and the threat of bankruptcy prompted managers to seek to reduce that risk by reorganizing assets into separate limited liability companies and engaging in debt for equity swaps with banks and creditor enterprises. A positive aspect of this process was the decentralization of decision-making to managers of the satellite enterprises and the possibility of the involvement of the new owners (banks, other enterprises) in promoting restructuring. On the other hand, an important motivation for these initiatives of managers was to protect the enterprise from the actions of the government – including any attempt to introduce competition-oriented restructuring.

The move to centralized privatization with the establishment of the Hungarian State Property Agency (SPA) in 1990 appears to have failed to raise the pace of top-down restructuring and to have slowed enterprise-initiated restructuring. The authorities sought to achieve the rapid *sale* of state firms as entities and without dealing with enterprise indebtedness. As the experience of the former GDR suggests (section 5.3), this was unlikely to be successful, except in the case where monopolies were for sale. With respect to monopolies, the clash between the objectives of rapid privatization, maximizing revenues for the state budget and competition-oriented restructuring is well-known from the UK privatization experience. It appears that the objectives and instruments of centralized privatization in Hungary have had the effect of increasing the degree of organizational centralization, inhibiting the break-up of SOEs necessary both for increased productive and allocative efficiency (section 5.4).

The most recent period in Hungary has seen policy increasingly dominated by the widening crisis of enterprise profitability. This has overwhelmed the shift in objectives of policy makers away from a policy based on maximizing the sales price to one of seeking to boost the demand for state assets from a nascent Hungarian middle class (by making available loans on preferential terms, promoting employee share ownership participation (ESOP) schemes and leasing arrangements) and the supply of suitable assets by splitting up the large SOEs.

The implementation of the bankruptcy law at the beginning of 1992 revealed the inappropriateness of such a procedure for dealing with an economy-wide problem. The subsequent attempts by the state to undertake organizational and financial restructuring have been poorly designed (section 5.4). It appears that financial assistance has been provided to enterprises (initially, the so-called "Big Thirteen") *without* requiring structural adjustments by management. The procedure for bank consolidation appears to have suffered from similar incentive and credibility problems. In a climate of weak enterprise financial performance, the use of such "fire-fighting" techniques is dangerous, with the circle of enterprises receiving preferential treatment spreading to a wider set of SOEs, from industry to agriculture, from SOEs to the private sector and from Hungarian enterprises to multinational firms now claiming preferential credits (section 5.4).

Experience in the *Czech Republic* suggests that the process of spontaneous restructuring underway was interrupted, as in Hungary, by the government's establishment of a formal privatization procedure. Whereas it has been argued in the Hungarian case that the centralization of privatization impeded restructuring, there is some evidence that the Czech centralized programme promoted continued adjustment (section 5.2).[476] Two possible reasons for this have been highlighted: first, the requirement that managers of enterprises in the large-scale privatization programme had to submit a privatization project focused attention on a forward-looking business plan; and second, the assumption by managers that voucher privatization would leave them with control of the

---

[474] Buchtikova and Flek (1993), Table 3.

[475] A group of four industries – coal and lignite mining, manufacture of coke and petroleum refining, manufacture of basic metals, and electricity, gas and water – have taken their share in total profits in industry from 34 per cent in 1989 to 68 per cent in 1992 (Buchtikova and Flek (1993), Table 3).

[476] See also Estrin et al. (1993).

enterprise heightened their interest in adjustments which would enhance its viability.

There are some interesting examples from the Czech Republic which suggest that the government has been engaged in undertaking financial restructuring of enterprises (e.g., debt reduction) and in providing financial assistance for compensation schemes *in exchange for* restructuring by management. In the case of Poldi Steel, the restructuring package arose from cooperation between the enterprise, local government and the Ministry of Labour.[477] It was necessary to shed some 6,000 jobs and to break up the enterprise. Labour shedding was made easier because of the availability of jobs in Prague, but the restructuring deal included the provision of several thousand jobs – including measures through which skilled work-groups could be kept together. The government and the enterprise have provided subsidies to support so-called "conversion units" which have been set up using surplus facilities and labour. Most such conversion units have subsequently become independent subcontractors.

A recent study of enterprise transformation in *Poland* has generated considerable interest because it suggested that Polish state-owned enterprises were adjusting in response to the hardening of the budget constraint. Moreover, in the set of enterprises investigated there was no correlation between the status of the enterprise (privatized, corporatized or SOE) and its profitability.[478]

A World Bank cross-country study of enterprise adjustment in transition countries helps to provide a comparative perspective on the Polish results.[479] Although the efficiency-oriented restructuring measures undertaken by the Polish enterprises in the World Bank sample appear broadly consistent with the results of the Pinto study, they seemingly display weaker adjustment than the Czech and Hungarian enterprises. The World Bank authors suggest that specifically Polish factors – especially the powerful role of employees in SOEs – have inhibited adjustment in Poland relative to the other two cases. They also claim that for *viable* enterprises, the development of long-term adjustment strategies is intimately connected with the existence of a functioning privatization programme and that this helps to explain the superior adjustment observed in Czech (and, to a lesser extent, Hungarian) as compared with Polish enterprises.

Only in the *former GDR* has the privatization programme been coordinated with enterprise evaluation and the decision for either financial restructuring or liquidation (section 5.3). Widespread privatization of loss-makers has been possible in that case by virtue of the extensive pre-privatization restructuring undertaken and the availability of compensation for the losers. Elsewhere, the privatization programmes cannot solve the problem of enterprises which are loss-makers. It is becoming clear that the bankruptcy law is also inappropriate.[480]

A key debate now facing the transition economies is how the loss-making enterprises should be dealt with. The importance of macroeconomic policy in containing the spread of loss-making enterprises has been stressed above. At the microeconomic level, the debate centres on the problem of creating a sound financial system as well as dealing with the enterprise sector.[481] Two contrasting proposals are (i) to use the banks as the agents of enterprise restructuring by creating incentives for them to undertake this task; and (ii) to isolate the banks from the loss-making enterprises by bringing the enterprises under the control of a special state agency and taking the bad loans off the banks' portfolios.

---

[477] McDermott (1993).
[478] Pinto et al. (1993).
[479] Estrin et al. (1993).

[480] See, e.g., Mizsei (1993); van Wijnbergen (1993).
[481] Begg and Portes (1993); van Wijnbergen (1993).

5.2 Restructuring of state-owned enterprises in the Czech Republic

(i) Key issues in the restructuring of large SOEs

The Czech Republic started the transformation in 1989 with several hundred large and highly integrated state-owned enterprises. These enterprises had for more than forty years been protected from competition not only from the outside, but also domestically. Protection against competition from the world markets was secured through the state monopoly of foreign trade and the non-convertible currency. Protection against domestic competitors was assured by legislative barriers to entry and to exit, by price regulation and lack of incentives for entrepreneurial activities.[482]

The main sources of enterprise restructuring and adjustment of state enterprises are *privatization* and *competition*, or at least potential competition. The Czech government relied on indirect participation of the state in enterprise restructuring, the progressive removal of existing barriers to entry into the industry and promoting of competition, and fast massive privatization. At the same time new start-ups and small enterprises establishment are being supported. The state considers itself unable to undertake efficient wider restructuring since there are thousands of enterprises which need restructuring. Therefore, restructuring is left mainly to the future private owners, and privatization is considered to be the main path to restructuring.

The managers of state companies, with pending privatization schemes for 1992-1993 challenging their positions, had little motivation to get involved in the process of restructuring. Many state managers preferred to pursue their own short-run benefits (e.g., to direct their attention to their future private capital holdings).

There exists only limited information about the internal restructuring of firms. Changes in quality of management, organizational structure, quality control, organization of work, etc., are difficult to identify. Most of the steps for internal restructuring are probably still waiting for future introduction.

During the first three years of transition, the break-up of large state enterprises and changes in property rights were the main visible patterns of restructuring. Future restructuring will be more related to mergers, bankruptcies (acquisitions and liquidations), and the functioning of the capital markets.

Restructuring refers to changes undertaken in order make or keep companies competitive. It is useful to distinguish the following aspects: organizational, legal, and financial restructuring, even if they are implemented simultaneously and are strongly interrelated.

(a) Major agents of restructuring

The two major actors in restructuring are the *state* and the *management of state-owned enterprises (SOEs)*. The state has to create rules for the transformation of enterprises and a fair and transparent privatization process. The management of SOEs has the best information on the financial and economic situation of the enterprise and its possible future developments. The state and the management have different motivations in restructuring and thus influence the process differently. The result must necessarily be a compromise.

State involvement in restructuring of SOEs

In dependence on the general philosophy of economic transformation and the role of state in the economy, two different concepts of restructuring can be adopted: "bottom-up" and "top-down". The former relies on an indirect participation of the state in enterprise restructuring and gives preference to the progressive removal of existing barriers to entry into the industry and the promotion of competition. The latter places more reliance on direct participation of the state authorities in the break-up of the big, organizationally concentrated state enterprises.

Governments adopting the first approach would seek to create a system of equal rules for all economic agents. State enterprises are to be exposed to competition. Domestically this involves the removal of entry barriers, deregulation and price liberalization. Foreign competition is furthered by foreign trade liberalization and the introduction of currency convertibility, to put domestic producers into competition with imports.

The expected effect of such policy is the spontaneous break-up or liquidation of existing state enterprises and changes in the industrial structure based on the market critera. A constituent component of this approach is the creation of a new legal and institutional framework suitable for a competitive market economy. Such an approach requires a relatively long time but avoids costly failures.

The Czech government adopted this first approach in the early phases of transformation policy towards restructuring. The development of the structures of some industries give evidence in favour of this approach.

A first wave of enterprise break-ups occurred in the early 1990s; in some industries, the number of enterprises doubled or tripled. Although approval for the break-up had to be given by the appropriate founding ministries, plant managements played a vital role in instigating deconcentration. Their primary motivating factor was dissatisfaction with unqualified decision-making at the enterprise level and by the power of enterprise managers to redistribute resources between plants. Also, plant management frequently had a vision of future privatization of their plant through management buy-out (MBO) or employee buy-out (EBO).

Usually only technically well-equipped plants with a good chance of economic prosperity requested

---

[482] Managers employed their inventiveness and energies in negotiations with the centre for softer plans and larger resource allotment, and in other non-productive activities.

independence. Poorer and weaker plants and enterprises tended to throw in their lot with the large enterprise unit, relying on power based on size and the open hand of the state.

These processes of spontaneous break-ups and deconcentration based on economic calculation and expectations of future privatization were held up by decision of the government in 1991. There were several reasons for stopping this break-up process.

One reason for this decision was fear of a total *collapse of the production of basic supplies*. But the government also was concerned about the consequences of uncontrolled transfers to domestic joint stock companies or to foreign firms. Managers, in pursuit of their own interests, were selling enterprise assets at very low prices. A second reason was the programme based on the Act on Large-Scale Privatization approved by Parliament in February 1991. In several cases the government has become involved in restructuring out of fear of a chain reaction of bankruptcies caused by interenterprise indebtedness.

The biggest problems have been posed by the restructuring of the large state enterprises in capital-intensive industries which are not capable of changing their production in a flexible manner. It is often asserted that their restructuring, i.e., the break-up of these enterprises, is connected with considerable social risks and thus also with political destabilization on the one hand, and with the loss of of economies of scale on the other. But the contrary is true: the longer these large enterprises are maintained, the higher are the social losses stemming from their monopoly position. Social and political commotions will thus be stronger and longer lasting if the monopolies are artificially protected.

The state now pursues a policy of restructuring large enterprises either by their founding ministry prior to privatization, or through the Privatization Ministry during privatization, or through large banks after privatization.

The government selectively restructures enterprise debts to facilitate privatization, particularly when financial restructuring – and perhaps reimbursement for environmental damages – creates a realistic chance that an enterprise will become internationally competitive.

During the early stage of transformation the government also continued to protect domestic markets from foreign competition. Until 1992 there existed, for instance, an 18 per cent, and later 15 per cent, surcharge on imported goods, import licensing and further limits of the foreign trade liberalization. A rather steep devaluation of the Czechoslovak currency at the end of 1990 (US $1 = Kc 30) also protected domestic producers.

Management role in restructuring of SOEs

The role of management as well as the role of employees was an important topic in the discussion between gradualists and radicals in the government at the early stage of transformation. While the conception and rules of the transformation programme were unclear, management acted spontaneously.

TABLE 5.2.1

Structure of privatization projects by originator, Czech Republic, 1992
(Per cent)

Project originator	Share in project	
	Submitted	Approved [a]
Enterprise management	21.3	81.8
Outsiders	48.2	7.4
Plant management	3.0	5.7
Consulting firms	2.3	1.9
Restitution beneficiaries [b]	2.7	0.9
Municipalities	7.2	0.4
Others [c]	15.3	1.8
Total	100.0	100.0

Source: Ministry of Privatization, 1992 and 1994.

[a] Structure as of end-December 1992.

[b] Individuals eligible for restitution or preferential treatment in the purchase of certain assets.

[c] Including district privatization committees, private persons, lessees, enterprise employees, liquidators, land owners, etc.

In 1991, enterprise managers understood that privatization is an issue which cannot be avoided. Their strategy therefore focused on either becoming future owners of the company or finding foreign owners who would allow them to keep positions, or to use voucher privatization (see below), which was expected to generate dispersed ownership not allowing for effective corporate governance to keep positions. These different strategies of management had different implications for company restructuring.

With respect to management restructuring, changes in enterprise management were not directed from above. After the 1989 revolution there was opposition to the old managements from both inside enterprises and from the public at large. Employees, through the workers' council, had the right to participate in management appointments. Later, a law prohibiting secret police agents from retaining high positions in the state and public sector led to changes in top management in several state enterprises.[483]

This was a significant factor encouraging management to engage in "hidden" MBOs to avoid public scrutiny (in table 5.2.1, such transactions most probably fell under the category "others"). In particular, the public does not want to see individuals who benefited during the centrally planned economy to benefit again during the transition and privatization. In many cases, however, these are the best qualified individuals.

---

[483] Nevertheless, one factor leading to changes in management "from above" by founding ministries was evidence of theft by state enterprise managers. For example, a SOE manager would take a high interest rate loan from a private company that he set up for this purpose. Because the SOE is unable to pay its obligations, its value falls (perhaps into bankruptcy), making the company cheaper for would-be buyers, namely the SOE manager. A debt for equity swap with the private company might allow the manager to own the enterprise more cheaply. Alternatively, rather than creating a new private company, the manager may work with a local bank where he has close personal connections.

The negative public attitude towards MBOs or EBOs was already apparent during the small-scale privatization, when shops, restaurants, hotels, and small production plants were privatized. Initially, parliament discussed the possibility of granting pre-emption rights to the employees rather than using public auction. Employees of shops and restaurants organized strikes, and an active discussion of the issue was conducted in the mass media. Largely under their influence, the public attitude assured that no privileges should be granted to the management or employees during small-scale privatization. The same principle was ultimately accepted for large-scale privatization. Accordingly, EBOs are viewed somewhat negatively, MBOs are not treated with preference, and no special privileges are officially granted to insiders during enterprise privatization.[484] Employee ownership based on preferential or free transfer is limited by law to 10 per cent of the capital according to Section 158 of the Commercial Code.

As shown in table 5.2.1, privatization projects proposed by enterprise managers were much more often successful than those put forward by other parties.[485] According to the Law on Large-Scale Privatization, acceptable projects have to satisfy certain formal and information requirements.[486] The management in place has a comparative advantage, relative to potential competitors intending to submit a privatization project, in access to accurate information about their enterprise. Moreover, management has the possibility to manipulate information about the enterprise and thus mislead potential competitors.

In cases where management decided to buy the enterprise, it had the possibility to influence the book value, and thus the purchase price since domestic entities must pay at least book value for assets.[487] Management was also in a position to deter potential competitors by various operations and transactions, such as manoeuvres to incur artificial indebtedness (take credits which in fact were not necessary), the provision of false information about production capabilities and the ability to cover costs, by leasing equipment through companies of which the managers are owners, or by undertaking large investments financed by bank credit.

Because of the great difference between the value of plants subject to privatization and the total savings of households in the economy,[488] only small and medium-sized firms were expected to be sold directly to domestic investors.

Managers generally tried to obtain full financing for their acquisition, and most MBOs have been financed with four-year (exceptionally five-year) commercial bank credit at nominal interest rates of 15-17 per cent.[489] Due to a discontinuity in the tax system, instalment payments cannot be treated as costs by the enterprise, but impinge on after-tax profits. Some enterprises solve this problem by "sale and lease-back" agreements, which are only possible when the share of real estate in the book value is not significant. Other MBOs face a constant threat of bankruptcy due to high indebtedness, and therefore cannot make large investments.

(b) Restructuring and privatization

Privatization is considered the basic road to restructuring in the Czech Republic. The Czech government is in the process of privatizing even industries which in a number of developed market economies remain in the public sector, such as telecommunications, energy distribution and production, gas production and distribution, water pipelines, and airlines.[490]

Czech privatization combines standard and non-standard methods. Standard methods include: restitution of property to its original owners or their heirs, the sale of property to domestic or foreign investors through public auctions and tenders, direct sales to designated owners, transformation into joint stock companies, and the free transfer of property to municipalities, pension funds and the like.

According to the Law on Large-Scale Privatization, each of the approximately 5,400 state enterprises involved had to submit a mandatory privatization project.[491] Generally, the mandatory or basic privatization project was elaborated by enterprise management. Any other juridical or physical person had the right to summit a competitive project for all or part of the enterprise assets.

After the privatization project is approved by the Ministry of Privatization (MP), it is passed to the Fund of National Property (FNP) for implementation. Table 5.2.2

---

[484] Special regulations apply for privatization of the health care sector. Doctors may buy equipment or clinics with credit provided under advantageous conditions from the Fund of National Property.

[485] These data do not suggest that 82 per cent of the accepted privatization projects proposed MBOs. But the data support the conclusion that enterprise management was able to influence the decision-making of the ministries, due to its contacts and the possession of the best information. A high number of projects were submitted by enterprise managers primarily because they were obligated to elaborate the mandatory privatization projects. Such projects often involve several components proposing different methods of privatization for different units or plants of the enterprise. It stands to reason that the enterprises privatized via MBO in this framework were the more efficient ones.

[486] Privatization projects must provide information on the economic and financial situation of the enterprise, number and structure of employees, technical and legal data, asset valuation, business plan, method of privatization, etc.

[487] As noted above, foreign investors can buy at the market price, which may be below the book value.

[488] In 1991 the book value of the 5,400 enterprises involved in large-scale privatization was estimated to be Kc 1,500 billion. The savings of the population amounted to less than one quarter of this amount.

[489] The interest rate is floating and is linked to the discount rate, which has risen significantly in the past eight months.

[490] Some enterprises in these industries are involved in the voucher privatization process. The state will retain ownership of the railways and the postal service. Some apartments will remain communal property.

[491] Small-scale privatization, which is realized through public auctions, serves the restructuring of the retail distribution network and, together with restitution, bridges the existing technical barriers to entry for small-scale entrepreneurship stemming from the lack of physical accommodations.

TABLE 5.2.2

Privatized units and property according to privatization method applied, Czech Republic, 1992-1993
(Per cent)

Privatization method	Privatized units [a]	Privatized property [b]
Auction	8.1	0.8
Joint-stock company [c]	21.5	89.3
Public tender	7.5	2.2
Direct sale	31.7	5.7
Free of charge transfer	31.2	2.0
Total	100.0	100.0

Source: Ministry of Privatization, 1992 and 1993.

[a] End-December 1993.
[b] End-December 1992, based on book value.
[c] About 80-90 per cent of these joint stock companies are involved in the voucher privatization.

TABLE 5.2.3

Number of industrial units before and after privatization project approval, Czech Republic, February 1994
(Number of enterprises engaged in privatization projects)

Industry	Prior to approval	After approval
Ferrous metallurgy	20	51
Non-ferrous metallurgy	16	50
Chemicals and rubber	57	131
Machinery	303	676
Electronics	74	212
Building materials	119	280
Wood-processing industry	81	230
Metal products	18	41
Paper and cellulose	22	84
Glass, china and ceramic	55	159
Textiles	94	409
Apparel	23	72
Leather	19	72
Printing and publishing	31	50
Food-processing	198	683
Others	49	93
Total	1 179	3 293

Source: Ministry of Privatization, February 1994.

shows the number of privatized units by privatization method applied.[492]

On average, four competitive projects were submitted per company.[493] Project selection and approval is based on a multi-criteria system which is not explicitly defined. The lack of strictly defined rules facilitates attempts to influence decision-making bodies, particularly because project negotiations remained closed to the public and the mass media. Frequently, scepticism related to the objectivity of the decision-making process resulted in personnel changes and in the enactment of new "rules of the game" to achieve higher transparency and less paperwork. Over time, however, the press has become more involved, which makes more information available to the public. Thus the privatization process appears to be flexible and capable of reacting to criticism.[494]

The Ministry of Privatization has to decide whether the enterprise will be privatized as a whole or restructured into several independently privatized units. Table 5.2.3 indicates the break-up of large enterprises during the process of privatization, which is strongly differentiated according to the industrial branch. In general, the Ministry of Privatization favoured projects that would break up larger units, but this was mitigated by the desire not to abandon immediately components of larger enterprises (usually the weakest plants) by allowing separation of the better parts. For this reason some enterprises were included undivided in voucher privatization despite viable alternatives for the separate privatization of some components.[495] An important non-price criterion was the perceived capability of the investor and his commitment to improve company performance.

Voucher privatization

The non-standard method is voucher privatization, the instrument of mass privatization. About 50-60 per cent of Czech national assets are to be distributed through voucher privatization.[496] The major rules of voucher privatization are as follows:

- state-owned enterprises are transformed into joint stock companies, and shares of these companies are offered for investment vouchers;

- during a certain period of time, every citizen over 18 years of age is allowed to buy a voucher book of 1,000 investment units for a symbolic price of Kc 1,000 ($35);

- the value of vouchers is denominated in "investment points", and the owner of a registered voucher book is entitled to spend 1,000 investment points during each privatization wave;

---

[492] The administrative structures for privatization seem to reflect the past 40 years of central planning: a hierarchical system with several levels of decision-making typical of the command economy, rather than a transparent, streamlined system. There are three levels of decision-making: on the first level, the privatization projects have to be submitted to relevant founding ministries (Ministry of Industry and Trade, Ministry of Economic Policy, Ministry of Agriculture, Ministry of Finance). The founding ministry sorts and reviews the projects. The Ministry of Privatization represents the second level in the hierarchy and has the power to approve privatization projects in all cases with the exception of direct sale to a buyer determined in advance, in which case Government approval is necessary, the Ministry only having the authority to issue recommendations. The third level is the Fund of National Property (FNP), which implements the approved privatization projects.

[493] Out of a total of 11,555 privatization projects, 5,830 were reviewed during the first wave. As of September 1992, 1,594 privatization projects were approved. These projects were not necessarily directly competing, but in many cases were proposals to take over a subset of enterprise assets, thereby leading to deconcentration. The highest number of privatization projects for a single enterprise was 128.

[494] See, for example, Klvacova (1992).

[495] Nevertheless, it is likely that once effective corporate governance has been established in these companies, they will often be forced to sell the more promising asset components to generate cash.

[496] The second most important privatization method (27 per cent of the book value of assets) was the transfer of equity to municipalities or other entities free of charge. Direct sale of equity to designated purchasers represents 15 per cent. On average, each privatization project combined two privatization methods.

- shares are offered and applied for in individual privatization rounds (there were five such rounds during the first wave);
- before the first round is launched, voucher holders can hand over part or all of their vouchers to an Investment Privatization Fund (IPF), which then acts on their behalf; the voucher holders become shareholders of the IPF when the privatization wave is completed.

Voucher privatization will be implemented in two waves, the first of which was completed in 1993. It involved 988 joint stock companies,[497] and property in the book value of about Kc 200 billion was sold. About 72 per cent of all investment points were entrusted to IPFs. The eleven largest IPFs accumulated more than one third of all investment points.[498] The shares of the joint stock companies privatized during the first wave were distributed to the citizens and the IPFs in May and June 1993 and are now being traded on the stock exchange and in the RM-system (see below).

The massive transfer of vouchers to the IPFs resulted in a rather concentrated ownership structure for most companies, with one or several core investors. However, these investors do not sufficiently exercise the ownership rights of monitoring management, on the one hand due to a lack of appropriate skills in the funds, and on the other hand because of a lack of other options, i.e., alternative managers that would be better than the old management.

The second wave of voucher privatization is scheduled for early 1994, the registration of Czech citizens entitled to participate having closed by mid-December 1993. Some 860 companies with assets valued at about Kc 150 billion are involved.

(ii) **Developments in restructuring during the period 1989-1993**

Important features of the development of the industrial structure in the Czech Republic are:

- low level of internal restructuring of state enterprises;
- decline of the number of employees in most state enterprises;
- substantial growth in the number of registered enterprises;
- diversification of enterprise size structure;
- expansion of small enterprises;
- decrease of concentration in most industrial branches;
- none the less, a rise in the concentration for industry as a whole;

TABLE 5.2.4

Number of industrial enterprises, Czech Republic, 1989-1993

	1989	1990	1991	1992	1993 [a]
Number of enterprises	430	937	1 223	2 416	3 084
Total output *(billion Kc)* [b]	647.4	550.2	472.4	425.2	391.2
Total number of employees *(thousands)*	1 880	1 542	1 596	1 522	1 413
Average number of employees per enterprise	2 586	1 645	1 305	630	458

Source: Computations based on data of the Czech Statistical Office.

[a] November 1993.
[b] Constant prices.

- diversification of legal forms;
- creation of the legal framework usual for the market economy;
- development of the banking sector and of stock markets.

(a) Organizational restructuring

State-owned enterprises in the Czech Republic were horizontally integrated to a high degree during the centrally planned economy period; an enterprise in manufacturing industry consisted on average of 8-9 plants producing similar products. Most of these plants became independent enterprises during 1989-1993. By 1992 the average enterprise had 1-2 plants, similar to the usual ratio in the market economies.

A multi-tier system of vertical management had been created under the centrally planned system. This organizational structure was to enable the central authorities to control the entire national economy by directives. The adjustment of firms to competitive market conditions requires disintegration, a flatter organizational structure and further changes in the internal structure of the firms to strengthen their capacities in the fields of distribution, marketing, and the control and organization of work.

In 1989 there were 430 industrial state enterprises in the Czech Republic, whereas by January 1994 there were 3,110 industrial firms with more than 25 employees registered by the Czech Statistical Office, including both new entrants and parts of former state enterprises (table 5.2.4).

It can be roughly estimated that up to the end of 1992 the former large state enterprises were broken up on average into three independent enterprises either prior to privatization or during the privatization process. But the change in the number of operating enterprises varies substantially between branches. In consequence of break-ups, the number of enterprises increased 45 times in the optical and medical instruments branch, 15 times in the production of communication equipment, 11 times in the production of cars and trailers, 8 times in the clothing branch and 7 times in furniture-making. On the other hand, the number of enterprises decreased sharply in the production of business machines and personal computers

---

[497] The share of company basic capital made available for the voucher privatization varied from 7 to 97 per cent. The remaining part of shares was sold to foreign investors, transferred without charge to municipalities, or left temporarily or permanently in the Fund of National Property.

[498] There were more than 400 IPFs active in the first wave of privatization, which covered properties in all of former Czechoslovakia, i.e., in both the Czech Republic and Slovakia.

TABLE 5.2.5

Size structure of industrial enterprises, Czech Republic, 1989-1992
(Per cent)

Enterprises according to number of employees	Number of enterprises	
	1989	1992 [a]
Less than 200	4.14	47.45
201-1,000	23.77	38.73
1,001 and more	72.09	13.82
Total	100.00	100.00

Source: Computations based on the data of the Czech Statistical Office.

[a] Only enterprises with more than 25 employees.

TABLE 5.2.6

Share of the largest companies in total industrial output, Czech Republic, 1989 and 1993
(Per cent) [a]

	1989	1993
Share of 100 largest companies	52.3	51.7
Share of 10 largest companies	15.5	24.6
Share of 5 largest companies	9.6	17.4
Share of the largest company	2.4	6.4

Source: Computation based on data of the Czech Statistical Office.

[a] Industrial output in current prices.

(from 19 to 4) and in oil refinery and coke manufacturing (from 6 to 4). The number of enterprises grew only slightly in technically highly-concentrated industries such as rubber, metal working and chemicals.

While industrial output decreased almost by 40 per cent since 1989, employment decreased only by 25 per cent, pointing to a fall in productivity. However, this is a rather simplified statement, because inventories decreased sharply during the same period and the performance of enterprises became strongly differentiated. The biggest declines were reported in industries such as electronics, ready-made clothing, mechanical engineering and equipment production and in non-ferrous metallurgy. On the other hand, already in 1992 there were signs of revival in textiles, paper, printing, metal and chemical products and fibres as well as in construction. A negative tendency in the evolution of industrial structure was a further strengthening of the weight of the fuel and energy and other material-intensive industries, whereas the weight of manufacturing industries, contrary to expectations, declined.

A positive feature of the structural development was the fact that exports were reoriented to developed world markets and that the construction sector adapted rapidly to the conditions of the market economy. It was estimated that about one quarter of all foreign firms which invested in the Czech Republic participate in construction. The number of employees in construction stabilized and the volume of construction work increased by 22 per cent in 1992.

A large number of small private enterprises have been established. The role of the private sector increased, its share in GDP rising from close to zero in 1989 to about 18 per cent in 1992 and some 50 per cent in 1993. The break-up of large SOEs, together with the new entry of private firms, has led to a more diversified size structure of Czech industrial enterprises, as illustrated in table 5.2.5.

The developments in the size structure of enterprises constitute a positive trend in the Czech industrial sector in the sense of its adjustment to market economy standards: on the one hand the small business sector is growing, but at the same time the share of the largest companies in total industrial output is rising (table 5.2.6). The share of the 100 largest companies did not change markedly over the last three years, but overall concentration rose because the share of the ten, five and single largest companies increased substantially despite the general growth in the number of enterprises.

The sector of small and medium-sized enterprises (SMEs) is growing fast. This is important for the restructuring of large enterprises which must meet potential competitors. Small enterprises with less than 25 employees, which are prevalently new starts-up, are beginning to play an important role in some manufacturing industries (table 5.2.7).[499]

Government policy, the legislation, and the policies of banks were favourable for the development of SMEs after the revolution of 1989. Existing barriers to entry were removed step by step, the approval process became less bureaucratic, and the state provided tax advantages for enterprises with less than 25 employees. During the period from the second half of 1990 through the first half of 1992 it was not difficult to obtain credit.[500] The banks did not require any other collateral than the assets on which the credit was provided, they did not ask for credit history, and the business plans required were simple, often elaborated by bank officials. The fact that the state lacked a strong and sophisticated internal revenue service provided opportunities for tax avoidance.

Together with the large potential for entrepreneurship, all these factors led to a boom of small business foundations in 1990-1992. In 1991 the number of private entrepreneurs increased from 379,000 to over 1 million. The underdeveloped small business sector grew through new start-ups, restitution, small-scale privatization, and the division of big state enterprises into smaller units. The prevailing monopolistic structures also provided niches for SME activities, as well as "empty" industries with great potential of growth. New start-ups often offered better than average employment conditions (salary regulation in the state sector favoured the transfer of labour to private enterprises).

---

[499] It should be noted that the available data shown in table 5.2.7 capture only a sample of SMEs; hence the actual share of such enterprises in sales is substantially higher.

[500] The ease of obtaining bank credit was related to the fact that the Central Bank provided large amounts to refinance credits and that the existing state banks did not consider the risk of providing credits to SMEs.

TABLE 5.2.7

Small enterprises by industrial branch, Czech Republic, 1992
(Units, per cent)

Industry	Number of enterprises with less than 25 employees	Share of small enterprises in total sales
Foodstuffs	360	2.3
Textile	95	1.4
Clothing	89	4.7
Leather and shoes	33	1.9
Wooden products	244	12.4
Paper	26	1.1
Printing and publishing	162	11.1
Oil refined, coke	4	0.1
Chemicals	64	0.9
Rubber and plastics	136	6.7
Non-metal	146	2.9
Metals	20	0.2
Metal construction	533	10.0
Machinery	329	4.1
Business machines	19	42.3
Electrical machines	147	5.1
Communications equipment	119	14.9
Optical, medical	105	11.2
Cars and trailers	49	0.7
Other transport	18	1.3
Furniture	254	7.6
Recycling	28	7.2
Total manufacturing	2 980	3.1

Source: Computation based on data of the Czech Statistical Office.

TABLE 5.2.8

Shares of four largest producers in the total output of manufacturing branches, Czech Republic, 1989 and 1992
(Per cent branch output)

Branch	1989	1992
Foodstuff	19.46	16.04
Tobacco	100.00	100.00
Textile	20.66	16.52
Clothing	60.74	49.79
Leather and shoes	79.80	50.55
Wooden products	56.43	29.78
Paper	67.45	54.60
Printing and publishing	47.01	35.22
Oil refinery, coke	98.46	100.00
Chemicals	45.71	39.42
Rubber and plastics	48.49	47.99
Non-metal	23.07	24.95
Metals	61.42	66.32
Metal construction	25.14	24.10
Machinery	19.28	13.15
Business machines	60.89	89.50
Electrical machines	30.43	22.48
Communications equipment	100.00	34.29
Optical, medical	100.00	30.49
Cars and trailers	100.00	75.04
Other transport	48.19	58.66
Furniture	49.96	24.36
Recycling	90.70	64.85

Source: Computation based on data of the Czech Statistical Office.

While overall concentration increased, as indicated in table 5.2.6, concentration in many industries decreased (table 5.2.8). Exceptions were the branches of other transport means, business machines, oil and refinery, metal working, non-metal products where the ratios rose, and the metal construction and rubber and plastic branches where they remained almost unchanged. Particularly sharp decreases in the share of the largest producers occurred in leather and shoes, communications equipment, wood-processing, optical and medical instruments, textiles, non-metal products, and furniture. Even bigger differences in changes of the market concentration are shown by concentration ratios at the three-digit level groups of products. All these indicate adjustment of the industrial structure to the market economy, as can be confirmed by a comparison with Austria (table 5.2.9). The comparison also reveals that the concentration ratio in some industries remains high (those which had grown during the central planning period), while in others (above all in traditional industries) the production capacities have most probably not yet reached the optimal level.

Adjustment of the inner structure of enterprises, such as the creation of divisions, the expansion of some departments and activities mainly oriented to sales and marketing, are limited to already privatized enterprises. Change in the management, ways of communication, incentive structure, manpower changes, and changes in production organization are often postponed during the run-up to privatization with its environment of uncertainty and the short decision horizon of the existing management, often oriented to survive until the privatization.

Strategic decisions, which would lead to profound internal company restructuring, can be observed only in cases where strong foreign investors exist (Nestlé-Cokoladovny, Phillip Morris and partially Skoda-VW), or when clearly defined domestic owner/managers are in place, as in the case of impending management buy-outs.

(b) Legal restructuring

Only one legal form existed during the centrally planned economy, that of the state enterprise, with some modification close to the concern or trust. Even the cooperatives were in fact very close to the state enterprises. Change of ownership and size is related to the creation of a wide variety of business forms and thus legal forms of enterprises. Most former SOEs have been converted into joint stock companies. Limited liability companies are the main legal form for newly-established firms.

In a broader sense, legal restructuring means the creation of an institutional framework similar to the one existing in the developed market economies. State enterprise status was still in 1992 the most prevalent form of ownership – 35 per cent of existing firms. In 1993, state enterprises represented only 18 per cent of the total number of industrial enterprises with more than 25 employees. The number of joint stock companies increased to 881 in 1993, and the number of limited liability companies to 1,220.

TABLE 5.2.9

Concentration ratios comparison: Austria, 1987 and Czech Republic, 1992

(Share of four largest producers in branch output, in per cent)

Branch	Austria 1987 Share	Ranking	Czech Rep. 1992 Share	Ranking
Mining and iron production	100.0	1	77.7	2
Oil and refinery	99.0	2	100.0	1
Glass industry	84.9	3	56.0	7
Transport means	60.6	4	60.4	5
Iron foundry (casting)	46.2	5	44.4	11
Paper production	45.9	6	77.4	4
Non-iron metallurgy	41.3	7	76.2	3
Leather industry	41.1	8	50.9	9
Paper processing	37.4	9	52.6	8
Electrotechnics	33.7	10	15.0	18
Ceramics	28.8	11	23.7	15
Clothing industry	26.3	12	49.8	10
Metal working	25.9	13	31.9	13
Chemical industry	19.0	14	39.4	12
Wood processing	16.9	15	28.0	14
Sawing, timber	13.1	16	57.1	6
Textile	11.9	17	16.5	16
Food processing	11.8	18	16.0	17
Mechanical engineering	11.2	19	10.5	19

Sources: Czech Statistical Office 1992, WIFO, *QENB*.

A comparison of various ownership forms used in the Czech economy by output, employment and export levels shows the joint stock companies on all these characteristics to be the most important form by the end of 1992 (table 5.2.10). SOEs still accounted for slightly more than one third of all units, but had smaller shares on all other indicators, probably reflecting the fact that there remained many "residual" enterprises among these state companies, holding what was left over after the more promising component plants had separated from the non-viable state colossi and become private companies. These residual lame ducks thus were the dumping place of all unsolved or disputed problems, e.g., concerning restitution, the debts or the litigation cases of the former state corporation. The most probable destiny of many residual enterprises is a liquidation settlement.

More than half a million private sole proprietorships were registered in the Czech Republic by the end of 1992. These are symptoms of thriving competition.

There is no explicit provision for restructuring in the Czech legislative framework, and the instruments for enterprise restructuring applied by the Czech government are primarily organizational and ownership change.[501] Generally, important aspects of the legal foundation for restructuring are contained in the antimonopoly law, the law on large-scale privatization and the bankruptcy law.

[501] In some cases, such as mining and armaments, the Government hired international consulting firms to assist with restructuring. There is no clear evidence regarding the effectiveness of this approach.

Bankruptcy law

The bankruptcy law should have begun the process of eliminating firms in October 1992, but its coming into force was postponed until April 1993. Because of the threat of a large number of bankruptcies of SOEs and a possible chain reaction as a consequence of interenterprise indebtedness, the law was amended with a mechanism to impede such a chain reaction. The Fund of National Property is expected to help selected firms by protecting them from bankruptcy through direct or indirect subsidies. Protection is likely to focus on large enterprises, while small or medium-sized enterprises will go bankrupt and become the property of the banks.

Insufficient and delayed implementation of the bankruptcy law is the major obstacle on the side of exit. In the meantime the process of bankruptcies is moving slowly. The fact that commercial courts are overloaded is one reason. A second one is the conflict of interests inside the banks which are at the same time creditors of the companies and owners through Investment Privatization Funds. None the less it is expected that in the near future bankruptcy will come to play a significant role in economic life.[502] However, because of the threat of domino effects and social tensions, large core companies cannot go bankrupt and must undergo restructuring.

Antimonopoly law

The heritage of the command economy was *highly concentrated market structures*, that is, most enterprises were multiplant companies with a dominant share of the output in their particular industry. However, in many cases the monopolistic or oligopolistic positions of enterprises were caused by *organizational* concentration, with technological origins of concentration prevalent only in chemicals, machinery and metallurgy.[503]

Accordingly, demonopolisation is a key issue at the microeconomic level. As mentioned above, many enterprises were broken up prior to privatization. Privatization itself provides a further possibility for breaking up large state enterprises. The process is differentiated according to industries. In capital-intensive industries, the process of deconcentration and demonopolisation is slow, if it occurs at all, whereas in labour-intensive industries such as services, textiles, glass, or leather processing there is substantial deconcentration. In highly concentrated industries however, such as automobile production, the only realistic source of demonopolisation is competition from imports.

The Competition Protection Act became effective in February 1991 and is similar to EC legislation and the German Anti-Cartel Law. An Office of Economic Competition was established and has begun operations. But the Competition Protection Act seems to be a weak vehicle to facilitate restructuring. Approval of mergers is formal and application of the law bureaucratic: enterprises are frequently "strong enough" to defeat the will of the Office.

[502] Some 1,600 requests by creditors to open bankruptcy proceedings against their debtors had been filed in the courts by February 1994.

[503] This concerns primarily heavy machinery and chemical enterprises built during the communist era.

TABLE 5.2.10

Ownership structure of industrial enterprises, Czech Republic, 1992-1993
(Enterprises with more than 25 employees)

Legal form	Number of firms end-1992	Number of employees end-1992 (thousands)	Output 1992 (Million Kc)	Exports 1993 (Million Kc)	Number of firms end-1993 (Million Kc)
Limited liability companies	462	68 728	31 531	5 590	1 220
Joint stock companies	776	878 457	492 203	126 496	881
Cooperatives	247	54 814	12 287	2 027	261
State enterprises	856	511 034	273 308	48 441	577
Others	75	8 761	3 211	929	45
Total	2 416	1 521 794	812 539	183 483	2 984

Source: Computations based on the enterprise data from the Czech Statistical Office.

Foreign consulting companies often suggest keeping the enterprises as big as they were during the centrally planned economy. For instance, in the paper industry the original 12 enterprises have been spontaneously – at their own request – broken up into 23 independent enterprises. A foreign consulting firm suggested the creation of three big enterprises through the merger of all existing enterprises.

In its first proposal, BATA asked for state protection of the domestic shoe market from foreign competition for several years. There were also attempts to monopolise the market for construction materials.

Generally, antimonopoly policy is a delicate issue. On the one hand it provides a threat inducing enterprises to limit their abuse of monopolistic positions. On the other hand, an overly active antimonopoly office can repel foreign investment.

(c) Financial restructuring

Privatization and the break-up of enterprises requires the division of assets and liabilities between the newly-established independent enterprises. The handling of debts poses the main issue in financial restructuring. The establishment of capital markets and their proper functioning is important for the restructuring of enterprise fixed assets.

Financial restructuring of the enterprise sphere in the Czech Republic began in February 1991 with the establishment of the Consolidation Bank, which was founded by the Ministry of Finance and the Fund of National Property. Approximately Kc 80 billion in *working capital* credits to about 4,500 enterprises were transferred from the balance sheets of Komercni Banka (the Commercial Bank) and Investicni Banka (the Investment Bank) to the Consolidation Bank.[504] As of mid-1993, approximately Kc 17 billion had been repaid, of which Kc 2.3 billion was paid by the Fund of National Property on behalf of about 40 (mostly large) enterprises. In 1991, payment discipline *vis-à-vis* the Consolidation Bank was relatively poor, but in 1992 collections improved dramatically: only 12 per cent of these debts had to be classified as non-performing. For the most part, better discipline was linked to improved enterprise management and the realization that creditworthiness is an important factor in market-based economic relationships. It helped that the Consolidation Bank could impose a penal interest rate of up to 30 per cent for non-payment.

The second aspect of financial restructuring was the write-down of Kc 15 billion in pre-1990 bank debt: the commercial banks were allowed to transfer the weakest parts of their portfolio to the Consolidation Bank at a 20 per cent discount.

With respect to *interenterprise credits*, at the beginning of 1991, overdue accounts receivable from domestic buyers amounted to Kc 50 billion in the Czech Republic. By the end of 1991, interenterprise credits had increased to Kc 160 billion but they remained at approximately that level as of mid-1993. Some of the increase may be attributable to the larger number of enterprises and to the reclassification of transactions that formerly had taken place within the larger enterprises.

In order to address the problem of interenterprise debt, the government engaged in a series of debt netting exercises. Participation was voluntary, and initial expectations were that the process would reduce secondary insolvency by about Kc 50 billion.[505] To date, the process has not been considered highly successful.

According to Czech policy, resources for financial restructuring of enterprises are not to come from the state budget, but primarily from FNP privatization revenues.[506] In order to acquire sufficient funds for the FNP to settle outstanding debts, it is likely that the Ministry of Privatization will require more frequent use of tenders and

---

[504] These debts were originally "perpetually revolving", and were transformed into debts with a repayment period of 8 years at 13 per cent interest. Unofficial estimates by the Czech authorities are that one quarter to one half of the debts held by the Consolidation Bank will be unrecoverable.

[505] Given the voluntary nature of the debt netting process, a selection bias emerges in that only those enterprises likely to benefit from participation have an incentive to do so.

[506] There is no underlying reason why bank and enterprise restructuring should be explicitly linked to the availability of FNP assets. On the one hand, privatization should be pursued in accordance with its own economic, political, and social goals, with revenue generation given appropriate weight in this process. On the other hand, necessary restructuring measures, particularly the recapitalization of banks, should not be postponed because financial resources are considered too scarce.

direct sales in the remaining privatizations. To some extent the government still finances large "important" enterprises, owing to their social and political leverage as well as to perceptions of a possible systemic impact, which ultimately has an adverse affect on smaller businesses that lack "importance". Steps to assist larger enterprises include selective debt reductions and government guarantees for credits.[507]

An important obstacle to the *restructuring of fixed capital* is the perception that credit is expensive.[508] Also, banks tend to be cautious in their lending policies. For example, banks are reluctant to provide credit to domestic entities for purchases in the large-scale privatization process because of high risks associated with future enterprise operations. Credit is usually medium term (three to five years) with a floating interest rate linked to the inter bank rate, currently between 13 and 17 per cent.

Reform of the banking system, which began in 1990, aims to reintroduce western-style banking practices. The law on commercial banks, adopted in February 1991, was an important step in that direction.[509] Nevertheless, the banking system remains dominated by a few major players who may collude in decision-making.[510]

Different types of banks hold different loan portfolios. Banks established in 1991 and later did not inherit loans from the previous system and therefore have more resources available,[511] although a few already have weak portfolios. Banks created through the division of the former monobank could not foreclose on "bad" loans to state sector enterprises, in part because some were based on long-term commitments and also out of fear that bankruptcies would damage their own balance sheets.[512]

More recently, an increase in provisions, as well as alternate options for partially realizing classified assets, may lead banks to change their behaviour.

Given the prudent policies of the banks, some firms are unable to obtain the credit they desire, particularly because of inadequate collateral or the lack of a credit history. It is interesting to note that banks often ask for 100-120 per cent collateral from private firms, whereas collateral requirements are often 200 per cent and more for state-owned firms.[513]

Securities markets

Two securities exchange organizers emerged in the Czech Republic: the Prague Stock Exchange and the RM-System. The *Prague Stock Exchange* officially started to operate in April 1993. It now trades two days a week. About 60 brokers obtained licences, and most are active on the exchange. It is a classical stock exchange, based on the membership principle, with listed and non-listed markets. By the end of 1993, only bank and government bonds and shares of three large banks and two companies (not yet traded) were listed.[514] Several hundred securities of companies sold in the voucher privatization are traded on the non-listed market.

The *RM-System* is an electronic system operating on a basis of trading rounds similar to voucher privatization, using the computer network which was established for that process which can be directly accessed by anyone who fulfils the conditions of the "RM-System Trading Rules". Customers have the option whether to make the sales or purchases directly by themselves or whether to use broker services. The number of securities traded increased with time on both securities markets. Prices of shares are on average lower in the RM-System, and the prices of particular companies' shares differ significantly between the two markets.

(iii) **Lessons from Czech restructuring**

It is not easy to draw lessons from any given experience. The requirements of restructuring and privatization are likely to be substantially different in different socio-political and cultural environments.

After 40 years of unsuccessful attempts to restructure companies "from above", the Czech government refuses to impose an explicit policy in this field. The government has argued that the state lacks sufficient information and resources. Rather, changes in ownership structure are expected to evoke changes in industry and in the internal structure of enterprises.

---

[507] Through mid-1993, the FNP had revenues of about Kc 37 billion, most of which has been spent or committed: Kc 22.2 billion for repayment of enterprise debts (to banks and to other enterprises) and compensation for non-performing assets (such as receivables from Russia, or AERO airplanes ordered by Nigeria but never delivered); Kc 7.8 billion for construction of an oil pipeline to Germany; Kc 1 billion for administrative overheads associated with the setting-up of a programme to net interenterprise debt; Kc 1 billion for the Czecho-Moravian Guarantee and Development Bank, which supports SMEs; a commitment to spend up to Kc 9 billion to pay off a portion of the claims held by suppliers to enterprises undergoing bankruptcy; reserves for environmental damages; and a commitment to partially finance the creation of an export development bank (EGAP).

[508] Current real interest rates on outstanding credits are not particularly high, but expectations of future inflation tend to be below current levels, so that expected real interest rates may appear excessive.

[509] For a comprehensive discussion of Czech banking reform, see Kerous (1993).

[510] For example, one branch of the AERO company found its relationship with its bank dramatically altered after one of the company's new owners – another major bank – indicated that it would decide how the company should seek financing. Most of these interactions were closely linked to personal connections between the individuals involved.

[511] The newly-created commercial banks lent over 60 per cent of their assets to the private sector, while banks that inherited their portfolio from the former monobank have lent less than half of their assets to the private sector.

[512] According to Kerous (1993), total banking assets in the former Czechoslovak federation at end-1992 stood at Kc 1,492.3 billion. Bank capital was Kc 33.5 billion; legally required reserve funds were Kc 37.0 billion, and other reserves Kc 26.5 billion. Classified assets were Kc 133.1 billion, of which Kc 86.1 were non-standard, Kc 29.5 were doubtful, and 17.5 were lost.

[513] See Bulir (1992). On the other hand, private firms tend to pay higher interest rates. To a certain extent higher rates to the private sector might be explained by the lower collateral requirement, short credit history, and the fact that some loans to state firms are based on long-term commitments. Higher collateral requirements for state enterprises probably reflects the tendency of book value to overstate the real value of assets.

[514] Starting January 1994, the shares of Nestlé-Cokoladovny and IPS (a construction company) will also be traded.

In general, the Czech government has been unwilling to support particular industries or companies and to suppress others, preferring to allow the market to pick winners and losers. Private business is expected to make these decisions; initiative and responsibility are left to the enterprise level. The government's role is to restructure the whole economy; it is not the particular enterprise or industry which should be the subject of the government programme. The state should be strong in influencing the transformation process of the Czech economy through securing a stable economy, establishing clear rules for the transformation of state enterprises into private units, in setting up the laws and binding principles and securing their observation.

The state can assist in the restructuring of selected enterprises but cannot handle this task for thousands of state enterprises. That is why the task of restructuring state enterprises has to be developed from the bottom up, i.e., left to future owners.

Nevertheless, the state has to create the conditions and environment to encourage competing concepts on restructuring already during privatization. Only competition can reveal the information for a decision on which approach should win: whether an enterprise should be broken up or held together in case there is a strong candidate for future ownership. In some cases it might be more efficient to keep the enterprise as a multiplant unit and allow it to restructure after privatization, as in the Cokoladovny-Nestlé case. In other cases it might be more efficient to opt for a division into several independent units even if this will leave over some non-viable units, which then have to be closed immediately.

The government must pay attention not only to the existing old state enterprises, but also to the newly-emerging businesses, private enterprises established from scratch. These new firms are believed to contribute more importantly to the restructuring of the economy than the old state enterprises. As a part of the restructuring effort, the government therefore has to adopt a programme supporting newly-emerging business; large-scale privatization is a part of such a programme.

In the context of privatization and restructuring, the question arises whether in selling enterprises priority should be assigned to higher price or to restructuring promises – e.g., investment commitments. Recent experience shows that such promises will not necessarily be kept.[515] On the other hand, if the investor is willing to pay a good price, he probably has a good business or restructuring plan for the firm. One lesson that can thus be taken from the Czech transformation experience is that governments should not prefer selection of only such buyers who make the best restructuring promises. It must be the new owners who will restructure the company after privatization.

The commercialization of SOEs should go hand in hand with privatization: the creation of state-owned joint stock companies can set up obstacles which thereafter impede the state from taking the best decisions, owing to the powers conferred on management. In several cases, state-owned joint stock companies or holdings had been created from former large integrated SOEs before the large-scale privatization programme was launched. Company managements then persuaded the government to keep these companies together and not to break them into several parts (using arguments based on the existence of similar large firms in the market economies, often with the counsel of foreign advisors). Even though competing privatization projects suggested the break-up of the existing holding or joint stock company, the Privatization Ministry could not approve them without violating the law, as once these companies had been created the state had the right to privatize only its own stake as a whole, and not parts of the company. The break-up of such enterprises was thus prevented, even though these companies were often inefficient, and the state had to find other solutions for their restructuring.[516]

Fast privatization is the precondition for an effective restructuring of state enterprises. Adoption of non-standard methods of privatization, such as voucher privatization, should accompany the standard privatization techniques. Voucher privatization can not only speed up the privatization process, but also contributes to the social learning of investment in capital stock and the creation of capital markets. The efficiency and speed of restructuring depends on the organization of the privatization process. Privatization, and thus restructuring, are rather vulnerable to certain sources of distortion:

- government bureaucrats will always attempt some type of rent seeking;
- competing entrepreneurs (domestic as well as foreign) will always use lobbying practices.

For these reasons, restructuring, the break-up of enterprises and market demonopolization should not be initiated by the state, i.e., from the top down, and government ministries should have only procedural and implementation powers, not the decision-making ones.

Restructuring of the economy can be launched only when capital goods markets are established, and capital markets can be established only when enterprises are privatized.

---

[515] E.g., recently Volkswagen decreased the investment plans in the Skoda MB car factory to one third.

[516] The prime example is the case of AERO, an aircraft producer with 15,000 employees, which is organized as a holding company with 11 daughter companies. A part of the AERO shares was included in the first wave of voucher privatization. Even though 18 privatization projects had been submitted for all or part of AERO, the company was privatized as a single entity at the request of the SOE management, against the will of some plant managers who wanted to separate their enterprises from the holding. Soon after privatization, a proposal was submitted to divide AERO into two legally and economically separate parts, a civilian and a military component. This division was not approved by the Ministry of Privatization owing to concerns that it would be illegal, as well as posing technical problems of dividing ownership among many small shareholders. In the face of continuing economic difficulties of the holding, a reorganization through a debt-equity swap under the auspices of Investicni Banka (the main creditor) was first contemplated, but in February 1994 the government took the decision to break up the holding after all, to sell viable components separately and to liquidate non-viable components.

5.3 Enterprise restructuring in eastern Germany

(i) Introduction

The general lessons from east Germany's experience are limited by the special circumstances of the transition in that country. These included, most importantly, the "off-the-shelf" importation of a new legal system and commercial institutions, and the availability of massive resource transfers to support the transition.

The fact that the great majority of east Germany's enterprises were loss-makers in the wake of the "Big Bang" of German unification suggests that east Germany is more instructive about the problematic end of the distribution of SOEs elsewhere than about profitable east European SOEs. An examination of the former GDR may refocus attention on the difficult cases and on the necessity to develop policies to complement those of privatization and closure.

Although the bulk of east German privatization has been carried out through the sale of enterprises to "competent outsiders" after a process of broad-brush restructuring, other methods have been developed. For example, the process of breaking enterprises up and the reduction of employment prompted the emergence of the Management Buy-Out (MBO) as a method for east Germans to acquire some assets of the SOE. Belatedly the Germans realized that sales to competent outsiders could not provide a solution for the entire SOE sector.

The initial premise that what could not be sold should be closed down was challenged. It seemed that enterprises which were potentially viable were unable to attract a buyer. The view began to emerge that there was a shortage of management capability available to undertake the strategic restructuring of firms even for east Germany. The highly concentrated structure of ownership of east German *privatized* firms can be interpreted as signalling that a large amount of restructuring remained to be done and that very close control over the management was therefore required.

In the light of this conclusion, it was necessary to seek a method of economizing on scarce managerial talent. The outcome was the creation of a type of holding company, the *Management KG*. Typically, an experienced western manager takes responsibility for turning the enterprises round and is highly rewarded for success. Ownership remains with the Treuhandanstalt (THA). The manager is given a strict time limit for success (3-4 years). Other forms of holding company with private, state (e.g., regional government) and mixed private and state ownership are also being developed.

"Top-down" versus "bottom-up" methods and sequencing

The east German experience can be summarized as one of *rapid privatization* to *competent outsiders* based on extensive *pre-privatization restructuring*. The original intention was for restructuring to be left to the new owners, but in the event *enterprises could not be sold without restructuring*. This has virtually been a process organized entirely from above. That procedure has almost certainly produced too rapid a rundown of employment.[517] It has, however, allowed considerations of both private and social efficiency to influence the restructuring and privatization process. Problems of monopoly and excessive vertical integration were dealt with prior to privatization. In unbundling and rebundling parts of enterprises, attempts were made to take account of the industrial and regional external effects of activities.[518]

"Top-down" breaking up of large enterprises has been the general pattern in east Germany, although some examples of initiatives from below can be found. The question of *top-down* versus *bottom-up* is related to the *sequencing* problem. If monopoly or environmental problems are to be dealt with prior to privatization, then there will have to be intervention to achieve this. It is clear that enterprises will not initiate the dissolution of their monopoly position voluntarily. An additional reason for top-down intervention is that managers at the top of an SOE organizational hierarchy can establish effective barriers to moves toward break-up initiated by lower-level managers. The east German case provides useful evidence on this phenomenon because of the phase of spontaneous reorganization of enterprises in 1990, before the west German authorities took over the Treuhand. Although widespread disintegration of the *Kombinate* occurred, there were many examples of the consolidation of the power of top managers through the creation of holding company structures.

East Germany was somewhat uncharacteristic among the transition economies in the extent to which giant combines (*Kombinate*) dominated industry and construction, but throughout the former command economies the average size of enterprises was much higher than in the market economies.[519] Although there are many unique features of the east German case, it helps to demonstrate the following advantages of breaking up large SOEs:[520]

- it hardens the budget constraint. The threat of closure is more credible for "unbundled" units because the political costs of closure are reduced and the risks to the banking system are lowered;

- the creation of smaller units makes viable the use of "yardstick competition" between managers. This raises incentives for greater managerial efficiency and management-initiated restructuring in the light of managerial career paths in the enterprise and in the private sector.

---

[517] See Carlin (1993) for the elaboration of this argument and Aghion and Blanchard (1993) for a theoretical model where excessively fast labour shedding can occur.

[518] See Carlin and Mayer (1992a) for a detailed analysis of the issue of sequencing privatization and restructuring in the transition.

[519] See, e.g., Newbery and Kattuman (1992).

[520] Aghion et al. (1993).

- it broadens the possibilities for effective corporate governance by creating units small enough for MBOs and joint-ventures with or purchases by medium-sized foreign firms;

- by reducing vertical integration, it increases the possibilities for the development of supply relationships between private and public sector firms. In addition, the monopsony power of large state sector firms is reduced, facilitating the entry of private firms.

The mode of restructuring and privatization in east Germany has been one in which a single agency has been charged with imposing hard budget constraints and providing compensation to reduce opposition to restructuring. The analysis below illustrates how the initial organizational structure of enterprises has influenced the adjustment process and highlights the strategies engaged in by management.

(ii) The starting point: The conglomerate in the GDR economy

When conceptualizing the transition, it is useful to have in mind the key characteristics of the modern industrial enterprise as it has evolved over the past century in the United States, Europe and Japan. Will the plant, enterprise or combine in the planned economy form the basis for a modern industrial enterprise in a market economy? Chandler explains how successful companies made three sets of investment: in large plants to take advantage of economies of scale and scope, in national and international marketing and distribution organizations, and in management capabilities (lower and middle managers to guide and monitor the flow of materials and products and higher level managers to coordinate and monitor current activities and to allocate resources for future activities).[521] He claims that:

> If these company-specific and industry-specific organizational capabilities continue to be enhanced by constant learning about products, processes, customers, suppliers, and other relationships between workers and managers within the firm, enterprises in capital-intensive industries are usually able to remain competitive and profitable. If not, they normally lose market share in domestic and international markets to those firms who do.[522]

He argues that the failure of the Soviet model to permit the development of organizational capabilities through the process of learning by managers has been at the heart of the failure of the planned economies. Yet, he believes that in the absence of other institutional bases "the existing production associations do provide a solid base on which to rest the restructuring of the new microeconomic environment".[523]

In the archetypal model of detailed national planning, the central planning bodies and the ministries decide on investment and also on operational matters, controlling for instance the flow of materials into and the flow of finished products out of the enterprise. The lack of decision-making power on the part of managers sharply constrained the possibilities for organizational learning. This is not simply a question of a lack of market-based incentives for managers – managers in large western (including Japanese) companies have not typically been remunerated according to high-powered incentives.

In many centrally planned economies, reorganizations were implemented in the 1970s which created large combines (USSR: 1973, GDR: 1979, Czechoslovakia: 1979). In other countries, such larger organizations were often confined to military and capital goods, and mining. These were horizontally integrated conglomerates pulling together enterprises and plants producing similar products. In addition, the combines tended toward autarky or self-sufficiency in the production of parts, intermediate goods and also plant.

In the analysis below of combine formation in the GDR and their dissolution since 1990, Chandler's view that the combines were a good vehicle from which to build capitalist firms is brought into question.

The creation of the Kombinate in the GDR

In 1979, the GDR implemented a change in the relationship between the "plan" and the "enterprise". A new form of enterprise organization was developed which marked a clear shift from the previous situation in which enterprises were grouped, for purely administrative convenience, into production associations according to branch. The new organization was the *Kombinat*, whose General Director (GD) was to have increased autonomy as compared with managers in the previous system. One observer went as far as to suggest that the General Director of the *Kombinat* combined the role of "minister's delegate" and "entrepreneur".[524] The *Kombinat* GD had the right to transfer production from one plant to another, close plants and remove incompetent junior managers.[525] However, it seems that the GDs made little use of their increased power to rationalize production between different sites. They had no incentive for closing sites, since in a shortage economy it was rational for an enterprise to hold on to its access to capacity. In spite of the potential for rationalization represented by the *Kombinat* reform, the result was a further ossification of the structure of production. Production was spread across a wide range of vintages of plant, and there is little evidence of an attempt to optimize plant size. *Kombinat*-autarky thus resulted in plants in the GDR that deviated in both directions from the optimal size and bequeathed this feature to the restructuring requirements of the transition period.

Whereas economic theory suggests that vertical integration can enhance efficiency in a market economy, for example where security of access to inputs is essential, the striking thing about the *Kombinat* programme in the GDR was that the logic of self-sufficiency was applied

---

[521] Chandler (1990); for a summary, see Chandler (1993).
[522] Chandler (1993), p.314.
[523] Chandler (1993), p.336.
[524] Melzer (1981).
[525] Boot (1983).

TABLE 5.3.1

The transformation of the Treuhand portfolio, 1990-1993
(Units)

	Objects
Treuhand's original portfolio *(1 July 1990)*	
Enterprises	8 500
Plants	44 000
Transformation of Treuhand's portfolio *(30 December 1993)*	
Privatized	13 223
of which:	
Enterprises	6 180
Parts of enterprises	7 043
Enterprises returned to former owner *(restitution)*	1 573
Enterprises transferred to local authority	261
Enterprises closed or in the process of closure	3 196
Total of transformed units	18 253
Enterprises remaining in Treuhand's portfolio	951
Other activities	
Transfer to local authorities of enterprises and other facilities	12 618
of which:	
Educational facilities	668
Kindergartens, crèches	930
Sports facilities	1 140
Agricultural and forestry land	4 714
Sales of real estate	18 813

Source: Treuhandanstalt, *Monatsinformation der THA*, Stand: 31 December 1993.

uniformly. There was a textiles *Kombinat*, a heavy machinery *Kombinat*, a household appliances *Kombinat*, a paper *Kombinat* and so on. Because the shortage phenomenon was general in the planned economy, a uniform organizational response seemed to have been rational. However, this contrast between the uniformity of the construction of *Kombinate*, as compared with the differentiated criteria of the efficient extent of vertical integration in a market economy, suggests that Chandler's injunction to use the *Kombinat* as the primary organizational form from which to build a market economy may be misguided. Examples from east Germany illustrate this.

Vertical integration was common to all *Kombinate*, but there was a variety of organizational forms, which later played a significant role in the process of restructuring of enterprises by the Treuhandanstalt. There were three basic types of *Kombinate*: (1) the single enterprise *Kombinat* (e.g., the chemical giant Leuna); (2) the *Kombinat* with a dominant enterprise in which the top manager of the latter was also the General Director of the *Kombinat* (*Stammbetrieb*-type); (3) the *Kombinat* in which the management board was not also the management of a dominant enterprise (holding company or *Leitbetrieb*-type). Type (2) was the most common.

(iii) Restructuring in eastern Germany: Principles, methods and results

There are two reasons why restructuring requirements would be larger in east Germany than elsewhere. On the one hand, it began with a very highly distorted industrial structure (even by the standards of the region). On the other, its period of adjustment was foreshortened by wage convergence to western Germany and the lack of protection, including the need for rapid adjustment to the demanding quality norms for production facilities and products fixed by the German and EC authorities.

When the German Federal authorities took over the Treuhandanstalt and its portfolio of over 8,000 enterprises in July 1990, the mandate was to sell off enterprises fast. It became clear that buyers for enterprises (as opposed to real estate) would be very few unless substantial restructuring of enterprises was carried out. In addition, steps would have to be taken to prevent the mass bankruptcy of the portfolio. The Treuhand had wide powers in these three fields: privatization, restructuring and managing the application of bankruptcy and liquidation procedures. A notable feature of the east German experience was that the management of these three processes was unified at the outset in a single, new institution.

Before the methods used by the Treuhand to coordinate privatization, restructuring and liquidation are outlined, a brief summary of the magnitude of the property transformation which has occurred is presented.

(a) The property transformation: Enterprises and asset sales, closures

There is general agreement that the Treuhand has been successful in one respect – it was set up with the objective of a rapid privatization, and this has been achieved. Table 5.3.1 highlights the run-down of its portfolio. The Treuhand began with over 8,000 enterprises comprising some 44,000 plants. Privatization has taken the form either of the sale of an enterprise as a legal entity or of part of an enterprise as a so-called asset deal. Some 6,000 sales of the former type and over 7,000 of the latter had occurred by end-1993. In addition to sales to the private sector, the Treuhand's stock of enterprises has been reduced through several other routes: more than 1,500 enterprises have been returned to those who owned them prior to their nationalization by the Communist authorities, and another set of enterprises – mainly public transport and utilities – have been transferred to local authorities. There are some 3,200 enterprises scheduled for closure. All in all, nearly 17,000 enterprises or parts of enterprises have been sold, returned to a previous owner, closed or transferred to a local authority. The Treuhand still has just under 1,000 enterprises on its books.

Measuring the Treuhand's progress in numbers of enterprises is very crude. The data available are still very poor but a clearer impression of the meaning of these numbers comes from an examination of the results of privatization in terms of the receipts from sales and the amount of investment and number of jobs guaranteed by the purchaser of the enterprise (table 5.3.2).

The cost of this transformation has been enormous.

In the Treuhand's opening balance sheet (published on the basis of information on the receipts from the sales of assets and the costs of restructuring to October 1992), the value of its initial portfolio was set at DM 81 billion and the cost of privatizating and restructuring them at DM 215 billion.[526]

---

[526] Treuhandanstalt (1992a).

TABLE 5.3.2

Treuhand activities: Enterprise sales, revenues, job and investment guarantees, 1990-1993
(Cumulative data from July 1990 to end-1993)

	Number of firms and parts of firms sold	Sales receipts (DM billion)	Employment guarantees (Thousands)	Investment guarantees (DM billion)
Main privatization activity [a]	13 223	32.5	1 089	124.6
Other major activities				
Sales of land released from enterprises [b]	..	14.1	238.8	39.1
Agricultural and forestry land	..	1.0	137	18.3
Total for Treuhand [c]	..	48.1	1 487	186.6

Source: Treuhandanstalt, 1993.

[a] Sales of enterprises and parts of enterprises.
[b] For example, business parks.
[c] Including minor activities.

TABLE 5.3.3

The role of foreigners and east Germans in privatization, end-June 1993

	Number of firms and parts of firms sold	Sales receipts (DM billion)	Employment guarantees (Thousands)	Investment guarantees (DM billion)
Total	13 223	32.5	1 089	124.6
of which:				
To foreigners	818	5.6	146	20.1
Per cent of total	6.2	17.2	14.2	16.1
MBOs [a]	2 591	..	..	..
Per cent of total	19.6	..	..	..

Source: Treuhandanstalt, 1993.

[a] In general these are sales to east German managers and/or employees. In 200-300 cases of MBOs, a west German manager has become the owner in a spinoff (see section 5.3(vi)). Two thirds of the 1,733 MBOs which had taken place by the end of 1992 concern firms with less than 50 employees. Treuhandanstalt, *NL Report*, December 1992, p.15.

New owners

Privatization in east Germany has produced an ownership structure quite different from that found elsewhere in the transition economies. As noted above, the basic type of privatization in east Germany shares key characteristics with foreign direct investment elsewhere – namely, the new owner with a majority ownership stake is a western enterprise. The most common form of ownership of larger privatized east German companies (with at least 100 employees) sold by the Treuhand is one in which there is a dominant owner (with a stake of at least 50 per cent) which is a west German company. In other words, privatization has created subsidiaries of west German companies.[527]

Table 5.3.3 indicates that some 800 firms or parts of firms have been sold to (non-German) foreigners – the larger-than-average size of these firms is clear from the comparison between the foreigners' 6.2 per cent share of sales compared with a share of 17.2 per cent of sales receipts and investment guarantees. The receipts from sales of Treuhand firms to foreigners is of the same order of magnitude as the foreign direct investment attracted by its most successful east European neighbours (Hungary and the former Czechoslovakia).

East Germans have played a very limited role in the purchase of larger enterprises. Their ownership of firms stemming from the activities of the Treuhand remained limited to so-called MBOs of usually small parts spun off from Treuhand firms (see table 5.3.3).

There has been only one case of stock market flotation, and even in that case a west German company in the same sector held 51 per cent of the equity. The east German company, Sachsenmilch AG, went into liquidation in July 1993. This case exemplifies the magnitude of the task faced by management in achieving a successful turnround of an east German firm. Even with a controlling interest held by a western firm and with the backing of Deutsche Bank, control of costs during the phase of new investment was not sufficient to prevent bankruptcy.

The equity of privatized east German companies is mainly held very tightly, indicating that even after privatization considerable control over management by the owners is viewed as necessary.

Employment in privatized firms

Employment in east Germany has fallen by 3 million, from over 9 million before reunification to 6.1 million in the second half of 1993. The great majority of lost jobs have been in industry, with a decline of 2 million. In manufacturing industry, sectors in which output has begun to recover are those which supply the construction industry and benefit from the modernization of the telecommunications and railway systems. Output has also recovered in branches supplying local consumers (printing, food and drink). Investment goods, especially machine-tools and electrical machinery, have been hardest hit, *inter alia* a reflection of high unit labour costs and the exposure to intense international competition. The weakness of demand has been aggravated by the sharp downturn of the investment cycle in western Europe. Output in mechanical engineering had fallen by nearly 70 per cent by autumn 1993 compared with the second half of 1990. For electrical machinery the corresponding figure was about 50 per cent. Table 5.3.4 presents more detail on the problem industries in east Germany and their concentration in the Treuhand.

The other notable characteristic of the firms still owned by the Treuhand in mid-1993 is that the bulk of remaining employment (300,000) is in very large firms: just under 50 per cent of jobs were in 29 mining and manufacturing firms with more than 1,500 employees.[528]

---

[527] See Carlin et al. (1993).

[528] Treuhand (1993).

TABLE 5.3.4

East German manufacturing industry: The importance of Treuhand, 1991-1993
(Per cent)

	Per cent of east German employment in THA-owned enterprises (End 1992)	Per cent of THA employment in enterprises with more than 1,000 employees (February 1993)	Profit or loss as per cent of turnover [a]		
			1991	1992	1993 QII
Manufacturing	31	41	..	..	..
Mechnical engineering	45	29	-18	-25	-24
Chemicals	47	87	-54	-41	-32
Iron and steel	44	54	-30	-7	-20
Vehicles and shipbuilding	38	53	-48	-25	-20
Electrical engineering and electronics	25	55	-46	-45	-20
Metal fabrication	21	41	4	-4	-1
Textiles and clothing	47	-	-67	-37	-30
Food and drink	10	-	-11	-6	-2
Mining	74	..	-27	-10	-4
Economy (including enterprises with less than 20 employees)	8		..	..	..
Manufacturing (including enterprises with less than 20 employees)	21		..	..	..

Sources: Column 1: Lichtblau (1993), Table 3, p.16; Column 2: *DIW* (1993) Table 6, p.139; Columns 3-5: *Jahresgutachten 1993/94 des Sachverständigenrates zur Begutachtung der gesamtwirtschaftlichen Entwicklung*, Deutscher Bundestag, Drucksache 12/6170, 15 November 1993, Table 20, p.90.

[a] From a sample of 2,647 enterprises in 1991 and 812 enterprises in 1992 (samples may not have been fully representative).

(b) The "primary method": Broad-brush restructuring and sale to outsiders

Privatization in east Germany has taken place almost exclusively from above. Compared with elsewhere in eastern Europe, it has been very fast and has involved much more restructuring ahead of privatization. Two objectives have dominated the process: speed and the matching of management to assets.

Spontaneous restructuring before Treuhand control

In the period before the Treuhand came under the control of the German Federal authorities in mid-1990, the process of corporatization in the last year of the GDR created the opportunity for enterprises belonging to *Kombinate* to separate themselves and become independent companies wholly owned by the Treuhand (subject of course to the agreement of the *Kombinat* General Director). In this process, three patterns can be discerned: (i) a "spontaneous" dissolution of the *Kombinat* by its splitting up; (ii) a confirmation of the existing *Kombinat* structure; and (iii) the creation of a selective holding or holdings from parts of the *Kombinat*. The existence of this "spontaneous" phase in the GDR provides a useful standard against which the ultimate "market-conforming" outcome can be compared. Were new structures set up which turned out to be a diversion on the road to a market-based industrial structure?

The first form of reorganization tended to occur where enterprises that had been reduced to the status of production units under the *Kombinat* structure were keen to take advantage of the chance for independence. This type of spontaneous break-up was particularly prevalent in conglomerates subordinated to local (*Bezirk*) authorities, which were frequently a mixture of enterprises with no connection whatever except the common *Kombinat* management. But a number of centrally-directed *Kombinate*, especially in light industry, were also dismembered at that time (for a counter-example, however, see the case of the clothing *Kombinat* discussed in section 5.3(iv) below). There have been frequent conflicts between the management of the enterprise seeking to leave the *Kombinat* structure and the *Kombinat*-management which sought to corporatize with a complete set of subsidiaries.

In a number of *Kombinate* the leadership argued that in order to survive it was essential to create a corporate form in which the holding was kept intact. This strategy was common in mining. For example, the Kali (potash) *Kombinat* formed the holding *Mitteldeutsche Kali AG*. In the Kali case, the creation of a unitary holding company was an explicit attempt to build a "solidarity community" which would secure the future of the industry in the interest of employees' welfare. The objective of the holding was to prevent any splitting off of plants or other activities except where this would serve to maintain jobs or improve the profitability of the holding.[529]

All-inclusive holdings were also formed in the complex vertically integrated capital goods industries, to bind suppliers into the holding and in reflection of the view of *Kombinat* management that the saleability of the output of different final-goods producers in the group was enhanced by their ability to offer a full palette of goods. In other cases it was a deliberate strategy to hold together a monopoly supplier – for example, the monopoly producer

---

[529] Gusinski (1993), p.19.

of electric motors, the *Kombinat Elektromaschinenbau Dresden*. Such producers were extremely powerful in the shortage economy.[530] Where competition from abroad is not feasible, the formation of such monopoly positions creates obvious welfare problems in a market economy. In the former GDR, the cementing of such monopoly structures engendered a false sense of security about the ability of the enterprise to withstand competition.

A third alternative to either complete dissolution or total confirmation of the former *Kombinat* structure in a new corporate holding was the creation of a selective holding.[531]

In aggregate, the spontaneous reorganization associated with corporatization led to the partial or complete dissolution of 200 of the original 430 *Kombinate*. In consumer goods industries, some four fifths of the enterprises did not join a new holding, whilst the corresponding proportion was two thirds in the investment goods industry. Of the Treuhand's over 8,000 enterprises, some 7,000 were independent and a further 1,100 belonged to holdings.[532] The GDR experience suggests that whilst spontaneous restructuring resulted in the collapse of the most artificial of the *Kombinate*, it served to entrench untenable strategies and inefficient structures such as monopolies.

Valuation of enterprises and financial restructuring

One of the Treuhand's initial tasks was to establish the realistic value of its portfolio. Enterprises were instructed to provide opening balance sheets in deutsche mark for 30 October 1990. This task turned into a major project of enterprise evaluation and financial restructuring which lasted two years. The Treuhand set up a team of western experts (managers, accountants, management consultants), formally employed by the Federal Ministry of Finance, not the Treuhand, to evaluate each enterprise.

Each enterprise was classified according to its potential viability in the market economy. The evaluation of potential viability depended on three key elements: the existence of a market for the enterprise's output, the capabilities of management, and the existence of partners in the west. The evaluation resulted in some 70 per cent of enterprises being deemed potentially viable – but this result must be interpreted with caution. It means that in 70 per cent of enterprises there was deemed to be at least one potentially viable core business. This may have comprised only a fraction of the firm's original employment.

Enterprises which were classed as "potentially viable" had their balance sheets restructured so as to give them a debt/equity structure similar to a west German firm with the same projected turnover in the same industry. Setting the gearing ratio to levels found in the west (rather than writing off all the debt) creates appropriate incentives for financial performance by the firm.[533] Financial restructuring was an integral part of the restructuring/privatization procedure, ensuring that the core business activities of enterprises judged to have a chance of survival were not penalized by inherited financial burdens.

Financial restructuring and liquidations or bankruptcies

The absence of a scrapping rule for equipment at the enterprise level in the planned economy was mirrored at the level of the economy in the absence of a concept of bankruptcy or enterprise failure. The development of a bankruptcy law was seen as a priority in the creation of a market economy. The fact that there were ready-made bankruptcy and liquidation laws available for east Germany after unification serves to highlight another notable feature of the transition. The straightforward application of such laws to enterprises in transition is quite inappropriate: the laws are appropriate to firms which have been operating under the market economy rules of the game and have failed in this endeavour, but not – at least not immediately – to enterprises formed under completely different rules. The existence of bankruptcy laws combined with the obvious insolvency of the great majority of east German enterprises made it very clear that a specific liquidation regime for the transition had to be developed.[534]

The long delays that have accompanied the implementation of market economy bankruptcy codes elsewhere in the transition economies,[535] and the problems consequent to the activation of the law in Hungary,[536] indicate that *standard market economy practices could not be applied to enterprises in the transition without great cost*. One recent study outlines the logic behind the amendment to the Czech bankruptcy law in the spring of 1993:[537] a procedure was required to provide a moratorium from bankruptcy proceedings for "promising" companies saddled with debts to the banking system and enmeshed in chains of interenterprise debt.

The solution in the case of Germany was to suspend the application of automatic bankruptcy of Treuhand enterprises until the viability of the firms had been determined – i.e., until a confirmed opening balance sheet had been agreed by the sole shareholder, the Treuhand. In other words, during the key restructuring phase of enterprise evaluation and the consequential financial restructuring for viable firms and closure decision for non-viable ones, there was a moratorium on bankruptcy. The problem of overindebtedness of enterprises arising from their inherited debts was dealt with in east Germany across the board by the adjustments to balance sheets discussed above in order that the insolvency and bankruptcy law could come into effect.

---

[530] For an insightful discussion of monopoly power in the command economy, see Newbery and Kattuman (1992).

[531] For example, the *Kombinat Zellstoff und Papier Heidenau* in the paper industry consisted originally of 19 enterprises plus the main enterprise (*Stammbetrieb*), of which nine became independent and the other eleven were pulled together around the *Stammbetrieb* into a new company, *Dresden Papier AG*.

[532] Gusinski (1993), p.21.

[533] Aghion et al. (1993).

[534] Hansel (1993).

[535] See, e.g., Frydman et al. (1993).

[536] See section 5.4 below.

[537] Takla (1993).

As a second stage, for enterprises which were deemed non-viable and were technically required to file for bankruptcy, another new law enabled the Treuhand to intervene to carry out a liquidation instead of a court-administered bankruptcy.[538] Once again, this deviation from standard west German practice was a function of transitional conditions. The logic was that whereas a court-supervised trustee is obliged to maximize the financial proceeds for the creditors (the main creditor being the Treuhand), Treuhand-appointed liquidators may well be able to save more jobs since they would have a more intimate knowledge of the "market". For example, a Treuhand liquidation can take advantage of knowledge of other privatization or liquidation deals and the possibilities of complementarities in projects such as business parks.

The record on closures is as follows: by September 1993, 3,151 enterprises had been closed, more than four fifths of which were Treuhand liquidations. Some 37 per cent of the jobs in companies entering liquidation were saved, as compared with 16 per cent of jobs when court-administered bankruptcy was carried out.[539]

Efficiency restructuring: Breaking up enterprises

In tandem with the evaluation of enterprises and financial restructuring, enterprises have been split up well beyond what had resulted from the phase of spontaneous reorganization. A new law was introduced in 1991 (the *Spaltungsgesetz* or splitting-up law) to enable managers of subsidiary enterprises to split from a holding structure. Since July 1990, the process of splitting up large concerns has continued with the result that the number of enterprises which are or were owned by the Treuhand continues to grow. It began with 8,100 enterprises but subsequently has risen to 16,671. In addition to simply splitting up the *Kombinate* and linking the former subsidiary enterprises directly to the Treuhand, a great deal of breaking up of individual enterprises has also taken place. An indicator of this is that in addition to the sale of enterprises as legal entities, over 6,000 parts of firms have been sold in asset deals.

The motivation for breaking up the *Kombinate* and for splitting up enterprises was to increase efficiency. Allocative efficiency requirements to reduce horizontal integration have played a relatively limited role in east Germany in the light of the strength of competition in the product markets from west German suppliers. As noted above, the attempt by managers to cement monopolistic structures in corporate holdings in 1990 was ineffective in the face of the power of west German competition.

The need to improve private productive efficiency has dominated the splitting up process. In many industries the *Kombinat* organizational structure was intimately linked with the mode of sale of enterprise output. Sales to the CMEA area often comprised orders for related products from a series of members of the *Kombinat*. The frequently discussed synergy between member enterprises of a *Kombinat* appears to have value only in the context of the now-defunct CMEA trade arrangements. The criteria for efficiency restructuring have been dominated by the need to create rough units which "make sense" in market-economy terms. As ever in the east German case, west German structures have formed the explicit standard of comparison.[540] As enterprises were broken up, land not required for business purposes was separated from the enterprise and made available for new activities.

Selling core business activities

The Treuhand has focused its sales strategy on finding investors able to complete the turnaround of a Treuhand enterprise by undertaking sufficient investment to give the firm a secure future. The strategy was therefore directed exclusively toward western investors.

As noted above, industrial employment in east Germany has not been preserved. Nevertheless, the sales strategy of the Treuhand was based on the preservation of the core activities of enterprises. Its aim was first to match the assets of east German enterprises – rebundling these assets where necessary – to the management skills of potential purchasers. A potential purchaser had to demonstrate knowledge of the industry and, in particular, to give evidence that there was a market for the enterprise's output. Secondly, the purchaser had to demonstrate that he had the financial and managerial resources necessary to carry out the remaining restructuring tasks, in particular strategic restructuring in the form of new investment and the development of new products.

Employment subsidies have been a key component of the sales strategy. Investors have been given a discount on the sales price of the enterprise according to the number of jobs guaranteed. There was no centrally determined scale of subsidies used in negotiations, but subsidies varied according to the availability of alternative job opportunities in the area and the external effects of employment in the firm on the local job market. For example, in the sales associated with enterprises from one *Kombinat*, discounts per job guaranteed varied from DM 10,000 for an enterprise on the outskirts of Berlin to DM 80,000 for one near the Polish border.[541] In addition, in industries identified as of strategic importance – such as microelectronics – or subject to particular political pressure – such as shipbuilding – larger subsidies were provided.[542]

The advantage of this approach is that regional and industrial external effects can be taken into account. The disadvantage is that investors face market wages and prices at which, in the absence of the contracts, they would *ex post* choose lower employment levels. Thus the Treuhand is required to monitor its employment and investment contracts and therefore to maintain contact with its former enterprises for the length of the contracts.

---

[538] Hansel (1993).

[539] Hansel (1993), pp. 5-8.

[540] For details of how this was effected in one case of restructuring see Bischof et al. (1993).

[541] Bischof et al. (1993).

[542] E.g., over DM 250,000 per job guaranteed in microelectronics; see Bischof et al. (1993).

TABLE 5.3.5

Investment per employee by Treuhand, privatized and newly-founded firms in east German manufacturing, 1991-1992
(DM)

	1991	1992
Treuhand firms	11 070	12 900
Privatized or reprivatized (former THA firms)	23 340	29 900
Enterprises founded since 1989	47 360	132 400

Source: DIW (1992b), Table 8, p.718.

(c) Alternative restructuring/privatization strategies

Enterprises which have been privatized have typically already undergone considerable restructuring under Treuhand ownership as described above. But usually, only once the enterprise was in the private sector has *strategic* restructuring begun. Until very recently, the view of the Treuhand has been that it should not carry out forward-looking or strategic restructuring. By strategic restructuring is meant the reorientation of an enterprise toward new markets requiring major investment in fixed capital and the development of new products. Such decisions should, in the view of the Treuhand, only be taken by agents who would bear some risk. This was reflected in the very limited willingness of the Treuhand to give permission for investment expenditure. It exercised tight control of enterprise access to finance for investment by rarely giving guarantees for investment credits. Banks were very unwilling to lend to Treuhand firms without such guarantees because of the extent of uncertainty hanging over their future.

Aggregate data reflect the fact that investment in Treuhand firms is much lower than in privatized firms. For firms owned by the Treuhand in October 1992, investment in 1992 was just DM 7 billion, with one quarter of enterprises carrying out no investment at all. In privatized firms, investment was DM 30.3 billion, representing three times as much investment per employee.[543] Table 5.3.5 shows the difference in investment per employee in manufacturing firms owned by the Treuhand, privatized and newly-founded firms.

MBOs: Sales to managers

As a consequence of the Treuhand's basic strategy – to *sell* enterprises to buyers who have western management expertise, knowledge of western markets and technology – east Germans have been largely excluded from participation, lacking access to finance as well as to western networks. The Treuhand failed to develop a strategy for promoting MBOs. East German involvement developed as the threat of unemployment prompted serving managers of Treuhand enterprises to propose that parts be spun off as independent firms. This is the clearest example in east Germany of "privatization from below", the initiative for a privatization project coming from the eastern management itself.

To date, there have been almost 2,400 MBOs, accounting for just under one fifth of the total number of sales of enterprises or parts of enterprises. Two thirds of MBOs have been small firms with less than 50 employees; 6 MBOs had between 500 and 1,000 employees. Some 45 per cent are in manufacturing.[544]

Strategic restructuring: The Management KGs

In the spring of 1992, the Treuhand embarked on an experiment by setting up two new companies to introduce market incentives into the restructuring and privatization process whilst retaining the ownership of enterprises in state (Treuhand) hands. The Treuhand believed that a new strategy was necessary because large numbers of "potentially viable" enterprises had failed to attract a buyer. Prolonged parking of enterprises in the Treuhand was undesirable, and new institutional forms for state ownership were required which would provide more time for the enterprise to prove its viability and clear incentives for effective restructuring, including the forward-looking strategic restructuring typically denied to Treuhand firms.

The outcome was the creation of a new institutional form for state ownership known as the *Management KG*. The German corporate form of the "limited partnership" was chosen as the vehicle for setting up a restructuring company since it permits the separation of management from ownership (which remains with the Treuhand). An individual experienced western manager takes on the responsibility for turning the group of enterprises round and can earn a large bonus from a successful privatization. The Treuhand provides the finance for restructuring needed in the *Management KG* and sets the budget constraint.

The *Management KG* was designed to deal with medium-sized enterprises and to effect privatization within three years. It is a channel through which public sector funds can be directed to new investment in enterprises within the context of a strategic restructuring of the firm. This is not a structure set up to provide for prolonged periods of maintenance in the state sector. Enterprises were chosen for the *Management KG* form by the Treuhand according to four criteria: judgement of potential viability, requirement for a large amount of restructuring, no immediate privatization prospect and a minimum of 250 employees.

(d) Enterprise restructuring and industrial policy

Policies for industries and, given the structure of the GDR economy, often also for regions were developed piecemeal, in response to political pressure. The *chemical industry* was the first to be openly identified as needing a "plan" in order to ensure its survival. The technological and economic indivisibility between the large enterprises in a single location meant that the standard Treuhand incremental approach was inappropriate.

---

[543] Kühl (1993), p.18.

[544] Treuhandanstalt (1992b).

Microelectronics was also identified by the Federal government as a sector which would be retained. But in this case, the likelihood of generating a coherent plan for the industry was much lower because (unlike the chemical industry) the key microelectronics plants were located in several of the new *Länder* and there was no supraregional body capable of coordinating the reorganization of the industry. The Treuhand had the capability for doing this, but would not intervene in such "structural" policy. The result was fragmentation and perhaps a greater down-scaling of the industry than necessary.[545]

By mid-1992, there was considerable public concern that the rapid pace of employment-shedding, apparently necessary to achieve rapid privatization, was denuding east Germany of its "industrial core". Even with large cuts in employment within the Treuhand, manufacturing enterprises were particularly hard to sell and prone to closure. This prompted the Federal government to announce its commitment to retaining the "industrial cores" of east Germany. One approach has been to set up a procedure for identifying enterprises still owned by the Treuhand which are considered essential to the maintenance of a minimum industrial core in a region.

For example, in Saxony the ATLAS project has been launched as a joint initiative of the *Land*, the unions and the Treuhand. The Saxony government will support the modernization of enterprises viewed as critical to the region's economy with the policy instruments available to it – funds for the improvement of the regional economy, guarantees for loans, and labour market policy instruments. Enterprises chosen must be judged by the Treuhand to be salvageable and the restructuring concept for the enterprise must maintain existing employment or create new jobs. Particular emphasis is given to enterprises with important links to other enterprises in Saxony.[546]

The pledge to "save the industrial core" has lent renewed momentum to the creation of holding companies at the *Länder* level to which the ownership of Treuhand enterprises would be transferred. The holding companies will take on enterprises with industrial and regional significance which are too large to be dealt with through a *Management KG* and too important to close. It appears that this is the institutional structure which will provide longer-term state ownership and within which strategic restructuring will take place. Several *Länder* have moved to set up such holding companies (e.g., Berlin-Brandenburg, Saxony). Joint private sector (bank) and public sector funds are also being formed (e.g., the *Sachsenfond* for Saxony).[547]

(iv) Examples from east German enterprise restructuring

An examination of how east German *Kombinate* and their original constituent enterprises have been reshaped to promote the survival of core business activities in the market economy reveals a wide variation of experience.[548] A number of brief examples will be presented to highlight the interplay between spontaneous and "top-down" restructuring processes.

(a) Mansfeld AG

This is one of the difficult cases in the former GDR.[549] It was a very large *Kombinat* with over 20,000 employees in 23 enterprises in mining and processing of aluminium and copper. As in all *Kombinate*, there were large numbers of peripheral activities – transport, wholesale trade, consultancy, light engineering – in addition to the social activities. Along with a minority of *Kombinate*, Mansfeld was a so-called *Leitbetrieb*, the General Director of which *was not* also the manager of a dominant main enterprise (*Stammbetrieb*). Mansfeld had two major divisions – copper and aluminium, located on sites away from the headquarters at Eisleben. This combination of activities is not found in the west. Moreover, this is an example in which plants in the former GDR were too small to be competitive in the west: the turnover of the copper division was one half and that of the aluminium division one third that of the smallest European producer in each sector. Given the existence of excess capacity in the west able to supply Mansfeld's former customers, the copper division has gone into liquidation.

The Mansfeld AG's top management had kept the *Kombinat* together in the corporatization phase and opposed the subsequent efforts of the Treuhand – acting on the advice of the independent evaluation team (the *Leitungsausschuß*) – to break apart the divisions and enterprises between which no economically justified synergies existed. After three years, the Treuhand has yet to succeed fully in its determination to separate out Mansfeld AG as a pure shell holding company in order to liquidate it.

The delicate balance between rapid restructuring and the labour-shedding associated with it, and the rise in organized resistance to restructuring as unemployment increases, has not been maintained in this case. A large element of the problem seems to be the very powerful position and limited opportunities for "side-payments" or "compensation in kind" in the form of career prospects to the top managers in a case where they are not also the managers of a dominant enterprise.

Exactly the same problem was encountered in the case of Baukema AG.[550] A variant of the problem has been characteristic of the more usual *Stammbetrieb Kombinat*, the case in which the main enterprise had very poor prospects.[551]

---

[545] See Bischof et al. (1993) for a detailed discussion.

[546] Nolte (1993a).

[547] Nolte (1993b).

[548] Case histories are provided in *Kombinate* ... (1993), Heidenreich (ed.) (1992), and Bischof et al. (1993).

[549] This case study follows closely the findings of Price (1993).

[550] Documented in Bischof et al. (1993).

[551] Examples are the brown coal and potash *Kombinate*.

(b) Gisag AG

Where a potentially viable core business existed in the *Stammbetrieb*, the commitment of the Treuhand to restructure the balance sheet (cleaning up the old debts and recapitalizing) and to provide a subsidy to a new owner has enabled the necessary pre-privatization restructuring to be accomplished. Examples of this are very common. One such case was that of Gisag AG.[552] This foundry enterprise was faced with enormous down-scaling of its activities and massive labour-shedding if it was to survive. Early recognition of the likely magnitude of down-scaling and restructuring came with the decision of the Gisag managers to seek a west German industry expert to head their supervisory board in the corporatization phase in 1990. By the end of 1990 the management was convinced that survival of the core businesses at Gisag depended on breaking up the holding and seeking buyers for individual foundries.

The Gisag case also illustrates the role of the government in assessing the external effects of the maintenance of industrial activities: although the private costs of closing Gisag were less than the costs of restructuring and selling the foundries, there were social costs of the loss of the industry to the Leipzig area. Local and regional governments were called on by the Treuhand to assist in financing the restructuring and privatization option.

Although no comprehensive data are available, there is an accumulation of evidence in the case studies that the information monopoly of incumbent managers about their enterprise furthered their retention of managerial positions after privatization, suggesting that the prospect of "survival" with the survival of the core business promotes their cooperation with the pre-privatization restructuring.

(c) Kombinat Zellstoff und Papier Heidenau

This is an example where spontaneous restructuring promoted a market-conforming solution.[553] The paper industry in the west is one with a simple structure in terms of the production process, the sourcing of inputs and the sale of output. Spontaneous restructuring in the corporatization phase led to the splitting off of nine enterprises from the original 20. The other 11 original enterprises plus the *Stammbetrieb* formed a public company (AG) with 12 subsidiaries, the Dresden Papier AG. It is striking that no viable producers of the input to the paper industry (cellulite) remained in Dresden Papier AG. The theory of vertical integration predicts that where a standard commodity is the input, one would expect market transactions to prevail, and this is just what has resulted. The management of Dresden Papier AG took up the advice of the Treuhand evaluation team to reorganize production sites to accomplish a 1:1:1 outcome (1 location, 1 plant, 1 paper machine), as is characteristic of the industry in the west. This is not a complex industry and the limited post-privatization restructuring requirements are confirmed by the sale of Dresden Papier AG to a Canadian investment bank with the incumbent management running the enterprise.

(d) Kombinat Oberkleidung Berlin

This was the most prestigious of the four clothing *Kombinate* in the GDR.[554] It was large – with 21,000 employees in 15 enterprises, seven of which had more than 1,000 employees. In a report on the prospects of the *Kombinat* in early 1990, the *Kombinat* management stated that only one of the enterprises was profitable. Nevertheless the manager developed a grandiose plan for the restructuring of the *Kombinat* into a holding company structure: the new holding consisted of 10 of the companies formed from the former main enterprise (*Stammbetrieb*) plus 6 other *Kombinat* enterprises. Almost 8,000 persons were employed. This holding included enterprises building textile machines and spare parts, as well as a training centre for clothing workers. The new structure reproduced the logic of the *Kombinat*.

Two years later, the Treuhand had imposed liquidation on the holding and most of the subsidiaries. Yet again the ability of the management to create and defend a holding structure postponed the necessary adjustment and inhibited more flexible responses.

The fate of one of the best enterprises in the holding is instructive in another respect. It highlights the learning required for success in the market economy and suggests that attempts to jump the learning stage hasten failure. A study of the firm provides evidence on the extensive learning which has taken place through contract work for west German enterprises.[555] It has functioned as a means of learning the contacts and structure of the industry in the west as well as essential managerial and work practice techniques. The product orientation of the planned economy led to the misconception that developing a new product line would bring success. In this case, the enterprise developed a new range of women's clothing which was favourably received at trade fairs and by fashion houses. Sales did not follow because of the weakness of contacts in the industry and the difficulty with obtaining and developing marketing expertise. The expectation that a good product would guarantee success led to the enterprise refusing to engage in what was viewed as the demeaning work of contract jobs for western companies. The enterprise entered liquidation in spring 1992.

(v) Lessons for other transition countries

An examination of the east German experience of restructuring of SOEs, which has been dominated by the problem of dealing with unprofitable enterprises, draws attention to the need to develop policies in the transition economies to salvage the combinations of assets from large SOEs which are of social value. The justifiable wish to depoliticize economic life after communism must be tempered by the recognition that failure to deal with problems of industrial structure and inherited problems of

---

[552] This case is described in detail in Carlin and Mayer (1992b).

[553] This case study follows closely the findings of Price (1993).

[554] Based on the description by Fritz (1993).

[555] Birnie et al. (1993).

enterprise viability prior to privatization may leave more intractable problems to be dealt with later.

It has been argued that the east European experience in attracting foreign direct investment is a useful weathervane of progress with restructuring. The slow pace of foreign involvement reflects the unwillingness of foreign companies to take on the task of extensive restructuring. Where foreign direct investment has been liveliest is where foreign companies see the opportunity of purchasing a monopoly stake in the market, highlighting once again the costs to the domestic economy of the failure to restructure. It is clear from east Germany that joint ventures with western partners, even at the level of contract work, are an important route to adjustment toward market economy norms.

There is now an accumulation of evidence that a hard enterprise budget constraint promotes adjustment. However, the need to impose a hard budget constraint by tightening the link between an enterprise's access to resources and its current financial performance is sometimes interpreted as "no involvement by the state in enterprise restructuring". Such a view can bias the government against policies which promote restructuring – for example, where the enterprise management agrees to labour shedding, the unbundling of the enterprise etc. in exchange for the rescheduling of debts, assistance with alternative job creation measures and retraining or a temporary moratorium on bankruptcy.

East Germany has had unique access to managerial and administrative expertise which has enabled a coordinated process of enterprise evaluation and restructuring to take place on a massive scale. This is not an option available to other transition economies. However, even with its privileged access to management expertise, even in east Germany it has become clear that techniques for economizing on scarce managerial talent must be used. This realization led to the creation of the *Management KGs* through which experienced managers are engaged with high-powered incentives to restructure a set of enterprises still in state ownership.

5.4 Restructuring of large state-owned enterprises in Hungary, 1988-1993

(i) Definitions and key issues

The restructuring of state-owned enterprises (SOEs) can be considered as a process in which firms created under, and geared to, a planned economy are enabled to successfully operate in a market economy – or, alternatively, as a process of adaptation of firms to the new environment.[556] In this sense the entire transformation process in the former centrally planned economies can be regarded as restructuring, and the term would encompass any corporate or state action whereby the old economic conditions are revised, including changes in ownership, organizational systems, and the competitive environment.

A narrower interpretation will be used in this paper: *restructuring is here defined as specific actions, outside the normal conduct of business, which are aimed at the survival of firms and saving them from liquidation*. In this context, direct state actions, corporate actions or those implemented through intermediaries will be distinguished, according to the level of decision making and sources of financing. Restructuring will be further classified according to methods (organizational, financial), and timing (before, parallel with or after privatization).[557]

Within this framework, the most critical issues of restructuring can be outlined. The first question is whether restructuring can or should be implemented *before* privatization, or whether it should be left to the new owners. A second decision set concerns the issue of who should be responsible for the costs of restructuring. Is it certain that these measures have to be taken by the state, and if so, which bodies of the state: the government, the state-owned lenders, the organizations representing the state as a shareholder, or specific restructuring departments? Alternatively, is it possible to establish an environment where the SOEs themselves are willing and able to implement the restructuring process?

These are increasingly pivotal issues of political and economic debate in Hungary. The official approach, and the practice of restructuring, has been modified several times in the last five years. The initial bottom-up approach was replaced by centrally controlled privatization, when restructuring was overshadowed, and finally by centrally controlled restructuring. Analysis of these three periods compares the terms, methods and consequences of the different approaches.

Following a brief review of the initial conditions (section 5.4(ii) below), these different phases of privatization policy will be reviewed in sections 5.4(iii)-(v). In this context, the motivations and methods of organizational and financial restructuring will be described. Section 5.4(vi) offers a summary of the pros and cons of the different types of restructuring, together with some conclusions derived from the analysis.

(ii) The starting point: Early enterprise reforms in Hungary

(a) Restructuring in the late 1980s

One of the important initial conditions was posed by the *high degree of organizational centralization of state-owned enterprises*. Following the mergers launched from the 1960s on central initiative, and subsequently on the initiative of the large organizations created in this process, a highly centralized structure was established (table 5.4.1). This degree of centralization was quite unique even in the planned economies.[558] Between 1970 and 1980, the share of SOEs with more than 1,000 employees rose from 35 to about 45 per cent of all industrial firms. An *"inverse pyramid"* was built with a heavy top layer of very large organizations and a shortage of small and medium-sized enterprises.[559] Centralization often amounted to monopolistic positions. According to a review of the Institute of Economic Planning covering 458 product categories, the leading manufacturers accounted for more than 50 per cent of the market in two thirds of these products.[560]

Conglomerates have not been typical in the Hungarian economy in recent decades; the last organizations of this type, called trusts in Hungary, were dissolved as almost the only result of a deconcentration campaign started in the early 1980s.[561] Most large organizations did not take the form of homogeneous, integrated enterprises. Most plants and factories of the large SOEs were merged administratively, but remained geographically and technologically separate units. They kept fighting with the enterprise centres, first for the preservation of their relative independence and decision-making rights and, from the 1980s onwards, for separation and organizational autonomy. However, in negotiations with third parties, including the government,

---

[556] "Restructuring during transition is a term used for manifold operations which change existing enterprise into viable companies capable of working in a market environment", including breaking up monopolies, technical reconstruction and financial rescue operations. WIIW (1993), p.48. A comparative research project defines enterprise restructuring as a complex process of "the adjustment of the enterprise sector to the new conditions", differentiating legal, organizational, commercial, industrial and financial restructuring. CEFRES (1993), pp.3-4.

[557] In principle, restructuring may include the changing of production systems, technology or markets. These areas, however, have been excluded here as being in the "normal course of business". As the paper focuses on restructuring of state-owned enterprises, it will not scrutinize restructuring after privatization, when the necessary measures are taken by the new (private) owners. The definition applied here is similar to that proposed by Carlin and Mayer (1992a), except for this last part.

[558] Czechoslovakia was the only country with a comparable degree of centralization.

[559] See Schweitzer (1982), p.130.

[560] Bertáné, Bod and Nagy (1990).

[561] For more details, see Voszka (1984). The majority of large SOEs, having strong negotiating positions and enjoying the support of branch ministries, managed to avoid being split up. Except for the trusts, mainly in the food processing industry, the committees set up by functional ministries managed to separate only a few plants from some SOEs.

TABLE 5.4.1

Structure of industrial enterprises by number of employees, Hungary, 1970-1991
(Percentage share of all enterprises)

	1970	1975	1980	1988	1989	1990	1991
Number of employees							
1-100	10.7	9.1	6.6	27.8	46.5	76.5	88.3
101-1,000	53.9	54.3	49.9	47.6	33.7	19.2	9.6
1,001-2,000	15.8	16.2	20.5	15.1	5.9	2.7	1.0
2,001-5,000	14.3	15.3	17.5	7.5	3.1	1.3	0.5
5,000 plus	5.3	5.1	5.5	2.0	0.8	0.3	0.1
Total	100.0	100.0	100.0	100.0	100.0	100.0	100.0

Source: Hungarian Central Statistical Office.

TABLE 5.4.2

Government subsidies by type, Hungary, 1987-1993
(Billion forint)

	1987	1988	1989	1990	1991	1992 [a]	1993 [b]
Consumption subsidies	56.4	42.5	42.5	36.8	40.4	19.1	20.4
Housing subsidies	17.4	32.7	81.8	83.4	72.8	73.0	61.6
Production subsidies	90.9	88.0	81.9	66.1	59.6	60.4	57.4
Total	164.7	163.2	206.2	186.3	172.8	152.6	139.4
Total without housing	147.3	130.5	124.4	104.9	100.0	79.6	78.8

Source: Yearly budgets of Hungary.

[a] Preliminary – 5.7 per cent of GDP.
[b] Projected – 4.2 per cent of GDP.

the large SOEs acted as integrated organizations. Their bargaining powers were based mainly on scale (volume of production, export and employees). In this position, and through their integration into the political system, they were able to achieve income redistribution in their own favour.[562]

Widespread income redistribution was the second important initial condition. Most large SOEs were used to regular budgetary subsidies to cover their losses or maintain exports (table 5.4.2). Investment funds were allocated in a predominantly central system through annual and five-year plans and lending policy guidelines. This system entailed a preferential bias in favour of the large organizations, irrespective of the credit risk, and thus increased their indebtedness.

Last but not least, and in addition to political intentions, the strong negotiating position of large SOEs was an important driving force in the relatively long and intense reform process. The basic objective of Hungarian reforms since the 1960s has been to increase the independence of enterprises. This process meant, *inter alia*, the decentralization of an increasing part of property rights from central bureaucratic organizations (ministries) to enterprise management. The inheritance from the former political system in this respect was not strong and stable state ownership, but a dispersed model where the property rights were divided among different organizations.[563]

The last step towards the decentralization of state property rights was the introduction of the so-called "self-governing enterprise" form in 1985. Enterprise councils were established for two thirds of the economic units. These bodies, which were in practice dominated by enterprise management, were given the right to determine the organizational structure, appoint the managing director, and make decisions on mergers and splitting up, and on the establishment of joint ventures and companies involving state property.

Companies were at first established according to laws enacted before 1945.[564] In 1988, a new Company Law was adopted,[565] giving a new legal framework for the setting up of corporations, but it did not provide any special rules for the transformation of state enterprises into company form (corporatization). This need was met by the so-called Transformation Law in 1989,[566] which declared that the decision to corporatize was the right of self-governing bodies; however, corporatization became subject to several conditions (the raising of capital, the entry of new, external owners), and the non-privatized shares were lodged with the state property administration as owner.

---

[562] For details see, *inter alia*, Antal (1985), Csanádi (1984) and Szalai (1989).

[563] For an excellent summary of this system see Szalai (1989).
[564] Law XXXVII of 1875.
[565] Law VI of 1988.
[566] Law XIII of 1989.

TABLE 5.4.3

Economic organizations by legal type, Hungary, 1988-1993
(Units)

	1988	1989	1990	1991	1992	September 1993	1993/1988
Economic organizations with "legal personality"	10 811	15 235	29 470	52 756	69 386	80 780	747.2
Company-forms without "legal personality"	29 657	24 143	34 095	52 136	70 932	92 459	311.8
Individual, non-incorporated business units	290 877	320 619	393 450	510 459	606 207	650 267	223.5
Budgetary and non-profit organizations	28 500	31 200	38 300	43 322	48 982	52 944	185.8
Total	359 845	391 197	495 315	658 673	795 507	876 450	243.6

Source: Hungarian Central Statistical Office.

TABLE 5.4.4

Economic organizations with "legal personality" by number of employees, Hungary, 1988-1993
(Per cent)

Year/employees	0-20	21-50	51-300	301 plus	No data	Total
1988	18.7	14.5	28.2	23.3	15.3	10 811
1989	33.5	18.7	22.7	17.2	10.9	15 235
1990	55.9	14.0	15.2	8.8	6.1	29 405
1991	69.8	11.7	10.2	4.5	3.8	52 756
1992	78.3	10.3	8.5	2.9	-	67 505 [a]
1993, September	80.9	9.5	7.5	2.1	-	78 948 [a]

Source: Hungarian Central Statistical Office.

[a] Excluding housing cooperatives and firms under liquidation.

The *need for restructuring* stems from two of the initial conditions: the high degree of centralization of the organizational system, and the high levels of subsidies and enterprise debts. The third condition mentioned above, the considerable formal and informal autonomy of large SOEs, provided *the possibility* for them to act as initiators in the transformation. Before analysing this process, the scale of the changes will be reviewed in the light of statistical data.

(b) Features of organizational change, 1988-1993

The rise in the number of market actors is one of the most dynamic processes of the Hungarian transition. By September 1993, the number of business organizations exceeded 800,000, as against some 360,000 five years earlier (table 5.4.3).

Individual entrepreneurships and unincorporated small businesses represent a numerical majority, but their share is smaller in terms of economic activity measures.[567] From the point of view of organizational change of the SOEs, however, the class of companies organized with the attribute of "legal personality" is the most relevant, because the successors (both private and state-owned) of the large units fall in this category. The number of organizations which have legal personality increased almost eight times between 1988 and autumn 1993.

The growth of this group was accompanied by structural change, and a proliferation of small firms and company forms. The proportion of organizations with less than 20 employees increased from some 18 per cent in 1988 to over 80 per cent in 1993 (table 5.4.4). It has to be mentioned, however, that employment concentration is considerably higher: in 1991, the most recent year of comprehensive data, only 1.6 per cent of industrial firms employed more than 1,000 people, but together they employed nearly the half the workforce (tables 5.4.1 and 5.4.5). The share of corporations with legal personality (limited-liability and joint-stock companies) grew from 9 to 88 per cent of all "legal personality" entities between 1988 and 1993 (table 5.4.6). Most of the small limited-liability firms presumably belong to the private sector which has emerged on this basis; that is, they were established independently of the privatization of state-owned enterprises.[568] Statistical data are not available to define the exact share of these two categories.[569]

---

[567] While employment in such firms increased from 300,000 in 1988 to over 700,000 in 1992, this only accounted for 16.7 per cent of the labour force at the end of the period according to data of the Labour Research Institute (Laky (ed.), 1993).

[568] Note that the growing number of registered economic organizations does not necessarily mean an equal increase in *new* market actors. Some units were transformed from previous private entrepreneurships which were not legal entities or from semi-legal units of the secondary economy. On the other hand, many small limited liability units are "shell" companies without any activities, created only to obtain tax preferences.

[569] According to an estimate for a previous period, among companies, state-owned assets were involved in some 6,500 organizations. See Voszka (1993).

TABLE 5.4.5

Structure of industrial employment in state-owned enterprises by firm size, Hungary, 1970-1991
(Per cent of total employment in state industry)

	1970	1975	1980	1988	1989	1990	1991
Number of employees							
1-100	0.4	0.2	0.2	1.1	4.5	8.5	12.8
101-1,000	16.6	17.3	16.3	26.4	30.5	35.4	39.6
1,001-2,000	16.8	16.8	18.4	25.9	22.2	21.3	18.8
2,001-5,000	32.7	33.0	33.8	26.3	24.8	21.4	18.8
5,000 plus	33.5	32.7	31.3	20.3	18.0	13.4	10.0
Total	100.0	100.0	100.0	100.0	100.0	100.0	100.0

Source: Hungarian Central Statistical Office.

TABLE 5.4.6

Structure of economic units with "legal personality" by organizational form, Hungary, 1988-1993
(Per cent of all units with "legal personality")

	1988	1989	1990	1991	1992	September 1993
State enterprises	22.0	15.8	8.0	4.3	2.5	1.6
Corporations	8.8	31.6	66.0	80.9	85.6	87.7
of which:						
Limited liability companies	4.2	29.6	62.3	78.1	82.5	84.6
Joint stock companies	1.1	2.0	2.2	2.0	2.5	2.7
Cooperatives	63.3	46.7	26.0	14.8	119.9	10.1
Other	5.9	5.9	-	-	-	0.6
Total number of units	10 811	15 169	29 405	53 765	69 386	80 780

Source: Hungarian Central Statistical Office.

Thus, the "inverse pyramid" of enterprise size clearly has been dismantled in the last five years. The establishment of small and medium-sized entrepreneurships also reflects the disintegration of big state-owned enterprises; spontaneous privatization was a crucial factor in this process.

(iii) Spontaneous privatization, 1988-1990: A bottom-up approach

The main aim of the process called "spontaneous privatization" in Hungary was the attempt to restructure large SOEs organizationally and financially, rather than ownership change and the promotion of former managers into the position of owners. The process started in 1988, in the last two years of the former political regime.[570] In one version of the process, firms contributed a (minor) part of their assets to new companies in which foreign investors also took a share, and the remaining part of the state enterprise continued to operate. But the basic form of "spontaneous privatization" was the "quasi-entire" transformation of a large SOE into a group of companies while the former enterprise centre took on the function of asset (stock) management. Although these units called themselves holding companies, they preserved the form of a state-owned enterprise.[571] SOEs set up companies on the basis of each of their factories, plants and even administrative departments.

The "holdings" usually retained the majority of shares in the new companies. In this type of company, new owners appeared as well, but apart from foreign investors these were state-owned organizations, such as banks and other enterprises, which were mainly business partners. Thus, in most cases "spontaneous privatization" did not mean privatization in the strict sense of the word, since private investors rarely bought shares in the new companies. The formal management buy-out (MBO) was rare in this period, although it is true that managers, like anybody else, were free to establish their own private firms. These firms often found it profitable to set up relations with the SOE as suppliers or customers, that is, SOE managers could pump revenue into their own businesses. This process, called "hidden" privatization, should be distinguished from the legal form of "spontaneous" privatization.[572]

---

[570] For details, see Móra (1990), Matolcsy (ed.) (1991), Tóth (1991), and Voszka (1991).

[571] There are no reliable data on the scope of various types of spontaneous privatization. Matolcsy (ed.) (1991) estimates that in the process of spontaneous privatization, some 250 large SOEs were partially or nearly fully transformed into companies, involving assets of some Ft 130 billion At that time the total volume of state assets to be privatized was estimated at Ft 2,000 billion.

[572] Kállai (1992) assumes that the scale of hidden privatization, applying these or other methods (not limited to SOE managers) was similar to the scale of official privatization.

The transformation into a group of companies was directly motivated by the changing economic and political environment. The main problems for firms in the late 1980s were insolvency or the lack of additional capital. This was mainly due to the restrictive economic policy, including the cut-back of budgetary subsidies (table 5.4.2). The traditional methods of survival, such as exerting pressure for more preferences and for the cancelling or rescheduling of debts, did not work any more. The state had become weak, both financially and politically, in a period when a large group of enterprises found itself in a critical situation as internal and external markets (first the CMEA) began to shrink, inflation and lending rates increased dramatically, and interenterprise debts accumulated.

In the case of enterprises in an unstable financial position, corporatization offered the advantage of a debt to equity swap with banks or other lenders and creditors. Another method of easing the financial burden was to assign all debts to the "holding" company; even if it were to go bankrupt, the spin-off companies, set up without debt, might survive.

The second motivation for spontaneous privatization, which applied beyond units on the verge of bankruptcy, was to meet the traditional desire of plants for independence: plants and factories, loosely integrated into the large unit, had not abandoned their efforts to achieve organizational autonomy. In the process of transformation into a group of companies, it was the bargaining between the enterprise centre and the factories that determined the organizational framework, and the distribution of assets and liabilities. (Workers organizations and local authorities played a marginal role in these deals.)[573] The formal independence of the subunits turned into separate companies was acceptable to the enterprise centres at this time because of the lack of resources for redistribution. The increasing need to find new markets and to change the production structure also played a role. The SOE centres knew from experience that the delegation of decision-making rights to internal units provided more incentives and flexibility. Yet, by retaining majority ownership of the former enterprise centre in the companies, the features of a large enterprise could also be kept. Moreover, as its previous administrative powers were replaced by legitimate ownership rights, the unit became more difficult to attack from inside or outside.

In fact, protection against external, governmental intervention was the third important motivation. Such intervention might result, for instance, in transfer under state control (the suspension of the self-governing bodies); in the splitting up of the enterprise; or in privatization initiated by state administrative bodies. The company form seemed to protect against most of these threats by creating shareholders other than governmental organizations.

As the example in box 5.4.1 illustrates, "spontaneous privatization" can be seen as a compromise between the state and the top management of large enterprises, and between the latter and the component plants. The lack of resources to be redistributed weakened both the state and the large enterprise centres in their bargaining position with their subordinates. In addition, the political standing of the government and the large state enterprises was undermined by that time.[574]

In this situation, the government understood that opening up the possibilities for firms to change their organizational and financial structure could well be of advantage to the state as well. Hence it was the state as a regulator that gave incentives – and at the same time legal options – to its enterprises to take this path. In the short run it might help enterprises to survive without restructuring efforts on the part of the state, and at the same time it economized on central resources and provided a potential for changing the economic structure.

From the point of view of SOE top managers, this opportunity could be perceived as a last gift from a politically weak and financially strapped government. It meant the final stage of decentralization of proprietary rights from the governmental to the enterprise level. The managers of the "holding" companies, and those of "normal" firms with majority ownership in several companies, extended their decision-making scope to the buying and selling of stocks and assets. Parallel with that, the former rights of the enterprise centres were transferred to the managers of the plants, that is, of the new companies, thus extending their decision-making power. So decentralization affected ever wider circles of managers, whose "quasi-owner" role, characteristic of the reformed planned economies, was strengthened. Without privatization in the strict sense of the term, however, they did not become legal owners. As directors of state-owned "holdings" or enterprises, they could be discharged by enterprise councils or government bodies at any time.

To sum up, the establishment of the new companies on the basis of state assets did mean some kind of financial restructuring (mainly through the elimination of old debt, to a much smaller degree through additional capital). The process led to organizational restructuring, too, although in a limited sense. As long as the majority of the shares was held by the state "holdings" (the SOE centres), organizational decentralization could remain a formal exercise. Where new owners were involved, however, the process turned into real decentralization. Thus, *the hardening of the budget constraint was more the precondition to than the consequence of enterprise restructuring.* Under the new circumstances of a handicapped state, as a compromise, managers of both large enterprises and their plants became willing and able to start the restructuring process.

"Spontaneous privatization" was criticized in 1989 by some opposition parties and reform economists, as well as by civil servants, because of the lack of both public (state) control and revenue for the state budget. As one of its last

---

[573] The strength of trade unions in Hungary was not comparable to that in Poland. The workers were represented in the enterprise councils, where they had some voice, but the self-governing bodies were in practice dominated by the enterprise and plant managements.

[574] Szalai (1991).

> **BOX 5.4.1**
>
> **A case study: Ganz-Danubius**
>
> These motivations for spontaneous privatization, and typical solutions, can be clearly observed in the experience of the shipyard company, Ganz-Danubius.[a] The firm, employing several thousand people, was among the top 100 Hungarian companies, ranking No.40 in production value and 14th in export volume in 1988. In 1985-1986, total debts including medium-term and short-term loans taken to finance its swollen inventories and span its cash-flow problems, were more than the value of its assets. In one of the first cases of spontaneous privatization, Ganz-Danubius divided itself on 1 January 1989 into seven share companies, forming independent legal entities from all its former factories. The headquarters, which employed a staff of nearly 700 people, was transformed into small limited liability companies, organized on the basis of the former functional departments (for example, trade and marketing, accounting, social services). One part continued to operate as a state-owned enterprise employing 50 persons. This "holding" company, led by the CEO of the former large enterprise, owned 89 to 99 per cent of the shares of the seven shipyard companies.
>
> Since neither additional external funds nor dividends from the companies could reasonably be expected, for debt management a debt-equity swap seemed to be the only alternative. The transaction was actually concluded with the key lender, the State Development Institute, and other state-owned commercial banks. After the swap of 1989, the holding company lost its majority ownership in four companies and its share fell below 75 per cent in the other three.
>
> The second main element of the strategy of the holding company consisted of the sale of one of the companies. The revenue from this transaction was supposed to cover the remaining debts, to provide Ganz-Danubius companies with some fresh capital, and to generate investment into other, more profitable, activities outside of the former large enterprise. The firm chosen for sale was located on one of the most valuable properties of the capital, an island in the Danube. The top management of the holding company carried out successful negotiations with a Danish investment trust, which planned to replace the traditional ship-building on the island with tourist establishments. However, the deal was not completed during the period of spontaneous privatization.
>
> The draft agreement to sell the company on the island was submitted to the SPA in August 1990, as required by the new laws then in force (see section 5.4(iv)); the Agency agreed that the area should not be used for industrial purposes, and that a foreign investor should be involved. Nevertheless, the holding was taken under direct state control and the CEO was fired. The Commissioner appointed by the SPA presented a new proposal regarding the island: first to build the infrastructure, then to sell the land in pieces. The factory on the island was closed, but given the lack of state and local government resources, no restructuring had started as of end-1993. Under the burden of old debt and in the absence of new capital, serious problems soon arose at other Ganz-Danubius companies too; four of the seven recorded losses in 1990. In 1991, all Ganz-Danubius plants registered losses, to a total of more than Ft 800 million. By summer 1992, four Ganz-Danubius companies were bankrupt or liquidated.
>
> ---
>
> [a] Described in detail in Voszka (1994).

measures, the former regime adopted a law to protect state assets and set up a central organization, the State Property Agency (SPA), to control corporatization and privatization transactions.[575] This was the starting point from which the new government changed the decision-making mechanisms after the parliamentary elections of March 1990.

(iv) Centralized privatization, 1990-1992: Insufficient restructuring

One of the first measures of the newly-elected government strengthened the protection of state assets, and centralized the selling decisions in an extension of the powers of the State Property Agency. The new laws prescribed for enterprises the obligation to report to the SPA any intentions of taking property into companies or selling or leasing it (above a low value threshold).[576] The SPA could request repeated assessments, require competitive bidding, or disapprove the contract. It had the right to take enterprises under direct state control, which meant the removal of the self-governing bodies of the firm and the recentralization of all ownership rights at governmental level.

In the years 1990-1991, economic management was based on tight monetary and fiscal policy. The government intended to sell the state-owned enterprises quickly, without any prior financial improvement,[577] through central privatization programmes.[578] In other words, the basic

---

[575] Laws VII and VIII, 1990.

[576] Law LIII, 1990.

[577] See Government of the Republic of Hungary (1990).

[578] At this time the First and Second Privatization Programmes were launched, which soon turned out to be failures. The first programme involved 20 large SOEs (book value Ft 54 billion); the second, 23 firms

assumption of this period was that *privatization was itself to be the tool of restructuring*: the state expected to sell these firms as they were (including debts) and leave it to the new private owners to transform them as necessary. The extension of the powers of the SPA resulted in the blocking of the earlier spontaneous processes, including restructuring initiated by the SOEs.

Enterprises which were not put under SPA control, however, could proceed with some restructuring. The method of spinning off departments and business units other than the core business was still widely used. It was also typical to sell properties and shares to maintain liquidity. These steps (above a low threshold) required the approval of the SPA, but this approval was not difficult to obtain. According to a report of the State Audit Office on the first year of the SPA (1992), 85 per cent of the 140 so-called "asset protection cases" submitted by companies (usually concerning shares to be sold or contributed to new companies) were approved without any change. This means that the SPA was not able effectively to control these restructuring steps and simply issued permits as a formal requirement.

In the centrally initiated privatization programmes, restructuring was characteristic only of the "small privatization" in retail trade and restaurant services (catering). The 366 SOEs covered by that programme were offered for sale divided into more than 10,000 individual units.[579]

The transformation of organizational structures was encouraged by the government also in other sectors. Until the end of 1991, the so-called Separation Law made it possible for plants to appoint the founding ministry as arbitrator if the enterprise council of the SOE concerned refused their request for separation.[580] The self-governing bodies usually rejected the split-up proposals of plants because the SOEs did not receive compensation for such shrinking of their domain. Moreover, most requests for separation were made by the most profitable units, and the big organization could be put in a critical position by their departure.

The Separation Law gave some impetus to the decentralization of organizational structures. Of the 118 requests for splitting-up that were submitted to the Ministry of Industry and Trade by the end of 1991, the ministry rejected only a few proposals, stating that the residual organization would not be viable.[581] Separation was successfully concluded in 70 per cent of the cases, and 81 new SOEs were founded. Most of the SOEs concerned belonged to the medium-sized group, not to the largest one. Agricultural machine production, textiles and the building industry were typical of this kind of splitting-up.

The Separation Law opened up opportunities for traditional, bottom-up organizational decentralization. In evaluating the actions of the government it should be remembered that there had been intensive discussions in Hungary since the early 1980s about the need for and methods of deconcentration. While it was generally agreed that the organizational system was overcentralized, most analysts argued that the large SOEs should not be disintegrated by administrative methods. The state bureaucracy was not considered well placed to assess technical efficiency or the effects of splitting-up on business, a view which was strengthened by the failure of the governmental decentralization campaign of the early 1980s mentioned above.

This generally accepted view was reflected in the Competition Law adopted in 1990.[582] This law encompasses every tool of competition policy used in market economies, including measures to control the abuse of a dominant market position, cartel agreements and acquisitions. Its philosophy focuses on the behaviour of firms, rather than on their organizational structure. Adopting the European (mainly the German) model, it provides sanctions against abuse, but does not oppose the development of a dominating or monopoly position. Thus, the law does not extend to the revision of the existing organizational system.

In the discussions of the draft bill it was proposed that the Competition Office should check for a potential dominating or monopolistic positions all organizations to be transformed into company form or privatized, and initiate splitting-up on the basis of criteria specified by the law (more than 30 per cent market share, higher than Ft 10 billion sales or acquisition of majority vote by one shareholder).[583] However, this formal linking of deconcentration and privatization was not implemented. While the requirement of encouraging competition has been generally noted in the privatization strategies and guidelines of the government, this is just one of the many objectives of privatization.[584]

Without any coercive law, the SPA had little interest in taking decisions to support separations. The SPA apparatus had neither the experience nor sufficient information to make decisions at the microlevel. Deconcentration takes time and is a labour-intensive task, which conflicted with the requirements of fast privatization. The SPA was also afraid that after "cherry picking" of the best business units it would be impossible to maintain or sell the remaining ones. It also seemed to be difficult to allocate the debts of the companies or to safeguard the interests of creditors. Finally, the dominant buyers (at that time foreign) insisted on large organizations and were willing to pay higher prices for substantial market shares. Under such circumstances, the option of consulting

---

(book value of Ft 24 billion). These programmes are described in detail by Matolcsy (1991).

[579] Law LXXIV, 1990.

[580] Law XXII, 1990.

[581] Data for other ministries are not available.

[582] Law LXXXVI, 1990.

[583] Alliance of Free Democrats (1990).

[584] As Tamás Sárközy, a key figure in economic legislation, said: "In the privatization process, too, efforts should be and can be made to decentralize organizations with unreasonable competitive powers. For the time being this is not addressed adequately by the existing laws and regulations". Sárközy (1991a).

the Competition Office and selling SOEs in separate units was rarely considered.[585]

As a general practice, efforts were made to sell state firms intact; moreover, substantial shares in more than one SOE in certain sectors were sold to the same buyer. Well-known examples include several networks of the retail sector in Budapest, as well as the glass and sugar industry. However, in some cases, such as cement production, it was realized only after the SPA decision had been made that the buyers, making their offers under different names, represented the same group of investors.

Thus, centrally controlled privatization has maintained, and often increased, the degree of organizational centralization. Partly for this reason, but mainly because of the slowness of finding private owners, the centralized approach to privatization and the excessive powers of the SPA were criticized after 1991, even by MPs of the coalition parties and by certain groups of the government (especially the Ministry of Finance). Consequently, centralization was slightly moderated and the SPA started the so-called self-privatization programme covering smaller companies. At the same time, a general revision of privatization policy, including restructuring, was initiated.

(v) Restructuring in 1992-1993: A top-down approach

(a) The motivation for restructuring

One of the starting points for revising the approach to restructuring was the modification of privatization policy. This modification meant enacting comprehensive laws and regulations on the one hand and changing priorities on the other.

The most important new feature of the so-called Privatization Laws of 1992 was the creation of the State Holding Company (SHC) to control state-owned firms that were not to be fully or partly privatized in the short run.[586] A total of 163 organizations with assets of about Ft 1,500 billion were assigned to the SHC. All other state-owned firms were put under the direct control of the SPA by compulsory corporatization.[587] This second important feature of the new laws meant the abolition of enterprise councils and the reclaiming of a "real" proprietary position by the state. If corporatization was not accompanied by immediate privatization, the shareholder of the firms would be the SPA. Thus, after the centralization of privatization decisions, the centralization of all ownership rights was enacted. The process was to be completed by the end of 1993.

The objectives of privatization have been changed accordingly. The establishment of the SHC has put the emphasis on asset management and the restructuring of state-owned firms. The other sign of a revised privatization policy was the adoption of a new privatization strategy at the end of 1992.[588] According to this document, the main goal of privatization is to be the creation of a broad and strong Hungarian property-holding middle class. The new policy requires modification of both the demand and the supply sides. The proposed instruments to increase domestic *demand* for state assets include preferential loans, an ESOP scheme and privatization leasing, and a voucher programme through the so-called "credit notes".[589] An adequate supply structure is to be created by organizational restructuring: i.e., the splitting-up of large units.

The pressure for financial restructuring was also partly due to the spread of distributional methods in privatization. The use of compensation notes in buying state assets, and the problem of giving assets worth Ft 300 billion to social security, acutely revealed the inability of most SOEs to operate profitably. They were unlikely to present any profitable offer against the credit notes either.

The other motivation for top-down restructuring was the increasingly critical financial position of the enterprises. According to an estimate of the Ministry of Industry and Trade (1993), losses of industrial enterprises in the first six months of 1991 alone reached the total loss of the previous year and 40 per cent of firms were loss-making. In this period, problems appeared first in a regional context. In several counties (especially in northern and eastern Hungary) where socialist industrial policies had created dependence on a single economic activity, like mining and iron and steel production, many large SOEs were on the verge of liquidation. In some counties the unemployment rate had already increased to 15-20 per cent in 1991-1992, which was double the then national average.[590]

This situation became even more threatening after the introduction of the new Bankruptcy Law on 1 January 1992.[591] The previous regulation on bankruptcies was almost inoperable; creditors were not usually interested in starting the liquidation process because it was unlikely that they could get back their money. The most important amendment of the new law mandated filing of bankruptcy for firms over 90 days delinquent. Creditors and debtors have the legal possibility of reaching an agreement during both bankruptcy and liquidation proceedings. This option itself is a tool of restructuring as it may mean the partial

---

[585] The rare exceptions included the case of the Oxygen and Gas Works. This organization, comprising five functionally separate but vertically integrated plants, enjoyed a strong monopoly in the Hungarian market. As a competent expert said, "... nobody wanted to buy OGW piece by piece. On the other hand the assessed worth of Ft 2 billion for the whole organization could be raised to Ft 4.5 billion. The buyer paid for the market share". In the similar case of the Herbal Oil and Detergent Works, the interested multinational firm insisted on buying the entire organization even though five of its six factories were loss-makers.

[586] Law LIII, 1992.

[587] Law LIV, 1992.

[588] Privatization Strategy Task Team (1992).

[589] According to the published proposals, "credit notes" up to Ft 100,000 can be obtained by all citizens, without any personal investment or collateral, for the purpose of acquiring minority shares in enterprises. The loans can be repaid from the income of the company. These credit notes were introduced in the guidelines of asset management policy for 1994 under the name of Small Shareholders Programme.

[590] Laky (ed.) (1993).

[591] Law IL, 1991.

TABLE 5.4.7

Number of firms concerned by bankruptcy and liquidation proceedings, Hungary, 1992-1993

	1992	August 1993	Total
Bankruptcies			
Applications filed	4 231	866	5 099
Public announcements	2 500	741	4 305
Agreements	682	306	968
Liquidation			
Applications filed	10 062	5 572	15 634
Public announcements	2 227	1 795	4 022
Completions	562	798	1 360

Source: Lamberger (1993).

cancelling or rescheduling of debt, or swapping of debt for equity. Up to August 1993, some 5,000 bankruptcy and more than 15,000 liquidation requests were filed.[592] Due to the excessive workload of the judiciary, only some of these cases were actually started (some 4,000 each of bankruptcy and liquidation proceedings – table 5.4.7). About one quarter of the bankruptcy proceedings started resulted in agreements with creditors, including state-owned commercial banks and other state or central institutions (tax office, customs, social security). Thus, restructuring processes implemented via bankruptcy amounted partly to agreements within the business sector and partly to the direct or indirect involvement of the state.

However, the government was concerned (reasonably, as it turned out) that these steps might not be sufficient to manage large-scale crisis situations. According to the new approach, the government could not withdraw from its own property; in other words, ministries could not neglect operational problems. At the same time, the drafting of a comprehensive and detailed *industrial policy* was begun, proposing underwriting by the state, interest rate discounts, cancellation of debts and debt to equity swaps.

To sum up, the arguments supporting state-controlled restructuring and rescue of companies were rooted partly in a desire to accelerate the privatization process by the sale and redistribution of the assets, and partly in the crisis of large enterprises with its concentration in certain regions. The process of liquidation, involving several hundred large organizations and monopolies, threatened rising unemployment, further shrinkage of the domestic market, declining exports, growing imports, and dwindling tax revenues. In short, the argument for top-down restructuring was that one cannot close down the entire economy of a country overnight. Thus, the state began to take action in both the *organizational* and *financial* areas.

(b) Organizational restructuring

Crisis management of SOEs through the merger of autonomous firms was widely practised in the planned economies. Such measures were rare in Hungary in the 1980s, but reappeared in the early 1990s. The "integration" of coal mines and electrical power plants is one of the most widely-known examples, a merger motivated by the loss-making and threatened bankruptcy of the mines. The government intended to overcome the financial and market problems by vertical integration, submerging the supplier/customer relations and the resulting disagreements inside a single organization with direct control and transfer prices. In this situation the acquired firms have a chance to survive, even though they complain about the loss of their independence. Budgetary subsidies are replaced by the resources of the acquiring units, while the latter become the controlling shareholder.

The splitting-up of big SOEs into smaller units became more widespread after organizational decentralization was declared a priority in the revised privatization policy in 1992. From the company point of view, the traditional form of decentralization upon central initiative is perceived as a hostile administrative decision resulting in cuts in the company's capacity, market shares and negotiating powers against business partners or government bodies, without any compensation. This type of splitting-up had so far concerned mainly the food industry and retail trade, as in the "small privatization" of the grocery networks in Budapest and in northern and southern Hungary, and of the baking industry.

In the 1990s, a new type of organizational decentralization occurred in Hungary. This splitting-up typically involves the sale of property, factories or plants on the initiative (or at least with the approval) of the large SOEs and with the consent of the SPA. Revenue from these transactions is recycled to the remaining units to consolidate their financial position, mainly through the repayment of their debts. According to experts, most of the recent decentralization falls into this category. The result of this process is similar to the "asset depleting" which was a criticism of spontaneous privatization. It is an important difference, however, that this time the final decision is made by government bodies. Permission to sell units and the granting of the revenue to the SOEs constitutes a government favour to them, as the privatization income of the SPA is significantly reduced by these measures.[593]

(c) Financial restructuring

Government management of the financial crises of firms started in 1991 with some exceptional, individual decisions. The three early cases of great concern included coal mining as well as metallurgy in Ozd and Diósgyör. The fate of these firms indicates that the measures amounted to no more than "fire fighting". They were elicited by mass demonstrations, strikes and other trade union actions. While several billion forints were spent, these amounts could only offer provisional and marginal relief to the firms concerned.

The "Big Thirteen"

The institutionalization of government financial restructuring started with the special treatment of thirteen firms (the *"Big Thirteen"*). According to a government

---

[592] Lamberger (1993).

[593] There is no registration of the revenue recycled to the SOEs. However, one of the SPA directors estimated the amount of this "reorganization fund" to be equal to the official privatization income (about Ft 130 billion between 1990 and July 1993).

resolution these organizations were short-listed on the basis of the following criteria: that the operation of these companies "on a competitive basis is a national economic interest and the prevention of their liquidation is supported by industrial policy considerations", such as significant weight in exports, and in regional employment the safeguarding of certain professional cultures.[594] Within this broad definition, central assistance should go to organizations producing competitive products or being able to change markets, at least in the longer run. It was also argued that the state would not actually suffer any real loss, the repayment of debts being unlikely anyway.

The Ministry of Industry and Trade (MIT) initially studied possibilities for special treatment of forty organizations. This list was reduced, not according to competitive potential, but on the basis of indebtedness criteria. The government would help firms which were indebted directly to the state (not to suppliers or commercial banks). The total asset value of the thirteen selected firms was assessed at nearly Ft 150 billion and their total debts at Ft 56 billion, not including supplier credits in the range of another Ft 25-30 billion; their gross sales plan for 1992 was Ft 230 billion; and together they employed more than 80,000 people.

It should be noted here that most of the firms concerned, just like other large SOEs, no longer operated within a traditional framework: they had been dismantled into sets of companies in the process of spontaneous privatization or later on, with SPA approval, and some of their plants had been transformed into joint ventures (Dunaferr, Rába, Hungalu, Ikarus, Pannonglas). In most cases their properties and departments had been divested, spun-off, sold or transformed, and their staff reduced, often by several thousand.

According to the ministry,[595] the debts of seven companies were cancelled, rescheduled or swapped in the total amount of Ft 11.1 billion. For some members of the group, Ft 3.1 billion of new credit was underwritten by the state. From privatization incomes, Ft 4.3 billion was allocated to reorganization, and Ft 3.5 billion of custom duties and tax debts were cancelled. Nearly half of the total cost of more than Ft 22 billion was received by one firm, Dunaferr Co.

The methods applied typically did not directly increase current budgetary expenditure; they implied instead lost revenue and deferred burdens. From the point of view of the companies concerned, the preferential treatment meant an opportunity to solve acute liquidity problems. Nevertheless, even according to the MIT evaluation the programme achieved only partial success, measured by the number of rescued companies, by the amount of the assets, or by the employees concerned, as well as by the stability of the results.[596] In other words,

crisis management, again, was no more than "fire-fighting", even in the most successful cases; it brought some temporary financial relief, without any structural adjustment.

Crisis management, even in this limited sense, proved to be successful where the debts directly concerned the state. Commercial banks could be put under informal pressure for some time by either the government or the companies themselves. Leading state-owned commercial banks rarely initiated any liquidation process, while they kept rolling over the loans to key debtors, so that, for example, the credits of the "Big Thirteen" were not recorded as non-performing.[597] The "permissive" banking attitude, combined with the poor inherited portfolios allocated to the banks at the time of their creation in 1987, and the uncertainty and recession, which equally hindered credit rating and repayment, meant that the capital structure and the liquidity position of leading banks were steadily eroded.[598] This is why the process of *debt consolidation* was launched.

Debt consolidation

In 1992, the state targeted improvement of the annual balance sheets of banks by cleaning the portfolios and by swapping bad debts against government bonds.[599] The first round included a package of Ft 102 billion face value and Ft 80 billion swap. This in itself amounted to redistribution as the interest on government bonds would be paid from the state budget. Redistribution occurred not only in favour of the bank sector, but also between banks. The highest gains were achieved by those who had accumulated most bad debts without building up adequate reserves, as now they could get rid of their non-performing loans cheaply. It was clear when the decision on debt consolidation was made that, in the absence of further change, another substantial part of debt would slip down to the non-performing category by 1993.[600] It was also predictable that the net benefits to the banks would be much smaller, because of the consolidation fees to be paid by them and the low interest rate on the government bonds. By international auditing standards, no appreciable improvement was achieved in capital-adequacy ratios.

---

[594] Government Resolution No. 3298/1992. For a detailed history of the "Big Thirteen", see Karsai (1993).

[595] MIT (1993).

[596] "Crisis management was successful in the case of eight companies and the position of one firm was improved as a result of earlier measures" the ministry states (MIT 1993). Looking beyond the number of SOEs,

the outcome seems even worse: according to calculations based on MIT data, only one third of the assets and employees of the "Thirteen" was rescued.

[597] In 1992, the year of the big bankruptcy and liquidation wave, only about 80 proceedings were initiated by banks, representing less than 1 per cent of all cases.

[598] Moreover, the new laws on banking and accounting adopted in 1992 introduced much more rigorous international standards. This in itself worsened the positions of banks or, more precisely, brought to the surface the hidden problems.

[599] At the beginning, consolidation concerned banks majority-owned by the state. In the course of 1993, 11 banks were involved, including banks with mixed ownership.

[600] As a result of consolidation in 1992, the amount of bad debts decreased by Ft 100 billion, only to increase again by Ft 30 billion in the first half of 1993 while the total qualified debts grew by more than twice this amount.

For these reasons, it was clear to all involved that consolidation would not remain a one-time opportunity. The 1993 plans focused on raising the capital base of the banks. The position of the banks was improved by swapping bonds for higher coupon-rate bonds and by abolishing debt consolidation fees, although these measures worsened the position of the state budget. Moreover, the amount to be invested in order to achieve at least a temporarily acceptable capital-adequacy ratio was estimated at nearly Ft 80 billion.[601] Increasing the minimum capital requirement adds additional burdens to the budget, and it may also alter relative positions by eliminating existing differences in performance. This step also modifies the ownership structure by reducing the weight of non-state shareholders (mainly SOEs, but also foreigners) and considerably increasing the share of the state.

All these measures have still not changed the position of the indebted firms. In 1993 the notion of "debt consolidation" was split into two branches: a narrower "bank consolidation" and the new "debtor consolidation". One of the main issues of debate at the governmental level has concerned the question of what kind of organization should manage the consolidated enterprise debts, since the solution initiated in 1992 (the predominant role of a new state organization, the Hungarian Investment and Development Corporation) proved to be non-viable. Under recent proposals, firms having bad loans in the consolidated banks may apply for participation in debtor consolidation;[602] they have to prepare reorganization plans to be evaluated first by a special interdepartmental committee, and then by the lending bank itself.[603]

As a consequence of consolidation, an issue of government bonds to the amount of Ft 200 billion through the end of 1993 increased the state debt, and the interest increased current budgetary expenditure. In return, the balance sheets of the banks involved in consolidation temporarily improved. Beside this, the intricate financial manoeuvre resulted in *renationalization*, this time literally, unlike in the case of compulsory corporatization: in 1993 the share of the state in the banks was increased.[604] Thus, *the state is restoring its decision-making sovereignty over both banks and their debtors.* By assuaging the banks' lack of interest in the cancellation or rescheduling of debts, the government removes the obstacles which had impeded the financial restructuring of the "Big Thirteen". Through debt consolidation concerning several thousand firms, the bank consolidation process is gradually turning into a comprehensive reorganization programme involving a major part of the economy.

As is often the case, class approaches are a two-edged sword and this applies to restructuring. While the implementation of a standard system can put a term to the endless process of negotiations, at the same time it sends the message to all economic actors that government eventually will come to the rescue. In other words, class solutions, instead of solving the problem may lead to its extension.

Spread of top-down restructuring

The spread of top-down restructuring over time has already been discussed above. It was gradually realized in both the bank sector and business that the methods used in 1992 and 1993 could not achieve any long-term, "final" solution. The partial portfolio cleaning was insufficient for bank consolidation, while the mitigation of direct indebtedness to the state was insufficient for reorganizing the big SOEs.[605] The government has declared that 1993 would be the last year of consolidation; the parties concerned, however, consider this statement, not without good reason, more a wish than reality. Many analysts agree that this follows from the nature of the problem: namely, not one group of banks or firms, but the entire economy is in a crisis situation. Successful treatment would mean the creation of a healthy economy, but such a huge and dynamic problem cannot be addressed by partial and static tools.

Besides the time dimension, the spread of restructuring to ever wider groups of companies is also striking. The initial exceptional cases have been followed by class solutions. The special treatment of 13 firms led on to proposals to rescue 40 large companies, as originally envisaged by the Ministry of Industry and Trade. If such measures are taken in industry, why leave out food processing or the agricultural sector as a whole? Of course, the Ministry of Agriculture came up with a comprehensive programme of restructuring. If there is help for sectors, there must be help also for depressed regions: accordingly, in 1993 the government approved a detailed project to manage the crisis situation of two counties in northern Hungary.

It has been noted before that state support may also be expected by private firms. The agricultural sector was the first to make a public suggestion to allow private farmers to bid for consolidation of their debts if their debt to equity ratio was higher than 25 per cent. The proposing ministry was aware of creating a precedent for the conversion of private into state debt. Nevertheless, in late 1993 it seemed to be a generally accepted idea to extend the debtor consolidation process to private business,

---

[601] This capital-adequacy ratio was set at 4 per cent. To reach international standards would require an investment of Ft 140 billion.

[602] "Bad" debtors of "good" banks are excluded from this opportunity.

[603] According to preliminary estimates, debtor consolidation may concern about 30,000 loan agreements, most of which involve private companies and not state-owned ones. More than half (2,300 out of 4,000) of the loan agreements entered into the consolidation process in 1992 were executed by private firms. The amount of these credits has not been published. However, the series of failures of private businesses which were considered to be sound until quite recently explains the growing importance of this sector for the banks.

[604] According to the latest proposals, these extended ownership rights of the state will be exercised not only by the present shareholder of the banks (the State Holding Company), but also by the Ministry of Finance, because of budgetary investments. The ministry wants to control 75 per cent of voting shares until the end of 1995, the termination date of the debt consolidation agreements.

---

[605] It is not hard to predict that the passive treatment, concentrating on existing credit burdens, will soon turn out to be insufficient; like the banking sector, the enterprises will also need fresh capital to cover their losses and to modernize their production systems.

irrespective of the field of operations. The main argument in favour of this approach is that the private sector cannot be subject to discrimination. This argument, once put forward to support the promotion of private business in the period of the planned economy, is now used in favour of extending state subsidies, effectively promoting nationalization. From the point of view of the entrepreneurial strata concerned, accepting this principle means no less than entrepreneurship without risk, courtesy of the taxpayers. Bank experts already claim that the possibilities for cancelling or rescheduling debts have discouraged repayment even among solvent debtors.

Private firms, mainly well-known international investors, are pioneers in the search for protection. In addition to privileged competitive positions, benefits sought can involve capital raised by the state or access to preferential funds. Many joint ventures with foreign participation hire Hungarian managers with a professional background in large SOEs or in the former administration precisely for their widespread personal contacts and good skills in governmental bargaining. The volume of their investment, employment or exports are arguments used by the (foreign) private firm to exert pressure, at times accompanied by threats to substitute imports for domestic suppliers, or to the shut down production either temporarily or for good.

Most of the preferences requested and obtained, including the regulation of foreign trade, entail the rearrangement of company positions by the state. In the case of the involvement of joint ventures, while their products are marketable and the companies are not hopeless cases, the income earned on the markets available is apparently not enough for profitable operation. Taking advantage of their favourable negotiating positions, foreign entrepreneurs do not always bring a market-style business culture to the Hungarian economy. Instead, for quite understandable reasons, they take the path of least resistance, adapting themselves to the prevailing business culture of milking the state budget.

(vi) Some lessons from Hungarian restructuring policies

While in comparative studies Hungary is usually considered as a country committed to fast privatization by sale, without restructuring, a closer analysis of the last five years reveals that restructuring was started in several forms and on several levels.

Advantages and disadvantages of the bottom-up approach

In the late 1980s organizational and financial restructuring processes were typically initiated and implemented by the SOEs themselves. Restrictive monetary and fiscal policy and the deregulation and liberalization of foreign trade and prices had hardened the budget constraint of the large SOEs. Thus, the most important lesson of the "spontaneous privatization" period is that, at least in the short run and under a specific constellation of power, it is possible to harden the budget constraint by changing the economic environment, without any restructuring implemented by the state. In this period *the hardening of the budget constraint was not a product of, but the most important motivation for restructuring.* But bottom-up restructuring also required that firms had the legal possibility to carry out the process of their own volition. This capacity was provided by the growing decentralization of ownership rights in consequence of the earlier and concurrent economic reforms.

Bottom-up restructuring seems to have several advantages. It is not based on administrative measures but on negotiations within the business sector. Decisions are made at the enterprise level, where most information is available and where the motivations are most immediate. The message of this situation is particularly important in the period when the market system is emerging: firms can no longer count on state assistance but have to solve their problems by reaching agreements with their business partners (customers, suppliers or lenders). In other words, bottom-up restructuring is a key element in the separation of economic units from the state and in the new orientation towards horizontal and competitive relations. It also has the considerable benefit of not putting direct burdens on budgetary resources.

On the other hand, bottom-up restructuring has had the disadvantage of often producing quasi-solutions. The process of splitting-up enterprises into a group of companies did not eliminate state ownership, nor did it attract additional capital, new technology or markets. The new (but still state) owners, the holding companies and the commercial banks, did not turn into successful owners. Efficient and long-term systems of corporate governance were not established. Partly for this reason, achievements such as better liquidity or cost reduction have proved to be temporary, or insufficient to prevent a decline of production and growth of unemployment. It is also true that while not increasing budgetary expenditures, bottom-up restructuring has not added to state revenues or aided in the reduction of deficits.

Motivations for top-down restructuring

The above-mentioned problems were not yet acute, however, when the new government extended direct central control to corporatization and privatization decisions. Bottom-up restructuring was blocked, and in the absence of any restructuring steps – except for a few specific sectors and firms – by the central authorities, this has slowed down privatization. These factors have played a significant role in the fall of the value of state assets and in the sharpening of macroeconomic tensions.

Thus, ironically, the centralization of privatization decisions and all ownership rights has contributed to the growing demand for centrally controlled restructuring both on the side of the government and the SOEs. The introduction and widening of the top-down restructuring approach has been clearly supported by the pressure of enterprises, afflicted by the shrinking of markets, growing competition, old and new debts, and growing costs including high interest rates and taxes. On the other hand, the attitude of the government is also understandable. It cannot be explained simply by ideological reasons or by the influence of forthcoming elections, even if these considerations should not be neglected. There is also a factor of heavy pressure: the government cannot allow the liquidation of dozens of large SOEs, a new surge of unemployment or a dramatic drop in exports. The fiscal and monetary authorities find it more and more difficult to neglect the pressure of the firms, which already enjoy the support of the new asset management organizations (State Property Agency and State Holding Company). The sole option of the financial administration is to use more and more hidden forms of subsidies, as it cannot increase budgetary expenditure.

Top-down restructuring and redistribution

In the absence of privatization, financial intermediaries, or new and solid methods of state asset management, several features of top-down restructuring seem to be similar to the characteristics of redistribution in a centrally planned economy.

First, the specific microlevel decisions defining company positions are made by central authorities (parliament, government or interministerial committees). Sub-centres of redistribution also continue to exist. In this group, the role of branch ministries is being taken over by organizations representing the state as owner (SPA and SHC). These organizations have developed the old ministry attitude in the representation of company interests.

Second, as far as the methods and criteria of decision-making are concerned, the old approach of central selection, and negotiations with individual companies or groups of companies, continues to persist. Decision-makers try harder to consider the competitive potential of a business or a product. While such evaluations can now be based on safer grounds, taking into account the judgement of the global market, the key criteria continue to include the size of the company (volume of production, sales or employment) and its monopolistic position.

Third, at the beginning, preferences were given to state-owned enterprises (and commercial banks). Several large SOEs, however, were left to their own devices, while on the other hand the group of those who might apply for rescue was swollen by foreign investors and domestic private entrepreneurs. This obviously reflects the shift of bargaining potential and negotiating positions within the company sector.

Fourth, the tools of central restructuring include the traditional methods of changing the organizational structure and the financial position of firms. Direct budgetary subsidies are replaced, however, by new forms, characterized rather by loss of budgetary income, postponed expenses and increased state debts than by current budgetary expenditure.

Advantages and disadvantages of top-down restructuring

From the point of view of the government and the firms concerned, the benefits of centrally controlled restructuring or redistribution are obvious. The process offers companies the chance to survive, temporarily decelerates recession, and contains the decline of certain macroeconomic indicators.

Paradoxically, four years after the collapse of the planned economy system, the question which was formerly posed by reform economists arises again: what are the disadvantages of central redistribution?

The costs include the preservation of a non-competitive production structure, the predictable surge of the budgetary deficit and foreign debts, as well as growing inflationary pressure. Since the unfavourable effects on equilibrium can be delayed but not eliminated, a redistribution spiral may be unleashed. Such costs will be financed, *inter alia*, by growing taxes that undermine entrepreneurship, simultaneously increasing the need for subsidy and reducing the funds available for distribution.

A still higher price has to be paid for the short-term relief of top-down restructuring in terms of a distorted orientation of business organizations and of the economic mechanism as a whole. At the end of 1993, it was clear that private business had successfully managed to insert itself into the SOE queue for state support. Consequently, *privatization in itself does not eliminate the redistributive economy*. Companies, including private firms, try to obtain governmental preferences in order to overcome their market problems. This leads to laziness, and prolongs disequilibrium. Therefore top-down restructuring does not remove but, on the contrary, restores the soft budget constraint characteristic of the planned economy, with all its implications. This approach is also hostile to competition, because the entry of new actors is hindered by the advantages of others and by non-transparent rules and regulations. It works against the interests of consumers by limiting choices and by keeping prices and taxes high in order to cover the costs of redistribution.

Alternatives to top-down enterprise restructuring

The extension of state-controlled restructuring and redistribution has been the logical consequence of the centralization of privatization decisions and of all state ownership rights. This does not mean, however, that redistribution has developed into the single decisive feature of the economic mechanism, nor that it has become impossible to put an end to the process. The companies do need to be restructured, and the state (the government) does have to play a role in this process.

If the argument that centrally controlled restructuring has extremely undesirable economy-wide features in the long run is convincing, then an alternative solution should be found. The starting point could be the liberal concept which proposes that the primary function of the state is to establish a sound system of laws and regulations and transparent rules of the game. The state should not influence the business environment except by indirect means, and it is not a responsibility of the state to define directly the positions of different companies or groups on a microeconomic level. Therefore, it is not a reasonable approach, either from the business point of view or in respect of overall economic efficiency, to assign the task of restructuring of companies before privatization to a central apparatus which lacks information, concern or responsibility.

A better alternative is offered by the bottom-up approach based on the survival drive and active efforts of enterprise management. This is not a flawless approach either, but as a general rule it seems to be reasonable to leave restructuring to the new owners replacing the state. *This means that privatization is the best way of restructuring.* Of course this is not simply a matter of governmental decisions to accelerate privatization of large SOEs. Hungarian experience indicates, however, that that process can be promoted by the active involvement of managers (that is, by decentralization of privatization decisions), and by not giving the highest priority to the sales price.

In the cases where this method cannot be applied, the tasks of restructuring should be assigned to special organizations established for this purpose. It is essential, however, to set up these organizations not as governmental bodies spending public funds, but as at least partly privately-owned agencies or ventures, risking private capital. The state should support the creation of such financial intermediaries by providing the necessary legal background and finance, while resisting involvement in any direct decision-making or imposing on them political considerations. While there is no promise of any quick and painless solution, this alternative may be expected to involve more reasonable methods of selection and treatment, and will mitigate the risk of a new invigoration and dominance of central redistribution.

5.5 Enterprise transformation in Poland

Restructuring the economy has been a key objective of the transformation programme initiated in Poland on 1 January 1990. At that time the Polish economy was dominated by large and medium-sized state-owned enterprises (SOEs) which enjoyed monopolistic positions in the domestic market, and many of them were very inefficient and unable to compete in foreign markets. It was therefore clear that the success of the programme would depend to a large degree on the breaking up of the large SOEs and their transformation, as quickly as possible, into private firms.

The purpose of this section is to examine the results of the restructuring process during the last four years. In the first part, the objectives of the restructuring are discussed, as is the legal and institutional framework in which the programme was pursued. The role of large SOEs in the Polish economy before transformation programme is reviewed in section 5.5(i), while the various approaches to restructuring are examined in section 5.5(ii). The progress actually achieved is summarized in section 5.5(iii).

(i) Restructuring of large state-owned enterprises: The main approaches

(a) Definition of restructuring

The radical transformation programme elaborated by the new, Solidarity-led, government formed by Prime Minister T. Mazowiecki in September 1989 consisted of two distinctive parts, namely, stabilization and restructuring. However, unlike the stabilization programme, which was a comprehensive and detailed short-term strategy aiming at restoring macroeconomic equilibrium in the Polish economy, the restructuring policy was never elaborated beyond a bare outline. In fact, the restructuring strategy has never been precisely defined by government ministers. Deputy Prime Minister L. Balcerowicz, the author of the transformation programme, simply stated that restructuring would be mainly achieved through privatization coupled with foreign direct investment.[606] He emphasized, however, that the macroeconomic stabilization of the Polish economy, which was then in a state of serious disequilibrium, was a necessary and prior condition for any restructuring.

The privatization of state-owned enterprises is the key element of the economic transformation programme. Indeed, the notions of privatization and economic restructuring have been treated as virtually synonymous by Polish policy makers. The transfer of state assets to private ownership was expected to result in a substantial improvement in enterprise efficiency by providing better incentives to labour, management and capital. The rapid privatization of state assets therefore seemed to be the simplest and most efficient way to move from a centrally planned regime to a free market system. According to the then Minister of Industry and Commerce, "the best industrial policy is no policy". Consequently, there was no industrial or restructuring policy to accompany the privatization programme. However, the rapid growth of the unemployment rate forced a change in this "hands-off" approach.

A set of medium-term, strategic goals for the privatization policy was outlined by the government at the beginning of 1991. According to this new programme, half of all state-owned enterprises would be in private hands by the beginning of 1994 and 85 per cent by 1996. The 85 per cent threshold was seen by the authorities as bringing the scale of private ownership in Poland into line with the western market economies. Furthermore, the government also emphasized its intention to ensure that the privatization process would be transparent and conform to the requirements of social justice.

When elaborating the detailed operational programme, the government listed the objectives of privatization. These were social and political as well as economic, but in general they were not very different from those in other transition economies.[607] The primary goal of privatization was to create a market economy dominated by the private sector. The specific, broad objectives were as follows:[608]

- a shift from a centrally planned system to a competitive market system, with an efficient private sector;
- an improvement in the performance of enterprises through a more efficient use of labour, capital and management skills;
- the fostering of private initiative;
- a reduction in the size of the public sector and, consequently, of the burden on the public budget and administration;
- the generation of funds from the sales of state assets to finance the restructuring of potentially viable firms;
- a wider distribution of private wealth;
- the development and proliferation of entrepreneurial and managerial skills;
- the breaking up of existing monopolies;

---

[606] "Poland's Economic Programme", Outline, Warsaw, October 1989. Published in Polish in *Rzeczpospolita*, 12 October 1989. Mr. Balcerowicz was then Deputy Prime Minister and Minister of Finance.

[607] For a detailed description of the motives and objectives of privatization see United Nations Economic Commission for Europe (1992), pp.191-216, and "Review of the country presentations in the light of a cross-country analysis by the secretariat on the design, implementation and results of privatization programmes", Report by the UNCTAD Secretariat, TD/B/WG.3/7/Rev. 1, 22 September 1993, part I.A.

[608] "Summary of the Work Plan for the Privatization Programme", Government of Poland, Ministry of Ownership Transformation, Warsaw, 22 September 1990.

- a start to the conversion of Poland's external debt into the equity of privatized enterprises (debt equity swaps).

The number and detail of the various objectives set by the authorities have turned out to be a constraint on the speed of privatization and thus on the restructuring of the economy. As the process of restructuring and privatization got under way, there was an increasing need for greater clarity in the concept and objectives of restructuring.

The need for financial restructuring emerged in the wake of the rapid growth in the indebtedness of state enterprises and banks. The Law on the Financial Restructuring of State Enterprises and Banks, passed by the Polish Parliament in February 1993,[609] provides enterprises with easier access to new credit and for debt rescheduling, on condition that they undertake a restructuring programme and that their banks reschedule bad credits via access to additional financing from the special fund. The new regulation allows for a market in debt and for debt-equity swaps. Banks involved in the programme will be capitalized with long-term Treasury bonds. This will in part be covered from the unused fund set up in 1989 with the aim of stabilizing the Polish zloty. Furthermore, the obligatory 10 per cent "dividend" charged so far on the founding capital of the state enterprises can be replaced by a dividend paid out of net profit. If an enterprise allocates one third of its profits to investment, its remaining profits can be distributed in equal parts as dividends to shareholders and as allowances for employees.

Negotiations addressing the social and financial issues were initiated on a tripartite basis in the second half of 1992.[610] The so-called Enterprise Pact addresses the problems encountered by state enterprises prior to and during privatization.[611] The pact deals with three distinct areas, namely, privatization, financial issues and social affairs. Certain financial regulations were adopted by Parliament under the Law on Financial Restructuring mentioned above; others were delayed by the Parliament's dissolution in May 1993.

The Enterprise Pact includes provisions aimed at easing the financial consolidation of a state enterprise before its privatization. The Pact tries to encourage initiative on the part of an enterprise's employees and management by giving them the chance to submit their own privatization proposal within six months of Parliament approving the new regulation. If the proposal is not acceptable on legal or budgetary grounds, it can be returned for amendment. If no such proposal is submitted, the Minister of Privatization or the appropriate founding organ is then free to determine the best way to privatize the enterprise. Enterprises in a poor financial situation will have to include restructuring measures in their programme.

The Pact also changes the rules for the preferential acquisition of company shares. So far, the Privatization Law assures employees of 20 per cent of the total shares at half the emission price. Under the new arrangement, 10 per cent of shares would be distributed to employees free of charge and another 10 per cent reserved for them at the market price.

The right of Workers' Councils to designate one third of the members of the Supervisory Council at the moment of privatization will be maintained, and employees will in addition have the additional right to designate a delegate to the board of firms employing over 2,500 people. The preferences currently granted to employees in the case of employee buy-outs are to be strengthened and income tax deductions for Polish citizens acquiring stocks or shares of privatized companies are to be introduced. The new government can still amend these proposals, but it seems likely that the general guidelines will be largely maintained if not extended in order to encourage employee participation in the privatization process.

(b) The relationship between restructuring and privatization

As already mentioned above, the notions of privatization and restructuring have been used by the Polish authorities virtually as synonymous. None the less, restructuring is also used to refer to the need for improving the financial situation of individual enterprises, as a *precondition* for their privatization. Restructuring is also required for enterprises with complex organizational structures. Under central planning there was a tendency to integrate, mainly horizontally but sometimes also vertically, independent plants and enterprises, thereby creating large conglomerates. Since 1989, there has been a tendency to break up many of these artificial creations.

In many cases it is not possible to avoid the closing down of firms. This problem raises the question of the relationship between consolidation and privatization, and notably the sequence in which they should occur.[612] Unlike Germany, the authorities in Poland have advocated, in principle, the restructuring of potentially viable companies before attempting to privatize them. The Industrial Development Agency, a government body, was created to assist such a process of restructuring before privatization.

(c) Role of the state in promoting restructuring

Although privatization means the withdrawal of the state from those activities which can be best done in the private sector, the initiation and management of the process needs an intensive and long-lasting effort by the government. In the countries of eastern Europe the engagement of the state has been all the more necessary because of the general lack, at the starting point, of an adequate legal and institutional framework. In order to meet this challenge the Polish authorities enacted, in July

---

[609] The Law, effective as of 3 February 1993, is published in *Dziennik ustaw*, No.18/93, item 82.

[610] The parties were the government, represented by the Minister of Labour and Social Policy, employers, represented by the Confederation of Polish Employers, and 10 major trade unions.

[611] The Pact was signed by all parties on 22 February 1993. Legislative proposals based on the Pact have been already drafted and submitted to Parliament.

[612] This question is raised in United Nations Economic Commission for Europe, *Economic Survey of Europe in 1990-1991*, New York, 1991, chapter 4.3, p.26.

1990, the Privatization Law for State-Owned Enterprises and created, in August 1990, the Ministry of Privatization.[613] The former constitutes the basic legal framework defining techniques, procedures and requirements for privatizing state-owned enterprises. The latter is the main operational office responsible for privatization. However, numerous issues quickly arose in the practice of privatization which needed to be addressed through specific regulations. Thus, more than twenty different laws and regulations now govern the privatization process.

In addition to the legal framework of rules, techniques and procedures, the Polish Parliament sets out each year, together with the annual budget, guidelines for privatization in the coming year. This programme is elaborated and submitted to Parliament by the Council of Ministers and subsequently becomes the constitutional basis for action by the Ministry of Privatization.[614]

Institutional framework

The central institution responsible for privatization is the Ministry of Privatization, which has its headquarters in Warsaw and 13 regional offices covering 43 *voivodships* (another 6 *voivodships* deal directly with headquarters). The Ministry collaborates very closely with the "founding organs" (supervising bodies which are assigned as state representatives at the moment of the creation of an enterprise). The role of the founding organ is assigned to the relevant ministry, usually the Ministry of Industry and Commerce in the case of industrial firms or to local authorities for municipal enterprises. The Agency for State-Owned Agricultural Property, which in turn is supervised by the Ministry of Agriculture and Food Economy, participates intensively in the process of privatizing state farms. The Ministry of Finance is involved in the privatization of banks and insurance companies and the Ministry for Foreign Economic Relations in dealing with the privatization of foreign trade enterprises, which are mainly state-controlled limited liability companies and thus are not covered by the principal Law on Privatization of July 1990.

The scope of ministerial initiative in restructuring

The principal functions of the Ministry of Privatization (MP) consist of initiating, monitoring and supervising the process of privatization as well as endorsing initiatives taken at the microeconomic level. It also provides legal and operational assistance in the privatization of enterprises at the municipal and cooperative level. The Ministry, as the body representing the interests of the State Treasury, actively participates in the process of corporatization, which consists of transforming state-owned enterprises into joint stock or limited liability companies owned solely, at the first stage of privatization, by the State Treasury. The MP's Department for Property Rights Supervision is responsible for more than 500 Treasury-Owned corporations. Its tasks include monitoring of each company's financial and economic situation and implementation of the necessary steps to final privatization.[615]

Training and education activities are also important functions of the MP. It organizes training for candidates to the Board of Directors of privatizing firms and for other people who are engaged in privatization operations, either in bodies collaborating directly with the Ministry or, like consulting firms, operating independently.

The MP is supported in its work by a number of specialized institutions, such as the Agency for Industrial Development, the Agency of State-Owned Agricultural Property, the Agricultural Fund for Restructuring and Debt Rescheduling, and so on. The important tasks of making preprivatization analyses and assisting firms in choosing the best route to privatization have been undertaken by consulting firms, foreign and domestic. The establishment of additional specialized bodies has been under discussion in recent months: among those most frequently envisaged are an Agency for the Development of Small and Medium-Sized Firms, a Credit Insurance Fund, an Agency for Technology Transfer and, currently being set up, National Investment Funds.

Role of the government in "pioneer" privatization

The MP wanted to acquire, as quickly as possible, practical experience of privatization and thus be able to transmit it to all the potential candidates. With this learning process in mind, seven firms were selected for the first wave of privatization through an initial public offering of shares. The process of analysis, auditing and valuation started in August 1990, with the assistance of foreign consulting firms to ensure that everything was done in accordance with international standards and requirements.[616] Two out of the seven selected firms were excluded from the first wave of privatization after the preliminary analysis of their economic and financial situation.[617] The shares of the remaining five companies were publicly offered for sale on 30 November 1990.[618]

---

[613] The literal translation of the Ministry's name is the Ministry for Ownership Transformation. The Law setting up this Ministry was published in *Dziennik ustaw*, No.51, 13 July 1990, item 299.

[614] Three such documents have been enacted so far by the Parliament: Programme of action for 1991, 23 February 1991, *Monitor Polski*, No.13/91; Programme of action for 1992, 5 June 1992, *Monitor Polski*, No.12/92 and Programme of action for 1993, 12 February 1993, *Monitor Polski*, No.9/93. The fourth document setting out guidelines for 1994 was submitted to Parliament at the end of 1993.

[615] The Department, in collaboration with the Central Statistical Office, issues a quarterly survey of financial and economic developments in all the corporations for which it is responsible.

[616] The participation of foreign consulting firms was partly financed from external sources. For example, the participation of British firms (Coopers & Lybrand, Deloitte, Barclays de Zoete Wedd, Baker McKenzie and Central European Trust) was co-financed by the British Government Know-How Fund.

[617] The rolling mill "Norblin" in Warsaw was finally sold a few months later through public invitation to tender and the meat processing factory, "Inowroclaw", was transformed into a limited liability company and then sold to 320 (of the total 350) employees through a leveraged buy-out. In the latter case, the employees offered 20 per cent of the firm's value in cash and obtained a five-year credit at a preferential interest rate.

[618] The companies were "Exbud", "Kable", "Krosno", "Prochnik" and "Tonsil".

There was an aggressive publicity campaign and the 4.33 million shares offered for 300 billion zlotys were over-subscribed by between 7 to 20 per cent (over 130,000 individual buyers applied for shares in the five companies).

The first privatizations were thus successful in terms of effective property rights transformation, but the process was technically difficult, time-consuming and expensive.[619] Given this experience of privatization through corporatization and public offering, the MP looked for more rapid ways of privatizing a wider range of firms. To that end the ministry launched the idea of mass-privatization, involving several hundred large and medium-sized enterprises.

To summarize, the state played an important role in establishing the legislative and an institutional framework for initiating the privatization process in Poland. It has also set operational guidelines and supervised the entire process in order to ensure that public interests are respected. Given the objectives of the initial programme and the slow progress in carrying it out, the government was driven to seek more efficient and speedy methods of privatization.

(d) The role of employees: Incentives and rights

Despite the very wide terms of reference of the MP and its omnipresence in the privatization process, plenty of room for initiative has been given to the workers and management of SOEs. In fact, the Law on Privatization of State-Owned Enterprises stipulates that a state enterprise may be privatized at the initiative of its own management and workers' council (see below).

The Law on Privatization also grants employees substantial rights in the process of property rights transformation. They are empowered to express their opinion and views via the workers' council or the general assembly of all employees (or, in the case of large firms, the general assembly of delegates). The employees together with the managing director may choose between corporatization or liquidation. In the case of corporatization, the appropriate request to the Minister of Privatization may be submitted by either: (a) the managing director together with the workers' council, provided that there is prior consultation with the general assembly of employees/delegates and the founding organ; or (b) the founding organ, provided that both the managing director and the workers' council have given their consent and that the general assembly of employees/delegates has expressed its opinion on the matter (the opinion does not necessarily have to be affirmative). In exceptional situations the decision to transform a SOE into a private company may be taken without the consent of the employees or the managing director.[620]

When the MP initiated the first mass-privatization, it selected, according to its own criteria, about 600 SOEs to participate in the exercise, but after a few months less than 200 firms had accepted to be included. Firms unwilling to take part applied for exclusion, arguing that they envisaged an alternative way to privatization.

In the alternative approach to privatization, i.e., through liquidation, according to Article 37 of the Privatization Law, the founding organ is empowered to make such a decision with the prior consent of the Minister of Privatization. The founding organ may proceed in this way on its own initiative or at the request of the workers' council. When the founding organ proceeds with its initiative, the workers' council and managing director have the right to appeal. Particular requirements apply in the case of liquidation with the intention of leasing the assets against cash payment.[621] Bearing in mind that this latter method of privatization has been the most frequent in Poland so far, the formal requirements defined in the Privatization Law do not appear to be too restrictive.

Employees of transformed firms also have the right to participate in choosing strategic investors interested in buying shares in their company[622] and, by virtue of Article 9 of the Privatization Law, the right to become employees of the new company. Finally, employees of the company are entitled to designate one third of the members of the board of directors.

A number of incentives have been introduced to stimulate "grass-roots" initiatives for privatization. These consist of two tax charges imposed only on state enterprises. The first is a punitive tax on wage increases above an administratively established ceiling, the so-called *popiwek*. The second is a tax imposed on the initial stock of fixed assets, the so-called *dividenda*, which is paid out of profits and thus diminishes the capacity to invest. The only way to escape these two fiscal charges is to transform the state firm into a private one. Surveys show that these negative incentives have in most cases been the dominant reason for seeking privatization.

There is also a positive incentive to privatize in Article 24 of the Privatization Law which, as already noted,

---

[619] Privatization of the first five firms cost $5.7 million, i.e., about 17 per cent of their estimated value.

[620] In such a case, Article 6 of the Law stipulates that only the Prime Minister is empowered to take such a decision, at the request of the Minister of Privatization, and only after obtaining the opinion of the managing director, the workers' council and the founding organ. If no opinion is expressed within a month, it is assumed that there are no objections to the decision to corporatize. So far, there has been no case of a state enterprise being corporatized, under Article 6, against the opinion of the workers' council.

[621] The general assembly of employees/delegates must give its consent and the majority of employees of the enterprise shall agree to join the staff of the new company leasing all or part of the assets of the firm under liquidation. Apart from this, the Privatization Law requires only that physical persons create a new company (who do not necessarily have to come only from the liquidated company) and, what is in practice more difficult to meet, that the minimum initial capital of the new company be equal to 20 per cent of the joint value of the founding fund and the value of the liquidated enterprise.

[622] A recent example of the exercise of such rights is provided by the confectionery plant "Goplana" of Poznan, in which two foreign investors — the British E.D. & Man and the Swiss-based "Nestlé" — competed to buy a strategic stake of shares. After several months of negotiation, the workers' council and the Managing Director opted for the Swiss partner because its offer was better, not only in cash terms but also in terms of guarantees for job security and improvements in salaries. For details of the offers see *BOSS – Rolnictwo*, 20 September 1993 and 29 October 1993, p.5.

gives employees the right to acquire, at half their emission price, up to 20 per cent of the shares of a company owned solely by the State Treasury. Initially, this incentive seems to have had little impact, but after the Warsaw Stock Exchange boom of 1993, it is likely to have a more positive influence on employees' attitudes toward privatization.

(e) First approaches

The first version of the Polish privatization law (autumn 1989) envisaged the transformation of all state-owned enterprises into joint-stock companies with all shares owned initially by the State Treasury; a public offering would follow, with a certain proportion being reserved for employees.[623] In the final version of the Law, approved by the Parliament in July 1990, the government, sensitive to political pressures and real constraints, diversified the methods of privatization.

The main provisions of the Law stipulate that SOEs can be privatized, on the initiative of their own management and workers' council, through either of two available tracks. The first, under Article 5 of the Privatization Law, consists of converting a SOE into a joint-stock or limited liability company, owned by the State Treasury, whose shares or stocks should be disposed of within two years.[624] The disposal of shares may occur through an initial public offering, straight auctions, an invitation to tender, or a combination of all three. The alternative track, under Article 37, provides for the liquidation of a SOE on the initiative of its workers' council and management and following approval by the Ministry of Privatization. This Article allows three methods, which may be used alone or in combination, for privatizing all or part of a SOE: assets may be sold, used as a contribution to a new company, or leased for a fixed period.

Where an enterprise can be sold in its entirety, and provided that the legal ownership of land and other fixed assets has been settled, a "fast track" privatization can be implemented. In this case there is a simplified liquidation procedure by which the value of assets is based on their book value and an estimate of annual profits. This method, launched in 1993, is open only to Polish investors in the first round of invitations to tender. If no buyer appears, in the second round foreign investors are allowed to participate on the same terms as Polish citizens.

For an enterprise in a poor financial situation a third track, allowed under Article 19 of the Law on SOEs of 25 September 1981 (with further amendments), is bankruptcy, the sale of assets, and the liquidation of the firm.

The choice of which privatization path to adopt depends on a number of factors including:
- the size of the SOE in terms of annual sales, number of workers and the degree of competition in the domestic market;
- current and foreseeable financial performance;
- the SOE's managerial structure;
- "grass roots" initiatives by local or foreign investors;
- the relationship between the SOE's management, workers' council and trade unions.

Transformation through corporatization is the preferred method for large and medium-sized firms in a good financial situation. In these cases the Ministry of Privatization tries to find strategic investors, preferably foreign, who will be interested in acquiring a strategic stake of shares and investing in the company with the aim of expansion.

The leasing of a liquidated enterprise is generally recommended for smaller firms, and so far, has proven to be the most popular method of privatization. The assets of a wound-up enterprise are typically leased to its employees, subject to their contributing share capital worth at least 20 per cent of the value of the liquidated SOE. The annual leasing fee is calculated on the basis of the value of the assets plus an interest rate equivalent to 75 per cent of the current refinancing rate of the National Bank of Poland, the upper limit being set at 30 per cent per annum. Purchase of the leased assets is possible at the end of the lease. Asset valuation has initially been based on discounted cash flow. However, it has been found that managers, interested in buying the enterprise, have deliberately reduced cash flows in order to depress asset values.

At the start of its operational activity the Ministry of Privatization tried to privatize the SOEs one by one, but the slow rate of progress forced it to seek a more rapid and efficient approach.

Mass privatization

The discussion of a mass-privatization programme started in the first half of 1991, but only after long governmental and parliamentary debates was the Mass-Privatization Programme (MPP) approved on 30 April 1993.[625] The MPP allows for the rapid privatization of several hundred large and medium-sized enterprises of relatively good financial standing. SOEs selected for the programme will be converted into joint-stock companies and their shares transferred to national investment funds (NIFs). The NIFs shall hire experienced management firms which will be responsible for the development of the companies (and for raising the inflow of foreign management skills and capital into Poland). There are expected to be about 20 funds, each of which will manage around 30 state firms. All normal types of business transaction – including management contracts, commercial arrangements, and investments in the company's shares (including large shareholdings of over 50 per cent) – will be allowed. It will be possible for any investor to acquire shares in any of the investment funds, which will be listed on the Warsaw Stock Exchange. Under the mass-privatization programme each company will initially have the same shareholding structure: 33 per cent will be held by a lead NIF; 27 per cent will be distributed equally to all other NIFs; 25 per cent will be retained by the State

---

[623] Grosfeld and Hare (1991), pp.141-142.

[624] According to information from the Ministry of Privatization, the time limit will be abolished under a new law which has been discussed recently.

[625] See the Law on National Investment Funds, published in *Dziennik ustaw*, No.44/1993, item 202.

Treasury; and 15 per cent will be distributed, free of charge, to employees.

According to the latest information, over 30 applications have been received from foreign-led consortia to manage NIFs. The applicants are now before a selection committee, which is expected to complete its work some time in the first quarter of 1994. The selection committee has also to choose some 120 fund supervisory board members from around 3,000 applicants.

So far the Ministry of Privatization has identified 367 state enterprises which are to be included in the scheme. Share certificates are expected to be distributed sometime in the summer of 1994 and the NIFs will be listed on the Warsaw Stock Exchange in the summer of 1995.[626]

Sectoral approach to privatization

In order to speed up the privatization and restructuring of specific sectors of the economy, a sectoral approach has also been launched. To some extent, this is a response to the specificity of particular activities. The approach will apply to a number of *industrial branches*, as well as sectors such as *agriculture*, *banking* and *foreign trade*. The MP is currently conducting 14 sector studies across a wide range of activities (from ball bearings to breweries and from construction to confectionery).

Studies of particular *industrial sectors* have been carried out by the Ministry of privatization since mid-1991 in order to help in the choice of the best privatization strategy and to develop a more effective policy towards foreign capital.

There are essentially two steps to the sectoral approach. Following the Ministry of Privatization's notification to firms in a sector that they should prepare for privatization, a consultancy or advisory firm, selected by competitive tender, prepares a domestic and international analysis of the sector, and of each company in it. At the same time, the advisers contact all potential investors in the sector to gauge their interest and requirements, and to solicit their ideas about developing the sector and making it profitable. Finally the adviser prepares a strategy for the sector and a plan of action for privatization and/or restructuring of its enterprises.

In *agriculture*, the privatization of state farms was, in principle, excluded from the competency of the Ministry of Privatization. Given the specificity of the sector, the Law on Privatization of State Agricultural Farms was enacted by the Parliament on 19 October 1991 and the Agency for State-Owned Agricultural Property was established to deal with the issue. The Agency, which became operational in 1992, was assigned the task of appropriating and privatizing over 2,000 large state farms (comprising 3.7 million hectares) and some 8 million hectares administered by the State Fund of Land. One of the major problems the Agency is facing is the dramatic indebtedness of state farms, their total debt being estimated at close to $1 billion. Debt rescheduling or forgiveness is thus a precondition for privatization, but the main barrier to dealing with this is a shortage of available financing.

In the *banking sector*, the government's long-term privatization programme includes nine state-owned commercial banks which were split from the National Bank of Poland in 1989. In 1993 two of them were privatized. The first, *Wielkopolski Bank Kredytowy* (WBK) in Poznan, was successfully privatized through its transformation into a joint-stock company and a subsequent public offering of shares. The WBK has been quoted on the Warsaw Stock Exchange since June 1993. The same procedure was repeated a few months later with *Bank Slaski* in Katowice: there was a public offering of shares in November-December 1993 and their price rose by 13.5 times when they were first traded on the Warsaw Stock Exchange on 25 January 1994. The privatization programme also includes the imminent sale of the Krakow-based *Bank Przemyslowo-Handlowy*.[627]

Other approaches

With a view to accelerating the transformation of state-owned enterprises, the Ministry of Privatization has developed a programme called "Privatization through restructuring". This approach is aimed at small and medium-sized firms where preliminary restructuring is likely to make them economically viable prior to privatization.

In principle, a management group (MG) is invited to manage, restructure and then privatize a company participating in the programme. In return, the MG receives a management fee, a share of annual profits and a commission on the transfer of the shares to private investors. The company is considered to be privatized when at least 51 per cent of its shares has been transferred to private hands. The management contract is for two years, or less if the transfer of 51 per cent of shares to private investors can be achieved earlier. The contract can be extended but not for more than two years.

(ii) The starting point and first results

(a) The role of the enterprise in the planned economy

Under the centrally planned regimes, an enterprise was a receiver of decisions made by ministries or by the Central Committee of the ruling communist party. In turn, the enterprise provided the centre with information about its productive capacity and its material needs. In these conditions, financial and economic indicators such as prices and profits had little relevance for the situation of state enterprise. There was no risk of bankruptcy and the management had no incentive to improve the financial position of the enterprise. If an enterprise went into deficit,

---

[626] The government is being advised on the scheme by SG Warburg, and the British Government Know-How Fund is co-financing the project.

[627] Another large bank previously state-controlled, the Bank for Export Development (*Bank Rozwoju Eksportu* – BRE), was privatized in 1992 and has been quoted on the Warsaw Stock Exchange since October 1992. BRE, however, had been created at the end of the 1980s as a joint-stock company controlled by the State Treasury and two other Ministries. Its final privatization was similar to that of the two banks mentioned above, except that being already a joint-stock company it was privatized under the provisions of the Commercial Code rather than the Privatization Law.

additional financial resources were easily forthcoming. Price or income equalization schemes were widespread, both for domestic and foreign transactions. Transactions which produced above-average profits were taxed at discretionary rates, those that produced losses were given subsidies. Thus there was no incentive to reduce costs or increase profits.

Under central planning, enterprises tended to be organized in a highly concentrated fashion. This was desirable for management, workers, and for the central administration. The bigger and stronger an enterprise was, the easier it was to negotiate with the central authorities on subsidies and other discretionary benefits. Big conglomerates were preferred by the central planners because they were considerably easier to deal with than a myriad of small firms. For these reasons enterprises tended to be merged into large, horizontally-integrated conglomerates, often including large social sections with no direct link to the main productive activity. The Polish economy consisted of about 8,000 large and medium-sized enterprises.

A process of deconcentration has been underway since 1989 (see table 5.5.1). In 1980 large SOEs employing more than 1,000 people represented 21 per cent of the total number of firms in the industrial sector and accounted for 71 per cent of industrial employment. Small enterprises, employing up to 200 workers, represented one quarter of all enterprises, but only 3.9 per cent of employment. By 1989 the share of large SOEs in the total number of firms had dropped to 17 per cent, and to 9 per cent by 1992. Their share of industrial employment declined respectively to 65 per cent and 55 per cent. At the same time, small SOEs increased to 41 and 58 per cent respectively of the total of industrial firms. In terms of their share of total industrial employment and output, the development was less spectacular. About one third of the total number of SOEs were active in industry in 1990 (table 5.5.2).

The growth of private enterprise by sector is given in tables 5.5.3 and 5.5.4. The growth of private firms has been rapid in all sectors of the Polish economy. Their number increased from 16,600 in March 1990 to 64,700 in September 1993. The largest number, 35 per cent of the total in September 1993, were operating in trade. There was similarly rapid growth for small private firms employing up to five people. Their number increased from 814,000 in December 1989 to 1.683 million in June 1993, 39 per cent of them operating in trade services.

The process of de-monopolization was initiated in 1989-1990 with the break-up of big SOEs. According to data from the Ministry of Industry, between 1989 and mid-1991, 106 conglomerates were broken up.[628] As a result, about 600 new enterprises were created. These data refer only to the process underway at the national level. A similar process was also initiated at the regional level where founding organs (voivodship administrations) were engaged in the process of demonopolization of enterprises under their responsibility.

TABLE 5.5.1

Structure of employment in state-owned industry, Poland, 1980-1992
(Percentages)

	1980	1989	1990	1992
Proportion of enterprises employing				
up to 200 workers	25.8	40.7	45.1	57.9
200 to 1,000	53.0	42.6	40.8	33.2
more than 1,000	21.2	16.7	14.1	8.9
Employment distribution in SOEs				
up to 200 workers	3.9	6.0	7.3	12.5
200 to 1,000	25.0	28.7	30.5	33.0
more than 1,000	71.1	65.3	62.2	54.5
Output distribution in SOEs				
up to 200 workers	..	4.7	7.9 [a]	8.2
200 to 1,000	..	30.0	31.4 [a]	33.0
more than 1,000	..	65.3	60.7 [a]	58.8

Sources: GUS, *Rocznik Statystyczny 1993*, Warsaw, table 11 (400), p.292 and previous issues.

[a] 1991.

As a result of the deconcentration process, the total number of SOEs continued to grow until mid-1991 (see table 5.5.2), since when it has been falling. At the end of September 1993 the number was nearly 30 per cent below its peak in mid-1991. The same basic tendency occurred in all state-owned sectors. However, the disappearance of SOEs from the official statistics is a bit misleading since it does not mean that those enterprises have been privatized. An enterprise is automatically deleted from the SOE register at the moment of either: (1) its transformation into a State Treasury-Owned company, or (2) its liquidation with the aim of eventual privatization or bankruptcy. Neither of these cases immediately entails the fact of privatization.

(b) Increasing role of the private sector

Despite slower than expected progress, the share of the private sector in Poland's economy has been growing steadily. This is apparent, in varying degrees, at all levels of economic activity. The share of the private sector in GDP, in current prices, increased from 29 per cent in 1989 to 47 per cent in 1992 and, most likely, passed the 50 per cent level in 1993 (see table 5.5.5). This growth is exclusively due to private activity in the non-agricultural sectors, where the share of private enterprise has risen from 19 per cent of GDP in 1989 to 42 per cent in 1992. At the same time, the share of the private agricultural sector, as a result of its general weakness and perhaps partly because of the rapid price and trade liberalization in 1990, has declined from 10 per cent to 5.5 per cent of GDP.

In terms of employment, the share of the private sector has risen from 44 per cent of the total in 1989 to 55 per cent in 1992. This relatively high figure is influenced by the still very high share of employment in private agriculture, a share which even increased between 1989 and 1992. The paradoxical trends in private agriculture, where the relative drop in sectoral output is coupled with increasing employment, reflects the high rate of unemployment in the economy as a whole, which has led to people returning from urban industrial centres to the countryside.

---

[628] "Zmiany w poziomie koncentracji produkcji przemyslowej w latach 1989-1990", *Studia i Analizy Statystyczne*, GUS, Warsaw, 1991.

TABLE 5.5.2

State firms in Poland, by sector, 1990-1993
(Number, end of period)

Period	State enterprises				State cooperatives controlled by	
	Total	Industry	Construction	Agriculture	State Treasury	State legal persons
1990						
March	7 647	2 604	1 555	1 433	227	..
June	7 908	2 731	1 574	1 474	232	..
September	8 345	2 830	1 590	1 509	237	..
December	8 453	2 860	1 595	1 543	248	1 135
1991						
March	8 578	2 890	1 580	1 588	282	..
June	8 591	3 000	1 512	1 686	283	..
September	8 419	3 061	1 430	1 750	308	..
December	8 228	3 009	1 367	1 833	376	909
1992						
March	8 273	2 905	1 293	2 018	504	..
June	8 180	2 805	1 266	2 097	650	803
September	7 773	2 770	1 216	1 823	732	826
December	7 245	2 739	1 164	1 516	764	794
1993						
March	6 838	2 718	1 126	1 193	792	784
June	6 327	2 617	1 075	951	842	799
September	6 118	2 550	1 046	868	902	821
December	5 924	2 495	1 016	806	958	830

Source: GUS, *Biuletyn Statystyczny*, Warsaw, various issues.

TABLE 5.5.3

Private firms in Poland, by sector, 1990-1993
(Number, end of period)

Period	Private companies				Joint ventures
	Total	Industry	Construction	Trade	
1990					
March	16 589	4 082	3 455	2 809	681
June	21 542	5 160	4 195	4 380	926
September	26 275	5 914	4 779	6 636	1 306
December	29 650	6 416	5 171	8 326	1 645
1991					
March	34 642	7 168	6 053	10 448	2 290
June	38 516	7 698	7 164	12 598	2 840
September	41 450	8 103	8 007	14 363	3 512
December	47 690	9 182	9 122	16 377	4 796
1992					
March	48 404	9 236	9 356	17 206	6 187
June	54 267	10 387	10 344	18 726	7 648
September	56 706	10 855	10 790	19 609	8 860
December	58 218	11 172	11 098	20 359	10 131
1993					
March	61 437	11 787	11 543	21 340	11 473
June	63 498	12 221	11 921	22 060	12 804
September	64 656	12 524	12 146	22 546	13 801
December	66 457	12 914	12 413	23 155	15 053

Source: GUS, *Biuletyn Statystyczny*, Warsaw, various issues.

TABLE 5.5.4

Private firms employing no more than five people, by sector, Poland, 1989-1993
(Thousands, end of period)

Period	Total	Industry	Construction	Trade	Services and other activities	Employees
1989	813.4	..	..	..	..	1 475.5
1990	1 135.5	334.6	165.5	346.3	289.1	1 915.5
1991						
June	1 272.4	339.3	165.4	456.8	310.9	2 338.6
December	1 420.0	348.9	171.7	550.3	349.1	2 591.1
1992						
June	1 523.4	344.2	183.8	572.1	423.3	2 800.4
December	1 630.6	347.2	187.8	626.1	469.5	2 600.0
1993						
June	1 689.1	340.6	191.1	661.1	496.3	2 664.3
December	1 783.9	345.2	195.9	708.6	534.2	..

Source: GUS, *Biuletyn Statystyczny*, Warsaw, various issues.

TABLE 5.5.5

Share of the private sector in the Polish economy, 1989-1993
(Percentages)

Variable	1989	1990	1991	1992	1993
GDP *(current prices)*	28.6	30.9	42.1	47.2	..
of which:					
Non-agricultural sector	19.0	25.0	36.9	41.7	..
Agriculture	9.6	5.9	5.2	5.5	..
Employment *(annual average)*	44.3	45.8	51.1	54.6	59.9 [a]
of which:					
Non-agricultural sector	21.7	22.6	26.7	29.8	..
Agriculture	22.6	23.2	24.4	24.8	..
Fixed assets [b]	33.7	34.7	35.2	36.8	..
of which:					
Non-agricultural sector	16.6	17.1	17.8	19.9	..
Agriculture	17.1	17.6	17.4	16.9	..
Investment *(current prices)*	35.3	41.3	40.8	44.0	..
of which:					
Non-agricultural sector	27.7	33.3	36.7	40.2	..
Agriculture	7.6	8.0	4.1	3.8	..

Sources: GUS, *Rocznik Statystyczny 1993*, Warsaw, table 1, p.XLIV, Central Statistical Office, *Information on the Social and Economic Situation in Poland I-IX 1993*, Warsaw, December 1993, pp.22-23.

[a] September 1993.
[b] Book value in current prices, at end of year.

The share of the private sector in total investment has been relatively less dynamic, with an increase from 35 per cent to 44 per cent between 1989 and 1993. The aggregate change, however, conceals a sharp decline of investment in agriculture and a faster than average rise in non-agricultural sectors. The latter should also be seen against the background of a continuing shortage in the availability of credit combined with discouraging credit terms.

The private sector's share in global fixed assets has also risen slowly, but this reflects two important factors in the private sector development. The first, is the tendency of the private sector to engage in relatively labour-intensive activities and the second, presumably, the tendency for a more efficient use of fixed assets in the private than in the public sector.

The share of the private sector in output and employment still varies significantly between different branches of the economy. This reflects a number of factors including the structures inherited from the previous regime and the ease with which privatization has been able to proceed in different activities. Thus, in agriculture and retail trade private activity was already dominant at the start of the transition process. Private concerns have expanded rapidly in the construction sector, but in industry, as noted already, the concentrated structures inherited from central planning have presented important, although not insuperable, obstacles to privatization (table 5.5.6).

The emerging private sector was already playing an important positive role during the recession which followed the start of the transformation of the Polish economy. In 1990, output collapsed in all areas of public and private activity, but since 1991 the private sector has grown rapidly while public sector output has continued to fall (table 5.5.7). However, it is not yet possible to determine the relative importance of privatization in the recovery of the private sector: the expansion of existing and of newly-created private businesses has also played a role. At the same time, private sector activity assumed a rapidly growing role in the foreign trade activities of the Polish economy (table 5.5.8).

(c) The financial performance of restructured enterprises

A major goal of the privatization programme is to achieve a more efficient allocation and utilization of resources. It is therefore to be expected that private firms should show a better financial performance than public ones. However, the relevant data are still too poor and the period for which they are available too short to allow for anything more than tentative conclusions in this respect.

TABLE 5.5.6

Share of private enterprises in output [a] and employment, by sector, Poland, 1989-1993
(Percentages, end of period)

	1989	1990	1991	1992	1993
Industry					
Output	16.2	18.3	24.6	30.8	37.4
Employment	29.1	31.2	35.8	40.9	46.9
Construction					
Output	33.0	41.8	62.6	78.7	85.8
Employment	37.4	42.1	59.5	71.8	80.9
Transport					
Services rendered	11.5	14.2	25.2	39.3	44.3
Employment	14.3	15.2	26.0	23.1	28.5
Trade					
Retail sales	59.3	63.7	82.8	90.0	87.8
Employment	72.7	82.2	88.3	90.5	92.5

Sources: GUS, *Rocznik Statystyczny 1993*, Warsaw, various pages; and Central Statistical Office, *Information on the Social and Economic Situation in Poland I-IX 1993*, Warsaw, December 1993, pp.22-23.

[a] In current prices.

TABLE 5.5.7

Output changes in state and private enterprises, by sector, Poland, 1990-1993 [a]
(Percentages, end of period)

	1990	1991	1992	1993
Industrial output				
Total	-24.2	-11.9	3.9	6.2
State sector	-23.7	-19.4	-3.3	-6.5
Private sector	-27.2	25.2	23.4	34.7
Construction				
Total	-17.9	8.9	8.0	8.6
State sector	-17.9	-30.0	-38.5	-30.4
Private sector	-18.7	63.2	35.0	19.5
Transport				
Total	-14.2	-14.1	-.3.3	-3.8
State sector	-12.9	-23.0	-16.9	-15.9
Private sector	-20.9	34.5	39.1	18.9
Trade				
Total	-9.3	7.7	8.3	..
State sector	-21.7	-49.2	-37.2	..
Private sector	-1.1	38.4	17.4	..

Sources: GUS, *Rocznik Statystyczny 1992*, Warsaw, various pages, and Central Statistical Office, *Information on the Social and Economic Situation in Poland 1993*, Warsaw, December 1993, pp.81, 88 and 92.

[a] At constant prices.

One approach is to compare changes in profitability in the private and public sectors between 1991 and 1993. As shown in table 5.5.9, the gross profitability ratio – defined as the ratio of gross profit (before tax) to costs – has been much lower in the private than in the state sector, a difference which holds for most branches of the economy. Construction and transport services were the only exceptions in 1992. These data raise a number of issues.

TABLE 5.5.8

Private sector share in exports and imports, [a] Poland, 1990-1992
(Percentages)

	1990	1991	1992
Exports	4.9	21.9	38.4
of which to:			
EC	5.8	27.8	41.0
Other transition economies [b]	1.8	16.5	45.7
Rest of world	5.4	13.2	28.5
Imports	14.4	49.9	54.5
of which to:			
EC	20.2	62.7	59.5
Other transition economies [b]	2.9	18.0	37.3
Rest of world	14.0	48.9	54.9

Source: GUS, *Rocznik Statystyczny 1992*, Warsaw, table 13, p.LVI and previous issues.

[a] At current prices.
[b] Eastern Europe and the former Soviet Union.

TABLE 5.5.9

Financial performance of state and private enterprises, Poland, 1991-1993
(Percentages)

	1991	1992		1993	
	QI-QII	QI-QII	QI-QIV	QI-QII	Jan.-Nov.
Gross profitability [a]					
Total economy	6.7	3.3	2.2	3.6	3.8
State sector	8.4	4.4	3.0	4.3	5.0
Private sector	2.3	0.4	-	2.0	1.5
Net profitability [b]					
Total economy	0.1	-0.9	-1.5	0.1	0.3
State sector	-0.1	-0.9	-1.6	-0.2	0.4
Private sector	-	-0.7	-1.2	0.8	0.2

Sources: GUS, *Biuletyn Statystyczny*, No.10/93, table 2, Warsaw. Data for January-November 1993, GUS, *Information on the Social and Economic Situation in Poland 1993*, January 1994, p.27, Warsaw.

[a] Ratio of gross profit (before taxation) to costs.
[b] Ratio of net profit (after profits tax and other charges paid from profits, such as punitive taxation on excess wage increases (*popiwek*), and charges imposed on fixed assets (*dividenda*)), to sales revenue.

There is insufficient information to determine whether the difference in financial performance between the two sectors reflects reality or merely differences or inadequacies in accounting practices. There are some grounds for believing that private firms tend to depress their recorded profits in order to avoid tax payments.[629] Among the various categories of costs there is one – "other costs" – which is not precisely defined and is twice as high in the private than in the state sector. This suggests that the new accounting practices have allowed private firms, particularly small ones, to overstate their costs and understate their profits.

However, not all categories of private firms are less profitable than state enterprises (on the basis of the

---

[629] Uplawa (1992), p.191.

TABLE 5.5.10

Financial performance in firms undergoing privatization, Poland, 1992-1993
(Percentages)

Category of firm	Gross profitability [a]		Net profitability [b]	
	1992	January-November 1993	1992	January-November 1993
Total economy average	1.6	3.8	-1.7	0.3
Firms undergoing privatization				
Companies being privatized under Article 5	5.1	7.6	2.3	6.2
Companies solely-owned by State Treasury	2.7	2.2	-3.5	-3.4
of which:				
Individual privatization approach	1.7	..	-4.6	..
Mass-privatization programme	6.1	..	0.1	..
Liquidated and corporatized with State Treasury participation	9.9	..	6.4	..
Liquidated and leased by workers	7.2	7.0	3.7	3.6
SOEs under liquidation	-28.6	-25.9	-39.0	-36.2
Through Law on State Enterprises	-44.7	-33.6	-66.1	-48.7
Through Privatization Law	-2.2	-1.6	-6.5	-3.8

Sources: GUS, *Rocznik Statystyczny 1993*, Warsaw, table 23, p.LX; Central Statistical Office, *Information on the Social and Economic Situation in Poland 1993*, Warsaw, January 1994, p.70.

[a] Ratio of gross profit (before taxation) to costs.

[b] Ratio of net profit (after profits tax and other charges paid from profits, such as punitive taxation on excess wage increases (*popiwek*), and charges imposed on founding assets (*dividenda*)), to sales revenue.

available statistics). At least two categories have reported higher than average profitability. These are state enterprises transformed into private companies under Article 5 of the Privatization Law and liquidated firms leased to workers' companies: in both, gross and net profitability ratios were considerably higher than the average rate for the Polish economy in 1992 and 1993 (table 5.5.10). In these two groups of firms some clear gains in efficiency have already been achieved, but this does not appear to be the case with other enterprises involved in the transformation process. Significant, albeit very different, rates of *loss* are recorded for SOEs undergoing liquidation according to the Law on State-Owned Enterprises (real bankruptcy) and the Privatization Law (liquidation with the aim of privatizing), differences which underpin the rationale for having two different approaches to liquidation.

The data also show that the transformation of SOEs into companies owned by the State Treasury (the process of "corporatization") has not yet changed their financial performance. However, a different picture is provided by statistics on the profitability of enterprises already privatized and quoted on the Warsaw Stock Exchange (see table 5.5.11). In most cases the profitability of each privatized company is considerably higher than the average for its respective industry.

(d) Privatization and restructuring

The privatization of large and medium-sized state enterprises started in Poland three-and-a-half years ago. Progress is illustrated in table 5.5.12, but it should be stressed that "involvement in the privatization process" does not mean that the transfer of property rights has been completed. In fact, to date, only a very small part of the SOE sector has been truly privatized.

Since the beginning of the privatization process and up to the end of September 1993, 2,467 SOEs – out of a total of 7,647 registered at the end of March 1990 and 8,591 at the end of June 1991 – had been subject to various actions aimed at transforming their property status. Most of them have been involved in the process of privatization through liquidation (79 per cent of all non-agricultural SOEs subject to various privatization procedures) and the rest (21 per cent) have been – or are being – transformed into legal companies under Article 5 of the Privatization Law.[630] Under the mass-privatization approach, 367 SOEs had been designated for transfer to the National Investments Funds.[631]

Liquidation under the Law on SOEs (i.e., real bankruptcy and the subsequent sale of assets) has been the dominant method of transformation. This approach, however, led to the full privatization of only 168 enterprises, i.e., 15 per cent of all firms being liquidated. Under the liquidation approach, which altogether has involved 845 SOEs, the most common technique is the leasing of the liquidated firm's assets by its workers (633 cases). This means that the usufruct of the liquidated firm's assets is enjoyed by the lessees for a fixed period, which in practice may extend to ten years. After that period, in principle, the lessees may become the owners of

---

[630] Only 86 out of 511 firms have so far been actually privatized via the latter approach, 22 of them being quoted on the Warsaw Stock Exchange at the end of 1993.

[631] The Government Ordinance of 14 September 1993 listed 165 SOEs designated for transformation into legal companies, and additionally 7 State Treasury companies designated to be transferred to National Investment Funds management (*Dziennik ustaw*, No.89/93, item 412). Prior to that date, the Council of Ministers had designated 195 Treasury companies whose shares were to be transferred to NIF management.

TABLE 5.5.11

Financial performance of joint-stock companies quoted on the Warsaw Stock Exchange, 1991-1993
(Per cent)

Branch/company	Gross profitability [a]			Net profitability [b]		
	1991	1992	1993 [c]	1991	1992	1993 [c]
Glass products industry	6.7	2.1	4.3	-1.0	-2.4	-0.5
IRENA	9.4	1.9	..	4.9	1.1	..
KROSNO	0.8	0.3	4.8	0.3	0.2	1.2
Clothing industry	3.5	3.3	7.3	0.3	0.1	3.4
PROCHNIK	6.6	19.4	..	3.3	8.0	..
WOLCZANKA	12.1	16.2	..	5.3	6.5	..
Food industry	8.0	3.1	3.5	2.1	-	0.8
WEDEL	41.3	23.6	..	15.6	15.8	..
OKOCIM	63.5	35.4	..	12.9	16.0	..
ZYWIECH	70.9	37.2	..	25.8	14.7	..
Wood industry	-0.3	-0.9	2.9	-4.3	-3.9	0.2
SWARZEDZ	-13.6	9.6	..	-11.2	4.9	..
Metal industry	4.8	3.0	4.2	-2.7	-2.3	-0.2
KABLE	2.0	3.4	..	-	0.2	..
Electronics industry	-1.1	-4.2	3.0	-7.5	-8.2	-0.8
TONSIL	-13.5	-17.8	2.0	-14.3	-19.4	2.0
Construction	13.3	4.8	3.5	3.5	0.8	0.4
EXBUD	11.5	9.0	..	8.1	6.8	..
MOSTOSTAL	33.5	33.3	..	9.0	19.6	..
Foreign trade	4.6	4.1	5.0	1.6	1.7	2.7
ELEKTRIM	13.1	15.4	8.1	2.4	4.2	3.4
UNIWERSAL	-0.4	0.7	..	-0.5	0.3	..

Sources: GUS, *Biuletyn Statystyczny*, Warsaw, No.10/93, table 19 for branch ratio, Central Planning Office data and company reports issued in BOSS for company ratios.

[a] Ratio of gross profit (before taxation) to costs.
[b] Ratio of net profit (after profits tax and other charges paid from profits, such as punitive taxation on excess wage increases (*popiwek*), and charges imposed on founding assets (*dividenda*)), to sales revenue.
[c] For branches, profitability ratio data for first ten months of 1993, for firm data, first eleven months.

the company provided that their financial commitments to the state are met.

Worker buy-outs are the next most popular method of transformation in those cases where a SOE is being liquidated. This method accounts for some 5 per cent of all the 2,467 non-agricultural SOEs being transformed or 14 per cent of those being liquidated. By October 1993, liquidations of SOEs had led to the creation of around 700 workers' companies employing 220,000 people.

Among the other relatively new approaches, so-called "fast-track sales" have been in operation for the last 15 months. Under this method, 166 SOEs have been selected to be sold either through public tenders or negotiation. By October 1993 only 69 of them had actually been sold. Another 21 had failed to find investors and subsequently were liquidated under Article 19 of the Law on SOEs, and 6 were withdrawn from the initial list. The rest are still on the list for sale.[632]

The pace of privatization in the period 1990-1993 has fluctuated quite sharply. After an intensive and broad-based advance in 1991, the privatization process lost momentum in the following two years. This observation applies to all the various methods of privatization. The slow-down was mainly due to a lack of consensus among the different political parties as to the best approach to privatization but also to the generally poor financial situation of the SOEs. The mass-privatization idea, which was suggested as a means of speeding up the process, raised concern across the political spectrum about its economic efficiency and political viability. Rapidly rising unemployment added to concerns about the social consequences of transformation, worries which could not be ignored by the authorities. Thus, there was a need to find an approach that would address these financial and social concerns, and this eventually led to the notions of financial restructuring and the Pact on Enterprise.

Privatization has generated government revenue, although the increase has not been as large as expected. Budget revenues from privatization through corporatization were Zl 1,636 billion in 1991, Zl 3,231 in 1992 and Zl 4,323 billion in the first 10 months of 1993. That income was generated by the privatization of, respectively, 28, 22 and 42 SOEs.

---

[632] According to Ministry of Privatization data in *BOSS*, 21 October 1993, p.7.

TABLE 5.5.12

Progress in the privatization process in Poland, 1990-1993
(Number and percentages)

Method of privatization	1990 [a]	1991	1992	1993 [b]	1990-1993 Number	1990-1993 Per cent
Enterprises involved in privatization						
Including state farms	130	1 128	1 333	1 122	3 714	-
Excluding state farms	130	1 128	794	414	2 467	100.0
Privatization into legal companies	58	250	172	31	511	20.7
of which:						
Individual approach	58	186	53	17	309	12.5
of which:						
Already privatized	6	24	22	42	86	3.5
Mass privatization	-	64	119	19	202	8.2
Privatization via liquidation	72	878	618	388	1 956	79.3
of which:						
Already privatized	15	247	355	196 [c]	813 [c]	33.0
(a) Privatization Law (Article 37)	44	372	299	130	845	34.3
of which:						
Already liquidated	13	222	278	132 [c]	645 [c]	26.1
Leased	(24)	(315)	..	..	(633)	25.7
Incorporated into other companies	(1)	(16)	..	..	(39)	1.6
Workers' buy-outs	(3)	(50)	..	..	(117)	4.7
Mixed approach	(5)	(16)	..	..	(63)	2.6
(b) Through bankruptcy [d]	28	506	319	258	1 111	45.0
of which:						
Already privatized	2	25	77	64 [c]	168 [c]	6.8
State farms taken over by the Agency of State Agricultural Property	-	-	539	708	1 247	..

Sources: GUS, *Rocznik Statystyczny 1993*, Warsaw, table 19-21, p.LIX; GUS, *Information on the Social and Economic Situation in Poland I-IX 1993*, Warsaw, December 1993, pp.27-28.

Note: Data in brackets are from the Ministry of Privatization and are not fully consistent with the GUS data.

[a] August-December.
[b] January-September.
[c] January-June.
[d] Under Article 19 of State Law on Enterprises.

Agriculture

By September 1993, the Agency for State-Owned Agricultural Property had taken over the administration of over 3.018 million hectares of state farm land. So far, progress in transforming agricultural farms is negligible: only 1.3 per cent of land has been sold to private farmers and 21.3 per cent has been leased to individual or collective producers.

Farmers' involvement in the privatization of food-processing firms, in which they are allowed to acquire shares on a preferential basis, has also been marginal. They have taken up only 4.3 per cent of the preference shares to which they were entitled.

Financial restructuring

By October 1993 banks had initiated investigations, under the Law on Financial Restructuring, into 11 companies solely- or majority-owned by the State Treasury. In seven cases these investigations had led to agreements in the fourth quarter of 1993.

Warsaw Stock Exchange

The stock market is supposed to be an important element in the process of property transformation. The Warsaw Stock Exchange (WSE) opened in April 1991, quoting shares of the first five privatized companies. Gradually, the number of quoted companies has increased. Until the early spring of 1993 the situation on the WSE was relatively quiet, but in the rest of 1993 there was a boom in terms of prices and turnover. Between the beginning and end of 1993, the Warsaw stock market index *WIG* rose more than twelvefold in zloty terms and about sevenfold in US dollar terms. No other emerging stock market in the world has produced anything comparable to the boom on the WSE. Daily turnover (stocks are traded currently three times a week) surged to an equivalent of $100 million, and the total market capitalization of the 22 companies listed reached $3 billion. Among the 22 listed companies, there are three banks, two breweries, two glass makers, two construction companies, three clothing producers and two trading companies.

Polish stocks, priced at an average of 2.3 times their earnings (P/E ratio) during April-October 1992, are now traded at an average P/E ratio of more than 20, i.e., not very different from US or west European stocks.

How far this boom in Polish equities is being driven by pure speculation is difficult to say. Nevertheless, recent developments are a clear sign of growing interest by small investors in the securities market and also in the privatization process. Unofficial estimates suggest that two thirds of share trading is done by domestic investors, the rest by foreigners who are free to operate and acquire shares on the WSE.

Foreign investment

Foreign investment ventures have grown rapidly since 1992. The number of joint ventures increased from 4,800 at the end of 1991 to 13,800 in September 1993 (see table 5.5.3).

According to estimates of the Polish State Foreign Trade Agency, for the period 1991-1993, 192 big foreign investors had engaged in projects amounting to $2,828 million. Moreover, they have also committed themselves to additional investments of up to $4,650 million.[633]

(iii) Four years of transformation: A summary

From this review of progress in the restructuring of the Polish economy, the following points may be retained.

First, prior to the start of the transformation programme the Polish economy was organized in a highly concentrated manner. About 8,000 large and medium-sized SOEs, often horizontally integrated, dominated the economy. It was easy to break up some of the biggest conglomerates, especially those in natural-resource-based sectors and in heavy industry. An immediate effect of this process was a rise in the number of SOEs in all sectors and branches.

Second, at the first stage of the transformation privatization and restructuring were treated as synonymous.

---

[633] The largest foreign investors are: Italian FIAT ($180 million already invested), Coca-Cola ($170 million), Polish-American Enterprise Fund ($164 million), IPC ($140 million), Austrian Warimpex ($100 million), ABB ($100 million), Curtis ($100 million), Unilever ($96 million). The principal countries involved are: the United States ($1,028 million) Italy ($270 million), the Netherlands ($233 million), Germany ($212 million), Austria ($195 million) and France ($177 million).

No industrial policy was thought necessary and it was widely expected that foreign investors would assist and stimulate the process of restructuring. However, it quickly became apparent that this approach was insufficient.

Third, after four years, progress is much less than was expected. One half of all SOEs were supposed to have been privatized within three years; in fact, less that 20 per cent have been involved in the various approaches to privatization and only 10 per cent have been actually transformed into private firms. Polish privatization has thus proved to be a slow and time-consuming process. A major problem is that there were very few SOEs which were suitable for public share offers, the method originally preferred by the authorities.

Fourth, the Polish authorities have tried to grapple with the problem of restructuring property rights in a variety of ways. The method of liquidation and the subsequent leasing of assets by workers' companies has been the most common approach, but this has led to some manipulation of asset values by the management and workers in the affected SOEs. The transformation of a SOE into a legal company and the subsequent disposal of its assets has proved difficult, expensive and time-consuming. Nevertheless, the latter approach does appear to provide the best results in terms of financial restructuring.

Fifth, privatization in Poland is hampered by the conflicting interests of the main domestic political groups represented by the state bureaucracy, management and workers' collectives. The idea of mass privatization, launched three years ago, has not yet produced concrete results in terms of successful privatization. Lengthy discussions of the idea by government and Parliament has significantly delayed its implementation. None the less, the NIFs have raised interest among managers in Poland and abroad, although Polish SOEs have expressed far less interest in the approach.

Finally, the boom in the Warsaw stock market in 1993 is a positive signal for the authorities, in so far as it indicates a growing interest on the part of quite a large number of small and medium-sized investors in buying shares and may suggest an emerging popular awareness of the need for privatization, general support for which is needed to keep the transformation programme on course.

References

P. Aghion and O. Blanchard (1993), "On the speed of transition in Eastern Europe", mimeo, MIT and EBRD.

P. Aghion, O. Blanchard and R. Burgess (1993). "The behaviour of state firms in Eastern Europe, pre-privatization", EBRD Discussion Paper.

Alliance of Free Democrats (1990), "Hozzászólás a Versenytörvény tervezetéhez" (Some remarks on the competition bill), January.

L. Antal (1985), *Gazdaságirányítási és pénzügyi rendszerünk a reform útján* (The Hungarian system of economic and financial regulation on the way of reform), Közgazdasági és Jogi Könyvkiadó.

A. Bertáné, P. Å. Bod and Z. Nagy (1990), "A monopólium és a versenypiac között" (Between monopolistic and competitive markets), *Közgazdasági Szemle*, No.6.

D. Begg and R. Portes (1993), "Enterprise debt and firm transformation: financial restructuring in Eastern Europe", in C. Mayer and X. Vives (eds.) (1993), *Capital Markets and Financial Intermediation*. Cambridge, CUP.

E. Birnie, D. Hitchens and K. Wagner (1993), "Productivity and competitiveness in East German manufacturing: a matched plant comparison"; paper presented to CEPR Workshop, 4/5 June, Berlin.

R. Bischof, G. von Bismarck and W. Carlin (1993), "From Kombinat to private enterprise: two case studies in East German privatization". UCL Discussion Paper 1993-02 (forthcoming in J. Heath (ed.), *Revitalizing Socialist Enterprise: A Race Against Time*, Routledge).

P. Boot (1983), "Continuity and change in the planning system of the German Democratic Republic", *Soviet Studies*, 35, 3.

A. Buchtíková and V. Flek (1993), "The impact of deconcentration and indirect industrial policy in structural development and export performance in the Czech Republic 1989-1992", mimeo, Czech National Bank.

Business International/Creditanstalt (1992). *1992 East European Investment Survey*.

A. Capek (1993), "Output Decline and the Dynamics of Privatisation in the Czech Republic", paper prepared for the conference on Output Decline in Eastern Europe, IASA, Laxenburg, November.

W. Carlin and C. Mayer (1992a), "Restructuring enterprises in Eastern Europe". *Economic Policy*, No.15, October.

W. Carlin and C. Mayer (1992b), "The Treuhandanstalt: privatization by state and market"; paper presented to NBER Conference on Transition in Eastern Europe, Boston 1992 (forthcoming in O. Blanchard, K. Froot and J. Sachs (eds.) (1993), *Transition in Eastern Europe*, University of Chicago Press).

W. Carlin, C. Mayer and P. von Richthofen (1993), "Ownership of large East German private enterprises". Unpublished data set, University College London.

W. Carlin (1993), "Privatization and Deindustrialization in East Germany", *CEPR Discussion Paper*, No.892.

CEFRES (1993), Centre Français de Recherche en Sciences Sociales, *Enterprise Restructuring at Different Stages of Ownership Transformation: The Czech Republic and Poland*, Research Project Manuscript.

A. D. Chandler (1990), *Scale and Scope: The Dynamics of Industrial Capitalism*. Cambridge Mass., Belknap/Harvard.

A. D. Chandler (1993), "Organizational capabilities and industrial restructuring: A historical analysis", *Journal of Comparative Economics* 17, 2.

J. Charap and A. Zemplinerova (1993a), "Restructuring in the Czech Economy", EBRD, *Working Paper*, No.2, London March.

J. Charap and A. Zemplinerova (1993b), "Management and Employee Buy-Outs in the Process of Privatization"; paper prepared for the 3rd plenary session of the OECD Advisory Group on Privatization, Budapest, March-April.

J. Charap and A. Zemplinerova (1993c), "Foreign investment in the privatization and restructuring of the Czech economy"; paper presented to conference "Economic Transformation in Central and Eastern Europe", WZB Berlin, September.

M. Csanádi (1993a), *Függöség, konszenzus és szelekció* (Dependence, consensus and selection), Pénzügykutatási Intézet.

M. Csanádi (1993b), *Rendszer-függöségeink: A párt-állam mûködésének és összeomlásának hatása az átalakulásra Magyarországon* (System dependencies: Effects of the activities and collapse of a party state on the Hungarian transformation process), MTA Közgazdaságtudományi Intézet.

Deutsches Institut für Wirtschaftsforschung (1993a), "Gesamtwirtschaftliche und unternehmerische Anpassungsprozesse in Ostdeutschland, Achter Bericht", in *DIW-Wochenbericht* 13/93, pp.131-158.

S. Estrin, A. Gelb and I. Singh (1993), "Restructuring, viability and privatization: a comparative study of enterprise adjustment in transition", mimeo, World Bank.

C. Fritz (1993), "Kombinat Oberbekleidung Berlin: Des Schneiders neue Kleider", in *Kombinate...* (1993).

R. Frydman, A. Rapaczunski, J.S. Earle et al. (1993), *The Privatization Process in Central Europe*, London: CEU Press.

Government of the Republic of Hungary (1990), *A nemzeti megújhodás programja* (Government programme of national revival).

Government of the Republic of Hungary (1993), *Beszámoló az Országyûlésnek az Állami Vagyonügynökség 1992. évi tevékenységéröl* (Report to the Parliament on the 1992 activity of the State Property Agency), September.

I. Grosfeld and P. Hare (1991), "Privatization in Hungary, Poland and Czechoslovakia", *European Economy*, Special Edition No.2.

G. Gusinski (1993), "Vom Plan zum Markt: Erfolge, die schmerzen" in *Kombinate ...* (1993).

F. Hansel (1993), "The liquidation regime during the transition: the German case and the role of the Treuhandanstalt"; paper prepared for conference "Privatization and Socioeconomic Policy in Central and Eastern Europe", Kraków, October.

P. Hare (1993), (KPMG Management Consulting, CERT Heriot-Watt University, SovEcon Moscow), *A Study of the Russian Privatization Process*, HM Treasury.

M. Heidenreich (ed.) (1992), *Krisen, Kader, Kombinate: Kontinuität und Wandel in ostdeutschen Betrieben*. Berlin: Edition Sigma.

B. Ickes and R. Ryterman (1993), "From enterprise to firm: notes for a theory of the enterprise in transition", mimeo, Pennsylvania State University.

L. Kállai (1992), "Variációk privatizációs törvénykezésre" (Variations on privatization legislation), *Magyar Hírlap*.

J. Karsai (1993), "Fedöneve: reorganizáció" (Code-name: reorganization), *Közgazdasági Szemle*, No.9.

M. Kerous (1993), "Czech and Slovak banking in the transition period". Paper prepared for the Institute of Development Studies, University of Sussex, October.

E. Klvacova (1992), "The current situation of privatization in Czechoslovakia"; discussion paper, Institute of Economics, Prague, October.

Kombinate ... (1993), *Kombinate: Was aus ihnen geworden ist: Reportagen aus den neuen Ländern*. Berlin, Verlag Die Wirtschaft.

J. Kühl (1993), "Unternehmensentwicklung von Treuhandunternehmen und privatisierten ehemaligen Treuhandfirmen vom Ende der DDR bis Ende 1992"; presented at ZEW workshop "Arbeitsdynamik und Unternehmensentwicklung in Ostdeutschland - Erfahrungen und Perspektiven des Transformationsprozesses", Mannheim.

T. Laky (ed.) (1993), *A munkaerőpiac keresletét és kínálatát alakító folymatok* (Processes influencing demand and supply on the labour market), Labour Research Institute, June.

G. Lamberger (1993), *A csödhullám hatásai a magyar iparban és mezögazdaságban, különös tekintettel a külgazdasági hatásokra* (Effects of bankruptcies on Hungarian industry and agriculture, with special respect to foreign trade), KOPINT-DATORG, November.

K. Lichtblau (1993), "Privatisierungs- und Sanierungsarbeit der Treuhandanstalt", *Beiträge zur Wirtschafts- und Sozialpolitik*, Institut der deutschen Wirtschaft Köln, No.209.

G. Matolcsy (ed.) (1991), *Lábadozásunk évei* (Years of recovery), Privatizációs Kutató Intézet.

G. A. McDermott (1993), "Rethinking the ties that bind: the limits of privatisation in the Czech Republic". Paper presented to conference "Economic Transformation in Central and Eastern Europe", WZB Berlin September 1993.

M. Melzer (1981), "Combine formation in the GDR", *Soviet Studies,* 33.

P. Mihályi (1993), "Privatization in Hungary: An overview", manuscript, May.

MIT (1993), Ministry of Industry and Trade, *Beszámoló az ipari válságkezelési program keretében elvégzett válságmenedzselés tapasztalatairól* (Report on the experiences of crisis management under the industrial crisis management project), May.

K. Mizsei (1993), "Bankruptcy and the post-communist economies of East Central Europe", mimeo, Advanced Summer School in the Economies of the Market, Stirin Castle, Czech Republic.

M. Móra (1990), *Az állami vállalatok (ál)privatizációja* (Quasi-privatization of state-owned enterprises), Gazdaságkutató Intézet.

D. Newbery and P. Kattuman (1992), "Market concentration and competition in Eastern Europe". Department of Applied Economics, Cambridge University, Discussion Paper.

D. Nolte (1993a), "Das "ATLAS"-Projekt – ein Modell zur Sicherung industrieller Kerne in Sachsen". Unpublished manuscript, WSI-Institut, Düsseldorf.

D. Nolte (1993b), "Zwischen Privatisierung und Sanierung: Die Arbeit der Treuhandanstalt", *WSI-Materialien*, No.32.

B. Pinto, M. Belka and S. Krajewski (1993), "Transforming state enterprises in Poland: microeconomic evidence on adjustment", *Brookings Papers on Economic Activity*, 1993/1.

T. Price (1993), "VEB-Treuhand-GmbH: the Kombinat and economic policy in the German Democratic Republic and during the transition to a market economy", MSc Dissertation, UCL.

Privatization Strategy Task Team (1992), *A magyar privatizáció áttörési koncepciója és kormányzati munkaprogramja* (The breakthrough plan and governmental working program of Hungarian privatization).

T. Sárközy (1991a), "A tisztességtelen piaci magatartás tilalmáról szóló törvény a magyar gazdasági jog fejlödésében" (The law prohibiting unfair competition in the development of Hungarian economic legislation), in *Verseny- és árszabályozás* (Competition and price control).

T. Sárközy (1991b), *A privatizáció joga Magyarországon* (The legal framework of privatization in Hungary), Unió Kiadó.

I. Schweitzer (1982), *A vállalatnagyság* (Size structure of enterprises), Közgazdasági és Jogi Könyvkiadó.

State Audit Office (1992), *Jelentés az Állami Vagyonügynökség mûködéséröl* (Report on the activities of the State Property Agency), April.

State Audit Office (1993), *Jelentés az Állami Vagyonügynökség 1992, évi tevékenységének ellenörzéséröl* (Report on the activities of the State Property Agency in 1992), July.

D. Stark (1993), "Recombinant property in East European capitalism. Organizational innovation in Hungary", Paper presented to conference "Economic Transformation in Central and Eastern Europe", WZB Berlin, September.

E. Szalai (1989), *Gazdasagi mechanizmus, reformtörekvések és nagyvállalati érdekek* (Economic mechanism, reform intentions and interests of large enterprises), Közgazdasági és Jogi Könyvkiadó.

E. Szalai (1991), "Integration of special interests in the Hungarian economy: The struggle between large companies and the party and state bureaucracy", *Journal of Comparative Economics*, Vol.15, No.2.

L. Takla (1993), "The relationship between privatization and the reform of the banking sector: the case of the Czech Republic and Slovakia", mimeo, LBS and Royal Institute of International Affairs.

I.J. Tóth (1991), "A spontán privatizáció mint kormányzati politika" (Spontaneous privatization as government policy), *Külgazdaság*, No.9.

Treuhandanstalt (1992a), *DM Opening Balance by July 1, 1990*, Berlin, October.

Treuhandanstalt (1992b), *NL-Berichte*, 12.92

Treuhandanstalt (1993), *Monatsinformationen der THA*, June.

United Nations Economic Commission for Europe (1992), *Economic Survey of Europe in 1991-1992*, New York.

United Nations Economic Commission for Europe (1993), "Progress in privatization 1990-1992", in *Economic Survey of Europe in 1992-1993*, New York.

S. Uplawa (1992), "Private Sector Development" in Instytut Rozwoju i Studiow Strategicznych, *Transforming the Polish Economy, 1992*, Warsaw.

S. van Wijnbergen (1993), "On the role of banks in enterprise restructuring: the Polish example", mimeo, University of Amsterdam.

É. Voszka (1984), *Érdek és kölcsönös függöség* (Interests and interdependence), Közgazdasági és Jogi Könyvkiadó.

É. Voszka (1991), "Homályból homályba" (From one twilight to another), *Társadalmi Szemle*, No.5.

É. Voszka (1993), "Spontaneous privatization in Hungary: Preconditions and real issues", in Earl, Frydman and Rapaczynski (eds.), *Privatization in the transition to a market economy*, St. Martin's Press and Pinter Publishers.

É. Voszka (1994), "An attempt at crisis management and the failure of spontaneous privatization", *Industrial and Environmental Crisis Quarterly*, Vol.8, No.1, (forthcoming).

WIIW (1993), Vienna Institute for Comparative Economic Studies, *Transition from the Command to the Market System: what went wrong and what to do now?*, March.

In addition to its regular review of recent economic developments in Europe and North America, the Division for Economic Analysis and Projections of the United Nations Economic Commission for Europe, in Geneva, also publishes research studies with a longer time perspective.

Recent publications include:

"A note on recent developments in east-west trade in services", *Economic Bulletin for Europe*, vol.41, (1989), Sales No. E.89.II.E.26

"East-west trade in investment goods, 1970-1987", ibid.

"Economic reform in the east: a framework for western support", *Economic Survey of Europe in 1989-1990*, New York, 1989, Sales No. E.90.II.E.1

"The broader policy framework for 1990 and beyond", ibid.

"Developments in the service sector", ibid.

"International initiative in support of eastern reforms", ibid.

"Some implications of a German monetary union", ibid.

"Economic integration and the export performance of west European countries outside the EC", ibid.

"Europe's trade in engineering goods: Specialization and technology", ibid.

"The broader policy framework for 1990 and beyond", ibid.

"The unification of Germany", *Economic Bulletin for Europe*, vol.42, 1990, Sales No. E.90.II.E.37

"The Free Trade Agreement between Canada and the United States", ibid.

"Explaining unemployment in the market economies: theories and evidence", *Economic Survey of Europe in 1990-1991*, New York, 1991, Sales No. E.91.II.E.1

"The hard road to the market economy: problems and policies", ibid.

"Developments in the service sector", ibid.

"External economic relations of the Baltic States", *Economic Bulletin for Europe*, vol.43(1991), Sales No. E.91.II.E.39

"International support for eastern transformation", *Economic Survey of Europe in 1991-1992*, New York, 1992, Sales No. E.92.II.E.1

"On property rights and privatization in the transition economies", ibid.

"Migration from east to west", ibid.

"International support for transition countries", *Economic Bulletin for Europe*, vol.44(1992), Sales No. E.93.II.E.3

"Finland's trade with the Soviet Union: its impact on the Finnish economy",

"Progress in privatization, 1990-1992", *Economic Survey of Europe in 1992-1993*, Sales No. E.93.II.E.1

"Recent trade performance of the Visegrad countries", *Economic Bulletin for Europe*, vol.45(1993), Sales No. E.94.II.E.2

"Does it matter if the Urumuay Round succeeds or fails", ibid.

"Reforms in foreign economic relations of eastern Europe and the Soviet Union", *Economic Studies No. 2*, Sales No. E.91.II.E.5

"Demographic causes and economic consequences of population aging" *Economic Studies No. 3*, Sales No. GV.E.92.0.4

"Comparative GDP levels: Physical indicators, Phase III" *Economic Studies No. 4*, Sales No. GV.E.95.0.5

"Economic growth in the market economies, 1950-2000", *Discussion Papers, Volume 1 (1991), No. 1*; Sales No. GV.E.91-0-15

"Five years of *Perestroika*: Results, problems, prospects", *Discussion Papers, Volume 1 (1991), No. 2*, Sales No. GV.E.91-0-22

"Managing reforms in the east European countries", *Discussion Papers, Volume 1 (1991), No. 3*, Sales No. GV.E-92-0-1

"Economic reforms and their significance for all-European cooperation", *Discussion Papers, Volume 1 (1991), No. 4*, Sales No. GV.E.92-0-2

"Personal and collective services: An international perspective", *Discussion Papers, Volume 2 (1992), No. 1*, Sales No. GV.E.92-0-22

"The conditions for economic recovery in central and eastern Europe", *Discussion Papers, Volume 2 (1992), No. 2*, Sales No. GV.E.92-0-24

"The scope for macroeconomic policy to alleviate unemployment in western Europe", *Discussion Papers, Volume 2 (1992), No. 3*, Sales No. GV.E.92-0-27

"Economics and environment in the former Soviet Union and Czechoslovakia", *Discussion Papers, Volume 2 (1992), No. 4*, Sales No. GV.E.93-0-11

"Structural change, employment and unemployment in the market and transition economies", *Discussion Papers, Volume 3 (1993), No. 1*, Sales No. GV.E.94-0-2

Back issues of the *Economic Survey of Europe* (from 1948) and the *Economic Bulletin for Europe* (from 1949) are available in microfiche form (which can be supplied as printed pages).

Your source of information: *United Nations publications*